The Clinic Seminar

■ ■ ■

by

Deborah Epstein
Professor of Law
Georgetown University Law Center

Jane H. Aiken
Associate Dean for Experiential Education
Georgetown University Law Center

Wallace J. Mlyniec
Lupo-Ricci Professor of Law
Georgetown University Law Center

AMERICAN CASEBOOK SERIES®

Mat #41127690

The publisher is not engaged in rendering legal or other professional advice, and this publication is not a substitute for the advice of an attorney. If you require legal or other expert advice, you should seek the services of a competent attorney or other professional.

American Casebook Series is a trademark registered in the U.S. Patent and Trademark Office.

© 2014 LEG, Inc. d/b/a West Academic
444 Cedar Street, Suite 700
St. Paul, MN 55101
1-877-888-1330

West, West Academic Publishing, and West Academic are trademarks of West Publishing Corporation, used under license.

Printed in the United States of America

ISBN: 978-0-314-27494-6

To Chris, who taught me that true love is worth waiting for;
To Adam and Rachel, who taught me to be a better
parent and thus a better teacher;
To Bea and Steve, my first teachers, from whom
I continue to learn so much

Deborah

To Lanier, Robert, Claire and Thomas, and to
The Carnegie Academy for the Scholarship of Teaching and
Learning where I first encountered UNDERSTANDING BY DESIGN
which has had a profound influence on this book

Jane

To Abby, Emma, and Casey, and to the students and fellows
with whom I have shared a love of learning
during my 40 years at Georgetown

Wally

ACKNOWLEDGMENTS

The ideas we explore in THE CLINIC SEMINAR have been influenced, directly and indirectly, by so many of our colleagues, friends, and mentors over the course of many, many years. Although there are too many to mention, we hope to name those who have played the most significant roles. First, we wish to thank each other. This book grew out of innumerable collaborative teaching experiences, and each one of us is a better teacher for having engaged in the process of writing it. Each of us has also had the incredible good fortune of sharing the responsibility of designing and teaching a clinic seminar with master teachers. For this privilege, from which we have learned so much, we thank Rachel Camp, John Copacino, Matthew Fraidin, Kristen Henning, Paul Holland, Margaret Johnson, Laurie Kohn, and Colleen Shanahan. All three of us grew as teachers in the process of designing the Georgetown Summer Institute on Clinical Teaching. Much of that learning came from our extensive collaboration with the other members of the core Institute faculty, Susan Bryant, Catherine Klein, and Ann Shalleck. The deeply insightful contributions of learning theorist Grant Wiggins fundamentally influenced much of the Summer Institute; his Backward Design methodology permeates our understanding of effective teaching and the learning theory that underlies it, and his influence can be clearly seen in this book. We also learned from all other members of the Institute faculty, including Muneer Ahmad, Alicia Alvarez, Sameer Ashar, Margaret Martin Barry, William Brendel, Stephen Brookfield, John Copacino, Matthew Fraidin, Conrad Johnson, Elliott Milstein, Jean Koh Peters, Abbe Smith, Tirien Steinbach, and Robert Stumberg. We all benefited enormously from several years of participating in a series of rounds on clinical teaching and supervision that Elliott Milstein and Ann Shalleck facilitated with Jane and Deborah, and which grew out of similar work in New York, facilitated by Susan Bryant and Elliott Milstein; we thank all of our D.C. area colleagues who brought their creative energy and insight to those sessions. We also wish to thank all of our colleagues at Georgetown, especially those with whom we have designed class sessions over the years: Rachel Camp, John Copacino, Steven Goldblatt, Kristen Henning, Susan Deller Ross, Colleen Shanahan, Abbe Smith, and Robert Stumberg, as well as the fellows and students who helped us experiment with teaching methods throughout our years at Georgetown. Finally, we are deeply grateful to the talented clinical teachers who patiently read and provided us with invaluable feedback on various chapters of this book: Rachel Camp, Bridgette Carr, Matthew Fraidin, Tammy Kuennen, Vivek Sankaren, David Santacroce, and Colleen Shanahan.

We are particularly grateful to Danielle Pelfrey Duryea, who worked tirelessly to collect a wide range of interdisciplinary reading materials for the THE CLINIC SEMINAR. Our copy editor, Susanna Fix, patiently reviewed chapter after chapter of text—we could not have done this without her. Professor Charles Rose III graciously allowed us to use extensive materials from his wonderful book, FUNDAMENTAL TRIAL ADVOCACY; we hold his work in extremely high regard and suggest its use for trial advocacy issues that are beyond our book. We are thankful to West Academic Publishing, and especially to its Acquisitions Editor, Jim Cahoy, who first proposed the idea of THE CLINIC SEMINAR and asked us to write this book.

We also wish to thank those who developed or contributed to the development of the teaching exercises contained in this book. In all instances where we know or have been able to discern the teacher who first created a particular exercise, we have included the attribution in the appropriate chapter. But in many instances, despite our best efforts, we have been unable to discern the origins of exercises we or other clinicians have been using for years. This attribution problem is a testament to the incredibly talented and connected clinical teaching community of which we are all privileged to be part. So many wonderful teaching ideas have been shaped by a long-ago presentation at a clinical conference, or a brilliant suggestion made by a forgotten source, and have evolved over time and through the layered contributions of so many clinicians that it is not possible to find someone to credit for the idea. So we thank the entire clinical community for their collective contributions to our thinking and our work. It reminds us of Woody Guthrie's comment when asked how he felt about a writer who had used his music without permission: "Oh, he just stole from me. I steal from everybody." We are all so fortunate to have each other to steal from and we hope you find many ideas to steal here. Thanks to you all.

TABLE OF CONTENTS

The Clinic Seminar

CHAPTER 1

INTENSIVE ORIENTATION

LEARNING GOALS

The learning goals for the overall clinic orientation include helping you to:

- Understand the role of a lawyer in the clinic
- Understand the substantive and procedural laws and rules that will guide your client representation work
- Learn and understand the goals and methods of clinical pedagogy
- Build community and establish a collective sense of trust

The learning goals for the segment on introducing ourselves to each other include helping you to:

- Build community and establish a collective sense of trust
- Gain insight into the experience of interviewing and being interviewed
- Understand the responsibility you bear when presenting another person's story to an audience
- Understand the complex experience of hearing another person present your personal story to an audience
- Learn about each other and about the faculty

The learning goals for the segments devoted to an introduction to clinical pedagogy include helping you to:

- Understand the clinical teaching model
- Recognize the differences between the clinical model and a typical law office supervisor-supervisee relationship
- Recognize how that difference is connected to your learning goals
- Understand the importance of goals to the clinical pedagogy methods

- Understand your ownership, role, and responsibility for your own learning
- Understand how supervision and client needs relate to your learning goals
- Begin to develop personal learning goals for your clinic experience
- Learn about each other's goals
- Learn how your goals relate to the lawyering process
- See connections and tensions between personal learning goals and client representation
- Understand the importance of goals to clinical pedagogy

The learning goals for the segments devoted to an introduction to the legal system and community organizations include helping you to:

- Build a community and establish a collective sense of trust
- Become familiar with the relevant legal systems and community organizations you will encounter in your client representation work
- Become familiar with typical operations of the forum in which the clinic works
- Witness how clients are treated in these fora

The learning goals for the segments devoted to games include helping you to:

- Build a community within the clinic and establish a collective sense of trust among your colleagues
- Learn about each other and about the faculty

DESCRIPTION OF THE INTENSIVE ORIENTATION

In this series of classes, we will introduce you to several fundamental aspects of the clinical program in which you are about to participate. Orientation will provide you with a frame of reference for understanding the goals and methods of clinical pedagogy and the responsibilities that come with assuming the role of a lawyer. We hope to create a strong sense of clinic community based on trust, collaboration, and shared experience that will help you grow personally and professionally and that will help prepare you to face similar challenges in post-graduation practice.

READING ASSIGNMENT

1. David Chavkin, *Clinical Methodology in* Clinical Legal Education: A Textbook for Law School Clinical Programs 7 (2002).
2. Supplemental materials will be provided by your clinical professor.

READING

David Chavkin
Clinical Methodology
CLINICAL LEGAL EDUCATION: A TEXTBOOK FOR LAW SCHOOL CLINICAL PROGRAMS 7 (2002)

As we have discussed, clinical legal education has pedagogical goals that differ from those in non-clinical courses. In order to achieve these unique goals, special teaching methods have been developed to maximize the opportunities for learning throughout your clinical experience. While the opportunity to work with real-life clients to address real-world problems under the "supervision" of a trained faculty member is at the heart of the clinical experience, clinical education also uses other techniques to help you develop as a reflective practitioner.

A. The Problem of the Kitchen Organizer

At its best, clinical methodology is subtle and often invisible. For that reason, we will start our discussion of clinical methodology indirectly.

Think back to the first time that you lived alone. Perhaps it occurred during your undergraduate education; perhaps it happened earlier or later in your life. One of your first tasks was to organize your kitchen—to decide where to place the dishes, the glasses, the pots and pans, and the silverware. And, imagine that a Professor of "Kitchen Organizing" was present as you began to unload your boxes. Several courses of action were available to the Professor.

First, the Professor could have told you to unpack your clothes in the bedroom while s/he unpacked your kitchen supplies. S/he would then have placed your items on the shelves based on well-established principles of "kitchen organization"—principles with which you would have had no familiarity.

The result would have been a well-organized kitchen. However, you would have learned nothing about the relevant theories of kitchen organizing and, because you had not "bought into" the theories reflected in the professor's system, it is unlikely that you would have maintained the kitchen using that model.

Second, the professor could have asked you to be present while s/he organized the kitchen. You could have interacted with the professor as s/he placed items on the shelves and in drawers—asking questions as appropriate—and perhaps you might even have placed a glass or plate or fork as directed. Similar to a well-designed externship, you might have learned some of the principles of good "kitchen organizing" and you would have learned something of the work of the professional "kitchen organizer."

A well-organized kitchen would also have been produced. However, you would not have "owned" your experience as a kitchen organizer and would not have internalized the principles of kitchen organizing in the same way as when you "own" your learning process. Moreover, the kitchen might have been organized in a manner appropriate for the professor, but not necessarily for you and your intended uses of the kitchen.

Third the professor could have taken out a blackboard and lectured on the principles of kitchen organizing. You might have had an opportunity to ask questions, although your lack of personal experience in kitchen organizing would have limited your ability to design effective questions and the lack of factual context would have limited the utility of the lecture. The professor would then have departed and you would have attempted to design an effective kitchen based on the abstract principles you had heard in the lecture.

This educational model, generally referred to as "exposition-application," is the model commonly used throughout law school (and has some role even in clinic). *To the extent* that you were able to understand the principles expounded in the lecture and *to the extent* that you were able to apply those principles in a specific factual context (your own kitchen), the result would have been a grounding in the principles of kitchen organization, an ability to apply them in context, and an effectively-organized kitchen. However, the inclusion of the words "to the extent" highlights the problems in translating the theory presented in lecture materials into the practical ability to apply that knowledge.

Fourth, the professor could have gone out to lunch and left you to organize the kitchen. You *might* have conducted research into the principles of kitchen organizing and you *might* have been successful in researching those principles. You *might* have asked yourself critical questions about your intended use of the kitchen, the locations of fixed kitchen appliances, and the kitchenware to distribute and *you might* have been successful in applying the principles you learned through research to the facts you gained through answering your questions. However, you would not have had anyone with whom to reflect on the process of research and application. And the results, emphasized by the word "might," would have been very hit or miss.

Finally, the professor could have taken a very different role. She could have first sat down with you in the kitchen and talked with you about the task of organizing a kitchen. S/he would have asked you a series of questions to help you identify the issues you would have to confront in the process of organization. S/he would have asked you questions to help you think about the relevant facts about kitchen uses and equipment you would have to identify and consider and the principles you would have to learn to design an efficient and effective kitchen. Through these questions you would have begun to grapple with the specific considerations necessary to design this particular kitchen for this particular user (you) in light of your intended uses.

S/he would then have stepped back to let you begin the process and might have observed your work at particular intervals. S/he would also have met with you periodically to ask questions and to help you focus on particular aspects of the process. After the process was completed, the professor would then have helped you reflect on the steps you had undertaken to investigate, research, and implement and to help you identify principles you had developed, choices you had made, and consequences you had experienced or were likely to experience from those choices.

Like some of the other options described, the result would have been a well-organized kitchen. However, there are a number of other benefits that would have been achieved through this model (often referred to as "guided discovery learning"). First, you would have learned how to develop principles of fact investigation and research relevant to kitchen organizing and you would have developed the capacity to apply those principles in a specific factual context. Second, you would have learned how to identify choices that must be made (either by making a conscious choice or by failing to make a choice at all) and you would have developed the capacity to improve your decisionmaking process by reflecting on those choices as they were confronted. Third you would have developed skills of kitchen organization from your ownership of this experience.

We capture all of these pedagogical goals (and many others) through the concept of the "reflective practitioner." What we hope to do through clinical methodology is to create a reflective practicum. In this setting, we will work together to help you develop into a practitioner who can identify the many moments in the lawyering process at which choices can be made ("choice moments"). And, we hope to help you develop into a practitioner who has a reason for every choice s/he makes and a process for making and implementing those choices that includes critical reflection through every step of your professional career.

B. Instructional Settings

We turn now to the specific settings we will use to try to achieve these pedagogical goals.

1. Live-Client Representation

It is difficult to over-emphasize the importance of the real-life aspects of clinical education. Justice Rosalie Wahl, a former chair of the ABA's Section of Legal Education and Admissions to the Bar and a member of the Minnesota Supreme Court, described the impact of live-client representation on student attorneys in the following terms: "I personally feel that the real consequences of working with a live client has a quality and an ethical responsibility to that person that you cannot experience by just listening about it." You will be given the opportunity to relate to people of backgrounds that will often be very different from your own. You will also find that you will have much to learn from your clients as you grapple with a model of representation in most legal clinics that maximizes client autonomy in decisionmaking.

Another benefit of real-life client clinical experiences relates to motivation. Many of you are familiar with the law school maxim—"First year they scare you; Second year they work you; Third year they bore you." Although you are likely to experience many feelings and emotions in clinic, boredom is not likely to be among them. You will be moving in clinic from the role of "spectator" to that of "actor." In doing so, the fact that you will have real people dependent on you will motivate you in powerful ways. Moreover, the fact that you will not want to be embarrassed before a judge, an adversary, or a supervising attorney necessarily means that you will approach your clinic responsibilities very differently from the ways that you approached class preparation in even the most demanding classroom settings.

Another significant benefit of live-client representation is the opportunity to identify and answer questions of professional responsibility that directly confront your role as a lawyer. Students are consistently amazed at how quickly ethical issues arise in their real-life cases and how the ethical rules come to life. You will also learn how difficult those issues often are to resolve in real-life practice.

2. Making and Evaluating Choices

Clinic also uses two other methodologies that may be new to you. First, you will be asked to have a reason for every action you take. While that may seem like a fairly simple requirement, such reasons as "That's what the form book says" or "That's the way they do it at the firm where I work" are not going to cut it. Instead you will be asked to critically examine every opportunity at which a choice can and should be made and to develop thoughtful reasons for every decision you make. This approach will not guarantee that every decision is the "right" one—assuming that there even is a "right" one in many contexts. However, this approach will increase the *likelihood* that you will identity "choice moments" and make the right decisions with your clients by improving both your decisionmaking process and your process for implementing those decisions.

Second, you will be asked to address ambiguous situations throughout your clinical practice. These situations are ambiguous in two senses. You will not always have all the facts or legal authority that you might like to have. Reality places limitations on how much you can "know" and you will therefore have to frame and/or make decisions based on ambiguous information. These situations are also ambiguous in the sense that the outcomes of particular choices will not always be clear; they require you to grapple with "indeterminacy."

* * *

3. Case Supervision

Students need to regularly interact with their supervisors in a setting in which faculty members have sufficient time and energy to discuss case-related and personal issues with their students in an unhurried and nondirective manner. This generally requires a small student-to-faculty ratio—a significant departure from the large classes most of us have experienced as the norm throughout law school.

Although supervision styles vary from clinic to clinic and from supervisor to supervisor, there are some common features that you will experience in your clinic work. Students need to invest in the quality of their decisions—to own their clinic experiences. This process is facilitated by having supervisors help students reflect on their experiences and not by displacing students as the lawyers for their clients. The word "supervision" is therefore something of a misnomer. We will use it because most student practice rules use this term to describe the role of the clinical teacher. However, to the extent that it suggests a model in which your supervisor simply tells you what to do, we will use the term cautiously.

Supervisors will usually meet a student question with a question of their own to help you learn to discover not merely the answer to your question, but a process for finding answers to questions when supervisors are not available. This means that your question. "What do you think I should do here?" will often be met with the questions: "Well, what are your options? What do you see as the benefits and disadvantages of each option?" The goal here is *not* to "hide the ball" from you, but rather to help you discover the feel of the ball for yourself.

Despite the pedagogical reasons for this approach, times may arise in which your anxiety may exceed productive levels—periods in which your anxiety may begin to become debilitating. A little anxiety can be helpful as a motivating tool and some anxiety is inherent in the practice of law. However, too much anxiety can be destructive and can even become paralyzing. At those moments, be sure to share your feelings with your supervisor. Ordinarily, your supervising attorney will have picked up on these issues. However, in the event that you feel somewhat out of control, be sure to share this fact with him/her.

4. Rounds

You are probably familiar, from doctor shows on television, with the technique of having interns and residents present client symptoms and treatment approaches to a physician and to other interns and residents, often at the patient's bedside. The goal of these "medical rounds" is to have others benefit from the experiences of the presenters to learn diagnostic tools and treatment approaches that may not be presented in their specific patient cases.

Although law clinic rounds take place out of the presence of clients, they serve a similar purpose. You will have the opportunity to learn from the experiences of other student attorneys in the clinic and to brainstorm and provide insights to others handling cases. You will also learn how to present your cases to others in a focused and accessible way—a skill that you will use in court and in dealing with adversaries.

5. Seminar

Many clinic courses also offer a seminar to accompany your casework, a seminar that may not look too different from other seminar courses you have taken in law school. This seminar gives you the chance to learn some basic skills and values through a combination of lectures, discussions, and exercises before you begin and while you are providing real-life client representation. The seminar provides a vehicle for the transmission of the skills and values that you can apply in your real-life cases.

6. Simulations

Many clinic courses also offer opportunities to engage in simulations. Simulations are exercises in which lawyering skills and values are developed and applied in a fictional factual context. These exercises are ordinarily based on real-life cases. However, because the exercises are artificial and because the interests of real-life clients are not at stake, you can be given wide latitude in the exercises and you can take risks and try techniques and styles of lawyering that you would not undertake with real-life client interests at stake.

Simulations are no substitute for live-client experiences. However, they offer benefits that make them a useful part of your clinical experience. Because simulated cases have controlled facts, simulations provide a uniformity of experience for all students in the class. Moreover, because real-life cases do not always develop in an orderly, controlled manner, simulations provide an opportunity for you to deal with discrete issues in a progressively more complex way. Videotape can also be used in simulations to allow you and your supervisor to critique your work in the simulated setting without disturbing the real-life lawyer-client relationship. Often these critiques are preceded by written self-evaluations.

Admittedly, simulations lack the factual complexity and uncertainty of real cases. Furthermore, it is hard to become emotionally involved or as motivated in simulation settings as in real-life. However, you will find that the more you can invest in the simulations and the learning opportunities they represent, the more you will gain from the opportunities presented.

C. Role of the Clients

Seminars, rounds, simulations, supervision. All of these methodologies are important parts of clinical education. However, no clinical methodology rivals in importance the role of clients and your work within the attorney-client relationship.

Professor Ann Shalleck described this phenomenon in her article, "Constructions of the Client in Legal Education."

> [T]he [clinical] model is based on a deeply contextualized understanding of who clients are and why they are significant. Students no longer see clients as abstract people with predetermined traits; rather, they see clients as unique individuals with particular characteristics situated within the real world.

Professor Shalleck went on to emphasize:

> [However,] [l]ive client clinics only present an opportunity, albeit a powerful one because of the immediacy and force of human relationships, to undermine the constructed client, as well as to develop and teach new methods for understanding and working with clients.

So, in clinic we will begin to undo the prevailing message of so much of law school—that cases are decided on "the law" and that clients can be reduced to a few "facts" excerpted in appellate decisions. Indeed, we will team the critical importance of clients and their stories in the resolution of client problems. And, we will learn how to develop and present our client stories in the most effective ways to achieve our client goals.

D. Efficiency

Finally, as is probably evident to you from the various components that make up clinical methodology, clinic is a fairly expensive and labor-intensive form of legal education. However, these costs are incurred and these faculty resources are committed because there are many things that students can only learn in a clinical environment and other things that students can learn so much better in a clinical setting that the costs and resource allocations are easily justified.

Whereas efficiency is a necessary part of law practice, it is not a value within the clinical context.

* * *

If efficiency in representation were important, all of the representation would be provided by clinical supervisors—lawyers with experience in the areas in which the clients are seeking legal assistance. Instead, the focus in clinic is on ensuring professional competency while advancing educational objectives. This means giving you the space to find your own answers and, more important, your own questions.

E. Being Vulnerable

Many people get the message during law school that it is unwise to share weaknesses, that one must simply "tough it out." In any academic year, it is likely that the parent of a clinic student will get sick, that the romantic relationship of a clinic student will self-destruct, that the health of a clinic student may be impaired, that personal issues may intrude on the ability of a clinic student to fulfill his/her responsibilities. Whatever your feelings about being vulnerable generally, clinic is not a place to try to "tough it out."

Share information with your supervisor. While your supervisor will not be able to achieve miracles and certainly will not be able to make everything "right," s/he may be able to help you process the events intruding on your personal and professional lives. S/he may also be able to help take some of the pressure off you by arranging coverage for some of your work on behalf of clients or by addressing other needs. Without information about the need to compensate for these intervening events, it will be impossible for your supervisor to help you work through this.

F. Trying It Out

As one student wrote at the end of her clinical practice, "I experienced virtually every emotion possible in my work (happiness, sadness, frustration, anxiety, elation, sorrow, nervousness, apathy, elation . . . the list goes on)." That comment is fairly typical for the range of feelings that most students experience. Boredom is seldom a part of clinical education.

Your time in clinic will be relatively brief and you will want to learn as much as you possibly can about yourself and about the process of lawyering. To maximize the benefits, engage the various teaching methodologies throughout your clinical experience. At the same time, critically examine the various approaches to lawyering discussed. The more enthusiastically you invest in the clinical model and the less defensively you engage in the process of self-evaluation and self-criticism, the more you will gain from the experience. For most of you, this clinic course will be your only chance to "lawyer" with the support, oversight, and insights of a trained clinical supervisor. Make the most of this opportunity!

CHAPTER 2

CLIENT COUNSELING

LEARNING GOALS

The learning goals for this class include helping you to:

- Recognize that lawyers not only advance and serve their clients' interests, but also advise and counsel them
- Explore different roles a lawyer might play in the client counseling process, and assess the merits and drawbacks of each
- Explore the various ways in which a client might participate in the counseling process, and assess the merits and drawbacks of various possibilities
- Understand that a client's legal issues exist within a broader, extra-legal context, about which the client generally has greater knowledge
- Understand that the particular context of a client's life, in terms of values, relationships, etc., may profoundly affect that client's preferences regarding legal solutions
- Understand that a client's decision must be made against the background of the law and the legal system, about which the lawyer generally has greater knowledge

---

DESCRIPTION OF CLASS

In this class, we will explore an approach to lawyering that has been dubbed "client-centered" counseling. We will consider the ways in which differences in individual values, needs, backgrounds, and goals affect client decision making, and the hazards of assuming that a lawyer knows the best outcomc for any particular client. We also will explore the various ways in which a lawyer can be respectful of a client's individual goals and values, while still adding substantial value, expertise, and wise counsel in the course of representation.

ASSIGNMENT IN PREPARATION FOR CLASS

Draft and submit a memorandum in response to the following assignment:

> Think of a time when you were dealing with a difficult problem and you sought advice from someone you considered knowledgeable about this issue. The context is not important—it could be a health issue, a friendship/family/relationship issue, or anything else. What is important here is that you asked for and received advice from someone whom you considered an "expert" on the topic at hand.
>
> Note your responses to the questions below:
>
> - Putting aside the specific course of action the advice-giver recommended (if any), what was the most helpful thing that person said or did?
>   - Why was it helpful?
> - What was the least helpful thing the advice-giver said or did?
>   - Why was it unhelpful?
> - Did the advice-giver fully understand the specifics of the difficulty you were facing?
>   - If so, how did that understanding affect the quality of their advice?
>   - If not, how did that lack of understanding affect the quality of their advice?
> - Did the advice-giver fully understand your personal goals in the situation under discussion?
>   - If so, how did that understanding affect the quality of their advice?
>   - If not, how did that lack of understanding affect the quality of their advice?
> - Would you seek advice from that person again?
>   - Why or why not?

READING ASSIGNMENT

1. David A. Binder, Paul Berman, Susan C. Price, & Paul R. Tremblay, *Principles Underlying Effective Counseling, in* LAWYERS AS COUNSELORS: A CLIENT-CENTERED APPROACH 270 (2d ed. 2004).
2. Edward A. Dauer, *Hurting Clients, in* THE AFFECTIVE ASSISTANCE OF COUNSEL 317 (Marjorie A. Silver ed., 2007).
3. Peter De Jong & Scott D. Miller, *How to Interview for Client Strengths*, 40 SOC. WORK 729 (1995).

READINGS

David A. Binder, Paul Berman, Susan C. Price, & Paul R. Tremblay *Principles Underlying Effective Counseling* LAWYERS AS COUNSELORS: A CLIENT-CENTERED APPROACH (2d ed., 2004)[1]

* * *

From what you tell me, Mr. Rodale, your objective is to get DataCo's auditing department operating efficiently as quickly as possible. Is that right?

Exactly. We've got to decide quickly whether it makes sense to let Ms. Jensen go as soon as possible.

Well, from what you've said, it seems clear that DataCo has every legal right to terminate Ms. Jensen. She has repeatedly ignored warnings about getting her work done on time and, given the problems that her repeated tardiness has caused, there is certainly good reason to fire her. What you need to do, however, is determine whether you want to go ahead and terminate her or whether you want to follow some other course of action, such as suspending her or having her agree to resign in exchange for some kind of a severance package. From what you said so far, it does not appear as though the decision is going to be an easy one. Terminating Ms. Jensen seems to have a number of possible downsides attached to it, such as lowering morale in the audit division. Am I correct?

Yes; that will certainly be one result.

Well, in that light, what I think we should do is to try to take a look at each of your options and try to figure out which one, on balance, will

---

[1] Footnotes and/or internal citations omitted.

probably best accomplish your overall objective. Why don't we start by focusing on outright termination?

* * *

Ms. Biggs, has our discussion given you a picture of what options the partnership could follow in setting up a bank account and the pros and cons of each?

Yes, but I'm somewhat conflicted. On the one hand, I want to make sure that once the partnership is going David won't be able to make bank withdrawals of more than $3500. On the other hand, I can see that asking for this kind of protective provision in our written agreement may really poison the negotiations and our future relationship. What do you think I should do?

* * *

1. INTRODUCTION

Numerous decisions usually have to be made as clients' matters move toward resolution. A decision may involve ultimate resolution of a client's principal problem: Should a settlement offer be accepted? Should a contract be signed, despite its failure to include an exclusive dealing provision? Often, however, decisions involve subsidiary considerations: Should discovery be undertaken immediately? Should the draft of a proposed agreement include an arbitration clause? Who should prepare the draft—you or the other party?

This chapter explores issues that arise when you counsel and advise clients with respect to both ultimate and intermediate decisions. Those issues include:

a. Who, as between you and clients, should generally have the final say?

b. What decisions regarding the handling of a matter should you explore with clients?

c. With respect to decisions that require client consultation,

    1. What information should you elicit from clients before decisions are made?

    2. What information should you make available to clients before decisions are made?

    3. When should you provide opinions as to what decision should be made?

    4. What criteria should you use in arriving at opinions as to what decision should be made?

5. Are you responsible for ensuring that clients fully understand the ramifications of their decisions?
6. Under what circumstances might you suggest that clients' decisions are wrong?

These are the questions that are central to your understanding of counseling, the process by which you help clients decide what courses of action to adopt in order to resolve problems. This chapter describes the essential client-centered principles that govern that process.

2. CLIENTS ARE PRIMARY DECISION-MAKERS

A central tenet of client-centeredness is that you should generally afford clients the opportunity to make decisions. Clients should have primary decision-making power in part because of the simple truth that *problems are theirs, not yours.* After all, clients and not you have to live with decisions' immediate and long term consequences. For example, deciding to take depositions may result in a client, not you, expending thousands of dollars. Similarly, clients will receive the benefits or suffer the losses attendant to decisions to hire an expert, leave an arbitration clause out of an agreement, or accept a settlement offer. Given that clients bear the brunt of decisions' consequences, clients presumptively should have the opportunity to determine what courses of action to take.

A second reason for clients having primary decision-making power is that decisions should be made on the basis of what choices are most likely to *provide clients with maximum satisfaction.* Presumptively, clients are better able than you to assess which potential decisions are most likely to prove satisfactory. For one thing . . ., resolving problems typically requires consideration of nonlegal consequences, as to which clients are likely to possess more expertise than you. Moreover, even if both you and a client agree precisely on a decision's likely consequences, you and a client will not necessarily weigh those consequences equally in making the decision. The relative importance of decisions' consequences depends largely on values that often vary from one person to another, and autonomy notions assign primary importance to clients' values.

The following example illustrates the interplay between decisions and subjective personal values. Assume that you represent Stephanie Kimmel, who has sued Badger Outlets for wrongful termination of employment. The case has been pending for over a year, and Badger has made a settlement offer of $35,000. So far as the legal consequences go, your opinion is that if the case were to proceed to trial, Kimmel would be likely to recover at least $65,000. At the same time, trial is still six months away, and there is a small chance, perhaps 20%, that at trial Kimmel will recover nothing. Should she accept the offer?

Your personal opinion may be that Kimmel should accept the offer. From your legal, "objective" standpoint, accepting the offer makes sense because Kimmel gets money at once that she needs, and she avoids the risk of losing altogether. However, *Kimmel* may assess the likely consequences differently. For example, she may attach little value to the offer because $35,000 would not allow her to improve her life style substantially. Moreover, non-legal consequences may be of equal or greater concern to Kimmel. For example, Kimmel may decide to reject the offer because she is angry and wants to air her grievances in a public courtroom, even at the risk of losing. Kimmel's state of mind might also be a relevant factor. For instance, if the pendency of the case makes her anxious and restless, she may choose to settle to gain peace of mind. Whatever Kimmel's bottom line, she like all clients may value likely consequences differently than do you, and therefore should have the opportunity to make the decision.

Clients' subjective assessments of likely consequences lie at the heart of determining maximum client satisfaction in transactional matters as well. Assume that you represent George Martino, the owner of several shopping centers, including a new mid-sized center. On Martino's behalf, you are negotiating a proposed lease with SafeBet Markets. Under the lease, SafeBet would become an anchor tenant in the new center. Per Martino's instructions, during negotiations with SafeBet you have repeatedly asked SafeBet's lawyer to agree to a lease provision obligating SafeBet to pay a pro-rata share of the maintenance costs for the upkeep of the center's common areas. Such a provision is typical in commercial leases in your area. During a prior negotiating session, SafeBet's lawyer told you that a common areas clause is unacceptable to SafeBet. Tomorrow you are scheduled to have your final negotiation meeting with SafeBet's lawyer. In your opinion, there is only a small possibility that SafeBet will accede to the common areas provision. The decision to be made is whether or not to continue to insist on that provision.

One likely consequence of continued insistence on the provision is that SafeBet will break off negotiations, and as a result Martino will not acquire income from the lease. How important is it to Martino to obtain rent? If immediate additional income is important, or if Safebet's tenancy will encourage other potential tenants to lease space, the alternative of dropping the common areas clause will seem attractive.

However, if Martino's dropping the demand for a common areas provision becomes generally known, his bargaining position in future lease deals might be harmed. Future potential tenants might assume that if Martino did not require a common areas provision in a lease with SafeBet, he probably is in some way desperate for tenants. As a consequence, such tenants might be more willing to push Martino for concessions, making future lease negotiations difficult. How important is it to Martino to avoid this risk? If he believes that the absence of such a clause in SafeBet's lease will become generally known and therefore influence future deals, Martino may conclude that maintaining the demand is of great importance.

While Martino might have to evaluate many other potential consequences before making a final decision about whether to drop the demand for a common areas provision, what should be clear is that an assessment of what choice is likely to produce maximum satisfaction for Martino requires Martino's subjective evaluation of the importance of the decision's likely ramifications.

Thus, in neither litigation nor transactional matters can you determine what decisions are likely to lead to maximum client satisfaction through reference to external standards or your own values. Sensible choices about important decisions should take account of decisions' likely economic, social, psychological and moral ramifications *and* their relative importance. While you may help clients identify decisions' likely ramifications, only clients can determine their relative importance.

As the above examples also suggest, the subjective factor of "risk aversion" often has a substantial impact on clients' decisions. This point was made succinctly nearly three centuries ago:

> Price and probability are not enough in determining what something is worth. Although the facts are the same for everyone, 'the utility ... is dependent on the particular circumstances of the person making the estimate. . . . There is no reason to assume that ... the risks anticipated by each [individual] must be deemed equal in value.' To each his own.

Thus, when choosing a course of action, neither you nor a client can do more than predict *likely* consequences. Every decision entails a risk that predicted consequences may not occur. So, if Martino abandons the common areas provision, it does not follow automatically that SafeBet will sign the lease; or that if the lease is signed, Martino will receive the projected net income; or that Martino's future negotiating position will be damaged if he decides not to insist on the provision with SafeBet. These consequences are, to paraphrase Charles Dickens' *A Christmas Carol,* shadows of what *may* be, not what *will* be. Hence, by conceding to SafeBet, Martino indicates a willingness to risk a weakened bargaining position with future tenants. A different Martino, aware of precisely the same potential consequence, might not be willing to take this risk, and as a result might not concede to SafeBet. The fact that two clients can make the same predictions about consequences, yet make different decisions depending on their willingness to run risks, is a strong factor in favor of clients being the primary decision-makers.

Moreover, even if you could become fully conversant with clients' value and preference structures, you perhaps ought not be trusted to make important decisions because of potential conflicts of interest. When it comes time to make decisions, your interests and those of a client frequently are adverse. For instance, in making decisions about what provisions to include in a deal, lawyers often want to include a great many more contingency provisions than do clients. Lawyers often want clients to agree to contingency provisions not only to protect the clients but also to make sure that if a contingency ultimately does arise, the lawyer cannot be sued for malpractice. Clients on the other hand are often more interested in making deals than in being fully protected if an agreement should ultimately break down. Clients often predict that insistence on a contingency provision may kill the deal and they are therefore willing to drop the provision and take the risk that the contingency will not arise.

That lawyers and clients often have conflicting interests suggests once again that decisions ought to remain in a client's hands. Even if you could determine a client's values and preferences, the temptation to decide the matter in a way that advances your personal interests is reason to allow a client to make the ultimate choice.

3. A STANDARD FOR CLIENT DECISIONMAKING: "SUBSTANTIAL LEGAL OR NON-LEGAL IMPACTS"

An emphasis on clients as primary decision-makers may suggest that clients should have the opportunity to make each and every decision. Some commentators, in fact, have urged such a position.

However, a "client makes all decisions" position is unworkable and, in fact, inconsistent with client-centeredness. If clients were to make all decisions, you would have to inform them of each time a decision were necessary and engage them in discussions of potential options and consequences. As even simple matters may require scores of decisions (including such seemingly picayune matters as whether to send documents by regular or overnight mail), total client decision-making would force you to be in nearly continuous communication with clients. Undoubtedly, most clients would not have the time, the desire or the financial resources to hire you under these conditions. And even if they did, you would undoubtedly soon regard practicing law under such conditions as a sentence to a career of virtually continuous communication with a small number of clients.

Moreover, insistence on client consultation on each decision would deprive clients of the option of leaving certain decisions to the lawyer. As a consequence, such insistence would be inconsistent with client-centered decision making.

If consultation about every decision is unacceptable, how might you decide what decisions to call to clients' attention, and which to make on your own? In the past, some authorities attempted to draw a distinction between matters' "substantive" and "procedural" aspects. They suggested that lawyers should review with clients' decisions affecting the objectives of representation, but need not do so with respect to decisions that only affect the means by which the objectives are secured. Some courts continue to echo this ends-means distinction.

However, in practice a distinction based on means-end reasoning is unworkable. One reason is that decisions about "means" may be so important that most clients would reasonably expect to make them. For example, the economic consequences attached to a decision about whether to pursue discovery vigorously or cautiously may be so large that a client should be the one to make it.

Moreover, what you regard as a "means" may for a client be an "end." Assume for instance that you represent a client charged with burglary, and a decision arises about whether or not to call the client's sister as an alibi witness. You believe that the sister will make an excellent and helpful witness, but the client insists that she not be called because in the client's view testifying will cause the sister undue stress. For you, the decision involves a means to an end, but for the client not calling the sister as a witness is itself an objective. Because personal values can so often affect a conclusion about whether decisions involve ends or means, the distinction will often be of little help to your thinking about whether decisions are for you or clients to make.

Asking clients early on to indicate what kinds of decisions they want to be consulted about is a potential approach to the issue of when you need to consult clients. However, this "informed consent" approach too is typically inadequate. For one thing, you cannot expect meaningful advanced directives from inexperienced clients. Such clients cannot realistically anticipate which upcoming choices will warrant consultation and input and which will not.

Moreover, except in the most routine of matters, advance directives are unlikely to be workable even with experienced clients. Changes in clients' circumstances, unanticipated reactions from adversaries and the difficulty of predicting in advance what categories of decisions will be appropriate for client decision-making are among the factors that detract from the viability of the informed consent approach.

A better approach to the question of when to involve clients in decision-making is to acknowledge explicitly that "bright line" approaches represented by the "ends-means" and "informed consent" tests simply are inadequate guidelines. In their place is what you may call the "substantial impact" standard. If this standard lacks the comfort of bright line approaches, it is a realistic one that honors the values of client-centeredness while providing "safe harbors" for appropriate lawyer decision-making. Explicitly stated, the "reasonable lawyer" standard is as follows:

> Lawyers should provide clients with the opportunity to make decisions whenever a reasonably prudent and diligent lawyer would or should know that a pending decision is likely to have a *substantial legal or non-legal impact, on clients.*

The "substantial impact" standard requires that you comport with professional norms with respect to decision-making. For example, you need to be aware of and comply with ethical rules governing decision-making. Similarly, you should be familiar with the kinds of decisions that competent lawyers generally afford clients the opportunity to make. In that regard, the "substantial impact" standard probably reflects the behavior of most practicing lawyers. That is, undoubtedly most practitioners do afford clients the opportunity to make decisions that are likely to substantially affect clients' legal or non-legal concerns. For example, litigators often consult clients about such matters as granting continuances, filing motions, taking depositions, and pursuing negotiation strategy. Indeed, a lawyer might even consult a client as to the wisdom of asking a question on cross examination in circumstances where the impact of a critical admission might be undercut by an explanation, and the lawyer believes that the client may know whether the witness will give that explanation. Likewise, when substantial impact decisions arise in transactional matters, lawyers commonly discuss with clients such issues as whether to ask corporate officers to personally guarantee payments that the corporation will be obligated to make under the terms of proposed deals, whether a seller of a factory will agree to clean up environmental contamination prior to closing, and which of various options for restructuring companies' debts best suit their needs.

The "substantial impact" standard also requires consideration of what you know about individual clients. That is, you may know from prior dealings or conversations that a decision that would not have a substantial impact on most clients will substantially affect a particular client. If so, the standard requires that you afford that client an opportunity to make the decision. The reverse is also true; prior dealings with a client may allow you to make decisions with respect to matters that have substantial impacts, even though the standard would in most circumstances require consultation. For example, if a client has authorized you to use your discretion with respect to how many depositions to take, you may not need to consult the client each time you notice a deposition unless you have reason to think that the client may want to reconsider the earlier authorization.

Like any norm grounded in reasonableness rather than bright-line rules, the "reasonable lawyer" standard cannot claim to offer a simple calculus neatly resolving all decision-making issues. Rather, the standard leaves room for practical decision-making. This should hardly be surprising; much about the practice of law calls for you to exercise practical judgment of the type set forth in the standard. Moreover, the standard is client-centered. It focuses on the likely impacts on individual clients, rather than on fuzzy distinctions between "ends" and "means."

For an example of how you might apply the "substantial impact" standard in practice, assume that you represent Gower "Tower of Power" Bower, a financially independent professional basketball player nearing the end of his career with the Smeltics. Gower is in the "option" (last) year of his current contract; you are negotiating an extension with the Smeltics. Gower's primary goal is a three year contract that would allow him to continue to receive his salary for three years even if he were injured or let go. (The Smeltics, he knows, have a history of not resigning former stars to save money once they are somewhat past their prime.) Gower would like a raise in his $1,800,000 per year salary, but is willing to forgo an increase in favor of a three-year deal. He is anxious to conclude the negotiations as quickly as possible, since a career-ending injury is always a possibility.

Early in the negotiations, the Smeltics' attorney asks that Gower consent to a thorough physical examination. Should you or Gower make this auxiliary decision? The standard allocates the decision to Gower if its consequences are likely to have a substantial impact on him. Here, the outcome of the physical might well determine whether the team makes a multiyear offer. Thus the decision is likely to have a substantial impact, and the decision is one for Gower to have the opportunity to make.

The Smeltics' attorney next reminds you that the team's usual policy is not to negotiate in midseason. However, the team is willing to negotiate with Gower if a new contract can be signed within two weeks. You understand that if Gower does sign quickly, he will probably not be eligible to benefit financially from royalties from a cable TV contract that you expect the Smeltics to conclude after the season concludes. If he were to sign a new contract *after* the Smeltics signed a cable TV contract, Tower would probably receive a salary bonus in the range of $50,000 to $75,000. The standard would probably permit you to decide whether to open negotiations immediately. Given that a three year deal is worth at least $3.6 million more than a one year deal, the decision is not likely to have a substantial impact on him.

Analyzing the likely impact of a decision in light of Gower's actual situation and his preferences, rather than using vague distinctions such as "ends" and "means," seems to be the best way to allocate decisionmaking responsibility. And, since it looks to the likely impact on clients, the standard comfortably satisfies rules governing your duty to allow clients to make decisions.

4. THE "SUBSTANTIAL IMPACT" STANDARD AND LAWYERING TACTICS

This section considers the issue of whether the substantial impact standard may unduly interfere with your exercise of professional judgment about tactics. For example, if a decision to pursue a certain line of questioning on cross examination is likely to have a substantial impact, are you therefore obligated to consult the client regarding cross examination questioning strategy?

Most clients, recognizing their own lack of expertise, undoubtedly assume that you will make such decisions and do not expect to be consulted about them. Think, by analogy, of the look you'd give a plumber who asked you what size pipe fitting you thought should be used under your bathroom sink. The customer's act of hiring the plumber signals the customer's desire for the plumber to make those decisions which are in the plumber's traditional domain. Similarly, a client's decision to hire you is tacit willingness for you to make lawyering tactics decisions free from consultation. Thus, such matters as how you cross examine, write briefs, or phrase contingency clauses are generally for you alone to decide, even though they may have a substantial impact. They involve primarily the exercise of the skills and crafts that are the special domain of lawyers.

However, "lawyering tactics" are often not a sufficient excuse for failure to consult clients. When decisions are likely to have an influence beyond that normally associated with the exercise of lawyering skills and crafts, the "substantial impact" standard requires that you consult with a client. For example, consider these situations:

(a) A witness you are considering calling on behalf of your client is the client's boss.

(b) You are considering phrasing a contingency clause in a purposely vague manner because you do not think the other party will agree to the precise language your client desires, and the vague wording may at a future date be interpreted in your client's favor.

(c) You are considering whether to remove an action from state to federal court.

(d) You are considering whether to defend an action vigorously, as opposed to passively countering the plaintiff's moves.

You probably should consult the client in each of these situations. The decisions carry effects beyond those normally associated with the use of professional skills and crafts.

Thus, in (a), developing a case-in-chief may usually be a matter entirely for your professional judgment. But calling a client's boss raises sensitive issues beyond those normally associated with direct examination. Hence, the need for client consultation.

Similarly, in (b), the question of how to phrase the contingency clause is not simply one of professional craft, but of risk aversion and of a client's willingness to live with uncertainty. That decision too does not involve primarily the craft of legal writing, but may have a substantial impact on the client's position in the event the contingency arises. Hence, the need for consultation.

In (c), whether an action is tried in state or federal court is likely to have many effects, such as what evidentiary rules apply, what the composition of the jury may be, and when the action may come to trial. Again, even though the decision rests in part on the exercise of professional judgment, the potential impacts suggest the need for client consultation.

Finally in (d), costs to a client may be very different depending on how vigorously a suit is defended. Costs of course are the type of impact which very much suggest the need for client consultation.

Again, determining the impact of the exercise of professional skills and craft maybe difficult. However, leaving all decisions that may be characterized as involving lawyering tactics in attorneys' hands alone is inconsistent with client-centeredness. As the four examples above demonstrate, many lawyering tactics decisions require client consultation.

5. YOUR ROLE IN THE COUNSELING AND ADVISING PROCESS

This section provides an overview of the counseling process, the process through which you and clients sort through possibilities and arrive at decisions. . . . The remainder of this chapter summarizes the major components of the counseling process:

- Exploring alternative courses of action and their likely consequences. Consideration of alternatives and their likely consequences allows clients to make informed decisions about which choice is most likely to provide maximum satisfaction. So far as reasonably possible, your role includes assisting clients to evaluate alternatives and likely consequences free from distorting biases.

- When appropriate, providing advice as to the choices you believe to be in clients' best interests and the reasons you think that those choices will maximize client satisfaction. The advice-giving function may also include intervening in clients' decisions with which you disagree.

A. EXPLORE ALTERNATIVES AND CONSEQUENCES

By definition, every decision encompasses at least two possible choices. For example, a decision as to whether to accept a settlement offer encompasses at least "accept" and "don't accept." Of course, many important decisions may encompass more than two choices. The choices when a client has to respond to a settlement offer, for example, may include (a) accept, (b) don't accept but make a counter-offer, and (c) don't accept and don't make a counter-offer. When they have the opportunity to make decisions, your obligation is to make clients aware of reasonable alternatives and the likely consequences of each possible choice.

When courts and professional bodies such as the American Bar Association refer to lawyers' legal obligations with respect to counseling, they speak principally in terms of disclosure of information that lawyers (experts) must provide to clients (non-experts). However, clients generally have a reasonable opportunity to make decisions only if you elicit information from them as well as provide it to them. Succinctly stated, counseling must typically be a two-way street.

1. *Information to Elicit from Clients*

The subsections below set forth the types of information you typically try to elicit from clients during counseling discussions.

a. Clients' Objectives

The best measure of decisions' quality is the extent to which they satisfy your clients' objectives. Thus, clients should evaluate alternatives in the context of relevant objectives. To the extent that those objectives are not already "on the table," you may want to clarify them at the outset of counseling discussions. For example, you might start off a discussion with a comment such as, "It's been awhile since we talked about what kind of business relationship you hope to have with the defendant after this case is over. Can you give me your current thinking on this before deciding whether to pursue discovery aggressively?"

b. Potential Solutions

Ask clients for their thoughts about potential solutions. Clients may well be able to identify workable alternatives that would not occur to you, in part because clients may have "industry experience" that you lack and because clients' proposals often reflect their unique non-legal concerns. Even if clients' proposals aren't fully workable from a legal standpoint, you often can combine aspects of their proposals with your ideas to end up with more satisfactory solutions. Thus, during counseling sessions you may often ask questions such as, "What possible lease terms do you have in mind?"

c. Potential Consequences

What is true for alternatives is also typically accurate for consequences—clients' experiences and non-legal concerns may enable them to anticipate consequences that you would have overlooked. Thus, whether you or clients identify alternatives, you should generally ask questions such as, "What do you see as the likely effects of including an insurance-funded buyout provision in the partnership agreement?"

d. Bases for Clients' Predictions

Assertions about likely consequences typically rest on predictions. For example, consider this brief exchange:

L: What do you see as the likely consequences of asking Johnson for a personal loan guarantee?

C: I think that Johnson will walk away from the deal if we even propose that.

Here, the client's perceived consequence is a prediction about Johnson's behavior. And the accuracy of predictions such as these can be a factor that clients may need to consider before making decisions. To help clients evaluate predictions' accuracy, you may ask clients to indicate the bases of their predictions. For instance, you might ask the client above, "What is your basis for saying that Johnson will walk away from the deal if we ask for a personal guarantee?" The prediction may be based on the client's past dealings with Johnson or other similarly strong indicators of Johnson's likely reaction, or it may be based on little more than a hunch or on what the client has heard about how others have reacted to similar requests. Clients' predictions may also be distorted by persistent psychological habits known as "heuristics and biases" that researchers often refer to as "psychological traps" or "cognitive illusions." Thus, by ferreting out clients' bases for predicting consequences, you can help them make more informed and hopefully more satisfactory decisions."

e. Questions and Concerns

Finally, remind clients that you welcome questions and want to know about any concerns relevant to the alternatives and consequences. Encouraging clients to raise current concerns and questions increases the likelihood of arriving at satisfactory problem resolutions.

2. *Information to Provide to Clients*

Since counseling is a two way street, here are essential topics that you typically communicate to clients.

a. *Potential Solutions*

Suggesting alternatives is often your most important counseling role. In many situations you are likely to be aware of sensible alternatives that clients would have neither the legal experience nor knowledge to know about. For example, in a litigation matter you may suggest pursuing injunctive relief or punitive damages, potential solutions of which a client may be unaware. And in a business transaction, you might know of tax reasons for structuring a deal in one form rather than another.

Often, alternatives that you suggest do not simply grow out of your knowledge of "the law." Rather, you also draw upon your professional experience, awareness of human behavior and "industry knowledge." For example, you may through your practice with real estate matters be able to offer for a client's consideration various rent-fixing formulas that are used in connection with the leasing of commercial buildings. Similarly, your experience in the criminal justice system may allow you to propose a diversion alternative that, by including a particular type of community service, permits a client to avoid a jail sentence.

Finally, your ability to identify additional solutions may simply be a product not of greater knowledge, but of greater emotional distance from a problem.

b. *Potential Consequences*

Identifying consequences (both legal and to the extent you can predict, non-legal as well) goes hand-in-hand with identifying alternatives. In other words, at appropriate points in counseling discussions you talk to clients about what you view as options' likely consequences. For example, if you suggest the possibility of naming a corporate trustee to a client for whom you are drafting an inter vivos trust, you might either at the same time or later in the conversation advise the client that corporate trustees charge fees while individual trustees who are a testator's personal friend often do not, and that a court is likely to hold a corporate trustee to a higher standard of care than an individual trustee (legal consequences). You might also mention that trust beneficiaries often have difficulty convincing corporate trustees to exercise discretion, compared to individual trustees who know the trust beneficiaries personally (a non-legal consequence).

c. *Advice*

Providing advice about decisions that clients ought to make is a traditional counseling role for attorneys. Advice-giving can be consistent with a client-centered approach, so long as it is preceded by a counseling process that affords clients a reasonable opportunity to consider alternatives and consequences.

B. PROVIDE AN OPPORTUNITY TO EVALUATE OPTIONS AND CONSEQUENCES

At bottom, counseling is the process of identifying and evaluating options and likely alternatives. Of course, counseling is a fluid process that may vary greatly in its particulars from one client to another. For example, one client may want to have all reasonable options "on the table" before evaluating any of them, while another client, may prefer to focus first on a single option and move on to others only if evaluation suggests that others may be more satisfactory. As you know, which solutions are "best" often rest largely on subjective factors unique to each client. Value preferences, degree of risk aversion, and beliefs about which consequences are most important are some factors that you may help clients think through before choosing a "best" solution.

For example, in the Gower-Smeltics matter, assume that two of the options that Gower and you have identified are opening negotiations immediately on a three-year contract at the same salary and forgoing negotiations until after the basketball season concludes. Assume further that among the likely consequences identified by you and Gower are the following: if Gower waits until after the season to negotiate a contract, "plus" consequences include the possibility that as a free agent open to competitive bidding from different teams, he will be offered an increased salary, and enhanced post-career opportunities resulting from the added publicity the competitive negotiations produce. On the "down" side, delay in signing a new contract subjects Gower to the risk that an injury will reduce or end his career before he can sign a new contract, and may hurt his post-career opportunities if the delay suggests that he is disloyal to the team and its fans.

During the process of evaluating the options, you need to afford Gower the opportunity to weigh the likely consequences. Which consequences seem most likely to occur, and which are most important to Gower? How risk averse is Gower? What are his personal values on the questions of franchise loyalty, his family's financial security, standing up to the team ownership, and the like? Only through engaging in a process by which he has an opportunity to compare and assess such factors can Gower make a decision that is most likely to satisfy him and his family.

C. AFFORD CLIENTS A REASONABLE OPPORTUNITY TO EVALUATE ALTERNATIVES AND CONSEQUENCES

How far does the obligation to discuss alternatives and consequences with clients extend? This question covers at least two issues. First, should you counsel clients with respect to every conceivable alternative and consequence? Second, how much understanding of alternatives and consequences should clients possess for you to have provided adequate counseling?

Answers to these questions ultimately rest on professional judgment in the context of individual clients and their problems. In general, however, the following standard articulates the extent of your counseling obligation:

> In your role as a counselor, provide clients with a reasonable opportunity to understand and evaluate those alternatives and consequences that similarly-situated clients would consider pivotal to the decision at hand. Consider what this standard entails.

1. *"Pivotal Alternatives and Consequences"*

Limiting your obligation to identifying and evaluating "pivotal" alternatives and consequences recognizes that it is virtually impossible to cxplore all possible alternatives and likely consequences. "Pivotal" alternatives and consequences are those that might alter or change clients' decisions, and are reasonably foreseeable or likely to occur.

For example, assume that a client based in the United States is negotiating a purchase of knives from a Chinese manufacturer, and that the manufacturer insists on payment upon delivery of the knives to a carrier in Shanghai. The client is willing to agree to this arrangement provided a way can be found to inspect the goods before they are shipped. However, the client has no offices in China and knows no one in China who could inspect the goods on the client's behalf. Accordingly, the client is considering abandoning the deal. An opportunity to have the goods inspected by a reputable Chinese inspection company would obviously be a "pivotal option" because it would make or break the client's decision to go ahead with the deal and is an alternative that most clients would probably want to consider. By contrast, the option of arranging for the client to play every state lottery game every day until the client wins enough money to pay for a private inspector to fly to China would not make the cut, based on your judgment that such an option is just plain silly.

2. *"Similarly-Situated Clients"*

The extent of your counseling obligation is measured not by a mythical "average" or "reasonable" client. Rather, your obligation is to make clients aware of the alternatives and consequences that "reasonable and similarly-situated" clients would want to know about. In other words, how extensively you counsel depends on such factors as:

- the economic or psychological significance of a decision;
- the probable importance of a decision to a matter's outcome;
- a client's experience, knowledge, personal values and concerns;
- a client's cultural identity, which may produce alternatives and consequences that are pivotal primarily for people who share that cultural identity.

Of course, each client is not a "tabula rasa." Your judgment about what alternatives or consequences are pivotal to a particular client will necessarily and legitimately be influenced by your past experiences with comparable clients.

3. "Reasonable Opportunity to Understand and Evaluate"

Since clients' actual levels of understanding are beyond your ken, the standard refers to the process that should precede decision-making. Your counseling responsibility is to afford clients a reasonable opportunity to *understand* and to *evaluate* options. Pursuant to this standard, you provide adequate counseling even if you cannot be fully certain that clients have fully understood and evaluated their options. So long as you have offered them a reasonable opportunity to do so, you have satisfied your obligations as a professional counselor. The prevailing ethical and doctrinal authority is consistent with this conception.

The primary justifications for a process standard rather than one based on clients' actual awareness is that the latter is frequently impossible to gauge accurately or even to attain at all. For instance, assume that you represent Garvey, a homeowner who purchased defective kitchen cabinets from the Highs Big Box Home Improvement Store. When his dispute with Highs failed to resolve informally, you filed suit to recover the cost of his cabinets and of the contractor's time required to remedy the defects. As trial approaches, Highs makes a settlement offer that you explore thoroughly with Garvey. You explain that the settlement offer is probably at least as good an outcome as Garvey is likely to obtain through a trial. Aware of the tensions that the dispute has created for Garvey and his family, you also advise Garvey that a likely consequence of refusing the offer and going to trial is that the trial will greatly exacerbate those tensions. Garvey participates in the counseling discussions and has no trouble understanding what you have said. Nevertheless, Garvey persists in what you consider an unsupportable belief that a jury will find Highs' conduct, to be outrageous and award him far more than Highs has offered. Moreover, Garvey denies that trial will be any more stressful than what he and his family have lived with so far.

This summary raises doubts that Garvey fully understands and appreciates the alternatives and their likely consequences. His desire to go to trial does not reflect a difference in values so much as it does a misunderstanding of how a group of neutral jurors will react to what happened. Moreover, no matter how clear and rational Garvey's thinking, he may never be able to anticipate in advance the additional stress of going to trial. Thus, were the counseling standard to demand actual client understanding, you would have cause to doubt whether you have achieved it in Garvey's case. However, you satisfy the process standard if you have afforded Garvey a reasonable opportunity to evaluate the options and likely consequences.

As you can no doubt appreciate, what a "reasonable opportunity" consists of depends on the unique facts of individual settings. Common situational factors that may help you feel comfortable that you have provided a "reasonable opportunity" include:

- A decision's likely impact. The greater a decision's potential legal or non-legal impact, the greater the amount of time and effort you may need to devote to counseling under a "reasonableness" standard.
- A decision's complexity. A reasonable opportunity may require a greater counseling effort when discussions involve complex legal doctrine or factually complicated alternatives and consequences.
- Clients' backgrounds. Such factors as clients' legal sophistication and experience and clients' levels of emotional involvement can affect what constitutes a reasonable opportunity.
- Time available for deciding. Counseling discussions may have to be curtailed when decisions must be made quickly.
- Clients' willingness to participate and pay. You cannot lock your office door and force clients to participate in counseling discussions. Still less can you force them to pay for your time if they are willing to make decisions despite greatly truncated counseling.

Recognize, however, that a reduced counseling effort may be unreasonable if a client faced with an important and complex problem wants to but is unable to explore alternatives and consequences only because the client cannot pay your full hourly fee.

D. PROVIDING ADVICE

When decision-making is at hand, clients may ask for your advice in a variety of ways. For example, clients may say such things as:

- "I'm leaning towards accepting the settlement offer. Do you think that's what I ought to do?"
- "I just don't know what to do. What do you recommend? What do think I should do?"

A radical interpretation of the client-centered approach might lead you to reject all such requests for advice in order to avoid influencing decisions. However, such an extreme interpretation demeans clients' ability to make independent judgments, deprives clients of the opportunity to get advice from a person who has professional expertise and emotional distance from problems, and directly frustrates clients' expectations. Client-centeredness does not require you to hide from giving advice. Far from it. Client-centeredness encompasses the notion that as a matter of autonomy, clients who seek your help are entitled to ask for and receive advice.

What client-centeredness does entail is that you generally respond to requests for advice only after you have counseled clients sufficiently to be familiar with their objectives, concerns and values. Having this information makes it more likely that any advice you may give will reflect clients' best interests and values. For example, assume that Cathy Gilliger consults you about terminating an employee who has become a problem at her company. The options you have discussed consist of firing the employee and asking the employee to resign upon several months' severance pay. When evaluating these options, the consequences that Gilliger deemed most important were (1) supporting the supervisor who gave the employee a poor evaluation; and (2) avoiding a lawsuit by the employee. Gilliger asks for your opinion about what she ought to do. Given the values and concerns that Gilliger expressed, you would probably advise her that the severance pay option seems the better course. You might say something like, "In my opinion, given what you have told me about what you want to achieve, you'd be better off with the severance pay option, since it would both support the supervisor and minimize the risk of a lawsuit." You may personally feel that it is wrong to "pay off" an employee simply to avoid a lawsuit, but your opinion should reflect the client's values, not yours.

While clients' objectives, concerns and values may emerge during any phase of your representation (e.g., during time line or theory development questioning), a counseling discussion of those matters in the context of the decision at hand may be necessary before you can feel confident that you understand a client's position. Hence, a sensible approach is to provide opinions only after you have counseled clients with respect to specific decisions that need to be made.

In a variant of the situation described above, clients' questions and actions may suggest that they want you to advise them as to what you *personally* would choose to do were you in their situations. For example, clients may say such things as:

"What would you do if you were in my shoes?"

"I'm leaning towards disinheriting my three sons. Is that what you would do?"

Again, respect for client autonomy and independence means that providing opinions about what you would do were you the decisionmaker is consistent with the values of client-centeredness. When you do provide such opinions, including the experiences or reasons underlying them reminds clients that their decisions may reasonably differ from yours. For instance, you may accompany opinions with comments such as:

> I've never personally been faced with having to decide whether to accept a settlement offer, especially in a situation that I've felt so strongly that I've been wronged. But frankly, I think that at this point I'd feel that I made my point and I'd want to get on with my life. So I'd probably take their offer, but I can understand if you come to a different conclusion.

To the extent that you can refer to the experiences of other clients in similar situations, you may refer to decisions that they've found satisfactory. For example, in the above situation your comments might go along these lines:

> I've represented a few clients whose situations were somewhat similar to yours, and talked to other attorneys too. Most of my clients and those of the attorneys I've talked to have decided to accept settlement offers that are as reasonable as this one, and at least personally I've never had a client contact me after a case has been settled and tell me that they regret their decision.

Clients may request your personal opinion because they want moral support for decisions they've more or less already made. In such situations, your response may again combine your moral stances with the reasons or experiences underlying them. For example, a conversation may go as follows:

C: So at this point, I'm leaning strongly towards disinheriting the lot of them. Do you personally think that's the right thing to do?

L: That's a tough judgment to make, and I certainly won't try to talk you out of your plans. I'm a "blood is thicker than

> water" type, so I'd have a really hard time disinheriting my children. At the same time, I'm fortunate that my family relationships haven't been as troubled as yours. I suppose that if I were in your situation, I might well make the same decision that you have.

As the above discussion implies, offering advice in the absence of clients' requesting it is generally inconsistent with the values of client-centeredness. Offering unsolicited advice fulfills one traditional image of lawyers as advice givers, an image that depicts them as telling clients what to do. ("If I'm going to be your lawyer, I'll expect you to follow my advice. Now here's what we're going to do first. . .") An attorney who regards counseling as presenting clients with "fait accompli" has no need even to review with clients options and likely consequences. Needless to say, the only noteworthy aspect of this approach is that it manages to violate just about every tenet of client-centered counseling, and a few rules of professional conduct to boot.

Taking a somewhat more nuanced approach with regard to giving unsolicited advice, you might review options and consequences and then advise clients as to what decisions they ought to make and why. For example, you might say something along these lines:

> To sum up then, Mr. Garvey, basically what you have to decide is whether to accept or reject High's settlement offer. We've talked about the plusses and minuses of each option. I'll be frank with you. I think you ought to accept the offer. If it were me, that's the decision I'd make. But of course, the decision is up to you. Are you prepared to make a decision now, or do you want to mull it over for a day or two?

Here, unsolicited advice follows discussions that presumably comply with the counseling standard of giving clients a reasonable opportunity to decide. However, many clients are apt to resent unsolicited advice and view it as paternalistic and demeaning, even if you do first engage in a counseling process. Moreover, clients are likely to interpret unsolicited advice as meaning that you and not they are the primary decisionmakers. Regardless of their legal sophistication, many clients think themselves quite capable of making decisions. Thus, giving unsolicited advice to clients is likely to impair rapport, weaken client confidence in you, and reduce client participation in the problem-solving process.

Apart from whether clients resent unsolicited advice, providing it generally violates client-centered norms. Client-centeredness presumes that clients are capable of acting autonomously. Unsolicited advice suggests that clients cannot recognize their own best interests and thereby overrides client autonomy. Finally, satisfactory decisions generally reflect both legal and non-legal concerns, and clients are the experts when it comes to recognizing and evaluating non-legal concerns.

Typically, then, unsolicited advice is inconsistent with client-centered lawyering. . . .

Edward A. Dauer
Hurting Clients
THE AFFECTIVE ASSISTANCE OF COUNSEL
(Marjorie A. Silver, ed. 2007)[2]

One of the most valuable lessons I learned in law school wasn't on the bar exam, and probably never will be. Nonetheless—even if I did not realize it at the time—its significance to the art of legal counseling outweighs everything the bar exam has ever asked about the Rule against Perpetuities, and about Evidence, and Secured Transactions, and nearly everything else. The lesson happened in Victor Brudney's Corporations class, on a Spring day about 40 years ago.

The case *du jour* involved a particularly truculent course of litigation between two shareholders unhappily trapped together in a closely-held corporation, one of whom was suing the other for some cause of action like self-dealing or misappropriation of corporate assets. After extracting the obligatory briefing of the case, Professor Brudney asked the class, "What is this lawsuit about?" A few students raised their hands. "The fiduciary obligation of directors is blah blah blah. . . ." "The plaintiff is representing the corporation in a derivative capacity, according to the rule in etc. etc. etc. . . ." One particularly perspicacious soul suggested that "The shareholders' agreement failed to specify any restrictions on the freedom of the shareholders to compete with the corporation, so that and so on and so on. . . ." None of this impressed Professor Brudney. He scowled, shook his head, and thundered at us, "What this case is about—is that *these two people hate each other.*"

I think about Victor Brudney every time I drive through Teller County, Colorado. Route 24 goes all the way across Teller County. It's a two-lane road for most of its length, winding through mountains and sparsely settled terrain on the edge of the Pike National Forest. But because it connects Colorado Springs with the ski areas in Summit County, for most of the year it carries a heavy flow of traffic. On property owned by Jineen McWherter, abutting Route 24 about 40 miles from the city and in plain view of all that traffic, there is a large billboard. It is twenty-two feet wide and sixteen feet high. It is mounted on three telephone poles sunk into deep concrete footings. The metal sign is bright crimson enamel with large, bright white letters. At night it is illuminated by a bank of flood lamps fed with a power line strung hundreds of feet

---

[2] Footnotes and/or internal citations omitted.

from the Rural Electric Cooperative Association poles for only this purpose. For more than three years the sign said,

We regret

doing business with

Hotchkiss Realty

Apparently that had some effect on Hotchkiss Realty, because the sign later sprouted what I can describe only as the billboard equivalent of pocket parts. The bottom of the sign was extended a couple of feet on each side and the third line of lettering was covered over with amended text, so that the sign read,

We regret

doing business with

A.J. and Lenore *Hotchkiss* Who Now Own Prudential *Realty*

Two years later, in July of 2005, almost overnight all of that disappeared. Sixteen feet wide, ten feet high, mounted on telephone pole pylons and illuminated with flood lamps, there is now Teller County's largest happy-face, and the legend,

We won the appeal.

Hotchkiss was 100% wrong!

I have long wondered what the real facts of that dispute were, but one doesn't just wander unarmed up to the door of someone who would deal with their enemies in that way. An outline, however, was available from the Internet: Apparently, the McWherters felt the Hotchkisses had done them harm as brokers in a deal between them and the Fletchers, in which McWherter lost some money and was out to recover it from the hides of Hotchkiss. For the Hotchkisses' part, A.J. still thinks the McWherters are "whacked out."

To some extent this kind of behavior is "irrational:" the financial, not to mention the emotional, costs of erecting and maintaining the sign must have been considerable. Its impact on the litigation could not have been helpful for Jineen McWherter. As economic behavior, this was preposterous. But, just as for the protagonists in Victor Brudney's corporations case, the emotional component was no less real and certainly no less motivating.

The lesson itself is a generalization from these kinds of examples. Most lawsuits seem to be about money. The plaintiff demands the defendant's money, and the defendant does whatever can be done to keep the plaintiff from having it. Money is not, however, what some clients who sue for money actually want. Lawsuits are about money only because, most of the time, money is the only thing a client can get from bringing a lawsuit. Anything else—like satisfaction and consolation and vindication (or their baser forms in revenge and retribution, *a/k/a* "justice")—is derivative, and money is only the surrogate. It is hard to measure exactly how often this is so; but for reasons to be offered anon, it is so often enough to be worth our careful attention: this client whom we represent in this matter on this day may well be motivated to bring an action for money not by the need for money, but by the need to accomplish something else. Without knowing about and knowing how to respond to whatever the something else is, we lawyers risk missing the opportunity to help that client find more satisfaction and wellbeing than a money lawsuit might bring. And at lower cost.

Lawyers don't always think about this deeply enough. Sometimes we commit clients to the path of litigation without questioning critically whether conventional litigation is what this client really wants or needs. Some clients, to be sure, come to us saying they want to sue for money; some lawyers don't know how to do anything else; and sometimes for whatever reason the lawyer-client counseling never gets to what else might matter more. Even when the suit is successful, the money judgment may be a poor substitute for the balm the hurting client might otherwise have had. And given the financial and emotional costs of bringing a lawsuit—even a successful one—the process and its outcome may in retrospect feel something like having burned the forest to catch the stag.

Law students don't always think about this enough either; and for that they cannot really be blamed. Bar exams ask about the Fertile Octogenarian variation on contingent remainders under the Rule Against Perpetuities; law school exams ask for instant recall of the eighth exception to the hearsay rule; all of most law students' casebooks are *casebooks;* and cases are for good reasons (but not for *really* good reasons) limited to the facts that the law makes germane—regardless of the facts that may be germane to the client. Some students, like those whose early instruction includes live-client clinics, gain a broader appreciation early on. The rest of us need to be reminded that sometimes clients hurt, that sometimes hurt matters, and that sometimes suing for money may not be the best way to help the client fix the hurt.

Clients Hurt and Hurt Matters

The field of medical malpractice has been a fertile one in which to study these phenomena. Perhaps because the data are better there (there is a patient record and an insurance file for every claim, and the judgments and settlements are all reported to a federal data bank), or maybe just because there has been intense public interest in the "malpractice liability crisis" which, some say, threatens to do in modern medicine, more data have been collected about patients and patient claims in medical malpractice than in any other part of civil litigation. What we see in all that data is that, at least among malpractice plaintiffs, Jineen McWherters abound.

Three significant investigations have been conducted into the needs and drives of people who feel themselves hurt by bad medicine and who bring legal claims against the doctors who, they believe, have hurt them. Although the studies were done at different times, in different countries, and with different methodologies, their results are remarkably consistent. People who allege injury from medical malpractice and who bring lawsuits demanding money *most of the time* are not suing because of money.

One of the three studies was done by Dr. Charles Vincent and his colleagues among patients and their families who brought malpractice claims in England. Vincent asked these people why they had brought their claims and what they hoped to achieve. In one part of the survey the respondents were asked to indicate which of a list of goals best described their motives to sue. Here are the results, edited from Vincent's Table 4:

	Agree %
So that it would not happen to anyone else	91.4
I wanted an explanation	90.7
I wanted the doctors to realise what they had done	90.4
To get an admission of negligence	86.7
So that the doctor would know how I felt	68.4
My feelings were ignored	66.8
I wanted financial compensation	65.6
Because I was angry	65.4
So that the doctor did not get away with it	54.7
So that the doctor would be disciplined	47.6
Because it was the only way I could cope with my feelings	45.8
Because of the attitude of the staff afterword	42.5
To get back at the doctor involved	23.2

Notice that while the desire for money did have significant salience, it mattered less frequently to these respondents than did explanation, prevention of further harm, and a host of other nonmonetary concerns. "So that the doctor would be disciplined" was not far behind, and "So that it would not happen to anyone else" was way ahead.

In another part of the study Vincent asked the question, "What could have been done that would have led you not to bring this claim?" These results were even more interesting. From Vincent's Table 5:

Explanation and apology	37
Correction of mistake	25
Pay compensation	17
Correct treatment at the time	15
Admission of negligence	14
Investigation by drug company/hospital	3
Disciplinary action	4
If listened to and not treated as neurotic	5
Honesty	4

Here we see "pay compensation" as one of the least significant factors. If the respondents were paying attention to the questions and answering accurately, the difference between the 65% compensation result for suits once begun and the 17% score for claims before they were filed suggests that, whatever the initial motivations may have been, they became transmogrified once the litigation began. People *brought* claims mostly to effect correction or recognition; they *pursued* claims once begun, they more frequently said, for money. It can't be proven just from these data, but it is certainly a tempting hypothesis that the litigation process itself changed the more authentic emotional motives into the more readily counted financial motives.

The second of the three studies was done in the United States by Dr. Gerald Hickson and his colleagues at Vanderbilt University, among families who had sued for neonatal birth injuries. These kinds of injuries—including what are sometimes called "bad babies"—are seldom if ever trivial. Yet Hickson, using a methodology different from Dr. Vincent's, found motivations strikingly consistent.

Hickson's group was interested in the factors that "prompted" claims-making, and so included within the response codes both motivations and influences, or precipitating events:

What motivated you to bring this lawsuit?	
Advice of a third person:	~33%
Physician not completely honest:	~25%
Needed compensation:	~24%
Only way to find out what happened:	~20%
Punish doctor / assure it won't happen again:	~20%

Once again the need for compensation played a relatively minor role, even among families who had suffered very significant traumas and injuries, and even though the data set included only closed money claims.

Moreover, the response rate for "punish doctor / assure it won't happen again" was 46% among families whose baby had *died*.

The methodologies and therefore the implications of both of these studies can, of course, be criticized. They were both surveys, and there is reason to believe that people responding to surveys will give responses that make them seem like good people—"I am doing this for the good of humanity, not to line my own pocket." No amount of methodological elegance can completely remove that concern. The third study, however, does very largely put that concern to rest. It is a remarkable piece of data collection just completed by Dr. Marie Bismark in New Zealand.

New Zealand differs from both the U.S. (Hickson's venue) and the U.K. (Vincent's) in that there is no civil liability for medical malpractice. A patient (or patient's family) who believes they were injured by medical care may bring a claim to the Accident Compensation Corporation (ACC) and will be compensated within that agency's scheme on a no-fault basis. It is not necessary to prove negligence, and the scheme has been described as the world's easiest compensation system for ordinary people to navigate. At the same time, the same people may if they wish bring a "complaint" to a wholly separate tribunal, the Health and Disability Commission (the HDC). Unlike the ACC, which can only award money damages, the HDC cannot award money damages at all. It can intervene in the doctor's practice; it can order corrective action; it can in a proper case suspend a physician's license. But it cannot order the doctor to pay the patient any money.

Bismark analyzed the self-reported reasons why people brought complaints to the HDC. In some senses these reports are purer than those of either Vincent's or Hickson's respondents. Because the HDC-complaint patients *cannot* be paid in money, and because the HDC process *cannot* have any impact on the ACC claim, these reports of motivation-to-complain are almost perfectly uncorrupted by the wish for money, however sublimated that wish may be.

Here, then, is what Bismark's respondents report:

Desired outcome	**Complainants (n=154)**
Lessons learned/system change	70 (45%)
Explanation	52 (34%)
Compensation for economic losses	28 (18%)
Discipline/punishment	18 (12%)
Apology/expression of responsibility	16 (10%)
Review of provider's competence	11 (7%)
Intervention with care or waiting lists	6 (4%)

Again we can see strong feelings toward punishing the wrongdoer, toward preventing whatever happened to the patient from ever happening to anyone else, toward having recognition of the hurt the patient endured. These feelings are *real*; and these feelings cause people to bring complaints and legal claims. But not for money, or at least not usually.

"Accountability"

The practical question is how we turn these sorts of empirical findings into useful observations about lawyering. But before we get there we can do some filtering and deepening of the meaning of the data, for it appears that there is a more organized way to understand what's going on. In a number of focus groups that Leonard Marcus and I conducted a few years ago, in which we had all of the interests involved in malpractice litigation assembled to talk about what they needed and wanted out of the process, the most frequently-voiced need of the patients and their representatives was the word "accountability." When doctors make errors and hurt other people, the injured people insist that the doctors must be "held accountable." Accountability is called for not only by the victims of medical malpractice, but by the families who lost loved ones in 9–11, by people "taken" by corporate accounting scandals, even by people who had donated their loved ones' cadavers to the UCLA Medical School only to discover that someone at UCLA was making money selling the corpses on the used body parts market. Its occurrence is so common, and seemingly so diverse, that it is tempting to consider the word "accountability" as having no distinctive meaning simply because it may have so many.

A closer examination of the med-mal data we just looked at, however, suggests a four-fold set of meanings that are broad enough to capture all the uses yet clear enough to be helpful. In particular, when people say they demand accountability, their demand may be for one (or more) of the following four kinds of things: *Sanction, Correction, Restoration, and Communication.* Here's what these four mean:

Sanction. People who do bad things should be punished. Punishment serves as vengeance; as expression of outrage, personal or social; as moral desert; as restoration of the equilibrium of good and evil that was upset by the wrongdoer's doing of the wrong. The effect of all of these is the same: Punishment means inflicting harm on a wrongdoer even when its infliction does not in any objective way necessarily benefit the victim. Like what Jineen McWherter was doing to A.J. and Lenore Hotchkiss, and what Victor Brudney thought the litigants were up to in his corporations case.

Restoration. In contrast to Sanction, which imposes a loss on the wrongdoer without necessarily achieving a gain for the victim,

Restoration focuses on compensation for the victim first, and only secondarily on its impact on the wrongdoer. "He messed up and now I have to pay all these bills, and I've lost income, and so he has to *pay me back.*" People who sue for money and really want the money are suing for Restoration. (Actually, there are two kinds of restoration—one is "fix what you broke." The other is "pay me money." The latter is usually called compensation.)

Correction. Someone who did the bad deed once just might do it again, unless something's done to prevent it. (Legal theorists call this "deterrence," and weave elaborate economic theories about it.) Punishment swift and sure should do the trick. Indeed, it would even be good if the punishment were public—behead one traitor in the public square and everyone might act better in the future. Accountability of this sort changes (if it doesn't kill) the wrongdoer; the threat of it guides the behavior of everyone else; and holding accountable today's wrongdoer (even if it does kill him) seems like a morally defensible way to make real the threat of doing the same to others. Recall here the commonly heard plaint in the malpractice complaints data, "I want to be sure what happened to me never happens to anyone else; that's why I'm suing *this* bastard."

Communication. This fourth aspect of accountability is the most difficult to define, but the most interesting in practice. It includes such familiar phrases as *"You owe me an explanation"* and *"Come clean."* and *"You let me down; come forward and "fess up."* and *"Take responsibility."* Common to all of those is the idea of disclosure and communication. It seems to be heard most often when one person (the victim) trusted or depended on another (the wrongdoer) who failed to live up to the expectations of that trust. Politicians are often "held accountable" in this way, as are employees and, notably, professionals who hold themselves out *as* caring as much for their clients as for themselves. The desire for accountability in the classic hit-and-run, or in a fraud committed by a total stranger, is seldom of this fourth type. But it is frequently this type of accountability that attends a breach of faith or an injury caused by the lack of care from someone in whom someone else placed their trust. Trustees are not allowed simply to offer restoration or to suffer a flogging stoically. They deserve more: they have to face the one they hurt and *explain* themselves. Later on we'll talk about apology and voluntary disclosure—two of the ways Communication gets expressed.

So, in short, out of any statistically sufficient group of people who were hurt through someone else's fault and who were moved to make a "legal claim" about it (for money, of course), we would find that some of them (probably a minority, though that can change from one setting to the next) demand the money because they want the money (Restoration); another group demand the money because they want to hurt the hurter back (Sanction); some demand the money because they care about the deterrent effect of bringing the claim (Correction); and a fourth group demand the money because the *process* of suing for the money requires the miscreant to recognize the hurt they caused, and to confront it if not confess it (Communication).

There are a couple of advantages to thinking about all of this in the way we just did—having four descriptions of what injured people want and one concept that embraces them all. For one, a lawyer consulting an injured client doesn't need an extensive knowledge of human psychology to be sensitive to what the client may really be saying they want. There is no question but that this four-fold way is simplistic, and would probably not earn a passing grade in an upper-level Psych course. But extensive taxonomies of mental states are more than what most lawyers ordinarily need. What we do need, however, is something that reminds us to think about the alternatives when a hurting client arrives demanding a lawsuit for money. Simple though it may be, the four-fold might be helpful in preventing us from clumsily hurting the client even more.

The second advantage is that having a unifying concept—Accountability—moves us closer to actually using these ideas in practice. Here's why: In what is probably a substantial number of all the cases, the four kinds of accountability people demand may just be four *seemingly* different facets of the same thing. To put that another way, injured people may have a real need for achieving accountability, and the four variations are just different ways by which they can do that. Now that's a hypothesis a Psych post-doc could get their teeth into, because saying that the four are really all the same means that if we satisfy one of them, we may well have slaked the thirst for any of the others.

That is not just a theoretical possibility. We know both anecdotally and systematically that among two groups of equally injured people, prompt full disclosure and recognition of the hurt offered to one group will result in that group producing fewer demands for any other kind of accountability. Medical patients to whom prompt disclosure of an error was made (Communication) are both less likely to sue for money (Restoration) *and* less likely to "report" the doctor to the licensing authorities (Sanction, Correction). We know from both ordinary experience and through methodologically rigorous experiments that offering apologies reduces not just the cash settlement value of a post-injury claim, but also causes the apologee to regard their injury as less serious than they would have without that balm. Something cognitively significant is going on—something important for lawyers who counsel hurting clients (and, as we'll see, for lawyers who counsel hurters as well as hurtees).

But one final digression. Although most of the studies that lead us to these ideas have been done in the setting of medical injuries, there is very good reason to believe that the same would be true almost everywhere when people injure other people. This drive toward effecting accountability, and each of the four guises that make it up, is a deeply rooted piece of human nature. It is, indeed, so basic to our make-up that we should expect to see it operating no matter the way or the setting or the device by which the hurt hurt. Victor Brudney's corporate antagonists, Jineen McWherter with her billboard, and all of the people in the U.S., the U.K., and New Zealand who suffered from medical error, may all have been acting from the same deeply basic motive.

Why People Act That Way

"Motive" isn't the right word now, because we are about to switch from Psych 101, where "motives" are valid concepts, to Evolutionary Biology, where the only things we are allowed to talk about are behavioral tendencies and traits. (Bear with me here. This is actually kind of fun.) So we'll call acting-to-effect-accountability a behavioral tendency, and its four guises a suite of behavioral traits.

You may have heard of the Darwin Awards. "The Darwin Awards salute the improvement of the human genome by honoring those who remove themselves from it in really stupid ways." Evolutionary theory holds that the genetic predispositions toward behaviors are selected for over time in the same way that physical traits are. If some behavioral tendency (such as eating) helps the individual survive long enough to breed, that gene has a higher chance of being passed to the next generation than does a gene that causes someone to act in a way that reduces their chances of breeding (such as having no fear of sabretooth tigers). "Useful" genes are accordingly selected for; self-destructive genes are accordingly selected against. So how did Jineen McWherter get hers?

We need to explain why people sometimes act in ways that seem to be contrary to their individual best interests. Why would anyone devote their time and resources to pursuing Correction, or any other aspect of Accountability other than individual Restoration? Why do the New Zealanders bring complaints to the HDC? An economist would find Jineen's actions "irrational"—she must have spent a great deal on a project that could not possibly have returned her anything. Yet many of us have experienced anger and the urge to get back at someone who cut us off on the highway, or who cheated us on the used car lot, even if following that urge might risk much and net nothing.

The answer, evolutionary theorists tell us, stems from the fact that humans, for good and sufficient physiological reasons, cannot survive as solitary animals. We evolved living in smallish groups; and we are dependent for our individual survival on the survival of the group—without it, we die. Without us, it dies. Cooperation is the key to group survival. The saga of the stag hunt tells it well. Hunting stag is a group activity; hunting hare can be done alone. Bagging a stag is better all around than catching a hare is. Is it better to hunt hare, or to contribute to hunting stag? If everyone cooperates in hunting stag, everyone—and the group—is better off. But if anyone "cheats" and goes off to hunt hare for themselves, the success of the stag hunt is endangered. So, will Tumak hunt hare, or help hunt stag? This is what game theorists call a prisoner's dilemma—if everyone cooperates, Tumak and everyone else win big; if Tumak "cheats" and hunts hare, Tumak wins a little; if Tumak cooperates in the stag hunt while others cheat, Tumak loses big. The "equilibrium solution" is for everyone to cheat. In a world of rational maximizers, where everyone does what maximizes their individual advantage, the equilibrium outcome is *less* positive for the group than it would be in a world where everyone cooperates.

But individual competition in a world of scarcity matters too (why else do law students care so much about graduating in the top 10% of the class?) In the whole of the environment, then, the behavior patterns that get selected for are some optimal blend of self-interest and group-interest, and thus (ethnologists believe) we see the evolution of altruism and reciprocity. Cheating, however, is still pretty tempting, and so backup systems also have survival value. One of those is called "strong reciprocity." Strong reciprocity is a behavioral tendency we have inherited, courtesy of both individual and group natural selection, to reward cooperators and punish cheaters even when doing that might cost the individual who does the punishing more than they could gain for themselves alone by doing it. It greatly improves the prospects for cooperation, and so contributes to the survival prospects for the group and, accordingly, for its members.

There is still, however, a "free rider" problem to get over. Why should anyone do such things? Why should I punish the miscreant who went off and hunted hare? Why should I run down and cut off the aggressive driver who cut me off? Punishing them is likely to be personally risky if not just costly. If someone else did it, I would be better off without risking anything of my own. Hence again the solution would be, that none of us would ever do anything to punish cheaters. But we do. Jineen McWherter sure did.

The mechanism for making "strong reciprocity" work is anger. Watching a cheater cheat makes Tumak angry. Anger, as the people back in Psych 101 tell us, results in cognitive distortions—angry people tend to *underestimate* the cost to themselves of the actions they are thinking of taking to get back at the object of their wrath; and they tend to *overestimate* the magnitude of the actual threat. Detecting a cheater produces anger, which in turn supports strong reciprocity and a system for enforcing group norms that overcomes the free rider problem. Tumak picks up his club, and the group is better off.

I am not suggesting that Jineen McWherter was driven inexorably by her DNA to risk her individual reproductive fitness by erecting an enormous billboard just to punish A. J. Hotchkiss for having cheated on the norms of Jineen's tribe. I am suggesting that the underlying behavioral trait that Jineen and most of the medical malpractice victims exhibit is an expression of a deeply rooted and very basic suite of behavioral propensities—to achieve accountability (now read, social cooperation) even when there is nothing in it for them alone. That makes what we see in the medical malpractice data far more likely to be a generalized phenomenon, happening across differences in time and setting and place. This is deep stuff.

Counseling

Suppose all of this is true. (It is.) The practical question is whether it matters. Does knowing about the origin and distribution of feelings a person experiences after an injury help at all, really? (It does.)

Let's take an anonymous version of a real case—one of many cases like it in which I have personally *seen* the value of knowing about these things. The year was 1985. Three years earlier a young mother of three children was injured in an accident, received three units of whole blood in the ER, and six months later was diagnosed with HIV. The virus moved rapidly to AIDS and the patient's condition deteriorated tragically. She and her husband sued the blood bank that collected the blood, the hospital where she received it, and the physicians who gave the orders to infuse it. The defendants mounted a staunch defense: until 1985, three years after this transfusion, there was no test for HIV, and no way for anyone to screen blood other than by screening donors for "life-style" risks. Blood, as every first-year Torts student should know, is not a product under Restatement Torts 402A, but a service. There is no strict liability for blood products. The plaintiff would have to prove that the blood center was negligent—that it failed to live up to the appropriate standard of care.

The lawsuit went to trial against the blood bank, and the blood bank won. The plaintiffs appealed, and the judgment was affirmed. The plaintiffs appealed to the state's supreme court where, on a narrow evidentiary point, the judgment was reversed and the case was remanded. The second trial began. We are now four years into the litigation. The plaintiff died while her attorney was making closing arguments to the jury. The second jury returned a verdict for the plaintiffs and this time the defendant appealed. While on appeal for the second time the case was settled. I do not know the amount of the settlement. My guess, knowing something about these cases in general, is that it cost the blood bank about as much to settle the case as it spent to that point defending it. The injured patient, meanwhile, died after spending her final years in litigation and in poverty. This was a legal tragedy that followed a medical tragedy. Should something else have been done?

The answer is obviously yes. But how could the case have gotten there?

I recognize that it is hard for contingency fee lawyers to live on 30% of an apology, but I think in most instances we guide our clients into litigation for better but still not very good reasons. That more likely cause of what I think of as counseling errors came to me some years later, in the form of a preposterous statement made by an otherwise decent member of the bar. I was arguing on that occasion for a greater use of ADR techniques such as mediation in civil claims, on the ground that mediation's flexibility of remedy could be more satisfying to at least some clients than a money judgment would be. The lawyer in question said, with a straight face, "My clients all want money. That's all the legal system can give them, and they know that. So when they come to see a lawyer, they have already decided that money is what they want."

"Baloney," I carefully explained.

These days I begin my own law school course in the subject of ADR by challenging my students with what I call Maslow's Dictum, after Abraham Maslow who is reported to have first uttered it:

If all you have is a hammer,

everything looks like a nail.

If all we lawyers know is litigation and its appurtenant histrionics, bargaining, threats, and bluster, then of course that's what we'll offer our clients. And the clients will respond with reinforcement of the choice. As Robert Redmount taught us many years ago, an injured client is often putty in the lawyers' hands. By selective questioning, by indicating what parts of the story are "relevant" and what parts aren't when we do our interviewing and counseling, by offering limited options for remedy, and in all by imposing on the client's facts what Leonard Riskin termed the "lawyer's standard philosophical map," lawyers tell clients what the lawyer expects the client to say. They dutifully respond and we call it authentic.

The patient, and her family, were really, really angry in this case. The infected blood carried a death sentence whether the blood center meant it to or not, and the whole medical apparatus was trusted to save her life, not to take it. Some lawyers consider their clients' emotions as problems to be managed as well as can be in the course of getting at the legal facts that really matter. In doing that they miss the point that feelings are facts just as much as physical wounds are, and in the process miss the chance to help their clients more effectively. In some cases, underestimating the affect of a matter can lead to results that make things worse, like this case.

The same thing is true for transactional lawyers. A colleague of mine was consulted once by a client for whom he had done some legal work in the past. He knew that this client owned a small corporation that was moderately successful, since he had formed the company and counseled with its owner on other things a few years before. On this day the client presented this question: "Is it possible for a corporation like mine to have two kinds of stock—one that has the right to vote on things and one that doesn't?"

The answer to that question is easy enough—classes of stock in closely-held corporations can be created with or without almost any voting rights one might want; and it is not a difficult matter to amend the By-laws to allow the issuance of new classes of stock even after the corporation has been formed. My friend the lawyer, however, wanted to know why the client wanted to know about this, and so he asked him, "Yes, we can do that; but tell me why you would want to?"

The client's answer was not unexpected; "Because I want to give someone who is going to work for the company an economic stake in the business but not the right to mess around with it." Ah, well, that's different. Now the possibilities widen. What seemed like the client's question was actually the client's answer to a question one layer down. Having discovered that, there became available to the lawyer a much wider array of possible answers—employee benefit plans funded with company stock but managed by a Trustee, incentive salaries tied to performance, and numerous other ways to link an employee's fortune to a company's without dealing in stock at all.

This lawyer was still curious. "Any particular employee?" The next answer was unexpected. After some hesitation the client revealed that his plan was to bring his son into the business—a son who, the father thought, had been misled in life by the blandishments of Boulder or Madison or Berkeley or wherever. That was the father's plan for repairing a badly frayed filial fabric. The young man's goals should be made consistent with those of the family business, which was how the father was going to relate to the wayward son; but he wasn't yet to be trusted with the right to vote.

Redrafting the corporation charter and issuing a new class of stock would have been a perfectly valid legal answer to a seemingly legal question, just as the plaintiffs' counsel in the blood case would not be faulted—under traditional standards—for having brought a well-framed and well-tried liability suit. But just creating the new class of stock would have been a very bad answer to the client's real question. Indeed, it is far from clear that the client's real question, of how to bond with the son he wished he had, is something a lawyer should have responded to at all. It is fair to suggest, however, that any such two-classes-of-stock plan would have been useless at best and, more likely, disastrous at worst.

Another example makes the same point in a more common setting. A commercial artist drew a new logo for a minor league baseball team and came, somehow, to an intellectual property lawyer to draft the contract, between him and the team, by which he would be compensated for giving the team the logo. The lawyer gave all the right advice about securing copyright protection, and laid out the pros and cons of the two major avenues for selling such things, *viz.* an outright sale of the artwork for some number of dollars, or a license agreement under which the artist would receive a royalty for every teeshirt or baseball cap sold that bore the logo. What the lawyer ignored throughout the interviewing and counseling of this client, however, was the half dozen times the client said, mostly in asides, how his love of baseball and of this team in particular came from his own childhood dream of playing on a professional baseball team some day, and how he might prefer the license deal because it would better make him feel that he was "part of the team," and how an outright sale would be just a commercial deal and that would be the end of it.

On the one hand, those feelings might indicate a preference for a license agreement over an outright sale. But the possibilities could go even deeper than that. How about his becoming the Art Director for the team; or (in this very different case) taking a small share of the ownership? What did this client really want? Money? I don't think so. Feelings matter.

Here's the point: To do the best for the HIV patient, and the artist, and the erring Dad, the lawyer has to have two things. One is the ability to hear what clients are saying, and to appreciate what they are saying might mean. The other is the willingness to believe that, even if all that emotional stuff doesn't fall neatly into the lawyer's standard philosophical map, it is the stuff of which good counseling is made—not stuff to be worked around while some satisfactory "legal" solution is conjured up.

With that, let's go back to the hard case—the infected blood—and see how that might have worked out. We can do it from two sides—the patient and the blood center. Blood center first.

One alternative approach, pretty familiar these days to any lawyer who has learned anything at all about "ADR" techniques such as mediation, would be to catalogue the blood center's interest, find out or guess what they could about the plaintiff's interests, and engage in either direct or mediated interest-based negotiation. That would have been an improvement over what actually happened; but the blood center could have done even more, and particularly so if they had gotten to it sooner than they did.

By the time the blood center responded to the problem, the plaintiff had already been through a longish process with her own lawyers, who very likely steered her toward voicing threats of a lawsuit *if* not the lawsuit itself. The blood center isn't necessarily to be blamed for that. It may well have been the long-standing advice of its counsel, or of its liability insurer, not to go looking for trouble. One liability insurer I know of, for example, has two general rules for its insured docs. Rule No. 1: If the doctor knows of an adverse event and hears a patient making rumbling noises, the doctor is not to speak with that patient until the insurance company appoints defense counsel. Rule No. 2: Defense counsel won't be appointed until the patient has actually filed a claim. So there we have a patient, disappointed or worse by the course of their care, maybe wanting the Communication part of accountability but unable even to *talk* with the doc until they file a formal claim. And of course once they file a formal claim the expectations everyone brings to the rest of the opera pretty much preclude any effective conversations from ever occurring thereafter.

Suppose, however, that the blood center had taken a different approach. Their counsel knows, let's say, all the stuff we've talked about in the first half of this essay, and particularly these facts: This patient is angry; people who entrusted their wellbeing to others and who feel abandoned get *really* angry; anger enhances the perceived gravity of the harm, it reduces the perception of the costs of responding to it, it drives people to put up big billboards along Route 24 (or the equivalent, to file very expensive and nasty lawsuits); and the patient's drive for, say, Sanction or Correction is one of the maybe-exchangeable guises of the more general motive to achieve Accountability. Suppose, then, the blood bank stepped up to the plate before the patient determined to file a claim; suppose it opened the books, so to speak, about what had happened, and how, and opened a conversation about what might be done about it; took care of the patient's immediate needs, expressed recognition of the patient's hurt and (gasp now, all ye traditional defense counsel) *apologized.*

As it happens, we *do* know what would probably have happened had they done all of that, because there are liability-management programs now going on across the country that tell us what happens. The data are there, and they are robust. The blood bank's liability costs would have gone down, the total number of claims for all transfusion-associated injuries would have gone way down, and the destruction of the blood centers public image attributable to avoidable litigation would have all but disappeared. Yes, it might have cost some money as well, but the evidence strongly suggests it would have cost much less than it actually did.

There you are, then, counsel to a blood center, or a hospital, or a doctor, or a retail store that sells things that can injure people if they're defective. Knowing all of this, how do you counsel the client? I'd tell them they should develop an early-intervention risk management system before the next injury happens. Runs counter to the scorch-the-earth approach of yesteryear? Right; but ya gotta believe it. Knowing why people sue rather than assuming you know why this person wants to sue, should at the very least open options to consider, for responding to other peoples' hurt.

To illustrate this practical point, I offer one more "war story." A few years ago the FDA ordered blood centers and hospitals to conduct "look-back" programs for Hepatitis C ("HCV"). Until 1990 or so there was no blood test for HCV, yet it was blood-transmissible. The disease itself could lurk undetected for many years, until it erupted in serious and even life-threatening liver disease. Some people who received transfused blood prior to 1990 might have HCV without knowing it. Most blood donors, however, are repeat players—if they donated today, they probably did years before as well. So, in 1993, when a blood donor shows up and—now that there is a good test—shows markers for HCV, it is possible to "look back" at all of that donor's pre-1990 donations, and to trace them to their recipients. The FDA ordered exactly that, and required that the hospitals contact those identified recipients and call them in for testing. Some would undoubtedly test positive for the disease.

How should a hospital blood bank deal with the legal risk of such a program? Conventional counsel gave the conventional defense advice: gird your loins, admit nothing, and fight the first few claims to victory at almost any cost. What we have just been discussing, however, counsels otherwise. What is likely to cause lawsuits is anger, and anger will come when the people called back feel not just injured, but abandoned—when they feel the blood center needs to be held accountable. Full disclosure, stepping up to the plate with explanation and care, should slake that demand for accountability (Sanction, Correction) by responding to other of its facets (Communication, Restoration.) That, fortunately, is what some blood centers decided to do; and, so far as I know, those centers have not had a single lawsuit filed.

Let's look at the harder side—the young mother with then-unmanageable AIDS. How might her lawyer have done better? Which brings up a question that should have been raised earlier: If it matters to know how a client feels, in addition to knowing "the facts" of how the matter happened, how does a lawyer do that? We needn't get deeply into the nuances of client counseling to see two very effective techniques. One is, just ask. In the case of the family corporation and the question about the shares of stock, the lawyer took the client's question as an answer to a question one layer down, and peeled that layer away: "Why do you want to do that?" Maybe something as straightforward as, "How do you feel about all of this?" And if that doesn't get anything, then it's still possible to pick up clues from the rest of the counseling dialogue—like the artist who let drop more than once that a licensing deal would help him feel like part of a baseball team—his childhood ambition. The critical *sine qua non* of hearing is listening, and that means believing that such things really can matter.

That may not always be as easy as it sounds. Asking Mrs. HIV how she feels is likely to open the sluice-gates to a torrent of emotions . . . emotions that many lawyers find uncomfortable, if not discomfiting. But those feelings are the facts, just as much as the facts are the facts, and knowing about them opens options on this side of the aisle as well.

The transfusion injury victim and her husband present themselves to the lawyer. Early on, the husband says something like, "They poisoned my wife and she's going to die and I want to see them bleed now." Knowing that a money judgment alone may not be as satisfying as something more sensitively tuned could be, and knowing that the anger is an appropriate and a deeply-rooted response, the lawyer decides to explore the emotional affect more. What is it that these people really want / need / might get from the object of their wrath? Surely money would be helpful, particularly for excess medical costs and lost wages, the lost value of household production, and whatever other economic consequences the family has suffered. There is neither need nor reason to avoid that part of it. But there could be more, and it may be that if the money claim is used only for what money can easily do, then the rest of the motivations might be addressed by something more efficient and less destructive to pursue. It would certainly make no sense to commit these people to a lawsuit as the dominant feature of their final months together, if their underlying needs can be met more effectively. Even the money items might not need money. Health care costs, for example, don't require money. What the plaintiff really needs is health care, and it may be that the blood center, if it is part of an integrated health care system, can provide that care more efficiently by providing it in kind.

Beyond that, and calling on what we know from the medical malpractice studies and from our recently-gained insights into anger and accountability, there may be a drive to have Communication, Sanction, or Prevention as well as Restoration. It is very likely that the family does want to prevent such a tragedy from happening again; that they do want recognition of the terrible harm they have suffered; that they do want the blood center to feel their pain if not its own. They might even want Restoration beyond compensation—lifestyle counseling, for example, for this extraordinary disease, or some public vindication that this case of HIV was the result of an innocent transfusion, not the lifestyle assignations that attended AIDS in its early days (the implication of illicit drug use or sexual promiscuity still).

Now the creative part: What could a blood center be asked to do to meet these kinds of needs? Name a fellowship residency after these victims and devote the residency to research in transfusion safety. Publicly appear hand in hand with the family, expressing sincere remorse. Communicate openly about the blood transfusion process rather than, as too many defense lawyers recommend, forcing the patient-now-plaintiff to go the wrong way through a funnel sieve to get basic information about what happened. And more, maybe much more.

But again, how does the lawyer know the client's authentic needs and wishes? Even assuming they are already formed (which Redmount tells us they usually are not), direct questions may be helpful but could be premature. One technique that can be used to good advantage is—again, listen first—to feed back to the client what you hear them say, and not just the facts. "What I hear in your voice is a real anger that you are innocent of everything yet your life has been so grossly affected." Or, "What I hear you saying is that you are terribly afraid of having your family impoverished by these enormous medical expenses." Let it come out. Then, when the time seems right, offer the client lots of options—including a full-bore lawsuit—while explaining the pros and cons of each. Pros and cons means suitability as measured not by each option's legal sufficiency, but by its resonance with what you have heard the clients say. Some ideas will be rejected, and in the explanation of *why* they are rejected there will often be a clearer description of the underlying *what*. "I don't want to do that, because what I really want to do is . . ."

* * *

This essay was not intended to be a how-to textbook for client counseling, though client interviewing and counseling is where the affective assistance of counsel, or its opposite, is most effectively given. Interviewing and counseling, of course, are subjects with deep and useful literatures: what causes clients to withhold saying what they mean or feel? What blocks lawyers from hearing the cues that reluctant clients are sending? How can these causes of interference be overcome? These are skills that require clinical experience to learn well. One essay won't do.

The point of this essay, however, is more foundational, or at least more straightforward—and, I hope, at least a little convincing in light of the discussion we have just explored. Remember Victor Brudney. When listening to what one of those mutually-hated victims of the other is saying, think of the legal or litigation categories into which those facts might be framed *if they need to go there*. But at the same time, listen to the affect of what the client is saying, with the possibility in mind that maybe those facts shouldn't go there.

I cannot resist one final personal tale. This year my niece entered medical school. My wife, a nurse with a lifetime of experience in medicine and in patients, bought her a stethoscope to celebrate the beginning of our niece's career. She wrote a card to go in the gift box: "When you use this stethoscope with your patients, listen not just with your ears, but with your heart."

The title of this essay was a double entendre, in case you hadn't noticed. If we lawyers are sensitive to the affect of injury as well as we are to its effect, we have the opportunity to be of immense assistance to our hurting clients. If we are not, then hurting clients is a greater risk in doing what we do.

Peter De Jong and Scott D. Miller
How to Interview for Client Strengths
40 SOC. WORK 729 (1995)[3]

Articles calling for a "strengths perspective" in social work practice have begun to appear in the professional literature. . . .

The strengths perspective rests on the following assumptions: First and foremost, despite life's problems, all people and environments possess strengths that can be marshalled to improve the quality of clients' lives. Practitioners should respect these strengths and the directions in which clients wish to apply them. Second, client motivation is fostered by a consistent emphasis on strengths as the client defines these. Third, discovering strengths requires a process of cooperative exploration between clients and workers; "expert" practitioners do not have the last word on what clients need. Fourth, focusing on strengths turns the practitioner's attention away from the temptation to "blame the victim" and toward discovering how clients have managed to survive even in the most inhospitable of circumstances. And, fifth, all environments—even the most bleak—contain resources.

These assumptions are grounded in the poststructural notion that social workers must increasingly respect and engage clients' ways of viewing themselves and their worlds in the helping process. Or, to put it differently, the strengths perspective asserts that the client's "meaning" must count for more in the helping process, and scientific labels and

---

[3] Footnotes and internal citations omitted.

theories must count for *less*. This shift toward a deeper respect for the frame of reference of a particular client is especially important in this era of practice with increasingly diverse groups. . . .

This article presents a set of interviewing questions that we believe are appropriate to the philosophy and practice principles of the strengths perspective, including the commitment to work within the client's frame of reference. These questions, collectively known as the solution-focused approach to interviewing, have evolved over 20 years of work by de Shazer and his colleagues at the Brief Family Therapy Center in Milwaukee. Although originally developed for use in individual, couples, and family therapy, the questions have evolved to the point where they are useful in a variety of practice settings and client concerns. Indeed, we are persuaded that they are useful alternatives in any practice setting previously calling for problem solving with clients. This article presents the two key concepts behind solution-focused interviewing, the questions themselves, and a discussion of how these questions fit with the key concepts of the strengths perspective.

Solution Focused Interviewing

Solution-focused interviewing turns on two practice activities. The first is the development of well-formed goals with the client within the client's frame of reference; the second is the development with the client of solutions based on "exceptions."

Well-Formed Goals

Berg and Miller, drawing on their practice experience, identified seven characteristics of well-formed goals:

1. Goals are important to the client. Goals are well formed when they belong to the client and are expressed in the client's language; they are not well formed when, first of all, they are thought appropriate by the worker and are expressed in the worker's categories. This characteristic constitutes a practice principle that rests on the belief that clients whose goals are respected are more motivated than those whose goals are overlooked. The principle is not compromised except in cases where the worker, after exploring for client strengths and coping capacities, is convinced that the client is overwhelmed or a danger to self or others.

2. The goals are small. Small goals are easier to achieve than large ones. For example, it is easier to "fill out one job application" than to "get a job."

3. The goals are concrete, specific, and behavioral. Goals so characterized help both client and worker know when progress is occurring. Accordingly, "going out to lunch with a friend twice a week" is preferable to "getting more involved with others."

4. The goals seek presence rather than absence. Clients, when asked about their goals, often tell workers what they want eliminated from their lives, for example, "feeling discouraged." Practice outcomes are improved when clients are helped to express their goals as the presence of something—for example, "taking walks"—rather than the absence of something.

5. The goals have beginnings rather than endings. Clients also tend initially to conceptualize their goals as end points, for example, "having a happy marriage." Workers, aware that achieving goals is a process, can help by encouraging clients to conceptualize the first steps to their desired ends, such as "asking my husband to pick a place for next summer's vacation."

6. The goals are realistic within the context of the client's life. This characteristic speaks for itself and is usually achieved automatically in the course of developing goals with the preceding characteristics. However, when uncertain, the worker can explore with the client what it is in the client's life that tells the client that this particular goal makes sense for him or her.

7. The goals are perceived by the client as involving "hard work." Encouraging clients to think about their goals in this way is both realistic and useful for protecting the client's dignity. It is realistic, because goals call for changes in the client, and change is difficult. It protects the client's dignity because, first, if the client achieves the goal, the achievement is noteworthy, and, second, if the client does not, it means only that there is still more hard work to be done.

This conceptualization of well-formed goals implies that they are negotiated between worker and client. It suggests that clients rarely enter the helping relationship with well-formed goals and that workers do not have the right or the power to determine which goals are appropriate for clients. Instead, practitioner and client must labor together to define achievable goals within the client's frame of reference.

Exceptions

Exploring for exceptions represents the second main interviewing activity in the solution-focused approach. Exceptions are those occasions in the client's life when the client's problem could have occurred but did not. For example, if a couple complains of a troubled relationship because of "constant fighting," the solution-focused worker asks the couple to describe those times when they were together during which they did not fight or, at least, fought less destructively.

Solution-focused questioning by workers is quite persistent, but it avoids in-depth exploration of client problems. Workers focus on the who, what, when, and where of exception times instead of the who, what, when, and where of problems. The consequence is a growing awareness in both workers and clients of the clients' strengths relative to their goals, rather than the clients' deficiencies relative to their problems. Once these strengths are brought to awareness and thereby made available, clients can mobilize them to create solutions tailor-made for their lives.

Interviewing Questions

In a solution-focused approach, interviewing for well-formed goals and interviewing for client strengths go hand-in-hand to increase the chances of uncovering those strengths most appropriate to the client's goals.

Interviewing for Well-Formed Goals

The relationship between client and social worker usually focuses first on the client's concerns or problems. Clients insist on telling their workers "what's wrong" with their lives. It is important for workers to listen to these concerns and then, once they have established that there is not an emergency, to turn the conversation toward developing well-formed goals. The "miracle" question is a good way to begin the negotiation. The worker might ask the following:

> Suppose while you are sleeping tonight a miracle happens. The miracle is that the problem that has you here talking to me is somehow solved. Only you don't know that because you are asleep. What will you notice different tomorrow morning that will tell you that a miracle has happened?

This question is the starting point for a whole series of satellite questions designed to take the client's attention away from difficulties and to focus it on imagining a future when the problem is solved. The following satellite questions might be used:

- What is the very first thing you will notice after the miracle happens?

- What might your husband (child, friend) notice about you that would give him the idea that things are better for you?
- When he notices that, what might he do differently?
- When he does that, what would you do?
- And when you do that, what will be different around your house?

The intent of these questions is to help the client formulate, in detail, what will be "different" in his or her life when the miracle happens. As the client struggles to describe these differences, the client also often develops both an expectation of change and a growing sense of the goals toward which to direct effort.

The satellite questions mirror the characteristics of well-formed goals. Thus, when a client responds to the miracle question, "I'd have a sense of peace," the worker might ask, "What might your husband notice different about you that would tell him that you are beginning to 'have a sense of peace'?" With this question, the worker is attempting to help the client develop more concrete goals that are more the beginning of something rather than the end and that respect the client's language. Or, to give another example, when a client responds to the miracle question with, "I'd cry less," the worker would ask, "What would be there instead of the crying?" recognizing that well-formed goals are the presence of something rather than the absence.

Interviewing for Client Strengths

Exception-Finding Questions. Exception-finding questions are used by the worker to discover a client's present and past successes in relation to the client's goals. Eventually these successes are used to build solutions. Examples of exception-finding questions are as follows:

> You said that when the "miracle" happens, you and your husband would notice yourselves "communicating more about your days and hug each other more." Are there times now or in the past when the two of you were able to do that?
>
> * * *
>
> Okay, if I remember correctly, you said you would know that you did not need to see me anymore when you were "drinking less and spending more time with your wife, kids, and nondrinking buddies." So, when was the last time you were "drinking less and . . ."?

Sometimes clients are not yet able to describe how their life will be different when the problem is solved; they can talk only about their problems. In these situations a worker can still explore for exceptions but must do so by working from the problem instead of from an answer to the miracle question:

> I'm wondering, are there days when you feel "less scared about the future" [client's definition of the problem]? When was the last time you had a better day? What was different about that day that made it better? Where did that happen? Who was there with you? What might [those people] have noticed you doing differently that would tell them that you were doing better?

Once exceptions are brought to light—in easily the majority of the cases—the worker then explores how they happened. In particular, the worker attempts to clarify, as concretely as possible, what the client may have contributed to making the exceptions happen. Whatever contributions the worker and client together can bring into the client's awareness represent client strengths. Here is an example of a conversation wherein a worker and a client uncover a client's contribution to making exceptions happen:

> *Worker:* I am curious about those days when you are "less scared about your future." What do you think you do differently on those days?
>
> *Client:* I'm not sure [pause], maybe wash the car and rake leaves.
>
> *Worker:* What else?
>
> *Client:* Well, yesterday I did check the want ads for another job.

When a worker and client together uncover an exception along with the client's strengths that contributed to the exception, the worker affirms and amplifies those strengths in a way that is consistent with the worker's individual style and sense of proportion:

> *Worker:* So on better days you do things like "washing the car, raking the yard, and checking the want ads for a better job." And those things help. They seem like a good idea. Where did you get the idea to do all that? [or: Was doing these things something new for you? Was it hard for you to do those things?]

Scaling Questions. Scaling questions are a clever way to make complex features of a client's life more concrete and accessible for both client and worker. They usually take the form of asking the client to give a number from 0 through 10 that best represents where the client is at some specified point. The worker usually designates 10 as the positive end of the scale, equating higher numbers with more positive outcomes and experiences. Here is an example;

> *Worker:* At this point, I want to ask you to rank something between 0 and 10. Let's say that 0 was where you were at with this problem when you first made the call to come in and see me

and 10 means your problem is solved. Give me a number that says where you are right now.

Client: Hmm. I guess about a 2 or 3.

Almost any aspect of a client's life can be scaled, including progress toward finding a solution, confidence about finding a solution, motivation to work on a solution, severity of a problem, the likelihood of hurting self or another person, self-esteem, and so on. Once the client answers with numbers greater than zero, the worker can follow up with questions that uncover, affirm, and amplify the client's strengths, as the continuation of the scaling question demonstrates:

Worker: So you are at a 2 or 3 right now. What's different that tells you that you're doing better now than when you first called?

Client: Well, I decided to come here, and I started thinking about how I might tell my boss that I *need* some time off.

Worker: [perceiving the client's sense of satisfaction] That's great. Was it hard for you to "decide to come here"? [also:] Where did you get the idea to "decide to come here"? Is that the way you start to find a solution—"to start thinking about" what you need to do differently?

Coping Questions. In the authors' practice experience, more than 80 percent of clients are able to work productively at developing goals and identifying exceptions. However, like all workers, we encounter clients who are feeling hopeless and seem able to talk only about how horrible their present is and how bleak their future looks. Sometimes these clients are experiencing an acute crisis that gives rise to their hopelessness, and at other times the hopelessness represents a persistent pattern of self-expression and relating to others. In both cases, coping questions can be helpful in uncovering client strengths.

These questions accept the client's perceptions and then move on to ask how the client is able to cope with such overwhelming circumstances and feelings. For example:

Worker: [empathizing and responding to a client who is describing a long-standing depression and one discouraging event after another in her life] I can see that you have many reasons to feel depressed; there have been so many things that haven't worked out the way you wished. I'm wondering how you have managed to keep going? How have you been able to get up each morning and face another day?

Client: I really don't know.

Worker: I'm amazed. With all . . . [worker refers to the discouragements in client's terms], I don't know how you make it. How do you do it?

Client: I surprise myself sometimes, too; sometimes I'd just like to end it all. But I can't. Who would take care of my kids?

Worker: Is that how you do it—think about how much your kids need you? You must care a lot about them. Tell me more about what you do to take care of them [worker explores for parenting strengths and motivation].

As the worker helps the client to uncover coping strengths, the client's mood and confidence usually rise. Sometimes new ideas for coping emerge that the client has never thought of before. However, it is also common for the client to return to problem descriptions and associated feelings of discouragement. As this occurs the worker respectfully listens, empathizes, and then gently returns the client to a focus on strengths exploration and affirmation.

"What's Better?" Questions. "What's better?" questions are not so much a distinct set of questions as an approach to beginning later sessions by continuing the work of building solutions and uncovering client strengths. Instead of beginning later sessions with a review of homework tasks assigned or even the client's estimate of progress, a solution-focused worker simply asks, "What's happening in your life that's better?" This is done for two reasons: First, it optimizes the chances of bringing to light exceptions that have occurred since the last visit with the worker. Second, it recognizes that the lives of clients, including their goals, are in process, not necessarily being the same today as yesterday. Consequently, the "what's better?" approach increases the chances of uncovering exceptions and associated strengths that are the most meaningful and useful to the client at the present moment.

Exploring for "what's better" is the same as exploring for exceptions. And, as with exceptions, clients may or may not have difficulty answering the questions. Therefore, workers will have to be more or less persistent, accordingly. The following is an example of an interaction involving a client seeking help with anxiety symptoms:

Worker: [first question of the second session] So, tell me, what's happening that's better?

Client: Well, I'm not sure; I mean, I still get the shakes. But maybe they're not quite as bad.

Worker: Oh, "not quite as bad." Some relief must feel good.

Client: Yeah, it does, but they still come back, and when they do, I'm miserable.

Worker: I'm sure you are—you've described to me how tough it can be for you to get through. [pause] Now, I'm wondering about when was the last time the "shakes" were "not quite as bad"? [also:] What was different about that time? How did it happen? What might [your friend] have noticed that you do differently that helped you [through that morning]? On a scale of 0 to 10 with 10 equal to "every chance," what are the chances of your having another morning like that in the next couple of days? What gives you that level of confidence? What's the most important thing for you to remember to increase the chances of having more mornings when the "shakes are not quite as bad"?

In solution-focused interviewing, it is customary for the worker to take a brief break before the end of an interview and prepare feedback for the client. The feedback consists mainly of affirming the client's well-formed goals (insofar as they exist) and highlighting thoughts, actions, and feelings of the client (gleaned from the exploration of exceptions) that already are contributing to either reaching the goals or coping with life's hardships or traumas. These thoughts, actions, and feelings constitute the client's strengths on the road to client-devised solutions expressed in the client's categories.

Fit between Solution-Focused Interviewing and the Strengths Perspective

There are six key concepts behind the strengths perspective to be operationalized in the worker-client relationship: empowerment, membership, regeneration and healing from within, synergy, dialogue and collaboration, and suspension of disbelief. Solution-focused clinicians must convey these concepts to their clients in practice.

Empowerment

. . . Saleebey explained that empowering clients means creating a context in which clients can "discover the considerable power within themselves" to handle their own problems, rather than—even with the best of intentions—telling clients what they need or ought to do to overcome their difficulties. The matter of whose "definitions of reality" take precedence in this process is critical. Those who practice social work from the strengths perspective try to empower their clients by encouraging them to define their own worlds, problems, aspirations, and strengths to create more satisfying lives.

Solution-focused interviewing honors a worker's commitment to use client meanings. For example, when a client states that her problem "might be depression," the solution-focused worker responds with, "What is happening in your life that tells you that you 'might be depressed'?" Similarly, the same worker would encourage the client to work at defining her own goals, exceptions, levels of confidence and motivation to solve her depression, and eventual degrees of progress—all in her own language. The client is empowered by the worker's creating a context that requires her to draw on two of her most important and unique human capacities: conceptualizing her own world and making decisions about how to live in it.

Membership

Frequently the clients of social workers are cut off from their cultural and geographic roots, feel vulnerable, experience discrimination, or are otherwise alienated; therefore, they lack a sense of belonging. In part because alienated people lack the sense of belonging, they are also out of touch with their strengths and possibilities. Consequently, in a beginning effort to foster a sense of membership in alienated clients, Saleebey wrote, "certain things are required of us [workers] at the outset:" (1) working collaboratively with clients, (2) affirming client perceptions and stories, (3) recognizing the survival efforts and successes of clients, and (4) fostering client links to contexts where client strengths can flourish.

The solution-focused interviewing questions discussed earlier demonstrate how practitioners can meet Saleebey's first three requirements. Regarding the fourth, we have found that in our work with clients, the miracle, exception-finding, "what's better?" and coping questions all uncover useful possibilities for linking clients to affirming contexts. . . .

Synergy

A synergic relationship is one in which the participants, by virtue of their interaction, are able to create a larger, more beneficial result than either could have created alone using individual resources. Such a relationship potentially can exist at or between any of the several levels at which people interact—from the level of individuals to that of large collectivities.

The strengths perspective asserts that both inner and outer human resources are expandable through synergic relationship. We believe that solution-focused interviewing increases the possibility of synergic relationship in two respects.

Between Client and Worker. First, in solution-focused work each party contributes differently to the interaction. The client provides content—a personal story, values, beliefs, perceptions, wishes, definitions of reality—expressed in his or her own way. The worker brings an understanding of the structure of the change process—the necessity of developing well-formed goals and building solutions from exceptions—along with the interviewing questions that reflect his or her understanding. The practitioner assists the client's participation by affirming the client's frame of reference and the strengths that emerge in the interaction. In the end, more often than not, the mix produces a synergic expansion of the client's inner resources.

Between Client and the Client's Context. Second, the strengths perspective is as committed to enhancing the relationships between clients and their contexts as it is to expanding the inner resources of clients (although the two often occur together). When solution-focused workers ask their questions, they always do so in relation to the social context of their clients. Satellite questioning opens up possibilities for different, more synergy-enhancing interactions between clients and their social contexts and thus contributes to creating "new and often unexpected patterns and resources."

Dialogue and Collaboration

To truly hold a dialogue with a client is to explore and affirm the "otherness" of the client. Solution-focused interviewing does just this. In drawing out the client's perceptions and strengths, the worker is continually respecting and affirming the client's otherness.

To collaborate with a client is to negotiate and consult with the client, not to provide expert answers. When clients insist on returning to problem talk or asking for answers from the worker, the worker listens, empathizes, and gently returns them to defining their goals for a more desirable future and examining the significance of exceptions in their lives.

Suspension of Disbelief

Although suspension of disbelief may seem to have drawbacks in the short run, it offers great hope of a synergic, empowering relationship between client and worker over the long haul. This concept of the strengths perspective challenges workers to avoid the long-standing tendency in the profession to distrust the perceptions and statements of clients about themselves and their circumstances. Solution-focused interviewing, too, is premised on a belief that respecting the client's perceptions and statements is the best antidote to what the profession calls "client resistance." Once the client experiences acceptance and affirmation from the worker, the likelihood of productive work increases.

Conclusion

It is hard to imagine a tighter fit between philosophy and practice than that between the strengths perspective and solution-focused interviewing questions. This article makes a case for that fit at the micro level of work with individuals, couples, and families, the level at which the interviewing questions were first developed and applied. Recently, applications have been made in work with groups and organizations.

Saleebey boiled the philosophy of the strengths perspective down to the following challenge:

> At the very least, the strengths perspective obligates workers to understand that, however downtrodden or sick, individuals have survived (and in some cases even thrived). They have taken steps, summoned up resources, and coped. We need to know what they have done, how they have done it, what they have learned from doing it, what resources (inner and outer) were available in their struggle to surmount their troubles. People are always working on their situations, even if just deciding to be resigned to them; as helpers we must tap into that work, elucidate it, find and build on its possibilities.

The miracle question, exception-finding questions, scaling questions, coping questions, and "what's better?" questions are invaluable resources for meeting Saleebey's challenge in day-to-day social work practice.

POST-CLASS REFLECTION MEMO

Draft and submit a memo in response to the questions below:

- How do the lessons you have learned in class today translate into the lawyering process in your clinic cases?
- How will your insights about the benefits (and the drawbacks) of client-centered counseling concretely affect your lawyering work in the clinic?
- When planning a counseling session, what checks can you put in place to ensure that you are:
  - crediting your client's values, rather than enforcing your own; and
  - offering your client your best professional advice, rather than making choices based on an effort to avoid conflict?

HANDOUTS

Client Counseling Exercise[4]

Facts:

Your rich aunt dies and leaves a will, making you one of several beneficiaries. The gift is $52,000 cash. However, a will contest has been filed by other close relatives not mentioned in the will. The case is set for trial in two years. If the will contest is successful, you will receive $0 (there is an earlier will in which you are not mentioned).

You have received a settlement offer of $9,500 after attorney fees, which would be paid next month.

Your lawyer tells you that there is a good chance that the will contest will be defeated, and that you will receive a net of $38,000 in two years (exclusive of attorney's fees), following the trial. The lawyer also tells you she believes the case will proceed to trial if you do not accept this settlement offer.

Instructions:

Write down whether you would accept the settlement or try the case. List the reasons for your decision.

You may respond to this hypothetical either by situating yourself in your own, actual family, or by imagining yourself as part of a different one. Either way, base your decision on your own values regarding money, risk, and value preference.

Client-Centered Counseling Model Development

Goals Group

- What categories of goals might be worth probing for, in terms of substance, time frame, legal, and extra-legal?
- How will you ensure that you move past generalities with Mrs. Dunlap?
- For example, assume that when you ask her what her goals are, she says, "I want to defeat my ex-husband's motion to modify custody." What follow-up questions might you ask?
- What strategies will you use to avoid making assumptions, à la Mr. Muth, about what is best for Mrs. Dunlap?

Options Generation Group

- How will you ensure that Mrs. Dunlap has a meaningful opportunity to participate in the process?

[4] This exercise is adapted from David A. Binder, Paul Bergman, Paul R. Tremblay & Ian S. Weinstein, LAWYERS AS COUNSELORS: A PROBLEM-SOLVING APPROACH (3rd ed., 2011).

- How will you make sure Mrs. Dunlap receives the benefit of your own legal expertise without silencing her or unduly influencing her thinking?
- What categories of options might be worth probing for, in terms of substance, time frame, legal, and extra-legal?
- What strategies will you employ to avoid making assumptions, à la Mr. Muth, about what is best for Mrs. Dunlap?

Options Evaluation Group

- How will you ensure that Mrs. Dunlap has a meaningful opportunity to participate in the process?
- How will you make sure Mrs. Dunlap receives the benefit of your own legal expertise without silencing her or unduly influencing her thinking?
- What strategies will you employ to avoid making assumptions, à la Mr. Muth, about what is best for Mrs. Dunlap?
- How will you ensure that the evaluation process is effectively tied in to Mrs. Dunlap's goals?

CHAPTER 3

COMMUNICATION AND ASSUMPTIONS

LEARNING GOALS

The learning goals for this class include helping you to:

- Understand how the ability to communicate well is essential to a lawyer's ability to effectively represent a client
- Analyze the role of audience in communication and explore the challenges inherent in the audience role
- Understand the role of unconscious assumptions in a lawyer's efforts to communicate

DESCRIPTION OF CLASS

We will engage in a series of exercises that are designed to surface ways in which our unconscious assumptions affect our ability to communicate to a target audience.

ASSIGNMENT IN PREPARATION FOR CLASS SESSION

Draft and submit a paragraph in response to the following:

Think of a time when you told a story or described a situation and the listener misunderstood what happened. In other words, the listener had a misimpression, a different understanding of what had happened than what you intended to convey.

Consider the following questions:

- What were the factual differences in the two understandings of the story or situation?

- What factors might have contributed to these different understandings?
- What strategies could the speaker and/or the listener have used to communicate more effectively?

READING ASSIGNMENT

1. Sue Bryant & Jean Koh Peters, *Five Habits for Cross Cultural Lawyering, in* RACE, CULTURE, PSYCHOLOGY AND LAW (Kimberly Holt Barnett & William H. George eds., 2005).
2. Jerome Groopman, *Introduction, in* HOW DOCTORS THINK 9 (2007).
3. Jennifer K. Robbennolt & Jean R. Sternlight, PSYCHOLOGY FOR LAWYERS: UNDERSTANDING THE HUMAN FACTORS IN NEGOTIATION, LITIGATION, AND DECISION MAKING (2012).

READINGS

Sue Bryant & Jean Koh Peters
Five Habits for Cross Cultural Lawyering
RACE, CULTURE, PSYCHOLOGY AND LAW (2005)[1]

Practicing law is often a cross-cultural experience. The law, as well as the legal system in which it operates, is a culture with strong professional norms that give meaning to and reinforce behaviors. The communication style of argument predominates, and competition is highly valued. Even when a lawyer and a non-law-trained client share a common culture, the client and the lawyer will likely experience the lawyer-client interaction as a cross-cultural experience because of the cultural differences that arise from the legal culture.

In addition to these cultural differences, we know that the global movement of people, as well as the multicultural nature of the United States, creates many situations where lawyers and clients will work in cross-cultural situations. To meet the challenges of cross-cultural representation, lawyers need to develop awareness, knowledge, and skills that enhance the lawyers' and clients' capacities to form meaningful relationships and to communicate accurately.

---

1 Endnotes and/or internal citations omitted.

This chapter, and the habits it introduces, prepares lawyers to engage in effective, accurate cross-cultural communication and to build trust and understanding between themselves and their clients. Section 1 identifies some ways that culture influences lawyering and the potential issues that may arise in cross-cultural lawyer-client interactions. Section 2 identifies the principles and habits that are skills and perspectives that can be used to identify our own cultural norms and those of our clients and to communicate effectively, knowing these differences. As one anthropologist has recognized, there is "a great distance between knowing that my gaze transforms and becoming aware of the ways that my gaze transforms." To help lawyers identify the ways their gaze transforms and the cultural bridges that are needed for joint work between lawyers and clients, we have developed five habits for cross-cultural lawyering.

CULTURE AND THE ROLE IT PLAYS IN LAWYERS' WORK

To become good cross-cultural lawyers, we must first become aware of the significance of culture in the ways in which we make sense out of the world. Culture is like the air we breathe; it is largely invisible, and yet we are dependent on it for our very being. Culture is the logic through which we give meaning to the world. Our culture is learned from our experiences, sights, books, songs, language, gestures, rewards, punishments, and relationships that come to us in our homes, schools, religious organizations, and communities. We learn our culture from what we are fed and how we are touched and judged by our families and significant others in our communities. Our culture gives us our values, attitudes, and norms of behavior.

Through our cultural lens, we make judgments about people based on what they are doing and saying. We may judge people to be truthful, rude, intelligent, or superstitious based on the attributions we make about the meaning of their behavior. Because culture gives us the tools to interpret meaning from behavior and words, we are constantly attaching culturally based meaning to what we see and hear, often without being aware that we are doing so.

In this chapter, when we talk about cross-cultural lawyering, we are referring to lawyering where the lawyer's and the client's ethnic or cultural heritage comes from different countries, as well as where their cultural heritage comes from socialization and identity in different groups within the same country. By this definition, everyone is multicultural to some degree. Cultural groups and cultural norms can be based on ethnicity, race, gender, nationality, age, economic status, social status, language, sexual orientation, physical characteristics, marital status, role in family, birth order, immigration status, religion, accent, skin color, or a variety of other characteristics.

This broad definition of culture is essential for effective cross-cultural lawyering because it teaches us that no one characteristic will completely define the lawyer's or the client's culture. For example, if we think about birth order alone as a cultural characteristic, we may not see any significance to this factor. Yet if the client (or lawyer) comes from a society where "oldest son" has special meaning in terms of responsibility and privilege, identification of the ethnicity, gender, or birth order alone will not be enough to alert the lawyer to the set of norms and expectations for how the oldest son ought to behave. Instead, the lawyer needs to appreciate the significance of all three characteristics to fully understand this aspect of the client's culture.

A broad definition of culture recognizes that no two people have had the exact same experiences and thus no two people will interpret or predict in precisely the same ways. People can be part of the same culture and make different decisions while rejecting norms and values from their culture. Understanding that culture develops shared meaning and, at the same time, allows for significant differences helps us to avoid stereotyping or assuming that we know that which we have not explored with the client. At the same time that we recognize these individual differences, we also know that if we share a common cultural heritage with a client, we are often better able to predict or interpret, and our mistakes are likely to be smaller misunderstandings.

When lawyers and clients come from different cultures, several aspects of the attorney-client interaction may be implicated. The capacities to form trusting relationships, to evaluate credibility, to develop client-centered case strategies and solutions, to gather information, and to attribute the intended meaning from behavior and expressions are all affected by cultural experiences. By using the framework of cross-cultural interaction, lawyers can learn to anticipate and name some of the difficulties they or their clients may be experiencing. By asking ourselves as part of the cross-cultural analysis to identify ways in which we are similar to clients, we identify the strengths of connection. Focusing on similarities also alerts us to pay special attention when we see ourselves as "the same" as the client so that we do not substitute our own judgment for the client's through overidentification and transference.

Establishing Trust

Lawyers and clients who do not share the same culture face special challenges in developing a trusting relationship where genuine, accurate communication occurs. Especially where the culture of the client is one with a significant distrust of outsiders or of the particular culture of the lawyer, the lawyer must work hard to earn trust in a culturally sensitive way. Similarly, cultural difference may cause the lawyer to mistrust the client. For example, when we find the client's story changing or new information coming to light as we investigate, we may experience the client as "lying" or "being unhelpful." Often this causes us to feel betrayed by our client's actions.

Sometimes when a client is reacting negatively to a lawyer or a lawyer's suggestions, lawyers label clients as "difficult." Professor Michelle Jacobs has warned that white lawyers interpreting clients' behavior may fail to understand the significance of racial differences, thereby erroneously labeling African American clients as "difficult." Instead, the lawyer may be sending signals to the client that reinforce racial stereotypes, may be interpreting behavior incorrectly, and therefore may be unconsciously failing to provide full advocacy.

In these situations, lawyers should assess whether the concept of insider-outsider status helps explain client reactions. Where insider-outsider status is implicated, lawyers must be patient and try to understand the complexities of the relationship and their communication while building trust slowly.

Accurate Understanding

Even in situations where trust is established, lawyers may still experience cultural differences that significantly interfere with lawyers' and clients' capacities to understand one another's goals, behaviors, and communications. Cultural differences often cause us to attribute different meanings to the same set of facts. Thus one important goal of cross-cultural competence is for lawyers to attribute to behavior and communication that which the actor or speaker intends.

Inaccurate attributions can cause lawyers to make significant errors in their representation of clients. Imagine a lawyer saying to a client, "If there is anything that you do not understand, please just ask me to explain" or "If I am not being clear, please just ask me any questions." Many cultural differences may explain a client's reluctance to either blame the lawyer for poor communication (the second question) or blame himself or herself for lack of understanding (the first question). Indeed clients from some cultures might find one or the other of these results to be rude and therefore be reluctant to ask for clarification for fear of offending the lawyer or embarrassing themselves.

Cultural differences may also cause lawyers and clients to misperceive body language and judge each other incorrectly. For an everyday example, take nodding while someone is speaking. In some cultures, the nodding indicates agreement with the speaker, whereas in others it simply indicates that the listener is hearing the speaker. Another common example involves eye contact. In some cultures, looking someone straight in the eye is a statement of open and honest communication, whereas a diversion of eyes signals dishonesty. In other cultures, however, a diversion of eyes is a sign of respect. Lawyers need to recognize these differences and plan for a representation strategy that takes them into account.

Organizing and Assessing Facts

More generally, our concepts of credibility are very culturally determined. In examining the credibility of a story, lawyers and judges often ask whether the story makes "sense" as if "sense" were neutral. Consider, for example, a client who explains that the reason she left her native country was that God appeared to her in a dream and told her it was time to leave. If the time of leaving is a critical element to the credibility of her story, how will the fact finder evaluate the credibility of that client's story? Does the fact finder come from a culture where dreams are valued, where an interventionist God is expected, or where major life decisions would be based on these expectations or values? Will the fact finder, as a result of differences, find the story incredible or evidence of a disturbed thought process or, alternatively, as a result of similarities, find the client credible?

The way different cultures conceptualize facts may cause lawyers and clients to see different information as relevant. Lawyers who experience clients as "wandering all over the place" may be working with clients who categorize information differently than the lawyer or the legal system. If a lawyer whose culture is oriented to hour, day, month, and year tries to get a time line from a client whose culture is not oriented that way, she may incorrectly interpret the client's failure to provide the information as uncooperative, lacking intelligence, or, worse, lying.[10] A client who is unable to tell a linear time-related story may also experience the same reaction from courts and juries if the client's culture is unknown to the fact finders.

Individual and Collective

In other settings, the distinction between individual and collective cultures has been called the most important concept to grasp in cross-cultural encounters. Understanding the differences between individual and collective cultures will help lawyers see how they and clients define problems, identify solutions, and determine who important players are in a decision.

Lawyers who explore differences in individual and collective cultures may see different communication styles, values, and views of the roles of the lawyer and client. In an individualistic culture, people are socialized to have individual goals and are praised for achieving these goals. They are encouraged to make their own plans and "do their own thing." Individualists need to assert themselves and do not find competition threatening. By contrast, in a collective culture, people are socialized to think in terms of the group, to work for the betterment of the group, and to integrate individual and group goals. Collectivists use group membership to predict behavior. Because collectivists are accepted for who they are and feel less need to talk, silence plays a more important role in their communication style.

Majority culture in the United States has been identified as the most individualistic culture in the world. Our legal culture reflects this commitment to individualism. For example, ethical rules of confidentiality often require a lawyer to communicate with an individual client in private if confidentiality is to be maintained and may prohibit the lawyer from representing the group or taking group concerns into account to avoid potential conflicts. Many client-empowerment models and client-centered models of practice are based on individualistic cultural values.

Here is an example of how a result that appeared successful to the lawyers can nevertheless be unacceptable when taken in the context of the client's collective culture. In this case, lawyers negotiated a plea to a misdemeanor assault with probation for a battered Chinese woman who had killed her husband and who faced a 25-year sentence if convicted of murder. The client, who had a strong self-defense claim, refused to plead to the misdemeanor charge because she did not want to humiliate herself, her ancestors, her children, and their children by acknowledging responsibility for the killing. Her attorneys did not fully comprehend the concept of shame that the client would experience until the client was able to explain that the possibility of 25 years in jail was far less offensive than the certain shame that would be experienced by her family (past, present, and future) if she pled guilty. These negative reactions to what the lawyers thought was an excellent result allowed the lawyers to examine the meaning of pleas, family, responsibility, and consequences within a collective cultural context that was far different than their own.

Legal Strategy and Decision Making

In another case, attorneys—whose client was a Somalian refugee seeking political asylum—had to change their strategy for presenting evidence in order to respect the client's cultural and religious norms. Soldiers had bayoneted her when she resisted rape, and she was scarred on a breast and an ankle. To show evidence of persecution, the plaintiff would have had to reveal parts of her body that she was committed, by religion and culture, to keeping private. Ultimately the client developed a strategy of showing the injury to the INS lawyer who was also female. This strategy, challenging conventional legal advocacy and violating cultural norms of the adversarial system, allowed the client to present a case that honored her values and norms.

Immigrant clients often bring with them prior experiences with courts or interactions with governments from their countries of origin that influence the choices they make in their cases. Strategies that worked in their country of origin may not be successful here. For example, clients from cultures that punish those challenging governmental action may be resistant to a lawyer's suggestion that a Supplemental Security Income (SSI) benefits appeal be taken, challenging the government's decision to deny a claim. Conversely, those who come from societies where refusal to follow government requirements is a successful strategy may be labeled as belligerent by the court when they consistently resist or challenge the court.

Finally, cultural differences may cause us to misjudge a client or to provide differential representation based on stereotype or bias. Few lawyers engage in explicit open racial or cultural hostility toward a client. However, if recent studies in the medical field have relevance for lawyers, we need to recognize that even lawyers of goodwill may engage in unconscious stereotyping that results in inferior representation. Studies in the medical field show that doctors are less likely to explain diagnoses to patients of color and less likely to gather significant information from them or to refer them for needed treatment. Although no studies of lawyers to our knowledge have focused on studying whether lawyers engage in discriminatory treatment, two recent studies have identified differential treatment by the legal system based on race. One study done by Child Welfare Watch shows that African American children are far more likely to be removed from their home, put in foster care, and left there longer than similarly situated white children. Another study showed that African American juveniles received disproportionate sentences when compared with similarly situated white youths. In each of these legal studies, lawyers—as prosecutors, representatives, and judges—were deeply implicated in the work that led to the differential treatment.

Once a cultural difference surfaces, we can see stark cultural contrasts with clear connections to lawyering choices. In hindsight, it is easy to see the cultural contrasts and their effect on the clients' and lawyers' challenges to find acceptable accommodations to the legal system. In the moment, however, cases are more difficult, and the differences and similarities are more subtle and, at times, invisible. The following sections give you some insights into how to make this more visible.

Culture-General and Culture-Specific Knowledge

In addition to developing awareness of the role that culture plays in attributing meaning to behaviors and communication, a competent cross-cultural lawyer also studies the specific culture and language of the client group the lawyer represents. Culture-specific knowledge, politics, geography, and history, especially information that might shed light on the client's legal issues, relationship with the lawyer, and process of decision making will assist the lawyer in representing the client better. As the lawyer develops culture-specific knowledge, he or she should apply this knowledge carefully and examine it on a case-by-case basis. Finally, a lawyer will have a greater capacity to build trust and connection if he or she speaks the client's language even if they do not share a common culture.

If the lawyer represents clients from a multitude of cultures, the lawyer can improve cross-cultural interactions by acquiring culture-general knowledge and skills. This culture-general information is also helpful to lawyers who are beginning to learn about a specific culture. Because learning any new culture is a complex endeavor (remember the number of years that we spent learning our own), the lawyer can use culture-general knowledge and skills while learning specifics about a new culture.

HABIT 1: DEGREES OF SEPARATION AND CONNECTION

The first part of Habit 1 encourages lawyers to consciously identify the similarities and differences between their clients and themselves and to assess their impact on the attorney-client relationship. The framework of similarities and differences helps assess lawyer-client interaction, professional distance, and information gathering.

The second part of the habit asks the lawyer to assess the significance of these similarities and differences. By identifying differences, we focus consciously on the possibility that cultural misunderstanding, bias, and stereotyping may occur. By focusing on similarities, we become conscious of the connections that we have with clients as well as the possibility that we may substitute our own judgment for the client's.

Pinpointing and Recording Similarities and Differences

To perform Habit 1, the lawyer brainstorms, as quickly as possible, as many similarities and differences between the client and himself as he can generate. This habit is rewarded for numerosity—the more differences and similarities the better. A typical list of similarities and differences might include the following:

Ethnicity	Economic Status	Marital Status
Race	Social Status	Role in Family
Gender	Language	Immigration Nationality
Sexual Orientation	Religion	Education
Age	Physical Characteristic	Time
Individualistic/ Collective	Direct or Indirect Communication	

With each client and case, you may identify different categories that will influence the case and your relationship. These lists will change as the relationship with the client and the client's case changes. Exhaustive lists help the lawyer make conscious the less obvious similarities and differences that may enhance or interfere with understanding.

Consciously identifying a long list of similarities and differences allows lawyers to see clients as individuals with personal, cultural, and social experiences that shape the clients' behavior and communications. In asking you to create long lists, we do not mean to suggest that all similarities and differences have the same order of importance for you or your client. For example, in interactions involving people of color and whites, race will likely play a significant role in the interaction given the discriminatory role that race plays in our society. In some cases, such as rape or domestic violence, gender differences may also play a greater role than in others. The connections that cause a lawyer to feel connected to a client may be insignificant to a client.

The most important thing is to make this list honestly and nonjudgmentally, thinking about what similarities and differences you perceive and suspect might affect your ability to hear and understand your client's story and your client's ability to tell it.

Another way to illustrate the degrees of connection and separation between client and lawyer is through the use of a simple Venn diagram. Draw two circles, overlapping broadly if the worlds of the client and of the lawyer largely coincide, or narrowly if they largely diverge. By creating a graphical representation of Habit 1, the lawyer can gain insight into the significance of the similarities and differences. For example, the list of similarities may be small, and yet the lawyer may feel "the same" as the client because of one shared similarity, or the lawyer may have many similarities and yet find herself feeling very distant from the client.

Analyzing the Effect of Similarities and Differences on Professional Distance and Judgment

After creating the lists and diagrams, the lawyer can identify where the cross-cultural challenges might occur. By naming the things that unite and distance us from our clients, we are able to identify relationships that need more or less professional distance because they are "too close" or "too far." No perfect degree of separation or connection exists between lawyer and client. However, where the list of similarities is long, the lawyer may usefully ask, "Are there differences that I am overlooking? Am I developing solutions to problems that may work for me but not for my client?" By pondering these questions, we recognize that even though similarities promote understanding, misunderstanding may flow from an assumption of precise congruence. Thus, in situations where lawyers and clients have circles that overlap, the lawyer should ask herself, "How do I develop proper professional distance with a client who is so similar to me?"

In other cases, where the list of differences is long, the question for the lawyer is "Are there any similarities that I am missing?" We know that negative judgments are more likely to occur when the client and lawyer see the other as an "outsider." Thus the lawyer who identities significant cultural differences between the client and herself will be less likely to judge the client if she also sees herself as similar to the client. Where large differences exist, the lawyer needs to consciously address the question "How do I bridge the huge gap between the client's experiences and mine?"

What does the analysis of connection and difference indicate about what we ought to share with clients about ourselves? Lawyers usually know far more about their clients than the clients know about the lawyers. Some information of similarity and difference will be obvious to a client, and other significant information will be known only if the lawyer chooses to tell the client. In thinking about establishing rapport with clients, lawyers often think about revealing information that will reveal similarities and establish connections to clients. Of course, exactly what information will cause the client to bond with the lawyer is difficult to know, as the significance of specific similarities and differences may be very different for the lawyer and the client.

Analyzing the Effect of Similarities and Differences on Gathering and Presenting Information

Differences and similarities or assumptions of similarity will significantly influence questioning and case theory. One example of how differences and similarities in the lawyer-client dyad may influence information gathering can be seen in the way lawyers probe for clarification in interviews. Lawyers usually ask questions based on differences that they perceive between their clients and themselves. Thus a lawyer, especially one with a direct communication style, tends to ask questions when a client makes choices that the lawyer would not have made or when he perceives an inconsistency between what the client is saying and the client's actions. A lawyer tends not to ask questions about choices that a client has made when the lawyer would have made the same choices; in such a situation, the lawyer usually assumes that the client's thought processes and reasoning are the same as his own.

For example, in working with a client who has fled her home because of spousal abuse and is living with extended family members, a lawyer might not explore the issue of family support. In contrast, had the client explained that she could not go to her family for support, the same lawyer might have explored that and developed housing alternatives. The probing occurs when the lawyer perceives the client's choices as different from the ones the lawyer might make, and therefore she tries to understand in this case why the client has failed to involve her family. The same lawyer might ask few questions about family support when she assumes that a client living with family had family support, because the lawyer would expect her own family to support her in a decision to leave an abusive spouse.

In her failure to ask questions of the first client, the lawyer is probably making a host of assumptions about cultural values that relate to the client's and the lawyer's family values. Assumptions of similarities that mask differences can lead the lawyer to solutions and legal theories that may not ultimately work for the client. For example, in assuming that the first client has family support, the lawyer in the previous example may neglect to explore other housing arrangements or supportive environments that the client needs. Family relationships are incredibly rich areas for cultural misunderstanding, and thus assumptions of similarity are perhaps even more problematic when issues of family are involved.

To identify the unexplored cultural assumptions that the lawyer may be making, the lawyer should ask what she has explored and what she has left unexplored. Reflection on the attorney-client interview allows the lawyer to identify areas where the lawyer may have missed relevant explanations of behavior.

HABIT 2: RINGS IN MOTION

If the key to Habit 1 is "identifying and analyzing the distance between me and my client," the key to Habit 2 is identifying and analyzing how cultural differences and similarities influence the interactions between the client, the legal decision makers, the opponents, and the lawyer.

Lawyers interview clients to gain an understanding of the client's problem from the client's perspective and to gather information that will help the lawyer identify potential solutions, particularly those that are available within the legal system or those that opponents will assent to.

What information is considered relevant and important is a mixture of the client's, opponent's, lawyer's, and legal system's perspectives.

If these perspectives are different in material ways, information will likely be presented, gathered, and weighed differently. Habit 2 examines these perspectives explicitly by asking the lawyer to identify and analyze the similarities and differences in different dyads and triads to assess the various cultural lenses that may affect the outcome of a client's case.

Like Habit 1, the lawyer is encouraged to name and/or diagram the differences and similarities first and then to analyze their effect on the case.

Pinpoint and Record Similarities and Differences in the Legal System-Client Dyad

The lawyer should identify the similarities and differences that may exist between client-law and legal decision maker-law. As in Habit 1, the similarities and differences can be listed or can be put on a Venn diagram. In many cases, multiple players will influence the outcome and should be included when identifying the similarities and differences. For example, a prosecutor, a prospective jury, a presentence probation officer, and a judge may all make decisions that influence how the client charged with a crime will be judged and sentenced. Or a forensic evaluator in a custody case may play a significant role in deciding the outcome of a case. Therefore, at various points in the representation, different, important players should be included in the diagram of similarities and differences.

For example, a forensic evaluator in examining a capacity to parent may look for signs of the parent's encouragement of separation of parent and child. In cultures that do not see this kind of separation as healthy for the child, the evaluator may find little that is positive to report. For example, the parent may be criticized for overinvolvement, for practices such as sharing beds with children, or for failing to tolerate "normal" disagreements between child and parent. Lawyers should identify the potential differences that exist between the client and decision makers and focus on how to explain the client's choices where they differ from the evaluator's norms.

In thinking about how differences and similarities might influence the decision makers, lawyers often try to help clients make connections to decision makers to lessen the negative judgments or stereotyping that may result from difference. To the extent that lawyers have choices, they may hire or suggest that the court use expert evaluators that share a common culture or language with the client. Cross-cultural misunderstandings and ethnocentric judgments are less likely to occur in these situations. By checking with others that have used this expert, lawyers can confirm that, despite their professional education, the expert has retained an understanding and acceptance of the cultural values of the client. When the client and decision makers come from different cultures, the lawyer should think creatively about similarities that the client shares with the decision makers. By encouraging clients and decision makers to see similarities in each other, connections can be made cross-culturally.

In addition to focusing on the decision makers, the lawyer should identify the cultural values and norms implicit in the law that will be applied to the client. Does the client share these values and norms, or do differences exist?

Pinpoint and Record Similarities and Differences in the Legal System-Lawyer Dyad

The lawyer should also focus on the legal system-lawyer dyad and assess the similarities and differences between herself and the legal system. To what extent does the lawyer adopt the values and norms of the law and legal decision makers? How acculturated to the law and legal culture has the lawyer become? In what ways does the lawyer see the "successful" client the same as the law and legal decision makers, and to what extent does the lawyer have different values and evaluations? Understanding the differences and similarities between the lawyer and the legal system players will help the lawyer assess whether her evaluation of the case is likely to match the legal decision maker.

Again the lawyer can list or create a diagram that indicates the similarities and differences. By studying these, the lawyer can develop strategies for translation between the client and the legal system that keeps the client and her concerns central to the case.

Pinpoint and Record Similarities and Differences of Opponents to Legal Decision Makers/Clients/Lawyers

The cultural background of an opposing party may also influence the outcome of a case. By listing or diagramming similarities and differences of the opponent with the various other players involved in a case, the lawyer can assess a case and design creative solutions. Often in settling cases, lawyers look for win-win solutions that meet the needs of clients and their adversaries. For example, in assessing the possibility of resolving a custody case, a lawyer may want to know what the norms of custody are in the opposing party's culture and the extent to which the opposing party still embraces these values. How might gender norms about who should have custody influence the opponent's capacity or willingness to settle the case? Will the opponent be the only decision maker in resolving the case, or might the extended family, especially the grandparents, be the people who need to be consulted for the settlement to take place. All these factors and more should be included in a lawyer's plan for negotiation.

Reading the Rings: Analyze the Effect of Similarities and Differences

After filling in the diagrams and/or making the lists of the different dyads, the lawyer can interpret the information to look for insights about the impact of culture on the case and potential successful strategies. The lawyer's goal in reading the rings is to consciously examine influences on the case that may be invisible but will nonetheless affect the case.

The following questions may help identify some of those insights:

Assessing the legal claim: How large is the area of overlap between the client and the law?

Assessing cultural differences that result in negative judgments: What are the cultural differences that may lead to different values or biases, causing decision makers to negatively judge the client or the opponent?

Identifying similarities that may establish connections and understanding: What does a successful client look like to this decision maker? How similar or different is the client from this successful client?

Assessing credibility: How credible is my client's story? Does it make "sense"? To what extent is knowledge of the client, her values, and her culture necessary for the sense of the story? How credible is my client? Are there cultural factors influencing the way the client tells the story that will affect her credibility?

Identifying legal strategies: Can I shift the law's perspective to encompass more of the client's claim and desired relief? Do my current strategies in the client's case require the law, the legal decision maker, or the client to adjust perspectives?

Identifying bones to pick with the law: How large is the area of overlap between the law and myself?

Identifying how my biases shape the inquiry: How large is the area of overlap between the lawyer-client, lawyer-law, and client-legal system circles? Notice that the overlap is now divided into two parts: the characteristics relevant to the legal case that the lawyer shares with the client and those relevant characteristics that the lawyer does not share with the client. Does my client have a plausible claim that is difficult for me to see because of these differences or similarities? Am I probing for clarity using multiple frames of reference—the client's, the legal system's, the opponent's, and mine? Or am I focused mostly on my own frame of reference?

Identifying hot-button issues: Of all the characteristics and perspectives listed on the rings, which loom largest for me? Are they the same ones that loom largest for the client? For the law?

Habit 2 is more cumbersome than Habit 1 and requires looking at multiple frames of reference at once. However, lawyers who have used Habit 2 find that it helps them to focus when a case or client is troubling them. The lawyer can identify why she has been focusing on a particular aspect of a case even when that aspect is not critical to the success of the case. She may gain insight into why a judge is bothered by a particular issue that is presented in the case. In addition, lawyers might gain insight into why clients are resisting the lawyer's advice or the court's directive and are "uncooperative." Lawyers might also begin to understand why clients often see the lawyer as part of a hostile legal system when a high degree of overlap between the lawyer and the legal system is identified.

What can the lawyer do with the insights gained from reading the rings or lists? Lawyers can ask whether the law and legal culture can be changed to legitimate the client, her perspective, and her claim. Can the lawyer push the law or should she persuade the client to adapt? Hopefully, by discovering some of these insights, the lawyer may be better able to explain the client to the legal system and the legal system to the client.

HABIT 3: PARALLEL UNIVERSES

Habit 3 helps a lawyer identify alternative explanations for her client's behavior. The habit of parallel universes invites the lawyer to explore multiple alternative interpretations of any client behavior. Although the lawyer can never exhaust the parallel universes that explain a client's behavior, in a matter of minutes the lawyer can explore multiple parallel universes to explain a client's behavior at a given moment.

For example, if a lawyer has a client in a custody dispute who has consistently failed to follow a court order to take her child for a psychiatric evaluation, the lawyer might assume that her client has something to hide. Although the client tells the lawyer she will do it, it remains undone. A lawyer using parallel universe thinking can imagine many different explanations for the client's behavior: the client has never gone to a psychiatrist and is frightened; in the client's experience, only people who are crazy see psychiatrists; going to a psychiatrist carries a lot of shame; the client has no insurance and is unable to pay for the evaluation; the client cannot accept that the court will ever give the child to her husband, who was not the primary child caretaker, the client may fear that she will be misinterpreted by the psychiatrist; or the client simply did not think that she needed to get it done so quickly.

Using parallel universe thinking, the lawyer for a client who fails to keep appointments can explore parallel universe explanations for her initial judgment that "she does not care about the case." The behavior may have occurred because the client lacked carfare, failed to receive the letter setting up the appointment, lost her way to the office, had not done what she promised the lawyer she would do before their next appointment, or simply forgot about her appointment because of a busy life.

The point of parallel universe thinking is to get used to challenging oneself to identify the many alternatives to the interpretations to which we may be tempted to leap on insufficient information. By doing so, we remind ourselves that we lack the facts to make the interpretation, and we identify the assumptions we are using. The process need not take a lot of time; it takes only a minute to generate a number of parallel universe explanations to the interpretation to which the lawyer is immediately drawn.

Parallel universe thinking would cause the lawyer in the introductory example to try to explore with the client why she is resistant or to talk to people who share the client's culture to explore possible cultural barriers to her following the court's order.

Parallel universe thinking is especially important when the lawyer is feeling judgmental about her client. If we are attributing negative inferences to a client's behavior, we should identify other reasons for the behavior. Knowledge about specific cultures may enlarge the number of explanations that we can develop for behavior. Parallel universe thinking lets us know that we may be relying on assumptions rather than facts to explain the client's behavior and allows the lawyer to explore further with the client or others the reasons for the behavior. This exploration may also be helpful in explaining the client's behavior to others.

By engaging in parallel universe thinking, lawyers are less likely to assume that they know why clients are doing what they are doing when they lack critical facts. Parallel universe thinking also allows the lawyer to follow the advice of a cross-cultural trainer who suggests that one way to reduce the stress in cross-cultural interactions is to ask, "I wonder if there is another piece of information that, if I had it, would help me interpret what is going on."

HABIT 4: RED FLAGS AND REMEDIES

The first three habits focus on ways to think like a lawyer, incorporating cross-cultural knowledge into analyzing how we think about cases, our clients, and the usefulness of the legal system. Habit 4 focuses on cross-cultural communication, identifying some tasks in normal attorney-client interaction that may be particularly problematic in cross-cultural encounters as well as alerting lawyers to signs of communication problems.

Good cross-cultural interaction requires mindful communication where the lawyer remains cognitively aware of the communication process and avoids using routine responses to clients. In cross-cultural communication, the lawyer must listen deeply, carefully attuned to the client and continuously monitoring whether the interaction is working and whether adjustments need to be made.

Habit 4 is accomplished in the moment and requires little planning for the experienced lawyer. The lawyer can identify ahead of time what she will look for to spot good communication and "red flags" that will tell her that accurate, genuine communication is probably not occurring.

In addition to paying attention to red flags and corrective measures, culturally sensitive exchanges with clients should pay special attention to four areas: (1) scripts, especially those describing the legal process; (2) introductory rituals; (3) client's understanding; and (4) culturally specific information about the client's problem.

Use Scripts Carefully

The more we do a particular activity, the more likely we are to have a "script." Lawyers often have scripts for the opening of interviews, explaining confidentiality, building rapport, explaining the legal system, and other topics common to the lawyer's practice. However, a mindful lawyer uses scripts carefully, especially in cross-cultural encounters, and instead develops a variety of communication strategies to replace scripts and explore understanding.

Pay Special Attention to Beginnings

A lawyer working with a client from another culture must pay special attention to the beginnings of communications with the client. Each culture has introduction rituals or scripts as well as trust-building exchanges that promote rapport and conversation. A lawyer who is unaware of the client's rituals must pay careful attention to the verbal and nonverbal signals the client is giving to the lawyer. How will the lawyer greet the client? What information will be exchanged before they "get down to business"? How do the client and lawyer define "getting down to business"? For one, the exchange of information about self, family, status, or background is an integral part of the business; for another, it may be introductory chitchat before the real conversation takes place. If an interpreter who is familiar with the client's culture will be involved with the interview, the lawyer can consult with the interpreter on appropriate introductory behavior.

Use Techniques That Confirm Understanding

Both clients and lawyers in cross-cultural exchanges will likely have high degrees of uncertainty and anxiety when they interact with someone they perceive to be different. The lack of predictability about how they will be received and their capacity to understand each other often leads to this uncertainty and anxiety. To lessen uncertainty and anxiety, both the lawyer and the client will be assisted by using techniques that consciously demonstrate that genuine understanding is occurring. Active listening techniques, including feedback to the client rephrasing his or her information, may be used to communicate to the client that the lawyer understands what the client is saying.

In addition to giving the client feedback, the lawyer should look for feedback from the client that she understands the lawyer or is willing to ask questions if she does not understand. Until the lawyer knows that the client is very comfortable with a direct style of communication, the lawyer should refrain from asking the client if she understands and instead probe for exactly what the client does understand.

Gather Culture-Sensitive Information

How do we gather information that helps us interpret the client within her cultural context? In the first instance, the lawyer should engage in "deep listening" to the client's story and voice. For reasons identified in Habit 1, the lawyer, in question mode, will often be too focused on his or her own context and perspective. When exploration of the client's values, perspective, and cultural context is the goal, the lawyer needs to reorient the conversation to the client's world, the client's understandings, the client's priorities, and the client's narrative. Questions that get the client in narrative mode are usually the most helpful.

Questions that ask the client how or what she thinks about the problem she is encountering may also expose differences that will be helpful for the lawyer to understand the client's worldview. What are the client's ideas about the problem? Who else has the client talked to and what advice did they give? What would a good solution look like? What are the most important results? Who else besides the client will be affected? Consulted? Are there other problems caused by the current problem? Does the client know anybody else who had this problem? How did they solve it? Does the client consider that effective?

If the client has come from another country, the lawyer should ask the client how this problem would be handled in the client's country of origin. For example, in many legal cultures, the lawyer is the "fixer" or the person in charge. In contrast, most law students in the United States are taught client-centered lawyering, which sees the lawyer as partner, and our professional code puts the client in charge of major decisions about resolving the case.

Look for Red Flags That the Interaction Is Not Working

What are the red flags that mindful lawyers pay attention to in assessing whether the conversation is working for the client and lawyer? Red flags that the lawyer can look for include the following:

The client appears bored, disengaged, or even actively uncomfortable;

the client has not spoken for many minutes, and the lawyer is dominating the conversation;

the lawyer has not taken any notes for many minutes;

the client is using the lawyer's terminology instead of the lawyer using the client's words;

the lawyer is judging the client negatively;

the client appears angry; or

the lawyer is distracted and bored.

Each lawyer and client and each lawyer-client pair will have their own red flags.

The first step is to see the red flag and be shaken out of complacency. "Uh-oh, something must be done." The next step is the corrective one. This must be done on the spot as soon as the red flag is seen. The general corrective is to do anything possible to return to the search for the client's voice and story.

Explore Corrective Measures

In creating a corrective, the lawyer should be careful to use a different approach than the one that has led to the red flag. For example, if the client is not responding to a direct approach, try an indirect approach. If the call for narrative is not working, ask the client some specific questions or ask for narrative on a different topic.

Other suggested correctives include

turning the conversation back to the client's stated priority;

seeking greater detail about the client's priority;

giving the client a chance to explain in greater depth her concerns;

asking for examples of critical encounters in the client's life that illustrate the problem area;

exploring one example in some depth;

asking the client to describe in some detail what a solution would look like; and

using the client's words.

Again, these are only a few examples of many correctives that can be fashioned. Encounter by encounter, the lawyer can build a sense of the red flags in this relationship and the correctives that "work" for this client. Client by client, the lawyer can gain self-understanding about her own emblematic red flags and correctives that specifically target those flags. Red flags can remind the lawyer to be aware of the client and to be focused on the client in the moment. With reflection, the red flags can help the lawyer avoid further problems in the future.

HABIT 5: THE CAMEL'S BACK

Like the proverbial straw that breaks the camel's back, Habit 5 recognizes that, in addition to bias and stereotype, there are innumerable factors that may negatively influence an attorney-client interaction. A lawyer who proactively addresses some of these other factors may limit the effect of the bias and stereotyping and prevent the interaction from reaching the breaking point. Once the breaking point has been reached, the lawyer should try to identify why the lawyer-client interaction derailed and take corrective actions or plan for future corrective action.

Consider the case of a woman client with a horrible story of torture, whom the lawyer had very limited time to prepare for in an asylum trial (she lived out of town). During their conversation, the woman spoke in a rambling fashion. The lawyer, just back from vacation, was thinking angry thoughts toward the client. In the extreme stress caused by time pressure and by listening to the client tell about some horrible rapes that she had suffered, the lawyer fell back on some awful, old conditioning: against people who are of a different race, people who are overweight, and people who "talk too much."

In the midst of these feelings, which were causing the lawyer shame, what can the lawyer do to put the interview back on track and prevent a collision? This lawyer, like all lawyers, had biases and stereotypes that he brought to this attorney-client interaction. Research on stereotypes indicates that we are more likely to stereotype when we are feeling stress and unable to monitor ourselves for bias. By identifying the factors contributing to the negative reactions and changing some of them, the lawyer could prevent himself, at least sometimes, from acting on the basis of his assumptions and biases.

For example, the lawyer in the previous situation can take a break, have some food and drink, and identify what is interfering with his capacity to be present with the client before he resumes the interview. This, however, requires that the lawyer accept his every thought, including the ugly ones, and find a way to investigate and control those factors that are simply unacceptable in the context of lawyering. Knowing oneself as a cultural being and identifying biases and preventing them from controlling the interview or case are keys to Habit 5 thinking.

Over time, lawyers can learn to incorporate the analysis that they are doing to explore bias and stereotype into the analysis done as part of Habit 1. In addition to biases and stereotypes, straws that break the lawyer's back frequently include stress, lack of control, poor self-care, and a nonresponsive legal system. Final factor analysis identifies the straws that break the lawyer's back in the particular case and corrective steps that may work to prevent this from happening.

For example, assume that a lawyer, after working with a few Russian clients, begins to stereotype Russians as people who intentionally communicate with a lack of candor with lawyers. Habit 5 encourages this lawyer to be extra mindful when interviewing a Russian client. Given her biases, there is a higher likelihood that the lawyer will not find herself fully present with this client. In addition to using the other habits, the lawyer can improve the communication by controlling other factors (hunger, thirst, time constraints, and resource constraints), knowing that she is at greater risk of misunderstanding this client.

The prudent lawyer identifies proactively factors that may impede full communication with the client. Some she cannot control: pressure from the court, lack of resources, bad timing, excessive caseload. But some she can: the language barrier (through a competent interpreter), her own stress (through self-care and adequate sleep, food, and water), and the amount of time spent with the client (increase as needed).

Habit 5 thinking asks the lawyer to engage in self-analysis rather than self-judgment. A lawyer who has noticed a red flag that recurs in interactions with clients can brainstorm ways to address it. Likewise, a lawyer who has noticed factors that tend to be present at particularly smooth encounters with clients can brainstorm ways to make more use of these advantages. By engaging in this reflective process, the lawyer is more likely to respond to and respect the individual clients.

Jerome Groopman
Introduction
HOW DOCTORS THINK (2007)[2]

ANNE DODGE HAD LOST COUNT of all the doctors she had seen over the past fifteen years. She guessed it was close to thirty. Now, two days after

[2] Footnotes and/or internal citations omitted.

Christmas 2004, on a surprisingly mild morning, she was driving again into Boston to see yet another physician. Her primary care doctor had opposed the trip, arguing that Anne's problems were so long-standing and so well defined that this consultation would be useless. But her boyfriend had stubbornly insisted. Anne told herself the visit would mollify her boyfriend and she would be back home by midday.

Anne is in her thirties, with sandy brown hair and soft blue eyes. She grew up in a small town in Massachusetts, one of four sisters. No one had had an illness like hers. Around age twenty, she found that food did not agree with her. After a meal, she would feel as if a hand were gripping her stomach and twisting it. The nausea and pain were so intense that occasionally she vomited. Her family doctor examined her and found nothing wrong. He gave her antacids. But the symptoms continued. Anne lost her appetite and had to force herself to eat; then she'd feel sick and quietly retreat to the bathroom to regurgitate. Her general practitioner suspected what was wrong, but to be sure he referred her to a psychiatrist, and the diagnosis was made: anorexia nervosa with bulimia, a disorder marked by vomiting and an aversion to food. If the condition was not corrected, she could starve to death.

Over the years, Anne had seen many internists for her primary care before settling on her current one, a woman whose practice was devoted to patients with eating disorders. Anne was also evaluated by numerous specialists: endocrinologists, orthopedists, hematologists, infectious disease doctors, and, of course, psychologists and psychiatrists. She had been treated with four different antidepressants and had undergone weekly talk therapy. Nutritionists closely monitored her daily caloric intake.

But Anne's health continued to deteriorate, and the past twelve months had been the most miserable of her life. Her red blood cell count and platelets had dropped to perilous levels. A bone marrow biopsy showed very few developing cells. The two hematologists Anne had consulted attributed the low blood counts to her nutritional deficiency. Anne also had severe osteoporosis. One endocrinologist said her bones were like those of a woman in her eighties, from a lack of vitamin D and calcium. An orthopedist diagnosed a hairline fracture of the metatarsal bone of her foot. There were also signs that her immune system was failing; she suffered a series of infections, including meningitis. She was hospitalized four times in 2004 in a mental health facility so she could try to gain weight under supervision.

To restore her system, her internist had told Anne to consume three thousand calories a day, mostly in easily digested carbohydrates like cereals and pasta. But the more Anne ate, the worse she felt. Not only was she seized by intense nausea and the urge to vomit, but recently she had severe intestinal cramps and diarrhea. Her doctor said she had developed irritable bowel syndrome, a disorder associated with psychological stress. By December, Anne's weight dropped to eighty-two pounds. Although she said she was forcing down close to three thousand calories, her internist and her psychiatrist took the steady loss of weight as a sure sign that Anne was not telling the truth.

That day Anne was seeing Dr. Myron Falchuk, a gastroenterologist. Falchuk had already gotten her medical records, and her internist had told him that Anne's irritable bowel syndrome was yet another manifestation of her deteriorating mental health. Falchuk heard in the doctors recitation of the case the implicit message that his role was to examine Anne's abdomen, which had been poked and prodded many times by many physicians, and to reassure her that irritable bowel syndrome, while uncomfortable and annoying, should be treated as the internist had recommended, with an appropriate diet and tranquilizers.

But that is exactly what Falchuk did not do. Instead, he began to question, and listen, and observe, and then to think differently about Anne's case. And by doing so, he saved her life, because for fifteen years a key aspect of her illness had been missed. . . .

Not long after Anne Dodge's visit to Dr. Myron Falchuk, I met with him in his office at Boston's Beth Israel Deaconess Medical Center. Falchuk is a compact man in his early sixties with a broad bald pate and lively eyes. His accent is hard to place, and his speech has an almost musical quality. He was born in rural Venezuela and grew up speaking Yiddish at home and Spanish in the streets of his village. As a young boy, he was sent to live with relatives in Brooklyn. There he quickly learned English. All this has made him particularly sensitive to language, its nuances and power. Falchuk left New York for Dartmouth College, and then attended Harvard Medical School; he trained at the Peter Bent Brigham Hospital in Boston, and for several years conducted research at the National Institutes of Health on diseases of the bowel. After nearly four decades, he has not lost his excitement about caring for patients. When he began to discuss Anne Dodge's case, he sat up in his chair as if a jolt of electricity had passed through him.

"She was emaciated and looked haggard," Falchuk told me. "Her face was creased with fatigue. And the way she sat in the waiting room—so still, her hands clasped together—I saw how timid she was." From the first, Falchuk was reading Anne Dodge's body language. Everything was a potential clue, telling him something about not only her physical condition but also her emotional state. This was a woman beaten down by her suffering. She would need to be drawn out, gently.

Medical students are taught that the evaluation of a patient should proceed in a discrete, linear way: you first take the patient's history, then perform a physical examination, order tests, and analyze the results. Only after all the data are compiled should you formulate hypotheses about what might be wrong. These hypotheses should be winnowed by assigning statistical probabilities, based on existing databases, to each symptom, physical abnormality, and laboratory test; then you calculate the likely diagnosis. This is Bayesian analysis, a method of decision-making favored by those who construct algorithms and strictly adhere to evidence-based practice. But, in fact, few if any physicians work with this mathematical paradigm. The physical examination begins with the first visual impression in the waiting room, and with the tactile feedback gained by shaking a person's hand. Hypotheses about the diagnosis come to a doctor's mind even before a word of the medical history is spoken. And in cases like Anne's, of course, the specialist had a diagnosis on the referral form from the internist, confirmed by the multitude of doctors' notes in her records.

Falchuk ushered Anne Dodge into his office, his hand on her elbow, lightly guiding her to the chair that faces his desk. She looked at a stack of papers some six inches high. It was the dossier she had seen on the desks of her endocrinologists, hematologists, infectious disease physicians, psychiatrists, and nutritionists. For fifteen years she'd watched it grow from visit to visit.

But then Dr. Falchuk did something that caught Anne's eye: he moved those records to the far side of his desk, withdrew a pen from the breast pocket of his white coat, and took a clean tablet of lined paper from his drawer. "Before we talk about why you are here today," Falchuk said, "let's go back to the beginning. Tell me about when you first didn't feel good."

For a moment, she was confused. Hadn't the doctor spoken with her internist and looked at her records? "I have bulimia and anorexia nervosa," she said softly. Her clasped hands tightened. "And now I have irritable bowel syndrome."

Falchuk offered a gentle smile. "I want to hear your story, in your own words."

Anne glanced at the clock on the wall, the steady sweep of the second hand ticking off precious time. Her internist had told her that Dr. Falchuk was a prominent specialist, that there was a long waiting list to see him. Her problem was hardly urgent, and she got an appointment in less than two months only because of a cancellation in his Christmas-week schedule. But she detected no hint of rush or impatience in the doctor. His calm made it seem as though he had all the time in the world.

So Anne began, as Dr. Falchuk requested, at the beginning, reciting the long and tortuous story of her initial symptoms, the many doctors she had seen, the tests she had undergone. As she spoke, Dr. Falchuk would nod or interject short phrases: "Uh-huh," "I'm with you," "Go on."

Occasionally Anne found herself losing track of the sequence of events. It was as if Dr. Falchuk had given her permission to open the floodgates, and a torrent of painful memories poured forth. Now she was tumbling forward, swept along as she had been as a child on Cape Cod when a powerful wave caught her unawares. She couldn't recall exactly when she had had the bone marrow biopsy for her anemia.

"Don't worry about exactly when," Falchuk said. For a long moment Anne sat mute, still searching for the date. "I'll check it later in your records. Let's talk about the past months. Specifically, what you have been doing to try to gain weight."

This was easier for Anne; the doctor had thrown her a rope and was slowly tugging her to the shore of the present. As she spoke, Falchuk focused on the details of her diet. "Now, tell me again what happens after each meal," he said.

Anne thought she had already explained this, that it all was detailed in her records. Surely her internist had told Dr. Falchuk about the diet she had been following. But she went on to say, "I try to get down as much cereal in the morning as possible, and then bread and pasta at lunch and dinner." Cramps and diarrhea followed nearly every meal, Anne explained. She was taking anti-nausea medication that had greatly reduced the frequency of her vomiting but did not help the diarrhea. "Each day, I calculate how many calories I'm keeping in, just like the nutritionist taught me to do. And it's close to three thousand."

Dr. Falchuk paused. Anne Dodge saw his eyes drift away from hers. Then his focus returned, and he brought her into the examining room across the hall. The physical exam was unlike any she'd had before. She had been expecting him to concentrate on her abdomen, to poke and prod her liver and spleen, to have her take deep breaths, and to look for any areas of tenderness. Instead, he looked carefully at her skin and then at her palms. Falchuk intently inspected the creases in her hands, as though he were a fortuneteller reading her lifelines and future. Anne felt a bit perplexed but didn't ask him why he was doing this. Nor did she question why he spent such a long while looking in her mouth with a flashlight, inspecting not only her tongue and palate but her gums and the glistening tissue behind her lips as well. He also spent a long time examining her nails, on both her hands and her feet. "Sometimes you can find clues in the skin or the lining of the mouth that point you to a diagnosis," Falchuk explained at last.

He also seemed to fix on the little loose stool that remained in her rectum. She told him she had had an early breakfast, and diarrhea before the car ride to Boston.

When the physical exam was over, he asked her to dress and return to his office. She felt tired. The energy she had mustered for the trip was waning. She steeled herself for yet another somber lecture on how she had to eat more, given her deteriorating condition.

"I'm not at all sure this is irritable bowel syndrome," Dr. Falchuk said, "or that your weight loss is only due to bulimia and anorexia nervosa."

She wasn't sure she had heard him correctly. Falchuk seemed to recognize her confusion. "There may be something else going on that explains why you can't restore your weight. I could be wrong, of course, but we need to be sure, given how frail you are and how much you are suffering."

Anne felt even more confused and fought off the urge to cry. Now was not the time to break down. She needed to concentrate on what the doctor was saying. He proposed more blood tests, which were simple enough, but then suggested a procedure called an endoscopy. She listened carefully as Falchuk described how he would pass a fiberoptic instrument, essentially a flexible telescope, down her esophagus and then into her stomach and small intestine. If he saw something abnormal, he would take a biopsy. She was exhausted from endless evaluations. She'd been through so much, so many tests, so many procedures: the x-rays, the bone density assessment, the painful bone marrow biopsy for her low blood counts, and multiple spinal taps when she had meningitis. Despite his assurances that she would be sedated, she doubted whether the endoscopy was worth the trouble and discomfort. She recalled her internist's reluctance to refer her to a gastroenterologist, and wondered whether the procedure was pointless, done for the sake of doing it, or, even worse, to make money.

Dodge was about to refuse, but then Falchuk repeated emphatically that something else might account for her condition. "Given how poorly you are doing, how much weight you've lost, what's happened to your blood, your bones, and your immune system over the years, we need to be absolutely certain of everything that's wrong. It may be that your body can't digest the food you're eating, that those three thousand calories are just passing through you, and that's why you're down to eighty-two pounds."

When I met with Anne Dodge one month after her first appointment with Dr. Falchuk, she said that he'd given her the greatest Christmas present ever. She had gained nearly twelve pounds. The intense nausea, the urge to vomit, the cramps and diarrhea that followed breakfast, lunch, and dinner as she struggled to fill her stomach with cereal, bread, and pasta had all abated. The blood tests and the endoscopy showed that she had celiac disease. This is an autoimmune disorder, in essence an allergy to gluten, a primary component of many grains. Once believed to be rare, the malady, also called celiac sprue, is now recognized more frequently thanks to sophisticated diagnostic tests. Moreover, it has become clear that celiac disease is not only a childhood illness, as previously thought; symptoms may not begin until late adolescence or early adulthood, as Falchuk believed occurred in Anne Dodge's case. Yes, she suffered from an eating disorder. But her body's reaction to gluten resulted in irritation and distortion of the lining of her bowel, so nutrients were not absorbed. The more cereal and pasta she added to her diet, the more her digestive tract was damaged, and even fewer calories and essential vitamins passed into her system.

Anne Dodge told me she was both elated and a bit dazed. After fifteen years of struggling to get better, she had begun to lose hope. Now she had a new chance to restore her health. It would take time, she said, to rebuild not only her body but her mind. Maybe one day she would be, as she put it, "whole" again.

Behind Myron Falchuk's desk, a large framed photograph occupies much of the wall. A group of austerely dressed men pose, some holding derby hats, some with thick drooping mustaches like Teddy Roosevelt's; the sepia tinge of the picture and the men's appearance date it to the early 1900s. It seems out of phase with Falchuk's outgoing demeanor and stylish clothes. But it is, he says, his touchstone.

"That photograph was taken in 1913, when they opened the Brigham Hospital," Falchuk explained. "William Osier gave the first grand rounds." A smile spread across his face. "It's a copy. I didn't steal the original when I was chief resident." Osier was acutely sensitive to the power and importance of words, and his writings greatly influenced Falchuk. "Osler essentially said that if you listen to the patient, he is telling you the diagnosis," Falchuk continued. "A lot of people look at a specialist like me as a technician. They come to you for a procedure. And there is no doubt that procedures are important, or that the specialized technology we have these days is vital in caring for a patient. But I believe that this technology also has taken us away from the patient's story." Falchuk paused. "And once you remove yourself from the patient's story, you no longer are truly a doctor."

How a doctor thinks can first be discerned by how he speaks and how he listens. In addition to words spoken and heard, there is nonverbal communication, his attention to the body language of his patient as well as his own body language—his expressions, his posture, his gestures. Debra Roter, a professor of health policy and management at Johns Hopkins University, works as a team with Judith Hall, a professor of social psychology at Northeastern University. They are among the most productive and insightful researchers studying medical communication. They have analyzed thousands of videotapes and live interactions between doctors of many types—internists, gynecologists, surgeons—and patients, parsing phrases and physical movements. They also have assayed the data from other researchers. They have shown that how a doctor asks questions and how he responds to his patient's emotions are both key to what they term "patient activation and engagement." The idea, as Roter put it when we spoke, is "to wake someone up" so that the patient feels free, if not eager, to speak and participate in a dialogue. That freedom of patient speech is necessary if the doctor is to get clues about the medical enigma before him. If the patient is inhibited, or cut off prematurely, or constrained into one path of discussion, then the doctor may not be told something vital. Observers have noted that, on average, physicians interrupt patients within eighteen seconds of when they begin telling their story.

Let's apply Roter's and Hall's insights to the case of Anne Dodge. Falchuk began their conversation with a general, open-ended question about when she first began to feel ill. "The way a doctor asks a question," Roter said, "structures the patient's answers." Had Falchuk asked a specific, close-ended question—"What kind of abdominal pain do you have, is it sharp or dull?"—he would have implicitly revealed a preconception that Anne Dodge had irritable bowel syndrome. "If you know where you are going," Roter said of doctors' efforts to pin down a diagnosis, "then close-ended questions are the most efficient. But if you are unsure of the diagnosis, then a close-ended question serves you ill, because it immediately, perhaps irrevocably, moves you along the wrong track." The great advantage of open-ended questioning is that it maximizes the opportunity for a doctor to hear new information.

"What does it take to succeed with open-ended questions?" Roter asked rhetorically. "The doctor has to make the patient feel that he is really interested in hearing what they have to say. And when a patient tells his story, the patient gives cues and clues to what the doctor may not be thinking about."

The type of question a doctor asks is only half of a successful medical dialogue. "The physician should respond to the patient's emotions," Roter continued. Most patients are gripped by fear and anxiety; some also carry a sense of shame about their disease. But a doctor gives more than psychological relief by responding empathetically to a patient. "The patient does not want to appear stupid or waste the doctor's time," Roter said. "Even if the doctor asks the right questions, the patient may not be forthcoming because of his emotional state. The goal of a physician is to get to the story, and to do so he has to understand the patient's emotions."

Falchuk immediately discerned emotions in Anne that would inhibit her from telling her tale. He tried to put her at ease by responding sympathetically to her history. He did something else that Roter believes is essential in eliciting information: he turned her anxiety and reticence around and engaged her by indicating that he was listening actively, that he wanted to hear more. His simple interjections—"uh-huh, I'm with you, go on"—implied to Anne Dodge that what she was saying was important to him.

Judy Hall, the social psychologist, has focused further on the emotional dimension of the dialogue between doctor and patient: whether the doctor appears to like the patient and whether the patient likes the doctor. She discovered that those feelings are hardly secret on either side of the table. In studies of primary care physicians and surgeons, patients knew remarkably accurately how the doctor actually felt about them. Much of this, of course, comes from nonverbal behavior: the physician's facial expressions, how he is seated, whether his gestures are warm and welcoming or formal and remote. "The doctor is supposed to be emotionally neutral and evenhanded with everybody." Hall said, "and we know that's not true."

Her research on rapport between doctors and patients bears on Anne Dodge's case. Hall discovered that the sickest patients are the least liked by doctors, and that very sick people sense this disaffection. Overall, doctors tend to like healthier people more. Why is this? "I am not a doctor-basher," Hall said. "Some doctors are averse to the very ill, and the reasons for this are quite forgivable," Many doctors have deep feelings of failure when dealing with diseases that resist even the best therapy; in such cases they become frustrated, because all their hard work seems in vain. So they stop trying. In fact, few physicians welcome patients like Anne Dodge warmly. Consider: fifteen years of anorexia nervosa and bulimia, a disorder with a social stigma, a malady that is often extremely difficult to remedy. Consider also how much time and attention Anne had been given over those fifteen years by so many caregivers, without a glimmer of improvement. And by December 2004, she was only getting worse.

Roter and Hall also studied the effect a doctor's bedside manner has on successful diagnosis and treatment. "We tend to remember the extremes," Hall said, "the genius surgeon with an autistic bedside manner, or the kindly GP who is not terribly competent. But the good stuff goes together—good doctoring generally requires both. Good doctoring is a total package." This is because "most of what doctors do is talk," Hall concluded, "and the communication piece is not separable from doing quality medicine. You need information to get at the diagnosis, and the best way to get that information is by establishing rapport with the patient. Competency is not separable from communication skills. It's not a tradeoff."

Falchuk conducts an inner monologue to guide his thinking. "She told me she was eating up to three thousand calories a day. Inside myself, I asked: Should I believe you? And if I do, then why aren't you gaining weight?" That simple possibility had to be carried to its logical end: that she was actually trying, that she really was putting the cereal, bread, and pasta in her mouth, chewing, swallowing, struggling not to vomit, and still wasting away, her blood counts still falling, her bones still decomposing, her immune system still failing. "I have to give her the benefit of a doubt," Falchuk told himself.

Keeping an open mind was reflected in Falchuk's open-ended line of questioning. The more he observed Anne Dodge, and the more he listened, the more disquiet he felt. "It just seemed impossible to absolutely conclude it was all psychiatric," he said. "Everyone had written her off as some neurotic case. But my intuition told me that the picture didn't entirely fit. And once I felt that way, I began to wonder: What was missing?"

Clinical intuition is a complex sense that becomes refined over years and years of practice, of listening to literally thousands of patients' stories, examining thousands of people, and most important, remembering when you were wrong. Falchuk had done research at the National Institutes of Health on patients with malabsorption, people who couldn't extract vital nutrients and calories from the food they ate. This background was key to recognizing that Anne Dodge might be suffering not only from anorexia nervosa or bulimia but also from some form of malabsorption. He told me that Anne reminded him that he had been fooled in the past by a patient who was also losing weight rapidly. That woman carried the diagnosis of malabsorption. She said she ate heartily and had terrible cramps and diarrhea, and her many doctors believed her. After more than a month of evaluation, with numerous blood tests and an endoscopy, by chance Falchuk found a bottle of laxatives under her hospital bed that she had forgotten to hide. Nothing was wrong with her gastrointestinal tract. Something was tragically wrong with her psyche. Falchuk learned that both mind and body have to be considered, at times independently, at times through their connections.

Different doctors . . ., achieve competency in remarkably similar ways, despite working in disparate fields. Primarily, they recognize and remember their mistakes and misjudgments, and incorporate those memories into their thinking. Studies show that expertise is largely acquired not only by sustained practice but by receiving feedback that helps you understand your technical errors and misguided decisions. During my training, I met a cardiologist who had a deserved reputation as one of the best in his field, not only a storehouse of knowledge but also a clinician with excellent judgment. He kept a log of all the mistakes he knew he had made over the decades, and at times revisited this compendium when trying to figure out a particularly difficult case. He was characterized by many of his colleagues as eccentric, an obsessive oddball. Only later did I realize his implicit message to us was to admit our mistakes to ourselves, then analyze them, and keep them accessible at all times if we wanted to be stellar clinicians. In Anne Dodge's case, Falchuk immediately recalled how he had taken at face value the statements of the patient at NIH who was secretly using laxatives. The opposite situation, he knew, could also apply. In either setting, the case demanded continued thought and investigation.

When Falchuk told me that "the picture didn't fit," his words were more than mere metaphor. Donald Redelmeier, a physician at Sunnybrook Health Sciences Centre in Toronto, has a particular interest in physician cognition and its relation to diagnosis. He refers to a phenomenon called the "eyeball test," the pivotal moment when a doctor identifies "something intangible yet unsettling in the patient's presentation." That instinct may, of course, be wrong. But it should not be ignored, because it can cause the physician to recognize that the information before him has been improperly "framed."

Doctors frame patients all the time using shorthand: "I'm sending you a case of diabetes and renal failure," or "I have a drug addict here in the ER with fever and a cough from pneumonia." Often a doctor chooses the correct frame and all the clinical data fit neatly within it. But a self-aware physician knows that accepting the frame as given can be a serious error. Anne Dodge was fitted into the single frame of bulimia and anorexia nervosa from the age of twenty. It was easily understandable that each of her doctors received her case in that one frame. All the data fit neatly within its borders. There was no apparent reason to redraw her clinical portrait, to look at it from another angle. Except one. "It's like DNA evidence at a crime," Falchuk explained. "The patient was saying 'I told you, I'm innocent.'" Here is the art of medicine, the sensitivity to language and emotion that makes for a superior clinician.

Falchuk almost rose from his chair when he showed me the pictures of Dodge's distorted small intestine taken through the endoscope. "I was so excited about this," he said. He had the sweet pleasure of the detective who cracks the mystery, a legitimate pride in identifying a culprit. But beyond intellectual excitement and satisfaction, he showed his joy in saving a life.

Intellect and intuition, careful attention to detail, active listening, and psychological insight all coalesced on that December day. It could have been otherwise. Anne Dodge, with her history of anorexia nervosa and bulimia, may then have developed irritable bowel syndrome. But Falchuk had asked himself, "What might I be missing in this case? And what would be the worst thing that could be missed?"

What if he had not asked himself these questions? Then Anne Dodge, her boyfriend, or a family member could have asked them—perhaps many years earlier. Of course, a patient or a loved one is not a doctor. They lack a doctor's training and experience. And many laymen feel inhibited about asking questions. But the questions are perfectly legitimate. Patients can learn to question and to think the way a doctor should.... In Anne Dodge's case, it was Falchuk who asked simple but ultimately life-saving questions, and to answer them he needed to go further. And Anne Dodge needed to agree to go further, to submit to more blood tests and an invasive procedure. For her to assent, she had to trust not only Falchuk's skill but also his sincerity and motivations. This is the other dimension of Roter's and Hall's studies: how language, spoken and unspoken, can give information essential to a correct diagnosis, and persuade a patient to comply with a doctor's advice. "Compliance" can have a negative connotation, smacking of paternalism, casting patients as passive players who do what the all-powerful physician tells them. But according to Roter's and Hall's research, without trust and a sense of mutual liking, Anne Dodge probably would have deflected Falchuk's suggestions of more blood tests and an endoscopy. She would have been "noncompliant," in pejorative clinical parlance. And she would still be struggling to persuade her doctors that she was eating three thousand calories a day while wasting away.

My admiration for Myron Falchuk increased when we went on from Anne Dodge's case to discuss not his clinical triumphs but his errors. Again, every doctor is fallible. No doctor is right all the time. Every physician, even the most brilliant, makes a misdiagnosis or chooses the wrong therapy. This is not a matter of "medical mistakes." Medical mistakes have been written about extensively in the lay press and analyzed in a report from the Institute of Medicine of the National Academy of Sciences. They involve prescribing the wrong dose of a drug or looking at an x-ray of a patient backward. Misdiagnosis is different. It is a window into the medical mind. It reveals why doctors fail to question their assumptions, why their thinking is sometimes closed or skewed, why they overlook the gaps in their knowledge. Experts studying misguided care have recently concluded that the majority of errors are due to flaws in physician thinking, not technical mistakes. In one study of misdiagnoses that caused serious harm to patients, some 80 percent could be accounted for by a cascade of cognitive errors, like the one in Anne Dodge's case, putting her into a narrow frame and ignoring information that contradicted a fixed notion. Another study of one hundred incorrect diagnoses found that inadequate medical knowledge was the reason for error in only four instances. The doctors didn't stumble because of their ignorance of clinical facts; rather, they missed diagnoses because they fell into cognitive traps. Such errors produce a distressingly high rate of misdiagnosis. As many as 15 percent of all diagnoses are inaccurate, according to a 1995 report in which doctors assessed written descriptions of patients' symptoms and examined actors simulating patients with various diseases. These findings match classical research, based on autopsies, which shows that 10 percent to 15 percent of all diagnoses are wrong.

I can recall every misdiagnosis I've made during my thirty-year career. The first occurred when I was a resident in internal medicine at the Massachusetts General Hospital; Roter's and Hall's research explains it. One of my patients was a middle-aged woman with seemingly endless complaints whose voice sounded to me like a nail scratching a blackboard. One day she had a new complaint, discomfort in her upper chest. I tried to pin down what caused the discomfort—eating, exercise, coughing—to no avail. Then I ordered routine tests, including a chest x-ray and a cardiogram. Both were normal. In desperation, I prescribed antacids. But her complaint persisted, and I became deaf to it. In essence, I couldn't think in a different way. Several weeks later, I was stat paged to the emergency room. My patient had a dissecting aortic aneurysm, a life-threatening tear of the large artery that carries blood from the heart to the rest of the body. She died. Although an aortic dissection is often fatal even when discovered, I have never forgiven myself for failing to diagnose it. There was a chance she could have been saved.

Roter's and Hall's work on liking and disliking illuminates in part what happened in the clinic three decades ago. I wish I had been taught, and had gained the self-awareness, to realize how emotion can blur a doctor's ability to listen and think. Physicians who dislike their patients regularly cut them off during the recitation of symptoms and fix on a convenient diagnosis and treatment. The doctor becomes increasingly convinced of the truth of his misjudgment, developing a psychological commitment to it. He becomes wedded to his distorted conclusion. His strong negative feelings about the patient make it harder for him to abandon that conclusion and reframe the clinical picture differently.

This skewing of physicians' thinking leads to poor care. What is remarkable is not merely the consequences of a doctor's negative emotions. Despite research showing that most patients pick up on the physician's negativity, few of them understand its effect on their medical care and rarely change doctors because of it. Rather, they often blame themselves for complaining and taxing the doctor's patience. Instead, patients should politely but freely broach the issue with their doctor. "I sense that we may not be communicating well," a patient can say. This signals the physician that there is a problem in compatibility. The problem may be resolvable with candor by a patient who wants to sustain the relationship. But when I asked other physicians what they would do if they, as patients, perceived a negative attitude from their doctor, each one flatly said he or she would find another doctor.

Jennifer K. Robbennolt and Jean R. Sternlight
PSYCHOLOGY FOR LAWYERS: UNDERSTANDING THE HUMAN FACTORS IN NEGOTIATION, LITIGATION, AND DECISION MAKING (2012)[3]

Perceiving and Understanding the World

Some of us tend to think of people as akin to seismographs, constantly and accurately recording sensory information from the world around them as it occurs. However, decades of psychological research reveal that "[t]he perceiver . . . is not simply a dutiful clerk who passively registers information. Rather, the perceiver is an active interpreter, one who resolves ambiguities, makes educated guesses about events that cannot be observed directly, and forms inferences about associations and causal relations." In the process of observing and constructing an understanding of the events and information to which we are exposed, we make assumptions and inferences, fill in gaps, impose patterns, change our perceptions (or not) in response to new information, and otherwise engage in interpretations that may differ from others' experiences of the same events.

These vagaries of perception and interpretation have important implications for the ways in which attorneys grapple with their clients' understandings of what they have experienced. Recognition of this active perception and construal process is useful for understanding the perceptions of witnesses, opposing parties and counsel, judges and jurors, and other actors in the legal system. Similarly, understanding how these processes affect attorneys' own perceptions can help attorneys to tread carefully in seeking to build a picture of their client and the case or transaction at issue.

. . .

In [a] recent study, researchers created a video in which one supermarket shopper walked behind a stack of boxes while another shopper emerged from behind the boxes; the second shopper then shoplifted a bottle of wine. Nearly two-thirds of people viewing the videotape failed to notice that a different person had appeared from behind the boxes, and those who did not notice the change commonly misidentified the first (innocent) shopper as the shoplifter.

These are just a few examples of the limits on people's ability to attend to stimuli. Psychologists call such failures to notice objects or

---

3 Footnotes and/or internal citations omitted.

substantial changes in objects *inattentional blindness* and *change blindness,* respectively. Interestingly, just as you may have done, people tend to incorrectly predict that they will be able to detect such changes—in one study, 90% of participants predicted that they would have seen the gorilla—a phenomenon known to psychologists as *inattentional blindness blindness* or *change blindness blindness.*

Once we stop and think about it, perhaps it should not be so surprising that we cannot attend to everything that we encounter. Our senses are constantly bombarded with an amazing array of information: sounds, sights, physical sensations, odors, and tastes. It would be virtually impossible to pay attention—let alone close attention—to all of the stimuli to which we are exposed. Accordingly, we attend to only a fraction of the possible features of the environment at any given moment. Features of both the stimuli themselves (for example, intensity, suddenness, unexpectedness, or movement) and the perceiver (for example, expectations or distractions) can influence what it is that gets noticed. But because "we vividly experience some aspects of our world, particularly those that are the focus of our attention," we mistakenly believe that we "process *all* of the detailed information around us." . . .

Even when we think we are looking carefully, there are limits to what we see. Consider radiologists, who are trained to spot abnormalities in medical scans such as X-rays and MRIs. When reading an image, radiologists "can't take in everything in the image, so they focus their attention on the critical aspects of the image." . . . Because their attentional capacity is limited, there is a tendency to miss features of the scan that are unexpected. Thus, a radiologist looking for a broken bone tends to be less likely to see a tumor. Similarly, the rarer and therefore, more unexpected, a particular abnormality is, the less likely it is to be detected. In addition, the radiologist is more likely to miss a particular abnormality in a scan when it is accompanied by an additional anomaly than when it is the only anomaly on the scan—a phenomenon known as *satisfaction of search.* The likelihood of detecting the target anomaly is decreased by the presence of a second anomaly even if the two anomalies are from the same category; for example, the presence of one tumor makes it less likely that another tumor will be detected.

These limits on attention also demonstrate how difficult it is to attend to and take in information from multiple sources simultaneously—a problem of divided attention. Indeed, when people attempt to pay attention to multiple things or to engage in multiple tasks at the same time, performance often suffers. This is an important realization for busy attorneys who must constantly manage multiple projects and deal with numerous interruptions. While we might think that we are effective multitaskers, it turns out that multitasking it not efficient.

Try the following exercise: Time how long it takes you to write down two lines of text on a piece of paper. On the first line, write this sentence: "Multitasking is not efficient." On the second line, write the numbers 1 through 26, one for each letter in the sentence on line 1. However, as you write, alternative between the two lines. Thus, after you write the letter *M* on the first line, you should write the number *1* on the second line; after you write the letter *u* on the first line, you should write the number *2* on the second line; and so on. Now, time yourself again. This time, however, simply write the sentence on the first line and then write the series of numbers on the next line.

When we attempt to do more than one task at the same time, our brain has to switch its attention back and forth between the tasks. And it turns out that there are costs to this task switching. Each time we turn our attention from one task to another—say, turning attention away from the motion being drafted to focus on answering the ringing phone or to look at e-mail or text messages—we are required to mentally change gears, calling to mind a new set of facts, relevant goals, decision rules, prior work, and a range of appropriate responses. Similarly, it may be difficult to leave behind the thoughts that were relevant to the prior task. And then when switching back to a prior task, we have to regain our train of thought and may even have to retrace our steps. Such mental reconfiguring takes time. Thus, people tend to process more slowly and to make more errors when switching between tasks than they do when they are able to perform one task at a time.

Interestingly, recent research has shown that people who report that they engage in a high degree of multitasking were actually more easily distracted by irrelevant stimuli and less efficient in switching tasks than people who multitasked less.

While many things escape our conscious awareness, many other things do capture our attention. It turns out that what we pay attention to and how we understand what we perceive are not determined at random. Rather, preexisting patterns of thinking direct our attention in predictable ways and color our interpretations of those stimuli to which we do attend.

In one famous experiment, students from rival schools watched a football game between the schools' teams. Students' assessments of the rule violations committed by each team and of the overall play were influenced (many would say biased) by which school they attended. Rather than simply recording the violations and the play, observers interpreted the action in accordance with their predispositions. Recent research that seems to reflect the same phenomenon found that NBA referees' foul calls were influenced by the race of the player and the race of the referee. In the case of both African American and Caucasian players, officiating crews called more fouls against opposite-race players.

Priming and Concept Accessibility

What we pay attention to and how we interpret it can be strongly affected by what else is currently on our conscious or unconscious minds. *Priming* occurs when exposure to a stimulus unconsciously influences perceptions or interpretations of a subsequent person or event. Because ideas that have been recently or repeatedly activated tend to be more accessible in our minds, such primed concepts can influence how we perceive new information.

Thus, people tend to judge their life satisfaction differently depending on whether they have just been thinking about some specific aspect of their lives such as their marriage or their job. Jurors primed with the concept of the presumption of innocence might be more likely to assert that they could ignore damaging pretrial publicity. News reports or campaign ads can prime people to think about particular issues such as crime, financial instability, or acts of heroism. Training in the law might prime lawyers to focus on issues of rights and responsibilities. And priming different character traits can influence interpretations of others' behavior, for example, a person's judgment about another's negotiation behavior might be influenced by whether notions of deception or trust are foremost in the observer's mind.

In similar ways, priming can even influence behavior. Thus, for example, people who have been primed with competitive concepts subsequently behave more competitively. Those who have been primed to think about university professors perform better in trivia games. Those who are primed with concepts related to being elderly tend to walk more slowly. And priming the concept of money leads people to behave less prosocially, to prefer to work alone, and to be less likely to ask for help on a difficult assignment.

Schemas, Scripts, and Stereotypes

Our construal of events and situations is also guided by basic knowledge structures known as *schemas.* Schemas define our expectations about how the world operates, fill in gaps in information, and facilitate an ability to "make inferences and judgments with heightened ease, speed, and subjective confidence." Thus, people have a schema for "baby" or for "lawyer" that provides them with certain expectations and assumptions. For example, when a client walks into a lawyer's office, he will have a set of preconceptions regarding how someone in the role of a lawyer should look and behave. Such schemas serve us well most of the time, allowing us to process vast amounts of information quickly. However, because schemas may not always accurately represent the state of the world in a particular instance, our schemas can sometimes lead us astray.

The fact that we rely on our schemas may have particular importance for lawyers, whose training and experience might lead them to pigeonhole clients and cases into readily accessible categories. For example, lawyers have schemas for concepts such as "real estate deal" or "divorce" that shape their perceptions of such cases.

> The chief danger that confronts a professional, in law or in any other field, is that he will tend to fill the gap with related informational material from other similar situations in his experience. Or, he may leap ahead and begin to anticipate information that may or may not actually be involved in the situation that now confronts him.

While lawyers' expertise facilitates the rapid integration of large amounts of information about the facts of their clients' cases and the relevant law, such expertise may also lead to incorrect assumptions and even erroneous memory for some distinct details.

Scripts are schemas for events. Scripts structure our understanding of the typical course of an episode. For example, if we hear that Bob went into a restaurant and ate dinner, we might infer that Bob both placed an order for his meal and paid the check at the end, even though these details were not explicitly recounted. If Chris and Mark are in a car accident, they might automatically exchange insurance information because that is part of their "car accident script." A party in a negotiation may expect that a concession offered by one party will be followed by a concession from the other party because they hold a "negotiation script" that characterizes the negotiation dance in this way."

Stereotypes are schemas that categorize people. Stereotypes consist of beliefs—favorable or unfavorable—about the characteristics of members of particular groups. People may hold stereotypes based on a person's race or ethnicity, gender, age, sexual orientation, weight, attractiveness, dress, athleticism, whether or not they smoke or drink, or other characteristics.

Most of us don't like to think of ourselves as making decisions grounded in stereotypes. Yet, research has shown that we all operate on the basis of stereotypes. To some extent, reliance on stereotypes is not necessarily bad. As with other schemas, stereotypes can facilitate the rapid categorization of people and allow us to preserve our mental resources for other tasks. Thus, while it is not true that all smokers get lung cancer, it is true that smokers are at higher risk of lung cancer than nonsmokers. Of course, some stereotypes may have no basis in fact, such as the idea that members of a certain race or ethnicity are less intelligent than members of another race or ethnicity. Moreover, even those stereotypes that have a basis in truth are not true in every case. For example, men are bigger and stronger than women in general, but there are plenty of women who are bigger and stronger than many men.

Social psychologists have shown that schemas and scripts can influence how we perceive and interpret information and that those interpretations, in turn, affect a range of understandings and behaviors. Specifically, preconceptions and expectations can influence how information is labeled and understood, how ambiguous information is interpreted, and the degree to which information is scrutinized. For example, when told that someone is "intelligent," we might understand the person to be "sensible, wise, insightful, and stimulating" if our impression of the person is otherwise positive. On the other hand, the same description—"intelligent"—might be understood as describing a person who is "cunning and scheming" and "detached" if we otherwise perceive that person negatively.

Similarly, stereotypes have been shown to influence how information is initially processed. For example, one study demonstrated that people asked to distinguish between tools and weapons were able to identify tools more quickly when they were primed with white faces and to identify weapons more quickly when they were primed with black faces. There is evidence that people pay more attention to information that is consistent with a stereotype and less attention to stereotype-inconsistent information, that people seek out information that is consistent with the stereotype, and that people are better able to remember information that is consistent with the stereotype. Such preferences for confirmation of stereotypes can make such views resistant to change.

We can, however, use a variety of strategies to minimize reliance on schemas in decision making. First, goals can influence the tendency to rely on particular schemas. For example, taking time and focusing attention on making an individuating assessment of another person can result in less stereotyping and increased attention to that person's distinct characteristics. Similarly, pausing to think about the unique features of a particular case may provide insight into the ways in which the case departs from the expected. On the other hand, time pressure and a focus on general impressions can increase the tendency to stereotype or to rely on other schemas.

Similarly, it can be helpful to acknowledge the reality that preexisting knowledge structures can influence perception and to actively question the basis for a particular understanding. In particular, we might reflect on our understanding and probe the assumptions that have been made, or we might solicit the insight of another person who may have a different set of schemas.

In addition, reliance on schemas tends to be reduced when counter-examples are available. For example, people are less likely to rely on negative stereotypes of African Americans or women when they have been exposed to instances of admired African Americans or famous women leaders. Such exposure can come from objects such as photos (who is on *your* "wall of fame"?), from personal connections with individuals within the stereotyped group, or even from simply creating mental images of counterstereotypes. . . .

Confirmation Bias and Biased Assimilation

Consider Marge, a supporter of capital punishment, and David, a death penalty opponent. Marge, it turns out, is likely to be more inclined than David to notice reports of studies showing that the death penalty deters crime. And David is likely to be more inclined to notice reports of studies showing no death penalty-deterrence link. Similarly, Marge and David are likely to differentially evaluate the quality of the different studies of capital punishment and deterrence: each is likely to perceive the studies with findings that are consistent with his or her beliefs to be of higher methodological quality and more persuasive than the studies that produced contrary results (even if the studies used similar methods).

Marge and David are not alone. We tend to exhibit *confirmation bias* in the ways in which we seek out and evaluate information. People tend to unconsciously seek out additional information that confirms their already existing views and to disregard conflicting information, rather than attempting to systematically gather accurate information. Moreover, when evaluating information once it is obtained, there is a tendency for assessments of the information to be influenced by the extent to which the information is consistent with the attitudes or expectations of the person doing the evaluation—a tendency known as *biased assimilation*. Information that is inconsistent with expectations or beliefs is discounted and scrutinized more carefully than is expectation-congruent data. In other words, "when we want to believe an argument, we tend to ask, 'Can I believe this?' When we do not want to believe an argument, we ask, '*Must* I believe this?' " . . .

Take, as an example, a recent study in which participants were asked to review a police file, evaluate the evidence, and make decisions about further investigation. Participants who were asked to name a suspect after reviewing the file demonstrated confirmation bias in seeking out and interpreting additional investigatory information. Specifically, they were more likely (than were participants who did not name a suspect) to remember evidence consistent with the named suspect's guilt, to discount evidence inconsistent with the named suspect's guilt, and to interpret ambiguous evidence in ways consistent with the named suspect's guilt. Importantly, naming a suspect not only affected how investigators interpreted the existing evidence but also influenced the information that they ultimately had available to them because they disproportionately chose to pursue additional lines of investigation that focused on the named suspect.

Interviewers have been shown to be subject to confirmation bias as well. Researchers have found that interviewers who are led to believe that an interviewee is likely guilty ask a higher proportion of questions that are consistent with the interviewee's guilt (*guilt-presumptive questions*), use more interrogation techniques early in the interview, and are more likely to judge the interviewee guilty than are interviewers who are led to believe that the interviewee is likely innocent. Interestingly, this approach to the interviews has consequences for the behavior of the interviewees as well: both guilty and *innocent* interviewees tend to display more defensive behaviors during the interview when they are questioned by someone who is predisposed to believe that they are guilty. Thus, the expectations of the interviewer elicited behavior from the interviewee that was consistent with those expectations—a self-fulfilling prophecy.

One strategy that has proven helpful in countering the effects of confirmation bias and biased assimilation is to explicitly *consider the opposite*. That is, when seeking out and evaluating information, consciously and explicitly reflecting on the possibility that our preconceptions are erroneous and seeking out disconfirming evidence can serve to reduce the bias. Thus, an investigator might make a point of looking for evidence that is inconsistent with a named suspect's guilt, or an interviewer might deliberately ask questions that could reveal evidence counter to her expectations. It can also be helpful to consult others who might hold different views or have different expectations. Psychological research has found that such overt consideration of alternatives is more effective in reducing reliance on preconceptions than is simply making a good-faith effort to be unbiased. . . .

Causal Attribution and Judgments of Responsibility

Why did the business manager fire the employee? Why did the supplier breach the contract? What led to the accident in which a schoolchild was injured? Did she hit him on purpose, or was it just an accident? Why did the investor's mutual fund balance drop so sharply?

One way in which people make sense of the world is by making causal judgments, that is, judgments about what caused an outcome. Such causal judgments—including making inferences of responsibility, weighing the relative contributions of potential causes, and making predictions about others' future behavior—are often central to legal situations. Attribution theory in psychology is the study of the ways in which people make attributions of causality or responsibility, particularly attributions that are focused on understanding another person's or our own behavior.

As an initial matter, it is clear that human beings often have a hard time distinguishing between patterns that are meaningful and those that are random. We frequently conclude that systematic patterns exist when they do not or see patterns that differ from those that actually exist. For example, most basketball fans are believers to the existence of what is known as the *hot-hand phenomenon,* wherein a player has a better chance of making his next shot when he has made his last several shots (that is, when he is "on a roll" or "in the zone") than when he has just missed a series of shots (that is, when he is "shooting cold"). Researchers who have studied the hot-hand phenomenon, however, have examined shooting percentages across large numbers of games and have found no evidence of streak shooting. Furthermore, just as we perceive patterns where there are none, we expect random events to be devoid of patterns. Consider the following example:

> When Apple first introduced the shuffle feature on its iPods, the shuffle was truly random; each song was equally as likely to get picked as any other. However, the randomness didn't *appear* random, since some songs were occasionally repeated, and customers concluded that the feature contained some secret patterns and preferences. As a result, Apple was forced to revise the algorithm. "We made it less random to make it feel more random," said Steve Jobs, the CEO of Apple.

Such *illusory correlations* can make discerning causal relationships challenging. When it comes to thinking about the causes of other people's behavior, we tend to discount the extent to which behavior is influenced by various aspects of the situation in which people find themselves. The phenomenon known as the *fundamental attribution error* (or *correspondence bias*) is the tendency of observers to attribute another person's behavior to dispositional factors (those internal to the person) rather than to situational (external) factors despite what we know to be the powerful influence of situational factors on behavior. Thus, if A runs into B with a grocery cart, B is apt to view the act as deliberate or careless on the part of A rather than to attribute the collision to a spill on the floor or a sticky wheel on the grocery cart. Similarly, people attribute the views contained in a speech (for example, defending or attacking the notion that marijuana should be legal) to the speaker even when they know that the person was assigned to speak on that side of the issue.

As an example of the fundamental attribution error, consider the following study: Researchers asked pairs of participants to negotiate the salary component of a job offer. Participants in the role of the job candidates were given information about their alternative to reaching an agreement with the employer, different groups of job candidates (assigned at random) were given alternatives that differed in value. It turns out that the behavior of the job candidates in the negotiation was primarily determined by the value of their alternative job. In the course of the negotiation, the negotiators in the role of the employer were able to discern these differences in the value of the candidates' alternatives. However, the employers appraised candidates with low-value alternatives as having more agreeable characters, appraised candidates with more risky alternatives as more emotionally unstable, and expressed preferences for the candidates' subsequent job assignments that were consistent with these appraisals. That is, the employers attributed candidates' use of hard bargaining to their internal personality traits rather than to the external differences in situations between candidates who did and did not have good alternative job opportunities. Thus, even when people grasp the nature of the situation, they may discount the influence of those situational factors on others' behavior.

Interestingly, there is cultural variation in people's tendency to make dispositional attributions. The fundamental attribution error is commonly found in independent cultures such as the United States. While this tendency is also found in more interdependent cultures, the effect is attenuated; in other words, people from more interdependent cultures are more likely to pay attention to the whole context and to make attributions that are more strongly influenced by situational factors. . . .

In an interesting turn, research has also shown that people view causation differently when evaluating their own acts as compared to the acts of others. In particular, while observers are likely to attribute others' behavior to dispositional factors, they are more likely to attribute their own behavior to situational factors—a phenomenon known as the *actor-observer effect*. That is, when someone else runs into a fire hydrant, we are likely to attribute the accident to careless driving. However, if we are the driver, we are more likely to blame the hydrant, its improper placement, or a faulty mirror.

The actor-observer effect works together with a number of other mechanisms to allow us to persuade ourselves that *we* did nothing wrong, or at least that we did the best that we could. Such self-justification is driven by the tension—a tension referred to as *cognitive dissonance*—that exists when a person holds two inconsistent cognitions: the belief that he is a good person who acts reasonably and the knowledge that he has engaged in an unreasonable act. The discomfort of simultaneously holding such incompatible beliefs can cause people to minimize their role in the behavior, discount the extent of the harm caused, derogate or blame the victim, or engage in other self-justificatory thinking in order to resolve the tension. The confirmation bias discussed above contributes by drawing our attention to evidence consistent with our self-justificatory view of events and allowing us to forget aspects of what happened that are inconsistent with our view of ourselves.

It is easy to see how conflict can result when actors justify their own behavior but attribute their counterpart's behavior to dispositional factors. Each party may see his own behavior as a reaction to the situation or to the other's behavior but see the other's behavior as unprovoked. Consider a set of people enacting the role of world leaders engaged in a discussion of nuclear strikes. Following the exchange, people were shown statements from the interchange and asked to recall the statements that immediately preceded and followed the statements. When evaluating their own statements, people were better able to recall what had been said immediately prior to the statement—that is, what led them to make the statement—than what the other's response had been. In contrast, when evaluating the counterpart's statements, people were better able to recall what was said immediately *after* the statement—that is, what they themselves had said in response to the statement—rather than what they had said leading up to the statement. As psychologist Dan Gilbert noted about such findings, "our reasons for punching will always be more salient to us than the punches themselves—but the opposite will be true of other people's reasons and other people's punches."

Research has also demonstrated a variety of additional influences on our judgments about the causes of an outcome. For example, we tend to attribute causal significance to factors that are near an outcome in space or in time, to factors that are prominent or salient, and to factors that are similar to the relevant outcome (for example, big effects are presumed to have big causes). We are more likely to assign responsibility to another person when we judge the cause to be internal to the person, controllable by the person, and stable. That is, we tend to hold others responsible for things we think they can control but not for events we think they could not have prevented or which occurred unpredictably. Moreover, we have a tendency to latch onto readily accessible single-factor explanations for particular effects rather than appreciating that there are often a host of causal factors underlying any given outcome.

Naïve Realism, False Consensus, and the Illusion of Asymmetric Insight

We have seen that people construct their reality based on where they focus their attention and as a function of how they construe information via their expectations and attributions. However, people often fail to appreciate the extent to which their own perceptions are affected by their preexisting knowledge and expectations or to recognize that other people may interpret the same basic circumstances very differently. This *naïve realism* results in the "feeling that [our] own take on the world enjoys particular authenticity, and that other actors will, or at least should, share that take, if they are attentive, rational, and objective perceivers of reality and open-minded seekers of truth.

To see just one example of this *naïve realism* at work in the law, consider the U.S. Supreme Court case of *Scott v. Harris*. Late one night in 2001, police officers clocked nineteen-year-old Victor Harris going seventy-three miles per hour in a fifty-five-mile-per-hour zone and attempted to stop him for speeding. But Harris sped away, and a high-speed chase ensued. The chase ended when police officer Timothy Scott rammed his cruiser into Harris's car, causing Harris to crash and rendering Harris a quadriplegic. Harris brought suit claiming that the police had used excessive force in the way in which they ended the chase and that this had violated his constitutional rights.

The chase and its aftermath were captured on videotape by cameras mounted in the various cruisers. This videotape evidence ended up being central to the Court's decision as to whether there was a genuine issue of material fact about whether Harris's conduct posed sufficient danger to the public to justify the officer's use of force. Consider how Justice Scalia, writing for the eight-justice majority, described what he saw on the tape:

> There we see respondent's vehicle racing down narrow, two-lane roads in the dead of night at speeds that are shockingly fast. We see it swerve around more than a dozen other cars, cross the double-yellow line, and force cars traveling in both directions to their respective shoulders to avoid being hit. We see it run multiple red lights and travel for considerable periods of time in the occasional center left-turn-only lane, chased by numerous police cars forced to engage in the same hazardous maneuvers just to keep up. Far from being the cautious and controlled driver the lower court depicts, what we see on the video more closely resembles a Hollywood-style car chase of the most frightening sort, placing police officers and innocent bystanders alike at great risk of serious injury.

Justice Stevens, however, disagreed with this characterization of the chase (as had the U.S. Court of Appeals for the Eleventh Circuit), describing the incident as "a nighttime chase on a lightly traveled road in Georgia where no pedestrians or other bystanders were present":

> At no point during the chase did respondent pull into the opposite lane other than to pass a car in front of him; he did the latter no more than five times and, on most of those occasions, used his turn signal. On none of these occasions was there a car traveling in the opposite direction. In fact, at one point, when respondent found himself behind a car in his own lane and there were cars traveling in the other direction, he slowed and waited for the cars traveling in the other direction to pass before

> overtaking the car in front of him while using his turn signal to do so. This is hardly the stuff of Hollywood. To the contrary, the video does not reveal any incidents that could even be remotely characterized as "close calls." . . . There is no evidence that he ever lost control of his vehicle. . . . It is apparent from the record (including the videotape) that local police had blocked off intersections to keep respondent from entering residential neighborhoods and possibly endangering other motorists. I would add that the videos also show that no pedestrians, parked cars, sidewalks, or residences were visible at any time during the chase. . . . "At the time of the ramming, apart from speeding and running two red lights, Harris was driving in a non-aggressive fashion (i.e., without trying to ram or run into the officers). Moreover, . . . Scott's path on the open highway was largely clear. The videos introduced into evidence show little to no vehicular (or pedestrian) traffic, allegedly because of the late hour and the police blockade of the nearby intersections. Finally, Scott issued absolutely no warning (e.g., over the loudspeaker or otherwise) prior to using deadly force."

The majority of justices, however, were "happy to let the videotape speak for itself and had "little difficulty in concluding" that Officer Scott's actions were objectively reasonable. Indeed, Justice Breyer, in concurrence, invited viewers to watch the tape for themselves:

> Because watching the video footage of the car chase made a difference to my own view of the case, I suggested that the interested reader take advantage of the link in the Court's opinion and watch it. Having done so, I do not believe a reasonable jury could, in this instance, find that Office Timothy Scott . . . acted in violation of the Constitution.

Was the Court right that the videotape spoke for itself? Following the decision in *Scott,* researchers showed a video of the chase to 1,350 people across the country and asked for their reactions. They found that a majority of respondents perceived the events in the videotape in ways that were consistent with the perceptions of the Supreme Court majority, including that Harris's driving posed a deadly risk to the public and to the police, that Harris was more at fault than were the police, and that deadly force was justified. There were, however, differences in how the tape was construed among different subgroups of respondents, with some viewers concluding that Harris's driving did not pose a deadly risk, that the police were more at fault than Harris, and that the use of deadly force was not justified. Certain groups—such as African Americans, those with lower incomes, and those with more egalitarian views—were more likely than others to depart from the Court's views. When the tape spoke, it did not say the same thing to everyone. Nonetheless, naïve realism means that any individual viewer is likely to believe that others, as long as they are objective, will see the tape in the same way that they do.

Naïve realism has a number of implications that have particular relevance to the practice of law. First, people tend to overestimate the degree to which others share their perspective. The *false consensus effect* "involves an overestimation of the commonness of one's own response and reactions." Thus, people believe that their behavior, choices, and beliefs are typical and, therefore, less indicative of their own character than are behaviors, choices, and beliefs to the contrary.

At the same time, however, when we are aware that others may have perceptions that differ from our own, those differences in perceptions can be magnified. In particular, we tend to overestimate the influence of factors such as ideology and self-interest on other people's attitudes and behavior, believing that such influences will cause people to have beliefs that differ wildly from our own. Thus, in one study, self-identified partisans and neutrals made judgments in a case involving interracial violence and made predictions about how their construals of the case would differ from those with other political viewpoints. While there were, in fact, differences in how the various groups perceived the case, these differences were relatively small compared to the large differences predicted by the participants. Similarly, people tend to overestimate the influence of self-interest on attitudes and to believe that others are more motivated by extrinsic incentives (such as money) and less motivated by intrinsic incentives (such as learning something new, facing a new challenge, or making a difference) than they are themselves. Overestimating such differences can result in unwarranted pessimism about working together and finding common ground.

Second, naïve realism has implications for the ways in which people convey information. For example, people have great difficulty conveying information with which they are familiar to someone who lacks their mental representation of the material. In one telling study, one group of people was asked to tap the rhythms of familiar songs for a second group to identify. The "tappers" (who had mental representations of the songs that included the melody and words) vastly overestimated the likelihood that the "listeners" (who heard only taps) would correctly recognize the songs. (As authors, we hope we have overcome this challenge in writing this book!)

Third, secure in the belief that they see the world accurately, people tend to be confident in their abilities to persuade those on the other side and neutral third parties of the merits of their position. However, when efforts to "enlighten" the other side are unsuccessful, people are likely to conclude that such others are unreasonable, biased, and driven by improper motives. Indeed, the more the other disagrees, the more he is thought to be displaying bias.

A recent series of studies demonstrated that people attribute bias to those with whom they disagree, based merely on the fact of their disagreement. Such attributions can have pernicious consequences. The studies found that once people make such attributions of bias, they are less likely to think that cooperation will be productive, less inclined to cooperate with the person with whom they disagree, and more likely to engage in highly competitive tactics when addressing the disagreement. The problem spirals and conflict escalates because when faced with such tactics, the other person is more likely to respond competitively as well, to view the disagreement as more conflictual, to be less hopeful that the conflict can be resolved, and to view the other as more biased.

Finally, believing that our own perceptions have particular legitimacy and that differing perceptions are the result of a lack of information, unreasonableness, or bias can also lead us to believe that we make more accurate judgments about other people than other people make about us. Indeed, "[w]e insist that our 'outsider perspective' affords us insights about our peers that they are denied by their defensiveness, egocentricity, or other sources of bias. By contrast, we rarely entertain the notion that others are seeing us more clearly and objectively than we see ourselves."

This *illusion of asymmetric insight*—the notion that we know others better than they know us—can incline us to "talk when we would do well to listen and to be less patient than we ought to be when others express the conviction that they are the ones who are being misunderstood or judged unfairly" and can make us "reluctant to take advice from others who cannot know our private thoughts, feelings, interpretations of events, or motives, but all too willing to give advice to others based on our views of their past behavior, without adequate attention to *their* thoughts, feelings, interpretations, and motives."

Perspective Taking

Given the challenges inherent in understanding the causes of other people's behavior and our tendency toward naïve realism, *perspective taking*—the ability to consider the viewpoints of other people and intuit their experiences, perceptions, interests, and feelings—is particularly important to the practice of law. Those who take the perspective of others are more likely to take into account situational influences on others' behavior, perceive others' interests and intentions more accurately, make less self-serving judgments of fairness, and engage in less stereotyping. As a result, considering the perspective of another helps in predicting their reactions and behavior. Such insight is likely to improve a lawyer's ability to negotiate successfully, to persuade a judge, or to give advice that is useful and palatable to a client.

However, perspective taking is not automatic or easy. First, even when we are motivated to figure out the perspective of another, it can be difficult to adjust away from the anchor of our own perspective. For example, when trying to judge how hungry and thirsty a group of lost hikers would be, we tend to be influenced by how hungry or thirsty *we* are. Similarly, those who behave competitively are more likely than those who behave cooperatively to expect others to also behave competitively.

Second, attempting to take the perspective of another sometimes serves to mistakenly amplify differences, real or imagined. When differences in perspective are particularly focal—as with plaintiffs and defendants, Democrats and Republicans, labor and management, or environmentalists and industry—"perspective takers [may] use their own beliefs as a point of *contrast* when stepping into the shoes of the opposing side. In these cases, it is possible for perspective takers to *overestimate* the extent to which the beliefs of opposing groups differ from their own."

In similar ways, at the same time that perspective taking tends to reduce self-serving biases, it can also result in more self-interested behavior in competitive situations. This can occur when the perspective taking focuses attention on the expectation that the other will act in a self-interested manner. Such a focus can result in the expectation that others will act less fairly and be more self-serving. When perspective taking highlights these expectations, perspective takers tend to respond by acting in more self-serving ways themselves. Conversely, in cooperative situations, perspective taking is more likely to draw attention to shared concerns and does not seem to result in more self-serving behavior.

Developing the ability to avoid these pitfalls and effectively take the perspective of others requires conscious attention. It takes effort to step outside of our own perspective and into the shoes of another. Indeed, attorneys may need to work even harder at taking the perspective of others because people in more powerful roles tend to be less likely to take another's perspective. Recent research has found that people with power, such as attorneys, are less likely to take into account another person's visual perspective, less likely to adjust for the fact that others do not have access to their private information, and less accurate at identifying emotions in others. But this work is likely to pay off in a better understanding of the influences on, interests, and intentions of others.

* * *

As we have now seen, there are many factors that can influence how we construct an understanding of the events we experience. How we focus our attention, the ways in which we construe our experiences, the ways in which we tend to attribute causation, our experience of naïve realism, and our use of (or failure to use) perspective taking all have an influence on how we perceive and respond to what happens to us. Importantly, however, while we tend to be willing to believe that others' views and behaviors are influenced by where they sit, we do not fully take into account this myriad of influences on our own understandings and actions. This asymmetry is known as the *bias blind spot.*

Understanding the ways in which people's understandings are shaped by the ways in which they perceive and understand the world can inform lawyers' approaches to eliciting information from clients and witnesses through interviews and depositions and reconciling the sometimes-conflicting information received, counseling clients about how to proceed, negotiating with others who have divergent perceptions, persuading others, and many other tasks. We will turn to a discussion of these implications in the second part of the book. . . .

Interpersonal Communication

In late 2001, attorney Kenneth Feinberg was selected to administer the September 11th Victim Compensation Fund that was created in the wake of the September 11 terrorist attacks. As Feinberg began the task of administering the fund and working with the families who were eligible for payment from the fund, he learned an important lesson about communication:

> Not surprisingly, the communication style I'd developed over the years proved less than ideal for this new challenge. I tend to be straightforward and businesslike, especially when I'm trying to explain a complex plan to a group of lawyers. My preferred approach is to dive in head first: "Hello, ladies and gentlemen, I'm here to explain how the 9/11 fund will work. Please hold your questions; we'll allow plenty of time for those later. Let's start at the beginning. The statute authorizes the following procedures . . ."
>
> I should have realized that this kind of neutral, authoritative, purely factual presentation would strike the 9/11 families as brusque and callous. Instead, it took me a while to realize the effect I was having and adjust my approach. Looking back, I should have started every meeting in a quieter, more empathetic way—expressing sympathy, offering words of respect and condolence, and inviting the families to start the conversation. . . .

Communication and interpersonal interaction are central to the work that attorneys do. Attorneys spend much of their time communicating in some form with clients, colleagues, witnesses, other attorneys, courts, insurance company representatives, and others. Attorneys who can communicate well with their clients will build better relationships with those clients, be better able to obtain relevant information from them, and be better able to provide information and advice to those clients. Such skills are crucial for effectively serving clients, sustaining client relationships, and developing business. Indeed, studies have found that clients independently value good relational skills in their attorneys. But the value of good communication is not limited to client relationships. Good communication with other attorneys can result in more effective negotiation and mediation. Effective communication with witnesses means more valuable depositions. And good communication with the court can mean the difference between a clear and persuasive argument and one that is confusing and fails to have the desired effect.

The Complexities of Human Communication

Many attorneys may wish that they could (or even believe that they can) communicate with others automatically and seamlessly, as if people were computers that could be networked. In this vein, Feinberg (quoted above) expressed his desire to be "straightforward and businesslike." But, for better or worse, human communication is not always so straightforward. Whereas computers communicate exclusively using strings of unambiguous numbers, human communicators rely on a jumble of information gleaned from inference, social convention, memory, body language, and shared knowledge, as well as from the relevant verbal or written expressions. The advantage of human communication, then, is that it can be saturated with meaning and rich with nuance. At the same time, human communication is rife with the ambiguities of language and dependent on interpretation. Understanding can be complicated by the use of humor, sarcasm, euphemisms, and idioms. Communication often depends on a shared base of knowledge, and the meaning of a communicative expression can change depending on the context. Communicators often have multiple, concurrent goals for their exchanges, goals that may include a clear exchange of information but that may also include impression management, persuasion, bluffing, puffery, monitoring the reactions of their audience, building relationships, and managing the flow of the conversation.

Given that the wish for computer-like communication is not going to be granted in the foreseeable future, it is important for attorneys to understand the ways in which humans communicate. We begin by describing some of the nuances of human communication before turning our attention to a number of ways in which attorneys can communicate more effectively.

Perspective Taking in Communication

Think about what it means to communicate with another person. In order to communicate effectively, it is useful to know how each person understands the situation and what information about the topic of conversation each person has and doesn't have. On the one hand, giving information that the other already has or explaining things that the other already understands can be tedious and even condescending. Children express this frustration to their parents frequently, not hesitating to note, "You told me that already." Assuming a shared base of understanding, however, when such a foundation doesn't exist can result in serious miscommunication. Imagine a mother who does not understand that her son needs to be hospitalized when the pediatrician says that he needs to be "admitted for a workup" or a child who doesn't understand that "look both ways" means to look to the left and the right to see whether cars are coming. . . .

Unfortunately, it can be very difficult to know what another person knows. And it can be particularly difficult to appreciate differences between what we ourselves know and what another knows. Because we often overestimate the degree to which others share our perspective and because we have difficulty ignoring what we know, we tend to overimpute our own knowledge and perspective to others. Therefore, even when we are aware that others have information that we do not, we fail to take into account their privileged knowledge. Conversely, even when we know that we possess relevant knowledge that others lack, we often fail to account for the others' lack of knowledge and expect those people to act as though they share our privileged information. This is known as the *curse of knowledge.*

Because we have such a deep knowledge of what we mean to say, we may gloss over key assumptions or fail to provide complete explanations. Given our own knowledge, what we say makes sense to us, and we assume that it will be understandable to others even when it is not. We saw an example of this in chapter 1 when we considered the difficulty experienced by people asked to estimate the likelihood that another person would be able to correctly identify a song whose rhythm they tapped. Recall that "tappers" were unable to set aside their own mental representations of the songs—representations that included words and melodies in addition to rhythm—and significantly overestimated their listeners' success. Similar results have been found in negotiation situations, with negotiators proving unable to ignore their privileged information in making predictions about their counterparts. Thus, in communicating with others, attorneys need to pay close attention to the details of their own knowledge and the extent to which it is shared—or not.

This self-monitoring, however, is complicated by the fact that communicators tend to misjudge how well they have conveyed their message. Writers of headlines surely believe that their captions clearly describe the underlying news story—even when the captions turn out to be fodder for comedy routines: "Drunk Gets Nine Months in Violin Case" or "Kids Make Nutritious Snacks" or "Red Tape Holds Up New Bridge." When speakers utter ambiguous sentences (for example, "Angela shot the man with the gun"), they have a particular meaning in mind (either that Angela used a gun to shoot the man or that Angela shot the man who had the gun). Consequently, they overestimate the extent to which a listener would understand the sentence in the way it was intended.

Conversational Norms

Successful communication often involves the exchange of information via conversation. Such exchanges typically rely on a set of mutually understood *conversational norms.* For example, participants in a conversation tend to expect that the information provided by a speaker will contribute to the ongoing conversation. Contributions are expected to be relevant. And contributions are expected to be informative, but not more informative than is needed. (We all know people who don't seem to "get" this norm and are therefore thought to be tedious.) Many legal discussions, however, including interviews, counseling sessions, depositions, and negotiations, deviate from typical conversations and the norms of such conversations in ways that have implications for attorneys' ability to maximize their effectiveness.

The above-listed conversational norms imply that a speaker does not need to contribute information that the other already has. Such information is an unnecessary contribution to the conversation. But attorneys often call upon clients or witnesses to violate this conversational norm by, for example, asking them to repeat themselves so that the attorneys can verify their understanding. Thus, attorneys will often ask questions to which they have already received an answer. However, "[u]nless the person asked has reason to believe that the questioner did not understand the answer given in response to the first question, he or she is likely to interpret the second question as a request for new information" and will provide an answer that differs in some way from the answer to the previous iteration of the question. Such inconsistencies can be problematic in many legal contexts. On the other hand, attorneys may attempt to capitalize on this conversational tendency by asking the same question again in the hope of eliciting inconsistent statements. Attorneys interviewing clients and preparing witnesses for depositions need to explain clearly what is expected from them.

Typical conversational norms also counsel that a speaker should not contribute to a conversation in a way that is uninformative. Such a norm may tempt people to provide responses that are more precise than their underlying knowledge would support and to hesitate to admit to a lack of knowledge. Accordingly . . ., attorneys should be alert to such pressures, encouraging clients to indicate when they are unsure or are merely offering a conjecture.

Similarly, in the context of an interview or a deposition, a client or witness will usually be expected to report information at a higher level of detail than would be expected in a typical conversation. In normal conversation, people tend to summarize their descriptions, emphasizing and sharpening some aspects and eliminating others. Whereas a client might simply tell her friends, "I was discriminated against," her attorney will need her to provide details as to when, where, how, and why she believes she was mistreated.

On other occasions, such as in the context of a deposition, however, a client might be advised to limit her answers in ways that would seem unnatural in typical conversation.

The classic example involves a simple request:

Q: Do you happen to have the time?

A: Sure, it's almost 2:30.

That is the wrong answer, of course, because it went beyond the actual question. In a deposition, if nowhere else in human interactions, the correct answer is simply "yes." If the lawyer wants more information, he will have to ask another question. In the world of litigation, this makes perfect sense.

Conversely, an attorney who is deposing an adverse witness might hope to get the witness to fall back into his normal patterns of conversation so that he will volunteer additional information or make inconsistent statements.

Nonverbal Communication

Human beings communicate volumes through body language, facial expressions, and voice. Indeed, it is virtually impossible not to communicate *something* nonverbally—even impassivity communicates. More actively, we wave, smile and frown, and use our hands to indicate distance or patterns of movement. We lean in or away from a conversation partner, make or break eye contact, tap our pens on the desk, nod or shake our heads, roll our eyes, cross our arms, give a thumbs-up, get tears in our eyes, and make a myriad of other movements or expressions. Such gestures, postures, and facial expressions all convey messages to others. Similarly, the ways in which words are spoken—for example, tone of voice, inflection, rate of speech, accent, or patterns of pausing—hold additional information. Other behaviors communicate as well: turning on loud music, arriving late for a meeting, and offering a cup of coffee all send a message.

Nonverbal displays can serve as an important source of information. By supplementing or illustrating a verbal expression, expressing emotion, or communicating expectations, nonverbal signals add to the messages conveyed by the words that are spoken. A facial expression, for example, may suggest uncertainty or anger even when the language used conveys confidence or agreement, and the use of air quotes may help to convey skepticism about the meaning or applicability of the words used. In addition, nonverbal signals can help to coordinate the communication interaction. For example, nonverbal displays facilitate turn taking and demonstrate that a person is paying attention. Similarly, as we will see, nonverbal displays, including mimicry, can facilitate the development of rapport. In these ways and more, nonverbal signals add richness and nuance to human communication.

* * *

Thin Slices and Malpractice

Psychologist Nalini Ambady and her colleagues conducted a clever study to explore the association between surgeons' tone of voice and whether they had been sued for malpractice.

First, the researchers recorded conversations between patients and their surgeons during a regular consultation. Half of the surgeons had been previously sued for malpractice and half had not. The researchers created four 10-second clips of each surgeon's voice. Each clip was "content filtered" so that the surgeons' vocal quality—tone of voice, speed, pitch, and cadence—was recognizable, but the substance of the conversation was not. Observers then listened to the clips and rated them on whether the surgeons' voices displayed various qualities—for example, warmth, concern, hostility, professional, competent, and dominance.

The researchers found that these ratings were associated with whether or not the surgeons had been previously sued. In particular, the more dominant and the less concerned the surgeon's tone was noted, the more likely the surgeon was to have been sued.

On the whole, we are able to discern a great deal from even thin slices of nonverbal behavior. For example, ratings of teachers given on the basis of just of few seconds of silent video of the teachers' classroom behavior are remarkably similar to evaluations by students in the teachers' classes. But people vary widely in their abilities to effectively read others or to project a desired impression. Indeed, facility with nonverbal communication involves a range of different skills, including noticing the nonverbal cues displayed by others; interpreting these perceived cues accurately, and expressing attitudes, emotions, and ideas through nonverbal cues accurately and effectively. Each of these facets of nonverbal communication can present complications.

In particular, it is important to remember that nonverbal displays are not necessarily a perfect window into a communicator's state of mind. First, consider that nonverbal cues seldom have a single evident interpretation. For example, a particular facial expression or shrug of the shoulders might be interpreted as disinterest when it really reflects confusion. "[N]o 'dictionary' of nonverbal cue meanings exists in which we can simply look up a cue and find out its meaning. Thus we must constantly be on guard against simple interpretations and simple cause-and-effect explanations of observed behavior." Similarly, there are cultural differences in the meanings that are attached to particular nonverbal displays. Gestures that are innocuous in some cultures may be obscene in others. For example, the U.S hand gesture for OK (with the thumb and forefinger forming a circle) has a sexual connotation in some European cultures. Likewise, the meanings of nonverbal behaviors such as eye gaze and facial expression can vary across cultures.

In addition, people routinely rely on theories about the association between particular nonverbal cues and particular mental states—theories that often turn out to be erroneous. For example, as we will see later in the chapter, in attempting to detect deception, people often rely on a variety of cues that they incorrectly think are associated with deception. And just as with interpretations of other sorts of information, our interpretations of nonverbal signals are colored by our moods, our prior expectations, and so on.

To complicate things further, nonverbal signals can be sent either unintentionally or intentionally by an individual. Sometimes nonverbal cues are automatic and unconscious. Indeed, sometimes nonverbal expressions belie a verbal message. For example, a negotiator might claim that he is not angry, but his red face suggests otherwise. At other times, nonverbal signals may be consciously controlled. For example, a speaker might intentionally adopt a particular expression or posture in order to accurately express his state of mind. On the other hand, a speaker might adopt a particular expression or posture in order to give a contrary impression, perhaps by exaggerating, minimizing, or masking a particular feeling. For example, a negotiator may attempt to effect a poker face to avoid giving away private information.

People may be more or less successful in such attempts to consciously control their nonverbal expressions. Some nonverbal behaviors (for example, crossing or uncrossing arms) are easier to control than others (for example, a spontaneous smile or a particular negative emotion). And people's ability to control their nonverbal expression may also depend on the intensity of the underlying experience: disguising intense anger is more difficult than covering up minor annoyance.

In addition, the conscious control of nonverbal behavior is complicated by the fact that nonverbal signals are more accessible to the receiver than to the one displaying the behaviors. "In interpersonal interactions . . . people never know as much about their own nonverbal behaviors as do the people with whom they are interacting." We do not see our own facial expressions or hear the tone of our own voices in exactly the same ways as others do. Nonetheless, the illusion of transparency means that we tend to believe that we can accurately read others' mental states and that our mental states are transparent to others. All of this makes it difficult to get an accurate read on how well we are communicating nonverbally. Indeed, "[p]eople high in sensitivity to nonverbal cues are not necessarily those who appraise their own skills highly." Thus, it is a good idea for all attorneys to pay close attention to how they express and interpret nonverbal communication.

Communication Mediums

We communicate through many different mediums: face-to-face, over the telephone, and in writing. In our high-tech society, electronic forms of communication have also become ubiquitous. E-mail, instant messaging, and text messaging are now used for an array of communication purposes ranging from a quick confirmation of the time of a meeting to extended and complex negotiations. Video calls and videoconferencing are common as well. The unique characteristics of these different forms of communication can have important implications for how a communication encounter unfolds. Thinking about these characteristics can help in deciding which medium to use for a particular communication and how best to use a particular medium. . . .

First, modes of communication differ in the extent to which they create a record of the exchange. Letters, e-mails, and even instant and text messages generate a running log of the communication. Such a "paper" trail, or archive, makes it possible to return to the text (though not other aspects) of the conversation. In contrast, unless they are recorded, face-to-face and phone conversations are less permanent.

Second, in contrast to communication in real time, some forms of communication, such as e-mails or letters, are asynchronous, lacking the immediate give-and-take of face-to-face conversation. Indeed, such exchanges can play out over hours, days, or longer. This inherent asynchrony can have its benefits. Asynchrony affords communicators the opportunity to think through their responses and to choose their words carefully, and it minimizes the likelihood that they will be dominated by quick-talking counterparts. For these reasons, e-mails and letters tend to facilitate the offering of more complex arguments or offers.

There are also, however, downsides to this asynchrony. Longer messages present the risk that attention will be focused on only part of the communication. In face-to-face conversations, there are constant opportunities to instantly self-correct errors, to ask for clarification, or to recognize and preempt potential disagreement. When communicating via e-mail or letter, in contrast, there are time lags between messages and fewer opportunities to quickly catch and clarify misunderstandings. Unfortunately, we do not always fully take into account this asynchrony—evidencing a *temporal synchrony bias*. Thus, people may expect immediate responses to e-mail messages even when such responses are impractical. They may make assumptions about meaning rather than clarifying. In addition, they may exchange less information. For example, one study found that people negotiating via e-mail were less likely to ask each other about their interests and capabilities and less likely to ask for clarification than those negotiating face-to-face. Similarly, people negotiating via e-mail have been found to exchange less information about preferences and capabilities than those negotiating via instant messaging, a communication medium that facilitates more frequent "speaking" turns.

Third, different forms of communication vary in the degree to which nonverbal and contextual information is available. For example, face-to-face conversation is a *rich* form of communication, one in which participants can draw on a range of verbal and nonverbal cues in helping them to navigate the communication encounter. In contrast, e-mail, text messaging, and instant messaging are *lean* forms of communication, relying on text and occasional emoticons to communicate. The myriad aspects of nonverbal communication on which people rely to understand each other—head nods, vocal inflection, body positioning, eye contact, and so on—are not available. Other forms of communication, such as phone communication, video calling, and videoconferencing, fall somewhere in between. Phone communication allows the possibility of vocal cues. And video-mediated communication further allows for the transmission of some additional nonverbal cues.

The absence of nonverbal cues can minimize the possibility of inadvertently and nonverbally communicating a message that was not intended. However, the same lack of nonverbal cues can make it difficult to establish rapport. In addition, a lack of nonverbal cues and the inhibition of efforts to seek clarification mean that the same statement can be more ambiguous in electronic than in face-to-face communication. Such ambiguity affords more room for preconceived expectations and stereotypes to influence how statements are interpreted.

Moreover, when the medium through which people are communicating provides little opportunity for signaling emotion through vocal inflection or body language, it can be particularly difficult to communicate about emotions. Consider e-mail. Studies of people attempting to communicate sarcasm, sadness, anger, and humor via e-mail have found that e-mail senders are overconfident about the receivers' ability to accurately determine the emotional content of the message. When they consider their own words, e-mailers hear them with the inflection that they would use if they were speaking them. Recipients do not have access to that additional information, but e-mailers fail to account for the lack of such cues to emotion that are inherent in the e-mail context. Even when they were allowed to use emotions, people continued to be overconfident about the degree to which they were able to communicate emotion.

Finally, communicators using different modes of communication experience different degrees of connectedness. In particular, those communicating via electronically mediated means tend to experience a greater sense of social distance, more anonymity, and less accountability than they do when interacting face-to-face or by phone. Some people may prefer to communicate via mechanisms that provide a greater sense of social distance, particularly those who are less extroverted. Interestingly, the relative anonymity of electronic communication can result, for better or worse, in greater disclosure.

The greater social distance associated with electronically mediated forms of communication can also result in a tendency to feel less constrained by social norms. Indeed, legal ethics experts have noted that "lawyers' tendency to be risk-averse seems to fade away on the Internet. 'They're disclosing confidences, talking about pending matters, they take potshots . . . like everyone else.' " Consistent with this observation, researchers have found that e-mail communicators engage in more negative communication behavior (such as flaming) than do those who communicate by less impersonal means. E-mail negotiators tend to develop relationships more slowly and expect to trust their opponents less. Consistent with these expectations, they do tend to perceive their opponents as less credible and trust them less. This lack of trust can lead to less cooperation and more deception. Hard bargaining tactics such as threats, ultimatum offers, and appeals to the other's obligations can be more damaging in electronic communication as the lack of nonverbal and contextual cues, lack of opportunity to clarify, and greater social distance contribute to an escalation of conflict. . . .

Attorneys should be aware of these dynamics when they engage in different forms of communication. In particular, when communicating electronically, attorneys should be vigilant for miscommunication, attempt to generate a back-and-forth flow of information to the extent possible, make a point of asking for information and clarification, and strive for good manners. In order to build rapport, it can be quite useful to engage in some non-task-focused communication prior to conducting business or negotiation via e-mail. In one study, half of a group of e-mail negotiators were asked to engage in a brief telephone call to get to know each other prior to beginning their electronic negotiation. Negotiators who "schmoozed" in this way developed better rapport. Consequently, they were able to consider a broader range of possible outcomes, were more likely to reach an agreement, and were more interested in working together in the future.

Culture and Communication

As we have already seen, cultural differences can be reflected in different styles of communication. For example, cultures differ in terms of the meaning that is attributed to silence in an interaction, the degree of formality that is expected, the appropriateness of interruptions, understandings of the meaning of eye contact, the contours of personal space, conceptions of time, the importance of perspective taking, and the appropriateness of self-disclosure.

One distinction that is commonly drawn is that between *low-context communication* and *high-context communication.* Low-context communication is associated with independent cultures and consists of communication in which the meaning is explicit in the words themselves and that can be understood without reference to the context in which the communication occurs. High-context communication, in contrast, is associated with interdependent cultures and tends to be indirect and highly dependent on context for its meaning. For example, low-context communicators will be more likely to say "no" when they mean "no," while a high-context communicator's refusal may be more implicit. Furthermore, in interpreting a contract, a low-context communicator might be more likely to rely on the text of the contract, while a high-context communicator might be more inclined to rely on what is known about the relationships between the parties to the contract and the circumstances under which the contract was signed. And . . ., low-context communicators are also more likely to appeal to logic, facts, and reasons to persuade; while high-context negotiators are more likely to appeal to emotion, social roles and obligations, and relationships as a basis of persuasion.

Consider how a negotiation interaction might differ for a low-context and a high-context negotiator trying to assess the other side's interests. A low-context negotiator would be more likely to follow the "script of asking the other party questions about his preferences and priorities, . . . reciprocating with information about [her] own preferences and priorities, and thereby slowly building a complete understanding of the tradeoffs in the negotiation and [then] formulating multi-issue proposals to capture those tradeoffs." On the other hand, a high-context negotiator would prefer to gather and disclose information more indirectly, making many, often multifaceted, proposals and drawing "inferences about the other parties' priorities from the patterning of proposals and counterproposals."

While there are broad cultural differences in communication style, different situations within a culture might also nudge an individual toward a particular communication style. For example, a person might tend toward more high-context communication when interacting with others with whom she shares a history, such as a family member or a close friend, as compared to a stranger.

Communication between those employing different styles of communication can be complicated. For example, "[h]igh-context people are apt to become impatient and irritated when low-context people insist on giving them information they don't need. Conversely, low-context people are at a loss when high-context people do not provide *enough* information." Attorneys who are sensitive to such possibilities are likely to get more out of a communication encounter and to be able to navigate such encounters more effectively.

Lying

Another difference between computerized and human communication is that computers don't lie. When a computer provides information to another computer, the information may be flawed, but the computer itself is simply conveying information. Humans, in contrast, may sometimes make deliberate misstatements. This means that effective communicators must be alert to and work to address the possibility of dissembling.

While there is a lot of folklore regarding how to distinguish liars from truth tellers, it turns out that identifying liars is extremely difficult, even for experts. Many of the cues that we think are associated with deception are not. Many of the cues that are actually associated with deception are subtle and not easily detectable. In addition, many cues to deception can also be associated with other states, such as stress, that are likely common to legal clients, witnesses, or negotiators. Indeed, across a variety of studies, psychological research has found that people are not very adept at distinguishing those who are lying from those who are telling the truth—performing at levels that are little or no better than chance. Moreover, there is little correlation between our degree of certainty that we have identified a liar and our accuracy. Apparent experts do not tend to perform any better than laypeople, though, ironically, they do tend to be more confident in their judgments. Thus, although many attorneys may believe that they are quite good at figuring out whether clients or opposing counsel are lying based on whether they blink, look away, or tap their fingers, they are probably wrong as often as they are right.

A primary reason why people are unable to reliably distinguish lies and truths is that we pay attention to the wrong things. Psychological research has identified a number of cues that people believe are related to deception. In particular, people strongly believe that liars avert their gaze, smile, engage in lots of movement (such as shifting positions, making hand and foot movements, and making gestures of illustration), and have more disturbed speech (including hesitation, pauses, and slower speech). Many of these anticipated cues are thought to be associated with nervousness and, hence, lying.

However, many of these purported indicators do not in fact prove reliable in distinguishing liars and truth tellers. For instance, the cue most commonly believed to indicate deception—averted gaze—has not been shown to distinguish liars from truth tellers. Similarly, while people anticipate that liars will display more movement, studies have shown either no differences or that liars tend to make fewer movements. A decrease in movement may result from attempts to compensate for the expectation that they will show an increase in motion or from a cognitive effort to carry out the lie. In the same way, higher rates of blinking and speech disturbances do not appear to distinguish liars from truth tellers. People also tend to incorrectly associate trustworthiness with attractiveness. The stereotype of the shifty-eyed, fidgety liar who looks like a weasel apparently does not serve us well. Accordingly, it is important that attorneys not rely on stereotypes about lying that do not accurately discriminate between liars and truth tellers.

All of this is made even more complicated by the fact that much of the time we are not dealing with others who are blatantly lying but instead with persons who hold varying versions of reality. As we saw in chapters 1 and 2, different factual accounts can result from, among other things, differences in what was attended to, differences in how events were construed or interpreted, and differences in what was remembered. In addition, self-presentational concerns can lead us to emphasize certain aspects of the story or gloss over others.

> Telling the whole truth and nothing but the truth is rarely possible or desirable. All self-presentations are edited. The question is one of whether the editing crosses the line from the honest highlighting of aspects of identity that are most relevant in the ongoing situation to a dishonest attempt to mislead.

In addition, because people tend to judge active conduct or commission more harshly than inaction or omission, *lies of omission* are not seen to be as serious as affirmatively false statements. Thus, it is likely that attorneys will more frequently encounter such misleading omissions than outright lies. For example, a client may fail to inform the attorney of particular details, or opposing counsel may gloss over certain specifics during a negotiation. Such omissions may simply be a function of a different understanding, a failure to remember, or a need to be viewed positively.

Some such omissions may be deliberate. Notwithstanding attorneys' incantation of the attorney-client privilege and exhortations to their clients to be forthright, some clients may believe that their attorneys will represent them more effectively if they are not aware of certain skeletons in the clients' closets. Clients may also fear that if they disclose damaging information to the attorney, the attorney will feel compelled to disclose it to the opposing side or to a finder of fact. If outright lies are difficult to discern, surely it is even more difficult to discern nuances of omission, shading, positive spin, or subtle editing.

While it is true that detecting lies is difficult, psychological research has more to teach regarding the detection of liars than simply admonishing us to be careful about our intuitions. There are some dimensions on which liars do tend to differ from those who are telling the truth. Liars tend to offer fewer details, give accounts that are less plausible and coherent, and speak with more vocal tension and higher pitch—though the size of these effects can be quite small. Unfortunately, these cues can also be present for other reasons; for example, a high pitch could be a sign of lying or a sign that the person is upset or nervous for some other reason (such as the stress of being questioned or being asked to talk about personal information). Similarly, lack of detail or coherency can reflect poor memory rather than lying. Thus, cues such as these should be seen as signals that are worth pursuing further in order to get more information or verification rather than as fail-safe indicators of lying.

Indeed, looking for inconsistencies between the interviewee's story and information obtained from other sources of information can be an effective way to identify areas for further probing. In attempting to distinguish truth from lies, people often rely on information from third parties, their own prior knowledge, any physical evidence, and so on. To the extent that an interviewer has access to other sources of information—for example, additional witnesses, documents, or physical evidence—such information can be used to craft more probing questions. Waiting to raise contrary information until late in an interview (or until a subsequent interview) provides an opportunity for such inconsistencies to surface and can lead to improved accuracy in detecting deception.

When dealing with multiple witnesses, inconsistencies in their reports may or may not indicate lying. It is clear from the research we have reviewed so far on perception, construal, and memory that two people's understanding and memory of a single event can vary widely. Similarly, complete consistency may not be a reliable indicator of deception either. Witnesses who tell harmonious stories may be providing accurate reports about an event, or they may have colluded to "get their stories straight." Psychological researchers have found it helpful to ask such witnesses questions that they might not have anticipated and, therefore, would have been less likely to have included in their discussion. Questions about unanticipated details tend to elicit more divergent answers from pairs of liars than they do from pairs of truth tellers. Similarly, asking an individual witness the same unanticipated question multiple times (perhaps in different ways) over the course of an interview or series of interviews can uncover contradictions because such details are less likely to be part of a rehearsed lie and have to be made up on the spot.

In addition, paying particular attention to changes in the behavior of the particular speaker may be revealing. While one individual's speech and behavior may simply differ from those of another person (for example, higher pitch) even when they are telling the truth, making distinctions among people difficult to draw, changes in an individual's behavior may be more predictive and worth following up with additional questions or verification. Thus, just as within-person confidence is more useful in assessing memory than are cross-person comparisons, within-person behavior is more useful in identifying lying.

Another strategy that has proven useful in separating liars from truth tellers is asking the person to recount the relevant information in reverse chronological order. Telling a story in reverse order is cognitively challenging, especially for those who are already laboring under the cognitive demands attendant to lying (formulating and remembering the lie, suppressing the truth, monitoring and attempting to control demeanor, and monitoring the listener's reactions). Indeed, there is evidence that liars telling their stories in reverse chronological order show more signs of cognitive load, providing fewer auditory details, speaking slower and with more hesitation, and demonstrating increased movement in the legs and feet. And, importantly, observers are somewhat better able to detect lies when people tell their story in reverse chronological order.

Finally, recent research has found that when people are asked direct questions, they are less likely to lie by omission. Instead, in responding to direct questions, people are more likely to answer with either the truth or with an express misstatement. In contrast, in the absence of a direct question, people tend to either tell the truth or to lie by omission. For example, the seller of a used car may fail to mention some sporadic *issues* with the car's brakes. When confronted with a direct question, however, a strategy of omission *is* more difficult to carry out. Some people who might have preferred to omit the relevant information will choose to tell the truth rather than tell a lie. Thus, while asking direct questions may increase the risk of a direct lie, such questions may also be more likely to produce clear statements that can then be subjected to verification or become the focus of warranties.

Ultimately, successful lie detection may depend on keeping an open mind as to whether someone is lying. Many people begin their assessment with a predisposition that influences their judgment. For example, laypeople tend to hold a bias in favor of judging statements to be truthful (*truth bias*), while law enforcement officers tend to hold a bias in favor of detecting deception. This is a form of ... confirmation bias.... In contrast, avoiding commitment to a conclusion about whether a person is lying until all of the available information has been processed allows a person to pay closer and more sophisticated attention to nonverbal cues, to focus closely on nuances of language, and to use corroborating or disconfirming information....

CHAPTER 4

INTERVIEWING

LEARNING GOALS

The learning goals for this class include helping you to:

- Understand the importance of and develop strategies for establishing rapport and communicating empathic understanding
- Learn how to obtain concrete, detailed facts from a client or potential witness
- Understand the importance of active listening, and the variety of factors that can serve as facilitators and inhibitors of conversation
- Overcome any instinctive avoidance of or awkwardness or embarrassment about difficult, uncomfortable, or negative facts
- Overcome concerns about bridging cultural and other differences between lawyer and client
- Understand the unconscious tendency to fill in gaps in factual knowledge with assumptions based on one's own experience
- Maintain client-centeredness, in part through ensuring adequate exploration of both legal and non-legal options
- Appreciate the rules of professional conduct as they apply to the lawyer-client relationship

DESCRIPTION OF CLASS

This class will focus on client interviewing techniques. Each student will be assigned to plan and role-play a portion of an interview with a potential client seeking clinic representation. We will take periodic breaks as the interview unfolds, to critique the process and to discuss topics that need to be covered, issues that may arise, and strategies for overcoming various challenges.

ASSIGNMENT IN PREPARATION FOR CLASS

Think of an experience you have had conducting an extended interview with someone you did not know well. Any context will do, including interviews of a subject for a research project, a candidate on behalf of your undergraduate admissions office, an applicant for membership in an organization to which you belong, or some kind of service provider. What is important here is that you were in a situation where you needed to ask an extended series of questions, in an effort to get a full understanding of a situation or story.

Note your responses to the questions below, and be prepared to discuss your thoughts in class.

- What was the most challenging aspect of the interview for you?
- What actions did you take (or what things did you say) that you believe facilitated the interview?
- What actions did you take (or what things did you say) that may have undermined the interview?
- What surprised you most about this experience?
- What did this experience teach you about successful interviewing techniques?
- What did this experience teach you about communicating effectively with a person whom you do not know well?

READING ASSIGNMENT

1. Jean R. Sternlight & Jennifer Robbennholt, *Good Lawyers Should Be Good Psychologists: Insights for Interviewing and Counseling Clients*, 23 OHIO ST. J. ON DISP. RESOL. 434 (2007–08).
2. Clark D. Cunningham, *What Clients Want From Their Lawyers* (2006), http://law.gsu.edu/Communication/WhatClientsWant.pdf.
3. Lisa Sanders, *The Facts and What Lies Beyond*, *in* EVERY PATIENT TELLS A STORY: MEDICAL MYSTERIES AND THE ART OF DIAGNOSIS 3 (2009).

4. Victoria Healey-Etten & Shane Sharp, *Teaching Undergraduates How to Do an In-Depth Interview: A Teaching Note with 12 Handy Tips,* 38 TEACHING SOCIOLOGY 157 (Apr. 2010).

READINGS

Jennifer Robbennholt and Jean Sternlight
Good Lawyers Should Be Good Psychologists: Insights for Interviewing and Counseling Clients
23 OHIO ST. J. ON DISP. RESOL. 434 (2007–08)[1]

I. Introduction

Practicing law means working with people. To be effective in working with clients, witnesses, judges, mediators, arbitrators, experts, jurors, and other lawyers, attorneys must have a good understanding of how people think and make decisions, and must possess good people skills Yet, law schools have tended to teach very little, directly, about how to be good with people . . . [In addition,] commonly graduate from law school understanding little if anything about perception, memory, communication, cognitive heuristics, or decisionmaking. While good lawyers ultimately pick up some of this information through experience, there is no reason to leave new lawyers to flounder based on a lack of understanding of these psychological principles. . . . While the best lawyers may have intuited some of what will be discussed here, some of the findings are counterintuitive, and even experienced lawyers can improve their approach to interviewing and counseling by drawing on relevant psychology.

In general, interviewing and counseling sessions have three main components. First, the attorney uses an interview to obtain information from the client. Second, the attorney uses the counseling portion of the initial session to provide information to the client. Third, throughout the session the attorney is concerned with establishing rapport between attorney and client. Success or failure in building rapport with the client will inevitably affect the attorney's ability to obtain and provide information, and to ethically and effectively counsel the client in this and future sessions.

Knowledge of the psychology of both client and attorney is highly relevant to all three facets of interviewing and counseling and is critically important as attorneys seek to build good rapport, obtain relevant

[1] Footnotes and/or internal citations omitted.

information from clients, retain that information, and guide clients regarding their options. . . .

III. Psychological Insights Relevant to Effective Interviewing and Counseling

. . .

Psychological scientists have studied many aspects of human cognition and behavior that are potentially relevant to interviewing and counseling clients. We focus here on empirical research—primarily from social and cognitive psychology—that has explored how people perceive, interpret, and make judgments about the world around them, how people remember and talk about such information, the influence of culture and notions of justice, and how people use that information to make decisions. Thus . . ., we consider the processes by which people remember and communicate about their experiences, exploring what the science of memory suggests about how to interview clients, whether liars can be reliably identified, and the role of several different aspects of communication in the effective transmission of information between attorney and client. [Then] we consider psychological research that finds broad differences among cultures in how people think, resolve disputes, and interact and research on the psychology of justice, both of which have additional implications for lawyer-client interaction. Finally, we explore a range of research findings related to understanding the ways in which people grapple with and make decisions. . . .

C. *Memory*

[M]any law students and . . . new attorneys believe human memories are better than they really are. Psychologists have demonstrated that both short-term and long-term memories are extremely frail. As in the movie *Rashomon,* different people's descriptions of the same event often vary significantly. It is not merely that people misremember whether someone was wearing a red or green shirt. We also do a poor job of remembering very significant events, their timing, the order in which events took place, or who was present:

> Our minds are not capable of making complete records of events; rather we encode features selectively. Even when we do remember events reasonably well, we do not come close to remembering all the fine details that are part of the event. We are not like video recorders, faithfully taking in and storing all the details in a scene.

Interviewers should be concerned with clients' ability to remember relevant information (i.e., quantity), with the degree to which the information reported by clients is accurate (i.e., quality), and with the interviewer's own ability to recall the content of the interview itself.

However, both clients and attorneys may be unable to provide relevant and accurate details because they did not attend to or encode such details accurately at the time the event occurred, because they have forgotten, or because their memories have become distorted since the event occurred.

1. *How Memory Works*

We [know] that not all details of an event attract our attention and that significant interpretation takes place as events occur. But even details that were noticed and could have been accurately reported immediately after the event may be forgotten. Working memory "holds on to small amounts of information for short periods of time—usually a few seconds—while people engage in such ongoing cognitive activities as reading, listening, problem solving, reasoning, or thinking." However, to be retained, this information must be transferred from short-term working memory to long-term memory: "the system must constantly discard what is no longer needed at the moment, and devote its resources to the temporary storage of incoming information. Unless special effort is made—such as repeating a sentence over and over again—information is lost from the system almost immediately after it enters."

Moreover, even memories that are stored in long-term memory tend to deteriorate as time passes:

> At relatively early points on the forgetting curve—minutes, hours, and days, sometimes more—memory preserves a relatively detailed record, allowing us to reproduce the past with reasonable if not perfect accuracy. But with the passing of time, the particulars fade and opportunities multiply for interference . . . to blur our recollections.

Test yourself, and you will likely find that you no longer remember things that were once deeply embedded in your memory, such as an old home phone number, how to drive to a particular location, or the name of grade school teachers or old friends.

In addition, there are a variety of "ways in which what is remembered can depart from what actually occurred." For example, people sometimes remember events in ways that are distorted from what actually happened, combine aspects of multiple events into a single memory, or remember events that did not happen.

One factor that leads to many of these errors is that people have difficulty with what is called "source monitoring." When people try to remember something they do not call up a perfectly accurate real-time recording of the event. Instead, they access a range of sources of information including their own "internal mental representation of the event," other basic information they have about how the world works, their schemas for how events such as this one typically happen, what they have been told by others about what happened, their experiences in other similar situations, stereotypes, what they imagined doing, and so on. A large body of psychological research has demonstrated that people have difficulty discriminating between these different sources of information. Thus, when someone tries to remember whether he turned off the stove before he left the house and seems to remember doing it, he may have difficulty determining whether he actually did it, or just thought about doing it, or remembered doing it on a different occasion.

One consequence of these difficulties in source monitoring is that people can be suggestible—exposure to information from sources other than what was actually observed can influence memories of what happened, altering details of memory or introducing new elements. For example, in one study participants viewed a videotape of an automobile accident. Next, they were asked a series of questions about the accident—including a question that asked about the speed of the car as it passed a barn. When asked questions about the accident one week later, 17% of participants reported having seen a barn, despite the fact that there had not been a barn in the video.

Finally, in a phenomenon with particular relevance to legal disputes, memories can be distorted when people make judgments that attribute blame. For example, in one study memory of an event—a customer leaving a restaurant without paying—was assessed one week after the event was described. As compared to participants who had been provided with a justification for the customer's behavior that tended to attenuate blame, participants who had been led to accentuate blame (i.e., were provided with negative information about the customer) remembered the price of the meal as being higher, were more likely to overestimate the price of the meal, and were more likely to incorrectly report that the customer had also failed to pay for a pre-dinner drink.

2. *Eliciting Memories*

Given the frailty of human memory, attorneys need to know how to help clients access their memories successfully. Anyone who has experienced the "tip of the tongue" phenomenon knows that having information available in memory is not the same as being able to access it on demand. Psychologists have explored a number of aspects of how people retrieve and report memories that have implications for interviewing clients. Importantly, since the interviewee is the one who possesses the information, the interviewee ought to be the focus of the interview. In particular, interviewers can help interviewees access their memories successfully by asking open-ended questions, avoiding leading questions, asking the interviewee to include details that may not seem important, and adopting interviewee-centered sequencing of questions.

First, psychological research suggests that interviewers ought to use open-ended questions when possible, following up with focused questions in areas in which more detail is needed. Asking open-ended questions "allows the interviewee time to collect his or her thoughts and consequently promotes more elaborate memory retrieval." Interviewees are able to focus their attention on remembering the event rather than being distracted from this task by a series of interviewer questions. Accordingly, open-ended questions can elicit more accurate information than do more focused questions.

In particular, open-ended questions also allow interviewees to control the level of detail they report in their initial responses. For example, a witness could choose to report that a particular event occurred "back in the spring" or that it happened "in April" or that it occurred "on April 10 during the morning break." Psychological research has shown that people intuitively adjust the level of detail that they report so as to choose a level of detail that favors accuracy (even at the expense of some precision) and that they therefore provide a higher proportion of accurate information. This finding is consistent with other research that finds that although people may not be able to completely recreate an event from memory, the information in people's unassisted reports does tend to be quite accurate. Thus, interviewees ought not to be initially forced to give specific answers to questions and, instead, should be given the opportunity to control the level of detail in their initial responses, and to indicate that they do not know the answer, are not sure, or cannot remember. A greater degree of confidence can be placed in the accuracy of such unaided, unpressed reports.

It may be inevitable, however, that a lawyer will ultimately have to press the client for further and more precise responses. Clients will likely be able to comply with such requests—people are able to adopt different accuracy and precision thresholds for their reports—although increasing the precision of the information provided can come at a cost to accuracy. One recent study found that when witnesses were forced to guess, more information was provided, but this information included both more correct information *and* more incorrect information. In addition, there is evidence that "guessing" can result in the same types of source misattribution errors described above, with the witness' conjectures later being remembered as having actually happened. The client, therefore, should be allowed to indicate where she is less sure of such details and both lawyer and client should keep in mind the potential for decreased accuracy.

By using open-ended questions and encouraging the interviewee to relay even unrequested information, the interviewer may also be able to minimize retrieval-induced forgetting. Retrieval induced forgetting occurs when "memory quantity for the reviewed items is enhanced, [but] memory quantity for related, non-reviewed items is reduced." For example, in one study, participants were asked to view pictures of two categories of items that had been stolen from two houses. Participants then answered questions about some of the items from one of the categories. Subsequently, participants were better able to recall the items about which they had been questioned than the other items. Thus, to the extent that focused, detailed questions are limited to specific aspects of the event or situation, they may inhibit memory for other related aspects of the dispute.

In contrast to open-ended questions, asking specific questions early in the interview—such as multiple choice questions or questions asking the interviewee to confirm or disconfirm a statement—can limit the range of information obtained, decrease accuracy, and increase the possibility that information contained in the question will be subsequently "remembered." Leading questions—questions that suggest or presuppose their answers—pose particular problems for memory. In one study, participants were shown a videotape of a car accident and asked to describe what they had seen. When asked about the speed of one of the cars, one group of participants was asked, "About how fast were the cars going when they hit each other?" Other groups of participants were asked the same question, but the word "hit" was replaced by one of the following: smashed, collided, bumped, or contacted. Estimates of speed varied depending on the descriptor used. In a follow-up experiment, participants who were asked about the speed of the cars when they "smashed into" each other were more likely to incorrectly remember that they saw broken glass than were participants who were asked about the speed of the cars when they "hit" each other. . . .

3. *Distinguishing Accurate and Inaccurate Memories*

As described above, some of our memories are erroneous. It turns out that people have an impressive ability to remember things incorrectly, and then to be certain that the incorrect memory is accurate. They are not lying, but rather just misremembering. What can attorneys do to distinguish accurate and inaccurate memories? Probably the best solution is to look for confirmation, particularly in contemporaneously prepared written materials or photos. While documents sometimes contain inaccuracies too, confirmation of human recollection by a document may at least decrease the likelihood of error.

. . . Psychological research has demonstrated that confident witnesses are not necessarily more accurate than non-confident witnesses. On the other hand, the relative confidence of a particular interviewee for different pieces of information can be a useful guide. As noted earlier, interviewees are reasonably good judges of the level of detail which they can accurately report. Accordingly, details for which the interviewee is confident do tend to be more accurate than details for which the same interviewee is less confident.

. . .

D. *Identifying Liars and Truth Tellers*

While there is a lot of folklore regarding how to distinguish liars from truth tellers, it turns out that identifying liars is extremely difficult, even for experts . . . [T]here is no particular cue or set of cues that can reliably be used to identify a lie. Many of the cues that could be associated with deception can also be associated with other states likely common to legal clients, such as stress. Indeed, across a variety of studies, psychological research has found that people are not adept at distinguishing those who are lying from those who are telling the truth—performing at levels that are little or no better than chance. Moreover, there is little correlation between our degree of certainty that we have identified a liar and our accuracy. Apparent experts do not tend to perform any better than lay people, though they do tend to be more confident in their determinations. . . .

A primary reason why people are unable to reliably distinguish lies and truths is that we pay attention to the wrong things. Psychological research has identified a number of cues that people *believe* are related to deception. In particular, people strongly believe that liars avert their gaze, engage in lots of movement (e.g., shifting position, hand movements, foot movements, gestures of illustration), smile, and have more disturbed speech (e.g., hesitation, pauses, slower speech). Many of these anticipated cues are thought to be associated with nervousness. However, many of these believed indicators do not in fact prove reliable in distinguishing liars and truth tellers. . . .

There are some dimensions[, however,] on which liars do tend to differ from those who are telling the truth. Liars tend to offer fewer details, give accounts that are less plausible and coherent, and speak with more vocal tension and higher pitch—though the size of these effects can be quite small. Unfortunately, these cues, too, can also be present for other reasons—for example, a high pitch could be a sign of lying or a sign that the person is upset or nervous for some other reason (such as the stress of being questioned or talking about personal information). Similarly, lack of detail or coherency can reflect poor memory rather than lying. Thus, cues such as these ought to be seen as signals that are worth pursuing further in order to get more information.

In addition, particular attention can be paid to *changes* in the behavior of the particular speaker. While one individual's speech and behavior may simply differ from another person's even when they are telling the truth, making distinctions difficult to draw, changes in an individual's behavior may be more predictive and worth following up.

Thus, just as within-person confidence is more useful in assessing memory than are cross-person comparisons, within-person behavior is more useful in identifying lying.

. . .

All of this is complicated by the fact that much of the time people are not dealing with others who are blatantly lying but instead who hold varying versions of reality.

> Telling the whole truth and nothing but the truth is rarely possible or desirable. All self-presentations are edited. The question is one of whether the editing crosses the line from the honest highlighting of aspects of identity that are most relevant in the ongoing situation to a dishonest attempt to mislead.

Probably the most common way in which clients lie to their attorneys is that they fail to inform the attorney of particular details. Such omissions may be deliberate. Notwithstanding attorneys' incantation of the attorney-client privilege and urging their clients to be forthright, some clients may believe that their attorneys will represent them more effectively if they are not aware of certain skeletons in the clients' closets. Clients may also fear that if they disclose damaging information to the attorney, the attorney will feel compelled to disclose it to the opposing side or to a finder of fact. In other instances, such omissions may simply be a function of misconstrual or a need to be viewed positively. If outright lies are difficult to discern, surely it is even more difficult to discern nuances of shading, positive spin, or editing.

. . .

1. *Listening*

It is important, psychologically, for attorneys to listen carefully and also to demonstrate to their clients that they are listening carefully. At a basic level, if the attorney does not pay attention to the information that the client is providing, she is likely to miss important data. Moreover, clients, like all other people, like to feel that someone is listening when they speak.

In order to both listen effectively and appear to clients to be listening effectively, lawyers should typically let their clients tell their initial stories without interruptions, follow up their accounts with clarifying questions, and then provide feedback and legal information that reflects that the attorney was listening carefully. Studies of interviewers, including lawyers, police interviewers, and physicians, have found that interviewers are prone to interrupt early and often. Research shows that interjecting a large number of specific questions can make it difficult for the interviewer to listen to the answers provided by the interviewee. "Directing those limited mental resources to formulating many questions—rather than listening intently to the witness's narrative response to open-ended questions—ought to increase the difficulty of understanding or notating the witness's responses." In addition, as we have already discussed, psychological research has documented the benefits to memory that come from listening to interviewees and not interrupting their answers to questions.

In addition, attorneys need to be conscious of messages they may inadvertently convey to their clients that signal a lack of attention to clients' answers. Studies have shown that people have a tendency to convey more detail in their answers when the listener is attentive and not distracted. . . .

2. *Conversational Norms*

Interviews deviate from typical conversations in ways that have implications for interviewers' ability to elicit information from interviewees. First, in the context of an interview, a client will usually be expected to report information. . . .

Second, the norms of everyday conversation posit that information provided by a speaker should contribute to the ongoing conversation—that it should not be information that the questioner already has. Accordingly, "[u]nless the person asked has reason to believe that the questioner did not understand the answer given in response to the first question, he or she is likely to interpret the second question as a request for new information" and will provide an answer that differs in some way from the answer to the previous iteration of the question. Thus, because attorneys often need their clients to violate this conversational norm, by either repeating themselves—so the attorney can verify her understanding—or providing additional detail, attorneys need to explain clearly what they need from their client.

. . .

3. *Perspective Taking and Empathy*

Perspective taking—the ability to take the perspective of other people and imagine their experiences, perceptions, and feelings—may be particularly important to the lawyer-client relationship. Importantly, people who take the perspective of another person have been shown to experience greater empathy towards that other—perceiving and sharing in the other's emotions. In addition, those who take the perspective of others engage in less stereotyping, make attributions about the other that are closer to the types of attributions they would make about themselves (i.e., giving more consideration to situational factors), perceive the interests and intentions of the other more accurately, and make less self-serving judgments of fairness. Thus, striving to take the perspective of another person may be important for lawyers. . . .

People in more powerful roles, however, tend to be less likely to take another's perspective. Recent research has found that people with power are less likely to "adopt another person's visual perspective," are less likely to "take into account that other people [do] not possess their privileged knowledge," and are less accurate in identifying emotions in others. Thus, attorneys—who occupy a position of power relative to their clients—may need to pay particular attention to the perspective of their clients.

. . . While lawyers may not want to try to become close friends with their clients, or to allow lawyering to drift into therapy, they do need to try to use their ears and eyes to better understand not only what their clients are saying but also what they mean and, sometimes, what they are *not* saying.

It may also be useful for lawyers to try to teach the importance of perspective taking and empathy to their clients. To the extent that clients can come to better understand a seeming adversary's perspective, clients may be able to better understand their likelihood of prevailing in litigation, to devise a mutually acceptable settlement, and to make an informed decision regarding whether it even makes sense to try to litigate a particular dispute. While attorneys cannot, of course, teach an actual class on empathy to their clients, they may want to help their clients imagine how the world might look through the eyes of the seeming adversary. In practice, it may be difficult for attorneys to engage in such discussions with clients. Clients often treasure the idea that their attorney is their advocate who would never see the world through anyone but the clients' eyes. However, to be truly effective in representing their clients' interests, attorneys must at times try to impart empathy.

4. *Trust and Rapport*

Trust is central to the attorney-client relationship. To trust is to "accept vulnerability based on positive expectations of the intentions or behavior of another." Clients, who are often in a vulnerable position, trust their attorney when they rely on the attorney to act in ways that are consistent with the clients' well-being—expecting both that the attorney will act with fidelity to their interests and will act competently in doing so.

Trust can further the attorney-client relationship by improving communication between attorney and client—promoting disclosure of important information by the client and facilitating the counseling process. Clients want to believe that their lawyer is their ally and advocate—and may hesitate to provide full information if they don't feel supported. In contrast, people tend to be more willing to share more information (particularly sensitive or personal information) with those whom they trust. In addition, if clients trust their attorneys, discussions regarding settlement and other options will be far more successful. Clients who trust their attorneys may be more willing to consider and follow the attorneys' advice. It is natural that when an attorney begins to discuss settlement, the client may feel let down or even abandoned. The lawyer who the client had seen as her knight in shining armor is now urging that the client's position may not be so strong after all. Is the lawyer perhaps looking out for her own interests rather than those of the client? However, if the client has real trust in her attorney, she is less likely to feel that the attorney misled her at any point.

Trust can be facilitated in a variety of ways. As an initial matter, existing reputations and institutional structures—such as the requirements and norms of professional responsibility—can lay a foundation for a relationship of trust. While lawyers often inform their clients that their communications are covered by the attorney-client privilege, urging clients to be forthcoming on this basis, merely informing clients of the existence of such a privilege may not be enough to create real trust. Beyond this, however, trust is influenced by patterns of communication and interpersonal interaction. Moreover, people can build trust through the ways in which they communicate openness and concern for the other's needs. . . .

F. *Cultural Differences*

. . .

In popular parlance, culture is often thought of as something exotic that other people have (special accents, food, dress), but that we do not. More properly, our culture provides a set of lenses through which we see the world. These lenses do not dictate our behavior, but may shape our perceptions and intuitive responses. While people tend to think of cultural differences as existing between groups who live in different parts of the world, significant cultural differences also exist within the United States. Cultural differences can be based not only on ethnicity, but also on differences in age, gender, world view, economic status, or religion. Thus, everyone operates from one or more different cultural perspectives. While culture affects many aspects of our world view, we will highlight several ways in which cultural differences may be particularly relevant to lawyers who are interviewing and counseling clients.

Cultures can differ in terms of their approach to dispute resolution. In particular, psychological research has shown that people from different cultures tend to differ in the importance they ascribe to the possible objectives of dispute resolution processes. Different cultures may place varying degrees of importance on goals such as maintaining relationships, achieving "justice," saving face, achieving economic gains, or laying a foundation for the future. Clients from more individualistic cultures may be primarily concerned with their own personal success. Clients from more collectivist cultures may be more highly attuned to how their behavior has affected or will affect the social standing of the broader group with which they identify, how they are viewed by that group, the joint success of the parties, or how relationships are affected. In addition, a client may be concerned about the "cultural consequences" of her actions—that is, the consequences of "taking steps that are out of her culture's norm."

Not surprisingly then, clients from different cultures also tend to display differing preferences for how to go about resolving disputes. For example, people from more individualistic cultures may prefer resolving disputes through strategies that focus on the immediate conflict, involve direct confrontation, and result in a determination of who is right and who is wrong. In contrast, those from more collectivist cultures tend to prefer more relational strategies that involve the use of intermediaries, mediation, collaboration, accommodation, or avoidance. In addition, cultural difference can influence whether one prefers resolving disputes by looking to universal principles or rules, or whether one prefers a case-by-case analysis of the particular circumstance involved. Culture may also influence the value placed on debate, and the inclination to take other perspectives or to consider counterarguments.

Culture may also be related to differences on a variety of other dimensions that have implications for client interviewing and counseling. For example, cultures differ in terms of the meaning that is attributed to silence in an interaction, the degree of formality that is expected, the appropriateness of interruptions, understandings of the meaning of eye contact, the contours of personal space, conceptions of time, conventions about the display of emotion, the appropriateness of self-disclosure, how agency is viewed, and attitudes toward authority. In addition, one's cultural background is related to the ways in which one perceives associations among people and events in the world. In particular, psychological research has shown cultural variation in people's tendency to make dispositional attributions—people from more interdependent cultures are more likely to pay attention to the whole context and to make attributions that are more strongly influenced by situational factors. Similarly, people from collectivist cultures have been shown to be less susceptible to making self-serving judgments.

In applying these insights the attorney's challenge is to recognize that persons from different cultures see the world differently, while at the same time avoiding the trap of assuming that all persons from a particular culture see the world the same way. That is,

> [t]he task here is to appreciate and respect the differences among your clients, but without resorting to stereotypes or stubborn myths about race, sex, ethnicity, and culture. To ignore

likely differences in culture is an invitation to malpractice in counseling; to presume you know what those differences will be once you know your client's race or sex or cultural background is an invitation to dehumanize or reify your client, and to assume generalizations that may not apply to him.

. . .

V. CONCLUSION

It has been said that "neither LAW nor HUMAN NATURE is an exact science," and surely many lawyers would agree. Nonetheless, the science of psychology has much to contribute to the art of legal practice and to the craft of interviewing and counseling clients. While we cannot provide an exact recipe for success, we hope that by reminding lawyers of the importance of psychological science and by highlighting some critical insights offered by that field, we have provided the tools to improve their representation of clients.

Clark D. Cunningham
What Clients Want From Their Lawyers
(August 2006)[2]

I went to [this solicitor] because of her reputation and expertise—she is a part-time registrar and has a big reputation as a specialist in this area—but she just doesn't listen. She listens for part of what I have to say, and then interrupts, saying something like: "OK, I've got the picture, what we'll do is . . ." and she hasn't really got the picture, she's only got half the picture. I think it's partly because she's so busy and also because she's simply not used to giving clients a voice. . . . [W]hat's more she has actually made me frightened of expressing my views. I am about to change to another solicitor.

In 1997–98 the Law Society of England and Wales commissioned a study of solicitors and clients regarding their perspectives on quality service. As part of this research project Hilary Sommerlad, a senior lecturer in law at Leeds Metropolitan University, interviewed 44 clients of 21 different solicitors in the north of England. 50% said that they had previously used a solicitor whom they did not like. Some, like the client quoted above, were also dissatisfied with their current solicitor.

It has become increasingly common to read in bar journals reports that "communication problems" are an important source of client dissatisfaction, but the examples given tend to assume that "bad

---

2 Footnotes and/or internal citations omitted.

communication" is just a matter of careless or sloppy practice: not putting initial instructions in writing, unreturned phone calls, not keeping clients up to date on their cases, and lack of clarity about fees. In contrast, the communication problems identified in the opening quote above do not arise from carelessness (although the lawyer is described as "busy") but instead seem to be related to a fundamental way the lawyer interacts with clients. This specialist with a "big reputation" interrupts the client precisely because she assumes from her expertise that she has heard enough to "get the picture" and decide what needs to be done. This behavior prevents the solicitor from learning what the client considers important information—not only because she cuts off the client at an important moment in the interview but because her attitude makes the client "frightened" of expressing her views throughout the representation.

Other clients in the Law Society Study also emphasized that a solicitor needs to be a good listener in order to learn necessary information:

> "One client explained that she had sacked her former solicitor because she wouldn't listen: 'that is absolutely fundamental; this was our case, only we knew the full circumstances.' "
>
> "They must be able to give you time. If solicitors haven't got enough time, they can't get enough out of you. You have to have time to be able to tell your story."
>
> "It's very important to be able to have trust and friendship with your solicitor because then you can talk about your case and you remember things."
>
> "Regular communication is key . . . the quality of being able to talk things through is very important. No one knows their problem as well as the plaintiff. . . . It's crucial that they enable you to talk it through. That listening and communication is crucial. So they have to be prepared to give you time, so that you can establish a personal relationship with them."

The clients wanted not only to be heard but also to understand what the solicitor said to them:

> "If they communicate clearly you feel on the same wavelength with each other. It has got to be a mutual rather than a one-way relationship."
>
> "At my first meeting with [my current solicitor] . . . I was impressed by his natural ability to talk about technical things with knowledge, but on a level that I could understand . . . . we actually talked and he explained in clear language. . . . Other people just had a job to do, but [he] took time to clearly explain technical things. . . . He explained how the system works."

> "She speaks of legal matters in a way that is knowledgeable and she explains it well."
>
> "She communicates clearly. She puts things in layman's terms."

Although the Law Society study focused on individual clients, it also appears that even the sophisticated business and institutional clients of major law firms also value the ability to translate legal issues into terms a lay person can understand. In its current rating of top Scottish law firms, Legal 500 makes a point of reporting the following client comments:

> "He has the knack of being able to present very complex situations comprehensibly to commercial managers"
>
> "[Their entire legal team is able to] provide a clear explanation to the layperson on sometimes complex legal issues"

The Law Society study showed that effective two-way communication—attentive and patient listening and clear explanations—was valued by clients not only because it improved the exchange of information but also was essential to the development of rapport, trust and mutual respect:

> "Just coming here and have someone listen to you, treat you with respect, be on your side . . . that's marvellous."
>
> "She talked to me as a person, with respect."
>
> "I wanted the law to be explained. . . . The way the solicitor views the client is important. He has to be interested in our views."
>
> "I felt I couldn't talk to him. He'd fob you off . . . didn't really sit and explain to you. It was just the lack of communication to me."
>
> "I never liked him [describing a former solicitor] . . . . we couldn't have had a solicitor like him for this; I think he was perfectly competent, but there was no sympathy . . ."
>
> "If you do not have communication you might as well go elsewhere. It was quite hard to get in touch with [my former solicitor] . . . he was a bit 'uppity' . . . But [my current solicitor] is excellent . . . we communicate . . I trust her"
>
> "[I like my current solicitor because] I can have a chat with her, I trust her. . . [she's] much better than other solicitors I've had. . . . The other solicitor—I was just a file for him, but for her I'm a real person and that comes across in court."
>
> "[My current solicitor is] very easy to talk to—some solicitors can be intimidating."

It is not unusual to hear lawyers describe such communication practices as patient listening and translation of legal issues into terms the client can understand as "hand-holding"—something to be done to make the client feel good if you have the time and inclination but not really essential to effective legal representation. For example, one of the solicitors interviewed in the Law Society study said:

> "Clients cannot assess the quality of the service. What they really need and respond to is reassurance. . . . They want to feel you care."

Sommerlad, though, reports that "for many clients, their engagement with the law was not simply about achieving a result; their responses indicated that ***the process itself was important***. . . [From the clients' perspective] the realization of their legal goals depended upon the establishment of an individualized relationship of trust with the practitioner. Thus clients tended to view the subjective aspects of quality, such as empathy and respect, ***not as luxury items but as fundamental to the service so that their absence would limit the solicitor's effectiveness even within the narrowest definition of his responsibilities as a legal adviser.***" Sommerlad's point is illustrated by the following pointed conclusion by one client about a former solicitor:

> "She was efficient but a total waste of space . . . I could not communicate with her."

Many lawyers equate client satisfaction with the outcome achieved, an assumption that might cause them to puzzle over a client's conclusion that a lawyer was "efficient" but nonetheless "a total waste of space." However, social science research over the past two decades has produced impressive evidence that clients evaluate their lawyers' competence more in terms of the process experienced by them in the representation than the outcome. Indeed the leading researcher in this area has made the following bold statement:

> "Clients care most about the process—having their problems or disputes settled in a way that they view as fair, second most important is achieving a fair settlement, least important factor is the number of assets they end up winning."

Tyler's research findings are consistent with two important studies conducted in Australia. Australia's largest indemnity insurer for lawyers, LawCover, commissioned a Risk Management Project to study a representative sample from over two thousand professional liability claims. The researchers interviewed each lawyer in the sample against whom a claim had been filed; these interviews were extensive and confidential. The researchers in most cases also interviewed the lawyer retained by LawCover to defend the claim.

The results of this unusually in-depth study were "clearly disturbing," showing how easy it was for the average lawyer—even the lawyer other lawyers would choose and trust—to become entangled in the events that often lead inexorably to a claim. The lawyers did not seem to understand the dynamics of the claims. The researchers concluded that most lawyers need help to see the patterns and to understand how they should act differently in future to reduce their inherent exposure. By far the most significant cause of professional negligence claims was *not* dissatisfaction with outcome but instead related to the handling of the client relationship; the most frequent problems were failure to listen to the client, ask appropriate questions and explain relevant aspects of the matter.

A different empirical study in Australia, an evaluation of specialist accreditation that included client focus groups and surveys, found that practitioners and their clients were selecting divergent indicators of performance with which to assess satisfaction with service. Although there was widespread client satisfaction with the specialists' legal knowledge and skills, the evaluators also found "consistent evidence of client dissatisfaction with the provision of services, and the quality of the service-delivery process." According to this study:

> Practitioners are concentrating on developing their knowledge and skills to deliver better outcomes; but their clients, expecting both technical competence and results, are being disappointed by the process of getting there. Clients complained about the quality of their lawyers' services in terms of inaccessibility, lack of communication, lack of empathy and understanding, and lack of respect. . . .
>
> The evaluators concluded that
>
> consideration should be given by the profession to introducing additional training to redress identified performance deficits in the related areas of *inter-personal skills* and *client management techniques*. This training should be client focused, rather than transaction focused; it should train practitioners to recognise that client needs are not confined to attaining objective outcomes; and it should help lawyers to listen to clients more attentively, diagnose their various levels of needs and demonstrate empathy.

Lisa Sanders
The Facts and What Lies Beyond
EVERY PATIENT TELLS A STORY: MEDICAL MYSTERIES AND THE ART OF DIAGNOSIS (2009)[3]

The young woman was hunched over a large pink basin when Dr. Amy Hsia, a resident in her first year of training, entered the patient's cubicle in the Emergency Department. The girl looked up at the doctor. Tears streamed down her face. "I don't know if I can take this any longer," twenty-two-year-old Maria Rogers sobbed. Since arriving at the emergency room early that morning, she'd already been given two medicines to stop the vomiting that had brought her there—medicines that clearly had not worked.

"I feel like I've spent most of the last nine months in a hospital or a doctor's office," Maria told the doctor quietly. And now, here she was again, back in the hospital. She'd been perfectly healthy until just after last Christmas. She'd come home from college to see her family and hang out with her friends, and as she prepared to head back to school this strange queasiness had come over her. She couldn't eat. Any odor—especially food—made her feel as if she might vomit. But she didn't. Not at first.

The next day, on the drive back up to school, she'd suddenly broken into a cold sweat and had to pull over to vomit. And once she got started, it seemed like she would never stop. "I don't know how I made it to school because it seems like I had to get out of the car to throw up every few minutes."

Back at school she spent the first few days of the semester in bed. Once she was back in class her friends joked that she was just trying to get rid of the extra pounds from the holidays. But she felt fine and she wasn't going to worry about it.

Until it happened again. And again. And again.

The attacks were always the same. She'd get that queasy feeling for a few hours, and then the vomiting would start and wouldn't let up for days. There was never any fever or diarrhea; no cramps or even any real pain. She tried everything she could find in the drugstore: Tums, Pepcid, Pepto-Bismol, Prilosec, Maalox. Nothing helped. Knowing that another attack could start at any moment, without warning, gnawed insistently in the back of her mind.

She went to the infirmary with each attack. The doctor there would get a pregnancy test and when it was negative, as it always was, he'd give her some intravenous fluids, a few doses of Compazine (a medicine to

---

3 Footnotes and/or internal citations omitted.

control nausea), and, after a day or two, send her back to the dorm. Halfway through the semester she withdrew from school and came home.

Maria went to see her regular doctor. He was stumped. So he sent her to a gastroenterologist, who ordered an upper endoscopy, a colonoscopy, a barium swallow, a CT scan of her abdomen, and another of her brain. She'd had her blood tested for liver disease, kidney disease, and a handful of strange inherited diseases she'd never heard of. Nothing was abnormal.

Another specialist thought these might be abdominal migraines. Migraine headaches are caused by abnormal blood flow to the brain. Less commonly, the same kind of abnormal blood flow to the gut can cause nausea and vomiting—a gastrointestinal equivalent of a migraine headache. That doctor gave Maria a medicine to prevent these abdominal "headaches" and another one to take if an attack came anyway. When those didn't help, he tried another regimen. When that one failed, she didn't go back.

The weird thing was, she told Hsia, the only time she felt even close to normal during these attacks was when she was standing in a hot shower. Couldn't be a cold shower; even a warm shower didn't quite do it. But if she could stand under a stream of water that was as hot as she could tolerate, the vomiting would stop and the nausea would slowly recede. A couple of times she had come to the hospital only because she'd run out of hot water at home.

Recently, a friend suggested that maybe this was a food allergy, so she gave up just about everything but ginger ale and saltines. And that seemed to work—for a while. But two days ago she'd woken up with that same bilious feeling. She'd been vomiting nonstop since yesterday.

Maria Rogers was a small woman, a little overweight with a mass of long brown hair now pinned back in a barrette. Her olive skin was clear though pale. Her eyes were puffy from crying and fatigue. She looked sick, and was clearly distressed, Hsia thought, but not chronically ill.

How often did she get these bouts of nausea? she asked the girl. Maybe once a month, she told her. Are they linked to your periods? Hsia offered hopefully. The girl grimaced and shook her head. Are they more common just after you eat? Or when you're hungry? Or tired? Or stressed? No, no, no, and no. She had no other medical problems, took no medicines. She was a social smoker—a pack of cigarettes might last a week, sometimes more. She drank—mostly beer, mostly on the weekends when she went out with her friends.

Her mother had been an alcoholic and died several years earlier. After leaving college she had been living with her father and sister but a few months ago moved into a nearby apartment with some friends. She had no pets, had not traveled within the past year. Had never been exposed to any toxins as far as she knew. Hsia examined her quickly. The gurgling noises of the abdominal exam were quieter than normal and her belly was mildly tender, but both findings could simply be due to the vomiting. There was no sign of an inflamed gallbladder. No evidence of an enlarged liver or spleen. The rest of the exam was completely unremarkable. "As I walked out that door," Hsia explained to me, "I knew I was missing something but I had no idea what it was. Or even what to look for."

More Than Just the Facts

Dr. Hsia was a resident in Yale's Primary Care Internal Medicine residency training program, where I now teach. She told me about Maria Rogers because she knew I collected interesting cases and sometimes wrote about them in my column in the *New York Times Magazine*. In thinking about this case, Amy told me she knew from the start that if she was going to figure out what was causing this patient to suffer so, it wasn't going to be because she had greater knowledge—because Maria Rogers had already seen lots of experts. No, if she was going to figure it out, it would be because she'd find a clue that others had overlooked.

The patient's story is often the best place to find that clue. It is our oldest diagnostic tool. And, as it turns out, it is one of the most reliable as well. Indeed, the great majority of medical diagnoses—anywhere from 70 to 90 percent—are made on the basis of the patient's story alone.

Although this is well established, far too often neither the doctor nor the patient seems to appreciate the importance of what the patient has to say in the making of a diagnosis. And yet this is crucial information. None of our high-tech tests has such a high batting average. Neither does the physical exam. Nor is there any other way to obtain this information. Talking to the patient more often than not provides the essential clues to making a diagnosis. Moreover, what we learn from this simple interview frequently plays an important role in the patient's health even after the diagnosis is made.

When you go to see a doctor, any doctor, there is a very good chance that she will ask you what brought you in that day. And most patients are prepared to answer that—they have a story to tell, one that they have already told to friends and family. But the odds are overwhelming that the patient won't have much of an opportunity to tell that story.

Doctors often see this first step in the diagnostic process as an interrogation—with Dr. Joe Friday getting "Just the facts, ma'am," and the patient, a passive bystander to the ongoing crime, providing a faltering and somewhat limited eyewitness account of what happened. From this perspective, the patient's story is important only as a vehicle for the facts of the case.

Because of that "facts only" attitude, doctors frequently interrupt patients before they get to tell their full story. In recordings of doctor-patient encounters, where both doctor and patient knew they were being taped, the doctor interrupted the patient in his initial description of his symptoms over 75 percent of the time. And it didn't take too long either. In one study doctors listened for an average of sixteen seconds before breaking in—some interrupting the patient after only three seconds:

And once the story was interrupted, patients were unlikely to resume it. In these recorded encounters fewer than 2 percent of the patients completed their story once the doctor broke in.

As a result, doctors and patients often have a very different understanding of the visit and the illness. Survey after survey has shown that when queried after an office visit, the doctor and patient often did not even agree on the purpose of the visit or the patient's problem. In one study, over half of the patients interviewed after seeing their doctor had symptoms that they were concerned about but did not have a chance to describe. In other studies doctor and patient disagreed about the chief complaint—the reason the patient came to see the doctor—between 25 to 50 percent of the time. This is information that can come only from the patient and yet, time after time, doctors fail to obtain it. Dr. George Balint, one of the earliest writers on this topic, cautioned: "If you ask questions you will get answers, and nothing else." "What you won't get is the patient's story, and that story will often provide not only the whats, wheres, and whens extracted by an interrogation, but often the whys and hows as well.

Moreover, the interrogation model makes assumptions about the elicited symptoms and diseases. And while these assumptions might be true for most of the people with those symptoms, they may not be true for this particular individual. The great fictional detective Sherlock Holmes talks at length about the difference between the actions and thoughts of the individual when contrasted to the average. Holmes tells Watson that while you may be able to say with precision what the average man will do, "you can never foretell what any one man will do." The differences between the average and the individual may not be revealed if the doctor doesn't ask.

"It is much more important to know what kind of patient has the disease than what sort of disease the person has," Osier instructed his trainees at the turn of the twentieth century. Even with all of our diagnostic technology and our far better understanding of the pathophysiology of disease, research suggests this remains true.

So getting a good history is a collaborative process. One doctor who writes frequently about these issues uses the metaphor of two writers collaborating on a manuscript, passing drafts of the story back and forth until both are satisfied. "What the patient brings to the process is unique: the particular and private facts of his life and illness." And what the physician brings is the knowledge and understanding that will help him order that story so that it makes sense both to the doctor—who uses it to make a diagnosis—and to the patient—who must then incorporate that subplot into the larger story of his life.

If getting a good history is so important to making an accurate diagnosis, why are we so bad at it? There are several reasons.

First, most researchers, doctors, and patients would agree that time pressures play an important role. A visit to a doctor's office lasts an average of twenty-two minutes. Although there is a sense that doctors are spending less time with their patients, that number has actually increased over the past twenty years. In 1989, the average doctor's appointment lasted only sixteen minutes. Despite this extra time, both doctors and patients frequently agree that their time together is still too short.

In response, doctors often depend on a few highly focused questions to extract the information they think will help them make a diagnosis quickly. Yet it is clear that this effort to reduce the time it takes to get a good history increases the risk of miscommunication and missed information. Like so many shortcuts, this information shortcut often ends up taking more time than those interviews in which patients are able to tell their stories in their own ways.

Studies suggest that getting a good history allows doctors to order fewer tests and make fewer referrals—without taking any more time. Indeed, some studies suggest that obtaining a good history can even reduce visit time. In addition, patient satisfaction is higher, adherence to therapy is higher, symptom resolution is faster, lawsuits are less frequent.

Lack of training may also contribute to the problem. Doctors spend two years in classrooms learning how to identify and categorize disease processes, matching symptoms to known disease entities, but until recently very few programs offered any training on how to obtain that essential information. The assumption seemed to be that this did not need to be taught. And there may have been an unspoken expectation that our improved diagnostic technology would reduce our dependence on this kind of personal information. Studies have shown that neither assumption is true, and now most medical schools offer classes in doctor-patient communication. Moreover, since 2004, medical students are required to demonstrate proficiency in their history-taking skills in order to become licensed physicians. A new generation of physicians may not use these tools, but at least they have them.

Finally, many doctors are uncomfortable with the emotions that are sometimes associated with illness. When patients present their stories, they often look for cues from the doctor as to what type of information they should give. The interrogation format tells the patient that what's needed from them are the facts and only the facts. And yet illness is often much more than a series of symptoms. The experience of being sick is frequently interlaced with feelings and meanings that shape and color a patient's experience and perception of a disease in ways that are unimaginable, and unanticipated, by the doctor. A family history of heart disease or cancer may lead a patient to minimize a symptom. I recently got a phone call from a friend, a man in his late fifties whose father had heart disease. My friend was having chest pains when he walked up a hill. He wondered if this was his childhood asthma returning. He was shocked when I suggested he see a cardiologist. He had two blocked arteries, which were opened with complete resolution of his pain. The same history might cause another to focus on a symptom well beyond its actual severity. I have a few patients who have had many stress tests because of their concerns over their chest pain. The fact that previous tests have not shown heart disease provides them with no comfort or reassurance. Financial concerns may likewise affect how patients tell their stories.

Worries about the social meaning of symptoms can complicate even a straightforward diagnosis. I learned this the hard way. A patient I saw when I was a resident came for a school physical. She was young and healthy. As I was finishing up and preparing to move on to the next patient, she suddenly asked me about a lesion on her buttocks. Could it be from doing sit-ups on the hard floor? she asked somewhat anxiously. I quickly looked at the lesion. It looked like a small blister, located in the cleft between the buttocks. Certainly, I reassured her, glancing at my watch. I noticed that she seemed worried about the lesion, but I didn't ask any further questions or do a more thorough exam because I was running behind schedule. Only when the lesion reappeared months later did she acknowledge that her boyfriend had had a breakout of genital herpes on a vacation they'd taken together and she hadn't insisted on his use of a condom. The reappearance of the lesions made herpes the likely culprit. I completely missed a straightforward diagnosis because I was too rushed to address her anxiety and she was too embarrassed to offer this other history. It happens all the time.

Everybody Lies

Several years ago I got a call from a producer named Paul Attanasio. He had created a television show based in part on my column in the *New York Times Magazine* and wanted to know if I would be interested in being a consultant for this new show. It was a drama, he told me, about an ornery doctor who was a brilliant diagnostician. I agreed to work on the show, thinking that it wasn't going to last long. The show, called *House M.D.,* quickly found an enthusiastic audience.

In this show, Dr. Gregory House doesn't value patient history. Indeed, he frequently tells his trainees that they should not believe a patient's version of his illness and symptoms, because "Everybody lies." In the context of the show, there is a certain truth in that. Patients frequently lie to House and sometimes his staff—not because the patients are intrinsically deceitful but because of who House is. As portrayed (brilliantly by Hugh Laurie), House is far from the kindly and gentle doctor whose presence invites trust and confidences. Instead, he is narcissistic and arrogant, a drug addict, and something of a pedant. He is a darker, more bitter version of Conan Doyle's brooding detective Sherlock Holmes. House's demeanor tells patients that the feelings and meanings illness may have for them are not important and so they don't tell him about them. As a result, House often gets only part of their story.

The mystery is solved only when the rest of their story is revealed—either from evidence found when his staff break into the patient's home (a quirky twist on getting a thorough history) or when the patient is finally forced to reveal his hidden truths. House acknowledges the importance of a thorough patient history but concludes that the problem is the patient who lies rather than the doctor who fails to establish a relationship in which difficult, embarrassing, or distressing truths can be told.

Amy Hsia knew from the start that if she was going to figure out the cause of Maria Rogers's cyclic episodes of vomiting, it would be because of some key piece of history that she was able to get that others had overlooked. But sitting outside the patient's room that afternoon, she wasn't sure she'd found it. She went through the thick charts, reading the notes and test results collected by all of the other doctors involved in the same exercise in previous hospitalizations, trying to make it all make sense. Nothing leaped out at her. The sketchy description of the symptoms and history provided nothing she hadn't already found out from the patient herself.

Hsia considered the differential diagnosis once more. Nausea and vomiting have a very long list of causes: ulcers, gallstones, obstruction, infection, Hepatitis, pancreatitis, colitis, strokes, and heart attacks. None of them seemed to fit in a case of a young woman with multiple episodes of vomiting and lots and lots of tests showing no abnormalities. Maybe she wasn't going to be able to figure this patient out either. She ordered a new medication to relieve the nausea and then moved on to see her next patient.

The next morning, when Dr. Hsia, her supervising resident, and the attending physician—the troika of the modern hospital medical patient care team—visited Ms. Rogers, the girl's bed was empty. The sound of the shower told them where she'd gone. That caught the young resident's attention. When she had come by a couple of hours earlier to examine the girl, she'd been in the shower then too. She remembered that Rogers had told her that her nausea improved when she took a shower. What kind of nausea didn't get better with the traditional nausea medications—by now she'd been on most of them—but improved with a hot shower?

Hsia posed the question to the team. Neither had heard of such a syndrome. So, after the team had finished seeing all the patients they were caring for, Hsia hurried to find a computer. She went to Google and entered "persistent nausea improved by hot showers." She hit the enter key and less than a second later the screen was filled with references to a disease Hsia had never heard of: cannabinoid hyperemesis—persistent and excessive vomiting (hyperemesis) associated with chronic marijuana use (cannabinoid).

The disorder was first described in 1996, in a case report from an Australian medical journal. Dr. J. H. Allen, a psychiatrist in Australia, described a patient admitted to his care with a diagnosis of psychogenic vomiting—vomiting due to psychological rather than physiological causes. Allen noticed that this patient's vomiting was associated with a bizarre behavior—repetitive showering. He took a dozen showers each day. Allen also noticed that the symptoms improved over the course of his hospitalization but recurred when the patient was sent home. The patient had a long history of chronic heavy marijuana use and Allen hypothesized that the vomiting might be triggered by the marijuana.

Over the next several years Allen noted similar patterns in other patients admitted with vomiting disorders, and in 2001 he published a paper reporting on ten patients with the disorder he named cannabinoid hyperemesis. Each patient in his series smoked marijuana daily; each had developed intermittent nausea and vomiting. All had used marijuana for years before they developed these episodic bouts of nausea and vomiting. And remarkably, nine of the ten patients reported that hot showers helped their symptoms when everything else failed. All symptoms resolved when these patients gave up marijuana. And then reappeared in three of the ten who resumed their cannabis use. Other case reports followed from around the world.

Could this be what was plaguing Hsia's patient? Did Maria Rogers even smoke marijuana? Hsia hurried back to the patient's room. She found the patient sitting in bed, a towel wrapped around her still wet hair. Yes, she did smoke marijuana frequently. Maybe not every day but most days. That clinched it—at least in Hsia's mind. The young doctor felt like cheering. She'd figured it out when even the experts had been stumped! This is really one of the great pleasures in medicine—to put the patient's story together in a way that reveals the diagnosis.

She excitedly explained to the patient what she'd found on the Internet—that there was a good chance that marijuana was causing her nausea. She got better in the hospital because she didn't use it when she was here. But when she got home and resumed her regular exposure to the drug, the nausea would once again be triggered. All she had to do was to give up smoking marijuana, Hsia concluded triumphantly, and her symptoms would be cured forever.

This story, which seemed so logical and reasonable from Hsia's perspective, did not make the same kind of sense to the woman who was living it every day. Rogers's response was immediate and emphatic and—to Hsia—shocking. "That is total bullshit. I don't buy it," the patient snapped angrily. She knew many people who used marijuana a lot more than she did and they didn't get sick like this. How could Hsia explain that? Huh? Besides, wasn't marijuana supposed to help people who were sick from chemotherapy? Why would it decrease nausea in that case and cause nausea in her? she demanded. Where was her proof? Where was her evidence?

Hsia was taken aback by the patient's anger. She thought the young woman would be thrilled by the news that simply stopping the marijuana use would cure her of this devastating illness. Why was she so angry?

Later that morning, Hsia told the attending and resident what she'd found and how angry the patient had become when she told her about this diagnosis. It made sense to the other doctors caring for the patient. The marijuana use, the cyclic nature of the symptoms, and the restorative powers of the hot shower made it seem like a slam dunk. But how were they going to convince the patient?

They never got the chance. Maria Rogers left the hospital the following day. When contacted several weeks later, Rogers reported that the nausea had recurred. Yes, she had resumed her usual practice of smoking marijuana most days because she still didn't believe there was a link. She had arranged for an evaluation by a gastroenterologist at Yale. When I spoke with Ms. Rogers afterward, she told me that the doctors there had ordered many of the same tests her previous doctors had gotten. Not surprisingly, the results were no different. From Maria's perspective, what she had was still a mystery.

In medicine, the patient tells the story of his illness to the doctor, who reshapes the elements of that story into a medical form, into the language of medicine. The doctor will usually add to the story, incorporating bits of information gleaned through questions, from the examination of the body, from the tests that have been performed—and the result should be a story that makes sense—where all pieces ultimately add up to a single, unifying diagnosis.

But the story of the illness can't stop there. Once the diagnosis is made, the doctor has to once again reshape the story she has created—the story that helped her make the diagnosis—into a story she can then give back to the patient. She has to translate the story back into the language and the context of the patient's life so that he can understand what has happened to him and then incorporate it into the larger story of his life. Only when a patient understands the disease, its causes, its treatment, its meaning, can he be expected to do what is needed to get well.

Studies have repeatedly shown that the greater the patient's understanding of his illness and treatment, the more likely it is that he will be able to carry out his part in the treatment. Much of this research has been done in patients who have been diagnosed with diabetes. Patients who understand their illness are far more likely to follow a doctor's advice about how to change their diet and how to take their medications than those who do not.

It's understandable. Taking medications on a regular basis isn't easy. It requires dedication on the part of the patient. Motivation. A desire to incorporate this inconvenient addition into a life that is already complicated. Greater understanding by the patient has been shown to dramatically improve adherence. This is where getting a good history—one that provides you with some insight into the patient and his feelings about his illness, his life, his treatment—can really pay off.

To go back to the story of Maria Rogers, Hsia told me how surprised she was when the patient didn't accept her explanation of her illness. That marijuana was linked to the nausea and vomiting seemed obvious to Dr. Hsia. It was not obvious to Ms. Rogers. Perhaps there was no way for Hsia to explain this to her that would have been acceptable. The story Hsia told to this patient was the doctor's story—the observations and research that allowed Hsia to make the diagnosis. What she didn't do was create the patient's version of the story—one that would make sense in the larger context of her life.

And then the patient left the hospital and with her their chance to figure out how to help her understand her illness. Dr. Hsia tried to stay in touch with Maria after she left the hospital, but after several months the cell phone number she gave was disconnected and a letter was returned. And so, having rejected one diagnosis and the treatment option it suggested, Maria Rogers still suffers from a malady for which she has no name and no cure.

Stories That Heal

One of the most important and powerful tools a doctor has lies in her ability to give a patient's story back to the patient, in a form that will allow him to understand what his illness is and what it means. Done successfully, this gift helps the patient incorporate that knowledge into the larger story of his life. Through understanding, the patient can regain some control over his affliction. If he cannot control the disease, he can at least have some control over his response to the disease. A story that can help a patient make sense of even a devastating illness is a story that can heal.

The primary work of a doctor is to treat pain and relieve suffering. We often speak of these two entities as if they were the same thing. Eric Cassell, a physician who writes frequently about the moral dimensions of medicine, argues, in a now classic paper, that pain and suffering are very different. Pain, according to Cassell, is an affliction of the body. Suffering is an affliction of the self. Suffering, writes Cassell, is a specific state of distress that occurs when the intactness or integrity of the person is threatened or disrupted. Thus, there are events in a life that can cause tremendous pain, and yet cause no suffering. Childbirth is perhaps the most obvious. Women often experience pain in labor but are rarely said to be suffering.

And those who are suffering may have no pain at all. A diagnosis of terminal cancer, even in the absence of pain, may cause terrible suffering. The fears of death and uncontrollable loss of autonomy and self combined with the fear of a pain that is overwhelming can cause suffering well before the symptoms begin. There are no drugs to treat suffering. But, says Cassell, giving meaning to an illness through the creation of a story is one way in which physicians can relieve suffering.

In the case of Maria Rogers, Dr. Hsia was able to gather the data necessary to make a diagnosis. She knew the disease the patient had. And yet she didn't know enough about the person who had the disease. The story she gave back to the patient was a reasonable one and a rational one, but it was not one the patient could accept. And when confronted with the vehement rejection of that story and the raw emotion displayed, Hsia retreated. Before she was able to regroup and try again, the patient left her care. Rogers rejected Hsia's story, rejected her diagnosis, and, when last I spoke with her, continued to search on her own for an end to her pain and suffering.

And yet the right story has nearly miraculous powers of healing. A couple of years ago I got an e-mail from a patient whose remarkable recovery highlighted the difference between pain and suffering and the healing power of the story. Randy Whittier is a twenty-seven-year-old computer programmer who was in perfect health and planning to get married when suddenly he began to forget everything. It started one weekend when he and his fiancée traveled to her hometown to begin making the final arrangements for their wedding the following spring. He had difficulty concentrating and was frequently confused about where they were going and whom they were talking with. He chalked it up to fatigue—he hadn't been sleeping well for some time—and didn't say anything to his fiancée. But on Monday morning, when he went back to work, he realized he was in trouble and sent an instant message to his fiancée, Leslie.

Leslie saw the flashing icon on her computer announcing that an instant message had arrived. She clicked on it eagerly.

"Something's wrong," the message read.

"What do you mean?" she shot back.

"My memory is all f'ed up. I can't remember anything," he wrote. Then added: "Like I can't tell you what we did this weekend."

Leslie's heart began to race. Her fiancé had seemed distracted lately. She thought maybe he was just tired. But he'd been strangely quiet on their trip to New York this weekend. He had been excited when they set up the trip, and she'd worried that he was getting cold feet.

"When is our wedding date?" she quizzed him. If he could remember anything, he'd be able to remember that. Planning this wedding had dominated their life for the past several months. "Can you tell me that?"

"No."

"Call the doctor. Do it now. Tell them this is an emergency."

Over the next half hour, Randy put in three calls to his doctor's office, but each time he had forgotten what they told him by the time he messaged his fiancée. Separated by miles of interstate and several suburbs, Leslie was frantic. Finally, at her insistence, Randy, now terrified, asked a friend to take him to the closest hospital.

A few hours later, her cell phone rang. At last. He was being discharged, he told her. The emergency room doctor thought his memory problems were caused by Ambien, the sleeping pill he was taking. The doctor said the symptoms would probably improve if he stopped taking the medication.

Leslie didn't buy that for a second. "Don't go anywhere," she instructed him. "I'll pick you up. I'm going to take you to your doctor." A half hour later she found Randy wandering down the street in front of the hospital, uncertain about why he was there and even what her name was. She hustled him into the car and drove to his doctor's office. From there they were sent to Brigham and Women's Hospital in Boston.

Late that night, the on-call resident phoned Dr. William Abend at home to discuss the newest admission. Abend, a sixty-one-year-old neurologist, scrolled through the patient's electronic medical record as the resident described the case. The patient, who had no history of any previous illnesses, had come in complaining of insomnia and severe memory loss. Psych had seen him—he wasn't crazy. His physical exam was normal except he didn't know the date and he couldn't recall the events of the week or even that day. The ER had ordered an MRI of his brain but it hadn't been done yet.

The patient needed a spinal tap, Abend instructed, to make sure this wasn't an infection, and an EEG, an electroencephalogram, to see if he was having seizures. Both could affect memory. He'd see the patient first thing the next morning.

Randy was alert and anxious when Abend came to see him. Tall and slender with earnest blue eyes, the young patient seemed embarrassed by all that he couldn't remember. His fiancée, had gone to get some rest, and so his mother provided the missing details. He'd first complained about some memory problems a couple of months earlier. The past weekend everything got much, much worse. He couldn't remember anything from the past few days. He couldn't even remember he was in the hospital. Overnight, he repeatedly pulled out his IV.

On exam, Abend found nothing out of the ordinary save the remarkable degree of short-term memory loss. When Abend asked the patient to remember three words—automobile, tank, and jealous—the patient could repeat them but thirty seconds later he could not recall even one. "It wasn't like—where did I put my car keys?" Abend told me. "He really couldn't remember anything." The neurologist knew he had to determine what was going on quickly, before further damage was done.

Abend checked the results of the spinal tap—there were no signs of infection. Then he headed over to radiology to review the MRI. There was no evidence of a tumor, stroke, or bleeding. What the MRI revealed were areas that appeared bright white in the normally uniform gray of the temporal lobe on both sides of the brain.

There are only a few diseases that would cause this kind of injury. Viral encephalitis—an infection of the brain that is often caused by herpes simplex—was certainly the most common. Autoimmune diseases like lupus could also cause these kinds of abnormalities. In lupus, the body's natural defenses mistakenly attack its own cells as if they were foreign invaders. Finally, certain cancers can do this too—it's usually lung cancer, usually in older smokers.

The young man's symptoms had been coming on gradually over two months. Abend thought that made an infection like herpes less likely. The patient had already been started on acyclovir—the drug usually used to treat herpes encephalitis—since the disease can be deadly when it infects the brain. Although Abend thought it unlikely, they would need to do additional tests of the spinal fluid to make sure there was no evidence of this dangerous viral infection.

Lupus seemed even more unlikely to Abend. It is a chronic disease that can attack virtually any organ in the body and is generally characterized by joint pains and rashes. The patient had none of these symptoms. Still, perhaps this was the first sign of this complex disease. It would be unusual, but so was the young man's extensive memory loss.

Although cancer was an uncommon cause of this kind of injury, it seemed to Abend the most credible in this patient. Even nonsmokers can get lung cancer. And other cancers can cause the same type of brain injury. Moreover, if these symptoms were caused by a cancer, there was a good chance that they would resolve once the cancer was treated. He ordered a CT of the chest, abdomen, and pelvis. Ordering all of these scans communicates uncertainty about what you are looking for and where it might be located, but Abend felt strongly that they didn't have time to be wrong.

Results from the tests trickled in over the next few days. He wasn't having seizures. It wasn't a virus. He didn't have lupus. But by the time those test results arrived they already had an answer. The CT of Randy's chest had shown a large mass—not in his lungs, but in the space between them, the area called the mediastinum. A biopsy revealed the final diagnosis—Hodgkin's lymphoma, a cancer that attacks the immune system. He had what is called a paraneoplastic syndrome, a rare complication in which antibodies to his cancer attacked the healthy cells in his brain.

Randy had surgery to reduce the size of the mass and then started chemotherapy. And slowly, remarkably, his memory began to improve. But the trip to New York remains vague, and his only memory of his weeklong hospital stay is his nurse telling him he was going home.

His fiancée remembers the day she realized he was getting better. It was several weeks after leaving the hospital. She reminded him that he wanted to get a haircut. He told her that he tried to go the day before but the line at the barbershop was too long.

She almost cried. "At that moment," she told me, "I finally knew that the man I loved was still in there and that he was coming back."

When I called Randy after receiving his e-mail, he still couldn't remember much of his ordeal, but he understood the illness and the prognosis. One doctor stood out from the crowd of physicians caring for him. Marc Wein was a medical student at Brigham, and he had become fascinated by Randy and his illness. He read voraciously about the disease, tracked down case reports of other patients with a similar manifestation of cancer, and came back again and again to explain it all to Randy and Leslie. Together Marc and Randy created the story of this remarkable diagnosis that made sense to both of them. And that made all the difference.

Randy tells me he was never in pain but he hated the way he became a clean slate every five minutes. He hated the worried looks he saw on the faces of those he loved. He hated the loss of a sense of who he even was.

He embraced the story that Wein put together for him. Leslie had to remind him frequently of the particulars of that story, but he remembered that he had a cancer and that curing that cancer would restore him to himself. He welcomed the surgery and never minded the pain from the incision down his chest. He even looked forward to chemotherapy. Watching the intravenous needle pierce his skin, he remembered it meant he was one step closer to getting better. I spoke with Randy several times as he faced his ordeal. His optimism never flagged. He is now disease free and his life has moved on. He returned to work five months after that strange weekend and got married the next year.

Randy's body may have been cured by the chemotherapy, but his mind was healed by a story.

Victoria Healey-Etten and Shane Sharp
Teaching Undergraduates How to Do an In-Depth Interview: A Teaching Note with 12 Handy Tips
38 TEACHING SOCIOLOGY 157 (April 2010)[4]

1. *Probe, Probe, Probe in a Nonalien Way:* The MOST IMPORTANT question for your interviews is probably not on your question sheet. Rather, the most important question is the probe, which is a question you ask in order to learn more about what an interviewee just told you. Probing more in depth makes the interviewee think more about his or her thoughts, feelings, and behaviors, and thus allows you to learn just what is behind these things. Sometimes you can anticipate what issues will need further probing. If so, then it is helpful to write down probing questions underneath your main questions to remind you to probe further. Some specific interview probes you might use include: "Can you describe what the place looked like?"; "How did that make you feel at the time?"; "Can you give me an example of that?"; and "What did you mean when you said_______?"

2. *Avoid $100 Words:* Don't ask questions like "What is your gender ideology?" or "Tell me about your role overload." Rather, phrase questions in a way that a generally educated respondent would understand. For instance, instead of asking "What is your gender ideology?," ask "What do you think the proper role for a woman [man]

---

[4] Footnotes and/or internal citations omitted.

is?" or "Who do you think should be responsible for housework?" The answers to these questions will let you know a person's gender ideology.

3. *Turn a Clark Kent Question into a Superman Question:* Many closed-ended questions can be turned into an open-ended question by beginning the question with a "why" or "how" instead of "what," or by following up the answer to a close-ended question with "Why?," "Why not?," "Why do you feel that way?," "How does that make you feel?," and other pithy phrases. For example, a question like "What chores do you do on a regular basis?" is rather closed-ended. However, adding the follow-up "Why do you do these chores in particular?" or "How did you and your spouse decide who does what chore?" opens up the question for further elaboration by the interviewee. In general, try to use "how" more than "why," since "why" questions sometimes cause interviewees to feel that you are judging them. When you feel that asking a "why" question is appropriate, make sure to ask this question in as nonjudgmental way as possible (see 5 and 11).

4. *Probe, Probe, Probe:* Did I mention this? Good. Don't forget it.

5. *Do a Homer Simpson:* Sometimes you will ask questions that seem very commonsensical to your interviewees. One tactic for handling this problem is just to "play dumb." Tell them that you really don't know what they are talking about. This will make your interviewees further explain things, which will provide you with much better data. Another way you can do this is blame it on the assignment and say that even though you know what they will say, the assignment and your mean old professor and teaching assistant requires them to say it. Playing stupid is also a good way for you to not seem judgmental when asking a "why" question, since you can say that you want to know "why" because you sincerely don't understand and not because you think they're wrong for feeling, thinking, or behaving in a certain way.

6. *Battle the "You Know What I Mean?" Demon:* You may find that your interviewees will end a statement by the phrase "You know what I mean?" or some other variant. Kill this demon every time you see it. Do not allow it to kill you by nodding your head and saying "Yep." Rather, say no, you don't know what they mean, or ask the interviewees to just clarify what they mean for your sake. This demon raises its ugly head especially with questions about thoughts and feelings. This is why this demon is especially evil, because unless you have the magical ability to know what's in a person's head, then you really don't know what they mean.

7. *Order Attention Pay to:* The questions that you ask should flow logically from one to another, or you should have transitions between

sets of questions to let the interviewee know that you are now going in a different direction. Asking questions that do not logically follow one another makes the interview process seem disjointed and artificial, and this can have a huge impact on the interview dynamic. Questions that seem orderly put the interviewee at ease and make the interview seem more conversation-like, and this practice will cause the interviewee to open up to you more. It will also make you seem as if you've got your act together, giving you legitimacy as an interviewer.

8. *Be a Good Ant and Don't Lead, Follow:* Try to avoid leading questions that may make interviewees feel obligated to answer in a particular way. "How did the division of housework make you upset?" is a leading question because it assumes that the person was upset about the issue. However, the question "How did the division of the housework make you feel?" gets at the same thing, but it does not lead the interviewee into a specific emotional direction.

9. *Probe, Probe, Probe:* Just in case it hasn't burrowed its way into your mind forever by now. I'm serious. Do it. You'll be sorry if you don't.

10. *Enjoy the Silence:* Oftentimes there will be "dead air" during the interview. Avoid the temptation to fill it. Give your interviewees time to think about the answers that they want to give. Don't worry. Interviewees are usually quick to tell you if they don't understand a question or if they don't have anything else to say about a topic.

11. *Don't Be a Judge Judy:* You may not agree with some or a lot of what your interviewees say. However, it is really not your job as an interviewer and researcher to morally judge your interviewees. Rather, your goal is to document, understand, and try to explain why they think and feel in certain ways. Therefore, during the interview try not to take a judgmental tone or stance toward what the interviewee says. Also remember that you can express judgment in nonverbal ways, such as how you look at a person when they give an answer or the critical tone you use when asking follow-up questions. Try to keep these nonverbal cues in check during the interview.

12. *Shut up:* Do not put words into people's mouths. Rather, let them say things in their own words, especially with questions that deal with thoughts, opinions, and feelings. Remember, if you say it, it's not data. It is only data when the interviewee says it. If you go back over an interview tape and you notice that you talk as much or more than the interviewee did, then it was probably not a good interview.

POST-CLASS REFLECTION MEMO

Draft and submit a memo in response to the question below:

Name at least one concrete way in which you will take the lessons you have learned in class today and apply them in your client representation, with respect to:

- Obtaining details;
- Avoiding the imposition of unconscious assumptions on gaps in a story;
- Prompting an interviewee's memory;
- Eliciting negative facts;
- Assessing a client's goals; and
- Educating a client about the legal system.

CHAPTER 5

INTERVIEWING TRANSACTIONAL OR PROJECT CLIENTS

LEARNING GOALS

The learning goals for this class include helping you to:

- Identify your goals for the first client meeting
- Identify and help prioritize client goals for the transaction or project
- Engage in the important exercise of planning and reflection
- Learn how to develop the attorney-client relationship
- Learn how to probe for information and manage client expectations

DESCRIPTION OF CLASS

In this class, we will begin the process of planning for your initial interview with your project client. Working with our project teams and in the whole group, we will attempt to gain clarity about our clients' and our own goals for the clinic work. We will also do an exercise in which we will simulate an initial client interview, working in stages to try to anticipate some of the issues that may arise when you meet with and interview your client.

ASSIGNMENT IN PREPARATION FOR CLASS

Before class, review any material that you believe might be useful to gain insight into your client, your client's particular goals for the work in the clinic, your client's larger goals and how your work might fit with the client's larger goals. Share this information and your thoughts about it with fellow team members before class. In class we will be planning an initial interview with your client. This information will help you frame how you will approach that interview.

READING ASSIGNMENT

Paul R. Tremblay, *Counseling Community Groups,* 17 CLIN. L.REV. 389 (2010).

READING

Paul R. Tremblay
Counseling Community Groups
17 CLINICAL L. REV. 389 (2010)

. . .

I. THE BENCHMARK: COUNSELING INDIVIDUAL CLIENTS

This section describes what has emerged as the "default" orientation to counseling clients—a meeting between a lawyer and her individual client to assist with a difficult legal matter regarding that client's personal or business affairs, and about which the client must make an important decision or choice. It is of some interest that the one-on-one individual client interaction serves as the baseline model for this lawyering skill, but that observation is a solid one.[19] That default understanding also tends to address a paradigmatic kind of counseling experience—assisting a client to make a definitive choice among a finite set of alternatives.[20] While a lawyer's counseling responsibilities include other kinds of interactions—including, for example, offering

---

19 The pioneering texts on the legal skills of interviewing and counseling tend to use individual clients as examples for their advice and models, and those examples tend to cover dispute resolution or litigation matters rather than transactional matters. The earliest and most influential book had that quality. *See* Binder & Price, *supra* note 12, at 53–103. While the collective understanding of effective counseling has grown in sophistication since the pathbreaking work of Binder & Price, the prevailing contexts within that literature continue to focus largely on individual clients with individual legal needs. *See, e.g.,* LAWYERS AS COUNSELORS, *supra* note 13; Robert F. Cochran Jr., John M. A. DiPippa, Martha M. Peters, THE COUNSELOR-AT-LAW: A COLLABORATIVE APPROACH TO CLIENT INTERVIEWING AND COUNSELING (2d ed. 2006); Stefan H. Krieger & Richard K. Newmann, Jr., ESSENTIAL LAWYERING SKILLS: INTERVIEWING, COUNSELING, NEGOTIATION, AND PERSUASIVE FACT ANALYSIS (3d ed. 2007).

20 *See, e.g.,* LAWYERS AS COUNSELORS, *supra* note 13, at 282 (describing counseling as comparing identified alternatives); COCHRAN ET AL., *supra* note 19, at 116–17 (same); Krieger & Newmann, *supra* note 19, at 236–54 (same).

straightforward advice about what the law is,[21] or assisting a client to develop some authority for the lawyer to use in negotiations[22]—those tasks receive less attention in the standard texts, and they are less relevant for our purposes.

For purposes of both respect and convenience, I will refer to the default understanding of individual counseling as the "Binder & Price" model,[23] while fully acknowledging that later writers, including David Binder and Susan Price themselves, have refined the early thinking about this skill set with tremendous insight and sophistication. But the basic conceptions offered by Binder & Price in 1977 remain valid today, even if they have generated considerable rich discussion about their implications.[24]

Two aspects of the Binder & Price approach concern us here, the two which have the most relevance to our comparisons between individual counseling and group client counseling. The first is the fundamental commitment to client-centeredness in the counseling process. The second is the elegance of the proffered structure of an effective counseling session. While both of these are quite familiar to those who teach about and engage in client counseling, they warrant a brief summary here.

Client-Centeredness: The Binder & Price approach to the lawyer/client interaction is expressly "client-centered," and their client-centered approach to lawyering has become the "predominant model" taught in law schools today.[25] A client-centered approach to lawyering respects an individual's autonomy, and warns against a lawyer's interference, either willingly or otherwise, with a client's full ownership of his legal matter.[26] Its basic premise is this: A lawyer must aim to assist a client to make choices and to proceed with his legal work in ways which reflect *the client's* preferences, values, goals, and commitments. It is profoundly anti-paternalist in its philosophy. It also makes a good deal of

---

[21] Lawyers of course often have simply to explain the law to a client in a didactic fashion, even when the client need not use it in a complicated way. For example, a lawyer might advise a client about the requirements for a nonprofit corporation to obtain 501(c)(3) status, simply as a list of legal requirements. While this task is often more challenging than one might expect, it tends not to be the focus of the more interesting writing about the counseling process.

[22] I have argued that this kind of counseling is far more prevalent, and far more difficult, than the standard texts admit. *See* Paul R. Tremblay, *Pre-Negotiation Counseling: An Alternative Model,* 13 CLINICAL L. REV. 541 (2006).

[23] *See* Binder & Price, *supra* note 12.

[24] See, e.g., Robert D. Dinerstein, Client-Centered Counseling: Reappraisal and Refinement, 32 ARIZ. L. REV. 501 (1990); Stephen Ellmann, Lawyers and Clients, 34 UCLA L. REV. 717 (1987); Michelle S. Jacobs, People from the Footnotes: The Missing Element in Client-Centered Counseling, 27 GOLDEN GATE U. L. REV. 345 (1997); Katherine R. Kruse, Fortress in the Sand: The Plural Values of Client Centered Representation, 12 CLINICAL L. REV. 369 (2006) [hereinafter Kruse, Fortress in the Sand].

[25] See Kruse, Fortress in the Sand, supra note 24, at 370.

[26] LAWYERS AS COUNSELORS, *supra* note 13, at 272–75; *see* Kruse, *Fortress in the Sand, supra* note 24, at 373 (noting but critiquing this analysis).

sense. A lawyer is an agent of a client, who is the principal in the relationship. Each lawyer brings to the interaction her own peculiar set of values, fears, likes and dislikes, and it is wrong, as a moral measure, for the lawyer, the professional with power and status, to make choices based upon the lawyer's preferences instead of the client's.[27]

A commitment to client-centeredness leads Binder & Price to craft counseling models imbued with *neutrality*. To understand why (and to appreciate the challenges of this stance), we should consider for a moment the expectation of a client seeking help from a lawyer on a complicated and serious legal matter. Imagine that the client has agreed to pay the lawyer a lot of money for the lawyer's services. The client might expect that for the high prices she charges, the lawyer will offer direct and definitive advice: "My expert, considered opinion is that you should do the following. . . ." The client-centeredness approach suggests that the lawyer will seldom provide that kind of direction to her clients. Why not?

The reason why not is grounded in what lawyers assist clients to do. Suppose that a client wants to know from his lawyer what legal device will accomplish Goal X, and that only one plausible legal maneuver, Device Z, will accomplish Goal X. In that case, the lawyer should and will offer her expert advice: "We'll use Device Z." But few legal matters have such straightforward and definitive solutions. Most legal matters—and virtually all of the legal matters that are interesting and challenging—involve multiple alternative actions, uncertainties about each, assessments of levels of risk, and imperfect predictions about what some other people are likely to do in the future. A smart and wise lawyer will recognize the relevant alternatives, describe the inherent uncertainties, offer reliable predictions about other participants' likely behaviors, and assess the risk levels. But then, once the lawyer has performed her role and communicated all of that critical information to her client, only the client can choose among the available alternatives based on factors peculiarly within the client's competence.

Perhaps like most of us, many clients will want the lawyer to go further, and to make the ultimate choices for them. But, while a lawyer is well equipped to perform the role just described, she is ill-equipped to understand *what choice meets the client's needs most fully*. The lawyer may know her client really well, but the odds are that she does not know the client as well as the client knows himself. Because of the risks and uncertainties involved, the "best" decision is the one which accommodates the client's preferences, values, and position on the risk-taking versus

[27] This fundamental objection to lawyer control, and its respect for the preferences of the client, is a well-accepted component of client-centered lawyering. For its early articulation, see Binder & Price, *supra* note 12, at 147–53; Spiegel, *supra* note 6; Marcy Strauss, *Toward a Revised Model of the Attorney-Client Relationship: The Argument for Autonomy,* 65 N.C. L. REV. 315 (1987); Richard Wasserstrom, *Lawyers as Professionals: Some Moral Issues,* 5 HUM. RTS. 1, 4 (1975).

risk-avoiding scale. It is also becoming more well-accepted that good decisionmaking is far more dependent on emotion than on reason.[28] A choice will be "right" not because of some reasoned, objective calculus, but because it meets the personal (and often unconscious[29]) needs of the person who will live with the results.

This description is almost embarrassingly oversimplified. It does not acknowledge the challenges of adhering to a client-centered approach in practice with our clients, or our students' clients.[30] It has not addressed those settings where the above arguments lack analytical power, such as in cases involving morally unacceptable conduct[31] or where the lawyer's client lacks sufficient capacity to make informed decisions, either because of a disabling mental or emotional impairment[32] or, as some have argued, because of political oppression that limits autonomous decisionmaking.[33] But those considerations aside, the client-centered approach is fundamentally *right,* and morally coherent.[34] Any counseling model or

---

[28] *See* Jonah Lehrer, HOW WE DECIDE 34–42 (2008).

[29] *Id.* at 237.

[30] Kate Kruse offers one of the more elegant of the critiques of the simplified view of the neutrality principle. *See* Kruse, *Fortress in the Sand, supra* note 24. Others question whether it inadvertently (or otherwise) privileges dominant cultural habits while overlooking less prevalent practices and patterns of relationships. *See* Jacobs, *supra* note 24, at 361–74; Ascanio Piomelli, *Cross-Cultural Lawyering by the Book: The Latest Clinical Texts and a Sketch of a Future Agenda,* 4 HASTINGS RACE & POVERTY L. J. 131 (2006).

[31] *See, e.g.,* LAWYERS AS COUNSELORS, *supra* note 13, at 391–93; Robert F. Cochran, Jr., Deborah L. Rhode, Paul R. Tremblay & Thomas L. Shaffer, *Symposium: Client Counseling and Moral Responsibility,* 30 PEPP. L. REV. 591 (2003); Kruse, *Fortress in the Sand, supra* note 24, at 431. Kruse has critiqued client-centeredness for its deafness to moral issues, *see id.* at 385, but in doing so she fails to afford the model sufficient credit. While it may be true that some of the early descriptions of the model may not have been sufficiently clear, it is equally evident that deference to client preferences may only be justified when those preferences are not morally troublesome. There is nothing paternalistic about a lawyer's resisting morally unacceptable schemes, and nothing within the Binder & Price theory would suggest that a lawyer must withhold judgments on those issues. *See* Paul R. Tremblay, *Client-Centered Counseling and Moral Activism,* 30 PEPP. L. REV. 615 (2003). Kruse's worries about the actual effectiveness of a lawyer's intervention (and the use of "moral dialogues"), on the other hand, are quite on target. *See* Kruse, *Fortress in the Sand, supra* note 24, at 431–33.

[32] See, e.g., David Luban, Paternalism and the Legal Profession, 1981 WISE. L. REV. 454; Paul R. Tremblay, On *Persuasion and Paternalism: Lawyer Decisionmaking and the Questionably Competent Client,* 1987 UTAH L. REV. 515.

[33] *See* Gary Bellow, *Steady Work,* 31 HARV. C.R.-C.L. L. REV. 297, 303 (1996) (recommending talking "seriously about purposive judgment—when and whether to intervene or to seek influence" with clients who are poor); Duncan Kennedy, *Distributive and Paternalist Motives in Contract and Tort Law, with Special Reference to Compulsory Terms and Unequal Bargaining Power,* 41 MD. L. REV. 563, 638 (1982) (discussing "false consciousness" as a possible justification for paternalism). This Article addresses that argument below. *See* text accompanying notes 282–307 *infra.*

[34] As we see below in our discussion of community group counseling (*see* text accompanying notes 286–88 *infra),* many critical scholars object to the "neutrality" framework emphasis within the Binder & Price model and its followers, particularly as applied to work with oppressed clients. *See, e.g.,* William H. Simon, *The Dark Secret of Progressive Lawyering: A Comment on Poverty Law Scholarship in the Post-Modern, Post-Reagan Era,* 48 U. MIAMI L. REV. 1099, 1099 [hereinafter Simon, *Dark Secret*] (scholars overstate domination of clients as an "overwhelming menace"). Those critics assert that neutrality is a false conception, because "lawyers will have to take sides" in their work with their clients. *Id.* at 1102. *See also* Kruse, *Fortress in the Sand,*

best practice must account for that commitment. While some adherents of what has come to be known in some contexts as a "collaborative" model of client representation assert that the arguments for lawyer neutrality are overstated,[35] their arguments continue to embrace a profound respect for the interests and the preferences of the clients.[36]

A Model or Structure: The second ground-breaking contribution from the first Binder & Price text is its outline of a *model* for conducting a counseling session.[37] While some may quibble about the propriety of using a model for a complex interactive lawyering experience such as a client counseling session,[38] as a pedagogical tool a model is a brilliant idea. The Binder & Price model is not a recipe, and it is not intended to be slavishly followed by students.[39] But its value as an orienting device to permit students (and, of course, lawyers) to understand the insights about effective counseling, and to arrange their time with their clients in a workable way, is considerable. Here, we review briefly the basic structure of a Binder & Price counseling session, to understand its underpinning and, later, to adapt it for a lawyer's work with a group, or with constituents of a group.

The basic counseling model from Binder & Price seeks to achieve the following goals:[40] The lawyer must appreciate the client's goals and needs; the client must understand in as meaningful way as possible what the

---

supra note 24, at 385 (neutrality is a psychologically flawed conception); Bellow, *supra* note 33, at 301 (the "practice of law always involves exercising power"). These critics do not, however, recommend that lawyers should, as a moral and tactical commitment, dominate their clients and assert their professional superiority over the clients. Not surprisingly, the progressive critics actively reject such an attitude, and urge far greater respect for the wisdom of the non-professional clients. *See, e.g.,* Alfieri, *Practicing Community, supra* note 3, at 1750 ("[Progressive lawyers] *take* people's dignity. The taking deprives them of the opportunity to demonstrate—in private and public spheres—their competence as autonomous, self-determining agents . . . [and] denies communities a crucial element of their solidarity (organization and mobilization).") (emphasis in original). Even the critics would agree, therefore, that a counseling model, whether with individual clients, group clients, or community groups, ought to seek to minimize the inadvertent domination by the lawyer of the client. In that spirit, and without rejecting the insights of the progressive critics, this Article proceeds with a baseline embrace of the neutrality principle.

[35] *See, e.g.,* Cochran et al., *supra* note 19, at 5 (a client-centered model of representation fails to account for the needs of third parties); Kruse, *Fortress in the Sand, supra* note 24, at 385–95 (client-centered model is too one-dimensional).

[36] *See* Cochran et al., *supra* note 19, at 11–25 (criticizing former lawyer-dominant practices); Kruse, *Fortress in the Sand, supra* note 24, at 421–24 (developing a more nuanced approach to recognizing and achieving client autonomy).

[37] *See* Binder & Price, *supra* note 12, at 157–87.

[38] *See, e.g.,* Jacobs, *supra* note 24, at 355–57 (critiquing the Binder & Price method for simplification of the complexity of client counseling); Linda Morton, *Teaching Creative Problem-Solving: A Paradigmatic Approach,* 34 CAL. W. L. REV. 375 (1998); Carrie Menkel-Meadow, *Narrowing the Gap by Narrowing the Field: What's Missing From the MacCrate Report—Of Skills, Legal Science and Being a Human Being,* 69 Wash. L. REV. 593, 604–05 (1994); Piomelli, *supra* note 30, at 179.

[39] *See* LAWYERS AS COUNSELORS, *supra* note 13, at 12–13.

[40] *Id.* at 281–92.

available alternatives represent, both objectively (as a matter of law and fact) and in how each alternative affects that particular client; the client must appreciate how the alternatives compare to one another, by exploring the relative advantages and disadvantages of the respective options; the lawyer must organize and present the preceding discussion in a way that does not attempt to influence the client to choose a result which the lawyer would choose based upon her own preferences or needs; the lawyer must understand and account for the heuristics and biases, or "cognitive illusions,"[41] which can distort a client's "rational" decisionmaking;[42] and, finally, the lawyer must then assist the client to make a choice or a decision that fits best the client's comfort with risk, his needs, his preferences, and his "values."[43]

The Binder & Price model aims to achieve those goals by suggesting the following structure of a counseling meeting between the lawyer and her individual client.[44]

A paradigmatic meeting might follow this scheme:[45]

- The lawyer and client review the client's goals and wishes;

---

[41] For an overview of cognitive illusions, see Persi Diaconis & David Freedman, *The Persistence of Cognitive Illusions,* 4 BEHAV. BRAIN SCI. 317 (1981); Robert E. Scott, *Error and Rationality in Individual Decisionmaking: An Essay on the Relationship Between Cognitive Illusions and the Management of Choices,* 59 S. CAL. L. REV. 329, 340–42 (1986).

[42] Early versions of client counseling models assumed that the lawyer and the client were economically rational actors seeking to maximize utility. In recent years both the lawyering skills community, as well as the greater legal and economic community, have come to appreciate the insights of the behavioral economists, who demonstrate how "predictably irrational" individuals tend to be in their decisionmaking. *See* LAWYERS AS COUNSELORS, *supra* note 13, at 382–91 (discussing the role of cognitive illusions in client counseling). For background in the increasingly popular literature on the topic of heuristics and biases, see, e.g., Amos Tversky & Daniel Kahneman, *Judgment Under Uncertainty: Heuristics and Biases,* in Daniel Kahneman, Paul Slovic & Amos Tversky, JUDGMENT UNDER UNCERTAINTY: HEURISTICS AND BIASES 14 (1st ed. 1982); Dan Ariely, PREDICTABLY IRRATIONAL: THE HIDDEN FORCES THAT SHAPE OUR DECISIONS (2008); Ori Brafman & Rom Brafman, SWAY: THE IRRESISTIBLE PULL OF IRRATIONAL BEHAVIOR (2009); Lehrer, *supra* note 28; Leonard Mlodinow, THE DRUNKARD'S WALK: HOW RANDOMNESS RULES OUR LIVES (2008); Richard H. Thaler & Cass R. Sunstein, NUDGE: IMPROVING DECISIONS ABOUT HEALTH, WEALTH, AND HAPPINESS (2008).

[43] It is quite common for writers addressing the counseling process to refer to the importance of the client's "values," using that term to capture the personal, internal commitments possessed by the client. *See, e.g.,* LAWYERS AS COUNSELORS, *supra* note 13, at 11–12; Ellmann, *supra* note 11, at 1164; Kruse, *Fortress in the Sand, supra* note 24, at 415. In my previous writing, I have resisted the use of that term, because of its implication that *moral* values are personal and idiosyncratic, and therefore essentially ungrounded outside of religious contexts. *See* Paul R. Tremblay, *Shared Norms, Bad Lawyers, and the Virtues of Casuistry,* 36 U.S.F. L. REV. 659, 680–86 (2002) (arguing that moral values are not personal and ungrounded). As I use the term "values" in this Article, I intend it to mean those commitments which are essentially idiosyncratic, and not as fundamental moral principles.

[44] While the following structure is, once again, not intended as a fixed orchestration and not a cookbook recipe, it does capture an elegance which makes a great deal of sense given the goals just identified.

[45] This scheme is a simplification of the model developed most recently in LAWYERS AS COUNSELORS, *supra* note 13, at 281–91. It is not inconsistent with the counseling advice contained in other texts, although other texts may rely less on models than Binder & Price and its successive iterations.

- The lawyer then *briefly* describes the available options, sufficiently so to permit the client to elect an order of discussion;
- The client then chooses which option to discuss first, second, and so forth;[46]
- The lawyer describes each option separately with great care and with elaborate detail, in an *objective* and non-normative fashion, to enable her client to understand the options and their respective levels of risk;[47]
- The lawyer and client engage in a *normative,* comparative discussion about the options, systematically and with explicit reference to advantages ("pros") and disadvantages ("cons") of each option as they apply to the client's specific circumstances;[48] and finally,
- The client, having understood the relative merits of each choice and the need to choose one, chooses one, through an active dialogue with the lawyer.

If a designer of lawyering protocols were to imagine a rational, value-maximizing actor wishing to make a deliberative decision in the most careful and thoughtful fashion, with a full appreciation for the risks involved and how those risks interact with the actor's peculiar brand of risk-taking (or risk-aversion), the designer would be hard pressed to arrive a better organizational protocol than the Binder & Price model just described.[49]

---

[46] The rationale for this step and that just preceding it is to minimize the lawyer's inadvertent (or advertent) skewing the decisionmaking process by choosing the order of topic discussion, signally thereby the lawyer's value judgments about the options. *See id.* at 309.

[47] As will remain apparent as this Article proceeds, the most important quality, and the most challenging factor, within a counseling meeting of this type concerns how the client will manage the relative risks involved in the available choices. In the paradigmatic circumstance, each alternative offers to the client some chance of good and some chance of bad, with the levels of risk, of good, and of bad different within each choice. The client's goal is not simply to choose the option that delivers the highest level of the good; he must instead grapple with his risk aversion sentiments to decide the types of gambles he is willing to take. For a discussion of this element of counseling, see, e.g., Donald C. Langevoort & Robert K. Rasmussen, *Skewing the Results: The Role of Lawyers in Transmitting Legal Rules,* 5 S. CAL. INTERDISC. L.J. 375, 379 (1997); Donald C. Langevoort, *The Epistemology of Corporate-Securities Lawyering: Beliefs, Biases and Organizational Behavior,* 63 BROOK. L. REV. 629, 655 (1997) [hereinafter Langevoort, *Epistemology*] (lawyers are motivated to overstate legal risk).

[48] The counseling texts often note the value of a chart to accomplish the systematic assessment of the competing alternatives. *See* LAWYERS AS COUNSELORS, *supra* note 13, at 236, 320; COCHRAN ET AL., *supra* note 19, at 167–68.

[49] The commentators tend to agree with this assessment. *See* Section of Legal Educ. and Admissions to the Bar, Am. Bar Ass'n, Legal Education and Professional Development—An Educational Continuum 179–83 (1992) [hereinafter The MacCrate Report]; Dinerstein, *supra* note 24, at 504 (noting "the extraordinary influence of the model within clinical education circles").

If such a scheme, with its dedication to neutrality and anti-paternalism, and its appreciation for personal risk-taking idiosyncrasy, works for an individual, value-maximizing actor, how, if at all, should it be adapted to fit the context of a member, representative, or constituent of an organization or group? That question serves as the basis for the remainder of this Article. To begin the inquiry, we must establish an understanding of the term "client group."

II. "GROUP" CLIENTS

We may start by recognizing that the conception of a "group" client easily separates into two distinct possibilities: (1) a group client might refer to a collection of clients whom the lawyer represents in the same matter—otherwise known in many circles as "joint clients"; and (2) a collection of individuals (or entities) who understand themselves to constitute a single organization—in other words, an entity, as commonly understood by Model Rule 1.13. Lawyer's responsibilities should be substantially different depending upon which kind of group the lawyer represents. Every instance of "group" representation falls into one of those two categories.

It might be the case that one's initial understanding of the task of counseling "group clients" would implicate only the former understanding, and not the latter, since, of course, an organizational client is a single client just as any individual person would be. Indeed, it is hard to consider a lawyer representing, say, Martha's Bakery, Inc. as representing a "group" client. In fact, for purposes of thinking about the lawyer's role as a counselor, the precise opposite understanding applies. A lawyer working with multiple individual clients is not counseling a "group client" at all, for the purposes of interest to this Article. A lawyer working with an entity, by contrast, is working with a "group client," almost all of the time. Given our ultimate goal of understanding a lawyer's responsibility in representing community groups, this contention is especially true.

The next section examines the differences in the counseling process between the two kinds of collective clients, but before we reach that examination we should add a bit of texture to this definitional introduction. . . .

III. COUNSELING GROUP CLIENTS

With the preceding definitional background in place, and with a reminder of the "baseline" counseling model emerging from the Binder & Price sources as an appropriate benchmark, this section will now consider the counseling responsibilities of a lawyer working with three kinds of group clients: (1) joint clients (even if they may not properly qualify as a "group"); (2) well-structured entity clients; and (3) loosely-structured entity clients. After having done so, Part IV will extrapolate from what we learn here to uncover the best practices considerations for working with community groups.

A. *Counseling Joint Clients*

As we have seen immediately above, a lawyer representing joint clients really has multiple *individual* clients. Given our plan to use the baseline Binder & Price individual-client model as a benchmark for comparison, there may not be very much of interest to consider when we explore how a lawyer ought to work with her multiple individual clients. Since the fact of joint representation does not deprive the respective individual clients of any rights within the lawyering relationship relevant to our purposes,[60] one might imagine that any counseling of the clients, whether together in one room or separately, would follow the default Binder & Price model. In other words, nothing in the joint representation itself requires the lawyer to alter the goals or the techniques of individual client counseling.

Understanding that, we ought to address here briefly the challenges faced by a lawyer when representing multiple individual clients with separable and potentially differing interests, especially since, as we shall see later, in some community group settings the lawyer might need to treat the collectivity as a form of joint representation.[61] The discussion here will be somewhat superficial, however, because the issues covered here are the subject of discussion in the conventional legal ethics literature.[62]

The most apt subject for our consideration here is the lawyer's preliminary but absolutely essential counseling responsibility—to advise her clients about the potential conflicts and obtain their informed consent to the joint representation.[63] This task is a paradigmatic Binder & Price counseling opportunity, with a finite set of alternatives (retain separate counsel, or accept joint representation) of which each client must choose only one, and not deciding (that is to say, being too uncertain or torn to arrive at a decision) means deciding on the "default" or status quo option,

---

[60] Joint clients do sacrifice some important confidentiality rights that non-joint clients own. With rare exceptions, a client jointly represented along with one or more co-clients cannot expect that any secrets he discloses to the lawyer will remain confidential as to the remaining co-clients. *See* MODEL RULES, *supra* note 52, at R. 1.7, cmt. 31; RESTATEMENT, *supra* note 50, at § 60, Cmt. *l*. That limitation on the attorney-client relationship does not affect the lawyer's counseling responsibilities, however.

[61] *See* text accompanying notes 77–80 *infra*.

[62] See, e.g., Multiple Representation, supra note 56.

[63] *See* MODEL RULES, *supra* note 52, at R. 1.7(c) and Cmts. 29 through 33.

which here would mean separate representation.[64] A lawyer's counseling meeting would seemingly look like the meeting described above, with the lawyer being neutral about which choice the client makes, and orchestrating the conversation to ensure a full descriptive component before an evaluative or normative discussion.[65]

There are two distinctive issues arising in a lawyer's effort to discern a client's informed consent to joint representation, however. Each warrants brief consideration here before we move on. The first issue has to do with whether the ethical obligations of the lawyer require her to meet separately with each of her potential clients for this informed consent talk, or whether the counseling may occur more efficiently by meeting with the potential clients together. The latter is both far more efficient and, one guesses, standard practice among lawyers.[66] Without probing the question in great depth here (and the topic perhaps warrants its own separate article[67]), we can at least tentatively conclude that neither prevailing legal ethics doctrine nor strategic wisdom would require separate meetings with each potential co-client. While some worry must exist that some subtle (or not-so-subtle) peer pressure could affect the voluntariness of any one potential client's decision to waive potential conflicts if made within a group meeting, that worry diminishes somewhat when one realizes that the result of the potential client's deliberation cannot help but be pretty apparent to the other potential clients, who will know with certainty whether the joint representation will go forward or not, and whether the others have waived conflicts or not.[68]

---

64 Because the lawyer must obtain an affirmative act from her client (a formal waiver of the potential conflicts) in order to proceed with the joint representation, the default arrangement is separate representation (or no representation).

65 *See* text accompanying notes 44–49 *supra*.

66 As my colleague Judy McMorrow notes, in practice this informed consent interaction often occurs by means of a letter, with no meeting about it at all. Conversation with Professor Judith McMorrow, February 26, 2010.

67 The topic receives attention in several published sources, usually in the context of estate planning, a practice field which may trigger its own special conflicts concerns. *See, e.g.*, AM. COLL. OF TRUST & ESTATE COUNSEL FOUND., COMMENTARIES ON THE MODEL RULES OF PROFESSIONAL CONDUCT 32 (4th ed. 2006) (known as the ACTEC Commentaries) ("A lawyer may wish to consider meeting with prospective clients separately, which would give each of them an opportunity to be more candid and, perhaps, reveal potentially serious conflicts of interest or objectives that would not otherwise be disclosed."); Geoffrey C. Hazard, Jr., *Conflict of Interest in Estate Planning for Husband and Wife,* 20 PROB. LAW. 1, 23 (1994) ("[I]f a multiple representation is being considered separate interviews should be held with each client, more than once if necessary. Separate interviews can reveal divergences in the clients' respective assumptions and purposes that otherwise would be masked by polite conversation.").

68 The explanation in the text is actually rather oversimplified, which again suggests the need for a separate treatment of this issue beyond what we may address here. If the lawyer needs to obtain informed consent to co-representation from *two* potential clients, then the reasoning in the text applies perfectly—each person will know which way the other has decided even if the counseling meetings are held separately and in private. But if the group of potential co-clients is three or more, that conclusion does not follow. None of the three will know which of

The second concern relates to, and actually undercuts the previous response to, the first. That concern relates to the lawyer's confidentiality obligations with her co-clients. It is itself doubly layered. Let us address the most obvious confidentiality layer first. The Model Rules,[69] and the doctrine surrounding the Model Rules,[70] establish that co-representation will normally include the understanding that there will be no secrets within the lawyer/client collectivity, and among the co-clients. This understanding emerges from the established doctrine within the attorney-client privilege[71] but also from the lawyer's obligations to each client under Rule 1.4 to keep her clients reasonably informed about developments material to the representation.[72] If the lawyer's counseling role were simply to announce to her clients that this concession is a necessary and inevitable by-product of joint representation (and therefore likely a disadvantage, a "con," to the idea of a joint endeavor), it would be of some interest but little more than that. In fact, however, the concession is neither inevitable nor necessary. It is a *choice* to be made by each prospective client.[73] While no doubt awkward in practice, the lawyer and her co-clients possess the right according to the substantive law of lawyering to opt not to share with one another all confidential information passing through the lawyer. Such an agreement will preserve the privilege waiver implications in the case of a later dispute between some co-clients,[74] just as it contractually limits the lawyer's obligations under Rule 1.4 and permits the lawyer to withhold otherwise material information from some of her clients.[75]

For our purposes, this insight complicates the lawyer's counseling strategy, and might influence whether she may perform her disclosure duties to the group as a whole. A competent informed consent discussion must address this issue with each affected prospective client. Each prospective client must have the lawyer's wise judgment about whether that client has information which ought not be shared with the others.[76]

---

the other two did not agree to joint representation if the lawyer does not obtain unanimity to the waivers.

69 MODEL RULES, *supra* note 52, at R. 1.7 cmt. 31.

70 *See, e.g.,* RESTATEMENT, *supra* note 50, at § 60; Ronald D. Rotunda & John S. Dzienkowski, PROFESSIONAL RESPONSIBILITY: A STUDENT'S GUIDE § 1.6–9, 262–64 (2008–09).

71 *See, e.g.,* RESTATEMENT, *supra* note 50, at § 75, Cmt. *d*; State v. Cascone, 487 A.2d 186, 189 (Conn. 1985); Waste Management, Inc. v. International Surplus Lines Ins. Co., 579 N.E.2d 322 (Ill. 1991); Ashcraft & Gerel v. Shaw, 728 A.2d 798 (Md. App. 1999).

72 MODEL RULES, *supra* note 52, at R. 1.4; A v. B. v. Hill Wallack, 726 A.2d 924 (N.J. 1999)(concluding that Rule 1.4 duties must be enforced even over objection of a co-client, because complaining co-client had warnings about shared secrets).

73 MODEL RULES, *supra* note 50, at R. 1.7, Cmt. 31; Rotunda & Dzienkowski, *supra* note 70, at § 1.6–9.

74 RESTATEMENT, *supra* note 50, at § 75, Cmt. *d*.

75 *See* MODEL RULES, *supra* note 52, at R. 1.7, Cmt. 31.

76 The example used in the legal ethics literature—the question of trade secrets—cleverly eludes this worry. *See* RESTATEMENT, *supra* note 50, at § 60, Cmt. *l*; MODEL RULES, *supra* note

The lawyer would be a more effective counselor to each prospective client if she could have that discussion outside of the earshot of the other potential co-client.

That concern is what was described a moment ago as the first of the two confidentiality layers. The second layer becomes apparent now, given our assessment of the lawyer's efforts to obtain intelligent, informed consent to the confidentiality waiver. While the lawyer is negotiating the contours of her relationships with the prospective clients (and potential co-clients), *those preliminary conversations* have their own confidentiality implications which the lawyer and her prospective clients must appreciate. Even if each prospective client opted not to retain the lawyer after the lawyer has explored the possible conflicts waivers, the discussions about whether to retain the lawyer are fully covered by the confidentiality protections of Rule 1.6.[77] Therefore, were the lawyer, in an explicit effort to be the best counselor to each person about whether that person would choose to waive confidentiality and to waive any other potential conflicts, to decide to meet separately with each person, all of her successive conversations would be imbued with the cloak of secrecy. The resulting constraint might then impair the lawyer's later representation of any client who chose to stay with the lawyer. More importantly, that reality might impair the lawyer's effectiveness in the next discussion with the next prospective co-client about whether to waive confidentiality and any possible conflicts of interest. . . .

This conversation captures the lawyer's responsibility, at least preliminarily, for seeking informed consent to multiple representation.[82] If some representation of community groups involves not entity representation but joint representation, as seems quite likely,[83] the lawyer working with the group must engage in some version of this conversation with those members of the community group who the lawyer understands will serve as formal clients.

52, at R. 1.7, Cmt. 31. One can easily imagine a lawyer working with two aligned but also competitor companies, where each would agree in front of the other that the lawyer will not reveal the respective client's trade secrets to the other. The fact of some valuable but extremely confidential information is not itself something to be kept from the other co-client.

77 MODEL RULES, *supra* note 52, at R. 1.18(b).

82 *See* ROTUNDA & DZIENKOWSKI, *supra* note 70, at § 1.7–2(d) (discussing the requirements for proper joint representation).

83 Some examples from the literature on community lawyering show groups which appear to be loosely combined collections of individual clients. *See, e.g.*, Bennett, *Embracing the Ill-Structured Problem*, *supra* note 9, at 58; Piomelli, *supra* note 1, at 401–02 (environmental justice story in which a lawyer represents three community members who partner with other residents as the story later develops). Indeed, Michael Diamond and Aaron O'Toole argue that the fluidity of community groups may be essential to their character, so that imposing the constraints of Rule 1.13's bureaucratic sensibility is harmful to the lawyer's work with such groups. *See* Diamond & O'Toole, *supra* note 2, at 523–24.

B. Counseling Well-Structured Group Clients

As we noted above, the concept of joint (but still individualized[84]) representation might qualify as the representation of a group, but more sensibly the latter would invoke the idea of representing the group *qua* group. While a collectivity may have an identity that makes the entity theory a coherent possibility, it of course does not have an intrinsic means of expressing itself. The lawyer representing the collectivity must discern how to gauge the intentions of the client in order to accomplish her purposes.[85]

Many group clients will have explicit and rigorous schemes in place for expressing the desires of the organization, and for making and implementing decisions. This subsection examines the responsibilities of a lawyer when working with that very typical type of client—typical, at least, outside of the community group context.

The question before us in this context might be summarized as follows: When a lawyer counsels a legitimate, authorized constituent of an entity, do the lawyer's responsibilities differ in any way from her working with an individual client (like, again, a woman in the middle of a contested divorce)? The answer to that question appears to be yes. The lawyer's role does differ, in a subtle but possibly important way. Given the goals of effective client counseling identified above, the entity's agent is not necessarily entitled to the same level of deference from the lawyer as the individual client in the divorce matter. This conclusion will be especially apparent in circumstances of internal organizational disagreement, of course, but it need not be that narrow. It will hold true even in conventional counseling interactions. . . .

The conventional neutral posture of a lawyer working with an individual stems from both the lawyer's moral duty to respect the preferences of the client, plus the realization that the lawyer lacks expertise to identify or unearth those preferences.[108] If one central goal of a counseling session is to arrive at a decision which bests satisfies the

---

[84] The legal ethics literature tends to refer to the joint representation as "aggregate," to distinguish that work from the conception adopted by the drafters of the Model Rules, which the literature refers to as the "entity" theory. *See* Hazard & Hodes, *supra* note 59, at § 17–3.

[85] This counseling question is a variation of the central ethical challenge faced by any corporate counsel—how to represent the entity through its "duly authorized constituents." While that question understandably has received considerable scholarly attention, scholars continue to struggle with the concept, and few if any address the quality of the actual interactions between the lawyer and her client's agents. For a sampling of the literature, see, e.g., Lawrence E. Mitchell, *Professional Responsibility and the Close Corporation: Toward a Realistic Ethic,* 74 CORNELL L. REV. 466 (1989); Nancy J. Moore, *Expanding Duties of Attorneys to "Non-Clients": Reconceptualizing the Attorney-Client Relationship in Entity Representation and Other Inherently Ambiguous Situations,* 45 S.C. L. REV. 659, 687–95 (1994); William H. Simon, *Whom (or What) Does the Organization's Lawyer Represent?: An Anatomy of Intraclient Conflict,* 91 CAL. L. REV. 57 (2003); Note, *An Expectations Approach to Client Identity,* 106 HARV. L. REV. 687 (1993).

[108] *See* LAWYERS AS COUNSELORS, *supra* note 13, at 368–69.

client's needs and preferences, a lawyer can never know as well as the client what those needs and, especially, preferences are.[109] The neutral stance is grounded in large part on what is essentially an epistemological insight, that the lawyer cannot know the things necessary for making the best decision.

That epistemological limitation simply is not as prevalent when the lawyer's client is a group client. Put another way, the epistemological challenge is a quite different one. With an individual client (say, the wife in the divorce matter), she may have great difficulty discerning what she wants to do,[110] but in the end only she can make that judgment in anything close to a reliable or sensible way.[111] With an organizational client, while it also may have great difficulty discerning what it wishes to do, its process of discernment is more open to examination and input. . . .

C. *Counseling Loosely-Structured Group Clients*

1. *Representation of a Loosely-Structured Group*

It is not uncommon for a community group to consist of a collection of concerned individuals who have not (yet) organized themselves into a structured corporation or similar entity.[113] We need to consider how a lawyer ought to work with such a group, especially as she considers her counseling responsibilities. Our review of this subject may be divided into two components. First, in this section, we consider the implications of establishing an attorney-client relationship with a group which does not possess a preexisting organizational structure. Then, in the following section, we review the counseling responsibilities of a lawyer working with such a group client.

The first question we confront—and it is a critical one—is whether a lawyer *may* represent a loosely-structured group, and enter into an attorney-client relationship with that group. Given, as we concluded above, that a lawyer may only represent a group either via a joint

---

[109] *Id. See also* Binny Miller, *Give Them Back Their Lives: Recognizing Client Narrative in Case Theory,* 93 MICH. L. REV. 485, 516–17 (1994) ("critical lawyers see the client's story as the only story worth telling"; lawyer should not presume to succeed in translating that narrative). Even the "collaborative model" theorists accept some limits on the lawyer's understanding of the client's unique personal story. *See, e.g.,* Cochran et al., *supra* note 19, at 20–25 (warning of the risks of lawyer translation).

[110] The interviewing and counseling scholarship respects an individual client's moral right to make choices about the direction of her life, but that literature does not pretend that individual clients find that task to be an easy one. Indeed, it can be frightfully difficult. *See, e.g.,* John Lande, *Possibilities for Collaborative Law: Ethics and Practice of Lawyer Disqualification and Process Control in a New Model of Lawyering,* 64 OHIO ST. L.J. 1315, 1357 (2003) ("[e]mpirical research indicates that many clients do have difficulty making decisions"); Spiegel, *supra* note 103, at 308 ("individual clients frequently have difficulty making decisions").

[111] One sensible way might be for her to delegate the decision to her lawyer, simply as a way to resolve some irreparable uncertainty. That choice, though, remains hers and hers alone.

[113] *See, e.g.,* Ellmann, *supra* note 11, at 1162 (noting that Ellmann's analysis concerns "relatively informal, democratic groups"); Diamond & O'Toole, *supra* note 2, at 488–92 (offering stories of loosely-structured groups but not treating them as aggregates of individual clients).

representation model or an entity representation model, it is essential to understand whether an unstructured, unincorporated collection of persons—aside from those who see themselves as a gathering of discrete if affiliated individuals—could serve as an "entity," for attorney representation purposes, without the presence of a formal organizational structure. This question is especially important in the community group context. If the entity representation model is not available with loosely-structured collectivities, then the lawyers working with such groups are left with the joint representation model. That latter model, as the preceding discussion showed and as later discussion here will amplify, is not well suited to the goals sought by community lawyers.[114]

The authorities are not at all clear regarding the legal status, within the attorney-client relationship, of a loosely-structured group, and the community lawyering literature has thus far elided this question.[115] The Restatement (Third) of the Law Governing Lawyers includes informal organizations in its definition of entities, and does not insist that the informal group otherwise have legal standing.[116] The Model Rules agree that Rule 1.13 applies to "unincorporated associations";[117] and, while the Rules also state that "[a]n organizational client is a legal entity,"[118] an ABA ethics opinion construes Rule 1.13 as not requiring the group to possess "a separate jural entity."[119] Hazard and Hodes's commentary

[114] *See* Raymond H. Brescia, *Line in the Sand: Progressive Lawyering, "Master Communities," and a Battle for Affordable Housing in New York City*, 73 ALBANY L. REV 715, 752 (2010) (describing the tension in community lawyering between the needs of the larger group and the interests of individual members).

[115] While several commentators have noted the applicability of Rule 1.13 to community group representation, none has confronted directly (or sufficiently in depth) the issue of the status of an informal group. *See, e.g.*, Bennett, *Embracing the Ill-Structured Problem, supra* note 9, at 70 (noting the persistence of the client identity question, but not attempting to resolve the issue); Diamond & O'Toole, *supra* note 2, at 512 (lamenting the lack of fit of Rule 1.13 to the fluid community group context); Ellmann, *supra* note 11, at 1160–61 (applying Rule 1.13 to an informal group without addressing the lawyer's capacity to establish the relationship with the apparent entity); Southworth, *supra* note 1, at 2465 (reporting empirical research showing that community groups often do not have any "duly authorized constituents" as Rule 1.13 contemplates).

[116] RESTATEMENT, *supra* note 50, at § 96, Cmt. *c* ("whether the organization is a formal legal entity is relevant but not determinative" to the entity conception). The Restatement offers as examples of such informal entities "a social club or an informal group that has established an investment pool." *Id.*

[117] MODEL RULES, *supra* note 52, at R. 1.13, Cmt. 1. When this Article addresses an unincorporated association, it refers to a group which has not formed a formal business entity in its jurisdiction, as would be the case for many community groups. In the business law world, an unincorporated association could include any business entity which is not a corporation, including any variety of partnership and limited liability companies. *See, e.g.,* Douglas M. Branson et al., BUSINESS ENTERPRISES: LEGAL STRUCTURES, GOVERNANCE AND POLICY 53–135 (2009) (addressing "unincorporated business entities" in that fashion); Larry E. Ribstein, THE RISE OF THE UNCORPORATION (2010) (describing the rise of unincorporated associations (for which Ribstein coins the term "uncorporation") such as LLCs).

[118] *Id.* Not every unincorporated association is a recognized legal entity for purposes of state law. *See* text accompanying notes 126–28 *infra*.

[119] ABA Comm. on Ethics & Prof'l Resp., Formal Op. 92–365 (1992) (concluding that an unincorporated trade association may be treated as an entity for purposes of conflicts of interest).

about the Rules offers an example of an ad hoc, informal group which qualifies as an entity for purposes of Rule 1.13: seventeen homeowners who choose to hire a single lawyer to represent them as a group, not as a collection of individuals, with the homeowners having agreed that the collectivity will be bound by a decision endorsed by twelve of the seventeen group members.[120] While the Hazard & Hodes example appears quite appropriate for the community group context, the commentators add a dramatic limitation to their understanding of the entity representation conception:

> It should be stressed, however, that if the "entity" [i.e., the homeowners association just described] is not sufficiently formal to have a *real legal existence,* such as having a charter and by-laws, then the representation will be considered to be of a series of individuals. . . .[121]

If the Hazard and Hodes commentary is correct,[122] then the responsibility of a lawyer working with an ad hoc community group would be very different from that described by most of the community lawyering scholarship, which generally assumes a commitment from the lawyer toward the community group.

It is not apparent that the Hazard and Hodes gloss is a necessary one. Contrary to their assertion, it appears to be the case that a lawyer might establish an attorney-client relationship with an informal group lacking a charter or formal by-laws. It is true, as Hazard and Hodes imply, that an unincorporated association does not have any distinct legal status in many states.[123] Several states have adopted a version of the Uniform Unincorporated Nonprofit Association Act, which provides otherwise informal associations with rights, duties and protections.[124] In

---

120 Hazard & Hodes, *supra* note 59, at § 17.4, pp. 17–15. *See also* Ellmann, *supra* note 11, at 1116 (discussing the Hazard & Hodes example).

121 Hazard & Hodes, *supra* note 59, at § 17.4, pp. 17–15—17–16 (emphasis supplied).

122 William Simon offers some historical support for the Hazard and Hodes assertion. *See* Simon, *supra* note 85, at 113 ("In the past, legal doctrine has tended to draw a sharp distinction between formally and informally organized associations. While formally organized ones were treated as entities, informal organizations were treated as joint individual representations.").

123 *See generally* Robert R. Keatinge, *The Implications of Fiduciary Relationships in Representing Limited Liability Companies and Other Unincorporated Associations and Their Partners or Members,* 25 STETSON L. REV. 389, 391 (1995) (some courts do not recognize an association as a legal entity separate from its constituents); United States v. American Radiator & Standard Sanitary Corp., 278 F. Supp. 608, 614 (W.D. Pa. 1967); Schwartz v. Broadcast Music, 16 F.R.D. 31, 32–33 (S.D. N.Y.1954).

124 *See* NATIONAL CONFERENCE OF COMMISSIONERS ON UNIFORM STATE LAWS, REVISED UNIFORM UNINCORPORATED NONPROFIT ASSOCIATION ACT (2008) [hereinafter "RUUNAA"]. For examples of state statutes implementing the Model Act or its 1996 predecessor, see Ala. Code §§ 10–3B–1 to 10–3B–18 (Alabama); D.C. Code § 29–971.12 (2001); N.C. Gen. Stat. § 59B–2 (2006) (North Carolina); Art. 1396–70–01 (Texas). The introductory comments to RUUNAA imply that it offers a codification of some common law principles and practices, which supports the conclusion that in some states without RUUNAA or its predecessor unincorporated associations have some legal status. *See* RUUNAA, *supra,* at "Prefatory Note."

those states, the compliant unincorporated associations will have recognizable status, and surely a lawyer may represent such an association as an entity. Similarly, there is little doubt that representation of a partnership implicates entity representation obligations,[125] and partnerships often emerge as unincorporated associations.[126] For associations lacking such discernable state law recognition, however, the traditional rule has held that the association's lawyer represents the association's members, since no "entity" exists.[127] But that traditional understanding is changing.[128]

The ABA's Committee on Ethics and Professional Responsibility, in Formal Opinion 92–365, offered a more nuanced understanding of the lawyer's duties to an informal group, although with less analysis than the issue deserves. The opinion concluded, without a great deal of discussion, that a lawyer representing an unincorporated trade association could serve as counsel to the organization and not to its members, even if the organization did not have any independent legal status.[129] Following that ethics opinion, the United States District Court for the Western District of Michigan in the *City of Kalamazoo v. Michigan Disposal Service Corp.* recognized a distinction between unincorporated associations "whose existence and interests are [so] intertwined with those of the individual members" as not to be treated as separate entities, and those with "operations, employees and continuing existence separate from its

---

[125] For examples of partnerships in which the lawyer was found to represent the entity and not the partners, see Chaiken v. Lewis, 754 So. 2d 118, 118 (Fla. Dist. Ct. App. 2000); Johnson v. Superior Court, 45 Cal. Rptr. 2d 312 (Ct. App. 1995); Morin v. Trupin, 778 F. Supp. 711 (S.D.N.Y. 1991); Mursau Corp. v. Fla. Penn Oil & Gas, Inc., 638 F. Supp. 259 (W.D. Pa. 1986). *See also* ABA Comm. on Ethics & Prof'l Resp., Formal Op. 91–361 (1991); Keatinge, *supra* note 123, at 403–04.

[126] *See, e.g.,* Scott B. Ehrlich & Douglas C. Michael, BUSINESS PLANNING 42 (2009) (general partnerships formed merely by associating in business activity, with no more formal measures needed); 1 Alan R. Bromberg & Larry E. Ribstein, BROMBERG & RIBSTEIN ON PARTNERSHIP §§ 1.20–1.21 (1996) (explaining partnership formation); UNIFORM PARTNERSHIP ACT (REVISED) § 202(a) (1997) ("the association of two or more persons to carry on as co-owners a business for profit forms a partnership, whether or not the persons intend to form a partnership," subject to certain exceptions).

[127] City of Kalamazoo v. Michigan Disposal Service Corp., 125 F.Supp. 2d 219, 236 (W.D. Mich. 2000) ("Because unincorporated associations had no separate legal existence, courts regularly held that attorneys for unincorporated associations had a direct attorney-client relationship with each of the members of the association.") *citing* Halverson v. Convenient Food Mart, Inc., 458 F.2d 927, 930 (7th Cir. 1972); Connelly v. Dun & Bradstreet, Inc., 96 F.R.D. 339, 341 (D. Mass. 1982); Philadelphia Housing Auth. v. American Radiator & Standard Sanitary Corp., 294 F. Supp. 1148, 1149 (E.D. Pa. 1969) ("Each individual member of an unincorporated association is a client of the association's lawyer.").

[128] City of Kalamazoo, 125 F. Supp.2d at 236. *See* Lawrence J. Fox & Susan R. Martyn, THE ETHICS OF REPRESENTING ORGANIZATIONS: LEGAL FICTIONS FOR CLIENTS 263–64 (2009) (applying Rule 1.13 to an unincorporated homeowners association).

[129] Formal Op. 92–365, *supra* note 119. The opinion relies upon Model Rule 1.13's comment stating that the Rule applies to unincorporated associations, but ignores an accompanying sentence in the same comment which states that an organization is a "legal entity." *See* MODEL RULES, *supra* note 52, at R. 1.13, Cmt. 1.

members," which a lawyer may treat as an entity.[130] While the definition offered by the District Court is close to question-begging,[131] it nevertheless grasps a reality of a group *qua* group, which captures the essence of much of the community lawyering literature.[132]

Given this evolving understanding of the status of unincorporated associations, we may proceed in our analysis by accepting, at least for the sake of our ethical deliberation, that a lawyer may have as a client a group of persons without a formal organization—say, the Hazard and Hodes homeowners[133]—whom the lawyer will treat as an entity. It is, of course, a very good thing that the substantive law evidences an emerging appreciation for the value of collectivity, given the importance that groups—including community groups—play in society.[134]

Before we address how the lawyer's counseling of such a client compares to the conventional Binder & Price model (or the variation we adduced above in the context of well-structured groups), we must recognize an important predicate, one which helps us address the counseling questions. A moment's reflection demonstrates that, while it is true that she may lawfully represent a loosely-structured group such as an unincorporated association, a lawyer *may not do so* within the constraints of the law of lawyering unless her client achieves many of the attributes of a well-structured organization. That insight seems indisputable, but it is not necessarily self-evident, nor accepted within the literature about counseling community groups.[135] Before a lawyer

---

[130] City of Kalamazoo, 125 F. Supp. 2d at 236. *See also* Franklin v. Callum, 804 A.2d 444 (N.H. 2002); Greate Bay Hotel & Casino, Inc. v. City of Atlantic City, 624 A.2d 102 (N.J. Super. 1993).

[131] The court's description fosters as many uncertainties as it resolves. The reference to "employees" (*see City of Kalamazoo,* 125 F. Supp. 2d at 236) is, seemingly, offered as an example and not as a condition. Similarly, the reference to "continuing existence separate from its members" (*id.*), when describing an unincorporated association, must be intended in a metaphorical and not a legal sense, for otherwise no unincorporated association, short of those covered by partnership law (*see* notes 125–26 *supra*) or the Uniform Nonprofit Act (*see* RUUNAA, *supra* note 124), would be covered by the description.

[132] A compelling, if perhaps unique, example of an unincorporated association possessing the quality of an entity is that of a labor union. While now addressed by federal legislation, historically the status of a labor union as an entity separate from its members was the subject of much disagreement. *See* Russell G. Pearce, *The Union Lawyer's Obligations to Bargaining Unit Members: A Case Study of the Interdependence of Legal Ethics and Substantive Law,* 37 S. TEX. L. REV. 1095, 1098–1100 (1996).

[133] *See* Hazard & Hodes, *supra* note 59, at § 17–4; *see* note 120 *supra.*

[134] *See, e.g.,* Aviam Soifer, LAW AND THE COMPANY WE KEEP (1995) (exploring the value of collectivity in our society); Lee Anne Fennel, *Properties of Concentration,* 73 U. CHI. L. REV. 1227 (2006) (exploring "associational" property benefits).

[135] *See, e.g.,* Diamond & O'Toole, *supra* note 2, at 510–11 (resisting the application of formal structures on an organic, fluid group); Diamond, *supra* note 1, at 70–72 (referring to well-structured collectivities as "bureaucratic groups," distinguishing them from "extemporaneous groups," and arguing that community groups fit the latter description much better than the former); Southworth, *supra* note 1, at 2465 (noting that community groups often have no duly authorized constituents). *But see* Michael J. Fox, *Some Rules for Community Lawyers,* 14 CLEARINGHOUSE REV. 1, 2 (1980) (suggesting that lawyers for community groups must find a formal set of structures before they may properly represent the groups).

establishes an attorney-client relationship with a group *qua* group, she must ensure several things, things which she would know with some confidence if her client were a formal entity such as an LLC or a corporation. The first of these is rather obvious: The lawyer must insure that the group members recognize themselves as a group. With a loosely-structured group this step is essential, but it is presumably readily accomplished (if perhaps a bit complex in its implementation[136]).

Second, the lawyer must identify which individuals are members of the group. Occasional stories of progressive lawyers representing community groups imply a looser identity of the client constituency,[137] but traditional understandings of privilege, confidentiality, fiduciary duty, conflicts of interest and malpractice require that the lawyer understand with some certainty which persons are her constituents and which are not.[138] A lawyer's conversation with a constituent of her entity client will usually be protected by the attorney-client privilege, while her conversation with a non-constituent (and thus non-client) will obviously

---

[136] Since this Article addresses a lawyer's counseling obligations and responsibilities, we ought to recognize that the lawyer will sometimes need to counsel the group about the benefits of proceeding as a group rather than as a collection of individuals. With a loosely-structured group, that choice is available, unlike with a formal entity such as an LLC, and it is more available if the population of the loosely-structured group is smaller and more easily identified. Of course, in her counseling conversations with the group members, the lawyer must attend to the status of her relationship with each member during that preliminary discussion. It seems inevitable that, for the preliminary purpose of determining how the collection of individuals will constitute themselves, the lawyer will owe some duties to each member individually, which is to say that she will have established a limited attorney-client relationship with each. This conclusion arises from the following reasoning: During her conversations with the group members about whether to proceed as an entity or as individuals (either jointly represented by the lawyer or through separate lawyers), the lawyer is representing *somebody*. She is offering legal advice to people who will use it and rely upon it. *See* RESTATEMENT, *supra* note 50, at § 14 (describing the factors necessary to establish an attorney-client relationship). Since the entity theory cannot yet apply to this interaction (that is the question for the membership to decide), the individual model serves as the default orientation. The lawyer may, then, have to engage in the same kind of conflict of interest warnings that we encountered above in our review of a client's agreement to joint representation. *See* text accompanying notes 63–75 *supra*.

[137] Most of the stories emerging from the community lawyering scholarship describe loosely organized and, as Michael Diamond describes them, "fluid" collectivities. Diamond, *supra* note 1, at 72 ("fluid membership" in community groups). *See also* Bennett, *Embracing the Ill-Structured Problem*, *supra* note 9, at 70 (noting her clinic's common "inquiry not merely into the client's professed goals but into the client's very composition"); Marshall, *supra* note 1, at 148 (describing an "unattached community advocate," without any formal attorney-client relationship); Piomelli, *supra* note 1, at 457 (describing community lawyers "engage[d] with clients and neighborhood residents as partners in a joint effort"); Seielstad, *supra* note 5, at 468–69, n.69 (discussing "moving forward without identifying and officially retaining a cognizable entity or individual as our client").

One apt example of the tension envisioned here is that of a lawyer's negotiating a "community benefits agreement" (CBA) on behalf of a "community" affected by planned development. *See* Patience A. Crowder, *More Than Merely Incidental: Third-Party Beneficiary Rights in Urban Redevelopment Contracts*, 17 GEO. J. ON POVERTY L. & POL'Y 287, 330–32 (2010) (exploring the enforceability of CBAs); Naved Sheikh, *Community Benefits Agreements: Can Private Contracts Replace Public Responsibility?*, 18 CORNELL J.L. & PUB. POL'Y 223, 233–34 (2008) (difficulties with CBAs because of the fluidity of the communities affected).

[138] *Compare* Keating, *supra* note 123, at 413–17 (discussing these issues in the context of representing unincorporated business associations).

not be privileged.[139] A lawyer who assumes incorrectly that a certain individual is a constituent risks revealing confidences to a non-client,[140] waiving an existing privilege,[141] and possibly triggering a conflict of interest.[142] The lawyer obviously needs to know to whom her duties of care lie, and which of the individuals—if any—might have claims against her for malpractice should the representation go awry.[143]

Finally, the lawyer must understand with considerable confidence the decisionmaking structure of the entity.[144] In this way, the notion of a lawyer representing a loosely-structured group almost approaches a tautology, because the lawyer cannot accept such a group as a client unless the group has become, at least in this fashion, well-structured. The reason for this conclusion should be clear. In order for the lawyer to apply the entity theory to her representation, she must accept the organization, not any of its constituents, as her client.[145] The organization, however, cannot advise the lawyer—and, indeed, the organization may not even

---

[139] *See, e.g.,* United States v. Upjohn, 449 U.S. 383 (1981) (organizational attorney-client privilege under federal law); Samaritan Foundation v. Goodfarb, 862 P.2d 870 (Ariz. 1993) (state organizational privilege); RESTATEMENT, *supra* note 50, at § 73 (offering a very broad organizational privilege).

[140] *See* MODEL RULES, *supra* note 52, at R. 1.6.

[141] A privileged communication may be waived by inadvertent disclosure to a non-party. *See* Calvin Klein Trademark Trust v. Wachner, 198 F.R.D. 53 (S.D.N.Y. 2000) (waiver by revelation to public relations firm).

[142] If the lawyer treats a seeming group member as a client, and offers him some legal advice about his circumstances, her representation of her entity client might be jeopardized if that person's interests conflicted with those of the entity. *See, e.g.,* E.F. Hutton v. Brown, 305 F. Supp. 371 (S.D. Tex. 1969) (firm disqualified from representing company after having offered legal services to a former officer).

[143] Some of the community lawyering scholarship envisions a lawyer connected to, and dedicated to, a diffuse community of affected individuals without explicit attention to the question of whether any of those persons could treat the community lawyer as *his* lawyer, and (should things turn out badly) sue the lawyer or law firm for malpractice. *See, e.g.,* Alfieri, *(Un)Covering Identity, supra* note 97, at 832 (describing subgroups within larger community groups); Diamond, *supra* note 1, at 127 (describing working with "resident leadership and its allies" in a community-based housing dispute); Ellmann, *supra* note 11, at 1152 (offering to meet with group members individually); Seielstad, *supra* note 5, at 505 (noting the ethical tensions in group representation but without identifying malpractice worries); *but see* Marshall, *supra* note 1, at 150–51 (addressing the question of client identity and conflicts of interest in community lawyering practices). Of course, if the entity theory applies, as we have assumed it does, none of the constituents of the organization would have a claim against the lawyer based upon a breach of duty of care theory, except through the entity's claims. *See, e.g.,* Palmer v. Fox Software, Inc., 107 F.3d 415 (6th Cir. 1997) (corporate constituent unable to recover against lawyer for malpractice); Waggoner v. Snow, Becker, Kroll, Klaris & Krauss, 991 F.2d 1501 (9th Cir. 1993) (same). That defense available to the lawyer does not, however, minimize her need to understand the status of the individuals with whom she has contact while she works with a loosely-structured group client. "[T]he large volume of case law . . . shows that, whether or not they ultimately win, lawyers for corporations are frequently sued by constituents who claim an attorney-client relationship." *Types of Practice: Client Identity,* Laws. Man. on Prof. Conduct (ABA/BNA) No. 91 at ¶ 10 (2004). While no such cases have arisen in the context of community groups, the potential for such claims is plain.

[144] *See* Bennett, *Little Engines that Could, supra* note 9, at 472–73; Fox, *supra* note 128, at 2.

[145] *See* MODEL RULES, *supra* note 52, at R. 1.13.

retain the lawyer[146]—unless it has an authority-generating voice emerging from some authority-generating process. . . .

2. *Counseling a Loosely-Structured Group*

The exploration thus far has concluded that a lawyer might indeed represent a loosely-defined group as an entity, subject to the guidance of Rule 1.13 and its accompanying substantive law. But, precisely because the group is ill-defined and possibly ambiguous in its membership and in its organizational decisionmaking schemes, the lawyer may not accept the group as a client until she is certain (a) that the group has agreed to proceed as an entity; (b) that the group has a defined an identifiable membership who serve as the constituents of the entity; and (c) that the group has adopted and agreed to a scheme by which to take actions and make binding decisions, including the act of giving authority to its lawyer to proceed with legal work. While stories appear within the public interest literature of lawyers working with collectivities of persons with common shared missions but with fuzzy membership identities and ambiguous leadership arrangements, and while undoubtedly lawyers work with such nebulous groups regularly, the conclusion here is that the laws of agency, professional responsibility and legal malpractice suggest some risks in such a practice. Only by transforming the loosely-defined group into a better-defined group may a lawyer proceed to represent its membership using entity representation principles. . . .

Since we concluded above that a lawyer working for a formal corporation should (or at least may) interact differently with a constituent client compared to an individual client, it is easy to discern here that, at minimum, the same reasoning would apply to a lawyer working with a constituent of an unincorporated association or similar nebulous group client. The more interesting question is whether the lack of a formal corporate-type structure changes the lawyer's role further, or whether we have already addressed this topic when we addressed the setting of the well-structured group. Put another way, our question as refined is this: Are the counseling protocols the same for well-defined and ill-defined group clients, or is there some difference caused by the fuzzier group structures in the latter case?

The fuzzier group structure does seem to create further differences for the lawyer in comparison to her work with a formal corporate structure. Those differences may be separated into two sorts, depending on whether the lawyer works through a constituent of the entity, or works

---

[146] This observation is an inevitable one, but its application in practice is subject to some uncertainty, given the fluidity of group work, especially within low-income communities. Some writers have assumed a lawyering relationship before the group has a decisionmaking structure in place. *See, e.g.,* Ellmann, *supra* note 11, at 1146–53 (discussing the lawyer's role in crafting the decisionmaking schemes with and for the group client).

with the unincorporated association membership as a whole. Let us review each of those areas in order.

Counseling a Loosely-Defined Entity Constituent: The discussion thus far has assumed that the lawyer will work with the unincorporated association through some constituent or constituents. Recall that this assumption departed from some of the writing about public interest lawyers working with community groups, but it seems a reasonable (if assuredly not exclusive) assumption. . . .

This more "activist" role for the lawyer representing a loosely-structured group stems from a number of considerations. The inherent doubts about the representativeness of the leadership in the loosely-structured group suggest a greater responsibility on Kendra's part as the entity's lawyer.[192] The nature of unincorporated associations themselves, and the relationship of a lawyer to such a group, also increases the lawyer's vigilance. It is not unfair to assume that loosely-structured groups tend to be newer and deserve enhanced fiduciary attention from their lawyers. In some respects, the role for the lawyer here resembles that of a lawyer for a class in a class action proceeding. While the considerable substantive and procedural protections governing class actions provide significantly better guidance to plaintiff class lawyers than to the unincorporated association lawyers discussed here,[193] the role of a lawyer for a class *pre-filing* is closer to the present context.[194] In that setting as well in the conventional post-filing context, a lawyer representing a plaintiff class has explicit responsibilities to the unnamed

[192] The analysis in the text rests on a premise which may be questionable. It presumes that in formal groups the lawyer may respect the quality of the leadership in some reasonably reliable way, given the leaders' formal delegation of authority. In practice, of course, organizational leaders' fidelity to organizational goals is intrinsically subject to question. *See, e.g.*, Donald C. Langevoort, *The Human Nature of Corporate Boards: Law, Norms, and the Unintended Consequences of Independence and Accountability*, 89 GEO. L. REV. 797 (2001).

[193] *See* Nancy J. Moore, *Who Should Regulate Class Action Lawyers?*, 2003 U. ILL. L. REV. 1477 (2003); Susan P. Koniak, *Feasting While the Widow Weeps:* Georgine v. Amchem Products, Inc., 80 CORNELL L. REV. 1045 (1995); Deborah L. Rhode, *Class Conflicts in Class Actions,* 34 STAN. L. REV. 1183 (1982).

[194] A lawyer who represents a purported class before a lawsuit is filed owes a duty to the class. *See* FED. R. CIV. P. 23(g)(2)(A), 2003 Advis. Comm. Notes ("Settlement may be discussed before certification. . . . Whether or not formally designated interim counsel, an attorney who acts on behalf of a class before certification must act in the best interests of the class as a whole. For example, an attorney who negotiates a pre-certification settlement must seek a settlement that is fair, reasonable, and adequate for the class."); MANUAL FOR COMPLEX LITIGATION § 21.12 at 337 & n. 753 (4th ed. 2007) ("Rule 23 and the case law make clear that, even before certification or a formal attorney-client relationship, an attorney acting on behalf of a putative class must act in the best interest of the class as a whole."); 2 Hazard & Hodes, *supra* note 59, at § 38.4, at 38–7 (lawyers for the proposed class owes class members "duties of loyalty and care"); Piambino v. Bailey, 757 F.2d 1112, 1144 (2d Cir. 1985) (duty triggered because counsel, by "asserting a representative role," "voluntarily accepted a fiduciary obligation towards the members of the putative class"); In re M&F Worldwide Corp. Shareholders Litig., 799 A.2d 1164, 1174 n.34 (Del. Ch. Ct. 2002) ("[I]t is well established that by asserting a representative role on behalf of a proposed class, representative plaintiffs and their counsel voluntarily accept a fiduciary obligation towards members of the putative class.").

class members, and may resist the suggestions of a named plaintiff whose choices are not deemed to be in the best interests of the collectivity.[195]

Especially when the loosely-structured group is large enough to make counseling the entire group impractical (likely a common phenomenon in neighborhood-based community group representation), the lawyer working with the group's leadership shares the responsibilities of a class lawyer to ensure that the leaders' views are consonant with the aims and goals of the larger group.[196] The lawyer's "activism" with the leadership will depend also on how well the lawyer herself understands the group's aims and goals. . . .

Counseling a Loosely-Defined Entity Through Its Membership: Stephen Ellmann has examined the dynamics of a lawyer counseling a group client without the use of constituents, and his analysis is invaluable on this topic. While Ellmann does not articulate a concern about the finite population of the group client, and in particular with the role of members (or purported members) absent from the meeting itself (a topic we discuss in a moment), and while he suggests a provocative tactic involving individual meetings between the lawyer and the members (which we also address below), his assessment of the counseling process is quite insightful for our purposes. Comparing that interaction with the conventional Binder & Price model of client counseling, Ellmann notes that the exploration with the client about goals and what he calls the client's "values" has to be different when working in a meeting of many individuals who likely do not share the same preferences and risk gauges. His wise conclusion is that the lawyer must be much more general and vague about that topic compared to the work a lawyer would engage in with an individual client. The traditional Binder & Price counseling model suggests that the lawyer explore with her client in some detail the client's goals and preferences as a necessary precursor to effective counseling. Ellmann observes that such a step is more challenging and likely to be less effective when working with a larger group. . . .

Ellmann views the problem of the group dynamics, and the participatory quality of the deliberations, as a central concern for the lawyer working with a loosely-structured group client.[210] He asserts that the lawyer has an obligation to "assur[e] a baseline of democratic and participative process within the group,"[211] even if doing so might be

---

[195] *See* In re M & F Worldwide Corp. Shareholders Litigation, 799 A.2d 1164, 1175 (2002) ("Counsel in class action . . . owed a duty to act in good faith on behalf of all interested beneficiaries of the representative action, and not simply at the direction of the named plaintiffs.").

[196] Michael Diamond and Aaron O'Toole make this point. *See* Diamond & O'Toole, *supra* note 2, at 512–15.

[210] Ellmann, *supra* note 11, at 1131–32.

[211] *Id.* at 1145.

understood as an exercise in benevolent paternalism.[212] To Ellmann, that means intervening in the group meeting to insure that those members who may be less vocal, or who may be intimidated by the group's leadership, have an opportunity to be heard.[213] He even suggests that the lawyer "might . . . make plain to each member of the group that she is always available to talk to any one of them *individually and in private*."[214] In this way, he argues, the lawyer can best serve her group client by fostering participatory, democratic decisionmaking.

Ellmann's observations trigger intriguing questions about the responsibilities of a lawyer for a loosely-structured group. While Ellmann's subject is explicitly community group representation,[215] his arguments raise important questions about group representation generally. Despite the power of his recommendations, it is difficult to accept them as best practices principles for group work outside of the community group setting.

Ellmann's insistence that a lawyer for an entity foster democratic and participatory processes for the client's deliberation seems to conflate the understanding of the lawyer for an aggregate of clients and that of the lawyer for an entity. Putting aside the difficulty with his quoted activist lawyer telling her group client members that she represents them individually, and not just the group's leadership,[216] the premise of the lawyer advising each constituent individually is difficult to square with the underlying conception of entity, rather than aggregate, representation. If we assume that Ellmann's lawyer would warn each such individual group member appropriately of the lawyer's fiduciary obligations toward the group as a whole and not to that individual, as Rule 1.13(f) requires, the arrangement he proposes only seems to work if

---

[212] *Id.* at 1146 n. 113.

[213] *Id.* at 1152. Ellmann refers to the silent group members as "victims within the group itself." *Id.*

[214] *Id.* (emphasis added). Ellmann describes a practicing lawyer's sentiments in support of this recommendation: "[The lawyer] wants the individual members to know 'that though I'm representing the group, the group is composed of individuals, and *I'm representing each individual* . . . and not, say, just the [group's] leaders.' " *Id.* (emphasis added) (quoting Ellmann's private interview with attorney Judith Whiting).

[215] *Id.* at 1104 (describing his context as "public interest lawyers' representation of groups," which I infer to refer to community groups).

[216] *See* text accompanying note 214 *supra*. The quote from Judith Whiting captures a sentiment which is at once understandable and, well, wrong as a matter of substantive law. Assuming (as seems to be the case given Ellmann's purposes in situating her quote) that she has opted for entity representation (under Rule 1.13) and not joint representation (under Rule 1.7), Whiting does not represent the individuals, just as she does not represent the leadership. Her desire to communicate to the rank and file of the community group the sense that she has no special allegiance to the leadership but instead has a commitment to the larger group is admirable, given the former's potential distrust of the group's hierarchy. But to say that she does not have a special representational relationship with the leadership is problematic, given the strictures of Rule 1.13. *See* MODEL RULES, *supra* note 52, at R. 1.13(a). Whiting's obligation as a lawyer would be to honor the wishes of the leadership if, in fact, the leadership served as the proxy for the group. *See* Fox & Martyn, *supra* note 128, at 76.

the group as an entity has agreed to that process for its decisionmaking. If Ellmann is advocating that the lawyer suggest such an arrangement on behalf of the group client, his argument is difficult to square with the usual commitment to client autonomy. . . .

Ellmann suggests that when engaged in that mediation the lawyer take pains not to be identified as supporting one faction over the other, while Diamond and O'Toole see that happenstance as often inevitable and not necessarily a bad thing. The underlying commitments of the Binder & Price counseling model tend to confirm Ellmann's worry about the lawyer's expressing her support for one bloc at the expense of another. But those commitments, as we have seen, have less clout in the organizational context. The mandate within Rule 1.13 that the organizational lawyer attend to "the best interest of the organization" informs the lawyer's duty to be a neutral, objective analyst, and might at times require her to resist the arguments of some subsection of the membership and to advocate the views of others. . . .

We are nearing the end of our examination of the lawyer's responsibilities when counseling a loosely-structured group client. We have one final topic awaiting us: What level of deference ought the lawyer pay to the group's deliberation? Put another way, how interventionist may the lawyer be when counseling the group as a whole? This question emerges from the context of our earlier discussions about neutrality and directiveness. We recognized the baseline moral commitment to neutrality when working with an individual client, out of respect for the individual client's personal preferences and risk aversion.[242] We then concluded that the moral calculus changes when the lawyer counsels a constituent of an entity client, with even less deference due when the constituent represents a loosely-structured group or unincorporated association.[243] Critical to the moral analysis was the recognition that the constituent, the person speaking with the lawyer, was not the client whose preferences need to be respected and only possessed a presumptive right to express the entity client's preferences and comfort level with risk. The fact that the constituent was at best an imperfect proxy for the true client served as a morally relevant consideration in discerning the responsibility of the lawyer during the counseling process.

When the lawyer counsels the group as a whole, the moral calculus changes again. The setting now resembles far more closely that of a lawyer with her individual client. The morally germane proxy element is now gone, and the group's choice—putting aside, for now, any consideration of its being a "community group" with whatever added commitments that designation might imply—accurately represents the

---

[242] *See* text accompanying notes 26–27 *supra.*

[243] *See* text accompanying notes 96–106 *supra.*

client's wishes. Note that this is a separate question from that of how the lawyer *discerns* the group's wishes, a matter we encountered above. But once discerned, or in the process of its development, the lawyer has little moral right to influence its direction.

Ellmann's review of the group counseling process concurs with this conclusion.[244] His arguments rest not only on the fact that the client as a whole is expressing its preferences,[245] but upon a more subtle realization as well, one that serves as a contrast to, rather than a similarity with, individual client counseling. With an individual client, once the lawyer understands the client's needs, preferences and comfort with risk, the lawyer might engage the client in a relatively active and even challenging fashion to account for any perceived disconnect between the strategy chosen by the client and the expressed commitments.[246] When working with a group client, Ellmann notes, the lawyer can never be confident enough about the group's commitments, preferences, and risk comfort, precisely because the group members will have a multitude of opinions and differing feelings. Lacking a sufficiently full understanding of the client's true commitments, the most effective role for the lawyer might be to oversee the decisionmaking *process* within the group to ensure that the membership's decisions are fair and coherent.[247] The lawyer, by this reasoning, would have little or no responsibility for the *content* of the group's decisions.

Two considerations might diminish the power of this conclusion, however. The first is equally applicable to a lawyer's work with an individual client. Most observers agree that lawyers bear some responsibility for the moral consequences of the work they perform for

---

[244] Ellmann, *supra* note 11, at 1164.

[245] Recall that Ellmann's analysis of group client decisionmaking treats the default orientation as a lawyer working with a group as a whole, rather than the default orientation adopted in this Article, which assumes that any functioning group client will need to have some rudimentary bureaucratic structure in place, and therefore the lawyer will work most often with constituent/leaders. Recall also the Diamond and O'Toole observation that most community groups will not be, and ought not be, "bureaucratic" groups as this Article suggests. *See* Diamond & O'Toole, *supra* note 2, at 514–15. For reasons developed throughout this article, that sanguine stance on the part of O'Toole and Diamond, while admirable, cannot square with the demands of the law of lawyering.

[246] *See, e.g.,* LAWYERS AS COUNSELORS, *supra* note 13, at 368–69; Krieger & Newmann, *supra* note 19, at 273–74; Cochran, DiPippa & Peters, *supra* note 19, at 155. The lawyer has no obligation to insist that the client choose the strategic option which best comports with the client's expressed preferences and penchants, of course, or to influence the client to do so. The client's actual choice may express those preferences more soundly than the client's *ex ante* articulation of them. *See* Lehrer, *supra* note 28, at 232–38; Kruse, *Fortress in the Sand, supra* note 24, at 422–23. But nor should the lawyer ignore an apparent inconsistency between what the client professes to want and what the client then chooses. *See* LAWYERS AS COUNSELORS, at 398–99.

[247] Ellmann, *supra* note 11, at 1164 ("the role of [the lawyer's] advice frequently may be more to inform further debate than to bring the [group] client to a quick resolution of uncertainty").

and with their clients.[248] The second consideration applies to organizational clients. As Richard Painter notes, because of the nature of entity clients operating through constituents, the relationship between the group's decisionmaking and the lawyer's input is quite "interdependent."[249] In Painter's words,

> [D]ebate over the relative merits of lawyer and client autonomy may be moot. Corporations are not autonomous, but rather corporate decisions are made by people standing behind the corporate entities: directors, officers, employees, and lawyers. Lawyers' choice is not whether to participate in making clients' decisions, but what type of participation theirs will be.[250]

IV. COUNSELING COMMUNITY GROUP CLIENTS

To appreciate adequately the counseling responsibilities for lawyers working with community groups, our preliminary aim has been to unpack those responsibilities as they apply to *group* clients generally. We have seen so far that a lawyer representing a group client must attend to a number of important strategic and ethical considerations. To complete our mission, we now inquire about the further special responsibilities, if any there are, for lawyers whose group clients are *community groups.*

This part concludes that the *community* quality matters. Once we articulate what we mean by the term "community group," we will see that a lawyer for such a group will find her role altered in three possible ways. First, because most community groups share (and often expressly commit to) a public mission, its counsel might assume responsibilities different from lawyers representing clients, whether group or individual, whose mission is principally private. Second, when representing a community group, including one that retains a private mission, a lawyer might need to attend in a different way to the oppression and structural power deficits of the group's members. Finally, and related to the second point but seemingly a different manner, a community group counsel might respond to her group client's experience of oppression in ways which appear less neutral and less deferential, in an effort to establish more

---

[248] A widely accepted exception to the standard conception of the lawyer's respecting client decisionmaking is when the client chooses an unlawful or an immoral course of action. In that setting, a lawyer has the responsibility to intervene, and that intervention, of course, is not an exercise in paternalism. *See, e.g.,* David Luban, LAWYERS AND JUSTICE: AN ETHICAL STUDY 160–74 (1988); Robert W. Gordon, *Why Lawyers Can't Just Be Hired Guns, in* ETHICS IN PRACTICE: LAWYERS' ROLES, RESPONSIBILITIES, AND REGULATION 42 (Deborah L. Rhode ed., 2000); Deborah L. Rhode, *Moral Counseling,* 75 FORDHAM L. REV. 1317 (2006). *See also* LAWYERS AS COUNSELORS, *supra* note 13, at 391–93 (counseling clients about moral issues).

[249] Richard W. Painter, The Moral Interdependence of Corporate Lawyers and Their Clients, 61 S. CAL. L. REV. 507 (1994).

[250] *Id.* at 517. Many observers agree, both in the conventional corporate arena, *see, e.g.,* Donald C. Langevoort, *Someplace Between Philosophy and Economics: Legitimacy and Good Corporate Lawyering,* 75 FORDHAM L. REV. 1615 (2006) [hereinafter, Langevoort, *Good Corporate Lawyering*], and in the community lawyering context, *see, e.g.,* Diamond & O'Toole, *supra* note 2.

favorable conditions for its members' eventual autonomy development. As the discussion below will show, these three observations are each quite tentative and contested. We begin, however, with the preliminary definitional question.

A. *Defining "Community Groups"*

For purposes of this discussion, we may consider a group client to constitute a "community group" if its members are economically and politically powerless and have joined together for collective aims related in some way to their plight of powerlessness.[251] This definition encompasses all kinds of underrepresented and oppressed groups. The counsel for the community groups most likely will be in some fashion "public interest" lawyers[252] (including law firm lawyers serving in a pro bono capacity[253]), but not necessarily so, as some groups fitting this description will hire private counsel for its legal work. For our purposes, it does not matter whether the lawyers whose work this part addresses are privately paid or publicly- or foundation-funded.

The definition here excludes, of course, most purely private groups which have banded together for private gain. While the earlier discussion of group representation applied equally well to profit-driven business entities and activist civic organizations, this discussion excludes the former organizations. Some groups banding together for private gain will fit within the definition, though, such as a low-income tenants' association[254] or even some merchants associations.[255] The critical question is whether the membership consists of those without a fair share of economic or political power, and whether the aims of the group include some increased share of assets, wealth, or power. The definition used here

---

[251] *See, e.g.*, Bennett, *Little Engines that Could, supra* note 1, at 472; Diamond & O'Toole, *supra* note 2, at 483; Richard G. Lorenz, *Good Fences Make Bad Neighbors,* 33 URB. LAW. 45, 79 (2001) (noting the powerlessness of community groups) (citing Laurence Susskind et al., NEGOTIATING ENVIRONMENTAL AGREEMENTS: HOW TO AVOID ESCALATING CONFRONTATION, NEEDLESS COSTS, AND UNNECESSARY LITIGATION 17, 21 (2000)).

[252] *See* Ellmann, *supra* note 11, at 1105 (focusing on public interest lawyers, whom he describes as "lawyers whose work is aimed at achieving social reform on behalf of people who would otherwise lack adequate representation").

[253] *See* Scott L. Cummings, *The Politics of Pro Bono,* 52 UCLA L. REV. 1 (2004); Scott L. Cummings & Deborah L. Rhode, *Public Interest Litigation: Insights from Theory and Practice*, 36 FORDHAM URB. L.J. 603, 621 (2009).

[254] *See, e.g.*, Diamond & O'Toole, *supra* note 2, at 490–91 (describing a building-wide group of tenants as a community group).

[255] *See* Bennett, *Little Engines that Could, supra* note 1, at 472 (noting that most merchant associations do not qualify as public charities despite their connection to community economic development). Several civic improvement organizations with "Main Streets Program"-related missions have qualified for 501(c)(3) status. *See, e.g.,* Matthew J. Parlow, *Civic Republicanism, Public Choice Theory, and Neighborhood Councils: A New Model for Civic Engagement,* 79 U. COLO. L. REV. 137, 175 (2008) (describing neighborhood councils organized as 501(c)(3) entities), *citing* Jeffrey M. Berry et al., THE REBIRTH OF URBAN DEMOCRACY 58–59 (1993); Treas. Reg. § 1.501(c)(3)–1(d)(2) (2004) (the term "charitable" includes "promotion of social welfare by organizations designed to accomplish [such] purposes . . . [as] (i) to lessen neighborhood tensions; . . . or (iv) to combat community deterioration").

easily includes the client groups which are the subject of the community lawyering literature.[256]

The definition articulated here elides many rich and fascinating debates within the community lawyering scholarship. At least for definitional purposes, it does not matter whether the community group is "representative" of the community for whom it purports to speak.[257] (That factor may matter, however, for some parts of our consideration of the lawyer's responsibilities.) Nor does it matter for our purposes what we define as a relevant "community"—whether a geographic locale or some other basis to apply that term.[258] The definition chosen here applies regardless of where one comes out on that issue.

With this understanding of a "community group," let us now investigate the role responsibilities for the counsel for such a group, building upon the previous development of group representation duties generally.

B. *Counseling Groups with a Public Mission*

Most (although clearly not all) community groups possess a public mission. For such a client, its membership has formed the entity[259] in order to attain some benefits beyond those of the individual entity's formal constituents. Many of those groups will have made their public missions explicit and non-negotiable, by forming a state nonprofit corporation and seeking tax exempt status from the Internal Revenue Service.[260] Not all nonprofits qualify as community groups, of course, and not all community groups qualify as nonprofits, but a significant subset of community groups will fit within this rubric. Let us consider, then, whether the fact of such a public mission affects the counseling strategies of the lawyer for the organization.

---

[256] For a sampling of that literature discussing the types of groups described here, see Alfieri, *(Un)Covering Identity, supra* note 97, at 831; Diamond, *supra* note 1, at 75; Ellmann, *supra* note 11, at 1111; Marshall, *supra* note 1, at 173; Rubenstein, *supra* note 240; Seielstad, *supra* note 5, at 449; Daniel Shah, *Lawyering for Empowerment: Community Development and Social Change*, 6 CLINICAL L. REV. 217, 233 (1999); White, *Facing South, supra* note 3, at 814.

[257] *See* Bennett, *Little Engines that Could, supra* note 1, at 474 (discussing that tension in her clinical work).

[258] As Nancy Cook has written, the concept of community is "vaguely defined and often only vaguely understood." Nancy Cook, *Looking for Justice on a Two-Way Street*, 20 WASH. U. J.L. & POL'Y 169, 191 (2006). For others who wrestle with this topic, see Sameer M. Ashar, *Law Clinics and Collective Mobilization*, 14 CLINICAL L. REV. 355, 356 (2008); Brodie, *supra* note 222, at 343–44; John O. Calmore, *A Call to Context: The Professional Challenges of Cause Lawyering at the Intersection of Race, Space, and Poverty*, 67 FORDHAM L. REV. 1927, 1937 (1999); Diamond, *supra* note 1, at 113–14; Robin S. Golden, *Toward a Model of Community Representation for Legal Assistance Lawyering: Examining the Role of Legal Assistance Agencies in Drug-Related Evictions from Public Housing*, 17 YALE L. & POL'Y REV. 527, 531 (1998).

[259] As the earlier discussion has shown, we must consider all community groups to be a form of "entity," even if the group is a loosely-structured entity. *See* text accompanying notes 123–34 *supra*.

[260] I.R.C. § 501(c)(3) (2006).

Given the analytical and moral premises upon which the previous counseling practices have been constructed—beginning with an individual client, and then comparing that to a constituent of an entity, and to the entity membership as a whole—a lawyer representing a community group client possesses some discretion, and perhaps an obligation, to intervene more actively in the decisionmaking of that client than in any of the previous contexts, in order to ensure the client's faithful pursuit of its public mission. The default commitment to deference and neutrality which characterizes the conventional counseling models rests on a coherent anti-paternalist sentiment, one grounded in deep respect for the autonomy of the private actor clients. The notion of respect for a client's "idiosyncrasies"[261] exemplifies that dedication to autonomy. With community groups devoted to an explicit public mission, the autonomy premise weakens considerably, as does the notion of honoring idiosyncrasy.[262]

The idea of a more activist lawyer role in this context garners support not just from the theories upon which counseling best practices are built, but on another public policy argument as well. William Simon, who advocates the more general position that entity lawyers ought to play a more activist role in discerning the most appropriate stance for the organizational client, points out that charitable organizations in particular can benefit from a lawyer's oversight.[263] Simon's point is that, because constituents of a charitable organization may not always be faithful to the charitable purpose of the entity, the lawyer's role ought to incorporate oversight of that commitment and intervention when necessary. He writes, "Given the relative weakness of monitoring [by the

[261] *See* text accompanying notes 26–27 *supra*.

[262] The arguments here intentionally distinguish a client's strategy to achieve *private* gain and a strategy to achieve *public* benefits. Several colleagues remain skeptical about that distinction. The arguments rest on a well-accepted premise within American law that individuals may act rashly or foolishly when their own property is at stake, and when they do so knowingly. That commitment is foundational to the anti-paternalist strain in American law. *See* Spiegel, *supra* note 6, at 74–77; Cass R. Sunstein, *Legal Interference with Private Preferences,* 53 U. CHI. L. REV. 1129, 1131–32 (1986). The argument then asserts a well-established converse proposition, holding that none of us may act rashly or foolishly with others' property to which we have been entrusted. *See, e.g.,* Joseph T. Walsh, *The Fiduciary Foundation of Corporate Law*, 27 J. CORP. L. 333, 333–35 (2002). The distinction, then, seems a sound one.

The difficulty arises from my applying that distinction to organizations. In organizations with shareholders distinct from management, the lawyer's responsibilities approach those I apply to community groups with public missions. *See, e.g.,* Einer Elhauge, *Sacrificing Corporate Profits in the Public Interest*, 80 N.Y.U. L. REV. 733, 756–76 (2005) (acknowledging the traditional commitment to shareholders but advocating a broader duty); Langevoort, *Good Corporate Lawyering, supra* note 250, at 1618–20. In smaller, close corporations, the right to act rashly might be more easily understood.

[263] Simon, *Intraclient Conflict, supra* note 85, at 112–13. For a discussion of Simon's "Framework of Dealing" approach to entity representation, see text accompanying note 107 *supra*.

IRS or state officials], it is arguable that the professional responsibilities of lawyers are exceptionally important in this sphere."[264]

In light of Simon's public policy argument, it is important to distinguish three counseling contexts for a lawyer representing a nonprofit community group. First, to fit Simon's argument into our analytic fabric, it is not terribly controversial to assert that the lawyer representing a tax-exempt organization may resist her client's constituents' plans when those plans breach the entity's duties under applicable IRS guidelines. All counseling models understand that respect for autonomy does not include respect for law-breaking,[265] and it is hard to imagine a best practices protocol which would discourage a lawyer from such resistance with charitable organizations.[266]

Second, to the extent that Simon's suggestion might be seen as applying to entity constituents' rather direct breach of fiduciary responsibility or federal law commitments, the proposal advanced here is broader than that. The intervention and diminished deference supported here are not triggered only by lawlessness. A lawyer representing a community group has discretion to intervene with, and engage, her client constituents about the wisdom of their pursuit of the entity's public mission. Unlike the case with an individual client, a community group lawyer need not be agnostic about issues of civic policy, community needs, or the public interest. It may be true, of course, that a lawyer may lack any such wisdom or expertise in any particular setting, in which case the lawyer would assume a conventional, neutral counseling stance.[267] But nothing in the theory underlying effective counseling strategy requires that neutrality as a matter of course. If the lawyer possesses expertise

---

[264] *Id.* at 113.

[265] See, e.g., LAWYERS AS COUNSELORS, supra note 13, at 328–30; KRIEGER & NEWMANN, supra note 19, at 277. See generally, Stephen L. Pepper, Counseling at the Limits of the Law: An Exercise in Jurisprudence and the Ethics of Lawyering, 104 YALE L.J. 1545 (1995).

[266] Some prominent law-and-economics scholars may disagree on this score, at least with for-profit organizations beholden to shareholders. Judge Frank Easterbrook and Professor Daniel Fischel famously argue that corporate management has a duty to violate the law when doing so benefits the firm. *See* Frank H. Easterbrook & Daniel R. Fischel, *Antitrust Suits by Targets of Tender Offers,* 80 MICH. L. REV. 1155, 1177 n.57 ("[M]anagers not only may but should violate the rules when it is profitable to do so."). For an in-depth critique of the Easterbrook & Fischel position, see Greenfield, *supra* note 209, at 73–75. The Easterbrook & Fischel thesis seems to have little applicability to management of a nonprofit organization, of course. That interesting theoretical debate notwithstanding, the substantive law of lawyering generally prohibits lawyer participation in wrongdoing, and certainly permits lawyer resistance of wrongdoing. *See, e.g.,* RESTATEMENT, *supra* note 50, at § 94(2); MODEL RULES, *supra* note 52, at R. 1.2 (lawyer may not assist client in crime or fraud); R. 2.1 (lawyer may counsel a client about moral and prudential considerations); Donald C. Langevoort, *Where Were the Lawyers?: A Behavioral Inquiry into Lawyers' Responsibility for Client Fraud,* 46 VAND. L. REV. 75 (1993).

[267] For a comparable protocol regarding ethical decisionmaking generally, see William H. Simon, *Ethical Discretion in Lawyering,* 101 HARV. L. REV. 1083 (1988) (arguing that the more reliable a law provision's purposes are, the less responsibility a lawyer possesses for achieving justice, and the less reliable the scheme, the greater the responsibility of the lawyer).

about the public mission strategy about which the constituents needs to decide, her client is better off having heard the lawyer's opinion.

The third point follows from the second to suggest a critical distinction, one related closely to the observations appearing in the next Subpart. There may exist a tension within the community group representation between the most effective pursuit of its public mission and the effectiveness, solidarity, or sustainability of the community group.[268] This tension is likely to arise especially within community groups whose members are poor, less sophisticated, or victims of structural oppression.[269] It is not at all implausible for a lawyer to conclude that her intervention on policy and mission issues adds substantial value to the group's deliberation about those issues. The counseling model outlined here permits such intervention on the "public mission" front, but such intervention may have serious disruptive consequences for the group process and cohesion.[270] A responsible lawyer will exercise her discretion delicately to minimize the latter effect while attempting to achieve the former goal.

C. Building Community

This subpart addresses from a "best practices" perspective a vibrant theme within the community lawyering literature—the responsibility of the counsel for community organizations to foster solidarity within the group, to promote democracy,[271] and to "build community."[272] Tellingly, but not surprisingly, one does not encounter those exhortations in the scholarship about corporate lawyering generally.[273] The question we

[268] I understand this to be the argument proffered by Diamond and O'Toole. *See* Diamond & O'Toole, *supra* note 2, at 482.

[269] This assertion requires delicate clarification, as well as acknowledgement of its tentative quality. To the extent that achievement of certain public policy objectives depends upon expertise, sophistication, and experience, it is neither unfair nor narrow-minded to predict that an educated lawyer is as likely to possess those qualities as persons with less education, sophistication, and experience. Recognizing that, though, does not imply a disrespect for the insights and experience of those community members who have suffered the most as a result of the policies which the group seeks to change. This is a central mission of Gerald López's writing. *See* López, *supra* note 1, at 66–74; *see also,* Anthony Alfieri, *Practicing Community, supra* note 2.

[270] *See* Diamond & O'Toole, *supra* note 2, at 483; Shah, *supra* note 256, at 236–40. For a thoughtful assessment of the lawyer's role in working with grass-roots organizations in the Third World, see David A. Wirth, *Legitimacy, Accountability, and Partnership: A Model for Advocacy on Third World Environmental Issues*, 100 YALE L.J. 2645 (1991).

[271] See Bennett, Little Engines that Could, supra note 1, at 479–82; Lucie White, "Democracy" in Development Practice: Essays on a Fugitive Theme, 64 TENN. L. REV. 1073, 1076 (1997).

[272] See Robert L. Bach, Building Community Among Diversity: Legal Services for Impoverished Immigrants, 27 U. MICH. J. L. REF. 639 (1994); Seielstad, supra note 5.

[273] In some respects, one encounters the opposite sentiments—that corporate clients have so much power as to be dangerous, and so corporate lawyers ought to serve as gatekeepers and monitors. *See, e.g.,* John C. Coffee, Jr., *Understanding Enron: "It's About the Gatekeepers, Stupid,"* 57 BUS. LAW. 1403 (2002); Roger C. Cramton, *Enron and the Corporate Lawyer: A Primer on Legal and Ethics Issues*, 58 BUS. LAW. 143 (2002); Robert W. Gordon, *A New Role for Lawyers?: The Corporate Counselor After Enron*, 35 CONN. L. REV. 1185 (2003); Susan P. Koniak, *Corporate Fraud: See, Lawyers*, 26 HARV. J.L. & PUB. POL'Y 195 (2003) (all commenting on that

confront here is whether what we might call for convenience this "empowerment theory"[274] affects in a tangible way the counseling responsibilities of a lawyer representing a community group. Note the difference between this issue and the previous one. This question applies to all community groups, including those which would not qualify for tax-exempt status because the membership aims to produce a form of "private inurement."[275] If the lawyer possesses some special commitments, they will not emerge from the public mission quality of the group client's existence.

It is useful to separate the strands of arguments in place within the empowerment theory claims. One central insight within the empowerment theory is the observation that community lawyers risk reproducing hierarchy and institutionalizing oppression by their habits of defining client needs within narrow legal categories, exploiting legal expertise to minimize the participation of citizens, and otherwise dominating or distorting group processes.[276] That insight is powerful, not terribly in dispute, and, seemingly, addressed conceptually by the strategic and moral considerations central to all of the preceding discussion. In that sense, it is easy to embrace this critical stance. Community lawyers will adopt a respectful and humble posture in their work with their clients.

But do the critics expect more? Consider one possible implication of the empowerment theory stance. Just as powerless group members ought not to be dominated by the professional lawyers in suits, it is similarly true (one might infer) that powerless group members ought not to be dominated by the more vocal and educated leaders within the

---

theme in the context of the Enron matter). Many observers perceive the Sarbanes-Oxley scheme as a manifestation of that worry. *See, e.g.*, Robert B. Ahdieh, *From "Federalization" to "Mixed Governance" in Corporate Law: A Defense of Sarbanes-Oxley*, 53 BUFF. L. REV. 721 (2005); James Fanto, *A Social Defense of Sarbanes-Oxley*, 52 N.Y.L. SCH. L. REV. 517 (2008); Peter Kostant, *From Lapdog to Watchdog: Sarbanes-Oxley Section 307 and a New Role for Corporate Lawyers*, 52 N.Y.L. SCH. L. REV. 535 (2008); Robert A. Prentice & David B. Spence, *Sarbanes-Oxley as Quack Corporate Governance: How Wise Is the Received Wisdom?*, 95 GEO. L.J. 1843 (2007).

[274] The "empowerment" term is commonly used as a moral commitment of progressive lawyers. See, e.g., Piomelli, supra note 1; Spencer Rand, Teaching Law Students to Practice Social Justice: An Interdisciplinary Search for Help Through Social Work's Empowerment Approach, 13 CLINICAL L. REV. 459 (2006); William P. Quigley, Reflections of Community Organizers: Lawyering for Empowerment of Community Organizations, 21 OHIO N.U. L. REV. 455 (1994); Shah, supra note 256.

[275] The Internal Revenue Service will deny tax exempt status to a purported nonprofits if the entity permits "private inurement"—that is, that constituents will receive some private gain from the entity's work. *See* I.R.C. § 501(c)(3) ("no part of the net earnings [may] inure[ ] to the benefit of any private shareholder or individual"); *see* Darryll K. Jones, *The Scintilla of Individual Profit: In Search of Private Inurement and Excess Benefit*, 19 VA. TAX REV. 575 (2000) (examining that factor).

[276] *See* Alfieri, *Impoverished Practices, supra* note 1, at 2592–95; Ascanio Piomelli, *Appreciating Collaborative Lawyering*, 6 CLINICAL L. REV. 427, 437–42 (2000).

community.[277] To the extent that corporate law principles applied to the community group setting require the lawyer to honor the instructions of the entity's "duly authorized constituents,"[278] the paradigmatic counseling responsibility of a community group lawyer might serve to "reproduce hierarchy,"[279] even when the lawyer adopts the respectful and humble posture just described. The empowerment theory might suggest to a community lawyer that she resist autocratic leadership (even if "duly authorized") and work more directly with the membership. Indeed, we have seen such suggestions before in the context of group clients generally, and rejected them as inconsistent with the governing ethical regime.[280]

We have now identified what seems to be a tension between the moral obligation of a community lawyer to foster membership power and the legal/ethical obligation that the lawyer respect the hierarchy within the organization. Of course, if leadership is committed to membership empowerment, the tension dissipates. If leadership is unreceptive to active membership involvement (whether for pragmatic or less honorable reasons), the principles we discerned above showing an entity's lawyer having greater discretion to intervene in counseling a constituent would apply here. The persistent critique of the empowerment theory serves a beneficial purpose for the community lawyer, serving as a constant reminder that her mission with her group client is both to respect the instructions of leadership but always with an eye toward increasing the felt stake of the membership in the resulting processes and decisions.

Let us, then, address one further implication of the empowerment theory critique before we move to our final subpart on the community group topic. The previous subpart noted that a lawyer working with a "public mission" community group (such as a recognized nonprofit) possesses both discretion and, at times, an arguable obligation to encourage the entity client to achieve its public mission, even if the constituents of the entity might disagree with the lawyer's proposals. That subpart noted the tension between that interventionist possibility and the empowerment theory stance, since lawyer intervention tends to imply some lawyer control and possible domination.[281] The present discussion regarding the tension between following the wishes of the entity's "duly authorized constituents" and empowering the membership invites further consideration of the "public mission" posture.

---

[277] Diamond & O'Toole recognize this risk. *See* Diamond & O'Toole, *supra* note 2, at 535–36.

[278] MODEL RULES, *supra* note 52, at R. 1.13(a).

[279] Brodie, *supra* note 222, at 375; Duncan Kennedy, *Legal Education and the Reproduction of Hierarchy, in* THE POLITICS OF LAW 40, 50 (David Kairys ed., 1982).

[280] *See* text accompanying notes 167–68 *supra*.

[281] *See* text accompanying notes 268–70 *supra*.

Imagine the following, then: The nonprofit entity's leadership recommends a certain action as the best avenue to achieve its public mission, but (as the lawyer discovers) many within the community group membership disagree. The lawyer, for her part, believes that leadership is correct on this call, and that the dissenting members, while acting in good faith, are wrong. The responsibility of the lawyer in this thin story is quite clear—her legal obligations and her moral obligations are in sync, and she may respect the instructions of leadership. In doing so, though, the lawyer has not fostered the power of the membership very well, and, indeed, has used her expertise and her professional position to exert some control over the members. She therefore accepts critique on the empowerment theory front. The point is that empowerment as a goal is one among many, and, while it will always serve as a critical factor in the lawyer's moral calculus, it is not a trump.

D. *Alienation, Oppression, and Positive Freedom*

A simplified view of the empowerment theory and the standard client-centered approach to client counseling shows substantial harmony among their respective goals. The Binder & Price model fundamentally resists techniques of lawyer control;[282] the critics espousing the empowerment theory rail against the persistence of lawyer domination, especially with poor and subordinated clients.[283] A more sophisticated perspective on the lawyer domination topic, however, questions that apparent symmetry. The "refined view" of the critical perspective understands the "autonomy" goals of both projects as not equating to what a client (whether group or individual) happens to choose. A good faith lawyer, as a fiduciary for her client's genuine needs and desires, may resist actively that client's immediate choices. If that sounds like a form of lawyer domination—well, perhaps it is, but it may not necessarily be morally troublesome.

Katherine Kruse is one commentator adopting the more sophisticated perspective.[284] In her critique of the client-centered model of counseling, Kruse notes the importance of both "negative liberty"[285]—the right to do as one chooses—and "positive freedom"[286]—the opportunity to exercise autonomy by reducing constraints on available choices. As Kruse explains, the Binder & Price model undersells autonomy if it only focuses on the negative freedom, aiming to create space for clients to make their own choices. A better practice, at times, would suggest that the lawyer *increase* a client's autonomy by actively working to alter the client's

---

[282] *See* LAWYERS AS COUNSELORS, *supra* note 13, at 4–8.

[283] *See* note 276 *supra*.

[284] Kruse, *Fortress in the Sand, supra* note 24, at 404–12.

[285] *Id.* at 410.

[286] *Id.* at 404.

"attitudes, beliefs, or unrealistic expectations."[287] In her development of the positive freedom conception, Kruse relies on the ideas of William Simon, a proponent of a more activist counseling model intended to augment the opportunities for oppressed clients.[288] Simon, in turn, builds upon the "refined" view of paternalism suggested by Duncan Kennedy.[289]

Both Kruse and Simon accept that lawyers working with community groups might have a professional obligation to intervene actively with their clients to assist the clients to get things *right.* As Kruse describes it, a "client empowerment" approach to representation (an approach Kruse finds as "particularly attractive to lawyers working with communities of poor client or of battered women"[290]) might, in appropriate contexts, reject a client's "[s]tated [w]ishes" to overcome "[c]lient misdiagnosis of what the client 'really wants.' "[291] Gary Bellow concurred in this outlook for lawyers working with oppressed communities. For Bellow, community lawyers are "not detached professionals offering advice and representation regardless of the consequences; we saw ourselves as responsible for, and committed to, shaping those consequences."[292]

We might call this version of the empowerment theory the "positive freedom" stance, using Kruse's term.[293] Note that much of the mainstream empowerment theory and community lawyering scholarship arguments are initially hard to square with the positive freedom stance.[294] A best-practices approach to counseling community groups must acknowledge the prevailing voice within progressive scholarship warning community lawyers against committing "interpretive violence" against poor clients[295] and "subordinating] their clients' perceptions of need to the lawyers' own agendas for reform,"[296] while noting that "quite a lot of oppression happens in the name of abstract humanist values such as democracy, autonomy and equality."[297] A best-practices approach must at once accept

[287] *Id.* at 420.

[288] *See* Simon, *Mrs. Jones's Case, supra* note 103, at 222–24; Simon, *Dark Secret, supra* note 34, at 1114.

[289] Kennedy, *supra* note 33.

[290] Kruse, *Fortress in the Sand, supra* note 24, at 423.

[291] *Id.* at 420.

[292] Bellow, *supra* note 33, at 300. Bellow elaborated: "Alliance is a better term than client-centered. It permits us to talk seriously about purposive judgment—when and whether to intervene or to seek influence." *Id.* at 303.

[293] Kruse, *Fortress in the Sand, supra* note 24, at 404.

[294] Indeed, for that very reason William Simon disdainfully refers to the positive freedom stance (although in quite different terms) as the "Dark Secret" of the progressive scholarship community. Simon, *Dark Secret, supra* note 34, at 1102.

[295] Anthony V. Alfieri, Reconstructive Poverty Law Practice: Learning the Lessons of Client Narrative, 100 YALE L. REV. 2107, 2123 (1991).

[296] Lucie E. White, Mobilizations on the Margins of the Lawsuit: Making Space for Clients to Speak, 16 N.Y.U. REV. L. & SOC. CHANGE 535, 545 (1987–88).

[297] Steven L. Winter, *Cursing the Darkness,* 48 U. MIAMI L. REV. 1115, 1129 (1994).

that "the practice of law always involves exercise of power,"[298] especially with marginalized clients, but that community lawyers must exercise that power without committing interpretive violence or "reproducing hierarchy."[299]

Advocates of a "collaborative" approach to community lawyering acknowledge this tension.[300] Missing from those accounts, though, are vivid *stories* of its practiced implementation. The accounts succeed in demonstrating collaboration, and respect for the views of client group members as more reliable than the purported expertise from the professionals.[301] But implicit in the collaborative models, and explicit in the positive freedom stance, is the understanding that marginalized clients might get things wrong, that their good-faith lawyers might discern the clients' "self deception"[302] and their "unrealistic" assessments of their "real needs and interests,"[303] and that those lawyers have an obligation to nurture the client's autonomy by resisting the client's expressed wishes. The literature needs more and better stories showing how the lawyer accomplishes that end without succumbing to the regnant ideas of the lawyer as expert and savior.

While the positive freedom stance may remain a relatively "thin" phenomenon within the critical lawyering scholarship, the proponents of collaborative lawyering (a group not necessarily aligned with the positive freedom advocates) do offer useful insights that might begin to shape a best-practices approach for working with community groups. The best collaborative lawyering writers stress the qualities of humility, transparency, and respect when working with marginalized clients. In a showing of deep respect for victims of oppression, the writers emphasize the strengths within the groups to hear honest opinions, recommendations and proposals from their lawyers without feebly surrendering to the experts' views. Those attributes may inform our effort to understand a practiced approach to the positive freedom stance. That stance tells us that community lawyers who discern "unrealistic" expectations and short-sighted choices within their client groups may possess a moral duty to persuade their clients to arrive at better decisions. In doing so, though, the lawyers need to exhibit humility and tentativeness—qualities which in a different context an observer has called "informed not-knowing."[304]

---

298 Bellow, *supra* note 33, at 301.

299 *See* note 276 *supra*.

300 *See, e.g.*, Piomelli, *supra* note 276, at 437–40.

301 *See, e.g.*, LÓPEZ, *supra* note 1; Alfieri, *Impoverished Practices, supra* note 1, at 2573–74; Shah, *supra* note 256, at 221.

302 Kruse, *Fortress in the Sand, supra* note 24, at 424.

303 *Id.* at 420, 423.

304 Joan Laird, *Theorizing Culture: Narrative Ideas and Practice Principles, in* RE-VISIONING FAMILY THERAPY: RACE, CULTURE, AND GENDER IN CLINICAL PRACTICE 21 (Monica McGoldrick,

A more intriguing question for the positive freedom stance considers the limits of a lawyer's manipulation in the interests of aiding clients who are "blinded by the passions of the moment to their long-term interest or deeper values,"[305] or "who are alienated from themselves, or in the grip of self-deception."[306] If we accept the premise that a lawyer owes her client (including, notably, a community group client) her assistance to increase the client's autonomy and positive freedom, and if we accept that lawyers have a reliable capacity to discern when those circumstances exist (and, further, to differentiate those contexts from the very different situations of the lawyer simply disagreeing about tactical issues, or having her own conflicting interests), then we must confront what it is that the lawyer may do to achieve the increase in client autonomy. If the collaborative techniques of honest conversation do not work, the lawyer might actively manipulate or cajole her client to proceed as the lawyer understands the client ought to proceed.

Here is where the positive freedom stance needs rich stories. Without thick narratives available, our instinct must be that manipulation is wrong, for a number of reasons. Manipulation—especially when contrasted with transparent conversation, as here—implies an element of deception, and deception is always presumptively troublesome. Manipulation also assumes a level of confidence on the part of the lawyer that she is *right,* and that confidence must be suspect, especially given the history of professional domination of marginalized persons.[307]

The best one could conclude, then, is the following. A lawyer representing a community group ought to appreciate her discretion to consider the positive freedom perspective, but with a strong burden of proof against its applicability. She might be correct that her client is succumbing to blind passions or short-sighted misunderstanding, but any such conclusion demands a great deal of confidence on the part of the lawyer. If she concludes that her client indeed fits the criteria for such intervention, then her professional discretion includes active and open challenging of her client's choices—but transparently so, without manipulation, and with considerable humility and tentativeness.

CONCLUSION

The training of lawyers for years has established ethical and practice protocols based upon an individual representation model, or, if they

---

ed. 1998) (quoting V. Shapiro, *Subjugated Knowledge and the Working Alliance: The Narratives of Russian Jewish Immigrants,* 1 IN SESSION: PSYCHOTHERAPY IN PRACTICE 9 (1995)).

[305] Kruse, *Fortress in the Sand, supra* note 24, at 424.

[306] *Id.*

[307] The lawyer's confidence might also be the result of common self-serving cognitive distortions. *See* Langevoort, *Epistemology, supra* note 47, at 654–57 (describing risks of lawyers' cognitive biases).

contemplated a form of collective representation, they have envisioned formal, structured entities with powerful constituents. The good lawyers who represent the dispossessed, the exploited, and the powerless need to craft different protocols, ones which accept messier, less organized, and often contentious group representation. Writing about the ethical and political mission of "community lawyers" has flourished, but that scholarship has tended to elide some knotty practical questions about the lawyers' professional responsibilities in their work with such groups. This Article is a beginning attempt to review community group representation through the lens of a traditional "law of lawyering" perspective.

A lawyer who accepts a "community group" as her client must attend to all of the professional ethical mandates applicable to more conventional corporate and partnership representation. She must distinguish with great care whether her client is an aggregate of community members, or an entity, and much will depend on the outcome of that discernment. The lawyer must engage the group members to assist them to decide which of those statuses will apply, and, in doing so, she must be clear about her relationship with the members as they make that choice.

If the community group lawyer accepts the *group* as her client, she must uncover, or create, an authority scheme on which she may rely for her direction. Once she has accomplished that, the community group lawyer may counsel her clients in ways different from how she would counsel an individual client with an individual legal matter. In representing any entity, the lawyer will owe to the entity constituents a different—one might say lesser—deference for their preferences and their leanings, because of their status as proxies for a larger client. The more loosely-structured the entity is (and there is much evidence that community group representation will involve many loosely-structured groups), the greater the responsibility of the lawyer to ensure that the constituent with whom she meets is a faithful proxy for the wishes of the group.

In addition to attending to her ethical responsibilities emerging from the very fact that her client is a group, the community lawyer must recognize further special duties from the fact that her client is not just a group, but a *community* group. This Article has uncovered three considerations peculiar to the community group representation context. For those groups with explicit public missions, the lawyer has a responsibility to attend to that mission, in ways she may not have permission to do for groups established to achieve purely private ends. At the same time (and often at odds with the prior commitment), the community group lawyer must attend with special care to the empowerment and group cohesion aspects of the group's work. Finally (and, again, at odds with the prior commitment), the community group lawyer may at times possess some moral duty to intervene with her group client to establish conditions, even if not chosen by the group, which are likely to increase the autonomy and the power of the group in the long run.

The ideas puzzled through in this Article emerge from the rich literature from so many progressive scholars over the past twenty-five years or more. The ideas need to be tested, nurtured and critiqued, though, especially by more stories from the field. The test of the ethical ideas will come from their usefulness in practice.[308]

POST-CLASS ASSIGNMENT

Now that you have given some thought to interviewing your project client, respond to the following questions, which are designed to provide a template for an initial client interview. After you have given them some thought, meet with your project team and work through them together to prepare for your initial client interview.

1. Think about your initial meeting with your transactional or project client from the client's perspective:
   a. What information does your client need from you in the context of this meeting?
   b. What value do you think your client wishes you to add to their work?
   c. What concerns or questions do you think your client will have regarding the client's relationship with your team?
   d. What questions or concerns is your client likely to share with you?
   e. What is your client less likely to share?
2. Think about your initial meeting with your project client from your own perspective:
   a. What are your top three goals for the meeting?
   b. What value do you think you will add for your client?

[308] As two noted pragmatists have written:

> Of one thing we may be sure. If inquiries are to have substantial basis, if they are not to be wholly in the air, the theorist must take his departure from the problems which men actually meet in their own conduct. He may define and refine these; he may divide and systematize; he may abstract the problems from their concrete contexts in individual lives, he may classify them when he has thus detached them; but if he gets away from them, he is talking about something his own brain has invented, not about moral realities.

John Dewey & James Tufts, ETHICS 212 (1908) (*quoted in* Paul R. Tremblay, *The New Casuistry*, 12 GEO. J. LEGAL ETHICS 489, 489 (1999)).

c. What concerns or questions do you have regarding your team's relationship with your client?

d. Think about questions or concerns you may share with the client, as well as those you may not share with your client.

e. What do you anticipate your next steps will be after this first meeting?

3. Identify who you are likely to be speaking with when you hold the transactional or project-based client interview.

   a. Who is this person in the context of the client organization?

   b. What is this person's stake in this project?

4. Identify what your client's likely goals for the project will be. Focus on the following:

   a. Goals that relate specifically to the problem or problems that your project seeks to address.

   b. Broader goals that your client is likely to have, including institutional and personal goals.

HANDOUT FOR GROUP PLANNING

Group 1: Opening and Identifying Role

- What will be the first thing you will say to your client?
- How will you describe your role?
- How will you ascertain who the "real" client is for purposes of this representation?
- How will you describe your ethical obligations as your client's lawyer?

Group 2: Eliciting Client Information about Goals

- What information is critical for you to understand your client's goals?
- What questions might you ask, and how might you ask them, in an effort to elicit this information?
- What assumptions, if any, might the client have that need to be addressed or deconstructed as part of the effort to understand the client's goals?

Group 3: Clarifying Client Priorities

Use the information provided to distill the goals and establish direction.

- How will you help the client identify what is most important to her?
- How will you ascertain whether this client speaks for the whole group as to priorities?
- How might you ensure that you and your client have similar expectations about the work you will be doing?

Group 4: Closing the Interview

- How do you plan to close the interview with your client?
- What do you expect will be the next steps?
- How do you address how much notice and control the client will want over contacts with others on his behalf?
- How do you expect to communicate with this client in the future?
- How will you plan for that future communication?

HANDOUT FOR OBSERVERS

Substance Feedback

- What difficult issues arose during this part of the interview?
- How did the students address the issues?
- Did the students appear to have or did they develop sufficient information to deal with the issues?
- Did the client seem satisfied?
- Did any ethical issues arise that needed to be addressed?
    - If so, how were they handled?

Process Feedback

- How are questions framed?
- Do the questions leave room for the client to respond?
- Are follow-up questions being asked?
- What role do you perceive the students to be taking on?
    - Are they acting as information gatherers?
    - Are they assisting in setting expectations?

- Are their questions helping the client identify and prioritize goals?
- What efforts are being made to bolster the attorney-client relationship?

CHAPTER 6

INFORMAL FACT INVESTIGATION

LEARNING GOALS

The learning goals for this class include helping you to:

- Recognize that information does not simply exist, fully-formed and ready to be uncovered, and understand the lawyer's role in obtaining, shaping, and expanding information
- Appreciate how case or project theory can guide fact investigation, and how fact investigation, in turn, can help refine case or project theory
- Appreciate the importance of planning and prioritizing when engaging in fact investigation
- Think creatively about ways to develop a fact investigation plan and identify potential sources for fact development
- Understand the importance of thinking through the time required as part of the prioritization process
- Understand the practical realities involved in moving from planning a fact investigation to actually gathering the information identified
- Understand the importance of both unpacking and testing the validity of factual conclusions

DESCRIPTION OF CLASS

In this class, we will discuss the importance of facts to the lawyering process, and begin to analyze how lawyers uncover and strategically shape facts in support of their client's goals. You will participate in an exercise that requires you to get out in the field and discover how to obtain factual information that is frequently needed in our clinic cases, and you will share your learning experiences with your clinic colleagues. Finally, we will explore ways in which lawyers can unpack factual conclusions into the component parts, and begin to discuss how to prioritize fact investigation tasks.

ASSIGNMENT IN PREPARATION FOR CLASS

In the Field: Real-World Lessons in Fact Investigation

Civil Clinic

Investigation tasks, to be completed prior to class on *[date]*, are set forth below. Please note that several of these assignments require you to gather information related to real people; you will need to obtain the actual records from real-world sources. In addition to accomplishing the investigation task you are assigned, your team will be expected to make a three- to five-minute in-class presentation to the class on *[date]* about the steps you took to make it happen, any obstacles you encountered, and any practical investigation tips your experience has taught you. You may use any method of presentation you believe will be effective and useful to your colleagues, and you should feel free to create and distribute handouts or any other educational materials.

> **Group 1:** You are representing a tenant whose landlord is trying to evict him from an apartment. He pays part of the rent through a Section 8 housing voucher, and part of it through his limited earnings. Your client has had trouble making his portions of the rent payments, due to a recurring physical illness. He received treatment at *[hospital]*. He also previously received medical care at *[second hospital]* in connection with another month when his rent payment was late. Learn and then walk your colleagues through how to obtain your (fictitious) client's medical records from these hospitals.
>
> **Group 2:** Your client signed a lease approved by the local Housing Authority that issues his Section 8 voucher, but he did not retain a copy. Learn and then walk your colleagues through how to obtain a copy of the lease from the agency.
>
> **Group 3:** You are representing the client identified for Group 1. While a friend from out of town was staying with your client, the friend got into a fist fight with a guy hanging out in front of the building. A neighbor called 911 to report the incident. Learn and then walk your colleagues through how to obtain the 911 recording.

Group 4: You are representing the client identified for Group 1. Police officers from the *[police district]* responded to the 911 call and wrote a report. Officers from the *[police district]* also wrote a report in connection with an incident that occurred approximately 12 months ago. Learn and then walk your colleagues through how to obtain a copy of both police reports.

Group 5: Assume you are representing *[former clinic client]* (a real person). Obtain a copy of the docket sheets of all landlord-tenant cases in which [same client] has been involved in our jurisdiction.

Group 6: Assume for purposes of this exercise that the most important supporting witness in your client's case is *[opposing party]* (a real person). You are worried about the effectiveness of his testimony, because your client believes the witness has several criminal convictions. Learn *[same opposing party]*'s criminal history, and gather any documentation required to describe it to your classmates.

Domestic Violence Clinic

Investigation tasks, to be completed prior to class on *[date]*, are set forth below. Please note that several of these assignments require you to gather information related to real people; you will need to obtain the actual records from real-world sources. In addition to accomplishing the investigation task you are assigned, your team will be expected to make a three- to five-minute in-class presentation to the class on *[date]* about the steps you took to make it happen, any obstacles you encountered, and any practical investigation tips your experience has taught you. You may use any method of presentation you believe will be effective and useful to your colleagues, and you should feel free to create and distribute handouts or any other educational materials.

Group 1: You are representing a woman seeking a protection order against her husband, who assaulted her one week ago. After last week's incident, your client received treatment at *[hospital]*. She also previously received medical care at *[second hospital]* in connection with a prior assault by her husband. You should learn and then walk your colleagues through how to obtain your (fictitious) client's medical records from these hospitals.

Group 2: You are representing the client identified for Group 1. Your client is seeking custody of her child who attends second grade at *[school]*. Learn and then walk your colleagues through how to obtain the child's records from this school.

Group 3: You are representing the client identified for Group 1. Your client called 911 during the incident. Learn and then walk your colleagues through how to obtain the 911 recording.

Group 4: You are representing the client identified for Group 1. Police officers from the *[police district]* responded to the 911 call and wrote a report. Officers from the *[police district]* also wrote a report in connection with an incident that occurred approximately 12 months ago. Learn and then walk your colleagues through how to obtain a copy of both police reports.

Group 5: Assume you are representing *[former clinic client]* (a real person). Obtain a copy of the docket sheets of all protection order cases in which *[same client]* has been involved in our jurisdiction.

Group 6: Assume for purposes of this exercise that the respondent in this case is *[opposing party]* (a real person). Learn *[same opposing party]*'s criminal history, and gather any documentation required to describe it to your classmates.

Criminal Defense or Juvenile Delinquency Clinic

Investigation tasks, to be completed prior to class on *[date]*, are set forth below. Please note that several of these assignments require you to gather information related to real people; you will need to obtain the actual records from real-world sources. In addition to accomplishing the investigation task you are assigned, your team will be expected to make a three- to five-minute in-class presentation to the class on *[date]* about the steps you took to make it happen, any obstacles you encountered, and any practical investigation tips your experience has taught you. You may use any method of presentation you believe will be effective and useful to your colleagues, and you should feel free to create and distribute handouts or any other educational materials.

Group 1: You are representing a woman charged with assaulting her husband one week ago. After last week's alleged incident, your client's husband received treatment at *[hospital]*. He also previously received medical care at *[second hospital]* in connection with a prior alleged assault by your client. You should learn and then walk your colleagues through how to obtain this (fictitious) complaining witness's medical records from these hospitals.

Group 2: You are representing the client identified for Group 1. Your client is seeking custody of her child who attends second grade at *[school]*. Learn and then walk your colleagues through how to obtain the child's records from this school.

Group 3: You are representing the client identified for Group 1. The complaining witness called 911 during the incident. Learn and then walk your colleagues through how to obtain the 911 recording.

Group 4: You are representing the client identified for Group 1. Police officers from the *[police district]* responded to the 911 call and wrote a report. Officers from the *[police district]* also wrote a report in connection with an incident that occurred approximately 12 months ago. Learn and then walk your colleagues through how to obtain a copy of both police reports.

Group 5: Assume you are representing *[former clinic client]* (a real person). Obtain a copy of the docket sheets of all criminal cases in which *[same client]* has been involved in our jurisdiction.

Group 6: Assume for purposes of this exercise that the complaining witness in this case is *[complaining witness]* (a real person). Learn *[complaining witness]*'s criminal history, and gather any documentation required to describe it to your classmates.

Transactional or Project-Based Clinic

Investigation tasks, to be completed prior to class on *[date]*, are set forth below. Please note that several of these assignments require you to gather information related to real people; you will need to obtain the actual records from real-world sources. In addition to accomplishing the investigation task you are assigned, your team will be expected to make a three- to five-minute in-class presentation to the class on *[date]* about the steps you took to make it happen, any obstacles you encountered, and any practical investigation tips your experience has taught you. You may use any method of presentation you believe will be effective and useful to your colleagues, and you should feel free to create and distribute handouts or any other educational materials.

Group 1: Your client is a group of women who are all survivors of domestic violence. You realize there is a pressing need for transitional housing for women who come to the end of a shelter stay but still need a place to be safe from violence. There are two houses that are in foreclosure in a local neighborhood *[neighborhood and cross streets]*, that will likely go up for auction in the next few months. The client group has approached a Women's Giving Circle about this need and the Circle is willing to put up the financing to purchase and rehab the two homes as transitional housing. Learn about and then walk your colleagues through the tax lien foreclosure process.

Group 2: You are representing the client group identified for Group 1. Identify one of the homes that are up for sale, visit it, and use the internet to determine what the appropriate purchasing price should be. Walk your colleagues through this process.

Group 3: You are representing the client group identified for Group 1. Go to a bank and discuss home financing with a bank officer. Walk your colleagues through the procedure for financing the purchase of a home.

Group 4: You are representing the client group identified for Group 1. Learn about and then walk your colleagues through what you can learn about the neighborhood surrounding the houses including the crime statistics and whether there are community centers or groups active in the community.

READING ASSIGNMENT

1. John Yarbrough, Jugues Herve, & Robert Harms, *The Sins of Interviewing: Errors Made by Investigative Interviewers and Suggestions for Redress, in* APPLIED ISSUES IN INVESTIGATIVE INTERVIEWING, EYEWITNESS MEMORY, AND CREDIBILITY ASSESSMENT 59 (Barry S. Cooper, Dorothee Driesel, & Marguerite Ternes eds., 2013).
2. Christopher Chabris & Daniel Simons, *I Think I Would Have Seen That, in* THE INVISIBLE GORILLA: AND OTHER WAYS OUR INTUITIONS DECEIVE US 5 (2010).
3. Benchmark Institute, *Case Planning, in* LEGAL SERVICES PRACTICE MANUAL: SKILLS 5 (2010).
4. Sir Arthur Conan Doyle, *The Boscombe Valley Mystery, in* THE ADVENTURES OF SHERLOCK HOLMES, FLORIDA CENTER FOR INSTRUCTIONAL TECHNOLOGY LIT2GO, http://etc.usf.edu/lit2go/32/the-adventures-of-sherlock-holmes/348/adventure-4-the-boscombe-valley-mystery.

READINGS

John Yarbrough, Jugues Herve, & Robert Harms
The Sins of Interviewing: Errors Made by Investigative Interviewers and Suggestions for Redress
APPLIED ISSUES IN INVESTIGATIVE INTERVIEWING, EYEWITNESS MEMORY, AND CREDIBILITY ASSESSMENT (2013)[1]

Introduction

Interviewing is the essence of law enforcement. The goal of an effective interview, be it with a victim, witness, informant, or suspect, is to elicit complete and accurate information. Of course, the gathering of complete and accurate information is not unique to law enforcement. Psychologists and psychiatrists rely on fact-finding interviews to—among other activities—diagnose and treat mental illness, assess malingering, and determine risk of violence. The retail loss prevention and other industries use investigative interviews to gather data to identify, neutralize, assess, and prevent thefts and frauds. Leaders of countries and politicians rely on accurate information to make geopolitical and economic decisions and to navigate diplomatic relationships. The gathering of intelligence has always been critical to the military in times of both peace and war. In other words, many important decisions are made on a daily basis that depends on information gathered by people through interviews.

The importance of interviewing notwithstanding, most professionals receive little training in effective interviewing (e.g., fact finding, reading people, and evaluating truthfulness); and the training that is provided is too often based on anecdotal experience and faulty concepts, assumptions, theories, and/or research findings based on inadequate or simplistic methodologies. As a result, interviewers are frequently left with an erroneous or simplistic view of human behavior when trying to design an interview strategy or evaluate the credibility of statements. . . .

This chapter examines the "Sins of Interviewing" that were identified as a result of the collaboration between law enforcement professionals, mental health professionals, and academics. . . . Fifteen sins are currently listed and they all have one variable in common: they detract from achieving the goal of an effective interview. That is, the goal of finding the truth—whatever it might be—and why the person believes it to be the truth. The 15 sins are not meant to be an exhaustive list, and the sins are not meant to be mutually exclusive. The listed sins simply reflect the most common errors committed by interviewers. The following describes

1 Footnotes, endnotes, and/or internal citations omitted.

these 15 sins and their causes, as well as practical solutions for overcoming them.

Sin Number 1: Imposing the "Me" Theory of Personality

The "me" theory is based on the concept that many of us believe that how we see the world, how we make decisions, or how we behave is necessarily the same for all other human beings. Clearly, this is not the case. Humans have variability in genetic expression, life experiences, and sociocultural backgrounds that impact thinking, feeling, and behavior. Despite the heterogeneous nature of human beings, we nevertheless often rely on the "me" theory to try to understand the people around us. This may be due to the fact that the "me" theory provides us with a simple, automatic heuristic for making sense of other people and their actions. That is, it is much easier (i.e., it requires less mental effort or cognitive load) to make interpretations based on one's own viewpoints and experiences than to gather relevant data and test multiple hypotheses to make an informed decision about the person under scrutiny. The end result is a predisposition to make quick (or automatic) and simplistic interpretations about other people based on our own belief system and experiences.

Obviously, relying on the "me" theory to make sense of other people has its limitations. First, it often leads to erroneous judgments about the thoughts, feelings and/or actions of others. This is especially true when trying to apply the "me" theory to people who are markedly different from us, such as individuals from different cultures or subgroups, with psychiatric problems, and/or with developmental delays. Second, when it leads to correct judgments, it typically reinforces poor interviewing skills (e.g., using automatic thought processes rather than critical thinking skills; believing that the behavior you share in common with the interviewee is a reliable sign of deception. In fact, when the "me" theory leads to a correct interpretation, it tells us more that the person being evaluated is similar to us than anything about our interpretation and related assumptions. . . .

Sin Number 2: Misunderstanding Memory

The second "sin" of interviewing relates to the lack of understanding that many law enforcement personnel have about memory. This is surprising given the importance of memory to police work. By definition, the goal of an investigative interview is to mine the interviewee's memory (i.e., the truth as s/he knows it). This holds true irrespective of whether the interviewee is a victim, witness, informant, or suspect. In many cases, particularly in child sexual abuse contexts, the victim's memory is often the only evidence that an alleged crime has been committed. Therefore, the importance of understanding how memory works cannot be overstated. In fact, it could be argued that investigators should treat offence-related memories as part of the crime scene. Would crime scene investigators (CSIs) be sent to a scene without any understanding of evidence collection? Would CSIs be allowed to contaminate the crime scene or only collect part of the evidence? The answers here are easy: no. Yet, investigative interviewers are often not held to the same standards with respect to collecting memory-based evidence.

The following provides the main properties/characteristics of memory that all investigative interviewers should know, as well as some of the common sins committed by memory-uninformed interviewers.

First, memory for personally experienced events is reconstructive, not reproductive. That is, we do not have an exact video recording of past events stored in our brains that we can freely play back at any time. If we did, we would have totally accurate recall but we would likely eventually run out of storage space for new memories. Instead, we only encode or store information that is important to us and reconstruct our memories piece by piece in a manner consistent with the cues that elicited or triggered them. The good news about this method is that we do not have any storage issues. The bad news is that this process is imperfect and prone to error. By imperfect, we mean that memory is incomplete because individuals simply cannot pay attention to everything of investigative importance (e.g., to the behaviors of all present during a crime). By prone to error, we mean that, each time a memory is recalled and, therefore, reconstructed, it is susceptible to being distorted by a host of factors. As Schacter notes, "in the process of reconstruction we add on feelings, beliefs, or even knowledge we obtained after the experience."

The knowledge that can distort one's memory need not be self-generated; in reality, it is often suggested by others, including interviewers. For example, when a witness to an event spontaneously recalls the details of an event or is interviewed and asked to recall the details of an event, the resulting product becomes a reconstruction of the stored parts and pieces of the memory being elicited, not a single reproduction of the memory. When the memory is reconstructed and verbalized, the quality and quantity of the actual memory becomes vulnerable to influences from external sources, such as the questions posed or information supplied to the witness that was not part of his/her original memory. Thereafter, this newly reconstructed memory is restored, only to be reconstructed and influenced again when the witness is re-interviewed at a later time.

Despite the fact that memory is reconstructive in nature and, therefore, incomplete and error prone, many inexperienced and experienced interviewers continue to believe that memory is like a video recording. As a result, they become frustrated when the results of an interview are not as expected (e.g., when a witness does not provide a smooth, linear "play back" of everything that happened during the offence). Many also fail to understand the malleable nature of memory and, therefore, the impact their own questions will have on the interviewee's memory, a sin further discussed below.

Second, our memory is best for events of personal significance. While most experiences are quickly forgotten because they are routine, mundane, or unimportant, events of personal significance, either positive or negative, may be retained for months or even years. This may be due to several factors, including the fact that events of personal significance are, by their very nature, emotional events and emotions serve as powerful memory cues. Furthermore, events of personal significance are more likely to be retold or discussed over and over again, a process that is known to reinforce memory.

One error made by improperly trained interviewers is in defining what is significant from their own perspective (i.e., according to the "me" theory) or from the perspective of the investigation (e.g., what evidence is "needed" to catch and convict the suspect), rather than from the perspective of the interviewee (i.e., what s/he found to be especially significant and, therefore, memorable). A victim of fraud, for example, may not know that s/he was being defrauded (i.e., at the time the fraud was being committed) and, therefore, may have little to no memory of the event (i.e., as it was not originally encoded as memorable). The longer the time between this type of event and its recall, the more likely it will be forgotten (e.g., in part or in whole). Unfortunately, a well-meaning interviewer may wrongly assume that the victim should recall the incident and consequently pressure the victim to provide information related to the fraud—information that is likely to be inaccurate and, therefore, lead the investigation down the wrong path.

Another error that novice and improperly trained interviewers sometimes make is changing topics when an interviewee becomes emotional during a retelling. This typically reflects the interviewer's discomfort dealing with emotional subjects and, unfortunately, serves to disrupt the reconstruction of memory. Emotions are a powerful cue to memory and, therefore, can serve to elicit important offence-related details. As such, the interviewer should allow the interviewee to express his/her emotions while providing their narrative. Of course, if a victim or witness becomes overwhelmed by their emotions (i.e., cries uncontrollably or is so angry or agitated that communication is disrupted), it would be appropriate to temporarily change topics.

Third, memory is not a discreet entity. Rather, it is a set of processes. There are, in fact, different types of processes and different types of memories, including the following: (1) Procedural memory (i.e., memory for psychomotor functioning, such as walking, sexual behavior, etc.); (2) Semantic memory (i.e., memory for general knowledge, such as math, physics, chemistry, geography, etc.); (3) Narrative memory (i.e., memory for personally experienced events, such as committing violence or being the victim of violence); (4) Script memory (i.e., memory for routine events, such as our typical morning routine); and (5) Prospective memory (i.e., memory for future events, such as going to a hockey game).

Narrative memory (also referred to as episodic or autobiographical memory) is typically the type of memory at the focus of most investigations. It may be about a single event at a single location, such as witnessing a car accident or a bank robbery; or it may be about a series of events, such as multiple meetings and discussions among conspirators to commit some type of action. In the latter case, multiple locations, multiple dates, multiple participants, and multiple acts could be involved and recalled. The second most likely type of memory to surface during an investigation is a script memory. We develop scripts for routine events, such as our typical drive to work or our typical family dinner. Likewise, some victims and offenders may develop scripts for repeated acts of violence that they interpret as routine (e.g., repeated acts of sexual or domestic violence). Remember not to fall prey to the "me" theory when it comes to the definition of routine. It is not what you believe to be routine, but what the interviewee believes to be routine.

The distinction between a narrative and script memory is often lost on improperly trained interviewers. However, the distinction is crucial. With all other factors being equal, the quality and quantity of information within a narrative memory will be greater than that in a script memory. For example, a victim who was sexually assaulted on one occasion may provide a great deal of information about the offender (e.g., what he was wearing, his approach behavior, and what he was saying), the offence (e.g., sequence of events, particular behaviors), and the location of the assault (e.g., place, time, and other contextual details) because of the uniqueness of the event. In contrast, a victim of repeated sexual assaults by the same perpetrator in the same context may only provide generalities about the offence script or how it "usually" happened because of the routine nature of these events (e.g., he used to come into my room at night, usually after drinking beer; he would start by turning off the light and taking my panties off). If the interviewer falsely believes that s/he is dealing with a narrative memory when, in fact, s/he is facing a script, s/he may become frustrated by the lack of details provided by the interviewee and perhaps become suspicious. Under this circumstance, the improperly trained interviewer may be at risk of asking leading or suggestive questions and, therefore, of contaminating the victim's memory. Instead, when dealing with a script memory, it is best to simply ask the interviewee how the offending typically occurred. Once the script is known, it may be possible to get information about a particular episode by asking if there was a time when the offending unfolded in a different manner (e.g., when an act of domestic violence is interrupted by the unexpected presence of a child; when a sexual offence of a child is interrupted by the non-offending parent unexpectedly returning home). This is called a script violation. Script violations are significant departures from how events typically unfold and, therefore, are memorable. The interviewer can use script violations to cue memory for a particular episode by asking the interviewee if s/he recalls anything more about the particular incident in which the script was violated. This process can be repeated until no further script violations and/or episodes come to mind.

Fourth, narrative memory is often piecemeal (i.e., only parts and pieces of the actual event are recalled). As noted above, when an event is unfolding, a witness cannot pay attention to every facet of the event, and different witnesses may focus on different parts of the event. Later, when recalling the event, the witness may fill in the holes in his/her memory with information that makes the memory seem complete but may, in fact, be inaccurate. Filling in the gaps is typical of social interactions and often relies on our semantic memory or our scripts. In other words, if a witness did not see a particular act during an event (e.g., the perpetrator's car swerve prior to hitting the victim), that witness might still assume that the particular act occurred (i.e., the car swerved prior to impact) based on his/her general knowledge and/or typical experiences with similar events (i.e., motor vehicle accidents). While an improperly trained interviewer would likely not stop (and may even sometimes encourage) witnesses to fill in the gaps, properly trained interviewers know to instruct witnesses to only report on what they saw and heard. Another effective way to avoid having a witness fill in the gaps is to first find out what s/he was paying attention to and then only ask questions about this information. Remember that many cooperative witnesses will provide information when questioned by officers, irrespective if they actually have a memory for what is being asked.

Fifth, memory is not formed in a vacuum. The memory for a significant event will have been surrounded by the memories for a whole array of relatively irrelevant events and experiences (e.g., from the perspective of the interviewer) that took place before, during, or after the event under investigation. The event in question may also trigger memories for other completely unrelated events. It is not uncommon for improperly trained interviewers to become frustrated when interviewees provide such information rather than focus on the details of the event under question (e.g., an alleged offence), which may lead the interviewer to interrupt the interviewee. This is a mistake for three reasons. First, this may negatively impact rapport, a sin discussed below. Second, this may disrupt the reconstructive process underway. Since memory is cued, personally significant but seemingly irrelevant details may assist in the reconstructive process of memory for the event in question. Third, since memory is cued, the emergence of "irrelevant" information during an investigative interview in which "relevant" information is also provided adds credibility to the witness' statement. In contrast, when such "irrelevant" information surfaces in the absence of any significant "relevant" information, the credibility of the witness' statement is diminished. A related issue is that memory of an event is a process in which some, if not all, of the five human senses are involved. Information is obtained and stored through sight, smell, hearing, taste, and tactile experience. While these senses do not equally contribute to memory encoding, those senses that were involved in the formation of the memory may serve as important cues for later recall. An interviewer can help the interviewee exhaust his/her memory by cueing the interviewee to recall what s/he saw, smelled, heard, tasted and/or touched to elicit further event-related details.

Sixth, memory reconstruction is impacted by several cognitive processes. Knowing these can help interviewers better understand why narrative memories are often imperfect and prone to error. It also helps them to avoid pursuing lines of question that may contaminate their witness' memory. Schacter describes seven cognitive/memory processes (i.e., "the seven sins of memory") that all interviewers should know: transience, absent-mindedness, blocking, misattribution, suggestibility, bias, and persistence. Transience, absent-mindedness and blocking are sins of omission: the inability to recall a particular piece of information. Misattribution, suggestibility, bias and persistence are sins of commission: some memory is present but it is either inaccurate or intrusive (e.g., unwanted). Each of these sins of memory and how they may impact an investigative interview are described below.

1. Transience refers to the decay of memory over time. This is the process behind normal forgetting. While a witness may have a detailed memory of an offence minutes after its occurrence, his/her memory may decay over time. This is why it is important to interview witnesses as quickly as possible following an event. We note that the memory "may" be prone to decay; that is, in some cases, a witness may have a remarkable memory for an event (i.e., a memory that evidences a great deal of detail, accuracy, and consistency over time). This may be due to, for example, frequent recollection of the event or to the nature of event (see persistence below for further details). Another important characteristic of transience is that different types of information may decay at different rates. In general, irrelevant or peripheral information (e.g., other witnesses) will decay at a faster rate than relevant or central information (e.g., what the perpetrator

was doing). Again, it is important to not fall prey to the "me" theory: what is peripheral and what is central information is in the eye of the beholder.

2. Absent-mindedness "involves a breakdown at the interface between attention and memory." As noted above, witnesses simply cannot focus on everything that happens in their environment. Absent-mindedness may also occur at the time of recall. In this case, the witness may focus only on some aspects of his/her memory and, therefore, not provide a full account of what s/he remembers. For example, a victim may only report on what she believes to be most important: the sexual assault. She may not, however, spontaneously provide information regarding how the offender gained access to her (e.g., grooming behavior) and/or what happened thereafter (e.g., how and where the ejaculate was disposed of). It is the job of the interviewer to cue these additional details.

3. Blocking refers to an inability to recall what one wants to and/or should recall. In this case, the witness may try to recall something that is in memory but is simply unable to retrieve it. Blocking may be involved in cases of dissociative amnesia (i.e., the inability to recall all or parts of a traumatic event). While issues concerning assessing the credibility of amnesia in victims, witnesses and offenders are beyond the scope of this chapter, it is important to note that a good understanding of memory is crucial to this task. There are two other types of blocking that are relevant to the interviewing context: retrieval inhibition and active forgetting. The former refers to the finding that selectively recalling certain events or parts of events can interfere with (or inhibit) the recall of the non-remembered information. This occurs when, for example, a victim or witness is questioned selectively about only certain aspects of the event in question (e.g., an offence) at the exclusion of other aspects of the event. Over time, the information that was not canvased may become more difficult to elicit. Active (or directed) forgetting occurs when a person consciously avoids cues that could elicit a memory. Although little is known about this phenomenon, it is a strategy reported by some victims of trauma. In cases of both retrieval inhibition and active forgetting, the end result is the weakening of the cues available to access a memory. While an improperly trained interviewer may become frustrated and leading when facing situations in which blocking occurs, the well trained investigator will know of and utilize memory enhancing techniques to overcome blocking. A knowledgeable and experienced interviewer will also know that spontaneous expressions of poor memory may be a clue to credibility. A good understanding of memory helps the interviewer to

differentiate likely true claims of poor memory from potentially false claims made to avoid discussing a particular topic.

4. Misattribution occurs when a person recalls aspects of an event correctly but misattributes the source (or origin) of the memory. For example, a bystander may believe s/he saw what the offender was wearing when, in fact, this information was provided by another witness. Alternatively, a witness may misattribute seeing someone during the event in question (e.g., an offence) when, in fact, s/he had seen him/her at some other time or place. In other words, interviewees may "have sketchy recollections of the precise details of previous experiences—when and where they encountered a person or object." According to Schacter, "A strong sense of general familiarity, together with an absence of specific recollections, adds up to a lethal recipe for misattribution." Fortunately, misattribution can be minimized by encouraging interviewees to only report what they specifically remember and by discouraging guessing and/or filling the gaps. Misattribution also points to the importance of both investigating the source of memories and corroborating this information. Otherwise, interviewers may risk focusing on false leads, including focusing on the wrong "suspect."

5. Suggestibility refers to the fact that memory can be contaminated by other people via leading questions, comments, or suggestions, or from misleading information from other sources (e.g., written materials, pictures, the media). Children and the developmentally delayed are especially susceptive to suggestions. Remember that memory is reconstructive and incomplete. Accordingly, each time a memory is reconstructed, it can be influenced by leading or suggestive questions or comments, particularly for information that was not encoded and/or that was affected by transience or blocking. It is imperative that interviewers avoid leading/suggestive questions (see Sin Number 9 below). The role of the interviewer should be to cue memory, not lead it. Suggestibility is also the reason why it is important to separate witnesses to an event as quickly as possible. Otherwise, they may discuss their personal experiences and contaminate each other's memories.

6. Bias reflects memory contamination of another kind, most notably that which is self-imposed. Our current knowledge and beliefs exert powerful influences on how we remember our past. In essence, our current thoughts, beliefs, and emotions serve as filters through which we interpret and potentially rewrite our past. "The result can be a skewed rending of a specific incident, or even of an extended period of our lives, which says more about how we feel *now* than about what happened *then*." The properly trained interviewer will know this and, therefore, focus on eliciting facts (e.g., who did what to whom) and

stay clear of (or at least place less weight on) subjective interpretations of past events. The properly trained interviewer will also know the significant influence of stereotypes on interviewees.

7. In the present context, persistence relates to the repeated recall of events/memories that we do not want to remember. Persistent memories are typically associated with experiences that the interviewee deems stressful/traumatic in nature and are, therefore, experienced as negative and intrusive. Although typically discussed in relation to victims and witnesses, it is important to note that offenders can be traumatized by their own offences and, therefore, experience persistence. This process accounts for why some interviewees have remarkable memories. When interviewing someone who experiences such intrusive, persistent memories, it would be important to monitor his/her emotional state. By definition, these memories are about traumatic events and their recollection could re-traumatize the individual. While a detailed review of trauma and memory is outside the scope of this chapter, it is important to note that trauma can have a variety of effects on memory, from amnesia to remarkable memories.

Seventh, in light of the above discussion on memory, it should now be clear that memory for past events should evidence variability over time, with memory for peripheral information being more variable than for central information. Yet, many improperly trained interviewers wrongly believe that memory should remain consistent over time and, consequently, view any deviations as a sign of deception. The reconstructive nature of memory in combination with the various sins of memory generally do not allow for perfect recollections from one time to another, although there are some exceptions to this (e.g., when an individual has retold the event numerous times or s/he experiences memory persistence). When there are no deviations from one retelling to another, then the memory should be viewed with suspicion as this may reflect rote memory (i.e., memorizing a story, such as when making a false claim of victimization or a false alibi). This raises another important topic to canvas during an interview: the history of the person's memory. This concerns how many times has the person thought about, dreamt about, written and/or discussed his/her memory for the event under investigation, as well as what kind of questions that were asked of him/her during retellings. This information may help the interviewer sift facts from fiction. Gaining the history of the interviewee's memory is especially important in the investigative interviewing context.

Finally, all investigative interviewers should be familiar with the Undeutsch hypothesis, which stipulates that the quality and quantity of memories for personally experienced events differ from the quality and quantity of fabricated events. This is why probing poorly prepared false accounts typically results in little to no additional details. Simply put, the person making a false claim cannot pull from memory the amount or type of details that are typical of personally experienced events. . . .

As the above discussion demonstrates, the more one knows about memory, the easier it is to elicit it and the easier it is to assess its credibility. In contrast, the less one knows about memory, the easier it is to contaminate it and/or the more likely one is to fail to elicit information crucial to the event in question.

Sin Number 3: Misunderstanding Lying and Truth Telling

As with the previous sin, the third "sin" of interviewing reflects the lack of understanding that many interviewers have about the nature and characteristics of lying and truth telling. Indeed, even though most people believe that they can accurately identify deception, research with professionals from various backgrounds (e.g., judges, lawyers, psychologists, and police) has shown that most people do no better than chance when trying to distinguish truth from lies in a standard laboratory task. This is especially problematic in the investigative interviewing context given that assessing the credibility of statements from victims, witnesses, informants, and suspects is central to the investigative process. The bottom line is that, to effectively assess credibility, interviewers need to understand what the truth looks like, what clues to lies looks like and how to assess these variables in their day-to-day work.

The "truth" is whatever information the person being interviewed believes to be true. Can a person who is being interviewed give information that is not true and yet not be lying? The answer, of course, is yes. Every day, many people provide false and erroneous information to others, information that they believe is true but, in fact, is not. As noted above, one's memory is fallible for a variety of reasons. Accordingly, it is important to understand that false information can be supplied quite innocently during an interview. For example, the interviewee may believe that some tidbit of information is correct and report it honestly, yet the information may ultimately prove to be false. Because the individual "believes" the information, s/he will not experience any of the emotional and/or cognitive consequences typically associated with lying. This is why it is important to understand the nature of memory, to cue memory and not lead it, and to stop interviewees from filling in the gaps.

A "lie" is whatever information the person being interviewed intentionally reports as truthful but knows to be false. While there are many contexts in which lying is of little consequence and/or acceptable (e.g., lying to your partner about a surprise birthday party; deception in laboratory research), this is not the case in the investigative interviewing context. This is important to note because "high stake" lies are likely to have more significant emotional and/or cognitive consequences for individuals than "low stake" lies.

People lie about a variety of issues. An emotional lie is an intentional misrepresentation of one's true emotional state. The suspect who states—with a red face, clenched teeth, and abrupt tone—that he "WASN'T ANGRY" at his missing spouse is an example. An opinion lie is an intentional misrepresentation of the true opinion held by the liar. A chronic spousal abuser who states, "It's wrong to hit women," is an example. Another example would be the suspect who, after being asked "What should happen to someone who committed this type of crime," timidly states, "I . . . I think that an apology and treatment would best serve everyone." A factual lie is a false denial of a fact, action, or experience or a false assertion of a fact, action, or experience, such as a false alibi or a false claim of victimization. An intent lie is a denial of an intention to do something in the future or a false claim that the liar will not do something in the future. Claims such as "I would never lie to you" have been made many times by many liars. National security professionals are especially concerned with intent lies—e.g., the terrorist who falsely claims that he/she is entering the country to attend a local auto show.

There are several methods used by interviewees to intentionally mislead interviewers. The two most common are concealment (i.e., leaving out true information) and falsification (i.e., presenting false information as if it were true). This is why witnesses are asked in court, "Do you swear to tell the truth, the whole truth, and nothing but the truth?" This oath implies that there are several ways that misleading information can be supplied by a witness to the trier of fact (i.e., judge or jury). Not only could a liar intentionally misstate a fact (". . . the truth"), but they could intentionally withhold truthful information (". . . the whole truth"), or they could also mix a lie in with a lot of truth (". . . and nothing but the truth"). Although various methods of lying exist, experience suggests that simply withholding truthful information is the method most used by successful liars. The reason for this is simple: it is much easier to say nothing than to invent a story. This is why it is often what is not said or what is skipped over that is often most revealing. When inventing, the liar has to create a credible story (e.g., an alibi) and then remember the false information in case the topic resurfaces later in the interview or in a subsequent interview. Moreover, if the lie is particularly complicated, there is a lot to remember the next time the same lie is told. This is why asking an interviewee who you suspect of lying via falsification to repeat his/her story can be a useful tool in assessing his/her credibility.

While certain types of lies may be easier to detect than others (e.g., emotional lie vs. factual lie; falsification vs. concealment), it is important to understand that the business of evaluating truthfulness is complex. The main reason for this is that there are no emotional, cognitive, behavioral and/or physiological signs that a person displays when lying that s/he does not also display under other circumstances (e.g., when stressed). That is, both truth-telling and lying have emotional and/or cognitive consequences. When telling the truth, the emotional and cognitive responses tend to be consistent with the content of the story and/or contextual demands. For example, the truthful witness who is being interviewed shortly after a robbery may display heightened emotional arousal stemming from his/her recent experience, while the truthful victim may display offence-related fear that has yet to dissipate. Over time, however, these emotions may no longer be present unless, for example, the event continues to have psychological impact. The person of interest who is, in fact, innocent may display stress, anxiety, or fear simply because s/he is being wrongly suspected of a crime, and this may be heightened if the interviewer uses an accusatory or challenging approach rather than an open-minded method. The truthful person may also show increased mental effort (or cognitive load) when telling his/her story because s/he is eager to provide as much detail as possible. However, when asked open-ended questions about his/her experience, the truthful person will generally display relatively mild cognitive load because s/he has an actual memory to rely on when answering questions.

In contrast, the liar's emotional and cognitive consequences tend to be inconsistent with the content of the story and/or contextual demands. As noted above, it is not uncommon for a suspect to claim that he has no anger/animosity towards a victim but nevertheless display signs of anger. In addition, the act of lying can trigger an emotion itself. For many, lying produces some internal emotions, such as the fear of being caught or guilt over deceiving someone. However, not everyone experiences negative emotions when lying. Some people, psychopaths, for example, habitually lie and can actually experience a thrill at the thought that they are fooling the interviewer. This is known as duping delight. With all other variables being equal, lying also requires greater mental effort than truth telling. A police officer conducting a routine roadside stop should have cause for concern if, for example, the driver stumbles or takes time to answer a question that s/he should know automatically, such as his/her name or birth date. Following a line of questioning, making up a plausible story and keeping one's story straight all requires more effort than simply telling the truth.

Knowing that truths and lies have emotional and cognitive responses is important but such represents only part of the process of evaluating truthfulness. How does someone know what someone else is feeling or thinking? While this is difficult to achieve with any certainty—hence why the business of evaluating truthfulness is complex—the good news is that the emotional and cognitive consequences associated with truth telling and lying tend to be displayed in behavior. This is referred to as "leakage." Leakage can be observed in a variety of behavioral channels, including the face, the body, in voice quality, verbal style, and in verbal content. Most of the time, when someone is telling the truth, his/her behaviors will be evidence that corroborates his/her claims and/or apparent emotional and cognitive load. In contrast, when someone is lying, his/her behaviors may betray him/her.

Leakage related to lying can be observed in two fashions: from a change in baseline and/or in light of inconsistencies across behavioral channels. Baseline refers to how someone typically behaves when telling the truth. With a good grasp of the interviewee's baseline behavior, the interviewer may then spot deviations from this baseline when discussing topics of importance. For example, the interviewee may suddenly evidence a change in posture, voice pitch and/or speech mannerisms (e.g., pauses or filled pauses) when asked about his whereabouts concerning a crime in question. This is the easiest way to identify leakage. Spotting inconsistencies takes more practice and skill but is also more revealing. Inconsistencies in behavioral channels, by definition, mean that the person is communicating different messages. For example, a person may say yes but nod no, or may shrug their shoulders when "confidently" verbally denying any wrongdoing.

Once leakage has been identified, it is the interviewer's job to explore, via effective interviewing techniques, its cause(s). Here lies another important point to understand about leakage. Emotional leakage by an interviewee only tells the interviewer that an emotion has occurred; it does not tell the interviewer the cause of that emotion. Similarly, seeing signs of cognitive load only tells the interviewer that the interviewee is exerting greater mental effort than is expected given the question or task. It is therefore crucial that interviewers not label leakage as a sign of deception. That decision is simply premature. Instead, the interviewer should note the information as it is important; that is, it is a "hot spot" (i.e., a clue to importance) to be further investigated. Otherwise, errors that could have been avoided will be made.

Wrongly judging a truth to be deception can have devastating consequences. The consequences of disbelieving the truth are exemplified by the phenomenon of false confessions. However, this is not the only example. Did a co-conspirator warn authorities of a pending hijacked airliner attack on the World Trade Center on September 11, 2011 and was the co-conspirator judged to be a lying? Wrongly believing the lie can also have dramatic consequences, particularly when the purpose of the interview is to determine some future activity. In 1938, British Prime Minister Chamberlain interviewed Hitler and erroneously believed that

Hitler was telling the truth about his peaceful intentions in parts of Czechoslovakia. History proved this to be a significant lie.

To summarize, while there are many other factors that influence our ability to differentiate truths from lies, evaluating truthfulness depends primarily on a good understanding of the nature and types of lies and of the psychology of truth telling and lying, and on skills in identifying, assessing, and interpreting behavioral leakage. Evaluating truthfulness should not be viewed as a single event or decision (i.e., deciding if person is being truthful or not) but rather as a process in which behavior is identified, hypotheses are generated, more questions are asked to test these hypotheses, and conclusions are data driven and logical.

Sin Number 4: Making the Pinocchio Error

Sin numbers 4–6 are by-products of Sin number 3: misunderstanding lying and truth telling. Making the Pinocchio error occurs when someone believes that there is a universal sign for lying: a specific type of leakage that always means a person is lying. This belief is propagated by a variety of factors, including erroneous theoretical perspectives (e.g., that looking up and to the left is associated with lying based on the theory of neuro-linguistic programming; see Mann et al., 2012), the mislabelling of signs of stress as signs of deception (e.g., as suggested by the developers of the voice stress analyser), simplistic portrayals in the media, and/or by well-meaning senior interviewers who were taught to believe in this myth. The bottom line is that there is no emotional, cognitive and/or physiological response in humans that equates to Pinocchio's nose growing. Research has consistently failed to find a single clue that means someone is lying across all people in all situations. In fact, it could be argued that there is greater variability than consistency when it comes to signs of deception across people. In the same way that the presence of a particular clue does not guarantee a lie, the absence of a particular clue does not mean someone is truthful.

Sin Number 5: Making the Othello Error

The Othello error occurs when a displayed emotion is wrongfully interpreted as evidence of lying. Othello was a character in Shakespeare's play, *Othello* and was led to believe that his wife, Desdemona, had been unfaithful. This was not true. However, when he confronted her with the accusation of infidelity, she was frightened because she knew how jealous he was. In fact, Othello had already killed the man he suspected was her lover, so she knew how dangerous his anger was and how hopeless was her situation. Nevertheless, Othello misinterpreted his wife's fear as evidence of her guilt, as opposed to her legitimate fear of being disbelieved. Remember that, when an interviewer sees an emotion, all the interviewer knows is that the emotion occurred. If an interviewee feels physically threatened, s/he may "leak" fear that could easily be misinterpreted as a clue to lying. For example, when a gang member who is corroborating with police shows fear, is this detection apprehension or fear of retaliation from fellow gang members? The Othello error cautions interviewers against relying too heavily on reactions/answers to specific questions as a sign of deception or guilt. The effective interviewer will note this as a hot spot to be probed further during the interview.

Sin Number 6: Making the Idiosyncrasy Error

The idiosyncrasy error reflects the failure to consider individual differences when interpreting the behaviors of others. There are a number of culturally dictated behaviors and idiosyncratic behavioral habits that are commonly misinterpreted as indications of deception but, in reality, have little meaning as hot spots without some understanding of the baseline rate of these behaviors. For example, some people never or rarely make eye contact; some people rub their noses a lot; some people frequently move their eyebrows; and so on. When a behavior is culturally sanctioned and/or habitual, its occurrence tells us little with regard to deception detection. For example, avoiding eye contact does not represent a hot spot during an interview if the person usually avoids eye contact. In this case, a more telling hot spot would be intimidating eye contact as such is inconsistent with the person's culture and baseline behavior.

The lesson here is that any leakage should be interpreted in relation to the person's baseline. The reasons behind individual behaviors are multifaceted and, among other factors, influenced by culture. For example, some cultures, such as certain Aboriginal or Asian cultures, tend to avoid eye contact, especially when talking with strangers or authority figures. However, experience suggests that some of these well-known culturally dictated behaviors are changing just as the world is changing. It may be that world-wide instant communication, such as e-mail communication or the availability of films on the Internet is breaking down these traditions. What we have always believed to be traditionally true may or may not be true any longer. This is another reason that no matter what you might assume about a person given his/her background (including culture), the best way to avoid errors is to compare the individuals' behavior to his/her baseline.

Sin Number 7: Not Being Self-Aware

One of the biggest impediments to effective interviewing is interviewer bias. That interviewers are susceptible to bias should not be a surprise in that all interviewers have one thing in common: they are human. Like other humans, they are subject to likes and dislikes, prejudices and fears, and personality traits that can bias their approach to the investigation and/or to the manner in which they interview others. While an effective interviewer will know his/her biases and attempt to minimize their impact, an ineffective interviewer unknowingly allows his/her biases to contaminate the investigation and/or interview. . . .

[B]iases affect the way we think about a particular subject, person or behavior. That is, biases reflect erroneous thoughts/beliefs. For example, as explained under Sin number 1, the "Me" Theory of Personality, interviewers often use their own thoughts, behaviors, and assumptions as a way of assessing the actions of victims, witnesses, informants, or suspects, or to judge the truthfulness of an interviewee's statement. Through improper training, an interviewer may also believe in a one-size-fits-all (or cookie-cutter) approach to interviewing. This type of approach "assumes" that all types of interviewees will respond identically to one interviewing style. This is too simplistic. Special populations, such as children, the development tally delayed and the mentally ill, for example, require tailored approaches that take into account their unique characteristics. . . . Thus, the skilled interviewer will always remember that effective interviewing requires a person-centered approach in which the interviewee's behaviors are interpreted from the interviewee's perspective rather than from the interviewers or in relation to other victims, witnesses, informants and/or suspects.

Sin Number 8: Not Considering Multiple Explanations

It is a common trap for any interviewer, experienced or not, to "know" what must have occurred and then set out to prove it. Magically, after the premature judgment has been made, much of the information that is gathered during the interview seems to support that judgment, even if the judgment was wrong. Jumping to conclusions is a consequence of being biased and this sin of interviewing emerges because the interviewer fails to maintain an open mind. Yuille has repeatedly testified on this issue in both Canadian and American courts, and commonly informs the triers of fact something to the effect of the following: the biggest single impediment to effective interviewing is when the interviewer has a single hypothesis about the fact pattern that he or she is dealing with. In contrast to that, the most effective approach to investigative interviewing is the alternative hypothesis method, where the interviewer entertains several alternative explanations as the interview/investigation unfolds. This way, the investigator is not blinded by one hypothesis. When there is only one hypothesis, there is a tendency to exaggerate the evidence that is consistent with it and minimize the evidence that is inconsistent. Keeping an open mind through multiple hypotheses testing reduces that problem.

Erroneous results are often produced when the interviewer assumes that any information provided by the interviewee that does not fit with the interviewer's single hypothesis must be false and, therefore, a lie. When this sin is being committed, the interview questions are generally worded in a biased fashion and the answers are generally interpreted in a manner favorable to the interviewer's biased hypothesis. Usually, this is not an intentionally malicious act. The "self-fulfilling prophecy" is the inevitable consequence of not keeping an open mind. Interviewers may also jump to the conclusion that an interviewee who lies about something or withholds information is guilty when the reason for this behavior may be something else altogether. For example, a woman being interviewed about her murdered husband may lie about her whereabouts not because she had something do to with his death but because she was having an affair. The interviewer who is locked into only one hypothesis will likely erroneously interpret her efforts to conceal the affair as a sign of guilt in the murder. This is why interviewers are encouraged to consider behavioral leakage a hot spot rather than a sign of deception or guilt. Remember that a hot spot may occur for a variety of reasons, of which lying is only one possibility. It may turn out that the interviewee has lied, but the process by which that conclusion has been reached should include identifying the hot spot, entertaining alternate hypotheses for the hot spot, probing the different alternate hypotheses about the hot spot with a variety of questions, considering other evidence in the case, and then making a decision. Considering multiple hypotheses for what we see and hear during an interview will go a long way to neutralizing interviewer biases and reducing errors in disbelieving the truth and believing the lie.

Sin Number 9: Not Planning Ahead

We have all heard the following edict: "A plan . . . even a bad plan . . . is better than no plan at all." Yet, it is not uncommon for an interviewer facing a heavy caseload to forgo planning an interview due to time management issues. Unfortunately, going into the interview without much preparation often leaves the interviewer frustrated that the interview produced very little information of value. . . .

Sin Number 10: Not Establishing Rapport

Rapport refers to the connection, harmony, confidence, or trust between the interviewer and interviewee. There is probably no other activity that can potentially influence the success of an interview to the same degree as establishing rapport. Positive rapport encourages people to talk and to talk honestly, including about topics they would otherwise not have talked about. Taking time to establish rapport further permits the interviewer the opportunity to establish a baseline and, therefore, contributes to evaluating truthfulness. Conversely, the failure to establish or maintain rapport can potentially jeopardize an interview. For example, an otherwise cooperative victim or witness may be put off and leave out crucial pieces of information, an informant may fail to report crime-related information, and a suspect may never feel comfortable enough to unload his burden onto the shoulders of the interviewer. If the interviewee reacts to the inability of the interviewer to establish rapport, his/her feelings may leak out and could potentially be misinterpreted as a sign of guilt. Moreover, if the interviewee is chronically stressed by the inability of the interviewer to establish rapport, the associated stress-related leakage could serve to mask more subtle hot spots elicited by offence-related questions. The importance of establishing rapport cannot be overstated. . . .

Sin Number 11: Not Actively Observing and Listening

Crucial information can be missed when one is distracted. Indeed, lies often succeed because the recipient of the lie was not paying attention. Unfortunately, there are many personal and professional demands that make distraction a reality within the interview context. An interviewer who is having problems at home or facing other personal problems will likely be distracted. Failure to attend to basic needs, such as food and sleep, can reduce our attentional capabilities. Acute and chronic pain further reduces our concentration, and some medications have known effects on attention and concentration. An interviewer facing a seemingly unmanageable case load or external pressures to find the suspect or identify the liar will likely be distracted. During the interview, the interviewer may be distracted by thinking about what question to ask next. This scenario is especially likely in novice interviewers and/or when the interviewer failed to prepare for the interview. The interviewer who is busy writing notes is, by definition, distracted. As well, the biased interviewer will also be distracted. His/her prejudices will likely surface into consciousness and, therefore, take away from limited attentional resources. The confession-seeking interviewer will be focused on navigating the interview to elicit a confession rather than focused on the here and now. The bottom line is that, the more one has on one's mind, the more likely one is to be distracted; and the more one is distracted, the less attention one has for the task at hand. Remember that attention is limited. This situation also sets the context by which corners are cut and poor interviewing techniques thrive (e.g., biases and not establishing rapport). For these reasons, distraction is the nemesis of the effective interviewer. . . .

Sin Number 12: Phrasing the Question Wrongly

One of the most frequent sins of interviewing is the improper phrasing of questions. This may be due, at least in part, to the fact that questions asked in the investigative interviewing context differ drastically from questions asked in the social context. The former requires a fact-finding mindset that avoids contaminating the interviewee's memory and/or distorting his/her self-report. These factors are not present in the social context which consequently promotes bad habits (e.g., phrasing questions to get a desirable answer or a story rather than just facts).

Within the investigative interviewing context, poorly phrased questions can have several unwanted consequences. Questions that are poorly worded can influence or contaminate how the interviewee answers the question, which itself may contaminate the interviewee's memory, or simply confuse the interviewee. At best, this reduces rapport and, at worst, it may serve as grounds to dismiss the case. An improperly worded question can also contain information that reveals what the interviewer already knows or, in some cases, does not know. Giving away your position is never a good plan. It matters not whether the questions are used in an interview (i.e., generally a non-confrontational solicitation of information from a cooperative interviewee) or an interrogation (i.e., generally a search for truthful or incriminating information from a reluctant or hostile interviewee)—the effects of a poorly worded question are the same. In order to recognize how often improperly worded questions are used in an interview, the interviewer should record the interview and then review the tape at a later date, critically listening for those questions that were confusing, leading, or otherwise supplied information to the interviewee, as well as the impact of such questions on the interviewee's self-report. . . .

Number 13: Timing the Question Wrongly

There are a number of ways that an interviewer can disrupt the tempo of an interview, cause the interviewee to forget to report vital information, or put the interviewee on the defensive by the timing of his/her questions. One of the most common examples of this sin is when the interviewer interrupts the interviewee. Interrupting any interviewee, deceptive or cooperative, is problematic more often than not. In many cases, an interviewer, after having established rapport, introduces the topic under investigation with a great opening statement, such as "Please describe everything that you can recall about the robbery yesterday." The mistake occurs when the interviewer quickly interrupts the interviewee with a second question. For example, the interviewer may stop the narrative and ask about specific characteristics of the perpetrator. With the cooperative interviewee, the interruption can disrupt the reconstructive process of memory and, therefore, result in less information being provided or key details being left out. The interruption can also be confusing and distracting to the interviewee, which may reduce rapport and/or implicitly communicate to the interviewee that the interviewer has an agenda that is not necessarily to get the interviewee's detailed account of what s/he knows. By definition, an interruption indicates that the interviewer was thinking of another line of questioning rather than actively paying attention to what was being said. . . .

Sin Number 14: Misunderstanding Coercion

History is filled with descriptions of torture tactics, from "the rack" to "the rubber hose." Defining some of these tactics as "torture" is often self-evident. But there are other, less brutal tactics that are designed to manipulate the interrogated person psychologically. Tactics such as exposure to loud sounds, prolonged isolation in extreme ambient environments, and degrading techniques are but a few. These are considered abusive in nature and are increasingly being shunned by the public, various professional groups and the courts. There are, however, other less abusive techniques that also aim to manipulate the interviewee who is being interrogated. These are viewed as coercive in that they are likely to render a confession that is not the product of the interviewee's free will regardless of whether free will was actually actively overcome. Coercive tactics include manipulation and deception (e.g., falsely claiming that evidence exists when it does not) and the failure to consider important individual difference factors (e.g., the limited cognitive abilities of the interviewee). Coercive tactics have been implicated in false confessions and the legal acceptability of these tactics depends on local policies (e.g., Canadian laws do not allow for the use of false evidence during interrogations that some other jurisdictions permit).

There are two major concerns with the use of coercive techniques. First, the probability is strong that memory, both in terms of content and accuracy, will be adversely affected in direct proportion to the amount/severity of the coercive techniques that are employed. The second concern relates to the possibility that the individual being interviewed or interrogated may not have engaged in the suspected activity or may not possess the knowledge being sought. This is not a statement of fact but a constant reminder that the purpose of the interview is to develop as much accurate information as possible from the interviewee without presupposing that the interviewee must know anything about what actually happened. By adopting this attitude, the interviewer is much more likely to consider alternate investigative hypotheses, ask more open-ended questions, allow the interviewee more narrative latitude, avoid coercive and unethical tactics, and consider lesser explanations for false or misleading information. In fact, this attitude forces the interviewer to work diligently at developing the information necessary to make accurate judgments about the interviewee. In contrast, the use of torture and other coercive or unethical tactics, by definition, presupposes that the individual has the information and that it is just a matter of breaking his or her will to withhold it.

Sin Number 15: Not Corroborating Information

The final sin of interviewing reviewed in this chapter occurs when the interviewer fails to corroborate the information gained in the interview. As noted above, the "truth" is whatever the interviewee believes to be true and there are a host of reasons why this "truth" may be historically wrong. It is, therefore, always important to find out why the interviewee believes the information to be true. It then becomes the responsibility of the interviewer to conduct a follow-up investigation to determine whether or not the information can be corroborated. Only then will the interviewer know for sure that what was said by the interviewee was, in fact, true or not. Corroborating statements would go a long way to reducing incidences of wrongful convictions due to false confessions and/or false claims of victimization.

Conclusion

This chapter covers 15 sins of interviewing that have been identified through practical experience and the collaboration between law enforcement professionals and academics/researchers. This chapter also provided practical suggestions for overcoming these sins. The first three sins are arguably the cardinal sins of interviewing in that they account for the development and/or maintenance of the remaining 12 sins. Avoiding these cardinal sins would, therefore, go a long way towards promoting effective interviewing skills. It seems only reasonable to assume that, if some of the major mistakes associated with the practice and research of interviewing could be identified and, therefore, avoided, the result would be more effective interviews and more complete and accurate information.

Many of these sins reflect insufficient or improper training, and point to the need for scientifically based training in investigative interviewing that is both practical and delivered in a way that maximizes learning and generalizing of skills to the real world. Arguably, the most effective training is developed through collaborative efforts between law enforcement professionals and academics, and delivered by subject matter experts who are also qualified instructors that can effectively communicate, demonstrate, and convey the training content. For now, the reader is reminded that the probability of conducting a successful interview that results in accurate information is enhanced when the following steps are followed:

1. Be **A**ware of the personality characteristics, traits, and background of the interviewer and the interviewee;
2. Determine the **B**aseline behavior of the interviewee;
3. Watch for **C**hanges in the interviewee's behavior during the interview;
4. Actively listen and watch for **D**iscrepancies between the interviewee's behavior and the verbal content of the statements;

5. Be willing to Engage and challenge the interviewee when deception possibly occurs; and,

6. Conduct a Follow-up investigation to corroborate the interviewee's statements.

Christopher Chabris & Daniel Simons
I Think I Would Have Seen That
THE INVISIBLE GORILLA: AND OTHER WAYS OUR INTUITIONS DECEIVE US (2010)[2]

The two of us met over a decade ago when Chris was a graduate student in the Harvard University psychology department and Dan had just arrived as a new assistant professor. Chris's office was down the hall from Dan's lab, and we soon discovered our mutual interest in how we perceive, remember, and think about our visual world. The Kenny Conley case was in full swing when Dan taught an undergraduate course in research methods with Chris as his teaching assistant. As part of their classwork, the students assisted us in conducting some experiments, one of which has become famous. It was based on an ingenious series of studies of visual attention and awareness conducted by the pioneering cognitive psychologist Ulric Neisser in the 1970s. Neisser had moved to Cornell University when Dan was in his final year of graduate school there, and their many conversations inspired Dan to build on Neisser's earlier, groundbreaking research.

With our students as actors and a temporarily vacant floor of the psychology building as a set, we made a short film of two teams of people moving around and passing basketballs. One team wore white shirts and the other wore black. Dan manned the camera and directed. Chris coordinated the action and kept track of which scenes we needed to shoot. We then digitally edited the film and copied it to videotapes, and our students fanned out across the Harvard campus to run the experiment.

They asked volunteers to silently count the number of passes made by the players wearing white while ignoring any passes by the players wearing black. The video lasted less than a minute. If you want to try the task yourself, stop reading now and go to the website for our book, www.theinvisiblegorilla.com, where we provide links to many of the experiments we discuss, including a short version of the basketball-passing video. Watch the video carefully, and be sure to include both aerial passes and bounce passes in your count.

---

2 Footnotes and/or internal citations omitted.

Immediately after the video ended, our students asked the subjects to report how many passes they'd counted. In the full-length version, the correct answer was thirty-four or maybe thirty-five. To be honest, it doesn't matter. The pass-counting task was intended to keep people engaged in doing something that demanded attention to the action on the screen, but we weren't really interested in pass-counting ability. We were actually testing something else: Halfway through the video, a female student wearing a full-body gorilla suit walked into the scene, stopped in the middle of the players, faced the camera, thumped her chest, and then walked off, spending about nine seconds onscreen. After asking subjects about the passes, we asked the more important questions:

Q: Did you notice anything unusual while you were doing the counting task?

A: No.

Q: Did you notice anything other than the players?

A: Well, there were some elevators, and S's painted on the wall. I don't know what the S's were there for.

Q: Did you notice *anyone* other than the players?

A: No.

Q: Did you notice a gorilla?

A: A what?!?

Amazingly, roughly half of the subjects in our study did not notice the gorilla! Since then the experiment has been repeated many times, under different conditions, with diverse audiences, and in multiple countries, but the results are always the same: About half the people fail to see the gorilla. How could people not see a gorilla walk directly in front of them, turn to face them, beat its chest, and walk away? What made the gorilla invisible? This error of perception results from a lack of attention to an unexpected object, so it goes by the scientific name "inattentional blindness." This name distinguishes it from forms of blindness resulting from a damaged visual system; here, people don't see the gorilla, but not because of a problem with their eyes. When people devote their attention to a particular area or aspect of their visual world, they tend not to notice unexpected objects, even when those unexpected objects are salient, potentially important, and appear right where they are looking. In other words, the subjects were concentrating so hard on counting the passes that they were "blind" to the gorilla right in front of their eyes.

What prompted us to write this book, however, was not inattentional blindness in general or the gorilla study in particular. The fact that people miss things is important, but what impressed us even more was the *surprise* people showed when they realized what they had missed.

When they watched the video again, this time without counting passes, they all saw the gorilla easily, and they were shocked. Some spontaneously said, "I missed that?!" or "No way!" A man who was tested later by the producers of *Dateline NBC* for their report on this research said, "I know that gorilla didn't come through there the first time." Other subjects accused us of switching the tape while they weren't looking.

The gorilla study illustrates, perhaps more dramatically than any other, the powerful and pervasive influence of the *illusion of attention*: We experience far less of our visual world than we think we do. If we were fully aware of the limits to attention, the illusion would vanish. While writing this book we hired the polling firm SurveyUSA to contact a representative sample of American adults and ask them a series of questions about how they think the mind works. We found that more than 75 percent of people agreed that they would notice such unexpected events, even when they were focused on something else. (We'll talk about other findings of this survey throughout the book.)

It's true that we vividly experience some aspects of our world, particularly those that are the focus of our attention. But this rich experience inevitably leads to the erroneous belief that we process *all* of the detailed information around us. In essence, we know how vividly we see some aspects of our world, but we are completely unaware of those aspects of our world that fall outside of that current focus of attention. Our vivid visual experience masks a striking mental blindness—we assume that visually distinctive or unusual objects will draw our attention, but in reality they often go completely unnoticed.

Since our experiment was published in the journal *Perception* in 1999, under the title "Gorillas in Our Midst," it has become one of the most widely demonstrated and discussed studies in all of psychology. It earned us an Ig Nobel Prize in 2004 (awarded for "achievements that first make people laugh, and then make them think") and was even discussed by characters in an episode of the television drama *CSI*. And we've lost count of the number of times people have asked us whether we have seen the video with the basketball players and the gorilla.

. . .

Who Notices the Unexpected?

Chris once demonstrated the gorilla experiment to students in a seminar he was teaching. One of them told him the next week that she'd shown the video to her family, and that her parents had both missed the gorilla but her older sister had seen it. The sister then proceeded to crow about her triumph in this gorilla-noticing competition, claiming that it showed how smart she was. Dan regularly receives e-mails from people he's never met asking why they missed the gorilla but their children saw it, or whether girls always notice but boys never do. A hedge fund manager found out about our study and had the people in her office do it. She tracked Chris down through a chain of acquaintances and interrogated him about the differences between people who notice the gorilla and people who don't.

Many people who have experienced the gorilla experiment see it as a sort of intelligence or ability test. The effect is so striking—and the balance so even between the number who notice and the number who don't—that people often assume that some important aspect of your personality determines whether or not you notice the gorilla. When Dan was working with *Dateline NBC* to create demonstrations, the show's producers speculated that employees in detail-oriented occupations would be more likely to notice the gorilla, and they asked most of their "subjects" what their jobs were. They assumed that how you perform on the task depends on what kind of person you are: a "noticer" or a "misser." This is the question of *individual differences*. If we could figure out whether some people consistently notice the gorilla and other unexpected events in laboratory tasks, then we could figure out whether they are immune to inattentional blindness more generally, and potentially train the missers to become noticers.

Despite the intuitive appeal of the gorilla video as a Rosetta stone for personality types, there is almost no evidence that individual differences in attention or other abilities affect inattentional blindness. In theory, people could differ in the total attentional resources they have available, and those with more resources (perhaps those with higher IQs) might have enough "left over" after allocating some to the primary task to be better at detecting unexpected objects. One argument against this possibility, though, is the consistency in the pattern of results we obtain with the gorilla demonstration. We conducted the original experiment on Harvard undergraduates—a fairly elite group—but the experiment works just as well at less prestigious institutions and with subjects who aren't students. In all cases, about half of the subjects see the gorilla and half don't. According to an online survey by Nokia, 60 percent of women *and* men think that women are better at multitasking. If you agree, you might also think that women would be more likely to notice the gorilla. Unfortunately, there is little experimental evidence to support the popular belief about multitasking, and we haven't found any evidence that men are more prone than women to miss the gorilla. In fact, the main conclusion from studies of multitasking is that virtually nobody does it well: As a rule, it is more efficient to do tasks one at a time rather than simultaneously.

It's still possible—even reasonable—to suspect that people differ in their ability to focus attention on a primary task, but that this ability isn't related to general intelligence or educational achievement. If individual differences in the ability to focus attention lead to differences in noticing unexpected objects, then people for whom the counting task is easier should be more likely to notice the gorilla—they are devoting fewer resources to the counting task and have more left over.

Dan and his graduate student Melinda Jensen recently conducted an experiment to test exactly this hypothesis. They first measured how well people could do a computer-based tracking task like the one we used in the "red gorilla" experiment and then looked to see whether those who performed the task well were more likely to notice an unexpected object. They weren't. Apparently, whether you detect unexpected objects and events doesn't depend on your capacity for attention. Consistent with this conclusion, Dan, and sports scientist Daniel Memmert, the researcher who tracked children's eye movements while they watched the gorilla video, found that who noticed and who missed an unexpected object was unrelated to several basic measures of attention capacity. These findings have an important practical implication: Training people to improve their attention abilities may do nothing to help them detect unexpected objects. If an object is truly unexpected, people are unlikely to notice it no matter how good (or bad) they are at focusing attention.

As far as we can tell, there are no such people as "noticers" and "missers"—at least, no people who consistently notice or consistently miss unexpected events in a variety of contexts and situations. There is one way, however, to predict how likely a person is to see the unexpected. But it is not a simple trait of the individual or a quality of the event; it is the combination of a fact about the individual and a fact about the situation in which the unexpected event occurs. Only seven people out of more than one thousand stopped to listen to Joshua Bell playing in the L'Enfant Plaza subway station. One had been to a concert Bell had given just three weeks earlier. Two of the remaining six were musicians themselves. Their expertise helped them recognize his skill—and the pieces he was playing—through the din. One, George Tindley, worked in a nearby Au Bon Pain restaurant. "You could tell in one second that this guy was good, that he was clearly a professional," he told Weingarten. The other, John Picarello, said, "This was a superb violinist. I've never heard anyone of that caliber. He was technically proficient, with very good phrasing. He had a good fiddle, too, with a big, lush sound."

Experiments support this observation. Experienced basketball players are more likely to notice the gorilla in the original basketball-passing video than are novice basketball players. In contrast, team handball players are no more likely to notice unexpected objects even though they are experts in a team sport that places demands on attention comparable to those of basketball. Expertise helps you notice unexpected events, but only when the event happens in the context of your expertise. Put experts in a situation where they have no special skill, and they are ordinary novices, taxing their attention just to keep up with the primary task. And no matter what the situation, experts are not immune to the illusory belief that people notice far more than they do. Gene Weingarten described John Picarello's behavior as he watched Bell play: "On the video, you can see Picarello look around him now and then, almost bewildered. 'Yeah, other people just were not getting it. It just wasn't registering. That was baffling to me.' "

How Many Doctors Does It Take . . .

Even within their field of specialty, experts are not immune to inattentional blindness or the illusion of attention. Radiologists are medical specialists responsible for reading x-rays, CT scans, MRIs, and other images in order to detect and diagnose tumors and other abnormalities. Radiologists perform this visual detection task under controlled conditions every day of their careers. In the United States, their training involves four years of medical school, followed by up to five years in residency at a teaching hospital. Those who specialize in specific body systems spend another year or two in fellowship training. In total, they often have more than ten years of post-undergraduate training, followed by on-the-job experience in studying dozens of films each day. Despite their extensive training, radiologists can still miss subtle problems when they "read" medical images.

Consider a recent case described by Frank Zwemer and his colleagues at the University of Rochester School of Medicine. An ambulance brought a woman in her forties to the emergency room with severe vaginal bleeding. Doctors attempted to insert an intravenous line in a peripheral vein, but failed, so they instead inserted a central line via a catheter in the femoral vein, the largest vein in the groin. Getting the line in correctly requires also inserting a guidewire, which is removed once the line is in place.

The line was introduced successfully, but due to an oversight, the physician neglected to remove the guidewire.[47] To address her blood loss, the patient was given transfusions, but she then developed difficulty breathing due to pulmonary edema (a swelling or fluid buildup in the lungs). She was intubated for respiratory support, and a chest x-ray was taken to confirm the diagnosis and make sure that the breathing tube was placed correctly. The ER doctor and the attending radiologist agreed on the diagnosis, but neither of them noticed the guidewire. The patient went next to the intensive care unit for several days of treatment, and after she improved she went to a standard unit. There she developed shortness of breath, which was caused by pulmonary embolism—a blood clot in her lung. During this time she received two more x-rays, as well as an echocardiogram and a CT scan. Only on the fifth day of her stay in the hospital did a physician happen to notice and remove the guidewire while performing a procedure to correct the pulmonary embolism. The patient then made a full recovery. (It was determined later that the guidewire probably didn't cause the embolism because it was constructed of so-called nonthrombogenic material specifically intended not to promote blood clotting.)

When the various medical images were examined afterward, the guidewire was clearly visible on all three x-rays and on the CT, but none of the many doctors on the case noticed it. Their failure to see the anomalous guidewire illustrates yet again the dangers of inattentional blindness. The radiologists and other physicians who reviewed the chest images looked at them carefully, but they did not see the guidewire because they did not expect to see it.

Radiologists have a tremendously difficult task. They often review a large number of images at a time, typically looking for a specific problem—a broken bone, a tumor, and so on. They can't take in everything in the image, so they focus their attention on the critical aspects of the image, just as the subjects in the gorilla study focused on counting the passes of one team of players. Due to the limits of attention, radiologists are unlikely to notice aspects of the image that are unexpected, like the presence of a guidewire. But people assume that radiologists should notice any problem in a medical image regardless of whether it is expected; any failure to do so must therefore be the result of the doctor's negligence. Radiologists are regularly sued for missing small tumors or other problems. These lawsuits are often based on the illusion of attention—people assume that radiologists will notice anything anomalous in an image, when in reality they, like the rest of us, tend to see best what they are looking for in the image. If you tell radiologists to find the guidewire in a chest x-ray, they will expect to see one and will notice it. But if you tell them to find a pulmonary embolism, they may not notice the guidewire. (It's also possible that when searching for the guidewire, they will miss more pulmonary embolisms.) An unexpected tumor that was missed during the original reading might seem obvious in hindsight.

Unfortunately, people often confuse what is easily noticed when it is expected with what should be noticed when it is unexpected. Moreover, the procedures frequently used in hospitals when reviewing radiographs are affected by the illusion of attention; doctors themselves also assume that they will notice unexpected problems in an image, even when they are looking for something else. To reduce the effects of inattentional blindness, one can deliberately reexamine the same images with an eye toward the unexpected. When participants in our studies know that something unexpected might happen, they consistently see the gorilla—the unexpected has become the target of focused attention. Devoting attention to the unexpected is not a cure-all, however. We have limited attention resources, and devoting some attention to unexpected events means that we have less attention available for our primary task. It would be imprudent to ask radiologists to take time and resources away from detecting the expected problem in an x-ray ("Doctor, can you confirm that this patient has a pulmonary embolism so that we can begin treatment?") to focus instead on things that are unlikely to be there ("Doctor, can you tell us whether we left anything behind in this patient's body?"). A more effective strategy would be for a second radiologist, unfamiliar with the case and the tentative diagnosis, to examine the images and to look for secondary problems that might not have been noticed the first time through.

So it turns out that even experts with a decade of training in their medical specialty can miss unexpected objects in their domain of expertise. Although radiologists are better able than laypeople to detect unusual aspects of radiographs, they suffer from the same limits on attention as everyone else. Their expertise lies not in greater attention, but in more precise expectations formed by their experience and training in perceiving the important features of the images. Experience guides them to look for common problems rather than rare anomalies, and in most cases, that strategy is wise.

. . .

Benchmark Institute
Case Planning
LEGAL SERVICES PRACTICE MANUAL: SKILLS (2010)[3]

Some form of case planning is needed for every case that you handle. Many advocates think that case planning means identifying the applicable law, learning some new facts and hoping that the entire case will hold together at the negotiation, hearing or trial. A great deal more is required to meet minimum standards of professional competence.

Case planning involves defining the client's problem, identifying possible solutions and selecting courses of action. It means constructing a complete picture of the client's situation from the facts, the applicable law, and the way in which the facts and law fit in the larger context in which they occur. It must include developing an overall theory of the case—a detailed, coherent and accurate story of what occurred which demonstrates the client's entitlement to relief. This picture requires projecting forward in time, imagining how the opposition will view the case and imagining how it will be viewed if it must be appealed.

---

[3] Footnotes and/or internal citations omitted.

Quality representation requires you to make things happen for your clients according to plan. Every step of your plan will influence the ultimate outcome and may even change the entire nature of the case. Advocates develop winning cases—they don't walk through the door.

This overview describes one approach to planning and preparing cases. It breaks out the various steps involved in case planning and presents in linear form that which is circular. It contains the elements common to all case planning models: defining the problem, generating and examining alternatives, locating facts, selecting and evaluating the facts and law, and devising a case theory to produce the result most favorable to the client's situation.

We have divided case planning into six major steps. In our case plan model, advocates must:

- Identify Client Objectives
- Analyze Facts, Possible Causes of Action, Remedies
- Analyze Cast of Characters
- Formulate a Theory of the Case
- Select Forum
- Formulate Workplan

These steps involve further tasks described below. . . .

1. **Identify the client's objectives.**

From the initial interview, what does the client want? Sometimes identifying the client's objectives requires probing beyond how the client first expresses what she wants. Sometimes the client needs help in articulating and framing exactly what she wants. It's every advocate's duty to find out at the initial interview what the client wants to achieve.

2. **Summarize the facts of the client's problem.**

What happened? Who said and did what? Who are the key players and what is their relationship to the client? This statement summarizes the facts but is specific enough so that someone unfamiliar with the problem could grasp it from reading this summary.

3. **Identify the legal issues in the case.**

What do you initially recognize as the issues in the case? For example: Is the father continually absent from the home? Are the premises habitable? This issue statement will be modified once further legal research and fact gathering are completed.

As you become familiar with particular areas of the law, initial issue identification becomes easier. Checklists of the types of issues presented by various factual situations can be helpful in areas with which you are unfamiliar or which are not in your area of expertise.

4. **List all possible solutions to the client's problem.**

This step involves brainstorming any and all solutions to the client's problem. The point is to generate as many possibilities as you can think of—no matter how crazy or far out. Quantity breeds quality. Include non-litigation strategies such as legislative, administrative, economic development and community education strategies.

This step also forces you to adopt a larger view of the client's problems. The larger implications of a case may relate to the client community as a whole thereby dictating other strategies. While cases often present a conflict between an individual and an agency, a broad range of other relationships and processes may touch on the client's problem in different ways. To generate possible solutions, you must understand some of what's actually occurring within the system where the dispute arises.

Example

The eligibility worker at the Welfare Department determines that the client and her children are no longer entitled to benefits because the children are not properly enrolled in school. Clearly related to the client's problem are the procedures and relationships between the Welfare Department and the school district and any government policies of the welfare department, the efforts to reduce welfare costs.

The client's problem is very involved in several relationships and processes. The way in which the advocate understands these relationships often determines how she identifies the alternative solutions to solve the client's problem. If action has been taken against the client because of a change in department policy, an administrative hearing for the client may not be an appropriate strategy and litigation to challenge the policy change may be more appropriate.

Understanding the larger context may suggest ideas for further research and fact investigation. Is the action taken against the client isolated or part of a larger change instituted by an institution or agency? How are decisions made within the institution and what are possible pressure points there? Is this behavior part of a pattern and practice that affects the client community? Is this a systemic problem that must be addressed?

Take advantage of the expertise within your program and legal services community in finding out about how institutions and systems function. Failure to examine the larger context within which the problems arise leads to decisions about handing a case which are not the most effective ones to achieve the client's desired goal.

5. **Identify any additional factual investigation that is needed *to formulate viable alternatives to present to the client.* Include the information needed, the possible sources of that information and the method you would use to get it.**

- WHAT
- SOURCE
- HOW

This step involves locating information needed to offer viable alternatives to the client. This information may be obtained by a quick call to an administrative agency or landlord or may involve more detailed information about an agency's or institution's usual practices. In any event, you should identify what information you need, the source of that information and how you will go about getting it.

6. **Identify any additional legal research that needs to be done to formulate viable alternatives to present to the client.**

What legal research must be completed in order to present viable options to your client? This step is critical to insure that you've identified all the potential legal issues and to determine which of any of the solutions generated in Step 4 are viable enough to present to the client.

In some cases the amount of legal research only may involve checking the language of a code section or regulation. In others it may involve reading narrative overviews of the subject, analyzing various statutes, regulations and court decisions. Write up the research and include it in the case file. Some offices require a legal memo to the file which includes this information.

7. **Formulate a timetable for action (what must be done, when it must be done and by whom).**

- WHAT
- WHEN
- WHO

This step incorporates what you have decided needs to be done for Steps 5–6 into a work plan. This step is particularly crucial when you are working with other people on a case.

8. **Identify the options that you will present to the client for his/her decision.**

This step assumes that you have completed the tasks in #7, refined the issues in #3 and have narrowed the solutions stated in #4 to realistic and viable solutions. Depending on the case, completing #1–8 could take minutes, days or even months.

9. **Construct a factual chronology of the case.**

Once the client has chosen which option to pursue, it's helpful to put together a detailed factual chronology of what happened when. You should begin as far back as needed to give a full background of the case. Doing the chronology will give you a good grasp on the case and make apparent factual gaps.

10. **Analyzing the case from a "non-legal" perspective:**

Looking at cases from a common sense perspective gives the advocate valuable insight into a case and usually contains the key to possible themes or theories of your case. To help you with this step, we suggest that you get the insight of people who are not in the legal business.

a) **What's the essential wrong or unfairness to the client?**

What isn't "right" about what's happened to your client?

b) **Does this unfairness suggest any causes of action or defenses that were not obvious to you?**

Be creative here. If the law doesn't recognize a real cause of action here, maybe it should.

c) **Identify any facts that makes the case special or more appealing.**

What stands out about your client, what happened to her or him, or the opponent which distinguishes this case?

d) **Identify any theme or unifying principle that these facts suggest.**

If this scenario was a painting, song, movie or TV show, how would you title it?

11. **Identify the legal theories of the case (causes of action or defenses/counterclaims).**

Formulating the legal theories may require continuing the legal research begun immediately after the initial interview. Expand your research until a firm decision is reached as to the nature of the substantive law governing the case.

Legal theories are the parties' legal arguments for why they should prevail. The plaintiff's legal theory is called a cause of action or claim. A cause of action is a legally acceptable theory for bringing a lawsuit which will be won if the facts support the elements of the theory.

For example, a tenant-plaintiff's theory in an affirmative action suit against a landlord-defendant might be that defendant had breached a statutory duty to keep a rented apartment in habitable condition, thus entitling the plaintiff to damages. In trying to evict a tenant, a landlord-plaintiff's theory might be that defendant tenant should be evicted because she had breached the lease by failing to pay the rent pursuant to state law. In a county action to cut off a family from AFDC, the family's theory for remaining on aid is that the children are deprived of parental support and care as defined in federal and state law.

The defendant's legal theory may be a defense designed to defeat the cause of action or a simple denial of facts that support the plaintiff's theory.

For example, in the habitability suit above, the defendant's theory might be that he did not breach the warranty of habitability. The defendant in the eviction suit might argue that she should not be evicted because she was entitled to not pay the rent because the landlord failed to make promised repairs. The welfare department's theory could be that the children are not deprived within the meaning of the law.

12. **Using the Legal Issues Form, identify the elements you must prove to prevail for each cause of action or defense, any legal arguments the opponent might make as to their validity, and your rebuttal.**

- Elements
- [Opponent's "O's"] Position
- Rebuttal

For each cause of action, claim and defense, list the elements that you must prove to prevail on that theory and the authority that supports your argument. Next indicate any arguments your opponent might make as to the validity of the element with applicable authority. Finally, state any legal arguments that you can make to rebut opponent's arguments.

The elements of a claim or defense are the conditions that must exist to sustain the claim or defense. Elements are found in the substantive law which governs the case, whether the law is embodied in statute, regulation or holding of a court opinion.

For example:

Assume that Section 123 provides: "An owner of real property may evict a tenant in possession of said property if the tenant has failed to pay agreed upon rent."

In order to evict pursuant to Section 123, these elements must be present: "*owner* of the *property*" "*tenant, fails* to *pay*" and "*agreed* upon *rent*." Parties can argue over what elements must exist or how elements should be defined. The arguments over the existence and definition of elements are legal arguments.

In the example above, the parties could disagree over the meaning of "tenant" in Section 123: whether a person who rents a room from the original tenant is a "tenant". Or suppose the welfare department alleges that Mother Jones is ineligible as an AFDC caretaker for three children because she was not a parent within the meaning of the law. As to the element of "parent", Mother Jones' position is that as a foster mother she meets the definition of parent. The Welfare Department's position is that "parent" only includes biological or adopted parent. Mother Jones' rebuttal would involve her legal argument in response to the department's argument.

13. **Using the Preliminary Fact Analysis Form, identify the facts that support the elements, O's rebuttal to those facts and additional facts that you need.**

- Elements
- Factual Bits
- O's Rebuttal
- Facts Needed
- Discovery Method

This step is the nitty gritty of analysis. It requires you to state the elements of each cause of action (transferred from the Legal Issues Form), list any facts or factual bits that you have to prove that element, state the opponent's rebuttal, identify additional facts that you *need* to prove the element, and indicate the method to collect that information.

For example, in order to prove the element "fails to pay" in the landlord-tenant example above, plaintiff lists these facts: rent was due on July 1st, landlord did not receive any money from tenant on July 1st or any other date since then. Under "opponent's rebuttal," plaintiff indicates that tenant alleges she mailed the rent on June 28th.

14. **Identify the "cast of characters" in the case. For each person or institution, list their strengths and weaknesses and any additional information you need about them.**

- Character
- Strengths
- Weaknesses

• Information

Err on the side of including all key players in the case including institutions and groups.

15. **Identify the theory of the case.**

16. **Identify the opponent's theory.**

At this point you have developed your legal theories of the case. From the material and evidence initially available, you must begin to develop a notion of how a particular course of events could have happened—a theory of the facts of the case. The theory of the facts must be grounded in your legal theories and the two enmeshed to formulate the theory of the case.

The theory of the case describes how you want the trier of fact to view the case. This picture involves a combination of your theory of the law and a theory of the facts, It is a dramatic appeal based upon the equities which appeals to the trier of fact's beliefs about what is right and what constitutes fair play.

A natural impulse is to rehash the facts and law developed in the preliminary analysis and to label the hash the case theory. A good case theory is based on this analysis, but is couched in a coherent framework which compels the conclusion that your client should prevail.

A good case theory:

• **Is based on strong facts and inferences which can be fairly drawn from these facts.**

• **Is built on facts not subject to much, if any, dispute,** such as documents which speak for themselves, admissions against interest, testimony from independent, reliable witnesses who have no stake in the outcome of the case; undisputed evidence from other areas. For example, assume undisputed evidence exists that a consulting physician who states that a disability claimant was not disabled examined the claimant for only 10 minutes. This evidence could strengthen the client's credibility and could become part of the hearing officer's reconstruction of the manner in which the SSA had handled the claimant's case.

• **Is not inconsistent with some incontestable fact.** A theory premised on the notion that the claimant visited certain doctors when the evidence indicates that she hasn't is not a good theory. A different theory must be developed which recognizes the existence of incontestable facts and provides a means for the recipient to prevail.

• **Takes into account and explains away as many unfavorable facts as possible.** It is rare that clients present a clean set of facts where no facts are unfavorable. Those clients will not need your help. As a result the theory you develop must take into account the unfavorable facts and have built into it an explanation for them. To be believable the theory has to explain their existence and has to be one which the trier of fact can reasonably believe.

• **Is accepted by the trier of fact without having to stretch the imagination—it is grounded in common sense and is consistent with what the trier of fact knows about how things happen in the world.** If it is too involved and requires too much imagination or belief in the way things are that is not generally accepted, it has little chance of being accepted.

This grounding in common experience is often the most difficult for advocates representing clients with little or no funds and living in poor communities. It is difficult to convince a trier of fact of a set of circumstances which are particular to the life situation of such individuals but not generally found in the life situation of the trier of fact.

In developing a theory consistent with this concern, you have to take into account this difference in perception and may well have to adopt the theory to deal with it. Advocates who fail to consider this are often surprised when a theory that seems very straightforward is not accepted by the trier of fact, because they find it unbelievable.

• **Is not based on wishful thinking about any aspect of the case.** The theory must be consistent with the facts and law which actually exist, not on what you wish them to be. At the same time, you must be creative. The history of legal services is full of creative theories, instances where the facts supported the theory being developed and there was reason to believe that the law could be developed in a certain way.

17. **Identify the forum where you will bring the case or whether the forum can or should be changed.**

If a choice of forums exists, some factors to consider are: resolution time, sympathetic judges, availability of jury trial, availability of discovery, available relief, and complexity, sophistication of procedures.

18. **Identify any provisional relief and motions that you will bring or anticipate the opponent bringing.**

19. **Do a discovery plan**

Building on your Preliminary Fact Analysis:

• Select the way each fact will be proved

• Determine Sequence

• Identify Problems

- Discovery Method
- Begin
- Complete
- O's Response
- Rebuttal

20. **Do case workplan**

- Identify the tasks that need to occur
- Identify who will do what
- List the support needed to accomplish the tasks
- State completion dates (over estimate)

Sir Arthur Conan Doyle
The Boscombe Valley Mystery
THE ADVENTURES OF SHERLOCK HOLMES

We were seated at breakfast one morning, my wife and I, when the maid brought in a telegram. It was from Sherlock Holmes and ran in this way:

"Have you a couple of days to spare? Have just been wired for from the west of England in connection with Boscombe Valley tragedy. Shall be glad if you will come with me. Air and scenery perfect. Leave Paddington by the 11:15."

"What do you say, dear?" said my wife, looking across at me. "Will you go?"

"I really don't know what to say. I have a fairly long list at present."

"Oh, Anstruther would do your work for you. You have been looking a little pale lately. I think that the change would do you good, and you are always so interested in Mr. Sherlock Holmes' cases."

"I should be ungrateful if I were not, seeing what I gained through one of them," I answered. "But if I am to go, I must pack at once, for I have only half an hour."

My experience of camp life in Afghanistan had at least had the effect of making me a prompt and ready traveller. My wants were few and simple, so that in less than the time stated I was in a cab with my valise, rattling away to Paddington Station. Sherlock Holmes was pacing up and down the platform, his tall, gaunt figure made even gaunter and taller by his long grey travelling-cloak and close-fitting cloth cap.

"It is really very good of you to come, Watson," said he. "It makes a considerable difference to me, having someone with me on whom I can thoroughly rely. Local aid is always either worthless or else biassed. If you will keep the two corner seats I shall get the tickets."

We had the carriage to ourselves save for an immense litter of papers which Holmes had brought with him. Among these he rummaged and read, with intervals of note-taking and of meditation, until we were past Reading. Then he suddenly rolled them all into a gigantic ball and tossed them up onto the rack.

"Have you heard anything of the case?" he asked.

"Not a word. I have not seen a paper for some days."

"The London press has not had very full accounts. I have just been looking through all the recent papers in order to master the particulars. It seems, from what I gather, to be one of those simple cases which are so extremely difficult."

"That sounds a little paradoxical."

"But it is profoundly true. Singularity is almost invariably a clue. The more featureless and commonplace a crime is, the more difficult it is to bring it home. In this case, however, they have established a very serious case against the son of the murdered man."

"It is a murder, then?"

"Well, it is conjectured to be so. I shall take nothing for granted until I have the opportunity of looking personally into it. I will explain the state of things to you, as far as I have been able to understand it, in a very few words.

"Boscombe Valley is a country district not very far from Ross, in Herefordshire. The largest landed proprietor in that part is a Mr. John Turner, who made his money in Australia and returned some years ago to the old country. One of the farms which he held, that of Hatherley, was let to Mr. Charles McCarthy, who was also an ex-Australian. The men had known each other in the colonies, so that it was not unnatural that when they came to settle down they should do so as near each other as possible. Turner was apparently the richer man, so McCarthy became his tenant but still remained, it seems, upon terms of perfect equality, as they were frequently together. McCarthy had one son, a lad of eighteen, and Turner had an only daughter of the same age, but neither of them had wives living. They appear to have avoided the society of the neighbouring English families and to have led retired lives, though both the McCarthys were fond of sport and were frequently seen at the race-meetings of the neighbourhood. McCarthy kept two servants—a man and a girl. Turner had a considerable household, some half-dozen at the least. That is as much as I have been able to gather about the families. Now for the facts.

"On June 3rd, that is, on Monday last, McCarthy left his house at Hatherley about three in the afternoon and walked down to the Boscombe Pool, which is a small lake formed by the spreading out of the stream which runs down the Boscombe Valley. He had been out with his serving-man in the morning at Ross, and he had told the man that he must hurry, as he had an appointment of importance to keep at three. From that appointment he never came back alive.

"From Hatherley Farm-house to the Boscombe Pool is a quarter of a mile, and two people saw him as he passed over this ground. One was an old woman, whose name is not mentioned, and the other was William Crowder, a game-keeper in the employ of Mr. Turner. Both these witnesses depose that Mr. McCarthy was walking alone. The game-keeper adds that within a few minutes of his seeing Mr. McCarthy pass he had seen his son, Mr. James McCarthy, going the same way with a gun under his arm. To the best of his belief, the father was actually in sight at the time, and the son was following him. He thought no more of the matter until he heard in the evening of the tragedy that had occurred.

"The two McCarthys were seen after the time when William Crowder, the game-keeper, lost sight of them. The Boscombe Pool is thickly wooded round, with just a fringe of grass and of reeds round the edge. A girl of fourteen, Patience Moran, who is the daughter of the lodge-keeper of the Boscombe Valley estate, was in one of the woods picking flowers. She states that while she was there she saw, at the border of the wood and close by the lake, Mr. McCarthy and his son, and that they appeared to be having a violent quarrel. She heard Mr. McCarthy the elder using very strong language to his son, and she saw the latter raise up his hand as if to strike his father. She was so frightened by their violence that she ran away and told her mother when she reached home that she had left the two McCarthys quarrelling near Boscombe Pool, and that she was afraid that they were going to fight. She had hardly said the words when young Mr. McCarthy came running up to the lodge to say that he had found his father dead in the wood, and to ask for the help of the lodge-keeper. He was much excited, without either his gun or his hat, and his right hand and sleeve were observed to be stained with fresh blood. On following him they found the dead body stretched out upon the grass beside the pool. The head had been beaten in by repeated blows of some heavy and blunt weapon. The injuries were such as might very well have been inflicted by the butt-end of his son's gun, which was found lying on the grass within a few paces of the body. Under these circumstances the young man was instantly arrested, and a verdict of 'wilful murder' having been returned at the inquest on Tuesday, he was on Wednesday brought before the magistrates at Ross, who have referred the case to the next Assizes. Those are the main facts of the case as they came out before the coroner and the police-court."

"I could hardly imagine a more damning case," I remarked. "If ever circumstantial evidence pointed to a criminal it does so here."

"Circumstantial evidence is a very tricky thing," answered Holmes thoughtfully. "It may seem to point very straight to one thing, but if you shift your own point of view a little, you may find it pointing in an equally uncompromising manner to something entirely different. It must be confessed, however, that the case looks exceedingly grave against the young man, and it is very possible that he is indeed the culprit. There are several people in the neighbourhood, however, and among them Miss Turner, the daughter of the neighbouring landowner, who believe in his innocence, and who have retained Lestrade, whom you may recollect in connection with the Study in Scarlet, to work out the case in his interest. Lestrade, being rather puzzled, has referred the case to me, and hence it is that two middle-aged gentlemen are flying westward at fifty miles an hour instead of quietly digesting their breakfasts at home."

"I am afraid," said I, "that the facts are so obvious that you will find little credit to be gained out of this case."

"There is nothing more deceptive than an obvious fact," he answered, laughing. "Besides, we may chance to hit upon some other obvious facts which may have been by no means obvious to Mr. Lestrade. You know me too well to think that I am boasting when I say that I shall either confirm or destroy his theory by means which he is quite incapable of employing, or even of understanding. To take the first example to hand, I very clearly perceive that in your bedroom the window is upon the right-hand side, and yet I question whether Mr. Lestrade would have noted even so self-evident a thing as that."

"How on earth—"

"My dear fellow, I know you well. I know the military neatness which characterises you. You shave every morning, and in this season you shave by the sunlight; but since your shaving is less and less complete as we get farther back on the left side, until it becomes positively slovenly as we get round the angle of the jaw, it is surely very clear that that side is less illuminated than the other. I could not imagine a man of your habits looking at himself in an equal light and being satisfied with such a result. I only quote this as a trivial example of observation and inference. Therein lies my mètier, and it is just possible that it may be of some service in the investigation which lies before us. There are one or two minor points which were brought out in the inquest, and which are worth considering."

"What are they?"

"It appears that his arrest did not take place at once, but after the return to Hatherley Farm. On the inspector of constabulary informing him that he was a prisoner, he remarked that he was not surprised to hear it, and that it was no more than his deserts. This observation of his had the natural effect of removing any traces of doubt which might have remained in the minds of the coroner's jury"

"It was a confession," I ejaculated.

"No, for it was followed by a protestation of innocence."

"Coming on the top of such a damning series of events, it was at least a most suspicious remark."

"On the contrary" said Holmes, "it is the brightest rift which I can at present see in the clouds. However innocent he might be, he could not be such an absolute imbecile as not to see that the circumstances were very black against him. Had he appeared surprised at his own arrest, or feigned indignation at it, I should have looked upon it as highly suspicious, because such surprise or anger would not be natural under the circumstances, and yet might appear to be the best policy to a scheming man. His frank acceptance of the situation marks him as either an innocent man, or else as a man of considerable self-restraint and firmness. As to his remark about his deserts, it was also not unnatural if you consider that he stood beside the dead body of his father, and that there is no doubt that he had that very day so far forgotten his filial duty as to bandy words with him, and even, according to the little girl whose evidence is so important, to raise his hand as if to strike him. The self-reproach and contrition which are displayed in his remark appear to me to be the signs of a healthy mind rather than of a guilty one."

I shook my head. "Many men have been hanged on far slighter evidence," I remarked.

"So they have. And many men have been wrongfully hanged."

"What is the young man's own account of the matter?"

"It is, I am afraid, not very encouraging to his supporters, though there are one or two points in it which are suggestive. You will find it here, and may read it for yourself."

He picked out from his bundle a copy of the local Herefordshire paper, and having turned down the sheet he pointed out the paragraph in which the unfortunate young man had given his own statement of what had occurred. I settled myself down in the corner of the carriage and read it very carefully. It ran in this way:

"Mr. James McCarthy, the only son of the deceased, was then called and gave evidence as follows: 'I had been away from home for three days at Bristol, and had only just returned upon the morning of last Monday, the 3rd. My father was absent from home at the time of my arrival, and I was informed by the maid that he had driven over to Ross with John Cobb, the groom. Shortly after my return I heard the wheels of his trap in the yard, and, looking out of my window, I saw him get out and walk rapidly out of the yard, though I was not aware in which direction he was going. I then took my gun and strolled out in the direction of the Boscombe Pool, with the intention of visiting the rabbit warren which is upon the other side. On my way I saw William Crowder, the game-keeper, as he had stated in his evidence; but he is mistaken in thinking that I was following my father. I had no idea that he was in front of me. When about a hundred yards from the pool I heard a cry of "Cooee!" which was a usual signal between my father and myself. I then hurried forward, and found him standing by the pool. He appeared to be much surprised at seeing me and asked me rather roughly what I was doing there. A conversation ensued which led to high words and almost to blows, for my father was a man of a very violent temper. Seeing that his passion was becoming ungovernable, I left him and returned towards Hatherley Farm. I had not gone more than 150 yards, however, when I heard a hideous outcry behind me, which caused me to run back again. I found my father expiring upon the ground, with his head terribly injured. I dropped my gun and held him in my arms, but he almost instantly expired. I knelt beside him for some minutes, and then made my way to Mr. Turner's lodge-keeper, his house being the nearest, to ask for assistance. I saw no one near my father when I returned, and I have no idea how he came by his injuries. He was not a popular man, being somewhat cold and forbidding in his manners, but he had, as far as I know, no active enemies. I know nothing further of the matter."

"The Coroner: Did your father make any statement to you before he died?

"Witness: He mumbled a few words, but I could only catch some allusion to a rat.

"The Coroner: What did you understand by that?

"Witness: It conveyed no meaning to me. I thought that he was delirious.

"The Coroner: What was the point upon which you and your father had this final quarrel?

"Witness: I should prefer not to answer.

"The Coroner: I am afraid that I must press it.

"Witness: It is really impossible for me to tell you. I can assure you that it has nothing to do with the sad tragedy which followed.

"The Coroner: That is for the court to decide. I need not point out to you that your refusal to answer will prejudice your case considerably in any future proceedings which may arise.

"Witness: I must still refuse.

"The Coroner: I understand that the cry of 'Cooee' was a common signal between you and your father?

"Witness: It was.

"The Coroner: How was it, then, that he uttered it before he saw you, and before he even knew that you had returned from Bristol?

"Witness (with considerable confusion): I do not know.

"A Juryman: Did you see nothing which aroused your suspicions when you returned on hearing the cry and found your father fatally injured?

"Witness: Nothing definite.

"The Coroner: What do you mean?

"Witness: I was so disturbed and excited as I rushed out into the open, that I could think of nothing except of my father. Yet I have a vague impression that as I ran forward something lay upon the ground to the left of me. It seemed to me to be something grey in colour, a coat of some sort, or a plaid perhaps. When I rose from my father I looked round for it, but it was gone.

" 'Do you mean that it disappeared before you went for help?'

" 'Yes, it was gone.'

" 'You cannot say what it was?'

" 'No, I had a feeling something was there.'

" 'How far from the body?'

" 'A dozen yards or so.'

" 'And how far from the edge of the wood?'

" 'About the same.'

" 'Then if it was removed it was while you were within a dozen yards of it?'

" 'Yes, but with my back towards it.'

"This concluded the examination of the witness."

"I see," said I as I glanced down the column, "that the coroner in his concluding remarks was rather severe upon young McCarthy. He calls attention, and with reason, to the discrepancy about his father having signalled to him before seeing him, also to his refusal to give details of his conversation with his father, and his singular account of his father's dying words. They are all, as he remarks, very much against the son."

Holmes laughed softly to himself and stretched himself out upon the cushioned seat. "Both you and the coroner have been at some pains," said he, "to single out the very strongest points in the young man's favour. Don't you see that you alternately give him credit for having too much imagination and too little? Too little, if he could not invent a cause of quarrel which would give him the sympathy of the jury; too much, if he evolved from his own inner consciousness anything so outrè as a dying reference to a rat, and the incident of the vanishing cloth. No, sir, I shall approach this case from the point of view that what this young man says is true, and we shall see whither that hypothesis will lead us. And now here is my pocket Petrarch, and not another word shall I say of this case until we are on the scene of action. We lunch at Swindon, and I see that we shall be there in twenty minutes."

It was nearly four o'clock when we at last, after passing through the beautiful Stroud Valley, and over the broad gleaming Severn, found ourselves at the pretty little country-town of Ross. A lean, ferret-like man, furtive and sly-looking, was waiting for us upon the platform. In spite of the light brown dustcoat and leather-leggings which he wore in deference to his rustic surroundings, I had no difficulty in recognising Lestrade, of Scotland Yard. With him we drove to the Hereford Arms where a room had already been engaged for us.

"I have ordered a carriage," said Lestrade as we sat over a cup of tea. "I knew your energetic nature, and that you would not be happy until you had been on the scene of the crime."

"It was very nice and complimentary of you," Holmes answered. "It is entirely a question of barometric pressure."

Lestrade looked startled. "I do not quite follow," he said.

"How is the glass? Twenty-nine, I see. No wind, and not a cloud in the sky. I have a caseful of cigarettes here which need smoking, and the sofa is very much superior to the usual country hotel abomination. I do not think that it is probable that I shall use the carriage to-night."

Lestrade laughed indulgently. "You have, no doubt, already formed your conclusions from the newspapers," he said. "The case is as plain as a pikestaff, and the more one goes into it the plainer it becomes. Still, of course, one can't refuse a lady, and such a very positive one, too. She has heard of you, and would have your opinion, though I repeatedly told her that there was nothing which you could do which I had not already done. Why, bless my soul! here is her carriage at the door."

He had hardly spoken before there rushed into the room one of the most lovely young women that I have ever seen in my life. Her violet eyes shining, her lips parted, a pink flush upon her cheeks, all thought of her natural reserve lost in her overpowering excitement and concern.

"Oh, Mr. Sherlock Holmes!" she cried, glancing from one to the other of us, and finally, with a woman's quick intuition, fastening upon my companion, "I am so glad that you have come. I have driven down to tell you so. I know that James didn't do it. I know it, and I want you to start upon your work knowing it, too. Never let yourself doubt upon that point. We have known each other since we were little children, and I know his faults as no one else does; but he is too tender-hearted to hurt a fly. Such a charge is absurd to anyone who really knows him."

"I hope we may clear him, Miss Turner," said Sherlock Holmes. "You may rely upon my doing all that I can."

"But you have read the evidence. You have formed some conclusion? Do you not see some loophole, some flaw? Do you not yourself think that he is innocent?"

"I think that it is very probable."

"There, now!" she cried, throwing back her head and looking defiantly at Lestrade. "You hear! He gives me hopes."

Lestrade shrugged his shoulders. "I am afraid that my colleague has been a little quick in forming his conclusions," he said.

"But he is right. Oh! I know that he is right. James never did it. And about his quarrel with his father, I am sure that the reason why he would not speak about it to the coroner was because I was concerned in it."

"In what way?" asked Holmes.

"It is no time for me to hide anything. James and his father had many disagreements about me. Mr. McCarthy was very anxious that there should be a marriage between us. James and I have always loved each other as brother and sister; but of course he is young and has seen very little of life yet, and—and—well, he naturally did not wish to do anything like that yet. So there were quarrels, and this, I am sure, was one of them."

"And your father?" asked Holmes. "Was he in favour of such a union?"

"No, he was averse to it also. No one but Mr. McCarthy was in favour of it." A quick blush passed over her fresh young face as Holmes shot one of his keen, questioning glances at her.

"Thank you for this information," said he. "May I see your father if I call to-morrow?"

"I am afraid the doctor won't allow it."

"The doctor?"

"Yes, have you not heard? Poor father has never been strong for years back, but this has broken him down completely. He has taken to his bed, and Dr. Willows says that he is a wreck and that his nervous system is shattered. Mr. McCarthy was the only man alive who had known dad in the old days in Victoria."

"Ha! In Victoria! That is important."

"Yes, at the mines."

"Quite so; at the gold-mines, where, as I understand, Mr. Turner made his money"

"Yes, certainly."

"Thank you, Miss Turner. You have been of material assistance to me."

"You will tell me if you have any news to-morrow. No doubt you will go to the prison to see James. Oh, if you do, Mr. Holmes, do tell him that I know him to be innocent."

"I will, Miss Turner."

"I must go home now, for dad is very ill, and he misses me so if I leave him. Good-bye, and God help you in your undertaking." She hurried from the room as impulsively as she had entered, and we heard the wheels of her carriage rattle off down the street.

"I am ashamed of you, Holmes," said Lestrade with dignity after a few minutes' silence. "Why should you raise up hopes which you are bound to disappoint? I am not over-tender of heart, but I call it cruel."

"I think that I see my way to clearing James McCarthy," said Holmes. "Have you an order to see him in prison?"

"Yes, but only for you and me."

"Then I shall reconsider my resolution about going out. We have still time to take a train to Hereford and see him to-night?"

"Ample."

"Then let us do so. Watson, I fear that you will find it very slow, but I shall only be away a couple of hours."

I walked down to the station with them, and then wandered through the streets of the little town, finally returning to the hotel, where I lay upon the sofa and tried to interest myself in a yellow-backed novel. The puny plot of the story was so thin, however, when compared to the deep mystery through which we were groping, and I found my attention wander so continually from the action to the fact, that I at last flung it across the room and gave myself up entirely to a consideration of the events of the day. Supposing that this unhappy young man's story were absolutely true, then what hellish thing, what absolutely unforeseen and extraordinary calamity could have occurred between the time when he parted from his father, and the moment when, drawn back by his screams, he rushed into the glade? It was something terrible and deadly. What could it be? Might not the nature of the injuries reveal something to my medical instincts? I rang the bell and called for the weekly county paper, which contained a verbatim account of the inquest. In the surgeon's deposition it was stated that the posterior third of the left parietal bone and the left half of the occipital bone had been shattered by a heavy blow from a blunt weapon. I marked the spot upon my own head. Clearly such a blow must have been struck from behind. That was to some extent in favour of the accused, as when seen quarrelling he was face to face with his father. Still, it did not go for very much, for the older man might have turned his back before the blow fell. Still, it might be worth while to call Holmes' attention to it. Then there was the peculiar dying reference to a rat. What could that mean? It could not be delirium. A man dying from a sudden blow does not commonly become delirious. No, it was more likely to be an attempt to explain how he met his fate. But what could it indicate? I cudgelled my brains to find some possible explanation. And then the incident of the grey cloth seen by young McCarthy. If that were true the murderer must have dropped some part of his dress, presumably his overcoat, in his flight, and must have had the hardihood to return and to carry it away at the instant when the son was kneeling with his back turned not a dozen paces off. What a tissue of mysteries and improbabilities the whole thing was! I did not wonder at Lestrade's opinion, and yet I had so much faith in Sherlock Holmes' insight that I could not lose hope as long as every fresh fact seemed to strengthen his conviction of young McCarthy's innocence.

It was late before Sherlock Holmes returned. He came back alone, for Lestrade was staying in lodgings in the town.

"The glass still keeps very high," he remarked as he sat down. "It is of importance that it should not rain before we are able to go over the ground. On the other hand, a man should be at his very best and keenest for such nice work as that, and I did not wish to do it when fagged by a long journey I have seen young McCarthy."

"And what did you learn from him?"

"Nothing."

"Could he throw no light?"

"None at all. I was inclined to think at one time that he knew who had done it and was screening him or her, but I am convinced now that he is as puzzled as everyone else. He is not a very quick-witted youth, though comely to look at and, I should think, sound at heart."

"I cannot admire his taste," I remarked, "if it is indeed a fact that he was averse to a marriage with so charming a young lady as this Miss Turner."

"Ah, thereby hangs a rather painful tale. This fellow is madly, insanely, in love with her, but some two years ago, when he was only a lad, and before he really knew her, for she had been away five years at a boarding-school, what does the idiot do but get into the clutches of a barmaid in Bristol and marry her at a registry office? No one knows a word of the matter, but you can imagine how maddening it must be to him to be upbraided for not doing what he would give his very eyes to do, but what he knows to be absolutely impossible. It was sheer frenzy of this sort which made him throw his hands up into the air when his father, at their last interview, was goading him on to propose to Miss Turner. On the other hand, he had no means of supporting himself, and his father, who was by all accounts a very hard man, would have thrown him over utterly had he known the truth. It was with his barmaid wife that he had spent the last three days in Bristol, and his father did not know where he was. Mark that point. It is of importance. Good has come out of evil, however, for the barmaid, finding from the papers that he is in serious trouble and likely to be hanged, has thrown him over utterly and has written to him to say that she has a husband already in the Bermuda Dockyard, so that there is really no tie between them. I think that that bit of news has consoled young McCarthy for all that he has suffered."

"But if he is innocent, who has done it?"

"Ah! Who? I would call your attention very particularly to two points. One is that the murdered man had an appointment with someone at the pool, and that the someone could not have been his son, for his son was away, and he did not know when he would return. The second is that the murdered man was heard to cry 'Cooee!' before he knew that his son had returned. Those are the crucial points upon which the case depends. And now let us talk about George Meredith, if you please, and we shall leave all minor matters until to-morrow."

There was no rain, as Holmes had foretold, and the morning broke bright and cloudless. At nine o'clock Lestrade called for us with the carriage, and we set off for Hatherley Farm and the Boscombe Pool.

"There is serious news this morning," Lestrade observed. "It is said that Mr. Turner, of the Hall, is so ill that his life is despaired of."

"An elderly man, I presume?" said Holmes.

"About sixty; but his constitution has been shattered by his life abroad, and he has been in failing health for some time. This business has had a very bad effect upon him. He was an old friend of McCarthy's, and,

I may add, a great benefactor to him, for I have learned that he gave him Hatherley Farm rent free."

"Indeed! That is interesting," said Holmes.

"Oh, yes! In a hundred other ways he has helped him. Everybody about here speaks of his kindness to him."

"Really! Does it not strike you as a little singular that this McCarthy, who appears to have had little of his own, and to have been under such obligations to Turner, should still talk of marrying his son to Turner's daughter, who is, presumably, heiress to the estate, and that in such a very cocksure manner, as if it were merely a case of a proposal and all else would follow? It is the more strange, since we know that Turner himself was averse to the idea. The daughter told us as much. Do you not deduce something from that?"

"We have got to the deductions and the inferences," said Lestrade, winking at me. "I find it hard enough to tackle facts, Holmes, without flying away after theories and fancies."

"You are right," said Holmes demurely; "you do find it very hard to tackle the facts."

"Anyhow, I have grasped one fact which you seem to find it difficult to get hold of," replied Lestrade with some warmth.

"And that is—"

"That McCarthy senior met his death from McCarthy junior and that all theories to the contrary are the merest moonshine."

"Well, moonshine is a brighter thing than fog," said Holmes, laughing. "But I am very much mistaken if this is not Hatherley Farm upon the left."

"Yes, that is it." It was a widespread, comfortable-looking building, two-storied, slate-roofed, with great yellow blotches of lichen upon the grey walls. The drawn blinds and the smokeless chimneys, however, gave it a stricken look, as though the weight of this horror still lay heavy upon it. We called at the door, when the maid, at Holmes' request, showed us the boots which her master wore at the time of his death, and also a pair of the son's, though not the pair which he had then had. Having measured these very carefully from seven or eight different points, Holmes desired to be led to the court-yard, from which we all followed the winding track which led to Boscombe Pool.

Sherlock Holmes was transformed when he was hot upon such a scent as this. Men who had only known the quiet thinker and logician of Baker Street would have failed to recognise him. His face flushed and darkened. His brows were drawn into two hard black lines, while his eyes shone out from beneath them with a steely glitter. His face was bent downward, his shoulders bowed, his lips compressed, and the veins stood out like whipcord in his long, sinewy neck. His nostrils seemed to dilate with a purely animal lust for the chase, and his mind was so absolutely concentrated upon the matter before him that a question or remark fell unheeded upon his ears, or, at the most, only provoked a quick, impatient snarl in reply. Swiftly and silently he made his way along the track which ran through the meadows, and so by way of the woods to the Boscombe Pool. It was damp, marshy ground, as is all that district, and there were marks of many feet, both upon the path and amid the short grass which bounded it on either side. Sometimes Holmes would hurry on, sometimes stop dead, and once he made quite a little detour into the meadow. Lestrade and I walked behind him, the detective indifferent and contemptuous, while I watched my friend with the interest which sprang from the conviction that every one of his actions was directed towards a definite end.

The Boscombe Pool, which is a little reed-girt sheet of water some fifty yards across, is situated at the boundary between the Hatherley Farm and the private park of the wealthy Mr. Turner. Above the woods which lined it upon the farther side we could see the red, jutting pinnacles which marked the site of the rich landowner's dwelling. On the Hatherley side of the pool the woods grew very thick, and there was a narrow belt of sodden grass twenty paces across between the edge of the trees and the reeds which lined the lake. Lestrade showed us the exact spot at which the body had been found, and, indeed, so moist was the ground, that I could plainly see the traces which had been left by the fall of the stricken man. To Holmes, as I could see by his eager face and peering eyes, very many other things were to be read upon the trampled grass. He ran round, like a dog who is picking up a scent, and then turned upon my companion.

"What did you go into the pool for?" he asked.

"I fished about with a rake. I thought there might be some weapon or other trace. But how on earth—"

"Oh, tut, tut! I have no time! That left foot of yours with its inward twist is all over the place. A mole could trace it, and there it vanishes among the reeds. Oh, how simple it would all have been had I been here before they came like a herd of buffalo and wallowed all over it. Here is where the party with the lodge-keeper came, and they have covered all tracks for six or eight feet round the body. But here are three separate tracks of the same feet." He drew out a lens and lay down upon his waterproof to have a better view, talking all the time rather to himself than to us. "These are young McCarthy's feet. Twice he was walking, and once he ran swiftly, so that the soles are deeply marked and the heels hardly visible. That bears out his story. He ran when he saw his father on the ground. Then here are the father's feet as he paced up and down. What is this, then? It is the butt-end of the gun as the son stood listening. And this? Ha, ha! What have we here? Tiptoes! tiptoes! Square, too, quite unusual boots! They come, they go, they come again—of course that was for the cloak. Now where did they come from?" He ran up and down, sometimes losing, sometimes finding the track until we were well within the edge of the wood and under the shadow of a great beech, the largest tree in the neighbourhood. Holmes traced his way to the farther side of this and lay down once more upon his face with a little cry of satisfaction. For a long time he remained there, turning over the leaves and dried sticks, gathering up what seemed to me to be dust into an envelope and examining with his lens not only the ground but even the bark of the tree as far as he could reach. A jagged stone was lying among the moss, and this also he carefully examined and retained. Then he followed a pathway through the wood until he came to the highroad, where all traces were lost.

"It has been a case of considerable interest," he remarked, returning to his natural manner. "I fancy that this grey house on the right must be the lodge. I think that I will go in and have a word with Moran, and perhaps write a little note. Having done that, we may drive back to our luncheon. You may walk to the cab, and I shall be with you presently."

It was about ten minutes before we regained our cab and drove back into Ross, Holmes still carrying with him the stone which he had picked up in the wood.

"This may interest you, Lestrade," he remarked, holding it out. "The murder was done with it."

"I see no marks."

"There are none."

"How do you know, then?"

"The grass was growing under it. It had only lain there a few days. There was no sign of a place whence it had been taken. It corresponds with the injuries. There is no sign of any other weapon."

"And the murderer?"

"Is a tall man, left-handed, limps with the right leg, wears thick-soled shooting-boots and a grey cloak, smokes Indian cigars, uses a cigar-holder, and carries a blunt pen-knife in his pocket. There are several other indications, but these may be enough to aid us in our search."

Lestrade laughed. "I am afraid that I am still a sceptic," he said. "Theories are all very well, but we have to deal with a hard-headed British jury."

"Nous verrons," answered Holmes calmly. "You work your own method, and I shall work mine. I shall be busy this afternoon, and shall probably return to London by the evening train."

"And leave your case unfinished?"

"No, finished."

"But the mystery?"

"It is solved."

"Who was the criminal, then?"

"The gentleman I describe."

"But who is he?"

"Surely it would not be difficult to find out. This is not such a populous neighbourhood."

Lestrade shrugged his shoulders. "I am a practical man," he said, "and I really cannot undertake to go about the country looking for a left-handed gentleman with a game leg. I should become the laughing-stock of Scotland Yard."

"All right," said Holmes quietly. "I have given you the chance. Here are your lodgings. Goodbye. I shall drop you a line before I leave."

Having left Lestrade at his rooms, we drove to our hotel, where we found lunch upon the table. Holmes was silent and buried in thought with a pained expression upon his face, as one who finds himself in a perplexing position.

"Look here, Watson," he said when the cloth was cleared "just sit down in this chair and let me preach to you for a little. I don't know quite what to do, and I should value your advice. Light a cigar and let me expound."

"Pray do so."

"Well, now, in considering this case there are two points about young McCarthy's narrative which struck us both instantly, although they impressed me in his favour and you against him. One was the fact that his father should, according to his account, cry 'Cooee!' before seeing him. The other was his singular dying reference to a rat. He mumbled several words, you understand, but that was all that caught the son's ear. Now from this double point our research must commence, and we will begin it by presuming that what the lad says is absolutely true."

"What of this 'Cooee!' then?"

"Well, obviously it could not have been meant for the son. The son, as far as he knew, was in Bristol. It was mere chance that he was within earshot. The 'Cooee!' was meant to attract the attention of whoever it was that he had the appointment with. But 'Cooee' is a distinctly Australian cry, and one which is used between Australians. There is a strong presumption that the person whom McCarthy expected to meet him at Boscombe Pool was someone who had been in Australia."

"What of the rat, then?"

Sherlock Holmes took a folded paper from his pocket and flattened it out on the table. "This is a map of the Colony of Victoria," he said. "I wired to Bristol for it last night." He put his hand over part of the map. "What do you read?"

"ARAT," I read.

"And now?" He raised his hand.

"BALLARAT."

"Quite so. That was the word the man uttered, and of which his son only caught the last two syllables. He was trying to utter the name of his murderer. So and so, of Ballarat."

"It is wonderful!" I exclaimed.

"It is obvious. And now, you see, I had narrowed the field down considerably. The possession of a grey garment was a third point which, granting the son's statement to be correct, was a certainty. We have come now out of mere vagueness to the definite conception of an Australian from Ballarat with a grey cloak."

"Certainly."

"And one who was at home in the district, for the pool can only be approached by the farm or by the estate, where strangers could hardly wander."

"Quite so."

"Then comes our expedition of to-day. By an examination of the ground I gained the trifling details which I gave to that imbecile Lestrade, as to the personality of the criminal."

"But how did you gain them?"

"You know my method. It is founded upon the observation of trifles."

"His height I know that you might roughly judge from the length of his stride. His boots, too, might be told from their traces."

"Yes, they were peculiar boots."

"But his lameness?"

"The impression of his right foot was always less distinct than his left. He put less weight upon it. Why? Because he limped—he was lame."

"But his left-handedness."

"You were yourself struck by the nature of the injury as recorded by the surgeon at the inquest. The blow was struck from immediately behind, and yet was upon the left side. Now, how can that be unless it were by a left-handed man? He had stood behind that tree during the interview between the father and son. He had even smoked there. I found the ash of a cigar, which my special knowledge of tobacco ashes enables me to pronounce as an Indian cigar. I have, as you know, devoted some attention to this, and written a little monograph on the ashes of 140 different varieties of pipe, cigar, and cigarette tobacco. Having found the ash, I then looked round and discovered the stump among the moss where he had tossed it. It was an Indian cigar, of the variety which are rolled in Rotterdam."

"And the cigar-holder?"

"I could see that the end had not been in his mouth. Therefore he used a holder. The tip had been cut off, not bitten off, but the cut was not a clean one, so I deduced a blunt pen-knife."

"Holmes," I said, "you have drawn a net round this man from which he cannot escape, and you have saved an innocent human life as truly as if you had cut the cord which was hanging him. I see the direction in which all this points. The culprit is—"

"Mr. John Turner," cried the hotel waiter, opening the door of our sitting-room, and ushering in a visitor.

The man who entered was a strange and impressive figure. His slow, limping step and bowed shoulders gave the appearance of decrepitude, and yet his hard, deep-lined, craggy features, and his enormous limbs showed that he was possessed of unusual strength of body and of character. His tangled beard, grizzled hair, and outstanding, drooping eyebrows combined to give an air of dignity and power to his appearance, but his face was of an ashen white, while his lips and the corners of his nostrils were tinged with a shade of blue. It was clear to me at a glance that he was in the grip of some deadly and chronic disease.

"Pray sit down on the sofa," said Holmes gently. "You had my note?"

"Yes, the lodge-keeper brought it up. You said that you wished to see me here to avoid scandal."

"I thought people would talk if I went to the Hall."

"And why did you wish to see me?" He looked across at my companion with despair in his weary eyes, as though his question was already answered.

"Yes," said Holmes, answering the look rather than the words. "It is so. I know all about McCarthy."

The old man sank his face in his hands. "God help me!" he cried. "But I would not have let the young man come to harm. I give you my word that I would have spoken out if it went against him at the Assizes."

"I am glad to hear you say so," said Holmes gravely.

"I would have spoken now had it not been for my dear girl. It would break her heart—it will break her heart when she hears that I am arrested."

"It may not come to that," said Holmes.

"What?"

"I am no official agent. I understand that it was your daughter who required my presence here, and I am acting in her interests. Young McCarthy must be got off, however."

"I am a dying man," said old Turner. "I have had diabetes for years. My doctor says it is a question whether I shall live a month. Yet I would rather die under my own roof than in a gaol."

Holmes rose and sat down at the table with his pen in his hand and a bundle of paper before him. "Just tell us the truth," he said. "I shall jot down the facts. You will sign it, and Watson here can witness it. Then I could produce your confession at the last extremity to save young McCarthy. I promise you that I shall not use it unless it is absolutely needed."

"It's as well," said the old man; "it's a question whether I shall live to the Assizes, so it matters little to me, but I should wish to spare Alice the shock. And now I will make the thing clear to you; it has been a long time in the acting, but will not take me long to tell.

"You didn't know this dead man, McCarthy. He was a devil incarnate. I tell you that. God keep you out of the clutches of such a man as he. His grip has been upon me these twenty years, and he has blasted my life. I'll tell you first how I came to be in his power.

"It was in the early '60's at the diggings. I was a young chap then, hot-blooded and reckless, ready to turn my hand at anything; I got among bad companions, took to drink, had no luck with my claim, took to the bush, and in a word became what you would call over here a highway robber. There were six of us, and we had a wild, free life of it, sticking up a station from time to time, or stopping the wagons on the road to the diggings. Blackjack of Ballarat was the name I went under, and our party is still remembered in the colony as the Ballarat Gang.

"One day a gold convoy came down from Ballarat to Melbourne, and we lay in wait for it and attacked it. There were six troopers and six of us, so it was a close thing, but we emptied four of their saddles at the first volley. Three of our boys were killed, however, before we got the swag. I put my pistol to the head of the wagon-driver, who was this very man McCarthy. I wish to the Lord that I had shot him then, but I spared him, though I saw his wicked little eyes fixed on my face, as though to remember every feature. We got away with the gold, became wealthy men, and made our way over to England without being suspected. There I parted from my old pals and determined to settle down to a quiet and respectable life. I bought this estate, which chanced to be in the market, and I set myself to do a little good with my money, to make up for the way in which I had earned it. I married, too, and though my wife died young she left me my dear little Alice. Even when she was just a baby her wee hand seemed to lead me down the right path as nothing else had ever done. In a word, I turned over a new leaf and did my best to make up for the past. All was going well when McCarthy laid his grip upon me.

"I had gone up to town about an investment, and I met him in Regent Street with hardly a coat to his back or a boot to his foot.

" 'Here we are, Jack,' says he, touching me on the arm; 'we'll be as good as a family to you. There's two of us, me and my son, and you can have the keeping of us. If you don't—it's a fine, law-abiding country is England, and there's always a policeman within hail.'

"Well, down they came to the west country, there was no shaking them off, and there they have lived rent free on my best land ever since. There was no rest for me, no peace, no forgetfulness; turn where I would, there was his cunning, grinning face at my elbow. It grew worse as Alice grew up, for he soon saw I was more afraid of her knowing my past than of the police. Whatever he wanted he must have, and whatever it was I gave him without question, land, money, houses, until at last he asked a thing which I could not give. He asked for Alice.

"His son, you see, had grown up, and so had my girl, and as I was known to be in weak health, it seemed a fine stroke to him that his lad should step into the whole property. But there I was firm. I would not have his cursed stock mixed with mine; not that I had any dislike to the lad, but his blood was in him, and that was enough. I stood firm. McCarthy threatened. I braved him to do his worst. We were to meet at the pool midway between our houses to talk it over.

"When I went down there I found him talking with his son, so I smoked a cigar and waited behind a tree until he should be alone. But as I listened to his talk all that was black and bitter in me seemed to come uppermost. He was urging his son to marry my daughter with as little regard for what she might think as if she were a slut from off the streets. It drove me mad to think that I and all that I held most dear should be in the power of such a man as this. Could I not snap the bond? I was already a dying and a desperate man. Though clear of mind and fairly strong of limb, I knew that my own fate was sealed. But my memory and my girl!

Both could be saved if I could but silence that foul tongue. I did it, Mr. Holmes. I would do it again. Deeply as I have sinned, I have led a life of martyrdom to atone for it. But that my girl should be entangled in the same meshes which held me was more than I could suffer. I struck him down with no more compunction than if he had been some foul and venomous beast. His cry brought back his son; but I had gained the cover of the wood, though I was forced to go back to fetch the cloak which I had dropped in my flight. That is the true story, gentlemen, of all that occurred."

"Well, it is not for me to judge you," said Holmes as the old man signed the statement which had been drawn out. "I pray that we may never be exposed to such a temptation."

"I pray not, sir. And what do you intend to do?"

"In view of your health, nothing. You are yourself aware that you will soon have to answer for your deed at a higher court than the Assizes. I will keep your confession, and if McCarthy is condemned I shall be forced to use it. If not, it shall never be seen by mortal eye; and your secret, whether you be alive or dead, shall be safe with us."

"Farewell, then," said the old man solemnly. "Your own deathbeds, when they come, will be the easier for the thought of the peace which you have given to mine." Tottering and shaking in all his giant frame, he stumbled slowly from the room.

"God help us!" said Holmes after a long silence. "Why does fate play such tricks with poor, helpless worms? I never hear of such a case as this that I do not think of Baxter's words, and say, 'There, but for the grace of God, goes Sherlock Holmes.' "

James McCarthy was acquitted at the Assizes on the strength of a number of objections which had been drawn out by Holmes and submitted to the defending counsel. Old Turner lived for seven months after our interview, but he is now dead; and there is every prospect that the son and daughter may come to live happily together in ignorance of the black cloud which rests upon their past.

POST-CLASS REFLECTION MEMO

Draft and submit a memo in response to the questions below:

- What are two or three concrete lessons about fact investigation you learned in class today that might help you change and improve your fact investigation in a current clinic case/project?

- What specific actions do you plan to take to implement those lessons?

CHAPTER 7

STORYTELLING

LEARNING GOALS

The learning goals for this class include helping you to:

- Explore and articulate initial ideas about what constitutes effective, high-impact storytelling
- Analyze the role of audience in storytelling and lawyering
- See connections between effective storytelling and effective lawyering
- Understand the elements, progression, and structure of stories, and how these factors both contribute to persuasive storytelling and expand a lawyer's ability to effectively represent a client
- Understand that facts do not exist in the world merely to be discovered, but are susceptible to development, differential emphasis, and organization through a lawyer's imposition of narrative
- Understand that multiple stories can be created from the same facts
- See that lawyers play a crucial role in the strategic shaping and rearranging of facts into stories in service of a client's goals
- Understand the role of unconscious assumptions in the ability to understand a client's story arising on the part of lawyers, fact finders, legislators, and any other system actor
- Analyze the benefits and risks of stock stories in the lawyering process
- Take responsibility for co-creating your own learning in clinic, and realize that you have much to learn from your fellow students

DESCRIPTION OF CLASS

In this class, we will explore the importance of storytelling to the lawyering process. We will create our own stories and assess what makes them most effective. We will review and analyze the essential elements of a persuasive story and consider the benefits and risks of trying to fit a client's situation into the confines of a culturally accepted "stock story." Next, we will consider our unconscious tendency to fill in actual facts with our own assumptions, and how that process can undermine a lawyer's ability to understand and communicate about a client's story. Finally, we will read a story together and analyze what contributes to its effectiveness and persuasive value.

ASSIGNMENT IN PREPARATION FOR CLASS

Storytelling I: The Creative Process and "Birds of a Feather"

Think of a time when someone told you a story. Draft and submit a paragraph in response to the following questions:

- What was the most memorable detail in the story?
- What made it so memorable?
- What aspects of the storyteller's body language, gestures, eye contact, pace, voice inflection, or other stylistic factor, contributed to the effectiveness of the story?

Storytelling II: The Essential Elements of a Persuasive, Compelling Story and the Risks of Unconscious Assumptions and Stock-Story Lawyering

Think of a story someone has recently told you.

- Was the story particularly memorable?
  - What made it so?
- Was the story compelling and believable?
  - Why or why not?
  - What was it about the story that caused it fall into either category?

READING ASSIGNMENT

1. Stephen Denning, *Telling Tales*, HARVARD BUSINESS REVIEW 115 (May 2004).
2. Tony L. Axam & Robert Altman, *The Picture Theory of Trial Advocacy*, LITIGATION 8 (April 1986).
3. Client Stories:
   a. ***Civil Clinic***: Andrea Elliott, *Girl in the Shadows: Dasani's Homeless Life*, NEW YORK TIMES (Dec. 9, 2013).
   b. ***Domestic Violence Clinic***: Donna St. George, *Murder in the Making*, WASHINGTON POST (Aug. 7, 2000).
   c. ***Criminal Defense or Juvenile Delinquency Clinic***: Sarah Burns, CENTRAL PARK FIVE (2001).
   d. ***Transactional Clinic***: Debbi Wilgoren, *Purchase of a Lifetime*, WASHINGTON POST (Dec. 14, 15, & 16, 2005).

READINGS

Stephen Denning
Telling Tales
HARVARD BUSINESS REVIEW 115 (May 2004)[1]

In 1998, I made a pilgrimage to the International Storytelling Center in Jonesborough, Tennessee, seeking some enlightenment. Several years earlier, as the program director of knowledge management at the World Bank, I had stumbled onto the power of storytelling. Despite a career of scoffing at such touchy-feely stuff—like most business executives, I knew that analytical was good, anecdotal was bad—I had changed my thinking because I'd seen stories help galvanize an organization around a defined business goal.

In the mid-1990s, that goal was to get people at the World Bank to support efforts at knowledge management—a pretty foreign notion within the organization at the time. I offered people cogent arguments about the need to gather the knowledge that was scattered throughout the organization. They didn't listen. I gave PowerPoint presentations that compellingly demonstrated the importance of sharing and leveraging this information. My audiences merely looked dazed. In desperation, I was ready to try almost anything.

---

1 Footnotes and/or internal citations omitted.

Then in 1996 I began telling people a story:

In June of 1995, a health worker in a tiny town in Zambia went to the Web site of the Centers for Disease Control and got the answer to a question about the treatment for malaria. Remember that this was in Zambia, one of the poorest countries in the world, and it happened in a tiny place 600 kilometers from the capital city. But the most striking thing about this picture, at least for us, is that the World Bank isn't in it. Despite our know-how on all kinds of poverty-related issues, that knowledge isn't available to the millions of people who could use it. Imagine if it were. Think what an organization we could become.

This simple story helped World Bank staff and managers envision a different kind of future for the organization. When knowledge management later became an official corporate priority, I used similar stories to maintain the momentum. So I began to wonder how the tool of narrative might be put to work even more effectively. Being a typically rational manager, I decided to consult the experts.

At the International Storytelling Center, I told the Zambia story to a professional storyteller, J.G. "Paw-Paw" Pinkerton, and asked the master what he thought. You can imagine my chagrin when he said he didn't hear a story at all. There was no real telling. There was no plot. There was no building up of the characters. Who was this health worker in Zambia? And what was her world like? What did it feel like to be in the exotic environment of Zambia, facing the problems she faced? My anecdote, he said, was a pathetic thing, not a story at all. I needed to start from scratch if I hoped to turn it into a "real story."

Was I surprised? Well, not exactly. The story was pretty bland. There was a problem with this advice from the expert, though. I knew in my heart it was wrong. And with that realization, I was on the brink of an important insight: Beware the well-told story!

The Power of Narrative

But let's back up a bit. Do stories really have a role to play in the business world? Believe me, I'm familiar with the skepticism about them. When you talk about "storytelling" to a group of hardheaded executives, you'd better be prepared for some eye rolling. If the group is polite as well as tough, don't be surprised if the eyes simply glaze over.

That's because most executives operate with a particular—and generally justified—mind-set. Analysis is what drives business thinking. It cuts through the fog of myth, gossip, and speculation to get to the hard facts. It goes wherever the observations and premises and conclusions take it, undistorted by the hopes or fears of the analyst. Its strength lies in its objectivity, its impersonality, its heartlessness.

Yet this strength is also a weakness. Analysis might excite the mind, but it hardly offers a route to the heart. And that's where we must go if we are to motivate people not only to take action but to do so with energy and enthusiasm. At a time when corporate survival often requires disruptive change, leadership involves inspiring people to act in unfamiliar, and often unwelcome, ways. Mind-numbing cascades of numbers or daze-inducing PowerPoint slides won't achieve this goal. Even the most logical arguments usually won't do the trick.

But effective storytelling often does. In fact, in certain situations nothing else works. Although good business arguments are developed through the use of numbers, they are typically approved on the basis of a story—that is, a narrative that links a set of events in some kind of causal sequence. Storytelling can translate those dry and abstract numbers into compelling pictures of a leader's goals. I saw this happen at the World Bank—by 2000, we were increasingly recognized as leaders in the area of knowledge management—and have seen it in numerous other large organizations since then.

So why was I having problems with the advice I had received from the professional storyteller in Jonesborough?

A "Poorly Told" Story

The timing of my trip to Tennessee was fortunate. If I had sought expert advice two years earlier, I might have taken the master's recommendations without question. But I'd had some time to approach the idea of organizational storytelling with a beginner's mind, free of strictures about "the right way" to tell a story.

It wasn't that I couldn't follow Paw-Paw Pinkerton's recommendations. I saw immediately how to flesh out my modest anecdote about the health worker in Zambia: You'd dramatically depict her life, the scourge of malaria that she faced in her work, and perhaps the pain and suffering of the patient she was treating that day. You'd describe the extraordinary set of events that had led to her being seated in front of a computer screen deep in the hinterland of Zambia. You'd describe the false leads she had followed before she came across the CDC Web site. You'd build up to the moment of triumph when she found the answer to her question about malaria and vividly describe how that answer was about to transform the life of her patient The story would be a veritable epic.

This "maximalist" account would be more engrossing than my relatively dry anecdote. But I had learned enough by then to realize that telling the story in this way to a corporate audience would not galvanize implementation of a strange new idea like knowledge management. I knew that in the modern workplace, people had neither the time nor the patience—remember executives' general skepticism about storytelling in the first place—to absorb a richly detailed narrative. If I was going to hold the attention of my audience, I had to make my point in seconds, not in minutes.

There was another problem. Even if my audience did take the time to listen to a fully developed tale, my telling it in that fashion would not allow listeners the mental space to relate the story to their own quite different worlds. Although I was describing a health worker in Zambia, I wanted everyone to focus not on Zambia but on their own situations. I hoped they would think, "If the CDC can reach a health worker in Zambia, why can't the World Bank? Why don't we put our knowledge on the Web and broaden our scope?" But if my listeners were immersed in a saga about that health worker and her patient, they might not have any attention left to ask themselves these questions—or to provide answers. In other words, I didn't want my audience too interested in Zambia. A minimalist narrative was effective, in fact, because it lacked detail and texture. The same characteristic that the professional storyteller saw as a flaw was, for my purposes, a strength.

On my return from Jonesborough, I educated myself about the principles of traditional storytelling. More than 2,000 years ago, Aristotle, in his *Poetics,* said stories should have a beginning, a middle, and an end. They should include complex characters as well as a plot that incorporates a reversal of fortune and a lesson learned. Furthermore, the storyteller should be so engaged with the story—visualizing the action, feeling what the characters *feel*—that the listeners become drawn into the narrative's world. Aristotle's formula has proved successful over the ages, from *The Arabian Nights* to *The Decameron* to *The Adventures of Tom Sawyer* and most Hollywood screenplays.

Despite the narrative power of the traditional story, I knew that it probably wouldn't spark action in an organization. In retrospect, though, I realize that my insight blinded me to something else. Believing that this wonderful and rich tradition had no place in the time-constrained world of modern business was as wrongheaded as thinking that all stories had to be full of detail and color. I would later see that the well-told story is relevant in a modern organization. Indeed, a number of surprises about the use of storytelling in organizations awaited me.

Tales of Success and Failure

In December 2000, I left the World Bank and began to consult with companies on their knowledge management and, by extension, their use of organizational stories. As part of this work, I once found myself in London with Dave Snowden, a director of IBM's Institute of Knowledge

Management, teaching a master class on storytelling to around 70 executives from private- and public-sector organizations.

During the class's morning session, I spoke about my experience at the World Bank and how a positive orientation was essential if a narrative like the one about Zambia was to be effective. But in the afternoon, to my dismay, my fellow presenter emphatically asserted the opposite. At IBM and elsewhere, Dave had found purely positive stories to be problematic. They were, he said, like the Janet and John children's stories in the united Kingdom or the Dick and Jane stories in the United States: The characters were so good they made you feel queasy. The naughtiest thing Janet and John would do was spill a bottle of water in the yard. Then they would go and tell their mother about it and promise never to do it again. Janet would volunteer to help out with the cleanup and John would offer to help wash the car. These stories for children reflected a desire to show things as they should be rather than as they are. In a corporate environment, Dave told his audience, listeners would respond to such rosy tales by conjuring up negative "antistories" about what must have actually happened. His message: Beware the positive story!

After the workshop, Dave and I discussed why his stories focused on the negative while mine accentuated the positive. I could see he had a point, that negative stories can be more powerful than positive ones. I'd used negative stories myself when trying to teach people the nitty-gritty of any subject. The fact is, people learn more from their mistakes than from their successes.

Eventually, however, it dawned on me that our points of view were complementary and that our stories served different purposes: My stories were crafted to motivate people, and Dave's were designed to share knowledge. His stories might describe how and why a team failed to accomplish an objective, with the aim of helping others avoid the same mistakes. (To elicit such stories, Dave often had to start by getting people to talk about their successes, even if these accounts were ultimately less useful vehicles for conveying knowledge.) It was then I began to realize that the purpose of telling a story might determine its form.

Granted, even optimistic stories have to be true and believable, since jaded corporate audiences know too well the experience of being presented with half-truths. Stories told in order to spur action need to make good on their promises and contain sufficient evidence of a positive outcome. But stories intended mainly to transfer knowledge must be more than true. Because their objective is to generate understanding and not action, they tend to highlight the pitfalls of ignorance; they are meant not to inspire people but to make them cautious. Just as the minimalist stories that I told to spark action were different from traditional entertainment stories, so effective knowledge-sharing stories would have negative rather than positive overtones.

A Collective Yawn

Once I saw that different narrative forms could further different business goals, I looked for other ways that managers could make stories work for them. A number of distinct story types began to emerge—ones that didn't necessarily follow Aristotelian guidelines but were nonetheless used to good effect in a variety of organizations. (For descriptions of some of them and the purposes for which they might be used, see the sidebar "A Storytelling Catalog.") I continued to come across unexpected insights about the nature of storytelling within organizations.

For instance, if negative stories have their place, so do "boring" ones. In his book *Talking about Machines,* Julian Orr recounts a number of stories that have circulated among Xerox repair technicians. While rich in detail, they are even less storylike than my little anecdote about the health care worker in Zambia. Most of these tales, which present solutions to technical problems, lack a plot and a distinct character. In fact, they are hardly stories at all, with little to hold the interest of anyone except those close to the often esoteric subject matter. Why are they compelling even to this limited audience? Because they are driven by a detailed explanation of the cause-and-effect relationship between an action and its consequence. For example:

> *You've got a malfunctioning copy machine with an E053 error code, which is supposed to mean a problem in the 24-volt Interlock Power Supply. But you could chase the source of that 24-volt Interlock problem forever, and you'd never, ever find out what it is. If you're lucky enough, you'll eventually get an F066 error code, which indicates the true source of the malfunction—namely, a shorted dicorotron. Apparently, this is happening because the circuitry in the XER board has been changed to prevent the damage that would otherwise occur when a dicorotron shorted. Before the change in circuitry, a shorted dicorotron would have fried the whole XER board. Changing the circuitry has prevented damage to the XER board, but its created a different issue. Now an E053 error message doesn't give you the true source of the machine's malfunction.*

This story, slightly condensed here, doesn't just describe the technician's accurate diagnosis of a problem; it also relates why things happened as they did. So the account, negative in tone and almost unintelligible to an outsider, is both informative and interesting to its intended audience.

As I continued my investigation, one area of particular interest to me was the link between storytelling and leadership. I already knew from personal experience how stories could be used as a catalyst for organizational action. And I had read in two influential books about leadership—*Leading Minds* by Howard Gardner and *The Leadership Engine* by Noel Tichy—how stories could help leaders define their personality for their followers, boosting others' confidence in the leaders' integrity and providing some idea of how they might act in a given situation.

I also had seen leaders using narrative to inculcate a positive set of corporate values and beliefs in the hearts and minds of their employees. Think, for example, of Tyco's effort to repair its battered value system. The company began by creating a straightforward manual that outlined new rules in such areas as sexual harassment, conflicts of interest, and fraud. But Eric Pillmore, senior vice president of corporate governance, quickly figured out that, as written, the booklet would merely gather dust on people's shelves. So he threw out what he had done and started again in an attempt to bring the principles alive through narrative. The story below became part of the revised guide, as a sidebar in the section on sexual harassment and other forms of intimidating behavior in the workplace:

> *The entire team jokes about Tom being gay. Tom has never complained and doesn't seem to mind, but when Mark is assigned to work with Tom, the jokes turn on Mark. Now that Mark receives the brunt of the jokes, he tells his supervisor he wants to be reassigned. His supervisor complies with Mark's request.*

While the guide clearly lays out the company's policy on harassment, the simple narrative helps bring the policy to life and provides a starting point for thinking about and discussing the complex issues involved. Dozens of similar stories illustrate an array of company policies.

An Enticing but Hazy Future

Although these types of stories furthered leadership goals in a relatively predictable way, others I came across were more quirky—particularly ones used to communicate vision. Noel Tichy writes in *The Leadership Engine* about the importance of preparing an organization for change. He notes that "the best way to get humans to venture into unknown terrain is to make that terrain familiar and desirable by taking them there first in their imaginations" Aha! I thought. Here is a place where storytelling, perhaps the most powerful route to people's imaginations, could prove indispensable.

But as I looked at examples of such stories in a number of arenas, I discovered that most of the successful ones were surprisingly sketchy about the details of the imagined future. Consider Winston Churchill's "We Shall Fight on the Beaches" speech and Martin Luther King, Jr.'s "I Have a Dream" speech. Neither of these famous addresses came close to describing the future in enough detail that it became, in listeners' minds, "familiar terrain."

Over time—and, in part, through my work in corporate scenario planning—I realized why. Specific predictions about the future are likely to be proved wrong. Because such predictions almost inevitably differ in major or minor ways from what eventually happens, leaders who proclaim them risk losing people's confidence. Consequently, a story designed to prepare people for change needs to evoke the future and conjure up a direction for getting there—but without being too precise. Think of the corporate future that was laid out in a famous mandate by Jack Welch: "General Electric will be either number one or number two in the field, or we will exit the sector." This is a clear, but general, description of where Welch wanted to take the company. Like my Zambia story, although for different reasons, this statement doesn't convey *too* much information.

I also came across stories used in somewhat unusual situations that called for reactive rather than proactive measures. These stories counteracted negative ones that circulated like a virus within an organization and threatened to infect the entire body. Dave Snowden of IBM first pointed out to me how stories could be used in this manner. His hypothesis was that you could attach a positive story to a negative one in order to defuse it, as an antibody would neutralize an antigen.

For example, at an IBM manufacturing site for laptop computers in the United Kingdom, stories circulated among the blue-collar workers about the facility's managers, who were accused of "not doing any real work," "being overpaid," and "having no idea what it's like on the manufacturing line." But an additional story was injected into the mix: One day, a new site director turned up in a white coat, unannounced and unaccompanied, and sat on the line making ThinkPads. He asked workers on the assembly line for help. In response, someone asked him, "Why do you earn so much more than I do?" His simple reply: "If you screw up badly, you lose your job. If I screw up badly, 3,000 people lose their jobs."

While not a story in the traditional sense, the manager's words—and actions—served as a seed for the story that eventually circulated in opposition to the one about managers' being lazy and overpaid. You can imagine the buzz: "Blimey, you should've seen how he fumbled with those circuit boards. I guess *he'll* never work on the line. But you know, he does have a point about his pay." The atmosphere at the facility began improving within weeks.

. . .

Much work remains to be done in developing a menu of narrative patterns that can be used for different purposes in an organizational setting. Although the handful of story types that I've identified is no more than a start, I hope it inspires leaders to consider the various ways storytelling might be used. Certainly, the ability to tell the right story at the right time is emerging as an essential leadership skill, one that can help managers cope with, and get business results in, the turbulent world of the twenty-first century.

Tony L. Axam and Robert Altman
The Picture Theory of Trial Advocacy
LITIGATION 8 (April 1986)[2]

Claus von Bulow stood accused of attempted murder. It was alleged that he had injected his wife with too much insulin, and she had become comatose and near death. The defense theory was that the maid had planted evidence against Mr. von Bulow to indicate his guilt. The defense lawyer developed his "Maria, the maid," theory with staccato questions and answers like these:

Q: I take it, it was *Maria, the maid,* who told you about the events that transpired on the 27th of December, 1975, is that right?

A: That's correct.

Q: And it was also, in February of the next year, *Maria, the maid,* who brought the black bag to your attention at the (von Bulow) residence of 960 Fifth Avenue, is that right?

A: It was early in the year, January or February, that's correct.

Q: But it was *Maria, the maid,* who brought the black bag to your attention, is that right?

A: That's correct.

Q: And later on that year, it was *Maria, the maid,* who brought the bag to your attention for the second time, is that right?

A: That's correct.

Q: And subsequently, around Thanksgiving of 1980, it was again *Maria, the maid,* who brought the bag to your attention, is that correct?

---

2 Footnotes and/or internal citations omitted.

A: That's correct.

That cross-examination shows the "Picture Theory of Trial Advocacy." The alliteration with "Maria, the maid," and the repetition of that phrase in several questions makes an indelible impression and a memorable picture.

The Picture Theory of Trial Advocacy means creating a picture in the courtroom without the use of demonstrative evidence. It is done with words. Word choice and its relationship to other words, phrases, and analogies are the foundation blocks of the Picture Theory of Trial Advocacy.

Most trial lawyers understand that jurors remember exhibits and pictures. Exhibits of colliding trains and cars are stronger than words. The Picture Theory of Trial Advocacy teaches that pictures can be created with words alone.

But why do this? Aren't real pictures better? There are short trials that do not lend themselves to large exhibits and elaborate presentations. Sometimes the pictures and exhibits are available but inappropriate. If you use the exhibit, you appear too polished. It's too much. Other times pictures are inadmissible.

The Picture Theory of Trial Advocacy teaches that words can create pictures as powerful and with as much impact as exhibits. With or without exhibits, lasting pictures can be created by words alone. Also, the Picture Theory of Trial Advocacy enhances the exhibits and adds another dimension to a well-prepared trial.

Anything from a single word to an entire story creates vivid pictures in the jury's mind. Choice of a single word can shape the course of an entire trial, and a careful choice of words throughout trial can make your theory of the case come alive.

Color, consistency, contrast, and closing are the touchstones that make it easier to create pictures in the courtroom with words alone.

We start with color. If someone walks into the courtroom wearing a polka-dot tie and red pants, you will remember that person because he is colorful. The same is true with colorful words and their arrangement. Certain words are more colorful or powerful than others and, thus, are likely to be remembered. Words have texture. Words have size, weight, shape, and color.

A young lawyer, in defending a man charged with rape, made the decision not to use the word rape. If not rape, then what? "Sexual intercourse" or "sexual relationship" comes the answer. The answer appears obvious. Rape connotes violence and lack of consent. Sexual intercourse connotes a consensual relationship rather than the unwillingness of rape. In most civil cases, the word choice begins with the complaint and in criminal cases, with voir dire. In the criminal case of rape, with consent as a defense, the following questions represent the preferred word choice during voir dire.

Q: Is there anyone who disapproves of two adults agreeing to *sexual intercourse?*

Q: Will you accept the judge's instruction on what the law says about *consensual sexual relationships?*

Q: Will you listen to what Don Williams says when he talks about the *sexual relationship* he had with the prosecutrix?

Q: Will you automatically reject what Don Williams tells you about his *relationship* with the prosecutrix?

The example with the words "rape" and "sexual relationship" are strong. The choice selection appears obvious with little debate. However, in most cases, the picture that the lawyer wants to create is painstaking because one must unlearn the legally familiar word and substitute a word of color.

In a case where a man was charged with murder, and the state was seeking the death penalty, the following questions were asked during voir dire of prospective jurors.

Q: You understand the state is asking for the death penalty?

A: Yes.

Q: You understand the state is asking you to agree on the outcome of what should happen to Mr. Howell?

A: Yes.

Q: Do you understand that the state is asking you to agree to have Mr. Howell *killed?*

A: . . .

When jurors were questioned individually, the impact of the word "killed" created frowns, flat affects, and uneasiness. The response of the jurors to the question gave the examining lawyer an additional index to select the juror. The examining lawyer reasoned that if the prospective juror showed an emotional response to such a powerful question and strong word, then it would be more difficult for that juror to vote for the death penalty than a juror who showed no response.

It is common for the plaintiff's lawyer in a car collision to ask the following questions during the direct examination of the plaintiff:

Q: Were you involved in an automobile accident?

Q: What kind of automobile were you driving?

Q: Was your automobile damaged?

Q: Were you injured?

Q: And did you see a doctor for your injury?

No! No! No! Instead, try these questions on direct examination of the plaintiff:

Q: Were you involved in a *car collision?*

Q: Were you *hurt?*

Q: Did you *bleed?*

Q: What did you think after you *heard* your arm *crack,* and you *saw* your *skin tear?*

Q: About your car—was it *hurt* also?

These questions add color. You think more money because collision was substituted for accident. Collision connotes injury and lack of mistake. Car is a better word than automobile because it is simpler. Hurt, bleed, crack, and tear have color. You *see* the blood, *hear* the crack, and *feel* the hurt.

Words of color appeal to the senses. They are the words of writers, directors, and artists. You feel the words, and the picture is indelible. Words of color should also be words of litigators.

You can use colorful words in opening; you can use colorful words in cross-examination; at every stage of the trial, you are in the process of selecting words that will have a positive feeling with the jury. Trials are psychological dramas usually limited to a courtroom. Trials are not decided on which side has the best evidence. They are more often decided on the deep emotions of the jurors. The music of one's voice and the lyrics should be colorful to appeal to the emotions of the jurors. One may spend hours selecting one word. The word might be mad; not angry, but mad. The word might be collision, sexual intercourse, or hurt.

Words, phrases, and stories help to create colorful pictures that the lawyer needs to persuade the jury.

The second touchstone for the Picture Theory of Trial Advocacy is consistency.

Consistency has to do with rhythm. We try to find a set of words that can be said and to which the jury will listen. And from listening, the jury becomes familiar with the pattern, the meter, or the words. The ear becomes accustomed to what is said. The juror anticipates and begins to make an association with the phrases, words, or metered speech. It sounds good to the ears. And because it sounds good to the ears, the jury is more likely to remember what was said.

One local lawyer closely studied the rhythms and cadence of various church sermons. He prided himself on being able to choose jurors who shared one religion and then preached a sermon with the proper rhythm and cadence in his closing argument.

With rhythm you create a set of words that become memorable. We think of nursery rhymes in that same way. "Jack Spratt could eat no fat. His wife could eat no lean." From remembering the sing-song alphabets to the alliteration and onomatopoeia of verse, the rules are common: if there is a consistent thread in length, choice of words or phrases, and similar sounds—one remembers.

The rhythm can easily be created by simply repeating or creatively arranging words. You can do it with the shortness of your sentences. You might arrange several sentences that have the same metered verse. You might not use the same words, but they might be the same meter, the same timing, or the same length. The jury will have a tendency to remember that set of questions more than any other set.

Consistency also refers to the need to create an overall trial theory reflected in the colors and rhythms you use. If you want to convince the jury that the other driver caused the collision, you should consistently stay away from the word, accident. If you can get opposing counsel to refer to the incident as a collision, you gain the benefit of having your opponent use the language you have chosen to define the facts of the case.

In a trial of colorful words and consistency, you are two steps ahead of your opponent even without exhibits and documentary evidence.

In the 1985 von Bulow trial, defense counsel used the phrase "Maria, the maid," to create an immediate and negative impression of the von Bulow maid, in support of the defense theory that the maid was engaged in a vendetta against Mr. von Bulow. The rhythm and repetition of the "Maria, the maid," questions resemble a child's chant with its simplicity and teasing.

Cross-examination is replete with examples of consistency and the use of the *same word* in a series of questions.

In a case where a police officer was cross-examined about a car and bus collision, the officer testified on behalf of the plaintiff to state and support the plaintiff's theory that their car was rear-ended by the bus. The defense lawyer believed the policeman had no way to remember what had happened two years before and that his report did not provide sufficient detail to support the defendant's liability. The following questions with the repetition of one word supported the defense theory.

Q: Now, you've indicated, Officer Hopper, that skid marks *appeared* to come from both the Pontiac and the bus?

A: Yes, sir.

Q: Officer Hopper, what tires on the Pontiac did the skid marks *appear* to come from?

A: Appeared to be the front tires, sir.

Q: They *appeared* to be the front tires?

A: Yes, sir.

Q: Officer Hopper, what tires on the bus did the skid marks *appear* to come from?

A: They *appeared* to come from the rear tires.

Q: You are not saying for a fact that they did?

A: No, sir.

Q: You are saying that they *appeared* to come from?

A: Yes, sir.

Q: Did the tire marks *appear* to come from both back tires of the bus?

A: Yes, sir.

Q: Officer Hopper, when testifying today you are only relying on your memory?

A: That's correct, sir.

Q: There's no indication whatsoever on your report about skid marks.

A: No, sir.

Q: Nothing about the location or what tires they *appeared* to come from?

A: No, sir.

Q: So when talking about skid marks, your report does not show what tires they *appeared* to have come from?

A: No, sir.

Q: Officer, you are not saying that the skid marks actually came from the tires that you indicated?

A: No, sir.

Q: Officer, your testimony is from memory and *appearance,* not a report and facts?

A: . . . (Silence.)

Cross-examination appears to be a natural format for repetition, the metered and short question, and colorful-sounding words. The creative lawyer may use consistency in direct examination or any part of trial. In a case where a man named Peter Spain was charged with malice murder after having shot and killed a man who had rammed his car, the following direct examination was developed to explain the shooting:

Q: What happened?

A: I stopped my car.

Q: And then?

A: I opened the door.

Q: And?

A: I got out.

Q: And then?

A: I reached for the gun. He was running at me. He was yelling.

Q: And?

A: I pulled the gun. I pointed it. The gun went off.

Q: And what happened?

A: He fell. I didn't intend to kill him.

The direct is short. The answers are simple. The sentences start with "I, he;" one sentence starts with "The." The questioning lawyer's voice is in a whisper while the answers are punchy, metered, and direct.

Experiencing consistency is akin to hearing a symphony. When the notes of a symphony are read, one does not hear the violins and the timpani. When "consistency" is read about, we don't hear the notes nor the meter nor the music. Consistency must be practiced orally. Consistency must be heard for the reader to appreciate its power.

The third touchstone of the Picture Theory of Trial Advocacy is contrast. Contrast by another name would be impeachment. But "color, consistency, and impeachment" is not memorable. We do not offer the legal definition of impeachment but the psychodramatic definition of impeachment. Impeachment: 1) when the witness squirms; 2) when the jury knows the witness squirms; 3) when the witness's believability is destroyed while the witness squirms.

But how does the Picture Theory of Trial Advocacy make impeachment an art form? All lawyers can be taught to memorize the mechanics of impeachment. One may ask the witness, "Are you a member of the Ku Klux Klan?" and receive an answer of "Yes." One may show a witness a document, have the document identified, and have the witness admit the document is inconsistent with his testimony on direct.

Contrast is created when opposites are placed next to each other. If you get on an elevator and someone is wearing one white shoe and one red shoe, the contrast will be something you remember. If a witness testifies that he is an angel, the greatest contrast can be created by immediately showing that he is satanic. Devil would be a better word.

If every other lawyer in the courtroom walks in wearing a blue pinstriped suit every day of the trial, my recommendation is that you walk in wearing a gray suit. Why? So you will be remembered.

The story goes that a female lawyer down in Mexico went before an elderly judge. That judge was sitting there on the bench with all these male lawyers just beating up on the female lawyer. She wore her best dress. The male lawyers were dressed like male lawyers. They had on their suits and their ties, and they fought hard. At the end of the motions hearing, the judge had to be aware of the contrast in the courtroom, that there were differences in the courtroom that he could remember. The way he ruled on that case showed that he saw the contrast. He looked down over at the men who were fighting against the one woman and said, "The lady wins."

The Picture Theory of Trial Advocacy teaches that words can effectively create contrast.

In a criminal murder case where the defendant was charged with having stabbed and killed a prison guard, an excellent example of contrast was developed. James Dickey, a prison inmate, identified the defendant as being chiefly responsible for the guard's death. Mr. Dickey was a small man with a soft voice and nonaggressive demeanor. Mr. Dickey took the oath like other witnesses and the following questions were asked during the middle of cross-examination:

Q: Do you know your IQ, Mr. Dickey?

A: Yes.

Q: What's your IQ, Mr. Dickey?

A: 125.

Q: You're not a dummy, Mr. Dickey?

A: No.

Q: A man with an IQ of 125 has a lot to think about?

A: Sure.

Q: You've used your 125 IQ to think of every legal and illegal means to get out of prison, Mr. Dickey?

A: Right.

Q: Mr. Dickey, you felt a sense of moral responsibility to say something against Mr. Collins (defendant)?

A: Yes.

Q: Are you the same James Edward Dickey convicted of forgery in Peach County?

A: Yes.

Q: Are you the same James Edward Dickey convicted of burglary in Crawford County?

A: Yes.

Q: Are you the same James Edward Dickey, alias Bunkum, convicted of murdering a policeman in DeKalb County?

A: Yes.

Q: And did you get a life sentence for killing a policeman in DeKalb County?

A: Yes.

Q: Did you feel a sense of moral responsibility when you were in Crawford, Peach, and DeKalb counties?

A: . . . (Silence.)

Q: Mr. Dickey, when was the last time you felt a sense of moral responsibility before this case happened?

A: . . . (Silence.)

Excellent. The witness squirmed, and the jury saw the witness squirm. The cross-examination created a contrasting image. A small, soft-spoken, nonaggressive man became the intelligent, plotting, police-killing witness. Moral responsibility as a reason to give a statement about someone accused of murder became unbelievable. The witness was impeached.

The art of "contrast" involves closely connecting the contrasting statements. In the last example, the connection with "moral responsibility" and being convicted of three crimes is vivid. Had the cross-examining lawyer asked about moral responsibility and never included the counties of the crimes, the effect of impeachment and contrast would be lost. Without careful preparation, the cross-examination of Mr. Dickey might have been:

Q: You have a 125 IQ?

Q: You're a smart man?

Q: You thought it was your moral responsibility to say something against Mr. Collins?

Q: You were convicted of forgery in Peach County?

Q: You were convicted of burglary in Crawford County?

Q: You were convicted of murder in DeKalb County?

Those are questions. The word choice is not colorful. The witness's name, Mr. Dickey, is not used for consistency. The contrast between the witness's cooperation with the police and his prior conviction in the shooting death of a policeman is not vivid. Contrast puts the impeaching material next to each other. Contrast uses colorful words and consistency to better impeach.

The fourth foundation of the Picture Theory of Trial Advocacy is closing.

Q: "Closing?" one asks "That's a part of the trial, it's so dissimilar from color, consistency, and contrast."

A: It starts with a "c."

Closing is where we usually try to use the most vivid pictures. Closing is the time for telling stories and creating analogies. Closings are high drama. When the lawyer talks with pictures that are created by analogies, then the story is complete. Stories are real and tangible, and that makes them memorable.

A defendant was charged with the murders of two men at the U.S. Post Office. He defended on the ground that he was insane. Prejudice against the insanity defense after the Hinckley verdict made for an appropriate story and analogy for the jury.

Trial counsel reasoned that the fear of the defendant's release was so strong that most jurors would not consider the insanity defense. The prejudice was attacked with the following picture:

> When I was young, I slept with a light on in the hall outside my bedroom. I believed in things that went 'bump' in the night. I believed in ghosts and other night creatures.
>
> I thought that something lived under the bed and inside the closet. And when the hall light was on, it cast shadows. Those shadows were creatures of the night. I was afraid when the light was on. I was afraid when the light was off. I was afraid when the bedroom door was closed. I eventually fell asleep every night. I'd wake the next morning relieved—not to have been reeled into the closet, or pulled under the bed by shadows.
>
> But my fear persisted. The same fear you have when you think about finding Mr. Brownlee not guilty by reason of

> insanity. The fear of not knowing what the verdict means. The fear of not knowing what's under the bed, in the closet, and in the shadows. Fear is not based on facts or law, but not guilty by reason of insanity is a fair verdict. Under the law and facts, Mr. Brownlee is a paranoid schizophrenic. He believed that the people who controlled the machines were going to kill him. Honor the law and facts instead of letting the fear of a little boy control you.

Color, consistency, contrast, and closing—The Picture Theory of Trial Advocacy.

Andrea Elliott
Girl in the Shadows: Dasani's Homeless Life
NEW YORK TIMES (Dec. 9, 2013)

She wakes to the sound of breathing. The smaller children lie tangled beside her, their chests rising and falling under winter coats and wool blankets. A few feet away, their mother and father sleep near the mop bucket they use as a toilet. Two other children share a mattress by the rotting wall where the mice live, opposite the baby, whose crib is warmed by a hair dryer perched on a milk crate.

Slipping out from her covers, the oldest girl sits at the window. On mornings like this, she can see all the way across Brooklyn to the Empire State Building, the first New York skyscraper to reach 100 floors. Her gaze always stops at that iconic temple of stone, its tip pointed celestially, its facade lit with promise.

"It makes me feel like there's something going on out there," says the 11-year-old girl, never one for patience. This child of New York is always running before she walks. She likes being first—the first to be born, the first to go to school, the first to make the honor roll.

Even her name, Dasani, speaks of a certain reach. The bottled water had come to Brooklyn's bodegas just before she was born, catching the fancy of her mother, who could not afford such indulgences. It hinted at a different, upwardly mobile clientele, a set of newcomers who over the next decade would transform the borough.

Dasani's own neighborhood, Fort Greene, is now one of gentrification's gems. Her family lives in the Auburn Family Residence, a decrepit city-run shelter for the homeless. It is a place where mold creeps up walls and roaches swarm, where feces and vomit plug communal toilets, where sexual predators have roamed and small children stand guard for their single mothers outside filthy showers.

It is no place for children. Yet Dasani is among 280 children at the shelter. Beyond its walls, she belongs to a vast and invisible tribe of more than 22,000 homeless children in New York, the highest number since the Great Depression, in the most unequal metropolis in America.

Nearly a quarter of Dasani's childhood has unfolded at Auburn, where she shares a 520-square-foot room with her parents and seven siblings. As they begin to stir on this frigid January day, Dasani sets about her chores.

Her mornings begin with Baby Lele, whom she changes, dresses and feeds, checking that the formula distributed by the shelter is not, once again, expired. She then wipes down the family's small refrigerator, stuffed with lukewarm milk, Tropicana grape juice and containers of leftover Chinese. After tidying the dresser drawers she shares with a sister, Dasani rushes her younger siblings onto the school bus.

"I have a lot on my plate," she says, taking inventory: The fork and spoon are her parents and the macaroni, her siblings—except for Baby Lele, who is a plump chicken breast.

"So that's a lot on my plate—with some corn bread," she says. "That's a lot on my plate."

Dasani guards her feelings closely, dispensing with anger through humor. Beneath it all is a child whose existence is defined by her siblings. Her small scrub-worn hands are always tying shoelaces or doling out peanut butter sandwiches, taking the ends of the loaf for herself. The bond is inescapable. In the presence of her brothers and sisters, Dasani has no peace. Without them, she is incomplete.

Dasani in the room at Auburn.

Today, Dasani rides the creaky elevator to the lobby and walks past the guards, the metal detector and the tall, iron fence that envelops what she calls "the jail." She steps into the light, and is met by the worn brick facade of the Walt Whitman projects across the street.

She heads east along Myrtle Avenue and, three blocks later, has crossed into another New York: the shaded, graceful abode of Fort Greene's brownstones, which fetch millions of dollars.

"Black is beautiful, black is me," she sings under her breath as her mother trails behind.

Dasani suddenly stops, puzzling at the pavement. Its condition, she notes, is clearly superior on this side of Myrtle.

"Worlds change real fast, don't it?" her mother says.

In the short span of Dasani's life, her city has been reborn. The skyline soars with luxury towers, beacons of a new gilded age. More than 200 miles of fresh bike lanes connect commuters to high-tech jobs, passing through upgraded parks and avant-garde projects like the High Line and Jane's Carousel. Posh retail has spread from its Manhattan roots to the city's other boroughs. These are the crown jewels of Mayor Michael R. Bloomberg's long reign, which began just seven months after Dasani was born.

In the shadows of this renewal, it is Dasani's population who have been left behind. The ranks of the poor have risen, with almost half of New Yorkers living near or below the poverty line. Their traditional anchors—affordable housing and jobs that pay a living wage—have weakened as the city reorders itself around the whims of the wealthy.

Long before Mayor-elect Bill de Blasio rose to power by denouncing the city's inequality, children like Dasani were being pushed further into the margins, and not just in New York. Cities across the nation have become flash points of polarization, as one population has bounced back from the recession while another continues to struggle. One in five American children is now living in poverty, giving the United States the highest child poverty rate of any developed nation except for Romania.

This bodes poorly for the future. Decades of research have shown the staggering societal costs of children in poverty. They grow up with less education and lower earning power. They are more likely to have drug addiction, psychological trauma and disease, or wind up in prison.

Dasani does not need the proof of abstract research. All of these plights run through her family. Her future is further threatened by the fact of her homelessness, which has been shown, even in short spells, to bring disastrous consequences.

Dasani's circumstances are largely the outcome of parental dysfunction. While nearly one-third of New York's homeless children are supported by a working adult, her mother and father are unemployed, have a history of arrests and are battling drug addiction.

Yet Dasani's trials are not solely of her parents' making. They are also the result of decisions made a world away, in the marble confines of City Hall. With the economy growing in 2004, the Bloomberg administration adopted sweeping new policies intended to push the homeless to become more self-reliant. They would no longer get priority access to public housing and other programs, but would receive short-term help with rent. Poor people would be empowered, the mayor argued, and homelessness would decline.

But the opposite happened. As rents steadily rose and low-income wages stagnated, chronically poor families like Dasani's found themselves stuck in a shelter system with fewer exits. Families are now languishing there longer than ever—a development that Mr. Bloomberg explained by saying shelters offered "a much more pleasurable experience than they ever had before."

Just three days before the mayor made that comment at a news conference in August 2012, an inspector at Auburn stopped by Dasani's crowded room, noting that a mouse was "running around and going into the walls," which had "many holes."

"Please assist," the inspector added. "There is infant in room."

Dasani was about to start sixth grade at a promising new school. This would be a pivotal year of her childhood—one already marked by more longing and loss than most adults ever see.

A tangle of three dramas had yet to unspool.

There was the question of whether Dasani's family would remain intact. Her mother had just been reunited with the children on the condition that she and her husband stay off drugs. The city's Administration for Children's Services was watching closely. Any slips, and the siblings could wind up in foster care, losing their parents and, most likely, one another.

The family's need for a home was also growing desperate. The longer they stayed in that one room, the more they seemed to fall apart. Yet rents were impossibly high in the city, and a quarter-million people were waiting for the rare vacancy in public housing. Families like Dasani's had been leaving the state. This was the year, then, that her parents made a promise: to save enough money to go somewhere else, maybe as far as the Pocono Mountains, in Pennsylvania.

Dasani could close her eyes and see it. "It's quiet and it's a lot of grass."

In the absence of this long-awaited home, there was only school. But it remained to be seen whether Dasani's new middle school, straining under budget cuts, could do enough to fill the voids of her life.

For children like Dasani, school is not just a place to cultivate a hungry mind. It is a refuge. The right school can provide routine, nourishment and the guiding hand of responsible adults.

But school also had its perils. Dasani was hitting the age when girls prove their worth through fighting. And she was her mother's daughter, a fearless fighter.

She was also on the cusp of becoming something more, something she could feel but not yet see, if only the right things happened and the right people came along.

Dasani is a short, wiry girl whose proud posture overwhelms her 4-foot-8 frame. She has a delicate, oval face and luminous brown eyes that watch everything, owl-like. Her expression veers from wonder to mischief.

Strangers often remark on her beauty—her high cheekbones and smooth skin—but the comments never seem to register.

What she knows is that she has been blessed with perfect teeth. In a family where braces are the stuff of fantasy, having good teeth is a lottery win.

On the subway, Dasani can blend in with children who are better off. It is an ironic fact of being poor in a rich city that the donated garments Dasani and her siblings wear lend them the veneer of affluence, at least from a distance. Used purple Uggs and Patagonia fleeces cover thinning socks and fraying jeans. A Phil & Teds rain cover, fished from a garbage bin, protects Baby Lele's rickety stroller.

Dasani and her family on the subway.

Dasani tells herself that brand names don't matter. She knows such yearnings will go unanswered, so better not to have them. But once in a while, when by some miracle her mother produces a new pair of Michael Jordan sneakers, Dasani finds herself succumbing to the same exercise: She wears them sparingly, and only indoors, hoping to keep them spotless. It never works.

Best to try to blend in, she tells herself, while not caring when you don't.

She likes being small because "I can slip through things." In the blur of her city's crowded streets, she is just another face. What people do not see is a homeless girl whose mother succumbed to crack more than once, whose father went to prison for selling drugs, and whose cousins and aunts have become the anonymous casualties of gang shootings, AIDS and domestic violence.

"That's not gonna be me," she says. "Nuh-uh. Nope."

Dasani speaks with certainty. She often begins a sentence with "Mommy say" before reciting, verbatim, some new bit of learned wisdom, such as "camomile tea cures a bad stomach" or "that lady is a dope fiend." She likes facts. She rarely wavers, or hints at doubt, even as her life is consumed by it.

When strangers are near, Dasani refers to Auburn as "that place." It is separate from her, and distant. But in the company of her siblings, she calls it "the house," transforming a crowded room into an imaginary home.

In reality, Auburn is neither. The forbidding, 10-story brick building, which dates back almost a century, was formerly Cumberland Hospital, one of seven public hospitals that closed because of the city's 1970s fiscal crisis.

In 1985, the city repurposed the former hospital into a shelter for families. This was the dawn of the period known as "modern homelessness," driven by wage stagnation, Reagan-era cutbacks and the rising cost of homes. By the time Mayor Bloomberg took office in 2002, New York's homeless population had reached 31,063—a record for the city, which is legally obligated to provide shelter.

Among the city's 152 family shelters, Auburn became known as a place of last resort, a dreaded destination for the chronically homeless.

City and state inspectors have repeatedly cited the shelter for deplorable conditions, including sexual misconduct by staff members, spoiled food, asbestos exposure, lead paint and vermin. Auburn has no certificate of occupancy, as required by law, and lacks an operational plan that meets state regulations. Most of the shelter's smoke detectors and alarms have been found to be inoperable.

There are few signs that children live at Auburn. Locked gates prevent them from setting foot on the front lawn. In a city that has invested millions of dollars in new "green spaces," Auburn's is often overrun with weeds.

Inside, prepackaged meals are served in a cafeteria where Dasani and her siblings wait in one line for their food before heading to another line to heat it in one of two microwaves that hundreds of residents share. Tempers fly and fights explode. The routine can last more than an hour before the children take their first bite.

The family's room is the scene of debilitating chaos: stacks of dirty laundry, shoes stuffed under a mattress, bicycles and coats piled high.

To the left of the door, beneath a decrepit sink where Baby Lele is bathed, the wall has rotted through, leaving a long, dark gap where mice congregate.

A few feet away, Dasani's legally blind, 10-year-old sister, Nijai, sleeps on a mattress that has come apart at the seams, its rusted coils splayed.

Hand-washed clothes line the guards on the windows, which are shaded by gray wool blankets strung from the ceiling. A sticky fly catcher dangles overhead, dotted with dead insects.

There is no desk or chair in the room—just a maze of mattresses and dressers. A flat-screen television rests on two orange milk crates.

To eat, the children sit on the cracked linoleum floor, which never feels clean no matter how much they mop. Homework is a challenge. The shelter's one recreation room can hardly accommodate Auburn's hundreds of children, leaving Dasani and her siblings to study, hunched over, on their mattresses.

Sometimes it feels like too many bodies sharing the same air. "There's no space to breathe 'cause they breathe up all the oxygen," Dasani says.

She carves out small, sacred spaces: a portion of the floor at mealtime, an upturned crate by the window, a bathroom stall.

The children spend hours at the playgrounds of the surrounding housing projects, where a subtle hierarchy is at work. If they are seen enough times emerging from Auburn, they are pegged as the neighborhood's outliers, the so-called shelter boogies.

Nothing gnaws at Dasani more.

A mucus-stained nose suggests a certain degradation, not just the absence of tissues, but of a parent willing to wipe or a home so unclean that a runny nose makes no difference. Dasani and her siblings can get hungry enough to lose their concentration in school, but they are forever wiping one another's noses.

When Dasani hears "shelter boogies," all she can think to say is what her mother always tells her—that Auburn is "just a pit stop."

"But you will live in the projects forever, as will your kids' kids, and your kids' kids' kids."

She knows the battle is asymmetrical.

The projects may represent all kinds of inertia. But to live at Auburn is to admit the ultimate failure: the inability of one's parents to meet that most basic need.

Dasani ticks through their faces, the girls from the projects who might turn up at this new school. Some are kind enough not to gossip about where she lives. The others might be distracted by the sheer noise of this first day—the start of sixth grade, the new uniform, the new faces. She will hopefully slip by those girls unseen.

She approaches the school's steps on a clear September morning. Fresh braids fall to one side of her face, clipped by bright yellow bows. Her required polo and khakis have been pressed with a hair straightener, since Auburn forbids irons.

Her heart is pounding. She will be sure to take a circuitous route home. She will focus in class and mind her manners in the schoolyard. She only has to climb those steps.

Minutes pass.

"Come on, there's nothing to be scared about," her 34-year-old mother, Chanel, finally says, nudging Dasani up the stairs.

She passes through the metal detector, joining 507 other middle and high school students at the Susan S. McKinney Secondary School of the Arts.

Housed in a faded brick building two blocks from Auburn, McKinney is a poor-kids' version of LaGuardia Arts, the elite Manhattan public school that inspired the television series "Fame." Threadbare curtains adorn its theater. Stage props are salvaged from a nearby trash bin. Dance class is so crowded that students practice in intervals.

An air of possibility permeates the school, named after the first African-American woman to become a physician in New York State.

There is Officer Jamion Andrews, the security guard who moonlights as a rap lyricist, and Zakiya Harris, the dance teacher who runs a studio on the side. And there is Faith Hester, the comedic, eyelash-batting humanities teacher who wrote a self-help book titled "Create a Life You Love Living" and fancies her own reality show.

The children also strive. Among them is a voice that periodically lifts the school with a "Madama Butterfly" aria. When the students hear it, they know that Jasmine, a sublimely gifted junior, is singing in the office of the principal, Paula Holmes.

The school matriarch closes her eyes as she listens. It may be her only tranquil moment.

Miss Holmes is a towering woman, by turns steely and soft. She wears a Bluetooth like a permanent earring and tends toward power suits. She has been at McKinney's helm for 15 years and runs the school like a naval ship, peering down its gleaming hallways as if searching the seas for enemy vessels.

Students stammer in her presence. She leaves her office door permanently open, like a giant, unblinking eye. A poster across the hall depicts a black man in sagging jeans standing before the White House, opposite President Obama. "To live in this crib," the poster reads, "you have to look the part."

Miss Holmes has no tolerance for sagging—sartorial, attitudinal or otherwise.

McKinney's roots run deep. Dasani's own grandmother studied there as a girl. Most of the middle school students are black, live in the surrounding projects and qualify for free or reduced meals. They eat in shifts in the school's basement cafeteria, watched over by the avuncular Frank Heyward, who blasts oldies from a boombox, telling students, "I got shoes older than you."

Most of the middle school students at the Susan S. McKinney Secondary School of the Arts qualify for free or reduced meals.

For all of McKinney's pluck, its burdens are great. In the last six years, the city has cut the school's budget by a quarter as its population declined. Fewer teachers share a greater load. After-school resources have thinned, but not the needs of students whose families are torn apart by gun violence and drug use. McKinney's staff psychologist shuttles between three schools like a firefighter.

And now, a charter school is angling to move in. If successful, it will eventually claim McKinney's treasured top floor, home to its theater class, dance studio and art lab. Teachers and parents are bracing for battle, announced by fliers warning against the "apartheid" effects of a charter co-location.

Dasani knows about charter schools. Her former school, P.S. 67, shared space with one. She never spoke to those children, whose classrooms were stocked with new computers. Dasani's own school was failing by the time she left.

At McKinney, Dasani quickly draws the notice of the older students, and not because she is short, though the nickname "Shorty" sticks. It is her electricity. When they dote on her, she giggles. But say the wrong thing and she turns fierce, letting the four-letter words fly.

It is still September when Dasani's temper lands her in the principal's office.

"Please don't call my mother," Dasani whispers.

Miss Holmes is seated in a rolling pleather chair held together by duct tape. She stares at the anguished girl. She has been at McKinney long enough to know when a child's transgressions at school might bring a beating at home.

The principal slowly scoots her chair up to Dasani and leans within inches of her face.

"O.K.," she says softly. "Let's make a deal."

From that day forward, Dasani will be on her best behavior. In turn, Miss Holmes will keep what happens at school in school.

With that, she waves Dasani off, fighting the urge to smile. She can't help but like this feisty little girl.

Dasani closes her eyes and tilts her head toward the ceiling of her classroom. She has missed breakfast again. ■ She tries to drift. She sees Florida. For a child who has never been to the beach, television ads are transporting. She is walking in the sand. She crashes into the waves.

"Dasaaaaaani!" her teacher sings out.

She opens her eyes.

There is Miss Hester, batting those lashes.

Both she and another teacher, Kenya Mabry, were raised in the projects. They dress and talk with a polish that impresses Dasani, who studies them.

Dasani in Faith Hester's class.

Miss Hester is also watching Dasani. She does not yet know where Dasani lives, or how hungry she gets. But Miss Hester finds two things striking: how late she arrives some mornings and how capable this girl is in spite of it. Without even trying, she keeps up.

Dasani possesses what adults at McKinney consider an intuitive approach to learning, the kind that comes when rare smarts combine with extreme life circumstances. Her intelligence is "uncanny" and "far surpasses peers her age," one counselor writes. "Student is continuously using critical analysis to reflect upon situations and interactions."

Principal Holmes is also taking note. She can already see in this "precocious little button" the kind of girl who could be anything—even a Supreme Court justice—if only she harnesses her gifts early enough. "Dasani has something that hasn't even been unleashed yet," Miss Holmes says. "It's still being cultivated."

For now, Dasani's most honed skill might be obfuscation. She works hard to hide her struggles, staying quiet as other children brag about their new cellphones or sleepovers with friends.

If there is one place she feels free, it is dance class. When she walks into McKinney's studio, and the music starts, her body releases whatever she is feeling.

"When I'm happy I dance fast," she says. "When I'm sad I dance slow. When I'm upset I dance both."

Dasani has been dancing for as long as she can remember, well before she earned her first dollar a few years ago break-dancing in Times Square. But the study of dance, as something practiced rather than spontaneous, this is new. She is learning to point her toes like a ballerina, and to fall back into a graceful bridge.

Perhaps it is no accident that amid the bedlam of Dasani's home life—the missed welfare appointments and piles of unwashed clothes—she is drawn to a craft of discipline.

Here, in this room, time is kept and routines are mapped with precision and focus.

Dasani never tires of rehearsing the same moves, or scrutinizing more experienced dancers. Her gaze is often fixed on a tall, limber eighth grader named Sahai.

Sahai is the middle school's valedictorian. A breathtaking dancer, she has long silky hair and carries herself like a newly crowned queen. She is a girl with enough means to accessorize elegantly. When Dasani looks at Sahai, she is taking the measure of all she is not.

You can be popular in one of three ways, Dasani's mother always says. Dress fly. Do good in school. Fight.

The first option is out of the question. While Dasani clings to her uniform, other students wear coveted Adidas hoodies and Doc Marten boots. In dance class, Dasani does not even have a leotard.

So she applies herself in school. "I have a lot of possibility," she says. "I do."

Her strongest subject is English, where a poem she writes is tacked to a teacher's wall.

By October, she is on the honor roll, just as her life at Auburn is coming apart.

It is something of an art to sleep among nine other people. One learns not to hear certain sounds or smell certain smells. ■ But some things still intrude on Dasani's sleep. There is the ceaseless drip of that decaying sink, and the scratching of hungry mice. It makes no difference when the family lays out traps and hangs its food from the ceiling in a plastic bag. Auburn's mice always return, as stubborn as the "ghetto squirrels," in Chanel's lingo, that forage the trash for Chinese fried chicken.

Dasani shares a twin mattress and three dresser drawers with her mischievous and portly sister, Avianna, only one year her junior. Their 35-year-old stepfather, Supreme, has raised them as his own. They consider him their father and call him Daddy.

Supreme married Chanel nine years earlier, bringing two children from a previous marriage. The boy, Khaliq, had trouble speaking. He had been trapped with his dead, pregnant mother after she fell down a flight of stairs. The girl, Nijai, had a rare genetic eye disease and was going blind. They were the same tender ages as Dasani and Avianna, forming a homeless Brady Bunch as Supreme and Chanel had four more children.

Two of Dasani's half-sisters, 7-year-old Maya and 6-year-old Hada, share the mattress to her right. The 5-year-old they call Papa sleeps by himself because he wets the bed. In the crib is Baby Lele, who is tended to by Dasani when her parents are listless from their daily dose of methadone.

Chanel and Supreme take the synthetic opioid as part of their drug treatment program. It has essentially become a substitute addiction.

The more time they spend in this room, the smaller it feels. Nothing stays in order. Everything is exposed—marital spats, frayed underwear, the onset of puberty, the mischief other children hide behind closed doors. Supreme paces erratically. Chanel cannot check her temper. For Dasani and her siblings, to act like rambunctious children is to risk a beating.

Dasani's siblings, clockwise from top left: Khaliq; Nijai; Papa; Baby Lele and Avianna; Hada and Maya.

By late fall, Chanel and Supreme are fighting daily about money.

It has been years since Supreme lost his job as a barber and Chanel stopped working as a janitor for the parks department. He cuts hair inside the shelter and sells pirated DVDs on the street while she hawks odds and ends from discount stores. In a good month, their combined efforts can bring in a few hundred dollars.

This is not one of those times. Supreme is keeping tight control of the family's welfare income—$1,285 in food stamps and $1,122 in survivor benefits for his first wife's death. He refuses to give Chanel cash for laundry.

Soon, all of Dasani's uniforms are stained. At school, she is now wearing donated clothes and her hair is unkempt, inviting the dreaded designation of "nappy." Rumors are circulating about where she lives. Only six of the middle school's 157 students reside in shelters.

When the truth about Dasani emerges, she does nothing to contradict it. She is a proud girl. She must find a way to turn the truth, like other unforeseeable calamities, in her favor.

She begins calling herself "ghetto." She dares the girls to fight her and challenges the boys to arm-wrestle, flexing the biceps she has built doing pull-ups in Fort Greene Park. The boys watch slack-jawed as Dasani demonstrates the push-ups she has also mastered, earning her the nickname "muscle girl."

Her teachers are flummoxed. They assume that she has shed her uniform because she is trying to act tough. In fact, the reverse is true.

A chilly, November wind whips across Auburn Place, rustling the plastic cover of a soiled mattress in a trash bin outside the shelter. ■ Chanel and Supreme stand nearby, waiting for their children to come from school. They are still short on cash. The children had pitched in $5.05, from collecting cans and bottles over the weekend.

Chanel inspects the mattress. Clean, it might fetch $10. But it is stained with feces. Janitors wearing masks and gloves had removed it from a squalid room where three small children lived, defecating on the floor. Their mother rarely bathed them, and they had no shoes on the day she gathered them in a hurry and left.

"You can smell it?" Chanel asks Supreme.

"No, I can see it," he says, curling his lip.

"Those are the people that they need to be calling A.C.S. on," Chanel says. At the shelter, the abbreviation for the Administration for Children's Services is uttered with the same kind of alarm that the C.I.A. can stoke overseas.

"Nasty girl," Chanel says, scrunching her nose.

Everyone knows Chanel. She weighs 215 pounds and her face is a constellation of freckles lit by a gaptoothed smile.

She wraps her copper-hued hair in a tubular scarf. The street is her domain. When she walks, people often step to the side—not in deference to her ample frame so much as her magisterial air.

Chanel is in everyone's business, scoping out snitches, offering homeopathic remedies, tattling on a girl's first kiss. A five-minute walk through Fulton Mall can take Chanel hours for all the greetings, gossip, recriminations and nostalgia. She has a remarkable nose for people, sniffing out phoniness in seconds. Those who smile too much are wearing "a frown turned upside down."

She is often spoiling for a fight, or leaving people in the stitches of laughter. While others want the life of the music mogul Jay-Z, Chanel would settle for being his pet. "Just let me be the dog. I don't care where you put me." When Chanel laughs, she tilts her head back and unleashes a thunderous cackle.

Dasani can detect her mother's laugh from blocks away. Today, she returns from school lugging a plastic bag of clothes donated by a security guard at McKinney.

Dasani begins rummaging through the bag. She pulls out a white Nautica ski jacket and holds it up to her shoulders. It is too wide, but she likes it. "It's dirty," she says forgivingly.

"Look, Mommy!" she says, modeling her new coat.

"That fits you real nice," Chanel coos.

Suddenly, Supreme leaps into the air. His monthly benefits have arrived, announced by a recording on his prepaid welfare phone. He sets off to reclaim his gold teeth from the pawnshop and buy new boots for the children at Cookie's, a favored discount store in Fulton Mall. The money will be gone by week's end.

Supreme and Chanel have been scolded about their lack of financial discipline in countless meetings with the city agencies that monitor the family.

But when that monthly check arrives, Supreme and Chanel do not think about abstractions like "responsibility" and "self-reliance." They lose themselves in the delirium that a round of ice creams brings. They feel the sudden, exquisite release born of wearing those gold fronts again—of appearing like a person who has rather than a person who lacks.

The next day, Dasani goes to school wearing her new Cookie's boots. Feeling amped, she gets into a verbal spat with some boys in gym class and must spend her lunch hour in the principal's office.

Miss Holmes glowers at Dasani, who tries to leaven the mood by bragging about her place on the honor roll. The principal is unmoved. Dasani still has a B average.

"I want the highest end of the honor roll," Miss Holmes says. "I want more. You have to want more, too."

Dasani stares at her tray. The discussion returns to her behavior in gym class.

"While we care for you, we're not going to take any crap," Miss Holmes says. "You understand?"

Trying not to cry, Dasani examines her food—a slice of cheese pizza, chocolate milk, a red apple. She wrinkles her nose. Miss Holmes has seen it before, the child too proud to show hunger.

"Can you hurry up?" Miss Holmes says. "The drama with the pizza is not working for me."

Silence.

"I'll feed you," Miss Holmes says. "I will feed you. You don't think I'll feed you? Bring the tray."

Dasani slowly lifts the pizza slice to her mouth, cracking a smile.

Miss Holmes has seen plenty of distressed children, but few have both the depth of Dasani's troubles and the height of her promise. There is not much Miss Holmes can do about life outside school. She knows this is a child who needs a sponsor, who "needs to see 'The Nutcracker,'" who needs her own computer. There are many such children.

Here at school, Miss Holmes must work with what she has.

"Apples are very good for you," she says, smiling. "Bananas are, too."

"I don't like those," Dasani says.

"Pretend you like them."

When Dasani is finished, she brings her empty tray to the principal for inspection. Miss Holmes gestures at Dasani's milk-stained mouth.

"Fix it," she says. "Go."

The tree is covered in Christmas lights that mask the lack of ornaments. The children gather around it inside a dilapidated, two-story rowhouse in East New York, Brooklyn—the closest thing they have to a home. It belongs to Chanel's ailing godmother, Sherry, whom the children call Grandma.

Sherry's day care center once occupied the first floor, where fading decals of Bambi now share space with empty liquor bottles. Chanel's two unemployed brothers, 22-year-old Josh and 39-year-old Lamont, stay in the dark, musty basement. When the children visit, they spend most of their time upstairs, sleeping on a drafty wooden floor beneath a Roman-numeral clock that is permanently stopped at 2:47.

Sherry's electricity has been cut, but the tree remains lit and the heat stays on, via a cable illicitly connected to a neighbor's power supply.

Christmas gifts are scarce: coloring books, a train set, stick-on tattoos, one doll for each girl.

A few nights later, the children are roused by shouts and a loud crash. Uncle Josh has punched his hand through a window and is threatening to kill Uncle Lamont.

Josh lunges at his brother with a knife. The men tumble to the floor as Chanel throws herself between them. Upstairs, the children cower and scream.

Dasani calls out orders: "Nobody move! Let the adults handle it!"

Sirens rattle the block. Josh is taken away in handcuffs as an ambulance races Lamont to the hospital with a battered eye. They had been fighting over a teenage girl.

January brings relief, but not because of the new year. It is the start of tax season, when Dasani's parents—and everyone they seem to know—rush to file for the earned-income tax credit, a kind of bonanza for the poor.

Their tax refunds can bring several thousand dollars, which could be enough to put down a rent deposit and leave the shelter.

On Jan. 7, the family heads to Manhattan for a rare outing. They take the Q train, which barrels high across the East River. The city's lights shimmer, making Chanel think of opportunity.

They will start looking for a home soon, she says.

"I wanna go somewhere where it's quiet," Dasani says.

"I wanna go somewhere where there's trees," Chanel says. "I just wanna see a bunch of trees and grass."

"Daddy say that he gonna buy this house with a lot of land with grass," Dasani says, "so that each of us would get a part, so that you can do whatever you want with that part of the land."

Supreme sits far-off, listening to music on his phone. Baby Lele wails.

Suddenly, Chanel spots Chinatown. The children squeal. Dasani mentions a book she read about the Great Wall of China.

"That's not this town," Chanel says.

"It's a big wall though," Dasani says.

"That's the real Chinatown," Chanel says. "This is the New York Chinatown, where they got Chinese people in Popeyes."

Dasani presses her forehead against the window and cups her hands around her eyes, as if preserving the view for herself.

Opportunity comes rarely, but Dasani is always waiting. She wakes early on Jan. 18, hours in advance of a track competition known for rescuing girls from the ghetto. ■ She has no running shoes, just a pair of imitation Converses. She is unknown in the rarefied world of athletic recruiters and private coaches. But ask anyone in her small corner of Brooklyn, from the crossing guards to the drunks, and they will say two things about this tiny girl with the wayward braids: She is strong like a boy and can run like the wind.

Dasani heads out in the icy cold with her mother and two of her sisters. They walk a mile before arriving at the manicured grounds of the Pratt Institute in the Brooklyn neighborhood of Clinton Hill, which is hosting the Colgate Women's Games.

The amateur track and field series is a magnet for athletic recruiters, and some of its champions have gone as far as the Olympics. Dasani will compete in the 200-meter dash. She heads to the bathroom to change.

"She got shorts to put on?" one of the organizers asks.

Dasani reaches for her leggings.

"Those are the sneakers?" the woman frowns.

Wearing no socks, Dasani ties her rainbow laces and walks to the track. When her number is called, she takes her place among four other girls.

The blank fires and she is off, ahead of the pack.

Win, Dasani tells herself. Win.

At the first bend, she trips and falls behind.

By the second turn, Dasani has caught up with the lead runner.

"Run, Dasani!" Chanel screams. "Run!"

They are in a dead heat for the finish line.

Dasani comes in second. It hardly matters that her time is insufficient to make it past the preliminaries. They leave the stadium feeling euphoric.

"My baby's going to the Olympics," Chanel crows. As they walk west along Willoughby Avenue, they talk of finding a trainer. Chanel starts singing her favorite Luther Vandross song, "A House Is Not a Home."

The girls have heard it enough times to sing along.

A chair is still a chair
Even when there's no one sittin' there
But a chair is not a house
And a house is not a home
When there's no one there
to hold you tight.

They turn north on Carlton Avenue, passing a renovated brick townhouse with sleek, metal window frames.

A skinny brunette is unloading her station wagon. At the sight of Dasani's family, she freezes. She smiles nervously and moves slowly to her car, grabbing an infant from the car seat.

The mood shifts.

"She thinks we gonna jump her," Chanel says as she keeps walking. The shelter is only three blocks away.

"Why do they feel like they're so apart? She's just two steps away from us. If you got jumped out here, a black man would be the first to save your ass. That's what I feel like telling her."

When they reach Myrtle Avenue, Chanel goes searching for a beer at her favorite corner store. Dasani trails her.

Inside, the short-order cook, a Mexican girl, stares at Chanel suspiciously.

"Don't look at me," Chanel says.

"You so nice, that's why I see you," the girl responds cockily.

"You better watch that grill," Chanel says. "I don't want to scare you."

"You think you scare me?" the girl yells.

"Let's fight right now!" Chanel shouts.

"Wait for me outside!" the girl calls back.

Chanel moves toward her, reaching for a mop.

"Mommy!" Dasani screams.

The owner, Salim, races toward Chanel.

"I'll crack her with a stick!" Chanel yells as Salim holds her back.

Dasani is frozen.

"I'ma wait for your ass when you come out," Chanel says. "What time she get off?"

"You run your mouth," Salim says, gently leading Chanel away, as he has done before.

As they leave, Dasani turns to the cook.

"She gonna knock you stupid, Chinese lady," Dasani says.

"Don't use those words," Salim cries out. "You're not supposed to turn out like your mother."

Donna St. George
Murder in the Making
WASHINGTON POST (Aug. 27, 2000)

On a Wednesday afternoon, in a quiet moment between cases, Judge Gary Gasparovic sat at his well-polished desk and read through a court motion, dense legal words on crisp white paper.

In the small Southern Maryland city of La Plata, Gasparovic had been a judge for 11 years, a towering, bespectacled man with salt-and-pepper hair and a reputation for being tough. He had, in his time on the bench, overseen hundreds of sad and contentious cases of domestic turmoil. This one did not strike him as extraordinary.

A woman named Janice Lancaster said her husband had struck her and threatened to kill her. She had given the court a letter he left on her dresser: "Time is running short for me and you. . . . I'm ready to go any time to lay my body to rest and [I am] not going to be the only one."

The judge reached for his pen and signed an order authorizing the husband's arrest.

It was but one decision—made in less than five minutes—for a judge who, on any given day, might hear 30 or 40 cases. It was a fitting decision under the circumstances, but it was not enough.

A day passed, and the paperwork lay untended in the court clerk's office. The bench warrant for the arrest was never prepared. Then the courthouse closed for a long New Year's weekend.

By the time the courthouse reopened on Monday morning, it was too late.

When her case reached the judge last Dec. 29, Janice Lancaster had long been a prisoner of her fear. She had bought a gun and taken to sleeping in a toolshed beside the house she shared with her husband and two children. At 33, she had selected a dress for her funeral.

Her terror was not a secret.

In one turbulent year, she had let a remarkable number of people inside her personal crisis: police, counselors, judges, lawyers, friends, relatives and co-workers. But her story came out to them in small and fleeting pieces—one night's ordeal, one ominous letter, one violent admonishment.

Never seeing the entire picture, never understanding the full gravity of events, people made decisions or gave advice: the judge in his chambers, the friend who gave her haven in a spare bedroom, the police officer who walked down her driveway, the lawyer who took on her case for divorce.

Her problems appeared as a jumble of disturbing snapshots that gave too little sense of the growing threat.

On the clear, cool morning of Jan. 3, James Steven Lancaster Sr. strode purposefully past the Christmas decorations and into their four-room home. He confronted Janice with a shotgun in the kitchen. They struggled.

Their teenage daughter yelled that she was going to call 911.

"I love you," Janice Lancaster pleaded.

He choked her. Then he pulled the trigger.

Twenty-five years after domestic violence emerged from the shadows of public discussion as a visible and vexing American pathology, the bodies of women like Janice Lancaster still are scattered in graveyards across the nation.

It remains the prevailing reason women are murdered in the United States. While the homicide rate is down overall, government experts say that one-third to one-half of slain women are victims of an intimate partner, about the same as in 1976, when the first wave of shelters opened for battered wives and girlfriends.

The primary reason is this: An array of new laws and programs developed during the last two decades has yet to overcome two obstacles. Those who most need help often feel conflicted about asking—ashamed, torn and frightened. And the system intended to protect them remains fragmented and uneven—almost impossible to comprehend and negotiate without an aggressive lawyer or advocate, which many women still do not have.

Janice Lancaster's case offers startling proof of both.

At times she was set back by her own ambivalence. She wanted to believe in the man she fell in love with as a teenager. "Stevie" was a brawny, soft-spoken man with roots in the rugged waterman's life in Southern Maryland. He was the father of their children, a boy now 13 and a girl 17.

Also, at its best, the system may not have been enough to save Janice Lancaster. But that's hard to know—the system was not at its best.

She willed, quite vividly, to help herself, engaging the system on so many levels. She took her husband to counseling. When he refused to continue, she went by herself. In hard times, she moved into friends' houses. At several junctures, she called on police. In court, she agreed to testify. At wit's end, she hired a private divorce lawyer.

In desperation, she learned to fire a .38.

As the violence escalated, she resolved to end the relationship. But he vowed to kill her—if she left him, if she got a protective order, if he faced time in jail.

Yet, somehow, her death still was widely unforeseen. In the anguish of the aftermath, many who had glimpses of her struggle recalled what they had seen. Taken together, these moments show a woman who understood the danger but not how to survive it.

Much of the story already existed in her own words. She took notes. She kept a journal. She recorded her husband's comings and goings.

Janice Lancaster, it should be said, wanted someone to know what had happened.

Nov. 14, 1998: He started swinging at me. . . . My daughter hollered, "Leave my mother alone. I'm going to call the police." . . . He went for her. . . . I jumped on his back. . . . He pushed me. He rammed my head into a picture. The glass cut me in my head.

CLOSE FRIEND TRACY DAWSON

February 1999

Tracy Dawson found it hard to imagine Steve Lancaster had grown menacing. She had gone to La Plata High School with the Lancasters. They seemed lucky at love—together 17 years, two good children; good to each other, too. She remembered cookouts when Janice cuddled on his lap, like the teenage sweethearts they once were.

Steve Lancaster seemed good-natured, well-mannered, an involved father. Dawson used to call him "Mr. Mom." He took his children crabbing, to watch basketball, to the racetrack. Every year, the family vacationed at Kings Dominion—rides, hotel rooms, dinners out.

Then again, Dawson thought, who knew what went on behind closed doors? Janice said Steve had changed. She said he was having an affair with a teenage girl, a girl younger than the couple's daughter. Steve insisted the relationship was not sexual, though he was at the girl's home day after day, often until 2 or 3 a.m.

At one point, the friends tried to convince themselves that Steve Lancaster, 36, was having an early midlife crisis.

Dawson tried to be supportive when Janice lamented: "He's just not my Steve anymore." It was harder, however, when Janice asked her what to do. Dawson begged off. "I don't live in your shoes," Dawson said. "You know more about the way he is than I do."

But when Janice phoned in early February to say Steve had threatened her life in a letter, Dawson thought: This is serious. Keep the letter, she advised. And this time Dawson needed to do more than offer support.

"You've got to tell someone," she insisted.

Feb. 5, 1999: He said if I leave I won't ever live in another home. Because he would kill me and him.

JUDGE RICHARD ALAN COOPER

Feb. 9, 1999

Judge Cooper sat in his high-back chair, overlooking the narrow courtroom where he had presided for three years. He was white-haired at 58, more stern in manner than in fact—the kind of judge, said one lawyer, "you would want as your grandfather."

Today, Cooper had a full load, and in addition to his scheduled cases was this one: 0402SP77, Janice Michelle Lancaster v. James Steven Lancaster. He did not know the couple, and he did not know it was Janice's first time in court, the beginning of what would become 11 months in the judicial system.

In Maryland, many domestic crises play out before a cast of judges. There is civil court, province of protection orders and divorce. There is criminal court, for assaults and other crimes.

Adding to the complexity, some cases end up in District Court and some go to Circuit Court. Each has its own files. Computer systems are not linked.

For Cooper, domestic turmoil was familiar territory. There were 262 domestic violence cases filed in Charles County District Court last year, in a state that recorded 17,489. Like many other women Cooper dealt with, the one before him wanted a protection order to forbid her husband to call or come near.

"Would you tell me what happened?" the judge asked.

Janice Lancaster began in a nervous rush of words: She was driving down the street when her husband sped up beside her and tried to cut her off. She managed to elude him for a time but finally made a panicked dash to the police station. He pursued her at top speed, stopping only when police officers surrounded him in the station parking lot.

"He left a note," she told Judge Cooper. ". . . I was scared that he would kill me because he had said he would do it if I leave him, and I left him."

"Are you and he living together at the present time?" the judge asked.

"We are, but I packed up and left Sunday."

"You want me to order him to leave the home?" he asked.

"Yes."

Cooper signed the papers. He did not ask to see the threatening note, the first public sign of what was on Steve Lancaster's mind.

Normally, more details would have emerged at a second hearing a week later. But Janice Lancaster, like nearly 50 percent of abused women in Maryland, changed her mind before the case returned to the courtroom.

"Are you ready to go forward on this case, ma'am?" a different judge asked when the day for the formal hearing came on Feb. 16. This time, her husband was in the courtroom.

"No, I would like to drop it," Janice Lancaster said.

"Can you tell me why you would like to do that?" the judge asked.

"We'd like to work out our differences," she said.

"And you do not feel you're in any danger?"

"No."

In her journal that day, Janice was more wary. Her husband, she said, had assured her "he wasn't trying to hurt me. He just wanted to talk. . . . But I didn't trust him."

TRACY DAWSON

Feb. 24, 1999

About the time she decided to give her husband another chance, Janice Lancaster went to Tracy Dawson to ask for help writing a will.

"Do you really think you need this?" Dawson asked her normally buoyant friend.

"The way he is," Janice replied, "I've got to be prepared."

Steve Lancaster had guns. He was a hunter—squirrels, rabbits, deer. Janice called the police the day of her first court appearance to ask that they take his guns away, but the officers got no answer when they came knocking at her home shortly afterward. So the guns remained.

And Steve Lancaster grew up under the influence of a violent father, a man who spent almost seven years in prison for assaulting his wife when Steve was 15 years old. After his release from prison, Steve's father shot a man near a tavern.

Now Janice worried that Steve might repeat his father's violence.

He really might try to kill her.

The detailed list of her belongings that Janice gave Dawson included family dishes, a crab cooker, a Dirt Devil upright, an armoire, a four-slice toaster, her class ring, her anniversary band, her 1990 Chevy Corsica, 24 folding chairs.

It was 79 lines long, three pages, her dearest possessions at 33 years old.

Janice mailed the will to her oldest brother, Joseph L. Tolson Jr., marked with the words "Open upon my death." He honored her wishes.

April 20, 1999: He paged me. I wouldn't answer him because I was mad. So when I came home from work that evening, he was pushing me and he choked me because I wouldn't answer when he paged.

POLICE CALL

May 8, 1999

The emergency call came at 5:56 a.m. The voice on the cellular phone was breathless: "Hi, my name is Janice Lancaster and I live on Popes Creek Road and right now I'm in the woods. My husband . . . he beat me up. . . . Oh."

Her voice broke.

She was hiding in the thickets off the road where she lived. Her husband was driving the streets, searching for her.

"Okay, where are you at right now?" the dispatcher asked.

I'm in the woods, beside Popes Creek Road, right beside a blue house. . . . Please hurry up."

"Okay, Janice. What is your home address?"

"Popes Creek Road, it's 10320. . . . But he's driving in the road."

"Okay, what is he driving, do you know?"

"It's a 280Z, it's gray. . . . But I'm in the woods. Please hurry."

"Hold on the phone with me a second."

She pleaded: "Please come and get me."

At 6:06 a.m., she waved down Officer Keith Moody.

Police had gotten to Steve Lancaster at 6:04 a.m.

In Charles County, police handled 4,888 domestic service calls in 1999. In Maryland, family violence calls have been the primary reason people dial 911, state officials say—and when police show up, they generally know only what the radio dispatcher's computer can tell them.

Janice Lancaster told the officers she had been out in the shed, gathering her things to flee, when Steve Lancaster confronted her. They argued. He punched her in the head and face.

Janice had tried to run to her car to escape, she noted in her journal. But her husband reached under the hood to yank something and said, "You won't drive this." She ran to her daughter's car. He followed her. Frantic, she fled into the woods.

Janice's lip was swollen, slightly bloody. That was enough for the police. Her husband was arrested at 6:20 a.m. on a charge of second-degree assault.

NOTE PINNED ON A DRESS:

When I die bury me in my long white dress. I want a pretty blue coffin. Please put socks on my feet because they are always cold. Put gloves on my hands too, white. I'm not a witch, I'm not a witch. I'm writing this because someone keeps saying they're going to kill me.

CLOSE FRIEND KIM CLEMENTS

June 12, 1999

Janice was having a yard sale, and she asked Kim Clements to come help. Clements was there at 8 a.m., working beneath the tall oaks in Janice's front yard.

Later, in the lull of the warm June day, Janice led Clements and a few relatives into her 8-by-12 toolshed. A pressed white dress, with big white buttons, hung off to the side in a plastic dry-cleaning bag.

"When I die," Janice said, "I want to be buried in this."

Clements and the other women gasped.

"Oh, Janice, no," Clements said.

But Janice was adamant. "You have to listen to me. You've got to be my voice."

The women quieted.

"I have a note attached," Janice went on, pointing to a small white paper pinned to the dress. Janice read aloud the alarming words about how to dress her for her funeral.

It was almost impossible to absorb.

Kim Clements had long been worried about her friend. The two women had been close for seven years, both residents of a rural crossroads called Faulkner, friends of the same age with the same girlish humor.

On several occasions during the late winter and spring, Janice had shown up at Clements's house with her children to seek refuge from her husband. Clements invited them to stay as long as they wished. But Janice always went back.

Clements finally urged her friend to move out for good. "You move into a shelter, and what happens after that?" Janice had asked her. "You're homeless." The nearest shelter, almost 20 miles away, served primarily homeless women and children.

Janice said she wanted more for her children, not less. She was about to be promoted to assistant kitchen manager at a nearby Catholic retreat where she worked as a cook. She had lived in her rented house 15 years. For her children, it was home. It had a tin roof and an outhouse, but Janice made it sweet-looking, with her bright flower beds, her lace-trimmed curtains, her matching country furniture. There were patio tables in the yard, tucked at the edge of the woods.

Besides, Janice had argued to her friend, why should she be the one to move? The lease was in her name. She paid the rent. It was Steve who created the havoc. And how far could she ever get from him, anyhow—without large sums of money and given his connection to their children? It seemed that he always would know where she was.

Aug. 3, 1999: He told the kids that he was going to kill your mother stone dead. They told this on 8–3–99.

LAWYER HOWARD M. SCHEMLER

Aug. 6, 1999

Howard M. Schemler was not alarmed by Janice Lancaster's story. It was another tale of marital infidelity, and he was a lawyer who'd carved out a niche in divorce.

Schemler worked in a solo practice in Fort Washington, a beefy man with a bristly mustache and a blunt manner. He did not have a secretary. His office was a cluttered three-room suite with paint the color of weak lemonade, file drawers ajar, dogeared folders cascading across his desk.

Janice poured out the details of her husband's affair, and they agreed she would file for divorce on grounds of adultery.

Adultery provided grounds for a speedier divorce, without the one-year separation required in more routine cases.

So did filing on grounds of domestic violence, but that option did not come up. On Aug. 6, Schemler was ready to file the paperwork. He met with Janice at 10 a.m., and as far as he could tell, she wasn't fearful. In cases where he noted a potential for violence, Schemler could combine divorce filings with requests for protection orders.

Today was different.

Schemler walked into the red-brick courthouse in La Plata, unaware that court records in the very same building contained critical facts about his client: Her husband had beaten her and tried to run her off the road on occasions when she tried to leave him.

The lawyer did not know violence was an issue.

Aug. 19, 1999: I came home from work. He said I was going to sleep with him tonight. And make love. He don't care what the lawyer said. If not, he will kill both of us. Later he left.

OFFICER WILLIAM R. JACKSON JR.

Sept. 19, 1999

The emergency call came at 11:43 p.m. Officer William R. Jackson Jr. steered his marked police cruiser down darkened Popes Creek Road, a well-traveled rural thoroughfare that led toward two of the area's fabled crab houses.

His sirens silent and flashers off, he slowed at a mailbox numbered 10320 and pulled onto a rutted dirt pathway, past two creaky barn stalls that looked abandoned. The house to his left was tiny, with a sloping foundation, a sagging porch, a nearby shed.

Jackson approached cautiously. Domestic calls, he knew, are hard to predict—charged and volatile and sometimes dangerous. He had been an officer for two years, and it was a rare night when he did not go out on one.

Now, pulling up, he saw Janice Lancaster: 5-foot-7, standing in the yard in a nightgown, alone and calm. She did not rush toward him. When Jackson approached, she answered each question. Quiet, he thought. Pleasant.

As they talked, Jackson recalled that this was the same woman he had met in February, when her husband had tried to run her off the road. He remembered she had been worried that her husband had a gun in his car.

Now, Janice told the officer that she had been sleeping in the shed when Steve came home and grabbed her by the chest. She resisted. He dragged her across the yard, back, into the house. They continued to argue. Her daughter called police.

Jackson asked if she had been hurt.

She showed him scratches on her neck and breast.

Then Steve Lancaster emerged from the house and told Jackson the same story. But he said he did not recall scratching his wife. Steve Lancaster was courteous, not the kind of mouthy, cursing offender he often confronted.

Steve Lancaster asked one question: "Who made the call?"

Jackson did not answer.

The arrest was an easy decision for Jackson: With a minor but discernible injury, this was second-degree assault. He led Steve Lancaster to his police car.

"Look, he might be out in a couple of hours," the police officer told Janice Lancaster before he left. "You might want to get a [protective order] or pack up and go someplace else."

"I don't want to leave my kids," she said.

DISTRICT COURT JUDGE RICHARD ALAN COOPER

Oct. 26, 1999

Judge Richard Alan Cooper was looking down from the bench at a man who—according to the paperwork before him—had punched his wife in the face and head one May evening. Today he was contrite and pleading guilty to second-degree assault.

Cooper did not remember the Lancasters from their protection order case nine months earlier. More significant, he did not know that Steve Lancaster had been arrested a second time for attacking his wife. He also did not know that Steve Lancaster had been ordered to stay away from Janice until that second case went to trial.

Nor did he know that Janice Lancaster had called police again Oct. 13, 1999—when no arrest was made. That night, she had pleaded to a dispatcher in a halting, fearful voice: "I need the police. . . . I think my husband's going to go get a gun. . . . Please hurry."

The prosecutor, Daniel Ginsburg, could not tell him. Ginsburg had not discerned the details, either.

Instead, Ginsburg told the judge: "This was a genuine incident of domestic violence, and too often victims aren't prepared to testify and she was prepared to do so today. She did sustain some injury. The state would recommend an active period of incarceration, perhaps weekends."

Then her husband's attorney, Frank Jenkins, made the other case.

"My client is 36 years of age. . . . He was having problems in his relationship; he simply overreacted. He realizes now that their marriage is in its final stages. He's very sorry, very embarrassed, about what has happened. It is out of character for him."

The judge inquired: "Mr. Lancaster, is there anything you want to say before I impose the sentence?"

"I'm sorry for what I've done," he said softly.

The judge asked about Lancaster's job on the water, and then went on: "You and your wife are no longer together?"

"We've seen each other once in a while," Steve Lancaster said.

"You don't live together?" the judge asked.

"Right."

This was a lie, Steve Lancaster had been living with his wife, in spite of her attempts to force him to leave, in spite of still spending many hours at his girlfriend's home.

"Well, Mr. Lancaster," the judge said, "these domestic violence incidents are taken seriously. . . . You're looking at up to 10 years on this particular charge."

The judge inquired: "Are there any domestic violence orders in effect? Are there protective orders in effect? A divorce case has been filed?"

"Oh, I don't know," Steve Lancaster said.

The judge made his decision without knowing that the trouble was escalating because no one involved—not the prosecutor, not police, not Janice Lancaster's attorney—had assembled all the incidents into a report or a file or a courtroom argument.

By the judge's calculations, the case looked like this: The injury meant he would give jail time. But because the injury was minor and this was a first-time domestic offender, the sentence would be minimal.

Steve Lancaster got five days behind bars. Eighty-five days of jail time would be suspended, the judge said, and probation would last 18 months. The judge ordered Lancaster to have no "harassing contact" with his wife and said probation would be unsupervised.

This meant no one would keep tabs on Steve Lancaster.

From start to finish, the sentencing took seven minutes.

Janice Lancaster sat confused and alone in the back of the courtroom. Why hadn't anyone called on her to speak? Why had her husband been allowed to lie? Why would he still be entitled to live in their house?

LETTER TO JANICE

Nov. 1, 1999

Steve Lancaster served three days in jail, getting out two days early for good behavior. A few days later, he left a letter on Janice's dresser. It asked whether Janice still wanted him in her life. Would she shun him after the divorce? And would she help get his assault case dropped?

He wrote: "I told you that I won't hit you know more. I can't touch you anymore because I got 18 months probation, that's that."

Then the tone shifted.

"Janice, I don't have anything left, so don't keep pushing me to the limit. . . . Be very careful with me. I'm right on the edge. . . . I know what I got to do to settle all of this . . . one way only and you know what I'm talking about."

He warned: "I'm ready to go any time to lay my body to rest and [I am] not going to be the only one."

FIRST COUSIN MARGARET LANDRY

Nov. 27, 1999

Janice's family was throwing a big party: a baby shower for one relative and birthday celebration for another. They had rented a party hall in St. Mary's County. Janice was among the first to arrive.

Margaret Landry, who had lived in Texas for a few years, was excited to see her first cousin again. They had grown up together, with Landry living next door much of Janice's childhood, something of a big sister. Janice had family living nearby in Charles County, but she was reluctant to draw them deeply into her volatile marriage.

Today, however, she confided in Landry. Her cousin was shocked when they stepped away from the festivities and Janice revealed that she had almost been stopped from coming.

She said Steve had insisted that she stay home. She had refused. So he forced her pants off and dropped them into a puddle. To get away, she grabbed her pants and jumped into her car.

"Huh? He did that?" Landry asked, stunned.

"You all just don't know," Janice said. "That fool is getting crazy."

Landry was blunt.

"You need to get out of there," she said.

"I am, I am," Janice replied. "I'm getting a house. I just need to wait until I get divorced."

FERN BROWN

COURT COORDINATOR FOR DOMESTIC RELATIONS

Dec. 20, 1999

Fern Brown is a calm and soothing personality, a retired computer analyst who, at 59, now passed her days explaining the forbidding language of the law to women who needed to use it to protect themselves.

Most people came to her courthouse office without a lawyer or money to spend on one. Brown explained the first step: how to fill out the form asking a judge for a temporary order of protection.

Brown did not follow their cases through the system, but she did what she could. Sometimes that meant walking someone into the courtroom. Sometimes it meant listening to a story for an hour or calling on a counselor.

The woman before Brown on Dec. 20, 1999, was wearing a Santa Claus hat with the name "Janice" written in glitter on the trim. Fern Brown smiled. She had never met Janice Lancaster before but liked the woman in her office—bright dark eyes, a generous humor.

On this quiet afternoon, five days before Christmas, Janice mentioned that she had just come from the prosecutor's office. There they were working to get her husband arrested for violating the order to stay away from her before trial.

The order had been issued by a court commissioner at a bail hearing in the criminal case, and no one had told Janice it existed. She had found out today. Now, she decided, she would push for as much protection as possible and seek a civil protective order, too. A civil order was more potent because it had criminal penalties and violators could be arrested without a warrant.

Her breaking point had come the night before. Steve had struck and threatened her because she attended a religious retreat that weekend.

She seemed to realize that another court order now might incense him. And, in fact, experts have concluded that this time of separating is highly charged and dangerous, with many a violent reprisal.

Brown took Janice upstairs to see a judge for a protective order that would last until Dec. 28, 1999, when her husband would come to court for a hearing.

When they said goodbye, Brown noticed an edgy expression on the face beneath the Santa's cap. Fear, Brown thought to herself. It gave her pause, and yet she saw it often in the women she helped. Probably one of four said her life had been threatened.

Brown never knew what became of most of them.

CIRCUIT COURT JUDGE STEVEN G. CHAPPELLE

Dec. 28, 1999

The proceeding before Judge Steven G. Chappelle the next week looked straightforward. It was the request for a civil protection order. Often, these hearings are heated and hard to sort out. But this time, the lawyers came in having already agreed to terms.

With no disputes before him, Chappelle asked few questions. He did not have all the couple's court files. Sometimes he got them, sometimes not.

So the judge heard nothing about the threatening letter, the nights in the toolshed, the wish for a pretty blue coffin. The way he saw it, his role was to make sure both sides understood the agreement they had reached, then give it the court's blessing.

"The terms of this order will be that it will remain in effect until one year from today," the judge said, ". . . That until that period of time, Mr. Lancaster will not abuse or threaten to abuse Mrs. Lancaster, That he will not contact [her] in person, by phone, in writing."

The judge asked the lawyers to review the order with their clients before the court.

"Is it your agreement not to have any type of contact with your wife whatsoever?" Steve Lancaster's attorney asked him.

"Yes," he said,

"You will leave the house on Popes Creek Road?"

"Yes."

"And the agreement is effective until the end of the year 2000, correct?"

"Yes."

No one asked about guns—though the question is posed on the protective order—and no one mentioned the violence counseling Janice had requested for her husband a week earlier.

Her attorney, Howard Schemler, was on vacation. The lawyer who stepped in to help, as a favor to her employer, had met Janice for the first time only the day before the proceeding.

In this critical moment, no one put the pieces together. No one saw the larger picture.

Elsewhere in the same small courthouse lay Janice's motion for Steve's arrest. It had been waiting seven days for a response from the other side. No one had remembered to alert the court clerk that the motion had urgency.

The motion for his arrest showed that Steve had repeatedly violated the only condition of his most recent bail: to stay away from his wife.

It showed he had gone so far as to strike her and threaten her life in a handwritten letter, which was included for the court to see.

This meant he had violated not only his bail but also his probation.

SUPERVISOR AND FRIEND FREDA WELLS

Jan. 1, 2000

Freda Wells felt Janice was in danger, but how much, she could not be sure. She was the manager in the kitchen of the Loyola Retreat House, a lush, rolling 240-acre preserve on the banks of the Potomac. The kitchen crew was like family, and after Janice's troubles became clear, Wells reminded her staff day after day: No one was to be left alone in the kitchen, and no one was to leave the wooded property without an escort.

It seemed one thing she could do to help.

Wells saw Steve Lancaster as "a walking time bomb." She had heard about his threats, his guns, his possessiveness, about nights when Janice fled him and he rousted his children out of bed to help him find her.

She remembered the warm autumn day when Janice told her Steve had showed the children a loaded shotgun and said: "This is for your mother. If you're not careful, it could be for you, too."

Sometimes, Janice got frustrated. Her stays at friends' houses could not go on forever. She wanted Steve locked up. She told Freda's sister-in-law Mary Wells that after being arrested and quickly released, Steve Lancaster had told her: "See, I'm back. They didn't keep me."

About Christmastime, Janice felt a new sense of hope. She told Freda that Steve was about to be arrested. Anyway, he had been barred from their home by a judge.

"I'm finally going to get my life together," she said with enthusiasm. "I just want peace."

Now, on Jan. 1, Freda and Janice were at the home of Mary Wells. The three friends turned on "The Bodyguard." They had seen the movie before, a Whitney Houston blockbuster in which the star is saved from an obsessed man.

Janice wanted to see it again.

Then, during a lull in the action, Janice brought up a curious telephone call she had had that day from her estranged husband's sister. Janice had once been close to Joan V. Swann.

"No matter what happens, Janice, I'll always love you," Swann had blurted out.

"What is this?" Janice had demanded. "A warning?"

The sister-in-law had hung up quickly.

Now the words nagged at Janice.

Freda Wells was definite.

"She's trying to tell you something," Freda said.

On Jan. 2, Janice Lancaster and Freda Wells worked much of the day at the Loyola Retreat House, baking crab cakes for visitors from a Catholic college. Janice mentioned that it had been two weeks and Steve hadn't been arrested. "I wonder why it's taking so long," she said. She worked until 8 that night, then drove home to her tiny frame house, one-third of a mile away.

Janice passed the evening with her two children, joking with them, laughing, ironing her work uniforms and their school clothes. They all went to bed.

Before dawn, Steve Lancaster parked his Datsun at the home of his father, about a mile from his wife's house. Wearing dark clothes and a stocking cap, he set out on foot to see Janice, carrying a 12-gauge shotgun close against his side.

At 6:15 a.m., he barged in as his son was leaving to catch a school bus and his daughter was letting the dog out.

He sent his son to the bus stop.

He followed Janice, dressed in a white nightgown and blue slippers, into the bedroom.

They struggled, and they argued.

Steve Lancaster wrested away her .38 revolver.

His daughter threatened to dial 911.

"Go on and call them," he said.

With one blast of the shotgun at 6:30 a.m., Janice's life ended. She collapsed in the kitchen.

Steve Lancaster walked to the front porch, pressed the shotgun muzzle to his chest and fired a second fatal shot.

His son heard the shots as his school bus rumbled down the road. He looked out the window and said, "I think that came from my house."

Helping the Survivors

The Lancasters' 13-year-old son and 17-year-old daughter are being cared for by their paternal grandmother, Mary Gloria Swann, in Charles County. A fund for their education has been established: The Janice

Lancaster Memorial Fund, Care of Citibank, Farragut North Financial Center, 1000 Connecticut Ave. NW, Washington, D.C. 20036.

Sarah Burns
CENTRAL PARK FIVE (2001)[3]

The day it happened, Wednesday, April 19, 1989, Raymond Santana, Jr., walked over to the Taft Houses in East Harlem to visit a friend. Raymond, whose family had moved to New York from Puerto Rico before he was born, lived with his father and grandmother in an apartment building on 119th Street, a few blocks north of the project, but he often hung out in the courtyard of the Taft Houses, where some of his friends lived. At fourteen, he was of average size—about five six and 130 pounds—with curly hair and small features. He was well liked at school, where his good sense of humor made him popular with girls. Even though there were always kids playing sports around the neighborhood, especially basketball and football in local school yards and the decrepit project courtyards, Raymond was more interested in drawing. He took art classes and spent a lot of his free time sketching.

As Raymond sat with his friend in the Taft courtyard that warm afternoon, a bunch of kids who lived there and in the surrounding buildings arrived. One of the boys in the group was Antron McCray, an exceptionally shy fifteen-year-old African-American from Harlem. Antron lived with his mother, Linda, and his stepfather, Bobby McCray, on 111th Street. He had adopted his stepfather's name at an early age and always considered Bobby his real father. The McCrays were devoted to their only son and were involved in his activities. Though he was a tiny five three and weighed only ninety-eight pounds, Antron was a good athlete and played shortstop on a neighborhood baseball team that his stepfather coached. They had gone to Puerto Rico together for an all-star tournament, a highlight of his Little League career. Antron was enrolled in a small public school program called Career Academy, where he enjoyed his social studies classes and got pretty good grades. Antron and Raymond had seen each other before, since they went to different schools housed within the same building, but didn't know each other well.

Over the next hour, the group in the Taft courtyard grew to about fifteen teenagers. Raymond and Antron joined them as they all began to wander south along Madison Avenue, then turned west onto 110th Street, heading toward Central Park. A block ahead, at the corner of the park, was an apartment complex called the Schomburg Plaza. The Schomburg is made up of two narrow thirty-five-story octagonal towers and, behind

---

3 Endnotes and internal citations omitted.

them, a large, squat, rectangular building. The two towers sit facing the northeast entrance to Central Park on a traffic circle centered at the intersection of Fifth Avenue and 110th Street. They are by far the tallest buildings in the vicinity and dominate, like sentinels, that corner of the park. Built in 1975 as a city development for middle- and low-income families, all three of the unsightly structures are constructed of beige concrete, with deep grooves running vertically like scars up and down the walls.

Yusef Salaam and Korey Wise, both African-Americans, lived in the northwest tower of the Schomburg Plaza complex. Yusef and Korey were good friends but could not have been more different. Yusef was skinny and tall, nearly six three, even at age fifteen. Korey, at sixteen, was only five five, and stockier. Yusef was a talented kid. He had been accepted at LaGuardia High School of Music and Art, a highly selective public school that requires the submission of an art portfolio for admission. Yusef, like Raymond Santana, had been drawing since he was five and was interested in jewelry making and wood sculpture. He also liked to take electronics apart to see how they worked and to try to put them back together. Korey, on the other hand, had had hearing problems from an early age and a learning disability that limited his achievement in school. He was in the ninth grade in April 1989, but his reading skills were nowhere near that level.

Yusef came from a strong family. His mother, a freelance fashion designer and part-time teacher at Parsons School of Design, raised three children on her own, and pushed them to succeed. Yusef was a practicing Muslim and followed the tenets of his religion closely. But he had been kicked out of LaGuardia when a knife was found in his locker. After his expulsion, Yusef switched schools several times; by April of 1989, his mother had placed him at Rice, a private Christian school in Harlem. She had also signed him up for the Big Brothers Big Sisters program, which paired him up with David Nocenti, an assistant U.S. attorney with whom he'd been spending time for the past four years. Yusef, who was gregarious and laid-back, prided himself on having friends from all over the neighborhood.

Korey Wise was also raised by a single mother, Deloris, who was pregnant in April 1989, and he had three older brothers. Korey was a good friend to Yusef, fiercely loyal, and well liked. At that time, he was dating a girl named Lisa Williams, who lived with a foster family in the same Schomburg tower. But his childhood had been especially difficult. Korey had only recently moved back in with his mother in the Schomburg Plaza; before that, he'd been living in foster care, at a group home in the Bronx. He moved there, he said, because his brothers were "coming and going," and he needed a more stable environment, but Aminah Carroll, a director at the Catholic foster agency that monitored Korey's case, remembered a much more troubled household. Carroll suspected that Korey's hearing problems had resulted from physical abuse, and when she tried to get him treatment, his mother refused to sign the necessary paperwork. A few years earlier, Korey had been on a trip to an amusement park, where he was molested by a group leader.

At sixteen, Korey was a gentle, emotionally stunted boy, his problems amplified by his hearing loss. Korey's development was severely delayed and his ability to comprehend his complicated and sometimes dangerous surroundings was woefully inadequate.

That afternoon, Yusef Salaam, Korey Wise, Korey's girlfriend, Lisa, and their friend Eddie were sitting on a bench near the entrance to Central Park. They were watching out for an older boy and his friends, who, they feared, were coming to start a fight. The young man wanted to date Eddie's sister, and Yusef and Korey were prepared to help Eddie fend him off. Korey, true to his loyal personality, had offered to fight the offender on Eddie's behalf. Eddie had taken a metal bar, at least a foot long, from Korey's apartment for protection, and it ended up in the pocket of Yusef's long coat. It was a solid piece of metal wrapped with black tape that was used in the Wise household to brace the apartment door against unwanted intruders.

As they headed back toward the Schomburg towers, Yusef noticed a large group of teenagers approaching along 110th Street from the other direction. He was certain it was the other kid and his gang coming back to fight, until he recognized a friend from his building, Al Morris. The group also included Raymond Santana, Antron McCray, and their friends from the Taft and other nearby housing projects.

Using Yusef's nickname, Al called out to him, "Yo, Kane!" and invited him to come hang out in the park. Yusef saw safety in numbers and joined them. He, in turn, invited Korey, who left Lisa behind and followed Yusef into the park. Still more Schomburg residents joined the crowd that was now headed into Central Park, including a fourteen-year-old African-American named Kevin Richardson.

Kevin lived with his mother, Grade Cuffee, in the same Schomburg building as Yusef and Korey. Their small apartment was on the thirty-fourth floor of the tower, with a spectacular view of Central Park laid out below the window. Kevin's parents had split up, but his four older sisters often visited. He was the baby of the family, the boy his mother had always wanted, and the women in his family doted on him and taught him to be polite and thoughtful. Kevin attended Jackie Robinson Junior High School on Madison Avenue at 106th Street, where he played the saxophone and participated in a hip-hop dance troupe called Show Stoppers.

Kevin had started playing football while living in Virginia for a few months when he was twelve, and he had dreams of making the team at Syracuse University. He was quiet and respectful at school and his teachers remembered him as having a good moral compass, though his grades showed that he was having trouble keeping up in class. Kevin looked young for his age, with a round baby face and large features. Kevin recognized Yusef and Korey from the building, but didn't know them well.

As the group, including Kevin Richardson, Korey Wise, Yusef Salaam, Antron McCray, and Raymond Santana, congregated at the northeast entrance to Central Park in the darkening twilight, Raymond counted thirty-three boys.

That same day, Patricia Ellen Meili woke up early, as she always did, so she could be at her office by 7:30 a.m. Trisha, as she was known to her family and friends, often worked long days at the office. She was employed at Salomon Brothers, an investment bank in downtown Manhattan, as an associate in the Corporate Finance Division. She had been at Salomon since moving to New York after finishing business school at Yale. At five o'clock, Meili decided that she would have to call off her dinner plans because she still had too much to do at the office that evening. She phoned her friend Michael Allen to cancel.

A few hours later, her colleague and former roommate Pat Garrett popped his head over from the adjacent cubicle. He wanted to know about the stereo system Meili had just gotten for her new apartment.

"Why not come over and take a look at it?" she said.

"Sure," he replied.

"Come around ten. That'll give me time to go for a run before you get there."

They made a plan to meet at 10:00 p.m. and Meili went home to her apartment on East Eighty-third Street, near York Avenue, where she lived alone. At ten minutes to nine, with the sky already dark, Meili left for her run, wearing black leggings, a long-sleeved white T-shirt over her sports bra, Saucony running shoes, and an AM/FM radio headset. Her keys were in a small Velcro pouch attached to one of her sneakers. She also wore a delicate gold ring in the shape of a bow.

On her way down the stairs from her apartment, she bumped into her neighbor James Lansing, who was on his way back from the gym. They chatted for a few minutes about jogging in the park, and then Meili left the building at five minutes to nine. She headed for Central Park.

The year 1989 had begun with New Yorkers still in shock over the news of a terrorist attack. A bomb smuggled into the luggage hold of Pan Am Flight 103 had detonated as the plane flew over Lockerbie, Scotland, on

December 21, 1988. The 747 had been on its way from London Heathrow to New York's JFK Airport, and all 259 people aboard, as well as eleven on the ground, were killed when the plane exploded in midair. It was clear from newspaper articles on January 1, 1989, which included obituaries for some of the victims, that people were still trying to piece together what had happened. Many of the passengers on the flight had been New Yorkers heading home.

The New York they were returning to that winter little resembled the prosperous, vibrant metropolis it had once been. Despite the charms that still made it the place of dreams for many, life in the city had become for others a nightmare that recalled the terrifying, gritty, crime-infested, and corrupt Gotham City of comic books. Over the past decades, New York City had experienced a staggering decline and had reached a low point in its history, with soaring crime rates, which no one had ever seen before or could have imagined just a few decades earlier. It was a place people wished they could leave, and in which today's relative wealth and safety seemed an inconceivable pipe dream.

In Harlem, where Antron, Raymond, Yusef, Kevin, and Korey lived, the streets were filled with thousands of abandoned and burned-out buildings. Bankruptcy for the city had been narrowly averted in the seventies, but funding for many services, especially those most valued by residents of poor neighborhoods, had been severely cut or eliminated. Fire stations, libraries, and rehab clinics had been shuttered. After-school programs disappeared and park maintenance faltered. Graffiti covered the subways and buildings throughout Harlem and other parts of the city. Empty lots became repositories for debris and garbage. New Yorkers, especially the poorest among them, mostly African-Americans and Latinos, were desperately in need of services and protection, but the city lacked the resources to fight the increasing challenges that its ghettos faced.

Citywide, muggings were regular events, and no one felt immune. Cars were broken into with startling regularity, often for prizes as minor as a shirt fresh from the dry cleaner's hanging inside the window. Falling asleep on the subway could mean waking up and finding that your pants pockets had been slashed with a box cutter and the contents removed by "lush workers," master pickpockets who preyed especially on drunks. Apartment doors were double-, triple-, and quadruple-bolted, and the "police lock," a piece of steel several feet long that was wedged diagonally between a lock on the inside of the door and a brace on the floor, was a standard protective measure. . . .

The violence and danger of the drug trade was especially present in the lives of the teenagers who lived in the Schomburg Plaza and the blocks surrounding it. Yusef watched one day from the window of his twenty-first-floor apartment in a Schomburg tower as cop cars screeched up to the front of one of the Taft buildings, just two blocks to the north. As people on the street scattered, he saw a man step out of the building with two guns and open fire on the police cars before running back inside the building. "Violence was a part of everyday life," Yusef recalled.

Many residents of Harlem and other minority neighborhoods saw the police as antagonists rather than protectors. . . . Many blacks and Latinos were fearful and mistrustful of a police force that seemed especially insensitive to their community. Parents would warn their children not to talk back to the police, for fear of them escalating a dangerous situation. Teenagers in Harlem were more likely to be harassed by the police, stopped and patted down or handcuffed in a subway station while the police "checked" on the validity of their transit passes, than to be protected from a gang who wanted to steal their coats or shoes. . . .

It was dark when Kevin Richardson, Korey Wise, Yusef Salaam, Antron McCray, Raymond Santana, and at least twenty-five other young African-American and Latino boys entered Central Park around 9:00 p.m. on April 19, 1989, but the moon was almost full and cast a bright glow on the quiet park. They meandered along a path that ran parallel to Fifth Avenue, heading south, laughing and playing around. Most of the boys were between thirteen and sixteen, and though many didn't know one another, they had the loose connections of their neighborhood, apartment buildings, and schools. Raymond, Antron, Yusef, Korey, and Kevin did not usually visit the park in such large numbers, and none had ever been arrested or been in serious trouble before, but there were some in the group who had more troublesome pursuits in mind. . . .

Just after nine o'clock on the evening of April 19, 1989, the series of events that would come to be known, in the following weeks and months, as "wilding" began.

First, the group of teenagers came across a Latino man, but someone indicated that he knew him, so they let him continue on his way. Then a couple walked by and one member of the group suggested that they leave the guy alone because he was with a "lady."

Officer Raymond Alvarez was driving through the park that night on his way to the West Side to deliver mail to another precinct when he spotted the group of boys around 106th Street. He shone his spotlight on them, and they scattered, heading south. Alvarez continued west on his errand.

As the teens began to regroup, a young man named Michael Vigna was riding a racing bike north on the East Drive, headed in their direction. It was 9:05 p.m. When they saw him, some spread out across the East Drive, forcing Vigna to swerve to his left to get around them. As he passed the group, one boy took a swing at him, narrowly missing his head as he sped by.

As the group of teenagers continued south along the East Drive, they came upon a middle-aged Latino man, Antonio Diaz, who was rumpled and dirty. They assumed he was homeless. Diaz was carrying a container of food and four bottles of beer. He was already drunk and still drinking from an open beer bottle as he stumbled through the park. Someone knocked him to the ground and a few of the boys started hitting and kicking him in the head and back. Many of the other teens were scattered around the same area but did not participate. Yusef Salaam stood nearby on a rocky outcropping across the road and saw another teenager eating. He asked him where he'd gotten the food. "From the bum," he said. After hitting and kicking and robbing him of his food, several boys dragged Diaz into the grass on the side of the road and left him there, bleeding from the head.

A few hundred feet farther south, the loose confederation of boys saw a couple on a tandem bike heading toward them along the East Drive. The group was in a grassy area just east of the road. At 9:12 p.m., as the cyclists, Gerry Malone and Patricia Dean, approached, several boys moved out onto the road, their backs to the bikers. The couple angled to their left, trying to avoid hitting anyone in the road, but as they got within one hundred feet, some of the teenagers scattered across the road, then turned around and faced the couple with their knees bent and their arms outstretched; some had hoods or hats pulled low over their faces.

With their arms spread, they spanned the entire roadway, and there was nowhere left for the riders to go. Malone and Dean started pedaling faster, heading to the far left. At the last moment, they swerved toward the group, heading straight for a taller boy in the middle. Just before they collided, the boys in the bikes immediate path jumped aside, and the couple flew past at nearly thirty-five miles per hour. One or two of the boys grabbed at them, but Malone and Dean managed to get away without being harmed.

The group of teenagers continued their southerly course. A few of them threw rocks at passing cars, including at a taxicab, whose driver got out and yelled at them. When they continued pelting him with rocks, he drove off. But now some worried that he would call the cops, so they moved off the road and walked through the North Meadow, south toward the Ninety-seventh Street Transverse. Another police car appeared to the north and shone a light on them. The group scattered again. Korey and some others left the park and went home, while some of the kids ran farther south, into the park. Yusef and several others climbed down the wall to the transverse, crossed the road, and climbed back up to the area just north of the reservoir. There, Yusef reconvened with some of the original group, who had also found their way to the reservoir. He recognized another boy who lived in his building, Steve Lopez.

At 9:25 p.m., Officer Alvarez was driving back through the park to the East Side. When he reached the East Drive, Antonio Diaz, the "bum," approached his car. Diaz explained that a few minutes earlier he had been assaulted by about five or so black and Hispanic youths. Diaz got into Officer Alvarez's radio car and they began driving around, looking for the group. A few minutes later, Michael Vigna, the bike racer, approached Alvarez and gave a similar description of the group that had harassed him on his previous lap. Alvarez then radioed other cars in the area with a description of the roving gang. Officers in and around Central Park now began looking for the boys.

Meanwhile, the smaller group of teenagers who had crossed the transverse reconvened just off the jogging path north of the reservoir. The Central Park Reservoir is a 106-acre pool encircled by a jogging track a little over a mile and a half long. Between the track and the water was a chain-link fence, built in the 1930s to keep people from committing suicide by jumping into the water during the Depression. It was still there in 1989.

At 9:25 p.m., David Lewis, a young man with blond hair, jogged by on a lap around the reservoir. By then, some of the boys had gathered near the tennis courts next to the running path. As Lewis approached, several boys assembled just off the path. One said, "Ready?" They were crouched, each with one arm to the ground, in the three-point stance of a football lineman. One threw a rock, which narrowly missed Lewis, bouncing off the fence just beyond him.

"Do you want to race?" Lewis asked.

"Yeah, we'll race all right," one of the boys replied.

Lewis then picked up his pace, unaware that up ahead about five more teens were coming out of the woods onto the path. Two stood in the middle of the path, blocking him. Lewis tried to run past, moving to the left, between one attacker and the chain-link fence along the reservoir. As he sprinted past, the boy hit him in the right arm. A couple of the other boys tried to run after him, but Lewis was too fast for them and was soon out of sight. He ran all the way to the Central Park Precinct along the Eighty-sixth Street Transverse, where he reported what had happened.

Over the next fifteen minutes, three more solitary male joggers ran by that same spot. About eight or ten boys were milling around on the path when a runner named David Good approached. As he neared the group, one said, "You better run faster than that." Seconds later, other teenagers in the group started throwing rocks and sticks at him. Good broke into a sprint, and as he ran past the last two boys in the group, one threw a heavy branch at him, hitting him squarely on the back of the leg. It hurt, but Good was able to continue running. Like David Lewis, he immediately headed for the Central Park Precinct to report the assault.

Just after 9:30 p.m., Robert Garner approached the group along the reservoir path. This time, fifteen or more boys ran out onto the track and surrounded him. They forced him off the path to the right and one boy started punching him. Garner asked what they wanted. The boy who had punched him replied, "Money, of course," and some of the others laughed. Garner told them he didn't have any money, then explained that the rattling sound of metal was coming from keys tied around his waist, not change in his pocket. One of the boys told him to leave, and he sprinted back to the edge of the park and then walked home.

As Garner was being surrounded, another runner approached the group. John Loughlin was wearing a green army jacket, camouflage pants, and a portable radio with headphones. He, too, was jogging around the reservoir when he saw from a distance what looked like a group of teenagers attacking someone on the ground. When the gang first saw him, some of the youths thought Loughlin was a cop, because of his army jacket and athletic build, and because he was running slowly and seemed to be watching them. At first, some were reluctant to harass him. But as Loughlin slowed to see what was going on, one of the boys, Jermain Robinson, got closer and asked, "What are you looking at? Are you some kind of vigilante?" Robinson then called out to some others who were nearer to Loughlin, telling them that this was "one of those vigilantes." Others picked up the mantra, referencing Bernhard Goetz.

Robinson ran up to Loughlin and threw him to the ground, where he and others started kicking and hitting him. At some point, the metal bar from Korey's house that Yusef had carried into the park was used to beat Loughlin. Jermain Robinson was the most aggressive assailant and some of the boys had to pull him off the battered jogger. He ran back for a few more punches, angry because his jacket had been ripped in the course of the attack. Eventually, they left Loughlin lying on the jogging path, bleeding.

He had been beaten badly and had cuts on his forehead and the back of his head. He had also been hit on his back and legs and had scrapes on his shins. A police officer who took Loughlin to the hospital said that he looked like he had been "dunked in a bucket of blood." His injuries were so serious that he spent two nights in the hospital.

After this attack, the teens still remaining in the park left, walking out in small groups onto Central Park West.

Just after 9:00 p.m., as the group of teenagers was winding its way south along paths in the park, Trisha Meili jogged into Central Park at the Eighty-fourth Street entrance. It was a clear, moonlit night, and warm for

April. She followed her typical route, turning north onto the East Drive. Though friends and family had expressed concern about her running alone in the park at night, Meili took pleasure in defying their warnings. This was her city, her park, and running was the one activity that was all her own. Her only compromise was to jog the northern part of her loop first, so that she would pass the area of the park that seemed more dangerous earlier in the night. She turned onto the 102nd Street Cross Drive, planning to head south again on the West Drive and run a loop back to Eighty-fourth Street south of the reservoir.

The 102nd Street Cross Drive, which connects the two main roads on the east and west sides of the park, is frequented by joggers and bicyclists, but is not open to regular traffic. The Cross Drive curves as it heads west, and much of the road is lined with trees. There are streetlamps along it, but they are far enough apart for much of the road to be dark and secluded. Trees and brush run along much of the north side of the path, and to the south the ground rises up over large boulders, so that the playing fields just on the other side are obscured. As one moves west, approaching the curve in the road, the trees are taller and grow on both sides, creating a canopy and making the road feel quieter and more isolated.

At approximately 9:15 p.m., about halfway between the East and West drives, Trisha Meili was attacked. The music coming from her headphones probably prevented any awareness of the imminent assault. She was hit on the back of the head with a large branch and fell forward. Her headphones skittered across the pavement. Bleeding from the head, she was then dragged off the road to the north, through a grassy area, and then into the woods that began forty feet from the road. She came to and began to fight back. Meili broke away and ran, but she fell and was beaten again. She was then raped and battered over and over about the face and head with a rock near an unpaved pathway north of the Cross Drive that meanders along a small body of water known as the Loch. Finally, Trisha Meili was tied up with her own shirt and abandoned, left there to die in one of the most secluded areas of the park.

Officers Eric Reynolds and Robert Powers were among those who had heard the radioed description of a gang of rowdy youths and were out looking for them in the park that night, patrolling in a Parks Department van. They saw the headlights of other police cars canvassing the area, and around 10:00 p.m., they decided to search for the gang around the outer edges of the park. As they drove north along Central Park West, they saw a small group of African-American and Latino teenagers slowly walking up the street across from the park. Officer Powers turned the van west onto 102nd Street, pulling directly into the path of the group. He and Reynolds jumped out of the van and yelled, "Stop! Police!" All but two of the boys scattered, some running back into Central Park. The two who remained, Raymond Santana and Steve Lopez, were arrested.

Officer Reynolds stayed with the two boys while Officer Powers followed the others, chasing them over the stone wall bordering the park and across some baseball fields. Powers, a stocky white officer, caught up to Kevin Richardson and tackled him, leaving a scratch on Kevin's left cheek.

Meanwhile, Lopez and Santana were taken to the Central Park Precinct. They were held there with Kevin Richardson and two other boys the police had arrested in the park, Lamont McCall and Clarence Thomas. . . .

Gracie Cuffee, Kevin's mother, still suffered from the lingering effects of a stroke she'd had seven years earlier. At the Central Park Precinct around 2:30 a.m., weak and tired, she asked again about when she could take her son home. By then, parents of three of the other young men had arrived; only Raymond Santana did not have a guardian present at the precinct. The police had tried to reach his father, but when he hadn't arrived within a few hours, they'd begun calling Raymond's older sister and grandmother, as well. Officer Reynolds explained to the waiting parents that as soon as all the family members had arrived, they would hand out tickets to appear in family court and then send them home. The parents continued to sit, believing that they would soon be able to leave with their sons.

The officers at the Central Park Precinct had actually intended to send the teenagers home with summonses, as they had told their parents. But at 3:00 a.m., Detective José Rosario, who had been dispatched to Metropolitan Hospital to check on the jogger, called the Central Park Precinct. He ordered the desk officer to continue holding the teenagers. A woman had been brutally raped and beaten in Central Park and she would probably die. . . .

Waiting in the clerical area of the Community Affairs office at the Central Park Precinct, Gracie Cuffee was exhausted and weak from staying awake all night, hoping that her son, Kevin Richardson, would be released. She'd seen Lamont McCall and Clarence Thomas sent home after interviews with the detectives in the youth room, so she pleaded that Kevin be allowed to go next. By then, members of the Central Park Precincts own detective squad were beginning their shifts, taking over from the Nightwatch detectives. At 9:40 a.m., eleven hours after his arrest, fourteen-year-old Kevin and his mother followed Detectives Carlos Gonzalez and John O'Sullivan of the Central Park Precinct into the juvenile room. The room was fairly small, with four desks and a few filing cabinets. Kevin and his mother were seated behind a desk in the back of the room. The detectives started by reading Kevin his Miranda rights and then began asking questions.

Because the rape had occurred in Central Park, Detective Humberto "Bert" Arroyo of the Central Park Detective Squad was placed in charge of the investigation. But soon, as word of the crime reached the upper echelons of the NYPD, elite detectives from the Manhattan North Homicide Squad began arriving at the Central Park Precinct. The Manhattan North unit is made up of the most experienced and effective detectives on the force, who are often called in on important cases to assist the local precincts in investigations. There was no homicide yet in this case, so typically Sex Crimes Unit detectives would have handled the case, but the joggers condition was so grave that she was not expected to survive.

Twenty minutes after Kevin Richardson's interview began with the Central Park detectives, Detectives John Hartigan and Scott Jaffer, both of the Manhattan North Homicide Squad, entered the juvenile room, joining Detectives Gonzalez and O'Sullivan. Detective Hartigan was one of the NYPD's very best, a veteran with twenty-five years on the force, twenty of them with a detective's shield. He excelled at interrogations, at convincing suspects to open up to him, and at getting them to confess under any circumstance.

The goal of any interrogation, by definition, is to elicit a confession from a guilty party, not to investigate the truth of a denial. The common tactics used to gain confessions are based on the idea that only guilty people are interrogated in the first place. In theory, when a suspect is brought in for questioning, detectives begin with an "interview," in which information is gathered and the police make an assessment as to the guilt or innocence of the party In this step, a nonaccusatory question-and-answer period is meant to allow the detective an opportunity to gather more information and to make observations about the suspect that might indicate that he is lying. Once they decide that they are speaking with a guilty party, the interrogation begins. Detectives often believe that they are experts at separating truth from lies, but studies have shown that this is a false confidence.

In this case, scientific evidence was not yet available to the detectives, so their decision to aggressively interrogate Kevin Richardson and others who were in the park that night was entirely based on their own instinctive assumptions about the young men.

. . . Kevin's interrogation was . . . becoming increasingly intimidating and aggressive, especially when his mother was called outside the room to speak with other detectives. At times, as many as five detectives were standing around him in the youth room. After a long night, Gracie Cuffee was not feeling well enough to stay there any longer. At 11:40 a.m., she signed a consent form that allowed her twenty-four-year-old daughter, Angela, to sit in with Kevin as the detectives continued their barrage of questions. Angela arrived having no idea of the kind of trouble her little brother was in.

At one point during the interrogation, the detectives noticed a scratch on Kevin's left cheek. Kevin explained that he'd gotten a bruise from the police officer who'd tackled him the night before, but the detectives didn't believe him. Detective Gonzalez said that he would call that officer, and he threatened that if the officer didn't back up Kevin's story, Kevin would have a problem.

Over the course of nearly three hours, the detectives convinced Kevin to provide a statement, admitting that he'd witnessed and even taken part in the rape of the female jogger. At 1:00 p.m., Kevin signed a statement that he'd handwritten. By then, his father, Paul Richardson, had arrived, so he and Angela signed the statement, as well. The statement described the night in the park, including the assault on an "old man," throwing rocks at a taxi, reaching for a couple on a two-person bicycle, and beating up a male jogger. Then he wrote about the rape:

> . . . she was knocked out thats when Antron, Raymond, and Steve took her close off. Before that happened when Mike hit her down I tried to grab her. I got scratch on my face, so I moved back and everybody started feeling on her I saw somebody (Raymond) pulling her pantys off, I saw somebody holden her arms and legs. Raymond had her arms and Steve had her legs and Antron had sex with her. Before, thats when she was yelling stop and help. She was unconscious when they had her on the floor. Before this happen they had dragged her into the bushes. Everybody left and she was still their. The cops stoped five of us and arrested us and I was the one that didn't rape her.

Though Kevin had not admitted to raping the jogger, the fact that he had placed himself at the scene, saying he had touched the jogger and witnessed others rape her, was legally just as significant. The law does not require someone to have committed a rape to be convicted of it, only to be "acting in concert" with those who did, though of course Kevin didn't understand that. The detectives had what they needed though Kevin had gotten many of the details wrong, most notably inventing shorts that the jogger had not been wearing, describing a tank top rather than a long-sleeved shirt, and mentioning that someone had ripped her "blouse."

Despite his statement, Kevin and his family still believed the officers when they said that he would soon be going home. After his statement was signed, officers moved Kevin and his family to the 20th Precinct, where the investigation was continuing. . . .

Just before five that morning, Kevin Richardson gave a videotaped statement to ADA Elizabeth Lederer. By then, Kevin's sister had left, and his father sat in as the guardian for the session.

On the videotape, Lederer repeatedly had to ask Kevin to speak up, as the obviously frightened boy often whispered his answers or merely shook his head. She methodically retraced his steps that evening, eliciting even greater detail about the events in the park than Kevin had previously related in his written statement to the detectives. By the end of the questioning, Kevin had described the attacks on Antonio Diaz, the couple on the tandem bike, John Loughlin, and lastly the female jogger. He denied actually having participated in any of the attacks, implicating instead some of the other kids, including Antron McCray, Raymond Santana, and Steve Lopez. Kevin said that he'd only grabbed the female joggers arm in an attempt to stop the rape.

As with the other statements, there were obvious problems and inconsistencies in the video that should have jumped out at an experienced prosecutor like Lederer. Kevin described the site of the attack on Meili as being on the same road where they'd attacked John Loughlin, along the northern side of the reservoir, and at Lederer's prompting, he said that the jogger had been moved just slightly off the road. In fact, Meili had been found almost half a mile to the north, above the 102nd Street Cross Drive, and she had been dragged nearly a hundred feet away from the road, into a secluded area near the Loch. Kevin had also incorrectly described her attire. In his statement, he said that she had been wearing gray shorts, black biking pants, and a white tank top, whereas Meili had actually been wearing black pants, not shorts, and a long-sleeved white shirt. Kevin said that he hadn't seen anyone tie up the jogger, even though she had been found gagged and bound, with her hands tied together in front of her face. Lederer asked Kevin multiple times whether the jogger was bleeding when they left her, and both times he said that he hadn't really been able to see. In fact, Meili was so covered in her own blood that the men who found her hadn't been able to tell whether she was male or female. Yet no one seemed to doubt the authenticity of Kevin's or any of the other teenagers' statements. . . .

The People v. Kevin Richardson and Korey Wise began on October 22, 1990. . . .

. . . Kevin's lawyer, Howard Diller, was a stout, white middle-aged defense attorney, who had been hired by the family for a five-thousand-dollar retainer, leaving him with little resources to invest in the case. But he loved all the media attention he got with such a high-profile defendant. When he'd released Kevin's videotaped statement to the media months earlier, he'd argued that Kevin never admitted to raping the jogger and that the tapes should actually exonerate his client. He followed the same tack in his opening statement. Rather than trying to convince the jury that Kevin's statement had been coerced, Diller suggested that the jury assume it was true, but he said that the jurors should note that Kevin described the events as a spectator, not as a participant. Diller's presentation was disjointed and unclear, and he went on to say, "There's nothing in the statement really that says that he did anything acting in concert with anybody, except the words. We submit that those were fed words." Other than this argument, which he undercut in the very same sentence, Diller provided little in the way of alternative theories or facts that might exonerate his client. . . .

The jury began their deliberations on Friday, November 30, and continued through the weekend. This jury was made up of seven women and five men and was just as diverse as the jury at the first trial, with five whites, four African-Americans, two Latinos, and one Asian-American. They deliberated for twelve consecutive days before reaching their verdict, which shocked both the defense and the prosecution. On December 11, 1990, as the verdict was read, the courtroom erupted into a frenzy. Kevin Richardson was convicted on every count, including attempted murder, rape, and sodomy. His mother fell to the ground as the verdict was read, and supporters screamed at the judge and prosecution, calling them racist, and yelled that the jogger was a "whore." The jury had to be removed to another courtroom to finish reading their verdict. . . .

When Kevin was released from Coxsackie Correctional Facility, his sisters and other family members came to pick him up. His mother had stayed in New York, too sick to make the trip, waiting for him to come home to the Schomburg Plaza. His sisters brought him nice new clothes to wear, and they cried and jumped for joy when he walked through the gates, finally a free man. He was so happy and relieved that he kissed the ground. . . .

Nancy Ryan . . . was assigned to reinvestigate Reyes's explosive confession and whether it had any impact on the convictions of the Central Park Five. . . .

Nancy Ryan and another ADA, Peter Casolaro, began the reinvestigation by looking back at the DNA evidence. When Reyes pleaded guilty in 1991 to his other crimes, DNA had connected him to several of the crime scenes, though no one had ever checked to see if his DNA matched the profile from the Central Park case.

This time, Reyes's DNA was compared to the single profile established in 1989 from a cervical swab and from Meili's sock. In May of 2002, they received the results: It was a match.

As soon as the DNA evidence gave credence to Reyes's claim, the district attorney's office moved ahead cautiously, checking his whole story and his assertion that he had raped the jogger alone. Until then, his confession had been kept under wraps, but once the DNA test connected Reyes to the case with certainty, the news began to leak out. In June 2002, *The New York Times* reported that the DA's office was investigating a claim by Reyes that he'd raped the Central Park Jogger, but there was still doubt as to what it meant for the teenagers who had already served their sentences. . . .

As the reinvestigation by the district attorney's office was concluding, lawyers working on behalf of the Central Park Five filed a motion in September 2002, asking a judge to vacate the original convictions based on Reyes's confession and the evidence that corroborated it. The defense attorneys had been alerted to Reyes's confession by the article in *The New York Times* in June and had set about getting an affidavit from Reyes that they could use as evidence to present with their motion.

ADAs Nancy Ryan and Peter Casolaro filed their affirmation on behalf of the People on December 5, joining with the defense lawyers' motion. The fifty-eight-page document outlined their reinvestigation in detail and concluded that, "based on the facts and for the reasons set forth below, the People consent to the defendants' motion to set aside the verdicts on all the charges of which they were convicted." The DA could have simply not opposed the defenses request, but he chose to submit the extensive report documenting exactly why the convictions should be vacated, explaining the facts that Reyes provided, the results of new forensic tests that exculpated the Central Park Five, and Nancy Ryan and Peter Casolaro's review of both the original case against the teenagers and Reyes's earlier crimes. Justice Galligan had retired from the New York State Supreme Court by then, so Justice Charles J. Tejada was assigned in his stead.

On December 19, 2002, Tejada called the lawyers into the courtroom. The Central Park Five were not in attendance, their lawyers having suggested they stay away. But many of their family members were there, including Kevin Richardson's sisters, Linda McCray, and Raymond Santana, Sr., who had stayed out of the courtroom during the original trial because he knew the outcome would be a bad one. This time, he had a good feeling. The judge took only a few minutes to announce that the motion to vacate the convictions was granted in full.

The ruling, which essentially affirmed that the defendants would not have been convicted at trial if Reyes's confession had been available at the time, fell short of truly exonerating them, leaving the district attorney free to reprosecute them for any and all of the charges in the original indictments. The DA's office quickly dispelled any fears of a new trial by immediately responding to Tejada's decision with an oral motion to dismiss the indictments. Tejada responded, "The motion is granted. Have a very Merry Christmas and a happy New Year."

The Central Park Five's convictions had been erased. The courtroom, filled with family members and other supporters, erupted into a joyous celebration, with weeping and shouting all around. Their families rejoiced, hardly able to believe that their hopes had finally been fulfilled.

———

Debbi Wilgoren
Purchase of a Lifetime
WASHINGTON POST (Dec. 14, 15, & 16, 2005)

The community room filled early that July night in 2002. The tenants of Capital Manor were about to learn how much it would cost to stay in their apartments.

Their century-old complex—three buildings with 34 units each—was a dilapidated eyesore in a gentrifying D.C. neighborhood. Its ceilings sagged, the window frames were cracking, the front-door intercom hadn't worked in years. In the summer, residents seeking refuge from stifling apartments shared the sidewalk with drug-dealing toughs.

Across the way was another threat—but also proof of what could be. Refurbished Victorian rowhouses lined the north side of the 1400 block of W Street NW, reminders of the wave of wealth sweeping up from U Street and pushing out poor and working-class residents. Rents in the new, nearby luxury apartments routinely topped $2,000, compared with Capital Manor's average $663.

These black and Latino tenants knew they had to buy their complex or risk being displaced by a new generation of city dwellers, most of them white.

They had chosen a developer to guide them through the process. His colored marker now squeaked across a whiteboard at the front of the room.

$1,500, he wrote. That's what each family would have to come up with in the next six weeks.

Looks of disbelief spread through the room. The 25 tenants gathered here were dishwashers, janitors, people on public assistance. They scrimped each summer to buy school supplies and saved for months for Christmas. To most of them, the number seemed astronomical.

"How many people do you actually think have that kind of money just sitting somewhere?" demanded tenant association President Deborah

Thomas, 48, who had spearheaded the purchase effort. "We were talking about making it so we could afford to stay here."

Their developer explained that the money was needed to show potential lenders that the tenants were committed to the project, as well as to pay for engineering and architectural studies.

Then Aaron W. O'Toole, the tenants' attorney, spoke up. "If 50 people can't sign a reservation form and put down a couple of hundred dollars," he said, "it's over."

Thomas returned to her apartment with trepidation. Within the hour, her phone started to ring. In Spanish and English, the callers had the same message.

No puedo pagar.

I can't pay.

After a year of hard work, of carwashes and raffles, of meetings and late-night phone calls, the whole plan seemed to be disintegrating before her eyes.

The saga of Capital Manor's rebirth as a tenant-owned cooperative played out over 4½ years, starting in spring 2001. It finished successfully last month, with the last original tenants moving into their freshly renovated apartments. In a neighborhood that has become one of the most sought after in the city, this was a rare accomplishment: the $12 million purchase and rehabilitation of three buildings by tenants whose average income hovered just under $20,000 a year.

The undertaking, one of the largest tenant purchases in the city, was a struggle all the way. The residents had to convince the District government that their plan was worthy of funding and prove to a bank that they were committed enough to handle a ban. Even then, work progressed at an excruciatingly slow pace. They faced opposition from wealthier neighbors, who wanted them gone, and defections within their own ranks. Their renovation plan changed drastically. The Washington Post has followed the project since the tenants first organized.

Why they succeeded starts with their leaders—longtime residents, led by Thomas, who passionately believed that they had earned the right to stay in their homes. They came to rely on two young men: their attorney, O'Toole, who worked at Georgetown University's nonprofit Harrison Institute, and their developer, Jair K. Lynch, who pulled the financing together and managed the project. They were lucky enough to find a sympathetic bank that took a chance on them and to make their move at a time when the city was under pressure to slow the hemorrhaging of affordable housing.

"The passion from the tenants was so obvious to us that we certainly had no option but to find a way to make it work," said Stanley Jackson, who was head of the city's housing development agency when the project was launched and now serves as a deputy mayor "People who otherwise would not be here will be able to be a part of all of the great development of this neighborhood."

The three buildings of Capital Manor originally housed middle-class families but were converted to low-income apartments through a federal program in the 1970s. Thirty years later, the federal subsidy—and the tax benefits that went with it—were about to expire. Besieged by developers, the company that owned Capital Manor put it on the market in March 2001 and eventually signed a contract to sell it for $3.4 million.

Thomas knew that D.C. law allows tenants of an apartment house to match any purchase offer—an unusual way to keep tenants from being displaced and to allow them to benefit when housing values climb. A decade earlier, the tenants of 1424 W St., just down the block, had converted their building into a cooperative. Now, Thomas thought, maybe she and her neighbors could do the same. She began to spread the word.

Meetings were held in the fluorescent-lit basement room, where men in work boots sat on mismatched chairs next to tired-looking women, some with squirming children on their laps. Everything was translated into Spanish, since many of the Latinos spoke little or no English.

They soon learned that buying the buildings would be only the starting point. The complex was badly in need of repair. Fixing it now would more than triple the price tag, their advisers told them, but would avert a crisis later.

The tenants formed an association and elected Thomas president. They could not have picked a more committed leader, or someone who had more at stake.

She'd lived on W Street for nearly 30 years. Her life, in dramatic ways, had paralleled the fortunes of the block.

When it was a respectable working-class haven, she was a church-going young woman who made good grades and followed the strict rules laid down by her mother, a hotel maid. By her mid-twenties, though, the 1400 block had become the city's largest open-air narcotics bazaar, so bad that police sometimes barricaded the street in a futile attempt to keep the addicts away. Thomas was living in an apartment a few doors down from Capital Manor, working a series of low-paying jobs. She steered clear of drugs for awhile but eventually tried crack cocaine and got hooked. Already the mother of two sons by two men, she gave birth three months early to a daughter who, she soon learned, was blind.

Thomas decided that she could not be both a mother and a crackhead. "I just stopped" using drugs, she said. She was working again and leading tree-planting efforts to beautify her battered neighborhood when an estranged boyfriend hurled a Molotov cocktail through the open window of her apartment, setting it ablaze and leaving her severely burned.

By this time, the U Street Metro station had opened, and the drug trade was melting away. Luxury developers were buying up long-empty lots.

Back on her feet, Thomas became immersed in the issues transforming W street and was elected an advisory neighborhood commissioner. With the help of a federal housing voucher, she rented a three-bedroom apartment in Capital Manor. When the complex was put on the market the next year, she saw her chance.

Ownership would mean stability—for her family and her neighbors. "I don't want my kids to have to grow up and struggle. I want them to have a place," Thomas would say. 'They'll never have to worry where they're going to live."

Thomas's top lieutenants were Peggy Fitzgerald, an old friend who was elected association vice president, and Osmin Rodriguez, a Salvadoran immigrant who had moved into the complex as resident manager five years earlier.

Fitzgerald, 59, had lived at Capital Manor for 28 years and had no intention of ever leaving. She'd raised three children and was now raising two grandchildren. Divorced for two decades, Fitzgerald had worked construction until her mid-fifties, then retired on disability after her back gave out. She struggled with diabetes and high blood pressure. Now she spent her time plotting strategy with Thomas and tracking tenant association dues and membership figures.

Rodriguez, 35, often worked alongside them, acting as a liaison to the Latino tenants. As resident manager, he earned more than most Capital Manor tenants, enough that a small house in the suburbs would not have been out of reach for him, his wife and their toddler son.

But Rodriguez was attached to Capital Manor. When he was hired in 1996, he'd been given a mandate to clean up the complex, at that time barely two-thirds full. In his first few weeks on the job, Rodriguez said, he initiated more than 20 evictions, many for drug-related reasons.

By 2001, when the complex went on the market, the drug dealers had moved down the street and the vacant apartments had been filled with new families. A community was being built here on W Street, Rodriguez felt. He did not want the overheated real estate market to blast it apart.

In those early months, the tenant leaders invited a parade of speakers—public interest advisers, city officials, developers—to educate them about the tenant purchase process.

Marian Siegel, a housing counselor, was one of the first. She provided a crash course in collaborative entrepreneurship. In a pronounced Long Island accent, her face shiny with perspiration, she reeled off a long list of suggestions and cautions, pausing every few sentences so Rodriguez could translate.

Interview at least three lawyers and three developers before picking one of each to work with you, she advised. Charge monthly dues to members of the tenants association, even if it's only $5 or $10. Organize fundraisers.

"If you don't do something out of your own pockets, it lessens your commitment," Siegel said. "And if you can't put together a yard sale, how are you going to buy this building?"

She left them with a warning: "Be patient. Because this will take a long time."

In fall 2001, while Washington was reeling from the Sept. 11 terrorist attacks, the tenants selected Georgetown's public-interest law clinic to represent them. The clinic assigned them O'Toole, a 29-year-old lawyer who spoke passable Spanish and had guided three smaller tenant-purchase efforts.

Next, the association interviewed developers. Most offered a package known as a low-income tax-credit deal, in which investors purchase and renovate a building in exchange for a federal tax break. After 15 years, the tenants can buy them out at a preset price.

But these tenants, who had been meeting for months, wanted to buy their buildings right away. Advocates including Siegel had told them that they could form a cooperative. That way the buildings could never be taken from them, and they, too, eventually could benefit from the soaring property values.

"This tenants association has already voted, and we want ownership," resident Nerissa Phillips snapped at one developer who offered a tax-credit deal. "So you can make your presentation, and we will listen. But that's our goal."

Only Lynch, 30, said he would find a way. He said he would seek financing from private lenders, foundations and government and obtain the help of a nonprofit housing development group.

Lynch grew up in the District, the son of a college professor from Trinidad and an economist from Colombia. A world-class gymnast, he graduated from Sidwell Friends School, then earned a degree in urban planning and engineering at Stanford University. In 1996, he won a silver medal at the Olympics in Atlanta. He returned to the District to launch his own development firm in a restored U Street rowhouse.

Capital Manor's tenants deserved to share in the corridor's rebirth, Lynch often said, because they had endured the worst of times. "They're survivors," he said. "They were here when things were tough."

Some tenants worried privately about Lynch's youth and relatively limited experience. But the March 2002 vote to retain his firm was unanimous.

One year into the ownership drive, Lynch and the tenants agreed on a plan: Refurbish and sell one of the three buildings as market-rate condos, then use the profits to repair the other buildings. Those biddings would become a low-income cooperative, collectively owned by the tenants. Lynch's firm would be paid about 10 percent of the cost of the project, conforming to the city's affordable-housing guidelines.

A few people expressed concern about giving up one building. But Lynch said it was doubtful that more than two-thirds of the tenants would commit to join the cooperative. Nowhere near that number had been paying monthly dues or showing up for meetings.

He pledged to help those who left the complex find decent places to live, as close by as possible, and the tenants agreed.

It was better, Thomas thought, than watching the entire complex soar beyond their reach.

Four more months had passed by the time Lynch announced the $1,500 deposit figure and people started bailing out. Thomas called an emergency meeting of the tenant board. They compared notes, tallied the number of tenants threatening to quit and started to panic.

Thomas appealed to O'Toole, the attorney, who said there was nothing sacred about the $1,500 amount—it was just Lynch's estimate of what would cover costs and impress the banks.

What's the smallest amount that would impress them? Thomas asked.

What's the most you think the tenants can give? came the reply.

Together, they agreed to gamble on $500, still a huge amount for most tenants and perhaps enough to convince the banks.

Only $100 would be due at the July 23 tenants meeting, less than two weeks away. Tenants would have until Sept. 15 to come up with the other $400. If they succeeded, the rest of the down payment would be due when renovations began.

The day of reckoning was a sweltering evening that felt even worse inside the community room. About 40 people showed up, many more than had been coming in recent weeks. Lynch sat in the front row, watching and waiting. He had received an e-mail from O'Toole with the revised numbers. If the smaller deposits meant enough people would sign up, he would find a way to make it work. "This is a partnership," he said later. "You ask and sometimes they say no."

The tenants listened to presentations about city-funded programs available to poor home buyers and classes to teach them ways to save.

Then O'Toole stepped forward, holding the reservation agreement, which guaranteed a spot to all who signed up and paid.

"This is critical for us. Absolutely critical. We need to demonstrate the commitment of this group to the lenders," O'Toole said. "We want enough money to show that people are serious. But hopefully an amount that they can come up with. And that's . . ."—he paused to glance at Lynch—". . . $500."

O'Toole reminded the tenants that they needed commitments from at least half of the 102 households by the end of the summer—but that more would be better. He began reviewing the four-page legal agreement clause by clause, in English and then Spanish.

The line formed before he finished the second page. Black and Latino, young and old, at least two dozen tenants in all. Some clutched live crisp, $20 bills; others held freshly inked money orders.

Over the next seven weeks, 55 households put down deposits of $500, or as close to that as they could manage.

The last payment came 40 minutes after the deadline of midnight Sept. 15, when a woman knocked on Peggy Fitzgerald's door, panicked that she might be too late. Smiling even though she had been roused from her bed, Fitzgerald assured her that she was not.

At Each Hurdle, Stronger Resolve

The message D.C. housing officials delivered to developer Jair K. Lynch was clear. His plan to keep Capital Manor Apartments affordable by selling one of its three buildings was a no-go. Mayor Anthony A. Williams would not fund a project that would eliminate some low-cost apartments, even in the interest of saving others.

The time was September 2002, the mayor was running for reelection and real estate prices were exploding. Critics were blasting Williams for doing too little to prevent the displacement of the poor from newly posh neighborhoods. The city had set $25 million aside for housing assistance, and Lynch was applying for $2 million to help the tenants of Capital Manor buy their complex, 102 crumbling apartments just off the trendy U Street corridor in Northwest.

The proposal relied on selling one building at market rate and using the profits to help renovate the others, which would become a low-income cooperative. Now that plan would have to change, Lynch told the five officers of the tenants association board. To improve their chances of winning city funds, all three buildings had to go co-op and remain affordable. Nobody would be able to cash in at market rates for at least a decade.

Worse, Lynch made it clear that even with these changes, the District could still turn Capital Manor down. Competition for city money was fierce, and because of the high-priced neighborhood, their project required a higher city subsidy per apartment than other proposals. The decision would not come until December—and an outside buyer was waiting to snap up the complex if the tenants did not close on their purchase by Jan. 15.

The news brought treasurer Kim Mitchell to her feet. "We're chasing and grabbing at something that we have no chance of getting," she snapped, her arms folded tight across her chest. "We keep meeting and we keep meeting, and we're not getting anywhere."

Resident manager Osmin Rodriguez was shaking his head, too. Revising the plan "doesn't work for me," he said flatly. He said he'd rather save for a home in an inexpensive suburb than continue fighting a losing battle, and he suspected other young Latinos in the complex might feel the same.

But the three others at the table were not willing to give up their dream. Association President Deborah Thomas, Treasurer Peggy Fitzgerald and Secretary Milagro Posada were older women, with deep roots in the neighborhood and few illusions about upward mobility. Their lives had been mostly scraping and struggling. They had never been comfortable with the idea of replacing one-third of their neighbors with rich newcomers, and they intended to leave their apartments to their children, not to sell them.

"I don't know about you, but I'm fighting for something," Thomas said. 'When we started this, we had not one penny. And guess what—we've been into this almost one year, and we're not outdoors yet. So that's enough for me to keep going. If we do nothing, we're going to end up with nothing."

Ultimately, the decision was up to the entire tenants association, which gathered in the basement community room a week later. Thomas, a former welfare recipient who now worked getting other women off the dole, stood in front.

"I thought we started this struggle to make sure we had a place to live," she thundered. "I've lived on this block for 30 years, and I'm not interested in being anywhere else."

Most of the tenants, including Mitchell's mother, were on limited or fixed incomes. They all knew of nearby apartment buildings that had been emptied and turned into condos none of them could afford. Changing the proposal was fine, one tenant after another said, if that would help keep their corner of the 1400 block of W Street populated by working-class families.

"A lot of people have worked really hard for this," tenant Danilo Nuez said in Spanish. "Let's get behind them."

In the end, the yes vote was unanimous.

"My mom wants to stay," Mitchell said afterward, by way of explanation. Rodriguez said he was committed to helping fellow tenants pursue their dreams.

"Don't group me with drugs. The faces they see here aren't the faces selling drugs on the street. And we were here first. And I'm not leaving."

While they waited for the city's decision, the tenants association worked on recruiting more residents to the project. Having more participants would bolster the application to the National Cooperative Bank, which had tentatively promised a $3.5 million acquisition loan and an $8.1 million construction loan. Nerissa Phillips and Solomon Moreno spent three hours one night preaching the gospel of collective home ownership door-to-door, offering tips in English and Spanish on how to save money for the down payments they hoped they would need. Give up chips and soda from the corner store, they suggested. Turn off your cell phone for a couple of months. Ask for cash for Christmas.

"We're all in the same boat. We all lose or we all win," Phillips said. "If someone is embarrassed because they're broke, well, we're all broke."

She and Moreno barely knew each other, although they'd lived three floors apart in the same building for years. Their joint effort was one of many small interactions unfolding across a cultural divide in the complex, which was about two-thirds Latino immigrants and one-third black residents. Until the tenant purchase effort, the two populations rarely mixed.

But the tenant board was chosen to include both. Meetings and documents were always translated. At a fundraising dinner, the $5 buffet featured chimichangas as well as chicken wings. Stereo speakers boomed hip-hop, then salsa, then hip-hop again. As the project moved forward, people who for years had passed each other in the dim hallways or concrete courtyards without speaking began exchanging polite greetings.

Arriving home one day loaded down with grocery bags, Fitzgerald noticed a Latino youth holding the door open for her—for the first time in her memory.

Little such camaraderie, however, developed with the mostly white residents of the 19 rowhouses across the street. Built early in the 20th century for well-off families, the houses had transformed over the decades along with the fortunes of W Street. When drugs and crime overtook the block in the early 1980s, only the poorest families remained. But with the U Street Metro station set to open in 1991, white-collar professionals started buying and upgrading the rowhouses. By the time Capital Manor went on the market in 2001, all but two had changed hands.

The northsiders said they liked the idea of living on a street that was racially and economically mixed. But some owners worried that Capital Manor's run-down appearance detracted from their property values. They complained about noise—Capital Manor's intercom system had stopped working years ago, so visitors often announced their arrival by blaring car horns. When Thomas proposed that the city build a playground on an empty lot between two rowhouses, the northsiders objected, saying it would become a magnet for thugs. The lot remains empty and has been put up for sale.

Kurt Ehrman, a government lawyer, said he was told when he bought his home in 2000 that the apartments across the street would soon be emptied and turned into condos. Instead, two years later, he saw fliers seeking community support for the tenant purchase. "I'm all for diversity," he said. "I don't want anybody across the street—except for those selling and buying drugs—moved elsewhere. But coming up with enough money to make sure those buildings are truly renovated, so that those of us who have a lot invested are satisfied, is going to be very difficult."

Council member Jim Graham (D-Ward 1) was hearing from constituents on both sides of the street. Thomas, a political ally who had campaigned for him, sought and received his strong support for funding the tenant purchase. The northsiders, many of whom had also backed Graham's 1998 council bid, kept asking if he could stop the project

In November 2002, Graham and Williams were elected to second terms. The next month, Graham called a meeting at the Reeves Municipal Center for his constituents on W Street. The topic quickly turned to crime. Rowhouse owners asked how the cooperative board would keep out drugs and violence.

"There was a shooting there. It didn't have anything to do with anyone in the building?" one man asked skeptically.

"Absolutely not," snapped Thomas. "Look around you." She gestured at Fitzgerald and several others. "We all have a lifetime of investment on this block. These are the people that are going to make the co-op what it is."

Graham ended the session after more than an hour, promising another soon. The tenants walked out to 14th Street, seething. The northsiders looked at them, they said, as if they were the drug dealers who sometimes loitered on W street.

"Don't group me with drugs," fumed Michelle Craig, a conventions concierge at a downtown Marriott. "The faces they see here aren't the faces selling drugs on the street. And we were here first. And I'm not leaving."

"We're trying to move the city forward. But we've got to bring everyone along, right?"

The stress was getting to Thomas. She remembers sniffling through a Dec. 21 doctor's appointment, sagging with anxiety about all that would be lost if financing did not come through. Then her cell phone rang. It was a co-worker. A fax had come in from the D.C. government. The tenants' application for $2 million had been approved. Thomas burst into tears.

Her doctor asked if she was okay.

"Now I am," she said.

The mayor announced the award the next day at a news conference at Plymouth Congregational United Church of Christ. In all, he said, the city would help fund 27 projects to create or protect about 1,850 low- and moderately priced apartments. "A safe, affordable home is a cornerstone of our community . . . a cornerstone of everything we're trying to do as a city," Williams said. "We're trying to move the city forward. But we've got to bring everyone along, right?"

Sitting shoulder to shoulder in the wooden pews, Thomas and Fitzgerald fervently nodded their heads.

Winning city money was supposed to help the loan application with the National Cooperative Bank, which specializes in affordable housing projects. The D.C.-based institution was considering financing the tenant purchase through its nonprofit affiliate and for-profit subsidiary. It, like most lenders, looked favorably on projects that had won support elsewhere.

But Alexandra Johns, a vice president at the bank's development corporation, called with some questions just before Christmas. She asked Lynch, the developer, why he hadn't conducted the usual engineering and architectural studies for a project of this nature. He explained that the previous summer, the tenants association had reduced the initial deposits to enable more people to join; the decision meant no money was available to pay for predevelopment work. Johns balked.

You've got to meet these tenants, Lynch told her. You've got to see the neighborhood, to understand what they're trying to do. The two set up a visit for Jan. 6, nine days before the purchase deadline. The president of the development corporation came, as did the bank's chief credit officer. They peppered the tenants and the project team with questions and toured one of the buildings.

But it wasn't enough. When members of the development corporation's loan committee met the next day, they decided that the deal was too risky. Unanticipated construction needs could send costs soaring. What's more, the funding letter from the city seemed tentatively worded. Committee members feared the $2 million in financing could fall through.

Lynch listened calmly to all the objections, Johns recalled. He quickly secured a new letter from the D.C. government, stressing the city's strong commitment. And he said that if costs climbed during the project, he would persuade the tenants to seek outside investors to preserve the complex as an affordable rental building.

On Jan. 14, loan-committee members reassembled.

They considered the U Street corridor, prices rising every month.

They considered the tenants, working toward the purchase for well over a year.

They considered the project team—attorney Aaron O'Toole, from Georgetown University Law School's Harrison Institute; Manna Inc., the affordable housing specialists who were playing a supporting role; and Lynch, the former Olympic gymnast whose office was just a few blocks away from Capital Manor, whose portfolio was dominated by projects that guaranteed poor people a place to live. Because the budget was so tight, Lynch had cut his fee by 20 percent.

"I found myself saying to people, 'silver medalist' " Johns recalled later. 'This is somebody with a history of focus and successful leadership, who's from this neighborhood and is committed to this project."

The committee approved the $3.5 million loan to buy the building and said details of the construction loan could be worked out later. The closing date was pushed to Jan. 24. Loan officer Renee Jakobs processed the paperwork faster than she had ever done before.

"Is there a piece of paper I can have that says we own? . . . I just want to walk away with something that says it."

Jakobs took a taxi to a Thomas Circle law office for the closing, a foot-high stack of papers in her arms. She didn't normally go to closings, she said, but she wanted to be there for this one. The room was crowded with people—among them Thomas, the tenants association president, in a bright-red wool coat; Treasurer Mitchell, equally vivid in a salmon-colored sweater; Lynch; O'Toole and his boss, Michael Diamond.

Rodriguez was there as well. He had quit his job as resident manager a few days earlier after a clash with the soon-to-be-former owners of the complex. He planned to move back into Capital Manor as soon as the tenants association assumed control and eventually launch his own small construction business.

Shyly, he unveiled a bottle of Moet & Chandon champagne and glass flutes. O'Toole then opened his own bag to reveal another bottle of bubbly and plastic cups. The attorneys reviewed the papers. Thomas began to sign. An hour later, the deal was done.

"Is there a piece of paper I can have that says we own?" Thomas asked. 'I know they're going to send us a big package, but I just want to walk away with something that says it."

The deed and the settlement statement were photocopied, the champagne was uncorked. The attorneys insisted that Thomas, Mitchell and Rodriguez drink from the glass flutes.

"Tenants get the real deal?" Thomas joked.

"Not tenants—owners," Diamond corrected her. "Owners get the real deal."

A Crash Course in Responsibility

For a victory party, the mood was dismal.

A few dozen residents of Capital Manor gathered under a neon-green "Congratulations!!" banner on a January evening in 2003 to toast their achievement: Nearly three-quarters of the people who lived in the low-income complex had signed reservation agreements and put down deposits to buy their apartments. They had staved off the gentrification sweeping the U Street corridor and hung on to three century-old buildings in the 1400 block of W Street.

But the complex they now owned was falling apart. Renovations had to be done and paid for. Vandalism had to stop. As home-baked cakes sat untouched at the front of the room, Deborah Thomas, the woman who had spearheaded the purchase effort, lectured her neighbors about taking responsibility.

"If you see your neighbor's kids hitting on the walls or breaking windows or dragging trash through the halls, don't forget that money to fix those things is coming out of your pocket," she said. 'We can no longer call the owner to say, 'This is broke, that's broke. . . . We *are* the owner. We're going to have to come up with the money to have it fixed."

Hands flew up. It's not so easy, one woman said in Spanish. Boys from down the block roamed the hallways of her building, smoking marijuana. They trailed residents into the building and slipped pennies into the door frame, jamming the lock so they could leave and reenter at will.

Call the police, urged Thomas, prompting an older man near the back to shake his head. He'd done that, he said, only to have the cops show up and let slip to the youths the apartment number from which the 911 call was made.

"The next day, I've got a problem," the man said.

Then Aaron O'Toole, the residents' young attorney, stood to remind them to save for their down payments, which would be due when renovations began. The payments—$2,300 for a one-bedroom, $3,200 for a two-bedroom—were cheap for the neighborhood but daunting for those in the room.

"I'm going to be eating a whole lot of hot dogs," sighed Michelle Craig, a single mother who worked for Marriott Corp.

"Hey," said the woman next to her, nodding. "Peanut butter and jelly."

The members of the newly named Capital Manor Cooperative were beginning to understand that entry into the ownership society also carries burdens.

The next 18 months were bleak. Renovations of the 102-unit complex, scheduled to start in September, were put on indefinite hold because the $8.1 million construction loan was delayed. With the operating budget already cut to the bone, basic repairs went undone. In one building, the boiler's pilot light kept going out, and co-op association Treasurer Peggy Fitzgerald got up twice each night to relight it.

O'Toole, who had shepherded the purchase effort for nearly three years, left Georgetown University's public-interest law clinic for a private firm. His boss, Michael Diamond, a stranger to most residents, took over.

Drug dealing and loitering continued outside the complex. One resident, Rafael Cruz, was robbed at gunpoint on Christmas Eve as he returned from a trip to the grocery store.

As the bad news mounted, several families announced plans to move. Cash flow withered each time one of them turned in their keys. There was no arrest in Cruz's robbery, and within a few months he left also.

"People are not seeing renovations take place. . . . People don't have heat or hot water. . . . People are frustrated," sighed Thomas, president of the cooperative association. Overwhelmed by the demands of the project, she'd given up her full-time job and was subsisting on part-time work counseling at-risk teenagers.

Gaining ownership did not guarantee success. Thomas constantly reminded her neighbors that what was happening at the other end of the block could happen to them, too.

She meant 1418 W Street, a building that had been condemned by the city a few years back. Thomas had lived there for decades, as had her parents. She moved to Capital Manor just six months before the city declared 1418 unlivable and charged its landlord with hundreds of housing code violations.

As part of a plea bargain, the landlord sold the building to the tenants for $1 in August 2000. Over the next three years, the former residents met endlessly with attorneys and consultants, trying to forge a renovation plan.

But condo developers kept calling, offering huge amounts to buy them out. Some resisted. But when in August 2003 a pair of developers offered $2.5 million, those people were outvoted. Each family received $114,000—a nice windfall, but not nearly enough to buy or rent at market rates in the neighborhood. Thomas's mother, Louise, who had voted against selling, secured an apartment at Capital Manor. Most of her former neighbors moved away.

Deborah Thomas was devastated by the loss of 1418 as a place where people of modest means could live. More than ever, she felt the importance of saving Capital Manor from a similar fate.

Longtime residents have "gone through dodging bullets and drugs and trash in the tree boxes," she said, "and then when it's all nice and clean everyone else wants to move in and push us out. Some of us are here by force. We couldn't afford to go anywhere else."

And yet, even as the residents pursued their goal, they found themselves frustrated by the project's limitations. Their pleas for fireplaces and walk-in closets were gently turned down. Jair K. Lynch, their developer, said construction funds would have to go toward the basics: sprinkler systems and new roofs, repairs to faulty wiring and worn-out heating and cooling systems. Residents pleaded for gas stoves; Lynch agreed but said they could not be individually metered. New washers and dryers would be ordered and installed—but in the same old basement laundry room, not in each unit. Kitchens got new cabinets, refrigerators and stoves, but not dishwashers.

Most of the work, Lynch explained, would take place behind the walls—"the heart and guts of the building that haven't been taken care of." It had to be that way, he insisted, even though "I don't know if the average person will appreciate a little sprinkler head poking out of the drywall." These homeowners could not afford major repairs down the road. They needed their buildings to be in top shape from the start.

Residents took to grousing about all the project lacked. "Amenities? What are we getting? Nothing," Sylvia Griffis said during a meeting.

No Internet connection. Not even a choice of paint color.

"What they're offering us is a place to stay that is affordable," countered Kim Mitchell. "A two-bedroom, two-bath in this neighborhood—that's a half-million dollars. I understand where you're coming from, but unless people are ready to sacrifice or to find new resources, we're not going to have no amenities."

Things began to improve in September 2004, after the construction loan from affiliates of the National Cooperative Bank finally came through. A year after the original start date, renovations could now begin.

To mark the occasion, a load of dirt was deposited outside the buildings one rainy afternoon. Mayor Anthony A. Williams joined Thomas, Lynch and others in donning a plastic hard hat and grabbing a shiny new shovel to plunge in.

Nerissa Phillips, now the association secretary, came to bear witness. "The only way we can lose it now is if we mess up," she said approvingly. 'We cannot be booted from the neighborhood, no matter how high the property values get."

Of the 102 households living at Capital Manor when it was put up for sale three years earlier, about 70 remained. Some families had never expressed interest in buying; others grew tired of waiting and left. Five senior citizens took advantage of a D.C. law allowing them to stay on as renters, and the board extended that same option to a developmentally disabled man. A few residents who failed to deliver their down payments had to be threatened with eviction before they agreed to leave.

The departures were unsettling, but there was a bright side: remaining members would not have to move away during construction. Those who lived in one building could relocate into empty units in the others while the work was being done.

The first round of moving was chaotic, with furniture broken and belongings lost. Renovations took longer than expected. But by mid-March of this year, 1436 W Street was reborn, with new windows, a working front-door intercom and fresh, brightly lit corridors. Every apartment had fresh off-white paint, new carpeting and a redone kitchen. Small sprinkler heads poked from the ceilings like sentries.

Once again, there were glitches. Peggy Fitzgerald's toilet overflowed all over her cream-colored carpet because a contractor had forgotten to flush out the pipes. The laundry machines didn't arrive on time, so Thomas, deluged with complaints, had the old machines temporarily reinstalled.

At the same time, there was a palpable sense of excitement.

Ingrid Campbell, the relocation manager, buzzed from apartment to apartment, hovering over residents as they packed up the temporary quarters and prepared to go home.

"I want you to vacuum out everything," she instructed Jose Diaz, 27. "And I want the refrigerator sparkling."

"It already is," Diaz countered, grinning. "You want to see?"

When Diaz mentioned that he would no longer have room for a pair of upholstered chairs, Campbell sifted through her mental list of residents and suggested offering it to a family on the third floor. "They don't hardly have furniture," she said.

Diaz had lived at Capital Manor almost exclusively since immigrating from El Salvador in 1995, first with his mother and sister, later with an uncle, Rafael Cruz, the victim of the armed robbery on Christmas Eve 2003. More recently, his girlfriend and her young son had moved in. It was a tight squeeze in his one-bedroom apartment, he acknowledged, but he would feel good knowing the space belonged to him.

"We all have a dream to own something," Diaz said. "I live here, and I don't see myself living someplace else."

With the first building completed, the second was emptied. This time, construction progressed more quickly, but some were not satisfied. Board Vice President Osmin Rodriguez, for one, complained that the floor of his apartment sagged just as it had before the renovations. Contractors said the building's foundation had sunk, but Rodriguez was not convinced.

"It hasn't gone half the way I wanted it to go. But . . . it's all right," he said shortly before moving back into his old apartment in mid-July. "It's still great, but it's not as great as I thought it would be."

Renovations of the last of Capital Manor's buildings were completed Thanksgiving week, and a ribbon-cutting is scheduled for this afternoon. But the transformation of the complex is still underway.

Thirty new households must be selected to fill empty apartments. Applicants cannot earn more than 80 percent of the area's median income (currently the income limit is $71,400 for a family of four). Their down payments will be $12,000 or $20,000, depending on unit size—much more than what the original residents paid. Lynch, the developer, calls the arrival of more moderate-income families "managed change."

A mix of incomes is a good thing, he said—"the middle ground between stagnation and gentrification." The next stage, he added, "is to really start building the bonds, the glue."

Lynch was talking about the new and old members of the co-op. But on W Street, the challenge also extends to forging ties with the mostly white, mostly affluent homeowners across the street—many of whom still regard Capital Manor as a blight. They hate the bright new security lights, which shine into their bedrooms, and they don't understand why there wasn't enough money to spruce up the facades.

"Their renovation hasn't been some great boon to the neighborhood," said Kurt Ehrman, a government lawyer who bought his rowhouse in 2000. "It hasn't been a boon to my home equity."

Concerned that he will be seen as "the complaining, rich, white neighbor," Ehrman hastens to add that he has befriended some of the older women across the street; one invited him in to see her renovated apartment. He has clashed with Thomas in the past but said last week that he hopes to build a relationship with her as well.

Residents of Capital Manor grouse that northsiders rarely come to their block parties and celebrations, or even greet them on the sidewalks when they pass. Orange Hat patrols of the block, launched by the Meridian Hill Neighborhood Association, are welcomed by many northsiders. But members of the cooperative find them intrusive.

The young men on the corner do not need to be shooed away, said Craig, 50, who has known many of them since they were in diapers. "They're not all drug dealers, they're not all going to rob you," she said impatiently. "Some of them are working for Metro. Some of them are doing construction. They have jobs, but they get together and hang."

At least one northsider is determined to bridge the two sides of the block. Sonal Sheth, 31, rents a room in a rowhouse and directs an afterschool youth program in nearby Petworth. One day last summer, she took a Frisbee across the street and asked the kids if anyone wanted to toss it. No one did. But she ended up sitting on the stoop with 15-year-old Jasmine Thomas, Deborah's younger daughter. Together, they sketched out a mentoring program in which residents of the rowhouses would tutor the children of Capital Manor and take them on field trips.

"It's two worlds that certainly can come together," Sheth said. "It didn't happen this fall, but I think it will happen next spring."

On a recent Sunday, on the way home from church, Thomas and her mother noticed balloons outside their old building, the one condemned by the District government years ago.

A smiling, smartly dressed woman stood in the entryway of 1418 W Street, handing out information about the newly rehabbed condominiums in "The Hamilton on W Street." Thomas and her mother looked at each other, then at the familiar building. They had to go in.

The kitchen cabinets were cherry, the countertops a dramatic, dark green sweep of granite. Appliances were shiny stainless steel. Prices started in the high $300,000s and topped out at $545,000.

Thomas drank in the hardwood floors and exposed brick, wondering how much it would cost to line a wall of her unit with similar masonry. She pictured a fireplace in her living room.

Then Thomas and her mother walked out of the building and down the block to Capital Manor. Thomas unlocked the door and entered the apartment she will one day leave to her children.

While the balloons flitted in the sunshine down the street, Thomas and her mother, part-owners of a multimillion-dollar cooperative, sat down to a Sunday dinner of macaroni and cheese, baked turkey wings and greens.

POST-CLASS REFLECTION MEMO

Draft and submit a memo in response to the questions below:

- How will the lessons you have learned in this class relate, in concrete terms, to your clinic client representation work?
- What specific actions will you take to ensure that you apply these lessons in service of your clinic clients?
- How will your insights about the following affect your client representation work?
    - The multiple options for shaping the same set of facts into stories
    - The elements, progression, and structure of stories
    - Character development
    - The role of audience.

CHAPTER 8

THEORY OF THE CASE OR LAWYERING PROJECT

LEARNING GOALS

The learning goals for this class include helping you to:

- Understand the role of theory of the case or project as a fact-centered explanation of events for the finder of fact, or as a way to frame the issues to elicit a favorable response from a decision maker or other stakeholders
- Understand the role that case theory plays as an organizing principle for lawyering work
- Understand the importance of client-specific particularities in developing an effective theory of the case or project
- Understand that both the broader context of the client's life and the perspective of the target audience(s) are important to the development of a case theory
- Achieve clarity about the need for flexibility in revising a theory of the case or project in response to changing factual and legal understandings

DESCRIPTION OF CLASS

In this class, we will explore the concept of the theory of the case or of the lawyering project. We will engage in a series of exercises designed to help you learn to develop a case or project theory. Next, we will think through the ways in which a theory of the case or project operates as a framework for every aspect of a lawyer's work. Finally, we will examine the need for a lawyer to remain flexible and open to revision of a case theory as a case or project develops over time.

ASSIGNMENT IN PREPARATION FOR CLASS

There is no assignment in preparation for this class.

READING ASSIGNMENT

1. David A. Binder, Paul Bergman, Paul R. Tremblay & Ian S. Weinstein, *Theory Development Questioning—Pursuing Helpful Evidence*, and *Theory Development Questioning Undermining Adversaries' Likely Contentions*, *in* LAWYERS AS COUNSELORS: A CLIENT-CENTERED APPROACH 151 (2012).
2. Steven Lubet, *Murder in the Streets of Tombstone: A Legendary Theory of the Case*, LITIGATION 35 (Fall 2000).
3. Roald Hoffman, *Why Buy That Theory?*, 91 AM. SCIENTIST 9 (Jan. 2003).

READINGS

David A. Binder, Paul Bergman, Paul R. Tremblay, Ian S. Weinstein
LAWYERS AS COUNSELORS: A CLIENT-CENTERED APPROACH (3d ed. 2012)[1]

Chapter 7: Theory Development Questioning—Pursuing Helpful Evidence

Bob, you've given me a quite clear picture of how this situation unfolded from the first day you met Ross right up to today. What I need to do now is to flesh out the story so that we can get a better picture of where you stand legally. We can get started on that today, but we may need another meeting before we can decide on the best way to proceed from here. However, before you leave today, we should be able to kick around some ideas about how you might best resolve this matter with Ross. How does that sound?

* * *

---

1 Footnotes and/or internal citations omitted.

1. INTRODUCTION

[Once you have the basic timeline of a client's story], you can turn your attention to the second major phase of initial information-gathering in litigation matters. This book refers to this phase of interviews as "theory development questioning," because during this phase you seek evidence to bolster your clients' legal contentions and vitiate those of your adversaries.

Theory development questioning generally places you in a more active questioning role than timeline questioning. The reason is that like gold ore, nuggets of useful evidence that may be present in clients' recollections often do not appear on the surface, waiting for you to scoop them up with a few open-ended timeline questions. Instead, you may have to dig down into clients' recollections with questions that reflect your analytical judgment. Thus, the orientation underlying this and the next chapter's approach is that information-gathering is more likely to be productive if you start out with some concrete ideas of what you're looking for.

2. THE PROCESS OF THEORY DEVELOPMENT QUESTIONING

Theory development questioning grows out of a quintessentially legal task, carrying out the analytic process of connecting concrete timeline stories to the abstract rules that constitute legal claims and defenses. This analytic process typically leads you to identify legal theories (claims or defenses) that timeline stories generate. You then work backwards from those legal theories to identify helpful potential evidence; that is, potential evidence tending to substantiate those theories. . . .

[T]heory development questioning often incorporates four separate kinds of tasks:

(a) pursuing helpful evidence;

(b) seeking to bolster the credibility of helpful evidence;

(c) seeking to rebut the impact of harmful evidence; and

(d) seeking to undermine adversaries' legal contentions. . . .

3. IDENTIFYING MATERIAL FACTS

The process of effectively and thoroughly probing timeline stories for additional helpful evidence usually begins with your identifying the material (ultimate) facts that you seek to prove. The subsections below describe a three step process for doing so. While you may depending on your experience sometimes be able to carry out this process automatically and perhaps subconsciously, this section explicates its component parts in order to aid your ability to gather helpful evidence when you are confronted with legal or factual situations with which you are unfamiliar. The three step process is as follows:

1. Identify applicable legal theories.
2. Parse legal theories into constituent elements.
3. Convert legal elements into factual propositions.

A. IDENTIFYING LEGAL THEORIES

The process of identifying the facts you want to prove begins by identifying the potentially-viable legal theories suggested by clients' time line stories. That is, evidence is "helpful" not in the abstract, but to the extent that it furthers a relevant legal claim or defense. For example, when interviewing a tenant in an unlawful detainer (eviction) case, you may seek evidence concerning illnesses suffered by the tenant's children not simply because illnesses would be "part of the story," but because the evidence would tend to show that lack of heating in the apartment rendered it "uninhabitable."

Often, and especially when you have received information about clients' problems before in-person interviews begin, you will have potentially-viable legal theories in mind at the conclusion of (and perhaps even at the start of) timeline questioning. If so, then an initial meeting may flow rather seamlessly from timeline to theory development questioning.

At times, however, you may be uncertain about the legal theories you can most profitably pursue during theory development questioning. For example, you may want to check on whether an established legal claim or defense applies to a client's timeline story. Or, you may be uncertain as to whether a potential theory is legally permissible in your jurisdiction. A third possibility, no doubt the most disquieting, is to simply draw a blank after listening to a timeline story.

In most cases, your general legal knowledge will be sufficient for you to probe timeline stories at least preliminarily as soon as that phase of interviews concludes. However, thorough theory development questioning may require a temporary adjournment of an initial meeting while you do legal research. The length of the postponement will, apart from other time commitments, typically depend on the amount of time you need to fully acquaint yourself with the applicable law. In all events where you lack full understanding of applicable law, theory development questioning may have to extend over at least two meetings.

The strategies for identifying helpful evidence to pursue during theory development begin with a specific legal claim or defense that you seek to prove or disprove. From this point on, therefore, the discussion assumes that you have identified a viable legal theory pursuant to which you want to identify helpful evidence.

B. PARSING LEGAL THEORIES INTO CONSTITUENT ELEMENTS

1. *Legal Theories Are Abstract Shells*

The earth probably did not move for you when you read that you should probe time line stories pursuant to legal theories. What other source would you use—theories of skeletal structure as set forth in Gray's Anatomy? However, you may feel at least a small tremor when you realize that legal theories are largely ephemeral. Most legal theories, be they criminal or civil, common law or statutory, are abstract shells that are not themselves provable. At a minimum, provable legal theories consist of bundles of elements that constitute the content of legal theories. For example, if you were asked what evidence you would offer to prove breach of contract or securities fraud, you would have to ask first what requirements (elements) you must satisfy to establish each legal theory. The legal theories standing alone are simply housings for elements, not concrete guides to proof.

2. *Elements Themselves Are Legal Abstractions*

Elements establish the requirements of legal theories. Nevertheless, elements themselves remain legal abstractions. As a result, even discrete elements are not a sufficient guide to case-specific questions.

For example, assume that a client's timeline story focuses on his near-decapitation by an exploding kitchen appliance. The story suggests to you a number of potentially-applicable legal theories, such as negligent manufacture of goods, breach of warranty, and strict liability on a theory of defective design. A quick riffle through your memory bank enables you to bring to the fore the following requisite elements of a claim for "strict liability/defective design:"

1. The defendant introduced a product into commerce.
2. The product when introduced contained a design defect.
3. The design defect was the actual cause of damages.
4. The design defect was the proximate cause of damages.
5. The design defect resulted in damages.

As you can see, these elements tell you nothing about what facts you must prove in your client's specific situation to succeed with this legal claim. For example, the elements are silent with respect to such basic facts as the type of product involved, its design, the client's injuries and other damages and what the defendant did to introduce the product into commerce. The elements are so broad that they can apply to an infinite number of stories. Indeed, elements are intentionally broad and abstract, for it is impossible to draft a specific rule for each set of factual circumstances that might arise in the context of a given legal element. Thus, abstract elements alone are not adequate guides to the facts that either you or an adversary may attempt to establish at trial, or to the questions you might ask to develop evidence of such facts.

3. Restating Elements as Factual Propositions

Converting abstract legal elements into provable "factual propositions" is the next step for identifying topics for theory development probing. Factual propositions meld abstract elements with legally salient facts in clients' timeline stories. That is, factual propositions tailor intangible elements to each client's concrete situation, so that proof of a factual proposition's accuracy establishes an element. Restating elements as factual propositions tells you what facts establish that element in a client's specific case. In turn, delineating factual propositions enables you to think concretely about what evidence in the existing story as well as what potential evidence is likely to establish the facts you need to prove. In addition to proving the elements of substantive legal theories, you may also have to prove miscellaneous facts such as those related to jurisdiction or a litigant's legal status.

To understand the process of converting legal theories into factual propositions, assume that you represent a personal injury client named Wilson. The interview thus far has revealed that Wilson was injured when the brakes in his car failed, causing the car to collide with another vehicle. Wilson's timeline story of this misadventure is as follows:

(1) On June 10, Wilson brought his car to a Goodstone Service Center to purchase two new tires.

(2) Goodstone's manager stated that the car needed new brakes and Wilson authorized Goodstone to do a brake job.

(3) The brake job took longer than anticipated, and Wilson was without a car for two days, which caused him hardship, including being late for work, needing friends to pick up children, etc.

(4) On June 12, Wilson picked up his car.

(5) During the following week Wilson noticed that the car pulled to the left whenever he applied the brakes,

(6) On June 20th, Wilson returned to Goodstone and explained his problem to a service representative and the mechanic who had originally worked on his car.

(7) Wilson left his car at Goodstone and picked it up later the same day after receiving a phone call indicating that the problem was with the brakes and that it had been fixed.

(8) The brakes worked fine for two days and then again the car began pulling to the left when Wilson applied the brakes.

(9) Wilson was returning to Goodstone on June 22nd to have the brakes checked when, approaching a red light at an intersection, Wilson applied the brakes and they failed totally.

(10) Wilson's car collided with the rear end of another car at a speed of about 35 mph.

(11) Wilson was in the hospital with head injuries for three days, incurring medical costs of about $58,000; over $17,000 in damages was done to Wilson's car.

(12) The insurance company for the driver of the car that Wilson collided with contacted Wilson and asked him for a statement. Wilson gave a statement to the insurance company.

(13) Six weeks after the accident, Wilson returned to Goodstone to talk to the mechanic who had worked on the brakes and learned that the mechanic was no longer employed by Goodstone.

Wilson's timeline story may suggest to you a number of potentially relevant legal theories by which Wilson might recover damages against Goodstone, including negligence, fraud and breach of warranty. For purposes of this discussion, focus on the negligence theory. In abstract terms, one element of this theory is "breach of the duty of reasonable care." Having heard Wilson's story and looked into how braking systems operate, you believe that Goodstone would have breached the duty of reasonable care if the mechanic had neglected to check the condition of the master brake cylinder. Thus, you might formulate the following factual proposition:

"Goodstone failed to check the master brake cylinder when repairing the brakes on Wilson's car."

As you can see, the factual proposition identifies a concrete fact, proof of which satisfies the element, "breach of the duty of reasonable care." Unlike the abstract element, the factual proposition enables you to identify case-specific topics likely to produce evidence establishing the proposition's accuracy. For example, using the strategies set forth below, you might pursue the following topics during theory development questioning of Wilson:

a. Whether Wilson was billed by Goodstone for inspection of the master brake cylinder.

b. Whether Wilson was billed by Goodstone for replacement of the master brake cylinder.

c. Whether Wilson was given any old parts when he picked up the car.

d. Whether the car's brake warning light came on before the accident.

a. Multiple Factual Propositions

Any single legal element may be satisfied by a virtually unlimited number of factual propositions. Across cases, this assertion is obvious. Two cases involving identical legal theories and elements will almost certainly lead to different factual propositions because of variations in their factual histories. For instance, the factual proposition that you might formulate for the element of "formation of contract" in a case involving breach of an employment contract will in all likelihood be very different from one that you might assert in a case involving breach of a construction contract.

Perhaps less obviously, you may want to formulate and pursue multiple factual propositions even for a single element in a single case. One reason is simply that a timeline story may give rise to multiple factual ways of satisfying the same abstract legal element. For instance, assume that you represent a plaintiff in a fraud case and your client states that the defendant made four different material misstatements. You therefore might formulate four different factual propositions, each one satisfying the element, "misrepresentation." Similarly, if you represent a defendant in an equitable action, a defendant's story may give rise to multiple factual propositions demonstrating the plaintiff's "unclean hands."

A second reason for formulating and pursuing multiple factual propositions for a single element in the same case is that a timeline story may leave you uncertain of an element's factual equivalent. For example, in the Wilson/Goodstone matter, Wilson's story may not enable you to pinpoint what Goodstone did wrong that constitutes "breach of the duty of reasonable care." Consider two common factors that often create uncertainty:

- Clients may be unaware of how events actually have transpired. For example, Wilson may have no idea why the brakes failed and may not know what the mechanic did or failed to do to his car.
- Clients who think they are aware of how events took place may be mistaken. For example, Wilson's story about why the brakes failed may be incorrect.

In such situations, often a sensible strategy is to formulate a number of factual propositions, each based on what seems to you a reasonable possibility. For example, factual propositions you might reasonably formulate on Wilson's behalf that would satisfy the element "breach of the duty of reasonable care" would include:

- Goodstone failed to replace the brake fluid in Wilson's car.
- Goodstone failed to install new brake linings properly.
- Goodstone installed discs not designed for Wilson's model of car.

When as in Wilson's case a number of propositions might reasonably support a timeline story, be reluctant to discard them out of hand before completing initial fact gathering. If you limit questioning to a single factual proposition, you are in trouble if down the road that solo proposition does not pan out with evidence. Searching feverishly for new factual propositions late in the game, you may instead be searching for a new client.

Especially if you are knowledgeable about cars, you might well be able to formulate additional factual propositions. But even the few alternatives above demonstrate how their creation increases the scope of potentially relevant evidence. Propositions about master cylinders, brake fluid, brake linings and discs each may be established by different evidence, and hence each suggests different lines of inquiry. For example, evidence that stepping on the brakes caused Wilson's car to pull to the left or right might suggest a problem with the discs or linings, rather than with the master brake cylinder or the brake fluid. The same might be said about evidence that the brakes were smoking prior to the accident.

Depending on your background and experience, in any given case you may feel that you lack the experience to develop alternative propositions. For example, as the subject probably was not covered in law school, you may know little about the potential causes of brake failure. Or, you might represent landowners who contend that a nearby dump contains illegal toxic wastes, and you may not be aware precisely of how toxic waste problems manifest themselves. In such situations, you may need to develop "industry knowledge" by involving an expert in the process of formulating factual propositions. For example assume you represent a person who was injured when a bridge collapsed. One thought you have is the collapse is due to the negligence of the company that designed the bridge or the company that erected it. If you have no experience in bridge design or construction, consulting an expert who does will help you identify factual propositions relating to negligence.

One note of caution: Judges and jurors do not award prizes to the side that produces the most factual propositions. Developing propositions to excess may prove the depth and breadth of your "industry knowledge" (e.g., that you are a master mechanic) as it drowns you in a sea of factual propositions. Do not be limited by the factual boundaries contained in a timeline story, but be reasonable in your creation of alternative ones.

b. Plaintiffs' and Defendants' Factual Propositions

The process of converting legal elements into one or more factual propositions appears to respond primarily to the way that plaintiffs' lawyers view the world. Plaintiffs normally pursue as many legal theories as are reasonably feasible, and they typically have the burden of proving each element of each alleged cause of action or criminal offense. Formulating a variety of provable propositions and trying to uncover evidence pursuant to each therefore well serves plaintiffs' interests.

Perhaps for less obvious reasons, defense counsel often have to identify the factual propositions on which their adversaries are likely to rely (at least for those elements that defense counsel plan to contest). Defense counsel cannot simply rely on the pleadings, because complaints typically do not specify the factual propositions by which plaintiffs may attempt to prove their various theories. For example, in the Wilson/Goodstone matter, Wilson's complaint may well allege little more than that Goodstone negligently serviced Wilson's car. Because Goodstone cannot attempt to negate every possible way in which its service might have been negligent, Goodstone's counsel must try to identify the factual propositions that Wilson will attempt to pursue.

At the same time, defendants often have to formulate their own factual propositions. Defendants may not typically have the burden of proving elements, and they may not contest each and every element of a claim. But as to those elements that defendants do contest, they often not only try to disprove plaintiffs' versions of events, but also offer their own affirmative stories. For example, Goodstone is likely to do more than pursue a factual proposition that "Goodstone did indeed check the master brake cylinder." In addition, Goodstone's counsel might formulate and try to identify evidence for the factual proposition "Wilson's driving at an excessive speed was the cause of the accident."

Still less are defense counsel simply naysayers when they allege affirmative defenses as to which they have the burden of proof. For instance, if in a criminal case the defense relies on an alibi, the defense is unlikely to limit itself to denying that the defendant was present at the scene of the crime. The defense will probably also try to prove defendant's actual whereabouts, and may even offer its own evidence as to the identity of the actual culprit. In such an instance, the defense might offer evidence to support at least two factual propositions, such as: (a)

"Defendant was actually in Miami Beach at the time of the robbery in Cleveland;" and (b) "The actual robber was Al Moore."

Hence, regardless of the burden of proof, defense attorneys also typically need to develop factual propositions before embarking on theory development questioning.

4. IDENTIFYING EMOTIVE (NON-MATERIAL) FACTUAL PROPOSITIONS

Litigation has both rational and emotive aspects. Hence you may also want to look for evidence tending to prove the accuracy of information that may lead a judge or juror to believe in the moral justness of your clients' causes. Assume for example that in providing a timeline story, Wilson told you that when he picked up his car on June 22nd, the service representative told him, "We've got it this time. You don't have to worry, your brakes are in perfect condition now." Proof that the service representative made this statement does not establish that Goodstone negligently serviced Wilson's brakes. At the same time, establishing that the service representative did make this remark may incline a judge or juror to want to decide the case in Wilson's favor. Thus, you may want to pursue proof of this "non-material" fact to the same extent as material facts.

Consider a second example in which you might want to pursue proof of a non-material fact. Assume that you represent a defendant tenant in an unlawful detainer (eviction) matter and have asserted a defense based on breach of the warranty of habitability because of the landlord's failure to keep the premises free of rodents. During her timeline story, the client indicated that when she was absent the landlord often entered her apartment to snoop around. Establishing this emotive fact that tends to cast the landlord as a "bad guy" might strengthen your claims with respect to the material facts.

5. IDENTIFYING HELPFUL EVIDENCE

Factual propositions, the case-specific counterparts of abstract elements, are the foundation for identifying helpful evidence tending to amplify the persuasive impact of time line stories. The subsections below explore strategies for identifying such evidence.

A. THE ROLE OF EXPERIENCE

Law school's emphasis on tools of legal analysis tends to obscure the extent to which the resolution of factual disputes depends on reasoning drawn from everyday experience. In reality, your own personal experience is often your primary source for identifying helpful evidence tending to support factual propositions. In other words, much of the helpful evidence you identify simply results from your use of the experience you've had in daily life, including observing and reading about how others live. Through your experiences you have undoubtedly internalized understandings about matters such as:

– how people typically behave

– how institutions typically behave

– how transactions commonly unfold

– how common mechanical and electronic devices operate

– how people typically think

– how people normally react in emotional situations

– the charm of the Rule Against Perpetuities.

How does experience enable you to identify helpful evidence based on factual propositions? Our everyday experiences lead us to expect that events usually unfold primarily according to recognizable patterns. Most of us accept, for example, that bystanders will be frightened when they witness violent crimes, that stockbrokers will stress the safety and growth potential of an investment when soliciting potential purchasers for newly issued stock, that people will be in a rush when late for an important meeting, and that cars with bad brakes may pull to the left or right when the brakes are applied. Because we accept that events occur in recognizable patterns, we can identify a variety of features that are likely to have been part of past events. Thus, when you employ personal experience to identify potential evidence topics, you identify happenings that are consistent with a factual proposition. Proof of those happenings in turn suggests a proposition's accuracy.

For example, assume that you want to identify topics likely to lead to evidence proving the proposition that "Store clerk Jones was afraid that the robber was going to shoot him." (This proposition satisfies a typical element of robbery, taking property "through means of force or fear.") Even knowing nothing about the robbery, you can undoubtedly use everyday personal experience to identify a number of topics that would establish this proposition's accuracy. You might include such topics as the realism of the gun's appearance, the robber's pointing it at Jones, the robber's nervousness, and the robber's use of threatening words. You can identify such evidence not simply because of any experience you have had with Jones or robberies but because your everyday experience provides you with a pattern of factors that are likely to make a robbery victim fearful of being shot.

You are undoubtedly familiar with the process of reasoning from evidence to legal conclusions. Judges and jurors engage in it routinely when weighing evidence pursuant to legal principles. Using experience to identify potential evidence is simply the converse of this familiar process.

During theory development questioning you begin with a conclusion (a factual proposition) and from that conclusion you identify topics that are likely to be present if the conclusion is accurate. Instead of piecing together evidence to reach conclusions, you start with a conclusion and reason backwards.

Despite its importance, everyday experience alone may not constitute a sufficient source of helpful topics. You may again need "industry knowledge"—that is, experience in the underlying context of a dispute. If a dispute centers on the language of a shopping center lease, it behooves you to know something not just about contracts in general or even about leases in general but specifically about lease agreements for shopping centers. If you represent a stockbroker who allegedly illegally "churned" an individual client's account, you must know not just about the stock market industry but about brokerage practices for non-institutional investors. If a client contends that she was negligently shot by a duck hunter, you must learn about guns and duck hunting. Experience with the underlying circumstances giving rise to clients' problems is critical for identifying helpful evidence topics tied directly to factual propositions. When you lack sufficient experience, you'll generally need to rely on others, often paid experts, to help you identify helpful evidence.

Obviously, one reason that lawyers develop specialized practices is to accumulate experiences in a particular industry or way of life. But even specialization is no guarantee of subject matter experience. For instance, though you may specialize in "wrongful termination" matters, your experience with matters that originate in government offices may be insufficient for a matter that arises in a restaurant. Even specialists, therefore, may need to call on experts.

Experience, then, both in general and in the activity involved in a particular dispute, is the bridge that connects legal principles and real world events. Remember, each and every day you use such experience to identify "evidence," if only subconsciously. Consider this sample dialogue:

Bo: "Why was the teacher smiling when we got to school today?"

Jo: "Probably because we did real well on the test yesterday."

Thus, identifying topics that might uncover helpful evidence pertaining to legal claims or defenses entails using the same thought processes you use in everyday life. Two organized approaches to applying experience to factual propositions are "Historical Reconstruction" and "Strengthening Generalizations." Both of these approaches rely on the importance and characteristics of circumstantial evidence.

B. CIRCUMSTANTIAL EVIDENCE

As you probably know, direct evidence establishes a proposition without the aid of an inference. In the Wilson/Goodstone hypothetical, the mechanic's admission that "I never did look at the master brake cylinder" is direct evidence in support of the factual proposition for breach of duty, "Goodstone failed to check the master brake cylinder." No inference (other than that the testimony is truthful) is required to go from the mechanic's testimony to the accuracy of the factual proposition.

By contrast, circumstantial evidence establishes a proposition with the aid of one or more inferences. For example, evidence that thick grease covered the master brake cylinder would constitute circumstantial evidence that the mechanic did not inspect it. From the presence of thick grease, one can infer that the cylinder was not touched; from that, one can infer that it was not inspected.

For a variety of reasons, most evidence that you uncover and offer at trial is circumstantial. However, the persuasiveness of circumstantial evidence to prove or disprove a factual proposition rests on the strength of an underlying premise. That is, circumstantial evidence has probative value only according to the strength of the premise that connects the evidence to a proposition. In the vast majority of cases, premises are generalizations about the behavior of people and objects. They are postulates about how people and objects typically behave. The probative value of evidence, then, typically depends on the strength of these underlying generalizations.

For example, assume that a factual proposition you are attempting to prove is, "Snider ran a red light and struck Mantle's car." Seeking to prove the accuracy of this proposition, Mantle's attorney calls Mays, who testifies, "I spoke to Snider 15 minutes before the collision, and he told me that he was very late for an important meeting across town." Mays's testimony is circumstantial evidence. And its probative value depends on the strength of the following two generalizations:

"People who are late for a meeting are often in a hurry."

"People who are in a hurry sometimes run red lights."

In the absence of such premises (generalizations), a trier of fact could make no inference connecting Mays' testimony about "lateness" and Snider's running the red light.

"Historical Reconstruction" and "Strengthening Generalizations" are two strategies for identifying topics that are likely to lead to helpful evidence. Each depends on your recognizing that generalizations connect items of circumstantial evidence to factual propositions. The difference is that you need not explicitly formulate generalizations when you employ the strategy of "historical reconstruction," whereas you do explicitly formulate generalizations when you employ the "strengthening generalizations" approach. Neither approach is necessarily better than the other. You may employ whichever one is more comfortable and helpful to you, and this may vary from one case to another or even from one proposition to another in the same case. If a case's complexity justifies it, you may even employ both reasoning methods.

C. HISTORICAL RECONSTRUCTION

1. In General

Historical reconstruction is a method of reasoning by which you combine experience with chronology to identify potential evidence. The notion behind historical reconstruction is that most events are neither isolated nor random but are parts of larger sequences of events. For instance, most of us can identify the kinds of problems that the owner of a small retail shop probably experienced when just starting out, and the activities of an apartment seeker who has two small children and who suddenly had to move. Experience can tell us a lot not just about how any discrete event may have unfolded, but how an entire sequence of events is likely to have unfolded.

To use historical reconstruction to identify topics likely to lead to helpful evidence, adopt the attitude that a factual proposition is accurate. Then ask yourself, in essence, "If this proposition is true, what else also would probably have occurred?" The "what else" will be topics consisting of potential evidence that, if confirmed, become circumstantial evidence tending to prove the accuracy of the proposition.

As an illustration of the use of historical reconstruction, assume that as counsel for Wilson, one factual proposition you have tentatively decided to pursue is that, "Goodstone failed to check the master brake cylinder when it repaired the brakes on Wilson's car." Start from the premise that this proposition is accurate. Then, using everyday experience, think about what actions or happenings are consistent with failure to check a master brake cylinder. Probably even the most mechanically inept among us can identify such indicators as:

a. the mechanic's worksheet did not indicate that the mechanic had inspected the master brake cylinder;

b. Wilson was not billed for inspection of the master brake cylinder;

c. When Wilson picked up the car, the mechanic said nothing to Wilson about the condition of the master cylinder;

d. Goodstone mechanics are paid according to how many cars they repair per day.

Though you need not explicitly formulate generalizations when using historical reconstruction, you can see that the potential evidence this technique identifies is circumstantial. That is, each item implicitly rests on an underlying generalization. For example, the generalization underlying item "c" is something like, "Mechanics who inspect master brake cylinders are likely to tell car owners that they did so." The generalization supporting item "d" is something like, "Mechanics who are paid according to the number of cars they repair are likely not to inspect cars thoroughly for latent problems." Try formulating generalizations for items "a" and "b" on your own.

2. *Chronology: Before, During and After*

As you know, events that culminate in litigation typically take place over a period of hours, days, months and even years. An alleged contract may follow lengthy negotiations; a traffic accident may follow a driver's attending a round of parties and engaging in social drinking; prolonged bitterness between a testator and a child may culminate in a will disinheriting the child. However, legal elements, and therefore factual propositions, nearly always bless particular moments in time with substantive importance. For example, a factual proposition asserting that a party breached a contract typically focuses on the specific moment in time that the breach occurred. Similarly, a factual proposition asserting a testator's incompetence to make a will focuses on the testator's state of mind at the moment the will was signed. In a legal contest, then, the parties battle over whose version of substantively critical events is accurate.

However, events that occur "before" and "after" the substantively critical ones often determine which party's version of substantively critical events is believed. For example, a testator's behavior in the months preceding and following the signing of a will may well be determinative on the issue of testamentary capacity. From a party's conduct before, during and after a long course of negotiations, a trier of fact is likely to infer whether or not the party agreed to enter into a contract. Evidence that a defendant has a lengthy drug habit and left town the day after a robbery may produce an inference that the defendant committed a crime. Thus, circumstantial evidence describing what happened before and after, as well as during, substantively critical moments in time often determines the outcomes of disputes.

Historical reconstruction encourages you to identify events that may have occurred before and after the substantively critical ones. The usual question is, "If a factual proposition is true, what events are likely to have preceded or followed the substantively critical ones?" For example, assume that a factual proposition you are trying to prove is, "Testator P.J. Giddy was competent to make a will in that at the time he signed his will

Giddy knew his children's names, ages and occupations." Potential "before" and "after" evidence suggesting that this proposition is true includes evidence that Giddy sent his children birthday and anniversary cards, telephoned them, and made statements to others about them both before and after the execution of the will.

Expanding the temporal scope of an interview through historical reconstruction typically expands the spectrum of potential sources of information. One goal of developing potential evidence is to learn of other people (or documents) that might either support your clients' accounts or provide evidence of which your clients are unaware. But often, the only people who can describe what occurred at a moment of substantive importance are the interested parties themselves. For instance, assume that a plaintiff investor seeks to establish that a defendant company knew that its prospectus was false when issued. In that situation, only the company officials who prepared the prospectus may know what knowledge they had concerning the statements in the prospectus. Likewise, no one other than the drivers may claim to know how an accident occurred; and only a lawyer and a couple of strangers who acted as witnesses may have been present when a will was signed. By identifying potential prior and subsequent events you typically uncover potential sources of evidence other than the parties themselves.

3. Multiple Perspectives

When using historical reconstruction, you may try to re-create events from the perspectives of the different actors who might have had roles in those events. Sometimes you will find that viewing events from the perspectives of different individuals leads you to think of potential evidence you might have overlooked had you been considering only one point of view. For example, return to the factual proposition, "Goodstone failed to check the master brake cylinder when it repaired the brakes on Wilson's car." The prior subsection briefly identified potential evidence that might support this proposition primarily from the standpoint of actions in which the mechanic might have engaged.

But further perspectives are possible. You might, for instance, think about how Wilson was likely to have behaved during the incident. Is Wilson generally experienced with cars? How do people who do have some expertise with brake repair describe a braking problem to a mechanic or service manager? How about someone without such expertise? Consider also the possible role of a Goodstone service manager. What does experience suggest about the potential behavior of service managers of automobile repair shops? Why might such a manager pressure employees to complete a high daily volume of brake jobs? For example, might a manager's job be on the line, or might there be competition among various Goodstone repair shops? If so, what kind of memoranda might indicate such pressure existed? Note that the store manager perspective produces not only new items of potential evidence but also another potential source of information (i.e., documents). Finally, think about the records of the parts department. What helpful information might you find there?

D. STRENGTHENING GENERALIZATIONS

Unlike historical reconstruction, identifying topics likely to lead to helpful evidence by using the approach of "strengthening generalizations" involves the explicit formulation of generalizations. Was any approach ever more aptly named?

To use this second technique, begin again with an assumption that a factual proposition is correct. Next, convert that proposition to a generalization. Lastly, identify topics by adding either "especially when" or "except when" to a generalization. "Especially whens" tend to add to a proposition's strength whereas "except whens" tend to detract from a proposition's strength. Thus, during theory development questioning you hope that clients can confirm "especially whens" and negate the occurrence of "except whens."

For example, assume that a factual proposition suggesting Goodstone's breach of the duty of reasonable care is that "Goodstone installed the wrong brake discs when it repaired the brakes in Wilson's car." Converting this factual proposition to a generalization produces an assertion such as, "Car mechanics sometimes install the wrong brake discs in a car." This generalization may be "especially true" when

- the mechanic is in a hurry;
- the brake discs that fit one model of car are quite similar to those that fit another;
- the mechanic is inexperienced;
- the mechanic is not closely supervised; or
- the mechanic is under the influence of alcohol or drugs.

On the other hand, the generalization may be true "except when"

- the mechanic is an expert in brake repair;
- the car is owned by an important customer;
- the brake discs come in a clearly marked package; or
- the brake discs had to be specially ordered.

As you can see, "except whens" may be simply the converse of "especially whens." For instance, the mechanic's lack of experience makes it more likely that the mechanic would have installed the wrong brake discs; the mechanic's having expertise makes it more likely that the mechanic would have installed the correct ones. However, you may well identify potential evidence in the context of one thought mode that you would not have identified in the other. For instance, only in the "except when" context did the authors identify the "important customer" item; the authors did not identify "when the customer is unknown to the mechanic" in the "especially when" context. Hence, you may want to think through generalizations with both perspectives in mind. . . .

Chapter 8: Theory Development Questioning Undermining Adversaries' Likely Contentions

1. INTRODUCTION

This chapter describes how you may . . . pursue two additional common theory development tasks. These tasks consist of searching for:

- Evidence tending to rebut (diminish the impact of) harmful information that clients have disclosed; and
- Evidence tending to rebut adversaries' likely contentions. . . .

[T]he order in which [this] book addresses the topics of pursuing helpful evidence and searching for evidence undermining adversaries' contentions in no way suggests that this is an order that you should follow rigidly during theory development questioning. You will often jump back and forth among these tasks as circumstances and your judgment dictate.

2. UNCOVERING EVIDENCE TENDING TO REBUT HARMFUL DISCLOSURES

You can reasonably expect that most information that clients provide to you will support their legal claims. However, clients often make disclosures that you recognize as harmful. For example, a client in an auto accident case may insist that she was driving carefully and within the speed limit, yet admit that at the time of the accident she was running late for an important meeting. Pursuing evidence that may undermine harmful disclosures is a primary theory development task because any information you uncover that tends to vitiate the impact of harmful information bears on your preliminary assessment of a client's position and helps you plan possible strategies for case investigation, settlement and trial.

A useful approach for seeking information that may vitiate the impact of harmful answers is to search for explanations that tend to rebut arguments that adversaries might put forward based on the harmful answers. Assume for example that in a breach of contract case you represent a defendant who claims that "That's my signature on that piece of paper all right, but I really didn't realize what I was agreeing to." In the face of the harmful disclosure ("that's my signature"), you may seek out additional information explaining why the client did not know what he was signing. Similarly, assume that your client in a wrongful termination matter contends that she was fired without good cause, yet admits to having been late to work on a number of occasions. You may seek out information tending to rebut the employer's likely argument that her being late to work was a factor in her termination.

Typically, what you seek to explain away is the inference that an adversary is likely to argue should be drawn from a harmful disclosure. For example, assume that your client Stephanie tells you that she was unaware of problems in her company's shipping department. However, she also reveals that she had previously signed an affidavit on the company's behalf asserting that she was aware of problems in the shipping department. Thus, the harmful evidence is that Stephanie has given inconsistent accounts of the same event, and you can reasonably anticipate that your adversary will use this inconsistency to argue that Stephanie's later account of events is false or mistaken. To counter this inference, you might seek to uncover credible explanations for the changed account. . . .

3. UNCONVERING ADVERSARIES' LIKELY CONTENTIONS

The fact-gathering portions of initial client meetings are of course devoted primarily to uncovering and strengthening the probative value of helpful evidence, as well as seeking explanations for harmful disclosures. However, you can further your ability to tentatively assess clients' legal positions and map out provisional case strategies if you have information about adversaries' likely legal contentions. Thus, if earlier phases of interviews, documents, pleadings or other sources haven't already provided you with a good picture of adversaries' likely stances, you might ask clients what they know about their adversaries' likely contentions and supporting evidence.

Just as you might ask clients for explanations that might vitiate their own harmful disclosures, you can also seek to uncover information rebutting adversaries' likely contentions. In this latter situation, your search can be twofold:

- Do clients have information undermining the credibility of the evidence on which their adversaries are likely to rely?
- Can clients offer explanations that vitiate the probative value of adversaries' likely evidence?

. . .

Steven Lubet
Murder in the Streets of Tombstone: A Legendary Theory of the Case
LITIGATION 35 (Fall 2000)[2]

Good trial lawyers are good storytellers, but they must be more than that. You can tell a terrific story but lose your case if you have failed to shape the evidence into a legally meaningful narrative that entitles your client to relief.

A theory of the case provides the necessary bridge between the drama of the story and the requirements of the law. A winning case theory has internal logical force, explaining why the discrete facts, however interesting they may be, actually add up to proof that your client should prevail. Popular imagination notwithstanding, a trial is something more than a play or a contest. It is a process in which the law is applied to the facts. Unless that link is supplied by a comprehensive theory of the case, even the most riproaringly exciting story can become nothing when the verdict is returned.

This is a story about a famous gunfight and a forgotten murder trial. The prosecution in the case presented an account that was well supported, gripping, and powerful. Unfortunately, the theory of the case fell short, and the defendants walked free.

On October 26, 1881, in the dusty town of Tombstone, Arizona, Wyatt Earp began his march toward immortality. Accompanied by his two brothers, Morgan and Virgil, as well as the infamous Doc Holliday, he faced down the wild Clanton and McLaury brothers in an alley behind the O.K. Corral. When the shooting was over and the smoke cleared, three men—Tom and Frank McLaury and Billy Clanton—lay dead or dying.

Wyatt and company constituted the police force of Tombstone: Virgil was the town marshal, and the others were his deputies. As the story goes, they believed they had no choice but to shoot it out with the outlaws who had spent the previous 24 hours loudly threatening to kill the Earps and Holliday. The Clantons and McLaurys were members of a loose gang of desperados called the Cowboys, who were notorious rustlers and suspected of worse. The Cowboys started the battle by drawing their weapons rather than relinquishing them at the Earps' command. That is the standard version, related in later years by Wyatt Earp, revered today as an American hero.

---

2 Footnotes and/or internal citations omitted.

But there is another side to the story: one in which the Earps are little more than brutal killers. According to multiple witnesses, including the county sheriff, the Cowboys had not resisted the Earps at all. In fact, they tried to surrender, only to be gunned down with their hands raised vainly in the air.

The Murder Charge

Sentiment in Tombstone was divided following the gunfight. The forces of law and order supported the Earps, extolling their bravery and courage under fire and emphasizing the need for a bold response to the Cowboy threat. Others were outraged, claiming that the Earps abused their badges in order to bring a bloody conclusion to a needless feud. The bodies of Tom, Frank, and Billy were on display outside the local undertaker's establishment, propped up beneath a sign that read "Murdered in the Streets of Tombstone." Thousands of mourners attended their funeral, and the town band led the cortege to the graveyard on Boot Hill.

Within a few days, the Earps and Holliday were charged with murder. Nine witnesses swore at the coroner's inquest that the Earps provoked the fight. The city council had already suspended Virgil as town marshal, pending the outcome of an investigation. Wyatt and Doc were arraigned, and bail was set at $10,000 for each of the defendants, including Virgil and Morgan, who were badly wounded and therefore excused from appearing in court. As required by territorial law, the initial step was a preliminary hearing, which began immediately. The sole legal question was whether the defendants would be held for trial in the district court.

The hearing convened before Judge Wells Spicer, who would eventually take the testimony of 30 witnesses in a proceeding that lasted nearly a month. Both sides approached the proceeding very much as though it were a full-scale trial. The prosecution called all of its available witnesses, subjecting them to cross-examination and apparently holding nothing in reserve. The defense responded in kind, going so far as to call two of the defendants, Wyatt and Virgil.

Ultimately, the charges were dismissed, allowing Hugh O'Brian, Kurt Russell, and Kevin Costner to grow wealthy through their exploitation of the life and legend of Wyatt Earp. During the actual trial, however, the outcome of the case was far from certain. In fact, at one point, Judge Spicer revoked bail for Wyatt and Doc and ordered them to jail on the prosecution's motion that "the proof so far was conclusive of murder."

Indeed, it is hard to understand how the prosecution could have failed to establish probable cause. To be sure, there was evidence of both guilt and innocence. As Judge Spicer put it, "witnesses of credibility" testified for both sides. Under those circumstances, a judge would ordinarily commit the case for trial and allow a jury to decide whom to believe. So where did the prosecutors go wrong? As it turns out, the answer lies in the theory of the case.

The prosecution started strong by calling William Allen, a friend of the McLaurys, who testified that he followed the Earps as they headed toward the corral. He heard one of them call out, "You sons of bitches, you have been looking for a fight." Allen went on to say that "Tom McLaury threw his coat open and said, 'I ain't got no arms.' " and that Billy Canton said, " 'I do not want to fight' and held his hands out in front of him."

The case against the Earps rapidly became clear. The Cowboys brandished no guns and posed no actual threat. Instead, it was the Earps who stalked the Cowboys, determined to have it out with them; the Earps fired before the Clantons and McLaurys even had a chance to surrender. As to the critical question of who shot first. Allen believed that Doc Holliday started the fight, stating that "the smoke came from him," and that the second shot also came from the Earp party.

Other damning witnesses followed, including Martha King, a Tombstone housewife who observed the lawmen on their way to the showdown. Before the fight ever started, she heard one of the Earps (probably Morgan) say, "Let them have it," to which Doc Holliday replied, "All right."

Perhaps the most compelling witness was Sheriff John Behan of Cochise County, a largely rural jurisdiction that included Tombstone. He was a well known rival of the Earps in politics and law enforcement, as well as a sometime associate of the Cowboys. Nonetheless, he was able to bring the prestige of his office to the witness stand. Testifying over a period of several days, Behan explained that he tried to stop the Earps from confronting the Cowboys, but they shoved him aside. Proceeding to the scene of the fight, he heard Wyatt yell, "You sons of bitches have been looking for a fight," and another of the Earps ordered the Cowboys to "throw up your hands." Then, according to Behan, the shooting began:

> I saw a nickelplated pistol in particular[,] [which] was pointed at one of the party. I think at Billy Clanton. My impression at the time was that Holliday had the nickelplated pistol. I will not say for certain that Holliday had it. These pistols I speak of were in the hands of the Earp party. When the order was [given] to "Throw up your hands," I heard Billy Clanton say, "Don't shoot me, I don't want to fight." Tom McLaury at the same time threw open his coat and said, "I have nothing" or "I am not armed," or something like that . . . My attention was directed to the nickelplated pistol for a couple of seconds. The nickelplated

> pistol was the first to fire, and instantaneously a second shot—two shots right together simultaneously—these two shots couldn't have been from the same pistol—they were too near together. The nickel-plated pistol was fired by the second man from the right, the third man from the right fired the second shot, if it can be called a second shot. Then the fight became general . . . The first two shots were fired by the Earp party.

(All quotations of the trial record are taken from *The O.K. Corral Inquest.* Edited by Alford Turner. College Station: Creative Publishing Co., 1981.)

Sheriff Behan added that at least two of the Cowboys, Ike Clanton (who survived) and Tom McLaury (who did not), were unarmed, and that "there was as many as eight or ten shots before I saw arms in the hands of any of the McLaury or Clanton party."

The capstone of the prosecution's case should have been the testimony of Ike Clanton, the only Cowboy who survived the gunfight. After giving his occupation as "stock raising and cattle dealer," he provided an account consistent with the other prosecution witnesses; a story filled with high drama and professions of personal courage. The Earps had bullied and intimidated the Clantons and McLaurys for nearly 24 hours before the battle, though Ike himself had "never threatened any of the Earps nor Holliday." Doc and Morgan fired the first shots; then Virgil and Wyatt loosed a barrage, despite the unarmed Cowboys' efforts to surrender. According to Ike, he heroically tried to take Wyatt out of the fight:

> He shoved his pistol up against my belly and told me to throw up my hands. He said, "You sonofabitch, you can have a fight!" I turned on my heel, taking Wyatt Earp's hand and pistol with my left hand and grabbed him around the shoulder with my right hand and held him for a few seconds. While I was holding him[,] he shot . . . I then went on across Allen Street . . . As I jumped into the door of the photograph gallery, I heard some bullets pass my head.

At this point, the prosecution's case was strong on details and weak on motive. A total of five separate witnesses had testified that the Earps started the fight and that the Cowboys were either unarmed, had tried to surrender, or both. Still, something was lacking.

It was truly unlikely that Judge Spicer, a law and order Republican, would conclude that the Earps were coldblooded killers who murdered the Cowboys for sport. After all, Virgil was a well respected lawman, holding the positions of both town and federal marshal, with no record of extravagant force. The other three men were his deputies and acted on his command. It was flatly unconvincing to claim that the lawmen were simply trigger-happy. The case against the defendants would be truly coherent only if the prosecution could explain why the Earps suddenly turned from peace officers into assassins. In other words, the prosecution needed a theory of the case.

At this point, it becomes necessary to digress. On March 15, 1881, the Tombstone-Benson stage was attacked by four bandits who killed the driver, Bud Philpot, as well as one of the passengers. A posse led by the Earps managed to track down and apprehend a man named Luther King, who confessed his involvement (though claiming he only held the horses) and implicated three others. The remaining three, still at large, were all known Cowboys: Harry Head, Billy Leonard, and Jim Crane.

Wyatt Earp's Deal

Some time later, Wyatt Earp made a deal with Ike Clanton. Suspecting that Ike might have information on the whereabouts of Jim Crane, Wyatt proposed to give Ike the hefty reward offered by Wells Fargo if Ike would snitch on his sometime pal. The deal had to be kept secret since Ike could hardly let it be known that he had agreed to inform on a fellow Cowboy. As for Wyatt, he was apparently willing to forego the reward money in exchange for an opportunity to arrest Crane. As Wyatt later explained, "I had an ambition to be sheriff of this county in the next election, and I thought it would be a great help to me with the people and businessmen if I could capture the man who killed Philpot."

The bargain between the Cowboy and the lawman fell through; nonetheless, it turned into a source of continuing friction between Wyatt and Ike. It also provided the missing link in the prosecution's case. Ike Clanton was therefore the only witness to offer an explanation of why the Earps would murder the Cowboys. He succeeding in filling the gap in the prosecution's theory, but his story was so incredible that it fatally undermined the prosecution's case.

Ike testified that Wyatt and Morgan had secretly confided in him that the Earps themselves, along with Leonard, Head, and Crane, were responsible for the stage holdup and the murder of Bud Philpot. Ike added that the Earps "piped off" $15,000 of stolen money to Doc Holliday (whom Ike later accused of being the man who actually shot Philpot). Wyatt, he continued, was fearful that Crane might squeal, and he therefore offered Ike $6,000 to help liquidate him. Unfortunately for Wyatt, Ike "would have nothing to do with helping to kill Crane."

Here was the missing motive. The Earps, having divulged their secret criminality to Ike Clanton, now had to eliminate him in order to avoid detection:

> I found out by Wyatt Earp's conversation that he was offering money to kill men that were in the attempted stage robbery, his confederates, for fear that Leonard, Crane and Head would be

> captured and tell on him, and I knew that ... some of them would murder me for what they had told me.

That explains why the Earps, and especially Holliday, fired so quickly, refusing the offer of surrender by the Clantons and McLaurys. It also explains Ike's earlier claim that Wyatt seemingly risked his life by firing at the unarmed, fleeing Ike Clanton rather than at the other Cowboys who drew their guns and returned fire. The validity of the prosecution's case now hung on the extraordinary tale of Ike Clanton.

The defense, of course, told a different story. Wyatt described the Clantons and McLaurys as dangerous criminals who contributed to the atmosphere of lawlessness in Tombstone. He outlined a long history of threats against the Earps by the Cowboys, many of which occurred in front of witnesses. "I knew all those men were desperate and dangerous men, that they were connected with outlaws, cattle thieves, robbers and murderers ... I was satisfied that Frank and Tom McLaury killed and robbed Mexicans in Skeleton Canyon." A prudent lawman could draw only one conclusion. "I naturally kept my eyes open and did not intend that any of the gang should get the drop on me if I could help it."

Wyatt was adamant that the Cowboys initiated the confrontation, repeatedly threatening the lives of Morgan, Doc, and Wyatt over a 24-hour period. Arriving at the lot behind the corral, Wyatt testified that "Frank McLaury's and Billy Clanton's six-shooters were in plain sight," and that Virgil yelled to the Cowboys "Throw up your hands, I have come to disarm you." Instead, according to Wyatt, Billy Clanton and both McLaury brothers went for their guns:

> I had my pistol in my overcoat pocket. When I saw Billy Clanton and Frank McLaury draw their pistols, I drew my pistol. Billy Canton leveled his pistol at me, but I did not aim at him. I knew that Frank McLaury had the reputation of being a good shot and a dangerous man, and I aimed at Frank McLaury. The first two shots which were fired were fired by Billy Clanton and myself, he shooting at me and I shooting at Frank McLaury. I don't know which was fired first. We fired almost together. The fight then became general.

Later, Wyatt became contemptuous: "The testimony of Isaac Clanton that I ever said to him that I had anything to do with any stage robbery ... or any improper communication whatever in any criminal enterprise is a tissue of lies from beginning to end."

Virgil's testimony was to the same effect. When he came in sight of the Cowboys, it was obvious that they were well armed. Billy Clanton and Frank McLaury had their hands on their six-shooters, and Tom McLaury was reaching for a Winchester rifle on a horse. Virgil called out, "Boys, throw up your hands. I want your guns." At that point, "Frank McLaury and Billy Clanton drew their six-shooters and commenced to cock them, and [I] heard them go 'click, click.' "

Virgil still attempted to avoid a fight "At that I said, throwing up both hands, with [a] cane in my right hand . . . 'Hold on, I don't want that.' " It was to no avail. Billy Clanton fired his pistol and Tom McLaury drew the rifle from its scabbard while using the horse as a shield. Virgil agreed that Wyatt had also fired an initial shot, simultaneously with Billy Clanton.

Judge Spicer delivered his opinion on November 30, 1881, and case theory made a great difference in his decision. Remarking that there were "witnesses of credibility" on both sides, Spicer nonetheless rejected the argument that the Cowboys were shot while trying to surrender. "Considering all the testimony together, I am of the opinion that the weight of the evidence sustains and corroborates the testimony of Wyatt Earp, that their demand for a surrender was met by William Clanton and Frank McLaury drawing, or making motions to draw[,] their pistols."

This conclusion alone should not have been sufficient to free the defendants. The proceeding was simply a preliminary hearing, held only for the purpose of determining whether there was sufficient evidence to warrant a full trial. Ordinarily, the existence of "witnesses of credibility" would be enough to allow the prosecution to go forward, with the weight of the evidence being left for decision by the jury. In this case, however, there was an added element. The Earps claimed lawful justification for the shootings. That, as Judge Spicer determined, was a legal defense well within his jurisdiction to decide:

> To constitute a crime of murder there must be proven, not only the killing, but the felonious intent. . . . [I]n looking over this mass of testimony for evidence upon this point I find that it is anything but clear.

Considering "the conditions of affairs incident to a frontier country," Judge Spicer required specific evidence of intent before he would order the lawmen to stand trial. Here, the prosecution faltered badly by offering only the allegations of Ike Clanton, which the judge rejected in their entirety:

> The testimony of Isaac Clanton that this tragedy was the result of a scheme on the part of the Earps to assassinate him and thereby bury in oblivion the confessions the Earps had made to him about "piping" away the shipment of coin by Wells, Fargo & Co. falls short of being sound theory, [on] account of the great fact most prominent in this matter, to wit: that Isaac Clanton was not injured at all and could have been killed first and easiest, if it was the object of the attack to kill him. He would have been first to fall, but as it was, he was known or believed to

be unarmed and was suffered, as Wyatt Earp testified, told to go away, and was not harmed.

This led inexorably to a single result. All charges against the Earps and Holliday were dismissed.

The prosecutors failed because they never presented a sustained counter-narrative to the Earps' story (and Spicer's evident assumption) of courageous law enforcement. To persuade Judge Spicer to rule against the "regularly or specially appointed" peace officers, contested assertions of partisan witnesses were bound to be insufficient. To win, the prosecution needed a compelling theory that explained not simply how but also why the Earps would murder the Cowboys.

One such theory has since been offered by historian Paula Mitchell Marks, who suggests that the fight may have grown out of the Earps' efforts to ingratiate themselves with Tombstone's financial interests, either to enhance Wyatt's chance of being elected county sheriff or simply to remain in the good graces of the local mine owners and businessmen. In either case, points could be made by coming down hard on the Cowboys and impressing the locals with their "tough brand of police work." Marks PM: *And Die in the West: The Story of the O.K. Corral Gunfight.* New York: William Morrow & Co., 1989.

So, when Ike Clanton showed up in Tombstone on October 26, mouthing threats and displaying his weapons, the Earps responded with force. The Clantons and McLaurys, however, did not have the good sense to get immediately out of town. Instead, they gathered at the O.K. Corral, two (and possibly three) of them armed, in seeming defiance of Virgil Earp's lawful, though excessive, authority. The Earps and Holliday then marched over to the lot on Fremont Street, perhaps intending only to intimidate the Cowboys or to administer beatings, but not with the settled purpose of committing murder. Unfortunately, things got out of hand: Either the Cowboys did not respond quickly enough, or the Earps and Holliday were too jumpy. Guns were drawn, and shots were fired—the first bullet coming from the volatile Doc Holliday. After that, the fight "became general," and the Cowboys' fate was sealed.

We will never know whether Marks's suppositions are historically true; they have been rejected by other researchers. As advocacy, however, her proffered theory has the advantage of plausibility. To sustain a finding of probable cause, Judge Spicer had to believe only that the Earps were overly aggressive and reckless, not that they were assassins. Consequently, Ike Clanton's wild charges would have been irrelevant to the case, making it far less likely that the prosecution would fall along with Ike's flimsy credibility. Of course, the great drawback to the theory is that it would only support a charge of manslaughter, not murder (at least against the Earps, a murder charge against Holliday might still have been a possibility). A tempered case was exactly what the prosecution needed in the first place. The murder charge was almost certain to fail, given the Earps' badges and Judge Spicer's predisposition.

The murder story was just too intricate, requiring that every dispute be determined in favor of the prosecution in order to justify a decision adverse to the Earps. Thus, the most cogent account of the Earps' guilt would have to focus on a lesser crime such as manslaughter—not as dramatic as outright murder, but still a serious felony.

In advocacy terms, the best cases are both simple and easy to believe, A simple story makes maximum use of undisputed facts while relying as little as possible on evidence that is either hotly controverted or inherently unbelievable. In the same sense, a story cannot be easy to believe if it depends on implausible arguments or if it requires proof that the opposing witnesses lied or falsified evidence. Trials can sometimes be won by stories that fail the tests of simplicity and ease, but it is an uphill struggle. The best and most effective trial theories encompass the entirety of the other side's case and still result in victory by sheer logical force.

A simple story actually seeks to narrow the scope of disagreement between the parties by incorporating (and accommodating) as many of the other side's facts as possible. No matter how vigorously presented, the murder case against the Earps and Holliday could never be simple. It required the resolution of too many contradictory facts: Who made the first move? How serious were the Cowboys' threats? If a judge were to believe Virgil and Wyatt on any one of these questions, any prosecution would fail. At trial, this is the cost of complexity.

A manslaughter prosecution, however, would have had the simple virtue of making most of those questions irrelevant. Indeed, it could have accommodated nearly all of Wyatt's and Virgil's testimony concerning Ike's threats, the march down Fremont Street, and even the eventual moment of truth. Imagine the prosecutor's final argument:

> Wyatt and Virgil Earp claim that the Clanton[s] and McLaury[s] reached for their guns, but sometimes you see what you want to see. After spending the previous night and morning brutalizing Ike Clanton and Tom McLaury, the Earps were ready for a showdown. They wanted to have it out with the Cowboys once and for all. So when Tom McLaury threw back his jacket to show that he was unarmed, the Earps and Holliday just couldn't wait to start shooting. Even a moment of calm hesitation would have shown that Tom had no weapon, but the defendants were all fired up. They didn't wait, they didn't think, they just started shooting. And that is manslaughter in this territory.

If the murder case was not simple, even less was it easy to believe, resting as it did on both implausible elements and the necessity of harsh judgments. Ike Clanton's outlandish story may have been the death knell of the prosecution's case. Of course, even improbable tales may sometimes be true, but it was just too much to ask Judge Spicer to believe that Deputy Marshal Wyatt Earp helped rob the Benson stage and confided the deed to the disreputable Ike.

The prosecution's case was not easy to believe for yet another reason. It required the judge to conclude that Wyatt and Virgil lied on the stand. In contrast, a manslaughter theory could have accommodated virtually all of the Earps' testimony, perhaps even turning it against them. For example, Wyatt testified that Frank McLaury and Billy Clanton had their six-shooters in "plain sight" as the Earps approached the Cowboys. When Virgil called for them to hold up their hands, "Billy Clanton and Frank McLaury commenced to draw their pistols." Wyatt continued, "I had my pistol in my overcoat pocket . . . When I saw Billy Clanton and Frank McLaury draw their pistols, I drew my pistol."

Wyatt also testified that he succeeded in getting off the first shot, an impressive achievement given that he had to pull his weapon out of his overcoat pocket, while Frank and Billy already had theirs out and in plain sight. Could it be that Wyatt was a bit readier to begin firing than he admitted or recalled? Perhaps the Cowboys were not really reaching for their pistols after all, as evidenced by the fact that Wyatt apparently had plenty of time to pull his six-shooter out of his pocket after he saw them move their hands. In either case, there is a feasible implication that Wyatt acted recklessly, shooting without thinking. Importantly, Judge Spicer could have come to that conclusion without assuming that Wyatt lied on the witness stand.

Trial lawyers understand how difficult it is to recreate the past even a few months or years following the events themselves. After nearly 120 years, it seems impossible to determine with exact certainty what happened in Tombstone that October afternoon. What does seem clear, however, is that the prosecution gambled on its theory choice—and lost.

Roald Hoffman
Why Buy That Theory?
91 AMERICAN SCIENTIST 9 (2003)[3]

The theory of theories goes like this: A theory will be accepted by a scientific community if it explains better (or more of) what is known, fits

[3] Footnotes and/or internal citations omitted.

at its fringes with what is known about other parts of our universe and makes verifiable, preferably risky predictions. . . .

But much that goes into the acceptance of theories has little to do with rationalization and prediction. Instead, I will claim, what matters is a heady mix of factors in which psychological attitudes figure prominently.

Simplicity

A simple equation describing a physical phenomenon (better still, many), the molecule shaped like a Platonic solid with regular geometry, the simple mechanism (A→B, in one step)—these have tremendous *aesthetic* appeal, a direct beeline into our soul. They are beautifully simple, and simply beautiful. Theories of this type are awesome in the original sense of the world—who would deny this of the theory of evolution, the Dirac equation or general relativity?

A little caution might be suggested from pondering the fact that political ads patently cater to our psychobiological predilection for simplicity. Is the world simple? Or do we just want it to be such? In the dreams of some, the beauty and simplicity of equations becomes a criterion for their truth. . . .

[T]here's no getting away from it; a theory that is simple yet explains a lot is usually accepted in a flash.

Storytelling

What if the world is complex? Here, symmetry is broken; there, the seemingly simplest of chemical reactions, hydrogen burning to water, has a messy mechanism. . . .

When things are complex yet understandable, human beings weave stories. We do so for several reasons: A→B requires no story. But A→B→C→D and not A→B→C→D *is* in itself a story. Second, as psychologist Jerome Bruner writes, "For there to be a story, something unforeseen must happen." In science the unforeseen lurks around the next experimental corner. Stories then "domesticate unexpectedness," to use Bruner's phrase.

Storytelling seems to be ingrained in our psyche. I would claim that with our gift of spoken and written language, this is the way we wrest pleasure, psychologically, from a messy world. . . .

Many theories are popular because they tell a rollicking good story, one that is sage in capturing the way the world works, and could be stored away to deal with the next trouble. . . .

Frameworks for Understanding

Stephen G. Brush has recently studied a range of fields and discoveries, to see what role predictions play in the acceptance of theories. Here's what he has to say about the new quantum mechanics: "Novel predictions played essentially no role in the acceptance of the most important physical theory of the 20th century, quantum mechanics. Physicists quickly accepted that theory because it provided a coherent deductive account of a large body of known empirical facts. . . ." Many theories predict relatively little (quantum mechanics actually did eventually) yet are accepted because they carry tremendous explanatory power. They do so by classification, providing a framework (for the mind) for ordering an immense amount of observation. . . .

The acceptance of theories depends as much on the psychology of human beings as on the content of the theories. It is human beings who decide, individually and as a community, whether a theory indeed has explanatory power or provides understanding. . . .

'Tis a Gift

The purpose of theory, Berson writes, is "to bring order, clarity, and predictability to a small corner of the world." That suffices. A theory is then a special gift, a gift for the mind in a society . . . where thought and understanding are preeminent. A gift from one human being to another, to us all.

POST-CLASS REFLECTION MEMO

Draft and submit a memo in response to the questions below:

- How will you take the lessons you have learned in class today about theory of the case or project and apply them to your work in representing clinic clients?
- How will your insights about the fundamental framing role of case theory affect your client representation over the next several days or weeks?

CHAPTER 9

COLLABORATION

LEARNING GOALS

The learning goals for this class include helping you to:

- Understand collaboration as an essential lawyering skill, and understand yourself as a contributor to a collaborative enterprise
- Understand and appreciate that individuals differ in terms of work styles and approaches to collaboration, and that every type of collaboration has both strengths and weaknesses
- Develop the capacity to plan for effective collaboration
- Recognize differences in approaches to collaboration and use those insights to develop effective collaboration plans
- Develop the capacity to identify collaboration challenges before they interfere with effective lawyering
- Develop a vocabulary that permits explicit conversations about challenges and potential improvements in a collaboration

DESCRIPTION OF CLASS

In this class, we will discuss collaboration as an essential lawyering skill. We will then engage in an exercise focused on exploring collaborative relationships within your clinic team and consider possible strengths, challenges, and concrete strategies for improvement.

ASSIGNMENT IN PREPARATION FOR CLASS

Take time to reflect on a collaborative experience you have had at work, in school, or in any other environment. Consider the following questions and jot down notes to bring to class (the notes are for yourself, to help guide your own thinking, and will not be distributed):

What did this experience teach you about the following:

- How you tend to approach working with a partner or team?
- The strengths you are likely to bring to a collaborative relationship?
- The weaknesses you are likely to bring to a collaborative relationship?
- How interpersonal differences affect collaboration?
- How interpersonal similarities affect collaboration?

READING ASSIGNMENT

1. *Collaborative Justice: How to Collaborate*, CENTER FOR EFFECTIVE PUBLIC POLICY, http://www.collaborativejustice.org/how.htm (2013).
2. Rhonda Muir, *The Importance of Emotional Intelligence in Law Firm Partners*, LAW PRACTICE MAGAZINE 60 (July/Aug. 2007).
3. Leigh Thompson, CREATIVE CONSPIRACY: THE NEW RULES OF BREAKTHROUGH COLLABORATION 120 (2013).

READINGS

Collaborative Justice: How to Collaborate
CENTER FOR EFFECTIVE PUBLIC POLICY (2013)

How to Collaborate

A Working Definition of the Term "Collaboration"

While we all recognize the challenges associated with collaboration, probably the one that receives the least amount of attention is the overuse of the [term], and therefore, the misinterpretation of the concept. The complexity of our work in the criminal justice field requires that we work together on a variety of issues—from offender management to community engagement and mobilization—and at a range of professional levels—from policy makers to front line staff. The fact that we call so many kinds of working together "collaboration" undervalues and underestimates the work involved in a genuine collaboration.

Chris Huxom [Creating Collaborative Advantage, London: Sage Publications (1996)] provides a helpful framework to describe the ways in which people engage work together.

- **Networking** is best described as exchanging information (i.e., agencies may meet to inform one another of their procedures, processes, restrictions, resources, and guidelines);
- **Coordinating** involves making slight alterations to activities to accommodate the needs of another (i.e., one agency might change their hours so that they have staff available to receive referrals from another agency); and
- **Cooperating** entails the sharing of resources (i.e., one agency may provide office space while another provides staff so that services can be co–located).

While these are all beneficial forms of working together, they are not the same as collaboration.

A working definition of collaboration is **joining together to make possible that which cannot be accomplished alone**. That is, collaboration allows partners to reach an aspiration that would be impossible to achieve without each member of the team working toward the same end. It requires the partnership and the commitment of all members working toward a common goal to succeed.

The Relationship Between Collaboration and Teamwork

[ ] Too often the problems we face are not reflections of a lack of knowledge or skill, but rather, a lack of understanding of the true nature of the problem to be addressed, and the resources at our disposal. Sometimes the necessary knowledge or resources rests with another—perhaps an individual, agency, or even a community—that could be mobilized in an effective way. But generally we fall short of identifying our assets, and even when we do know what their potential is, we have difficulty marshalling them in an effective way.

The information and tools that follow, therefore, are designed to help individuals and teams to understand clearly the work they are engaged in: the outcomes they seek, the values that guide them; the partnerships that will make success possible; the structures and methodologies that hold the greatest possibility for success; and the management of the relationships that are key to making the endeavor possible.

The Research on Effective Teams

In their pioneering work, Carl Larson and Frank LaFasto [TeamWork: What Must Go Right/What Can Go Wrong, Newbury Park, CA: Sage Publications (1989)] set out to understand the workings of effective teams. In conducting their research, they identified a variety of teams in a range of different environments—such as community action teams, project teams, sports teams, tactical teams, surgical teams, public health teams established to fight epidemics, and executive management teams. Their research process examined three distinct sample groups—a broad and varied group, a narrower and deeper hypothesis testing group, and a broader and more unusual saturation group—to find the answer to the question: "What do those teams that are highly successful have in common?" From this investigation, Larson and LaFasto developed a paradigm which involves eight characteristics that must be present for a team to be successful.

In our work with collaborating teams, the Larson and LaFasto paradigm of effective teamwork has proven to be exceptionally helpful in assessing a team's effectiveness, analyzing strengths, and identifying strategies to enhance collaboration. While their work did not focus specifically or even directly on criminal justice teams, it has demonstrated itself time and again as effective and useful with criminal justice teams of all varieties.

The Eight Characteristics of Highly Effective Teams

A Clear and Elevating Goal (Vision)

High performance teams have both a clear understanding of the goal to be achieved and a belief that the goal embodies a worthwhile or important result; teams with a 'clear and elevating goal' understand that whether the team succeeds clearly makes a difference.

Results-Driven Structure

The importance of structure is not in its presence or absence. More important is whether a structure is in place that is appropriate for the achievement of the performance objectives. To be successful, a team's structure should be designed around the results to be achieved.

There are three kinds of teams:

- *Problem resolution teams*—are established to resolve problems on an ongoing basis. Their most necessary feature is trust; members must believe in the integrity of their colleagues and feel secure in an atmosphere of collegiality and respect;

- *Creative teams*—are established to innovate. Their necessary feature is autonomy from systems and procedures. In other words, they must have the latitude to explore new possibilities and alternatives, be willing and able to abandon normative thinking, and serve as the incubator for new ideas; and
- *Tactical teams*—are established to execute a well-defined plan. Their most essential feature is clarity in task and an unambiguous role in the carrying out of the plan.

There are four necessary features to team structure:

- *Clear roles and accountabilities*—each member's relationship to the team is defined in terms of the role to be assumed and the results the role is to produce;
- *An effective communication system*—opportunities for team members to discuss team issues in a relaxed environment (social and informal interaction opportunities) are essential; methods for documenting issues raised and decisions made are important as well;
- *Monitoring performance and providing feedback*—establishing systems of checks and balances to assure that performance meets expectations is a must; and
- *Fact-based judgments*—objective and factual data should be the basis of the team's sound decision-making.

Competent Team Members

Competency is defined as the necessary skills and abilities to achieve the desired objective (technical competencies) and the personal characteristics required to achieve excellence while working well with others (personal competencies).

- Technical competencies are minimal requirements of any team. They include substantive knowledge, skills, and abilities related to the specific tasks to be accomplished.
- Personal competencies refer to the qualities, skills, and abilities necessary for individual team members to identify, address, and resolve issues.

There are three common features of competent team members:

- The essential skills and abilities to conduct the work;
- A strong desire to contribute; and
- The capacity to collaborate effectively.

Unified Commitment

A unified commitment is best characterized by "team spirit," or a sense of loyalty and dedication to the team. It is often exhibited by an unrestrained sense of excitement and enthusiasm for the team and its work; a willingness to do anything that has to be done to help the team succeed; and an intense identification with the people who are on the team.

There are two significant features of this characteristic:

- *Commitment to the effort*—teams do not excel without significant investment of individual time and energy; and
- *Unity*—group spirit and teamwork are indispensable to superior performance.

Collaborative Climate

A collaborative climate is most commonly described in the adage, "The whole is greater than the sum of its parts." Teams operating in a truly collaborative climate work well together, and trust is a mainstay virtue.

Trust is produced in a climate that includes three elements:

- Honesty (i.e., integrity and truthfulness);
- Consistency (i.e., predictable behavior and responses); and
- Respect (i.e., treating people with dignity and fairness).

Standards of Excellence

Standards define those expectations that eventually determine the level of performance a team deems acceptable. Standards determine the type of technical competency required, the amount of initiative and effort required, how people are expected to behave with one another, how firm the deadlines are, and how the results will be achieved. Ultimately, standards dictate the rewards for success and the consequences for failure.

Pressure to perform can come from a variety of sources:

- Individual standards;
- Team pressure;
- The consequences of success or failure (i.e., reaching the clear and elevating goal/vision);
- External pressure; and
- The team leader.

Three variables are integral to establishing and sustaining standards of excellence. They are the extent to which:

- Standards are clearly and concretely articulated;
- Team members require one another to perform according to the established standards of excellence; and
- A team exerts pressure on itself to improve.

External Support and Recognition

External support and recognition is measured by the extent to which those individuals and agencies outside the team who are capable of contributing to the team's success acknowledge and support the work of the team. (Interestingly, the external support and recognition factor seems to be more an effect of team success than a cause of it. It is noted more for its absence in poorly functioning teams than its presence in highly effective teams.)

Principled Leadership

Leadership can add tremendous value to any collaborative endeavor, even to the point of sparking the outcome with an intangible kind of magic. Effective leaders draw together the team's vision, a belief in the opportunity for change, and the ability to meaningfully involve others.

Effective leaders:

- Enlist others to embrace the vision;
- Create change; and
- Unleash the energy and talent of contributing members.

Rhonda Muir
The Importance of Emotional Intelligence in Law Firm Partners
LAW PRACTICE MAGAZINE 60 (July/Aug. 2007)[1]

"Law is human interaction in emotionally evocative climates. Any lawyer who can understand what emotions are present and why is at a tremendous advantage."□—Peter Salovey, President of Yale College and original Yale researcher on emotional intelligence

Law firms usually have a number of criteria for choosing who to invite into the partnership, but a traditionally sacrosanct factor is technical competence. In other words, the main concern is that partners be very

1 Footnotes and/or internal citations omitted.

good lawyers. So most firms try to hire the smartest law school graduates and then make the smartest of them partners, hoping thereby to secure the firm's reputation and future. Corporate America, however, has realized for nearly two decades that there is another type of competence involved in producing the highest bottom-line performance in organizations and it is not intellectual or analytical expertise but relational skills—in essence, managing emotions.

That conclusion has been supported by astonishing research in the fields of neuroscience and psychology, which demonstrates that emotional savvy enhances intellectual functioning and also opens access to critical additional abilities. In 1990 Yale researchers John D. Mayer and Peter Salovey published the first formal definition and experimental measurement of emotional intelligence (EI). Their research concluded that a combination of using emotion and thinking produces the most sophisticated analyses and decision making. Their findings were popularized by Daniel Goleman in his 1995 runaway best-seller, Emotional Intelligence: Why It Can Matter More than IQ.

EI involves recognizing your own and others' emotions, accessing the appropriate emotions at the appropriate time, understanding how emotions affect behavior, and knowing the best strategies for managing emotional situations.

So how do you recognize EI? It does not correlate with any particular personality trait, or translate into "being nice" or "liking people." But the lawyer who engenders strong loyalty from clients, associates and staff or those to whom others in the firm go for counsel on personal issues, conflicts and client imbroglios probably have higher EI. From management's standpoint, they are the ones who can truly hear what you are saying, including criticism, and respond reasonably. These kinds of partners are highly valuable assets that are not easily replaced by law firms.

Both the research and the experience of the corporate world offer valuable insights into how including EI as a criteria in making partners can improve your partnership and your firm in many ways.

Better Judgment and Higher Productivity

EI arguably accounts for as much as 80 percent of an individual's workplace success, more than raw intelligence and expertise combined. Studies at Harvard and elsewhere have shown that high IQ does not necessarily translate into high productivity, while the ability to "get along with people" has been found to be more critical than intelligence, decisiveness or job expertise in achieving bottom-line results. This indicates that emotionally intelligent partners will be among your strongest performers.

EI can also help lawyers quickly make accurate assessments. We feel before we think, and that feeling can be powerfully insightful, if it is accessible. A study involving a card game with four decks, two rigged to produce bad results, illustrates this beautifully. Most people take an average of 50 card tricks to identify the unlucky decks and 80 tricks before they can articulate that. However, it is clear from the participants' pulse and perspiration rates that they emotionally identify the problematic decks by the 10th card, 40 cards before their intellect does. The conclusion we can draw from this is that limited access to emotional data can leave lawyers out of touch with important information.

Data compiled from other studies across various industries also shows that high EI clearly hits the bottom line:

> Ninety percent of top performers across industries have high EI, whereas only 20 percent of low performers do.
>
> Insurance agents who score high on EI tests sell twice as much in policy premiums as agents who score lower.
>
> Managers at American Express Financial Advisors who complete an emotions training program achieve significantly higher rates of growth in funds under their management than do their untrained peers.
>
> Those who raise their EI are roughly 25 percent more productive than before.

Data also suggests that the emotionally intelligent are more likely to listen to and use feedback, helping them achieve even more over time.

Enhanced Business Development and Client Relationships

Both "finders" and "minders" can clearly benefit from higher levels of EI. According to professional services guru David Maister, "Ultimately, hiring a [law firm] is about confidence and trust. It is an emotional act." Supporting this, In-House Counsel magazine's 2006 ACC/Serengeti Managing Outside Counsel Survey reported that of the four reasons companies fire outside counsel, two are for deficiencies in "soft" skills—responsiveness and personality issues.

Thus, it follows that the advantage in both getting and keeping clients goes to the competent lawyer who can operate on a level of interpersonal interaction above the norm. Having emotionally intelligent partners courting your hoped-for clients provides the best chance of success, since these are the lawyers who are more likely to correctly identify client values, hear and respond to clients' stated and unstated concerns, and build a loyal relationship over time.

The Strength of 21st Century Leaders

Leadership, particularly of a business whose assets can walk out the door, is mostly a matter of influence. And influence in a law practice is built through individual relationships. Getting partners to work together, for example, cannot be done by fiat. The leader who can access, understand and manage his or her own emotions and those of others will be the one who can get optimal performance from the firm, making EI a very powerful driver of effective leadership.

A 2006 Altman Weil article identified five critical concerns of law firms, with people management being one of the highest. But the other four concerns—growth, competition, client service and pricing—also each require effective people management. Growth requires strong leadership and culture, office and practice integration. Competition is felt most dramatically in the war for talent, with quality people giving firms a competitive edge. Client service requires superior relationship skills. And even pricing is a function of service, which general counsels have consistently linked to people skills. It is the emotionally intelligent leader who is best equipped to make progress on all these fronts.

Managing a firm's people assets when they have the personality traits lawyers tend to exhibit is particularly challenging. High autonomy, skepticism and competitiveness are more likely to produce lone wolves than collaborators. The emotionally intelligent leader can help offset that tendency by connecting with others and supporting and promoting their success. In addition, EI at the top can be contagious—a positive managerial mood and the resultant enhanced general mood can go far both in improving employee performance and retention and reducing conflict.

As firms expand, EI will be even more critical. A recent study conducted by the Center for Creative Leadership found that the concept of effective leadership has changed over the past five years: 84 percent of those polled said leaders today are valued for collaboration skills, such as building and mending relationships, rather than solitary heroics, the standard five years ago. Specifically important is being able to "enhance co-worker relationships." This change is due, according to those surveyed, to the broader demands of leadership, which now go beyond one individual's capability and require collaboration across various boundaries.

More Effective Team Building

Perhaps the only need more pressing for law firms than identifying emotionally intelligent leaders is building emotionally intelligent teams. Having more emotionally intelligent partners puts firms farther along that path.

There is a revolution in law firms today toward an expanding use of teams—management, client, industry and marketing teams. Team effort produces happier clients, since the likelihood of someone connecting with the client on a personal level is enhanced, and there is more comprehensive expertise owing to the cross-fertilization of minds. Perhaps less obviously, members of teams report being happier than lone wolves, which in turn means more-dedicated, harder working teams.

Teams are more creative and productive when they achieve high levels of participation, cooperation and collaboration among their members. And at the heart of these conditions are emotions—bringing emotions to the surface, understanding how they affect the team's work, and encouraging behavior that builds relationships inside and outside the team. Consequently, team leaders with high EI are most likely to achieve the most collaborative and productive results.

Achieving the Edge Over the Competition

Ultimately, though, isn't it still essential to a firm's success that its partners be good at lawyering? Yes, of course. But in addition to being "good lawyers," emotionally intelligent partners have the interpersonal support and resilience to make unpopular but necessary decisions. They are able to hear bad news—from clients, litigants, regulators, other partners, associates and staff—and respond in an appropriate way so as to quickly reposition your case or deal, client, leadership or firm. They can glean the kind of information that could bring the firm to the next level, and they can model for younger lawyers the appropriate behavior, building the firm's EI capacity over time. Their ability to lead teams that identify the client's concerns, establish a strong relationship and get matters completed well, on time and on budget can mean the difference between success and failure in an increasingly competitive and global legal market.

Leigh Thompson
CREATIVE CONSPIRACY: THE NEW RULES OF BREAKTHROUGH COLLABORATION
(2013)[2]

Bono is a superstar in the music world. In 2011, he wrote the music and lyrics for the musical *Spider Man: Turn Off the Dark*—at $75 million dollars, the most expensive show ever produced on Broadway. However, Bono is not used to failure. And that was a big problem when *Spider Man* was declared a

2 Footnotes and/or internal citations omitted.

spectacular flop in early reviews. Bono and his U2 bandmate, The Edge, first began collaborating with renowned director Julie Taymor on the music for the show in 2002. But Bono came to regret this collaboration. "The hours and weeks and months . . . If we thought it would take this long, there is not a chance on earth we would have done it." However, throughout the collaboration, Bono retained faith in Taymor and her talent. But when the show opened in preview, critics savaged its plot as "incoherent" and "boring," which cut Bono to the core. In hindsight, Bono wishes he had spoken up about his doubts. However, he self-silenced because he feared that Taymor would walk out of the show if he criticized her—he felt that he could not be open with her.

The opening example reveals how people—even superstars—are terribly afraid of conflict. They don't want to rock the boat, even when millions of dollars are on the line and their inner voice is screaming for them to say something. As it turns out, *Spider Man* recovered from its early failures and has since been breaking box office records. So this is also a case in point that teams can recover from early failures—if they are willing to engage in the process of healthy conflict.

Conflict in a team is inevitable. But recognizing it and making it work for you in a team is anything but easy. Most people don't like conflict and so they don't want to deal with it; and when they do, they immediately want to extinguish it. So, repeat after me: *conflict is a sign of a high-performing team.* Now, say it like you mean it!

When I was a young assistant professor at the University of Washington, one of my dearest colleagues was John Gottman; you may know him as the world-renowned marriage and parenting researcher. In his long-term, cutting-edge studies, Gottman found that the couples with the strongest marriages—the ones that endure over time—are the couples that fight. Yes, that's right. They fight; they don't avoid conflict. However, there is a particular *way* these couples fight. They fight *fairly.* For example, consider the difference between one partner saying, "*I don't trust you. You are a creep*!" versus, "*I am really angry and I feel that I have lost trust*!" The first example is a personal attack; one spouse calls the other a name ("creep"). In the second example, the spouse has communicated anger *without* a personal attack. For Gottman, one of the keys to a successful marriage is the separation of pure anger from personal attacks. I argue that there is a parallel for teams—people in teams spend a lot of time with each other and get in each other's way, just as the partners in a long-term relationship.

Similarly, in my studies of negotiation, I have discovered that win-win outcomes result when negotiators are tough, ask penetrating questions, drill down for the core issues, and are hard on the problem, not the people. In fact, when negotiators are too polite and avoid sensitive topics, they are more likely to settle upon lose-lose outcomes.

In one of my research projects with Erika Peterson, we observed how teams of friends negotiate and compared them with teams composed of strangers. At first blush, it would seem that teams of friends would have a distinct advantage over teams composed of people who had no working relationship. Well, we were wrong. Teams of friends were excessively preoccupied about their relationships, and this interfered with their ability to focus on the task of negotiating. Things got even worse when the friends needed to depend on one other for information and when they had to report to a boss. In this case, teams composed of complete strangers actually reached more win-win agreements than did the teams of friends. Excessive concern for the relationship effectively shut down the ability of the teams to search for and integrate valuable information. Being polite is not conducive to the creative crafting of win-win negotiations.

The same is true for creative teamwork. In a study of seventy-one IT project teams, creativity was highest at moderate levels of *task conflict*—differences and disagreements on ideas, opinions, and interpretations of facts within the team. In contrast, *relationship conflict* deals with interpersonal conflict between the people in the group rather than the task they are working on. The importance of a moderate amount of task conflict in a team is particularly important when the group is in an early phase. Thus, it is important to set the stage for disagreement early on in the life of a team.

Fear of Conflict

Unfortunately, most people, particularly Americans, are afraid of conflict. Why? There are two major reasons.

First, we don't know how to separate the people from the problem. When we are attacked or threatened, our defense systems go into overdrive, and we usually respond by attacking the person who attacked us. This, of course, leads to an escalating spiral of tensions. To combat this pattern, we need some lessons on how to attack the *problem*, not the *person*. One of my colleagues has an effective behavioral technique for dealing with conflict. Whenever she feels that someone is attacking her, she takes one small step to the side and visualizes the angry words from the attacker going over her shoulder, rather than in her face.

Apparently, she is onto something big. My colleague Roderick Swaab at INSEAD suspected that visual contact between men who are on opposite sides of a negotiation table would lead to more aggression than if these men did not have visual access to each other. So, Swaab had men negotiate with either direct visual contact or no visual contact. All men then engaged in the same negotiation, with the same stakes, bottom lines, and so on, to ensure that any differences in the negotiated outcomes would not be due to economic factors, but rather psychological factors. As it turned out, the men who were in visual contact experienced an increase in testosterone levels.

Apparently, this physiological effect occurs because people, and men in particular, are hardwired to go into fight mode when they face a competitor. So, men who had direct visual contact essentially initiated an animal-stare-down with one another, tensions rising. The increases in testosterone led to more aggressive behavior and less mutually beneficial, creative outcomes. In contrast, the absence of direct visual contact paved the path toward more mutually beneficial agreements.

A second reason we avoid conflict is that we want to be liked. In this regard, most people subconsciously (and, as it turns out, mistakenly) assume that if they initiate conflict, others won't like them.

Code Cracking

Because of the inherent difficulties in navigating conflict, people often use indirect forms of communication rather than direct communication to convey what they mean. I refer to the use of indirect communication in conflict as *conflict code.* Conflict code is like a different language—if you don't know the code, something is certainly going to be lost in interpretation. The problem with using conflict code is that people on the receiving end are required to engage in several mental contortions to attempt to figure out what the other person means. This requires a lot of needless information processing, and receivers become exasperated or just downright confused. In short, they don't know how to crack the code. For example, consider a conflict in a work group in which one person really wants "Dan" to leave the team. There are at least nine different ways to communicate this to Dan, ranging from the blunt and direct to the nuanced and indirect:

1. Dan, leave the project team.
2. Dan, we're wondering whether it might be best if you left the team.
3. Dan, we're thinking that we don't need your involvement in the team at this point.
4. Dan, we're wondering if your talents might be best utilized elsewhere.
5. Dan, we're thinking that the team is ahead of schedule and does not require its original staffing.

6. Dan, have you thought about involving yourself in some of the new projects and lessening your involvement in others?
7. Dan, many of the original projects are being reconfigured; yours might be one that is affected.
8. Dan, the team has been able to take on the project, thanks to your early involvement.
9. Dan, we were hoping you would help us out with some of these new projects.

The first statement is direct and to the point; the subsequent statements are increasingly indirect, requiring Dan to have greater and greater insight into the unspoken intentions of the speaker. We have found that most people prefer to receive direct communication, but (falsely) believe that others are best served by using indirect, softer messages. Thus, there is a double standard.

According to Kellogg professor Vicki Medvec, *the illusion of transparency* is the belief that our thoughts, feelings, and intentions are clearer than they actually are. Most people believe that they are better communicators than they really are. Similarly, most people believe that their intentions and goals are more apparent than is actually the case. The illusion of transparency leads to problems for creative collaboration when team members are confused about what others are communicating. As a case in point, consider the failed launch of the *Mars Climate Orbiter* in 1999, in which a failure to communicate cost NASA's Jet Propulsion Laboratory (JPL) $125 million. Lockheed Martin engineers sent the orbiter's navigation information to JPL in Pasadena using the English measurement—*pounds of force*. But JPL had programmed its computers to calculate orbital navigation parameters and thruster firings using metric *newtons of force*. Neither group saw this problem because they thought their communications were transparent!

The remedy is to use more direct forms of communication and constantly check your understanding. Successful collaboration requires that people be in a heightened state of communication. In my own work with clients and students, I have gotten into the habit of summarizing what I think we have agreed to and have repeatedly found that my understanding is sometimes sorely lacking. Fortunately, this is quickly rectified at the end of the conversation, but could create a collaboration nightmare if too much time has passed!

The Mismanagement of Agreement

As a native Texan, since the first time I heard the fateful story of Jerry Harvey's trip to Abilene, I have been wary of team decision making. While spending quality time with his in-laws and extended family in

Coleman, Texas, one hot July day, management scientist Jerry Harvey witnessed a curious group dysfunction. Things started very innocently. Everybody was enjoying cold lemonade and the company of family on the porch. Suddenly, someone casually suggested that the entire family could drive to Abilene for ice cream. Despite the fact that Abilene was over fifty miles away and the only means of transportation was an unairconditioned car, the family members each nodded their heads slowly, saying they thought the idea was just fine. Several hours later, after a sweat-soaked crammed car ride across the Texas desert, the family returned to the comfort of their porch. After a long silence, somebody finally said, "That was fun . . ." That apparently was the last straw. One person finally spoke up and said, "Actually I was miserable." Eventually everybody confessed that they had thought taking the drive was a terrible idea and didn't want to go at all, but didn't want to rock the boat. Why didn't they say anything hours earlier—before packing into the car and driving? According to Harvey, everyone falsely assumed that others wanted to go—a form of *pluralistic ignorance.* If the creative team does not speak up, they are also doomed to make arduous trips to Abilene.

Harvey's experience reveals the common tendency for groups to make less-than-optimal decisions. It also points to the fact that people in teams don't speak up and challenge one another because they are afraid of rocking the boat. When it comes to creative thinking, the last thing we want is to drive to Abilene. The group would have been much better off enjoying the porch and the lemonade. Yet so often, organizations and teams repress their reservations, agree for the sake of avoiding feared conflict, and end up with a less-than-rewarding process—and often a collectively disastrous decision.

Neutralizing Alpha-Dominant People

Another reason teams often experience conflict is that people are unhappy with the allocation of the scarcest of team resources: time. The next time you go to a team meeting, surreptitiously get out a sheet of paper and bring a watch. Record who talks and for how long, and at the end of the meeting, add up how many minutes each person had the floor. If your meetings are anything like the hundreds studied by management scientists, you probably noticed that a minority of people did a majority of the talking, The rest of the folks did not get a word in edgewise!

This problem is known as the *uneven communication problem.* There are a few dominant people in most groups who control and monopolize the discussion. For example, in a typical four-person group, two people do 62 percent of the talking. In a six-person group, three people do 70 percent of the talking; and in an eight-person group, three people do 70 percent of the talking. The topper is that the dominant people do not realize this. In fact, they vehemently argue that the meetings are egalitarian. They lack self-awareness.

The question becomes: Why are the rest of us here? A dysfunctional self-fulfilling prophecy starts to unfold week after week in these meetings: the dominant people begin to feel that the silent people are unprepared or simply don't have any opinions, so they dominate more; similarly, the quiet folks feel that it is futile to try to be heard, so they stop trying. Left unchecked, this creates a self-perpetuating doom loop in the group. Team members may blame one another for the unsatisfactory team meeting. In order to get the most out of collaboration, it is important to neutralize the too-dominant people and encourage the too-submissive people. However, just saying, "Shut up" or "Speak up" does not work. We need a more effective technique. . . .

Conflict Sweet Spot

As you might sense, relationship conflict is generally not productive. Task conflict is often (but not always) productive. However, although too little or too much task conflict can thwart effectiveness, there is a "sweet spot" where moderate amounts of task conflict have beneficial effects. In one investigation, top management teams in 109 US hospitals examined the relationship between the amount of task conflict on the team and the teams' decision quality and found teams with moderate amounts of conflict were the most effective. This section introduces methods to ensure that teams engage in the right amount of conflict.

There is an apparent contradiction in the advice given to team leaders. On the one hand, teams and leaders are strongly advised by decision scholars to introduce devil's advocates, debate, and critical thinking into group meetings. On the other hand, creativity researchers admonish teams to set aside all evaluation and judgment and banish devil's advocates. Indeed, one of Alex Osborn's cardinal rules of effective brainstorming was to eliminate judgment and evaluation of ideas. Thus, leaders are the victims of a mixed message: "*Don't criticize others, yet engage in dissent!*" Which is correct? As it turns out, debate and competing views have positive value and stimulate divergent, creative ideas. . . .

What's Your "Tell"?

Most people have a characteristic style of dealing with conflict in their personal and professional lives. I call this your *conflict tell.* Frankly, the way we deal with conflict with a boss is not likely to be dramatically different from how we deal with conflict with a spouse. To begin your self-discovery process, think of a significant conflict you have recently had with someone you care about (i.e., not a one-off conflict with an airline attendant or service manager at a hotel, etc.). Rather, think about a long-term coworker, teammate, or superior. If necessary, think about your spouse! Of the four following behaviors, which would you say best characterizes how you behaved during that conflict?

> **Avoid:** You ignored the conflict; avoided the other person to the extent you were able to do so; wrote the other person off; circumvented a discussion because it seemed fruitless, hopeless, too painful, not worth your time, etc.
>
> **Rationalize:** You tolerated the relationship; rationalized the other person's behaviors; hoped the situation would resolve itself; tried to be understanding and accepting of the difficult situation; maybe even made excuses for the other person (e.g., "If he was not jetlagged, I'm sure that he would have thanked me for getting the project done on time.").
>
> **Attack:** You engaged in direct combat; stepped right up and told the other person off; recruited whatever resources were necessary to stand your ground and block or thwart the other person.
>
> **Engage:** You attempted to initiate a clarifying discussion with the other person; talked about your goals; acknowledged your own faults; separated the past from the future.

These four patterns represent how people often deal with interpersonal conflict. And your signature conflict style at home is often what you bring to work. Thus, if you often retreat from conflict at work or attempt to tune the other person out, you are probably doing this at home as well. The key thing to think about is: what behavior are you reinforcing in the other party? In other words, if you are engaging in avoidance, the other person has no doubt gotten the message that you are unavailable.

Conversely, if you use attack mode, chances are you have created a boxing match with the other party. This is what is meant by an *escalating conflict spiral.*

If you have rationalized the conflict and tried to keep a stiff upper lip, you have not been honest with yourself or the other party. There is never a right time for conflict. Conflict is always inconvenient. But if you don't take care of it, it is going to rear its head in an ugly way.

So, what course of action is best to take? An abundance of evidence suggests that it is only through engagement that conflict can result in productive outcomes. Avoidance, rationalization, or outright attacks are not optimal for solving conflict. People who use avoidance suppress conflict. If you suppress conflict, it often manifests itself in very unpleasant ways, such as poor health, passive-aggressive behavior, and the deterioration of relationships. Those who rationalize conflict are bound to eventually reach their breaking point. By making excuses for the other party, we are not treating them with the respect they ultimately deserve. The problem is that most people don't know how to start productive engagement because they are afraid or quite simply, have given up hope.

One of my favorite interview questions is, "Tell me about a conflict you had with someone at work and what you did to resolve it." If the job candidate answers, "I don't have conflicts with people," then I'm immediately suspicious. If they say that the people with whom they have had conflict with in their organizational career have been psychopaths (and proceed to give me full-blown personality profiles), then they lack self-awareness. If they say that they ignored these people, hoped they would change, or attacked them, I also score them below average. Why? People who are emotionally intelligent realize that conflict is inevitable in the workplace and they deal proactively with conflict (rather than reactively, passively, or aggressively).

The key to successful conflict management begins with self-awareness. If you are unaware that you are feeling angry, misunderstood, unappreciated, or defiant, you will be unable to move forward with proactive conflict management.

Once you have become self-aware, the next step is to inform the team of what is going on. The main principle to keep in mind here is that you need to take ownership of your beef with the team and avoid making the assertion that they have "caused" your problem.

To make this concrete, let's take the case of Lisa, who feels that the team makes an inordinate number of requests and demands of her and does not ask her about how this will affect her workload. In short, Lisa feels unappreciated, not respected, and "dumped on." What should Lisa do?

> **Don't say:** "I am fed up with how you guys are dumping on me. You don't show me any respect and you don't appreciate all that I do and I'm at the end of my rope and I won't take it anymore."
>
> **Do say:** "I feel frustrated and unappreciated when I get requests to do work that is in addition to what we have previously discussed. I want to discuss how to make things work better."

Engagement

Let's suppose you have decided to not avoid conflict and not rationalize it away. You feel like attacking, but instead you have committed yourself to having a real conversation. How do you begin? The phrase "Talk to Joe productively about our conflict" is not in anyone's Outlook calendar!

You don't want to ambush the other party. Instead, you need a *lead-in* to initiate engagement. Some of my favorite lead-ins, which have been pilot-tested by plenty of my clients and students, are:

- Harry, I would like to have a level two conversation about the project and check signals. What is a good time? I will work around your schedule.
- Susan, I feel uncomfortable talking about the project, but I'm unhappy with the current situation and suspect you might feel the same way. I'm hoping we can work out a time to check signals.
- Chris, I need to talk to you about something that is bothering me. I want to try to work this out before I start feeling resentful.

Once you have led into the conversation and carved out a time to talk, make sure you speak to this person, keeping to the following guidelines:

- **Use verbs, forget the adjectives:** Adjectives get us into trouble. It is much better to use verbs or behavioral descriptions. For example, compare phrases like "You are controlling" and "You are judgmental" (adjectives) with "I was upset when you did not consult me" and "I was taken aback when you criticized me in the meeting last Thursday," which reference an action or behavior. So, be descriptive via referencing behaviors and actions rather than evaluative. By focusing on behaviors and actions rather than internal states, the receiver of feedback is able to better change their behavior. Consider the difference between, "You seem lazy and uninvolved at work" versus "You arrive fifteen minutes late and you don't ask for others' help in projects." The former is blaming and immediately puts the other person on the defensive. The second is fact-based.
- **Be specific, not general:** Do not use the terms, "You always . . ." or "You never . . ." but rather, "Sometimes . . ." or preferably, "Last Wednesday . . ."
- **Speak for yourself:** We often show our anger and resentment by forming coalitions against someone. For example, consider a colleague who approaches a business associate and says, "You know, several people were talking about how we don't like how you are allocating the budget . . ." It is important to speak only for yourself. Otherwise, the person might become so defensive that he or she will be unable to hear the substance of your message. Do not say,

"Everybody thinks . . ." or "Everybody feels the same way I do." Instead, speak for yourself.

- **Ideally, find something positive to say:** People don't get enough positive feedback. So find something you actually do admire about this person—or something she does better than others—and compliment her.
- **Express optimism about change:** It is very important to emphasize that you not only care about the other person, but you believe that he has the power and ability to change and develop. Carol Dweck cites the belief in one's own ability to adapt and learn as the single most important key to success. For this reason, people who believe their skills are innately determined are less resilient than people who believe their skills are malleable.

Your Brain on Feedback

Most people say they want to hear the truth about how they are perceived, but in fact, it is often so frightening to get feedback that we don't react in a way that allows us to benefit. We often go into a flight-or-fight mode.

I get more questions about *giving* feedback than almost any other topic. What is interesting, however, is that I get very few questions about *receiving* feedback. One of the first principles I teach my students is that to be entitled to offer feedback to someone, you must be open to receiving feedback. The first principle when someone offers you feedback is to *thank them*. Think of it this way: someone cares enough or thinks you are important enough to bother to do something about. So, express gratitude when someone offers you feedback. Feedback is a gift, so say thank you or, even better, send a note or card.

The second principle is to be open to feedback. Don't ask, "How am I doing?"; ask "What can I work on?" Signal openness to feedback. However, just because you might see yourself as a person who can accept feedback, it in no sense guarantees that you are signaling that you are open to receiving feedback. And if you are hoping that your casual remark to your staff and subordinates that they should let you know if they have any feedback will get them to really speak their minds—well, just forget that. Rather, the burden is squarely on you to set the appropriate stage to receive feedback.

For example, Leo Babauta asked his readers for feedback to improve his blog, *Zen Habits*. After receiving a heavy dose of critical feedback, he returned all e-mails and thanked the readers for their comments. Similarly, Ken Mills, CEO of creative media company Mills James, solicited direct feedback from his employees when the company began expanding. He instituted a series of nonmanagerial employee meetings where feedback (and criticism) could be leveled without fear of reprisal. He admits that criticism of a personal nature, though sometimes necessary, can be a tough pill to swallow. "Sometimes I get depressed after these meetings. But I think the main thing is, that even more than what you do, is that the people feel like they are being heard. That goes a long way."

Here are three guidelines that will help you process feedback:

- **Ask for examples:** Remember that the people offering you feedback may not follow the guidelines of constructive (informational) feedback. That's okay. So, if they are using evaluative language, then don't lecture them about the importance of using behavioral examples, just ask them to give you examples. If they can't come up with any, then refer to meetings in the recent past and ask for them to give feedback pertaining to that situation or meeting.
- **Separate agreement from understanding:** Just because a person is offering you feedback does not mean you need to agree with it. It also does not mean you need to argue with this person. Rather, you can probe for understanding and set aside the question of whether you agree or not. I will warn you that this is hard to do, but think about these sentence stems, "I'm not sure I can agree with that or not, at least until I get some more examples of the controlling behavior you are referring to. Can we talk about whether you saw such behavior in the new program launch?" or perhaps, "I'm not sure I see it the same way you do, but can you give me some more examples that I can think about?"
- **Focus on the future; do not attempt to justify the past:** Most of the time, people become very defensive about the criticism that others offer them. Thus, they tend to dig up the past, explain and justify and rationalize their behavior, which really serves no purpose. However, it is a far more effective use of everybody's time to focus on what can be done in the future so as not to repeat past missteps.

Trust and Respect

People on teams need to care and to trust each other. Trust and respect are both important for teams, but they are not the same thing. *Trust* is the willingness of a person to rely on another person in the absence of monitoring or supervision. Conversely, *respect* is the level of esteem a person has for another.

To measure the amount of *trust* you have in your team, how much do you agree with the following statements?

1. I trust my teammates.
2. I have little faith that my teammates will consider my needs when making decisions.
3. I believe that my teammates are truthful and honest.

If you answered yes to items 1 and 3, but no to item 2, then you have high trust in your team.

To assess the amount of *respect* for your team, indicate how much you agree or disagree with these statements:

1. I think highly of my teammates' character.
2. This team sets a good example.
3. Our team does things the right way.
4. My team deserves my consideration.
5. I admire my teammates.
6. I am proud to be part of my team.
7. I think my teammates have useful perspectives.
8. My teammates usually have good reasons for their beliefs.
9. People on my team have well-founded ideas.
10. I hold my team in high regard.
11. I think highly of my team members.
12. Our team has reason to be proud.
13. I respect my teammates.

If you answered the majority of these questions with "true" or "I highly agree," that is a good indication that you have respect for your teammates. If you answered the majority of questions with "false" or "I disagree," that is an indication that respect is lacking.

Here's another way to think of the difference between trust and respect: suppose your colleague has failed his pilot's license test three times because he has an uncorrectable vision problem. However, he is a wonderful, generous person who is very smart. Most rational people would never get in a plane with him if he were to fly it because he lacks competence. We trust his intentions, but we don't respect his competence. We are (wisely) unwilling to make ourselves vulnerable when we don't respect someone's competence. Now, imagine you have another colleague who is an expert, decorated pilot, but knows that you have queasy stomach. You have occasionally wondered whether this person wishes to intimidate you or make you sick to your stomach. You would most likely not board her plane—not because of a competence issue, but because you don't trust her intentions. The first example is a respect issue; the second example is a trust issue. Ideally, we need both trust and respect in our teams. Teams high in respect but low in trust often appear as collections of individualists, afraid of exposing their vulnerabilities for fear they might be exploited. Conversely, teams high in trust but low in respect are safe but ineffective because they don't see much value in the contributions of their teammates, even if they are well intentioned.

People need to recognize the expertise of others (respect others' competence) and also trust their intentions. Trust is the willingness to make yourself vulnerable to achieve a greater goal. People in teams size up how "safe" they feel in bringing up certain subjects and seeking assistance from their team. *Psychological safety* is the extent to which people feel that they can raise issues and questions without fear of being criticized, scorned, or rebuffed.

What does it take to develop the collaborative spirit in people? Trust is critical for effective collaboration. Trust occurs when people are willing to be *vulnerable* in their relationships with others.

Many people have a difficult time being vulnerable with their teams. When we depend on others, we need to trust their skill and we need to trust their intentions. That is the only way we really learn. However, just like the airplane pilot example, we need to be judicious about whom we put our trust in.

There appears to be at least one caveat to the trust-is-good-for-creativity mandate. In one investigation, people were either exposed to subliminal distrust messages—below the threshold of their conscious awareness or subliminal trust messages—again, below the threshold of their awareness. If you ask these folks, they will tell you they were not aware of seeing anything. However, their brain took in the subliminal message and this led to an interesting twist: those who had been exposed to the subliminal distrust message were more likely to display cognitive flexibility—the opposite of rigid thinking! Why? Distrust provokes people to think about nonobvious alternatives to potentially deceptive appearances. Thus, even though people were not even consciously aware that they had been subliminally exposed to distrust, their brains started to spontaneously solve a problem by thinking outside of the boundaries!

POST-CLASS REFLECTION MEMO

Draft and submit a memo in response to the questions below:

What are three concrete strategies, in addition to those you identified with your partner(s) in class, that you will consider using to improve your collaborative relationship as you represent clinic clients?

HANDOUTS

Collaboration Spectrum Sheet

A	Harmony	1	2	3	4	5	Surfacing and Resolving Differences
B	Group Performance	1	2	3	4	5	Individual Performance
C	Internal Control	1	2	3	4	5	External Control
D	Creative/Intuitive	1	2	3	4	5	Logical/Planner
E	Task/Product	1	2	3	4	5	Relationship/Process
F	Tradition	1	2	3	4	5	Change
G	Introverted Thinker	1	2	3	4	5	Extraverted Thinker
H	Oral Communication	1	2	3	4	5	Written Communication
I	"Yes, but . . . "	1	2	3	4	5	"Yes, and . . . "
J	Deliberative Space	1	2	3	4	5	Interruption
K	Quick	1	2	3	4	5	Deliberative
L	Deadline Critical	1	2	3	4	5	Deadline Advisory
M	Detail-Oriented	1	2	3	4	5	Big-Picture Oriented
N	Humorous	1	2	3	4	5	Serious
O	Commit	1	2	3	4	5	Keep Options Open
P	Private	1	2	3	4	5	Open Book
Q	Instinct	1	2	3	4	5	Analysis
R	Visual	1	2	3	4	5	Oral
S	Earnest	1	2	3	4	5	Sarcastic

Guide for Completing Collaboration Spectrum Sheet

Please circle the answer that is closest to your point of view in each of the five areas.

A. Harmony or Surfacing and Resolving Differences

1. Disagreement is to be avoided at all costs.
2. Maintaining harmony is the primary value; anything can be worked out through the informal network without verbal conflict or embarrassment.
3. I don't like conflict, but I am willing to engage in it when it is necessary to get the job done.
4. Conflict can be creative and productive, but it should be well managed.
5. Disagreements must be aired; harmony is secondary and is restored through direct verbal resolution.

B. Group or Individual Performance

1. I strongly prefer working in groups, and I am always careful to include people who need to be there or who may feel that they are being left out.
2. I like group work because of the broad range of input it brings to the issues.
3. I think sometimes group work is useful, depending on the task.
4. We can spend too much time in groups, losing focus and clouding the issues.
5. Groups are time wasters; I'd far rather work alone.

C. Internal or External Control

1. Fate is in our hands; we can identify and solve any problem with the assistance of analytical techniques and formalized problem-solving skills.
2. I can usually have an effect on my environment.
3. About half the time I have control over a situation, and half the time I just have to live with it.
4. The plan is pretty well set, but I can control how I respond to it.

5. Most issues are resolved by someone more senior than I; my job is to make the best of the plan.

D. Creative/Intuitive or Logical/Planner

1. Making a plan at an early stage stifles creativity.
2. Usually plans emerge as I learn more about what work is needed.
3. Plans should not be set in stone and should be easily and regularly evaluated and revised.
4. Established project/case goals should guide the progress of all work.
5. It is essential to create a plan before beginning a project/case.

E. Task/Product or Relationship/Process

1. We're here to do a job. If we are to be competitive, we have to focus on the task.
2. We try to move quickly and get the job done, even if we also have to work with people we don't much care for.
3. How we interact with other team members has an impact on the product; I try to consider both.
4. We can't do anything without people; the best decision must first take people into consideration.
5. It isn't what we do but how we do it that counts. The best decision is useless if the process has been bad; it won't work.

F. Tradition or Change

1. If something isn't broken, don't fix it.
2. If something isn't working, we should fix it but only after we are really sure it won't work.
3. If something is broken, it will take care of itself. All things seek balance if we don't tinker with them.
4. Change is usually creative and good; the status quo makes us lazy thinkers.
5. Change is almost always productive. It generates fresh ideas, products, and programs.

G. Introverted Thinker or Extraverted Thinker

1. Before I offer suggestions or ideas, I work them out so that I am sure about what I mean. Brainstorming is usually not fun for me.
2. Once I have thought through a problem, I am fairly sure that I have considered all of the options and am pretty attached to my idea.
3. I enjoy discussing ideas with others but worry when some of those ideas are half-baked.
4. I enjoy thinking through issues with others and feel comfortable having tentative ideas that I can easily reject.
5. I use the communication process to develop my ideas. I love to brainstorm.

H. Oral Communication or Written Communication

1. Communicating orally is the best way to ensure that I am understood because I can answer any questions that I might not have anticipated.
2. Being forced to write out my ideas is often difficult because it slows down the process and can be cumbersome.
3. Both oral and written communication come easily to me.
4. I enjoy the process of writing because it helps me think more precisely. If I write it, I know it.
5. Writing controls outcomes so it is essential to any meaningful communication.

I. "Yes, but . . . " or "Yes, and . . . "

1. An unwillingness to argue signals a weak mind.
2. Debate is the best way to come to decisions. It ensures that we are prepared for all possibilities.
3. I am comfortable with both debating and discussing.
4. Discussion is the best way to come to decisions. Playing with an idea before we tear it down ensures that we give it a fair hearing.
5. Arguing signals an inflexible commitment to an idea.

J. Deliberative Space or Interruption

1. People who interrupt are rude and disrespectful.

2. A truly interested person will provide sufficient airtime and appreciate silence in a conversation.

3. Ideally, one should only interrupt when necessary because the other person has not provided a break in the conversation for other comments.

4. I sometimes interrupt and do not mind interruption if the conversation stays on topic.

5. Interruption signals an engaged and free-flowing conversation.

K. Quick Decision Maker or Deliberative Decision Maker

1. It is critical to come to a decision as quickly as possible and move on. Ninety-nine percent of the time, that initial decision will be the right one.

2. Being able to make quicker decisions along the way allows more time for planning subsequent steps.

3. I have difficulty making decisions.

4. Postponing the decision process creates the likelihood of more creative solutions.

5. Making a decision at the last possible moment ensures that the best possible decision has been made.

L. Deadline Critical or Deadline Advisory

1. Time is the primary criterion for assessing the work that can and should be done.

2. A person who does not honor a deadline is disrespectful to his or her fellow teammates.

3. Deadlines are important but it is often necessary to revisit them.

4. A lawyer who focuses too narrowly on deadlines may miss opportunities and risks being professionally irresponsible.

5. It is important to focus on the tasks that need to be done without considering time as a factor.

M. Detail-Oriented or Big Picture-Oriented

1. I love having everything organized and approaching perfection.

2. The devil is in the details and a failure to appreciate that is a sign of laziness.

3. I am both big picture and detail-oriented. I enjoy producing a perfected product that moves toward my ultimate goal.

4. Knowing what the overall goal is will help make the detail work more bearable.

5. The details will figure themselves out. It is critical to have a sense of where all of this work is headed.

N. Humorous or Serious

1. I need to be able to make jokes when I work to relieve tension, and I have trouble when I work with people who are overly serious.

2. A sense of humor is important when doing legal work because otherwise it is no fun and when work is fun, it is sustaining.

3. Humor has its place in collaborative work as long as it does not distract from the work at hand.

4. Humor is a defense mechanism often used to defuse conflict that needs to happen to move the project to a deeper place.

5. Humor has no place in the workplace. It is just not professional to joke around.

O. Commit or Keep Options Open

1. The act of making a decision is important in itself.

2. Decisions permit you to assess your progress. Spending time keeping options open permits collaborators to avoid really working on what needs to be done.

3. It is important to make decisions but with an eye that the decision could change.

4. It is important not to cut off other options so that there is maximum flexibility in a project.

5. A decision is really advisory. We should always have other options that we can go to in case things change.

P. Private or Open Book

1. Work is work and private life is private life. They should never be mixed.

2. Sharing details of your private life derails the real work of the collaboration. Adding personal drama to the work gets in the way.

3. Team members should feel that they can share their personal issues with the team so that appropriate accommodations can be made.

4. Sharing details of one's personal life can build trust among the collaborators and ultimately make the result more dynamic.

5. It is essential to know about the personal life of every team member because it is ridiculous to make such stark decisions between work and personal life. Intimacy is always good. The work ends. The personal relationships do not.

Q. Instinct or Analysis

1. People should trust their instincts because usually your instinct is always right.

2. The goal of legal education is to develop appropriate instincts about a wide array of topics and then to act on them.

3. Instincts are generally right but should not be acted on until there has been appropriate analysis.

4. Analysis in law is a powerful tool and going by instinct is often the lazy person's out.

5. Instincts are often wrong and professionals should never rely on them. The goal of legal education should be to have lawyers appreciate the importance of careful analysis.

R. Visual or Oral

1. Oral instructions are easily misconstrued and should not be relied upon. It is only through written materials that I really understand.

2. I understand best when I can see or read documents or work plans. It is through seeing them and marking them up that I can be sure that I am going in the right direction.

3. I enjoy hashing out ideas orally but also like to see them in writing before I move forward.

4. I like discussing plans and feel comfortable moving forward after a full discussion without having to commit the plan to writing before I act.

5. Oral instructions are better than written ones since they provide a chance to explore what the person means. Always having to commit things to writing can bog a team down.

S. Earnest or Sarcastic

1. When someone uses sarcasm, it is intended to hurt.
2. Although sarcasm may have its place in human interaction, generally it is mean, and the person using it may not be aware of its hurtfulness.
3. I appreciate sarcasm but think it should be used sparingly and with people who understand the humor.
4. Sarcasm is a useful mechanism to highlight irony, inspire laughter, and quickly give insight into the weakness of an argument without direct and hurtful confrontation.
5. Earnest people who fail to appreciate sarcasm are not very smart.

CHAPTER 10

DIRECT EXAMINATION

LEARNING GOALS

The learning goals for this class include helping you to:

- Think strategically about the relationship between the applicable law, the theory of the case, and the direct exam "story"
- Understand your role in and responsibility for shaping a witness's story
- Think strategically about the choice of witnesses and the facts to elicit from each witness
- Understand the potential strategic impact of dramatic details
- Think through the advantages of flexibility and the limitations of scripting a witness, as well as your options when an exam does not go as planned in court
- Understand the importance of listening to a witness's answers
- Understand how to avoid and respond appropriately to objections

DESCRIPTION OF CLASS

We will discuss the basic principles of crafting an effective direct examination to help you prepare for drafting and presenting witness testimony in your clinic cases. Next, each student will participate in drafting a portion of a direct examination, based on a movie scene. Students will role-play their direct examinations for the full class and participate in reflection and critiquing in terms of form, substance, and effectiveness.

READING ASSIGNMENT

Charles H. Rose III, *Direct Examination, in* FUNDAMENTAL TRIAL ADVOCACY (2d ed. 2011).

READING

Charles H. Rose III
Direct Examination
FUNDAMENTAL TRIAL ADVOCACY (2nd ed. 2011)[1]

. . .

A. The Skill of Direct Examination

1. Understanding Direct Examination

We have all watched movies where a witness is called and enters the courtroom, walking slowly to the witness stand. All eyes in the courtroom are drawn to the witness as the bailiff swears them in and they take a seat in the witness chair. Sometimes the camera angle shifts or pans outward, taking in the full panoply of the courtroom. The witness looks to the advocate and the direct examination begins.

> Open-ended questions may be used during all portions of the trial, but *must* be used by attorneys when performing a direct examination of their own witness. Attorneys are *not allowed* to ask leading or closed questions of their own witnesses on issues that are in dispute.

In that moment the witness is the focus of the entire courtroom. The manner in which the advocate chooses to conduct the direct examination determines whether the witness remains the focus of everyone's attention. One of the primary jobs of the direct examination is to ensure that the attention of the jury remains upon the witness and does not wander away. This is the moment in the trial where the focus of the jury should be on the witness, not the lawyer. You are merely the tool

---

1 Some footnotes and illustrations have been omitted or realigned. Unless otherwise specifically indicated, all professional conduct rules referenced are taken from the Delaware Supreme Court's professional responsibility rules. Those rules are almost identical to the model rules promulgated by the American Bar Association and are public domain documents.

empowering the witness to tell their story in a way that is understandable and believable.

There are certain things that advocates can do to maximize the focus on the witness. Consider the seven steps to a superior direct examination and how they help focus attention on the witness:

Seven Steps to a Superior Direct Examination:

- Start and end direct preparation with case analysis
- Organize logically. Be brief, but sufficient
- Simple language—vary pace with tone, body position, movement
- Exhibits—use them
- Use headlines, orientations, transitions, and coupling questions
- Set the scene though background, descriptive words, action words
- Listen to your witness—build your next question on their response—remember to ask the questions you planted in the juror's mind during voir dire and opening statement.

Advocates primarily use open-ended questions during direct examination to place the facts of their case before the jury. This focused approach to direct examination is predicated on the idea that direct examination showcases the witness, not the attorney. The effectiveness of the information delivered to, and accepted by, the jury is much greater when it comes from the witness and not the advocate.

A deft touch is required to manage the flow of information from the witness to the jury without impeding believability. Your goal is to elicit from your witness, in a clear and logical progression, their observations and activities so that the jury understands, accepts, and remembers the testimony. Direct examination lays the foundation for the admission of physical or demonstrative evidence and begins the preparation for your closing argument. As part of this process you should make a checklist for each witness identifying the facts and exhibits needed to make an effective closing argument that bookends the opening statement. The source materials for that checklist are found in your case analysis.

Your opening statement lays the foundation for the relevancy of the witness's testimony. Direct examination provides the jury the information it must have in order to decide the case. How should you take the facts from the witness and package them for presentation in a way that the jury will accept? Experienced attorneys consistently advise that the key to success in the courtroom is preparation, preparation, and more preparation—of both the trial lawyer and the witness. Hopefully the attorney has been in court before; the witness probably has not. It is critical for the witness to be comfortable and confident enough to tell the facts as they occurred, without becoming overly nervous and unsettled to the point where serious mistakes occur. You must first prepare yourself in order to properly and effectively prepare the witness. That preparation begins with applying the Rule of Threes to case analysis and then applying that same paradigm to each witness.

> Direct examination involves the management of information—analyzing, arranging & presenting.

Perform a thorough case analysis for each witness, determining which factual and legal theories are supported by their testimony. After identifying facts to witnesses, schedule a witness preparation session with each witness individually. The goal for each witness preparation session is to make the witness more comfortable and to clarify which facts each witness can, or cannot, testify about. This is an excellent time to determine potential conflicts between witnesses and to begin to identify potential areas of possible cross examination. While we will discuss the impeachment of witnesses in a later chapter, rely upon the following general areas of potential impeachment when interviewing witnesses: (1) ability to take an oath or make an affirmation, (2) perceptions, (3) memory, (4) narrative ability, (5) bias, (6) corruption, (7) hostility, (8) interest, (9) motive, (10) prejudice, (11) criminal convictions, (12) prior bad acts, (13) prior inconsistent statements, and (14) bad character for truthfulness.

2. *Structuring Direct Examination*

Direct examination is an educational opportunity. You are teaching the members of the jury a set of facts. Determining which facts and how to present them is the crux of the matter. Your initial case analysis drives the structure and substance of each direct examination, including the subsequent witness case analysis you must perform for each witness called. You build your directs upon the bones of those facts and issues already identified.

Before you begin to create a direct, take the time to sit down and review your earlier case analysis. What facts do your theme and theory require you to get out of this witness? What weaknesses did you identify?

Three Steps to Identify Topics on Direct:

- List all factual theories for the witness with supporting facts
- Decide whether to avoid any factual theories for the witness based upon your case analysis—create a final list of topics addressing the best and worst facts for each witness
- Organize the presentation order for each topic in direct examination

To accomplish this, prepare an outline of all topics relevant to your moral theme, legal theory, and factual theory of the case and use that overarching outline to determine which portions the testimony of the witness supports. This outline must address the in-court oral testimony on direct examination, the anticipated cross-examination of the witness, and possible redirect examination based upon the anticipated cross. Part of this process includes a review of all documentary evidence relating to each witness, including depositions or prior statements, and a personal interview of each witness that forms the basis for initial witness preparation. As a general rule you only prepare a witness after you know where you intend to go with that witness.

The initial witness interview may well alert you to issues that you otherwise may have missed. You must now perform a specific case analysis for the direct of that witness. This case analysis is a subset of the overall case analysis, identifying those disputed and undisputed facts from the witness that supports the overall theme and theory of the case. Once you know what the witness can and should relate, decide when and how they will testify. The tool that maximizes your success in determining what will be said, when it will be said, and how it will said is an outline of topics, key facts, and sources for the facts for each witness.

List All Factual Theories

- Documents authored by the witness
- Documents associated with the witness
- Other exhibits associated with the witness
- Other witnesses
- The witness

Meet with your witness for preparation sessions after creating the topic and key facts outline. The number of sessions will depend upon the complexity of the issues identified in your witness case analysis and the abilities of the witness and attorney. Eventually you will be prepared for one final session. During that final session go over possible testimony at trial to make sure that both you and the witness are comfortable with the process and, most importantly, that the witness understands what is going to happen. Make certain the witness knows and believes that their primary duty while on the stand is to tell the truth as they remember it, free from the influence of others, yourself included.

The surest way to conduct a poor direct examination is to attempt to massage the testimony of the witness in a particular direction. The witness must understand, accept, and internalize the belief that their primary duty is to simply and effectively tell the truth. You do not want the witness to become an advocate. When the witness believes this it frees them to have a conversation with the attorney for the benefit of the jury. It is a directed conversation, but the believability of what the witness says and the manner in which they say it will be greatly enhanced if the attorney has created a careful topic outline based upon a thorough case analysis, especially when the witness is committed to the truth as they remember it.

After you have identified which topics the witness will cover, you still must decide how the topics should bc organized for the most effective presentation of the witness and the case. Maximum persuasion is the desired result and, again, case analysis should drive these decisions. That analysis must include how each witness supports the factual theory, legal theory and moral theme of the case. Of paramount importance is whether or not the witness's testimony will answer any of the deciding questions of fact faced by the jury. The topic outlines for each witness should contain the parts of your overall case analysis that the witness supports. A well-prepared case analysis provides specific topics that can be lifted and reorganized for each witness, supporting your overall case theme and theory. The ultimate goal for every direct, cross, and redirect examination is to persuade the jury to accept your answers to the deciding questions of fact, as well as the underlying contested fact questions.

Organize the Presentation Order

- Have a structure
- Consider using time lines or chronologies
- Presentation must make logical sense to a first-time listener
- Organize to maximize persuasion

Never lose sight of the fact that the jury is hearing this for the first time. You cannot expect them to make the leaps of inference and logic that you have trained yourself to make through constant exposure to the witness and the case as a whole. Jurors are not incapable of understanding concepts, but they have not been exposed to the information in the way that you have. Do not make the mistake that many advocates make: do not assume the jury is stupid because they lack knowledge—educate them and you will reap the benefits.

When trying to determine what topics will accomplish this ultimate goal, consider what it is that you want to say in your closing. You must understand the connection between your witness's testimony and your closing argument. This should include issues that address both the strengths and weaknesses of your case. You can accomplish this through organization. Utilize the same tools that others use when they receive and digest information. Examples include structure (so that each direct tells a story with a beginning, middle, and end), time lines, and chronologies (either by time or event). The important consideration is to use tools for organization that increase the ability of a new listener to understand your presentation.

3. Questioning Techniques

Unless you are laying a foundation or discussing preliminary or introductory matters, you are generally not allowed to lead witnesses on direct examination. The purpose of direct examination for most witnesses is to get evidence supporting your version of the facts from the individuals who have firsthand knowledge of the event. In order to ensure that the information comes from the witness and not the attorney, open or non-leading questions are required. If the information does not come from the witness and their own observations, it is not sufficiently reliable to allow the finder of fact to consider it, and may not be either logically or legally relevant under the Federal Rules of Evidence (FRE). FRE 611 states that cross examination will be conducted by leading questions, and most jurisdictions have inverted that rule to require open-ended questioning during direct examination for the reasons stated here. This has immediate structural implications for direct examination. The questioning techniques used during direct examination are designed to focus the attention on the witness while minimizing the presence of the lawyer and meeting the requirements of local practice and the rules.

Examples of Open-Ended Questions:

- Wide-open questions
- Directive questions
- Open questions
- Probing or testing questions
- Coupling questions

Open-ended questions allow the witness to provide a complete answer on topics chosen by the advocate without the form of the question suggesting the answer to the witness. They work by identifying a topic of interest to the questioner and inviting the witness to testify fully regarding that topic. The quality and specificity of the answer is controlled by the nature of the open-ended question. A variety of open-ended questions are normally used when conducting a direct examination. The type of open-ended question depends upon the demeanor and knowledge of the witness, what the attorney wants to discuss and the discretion of the presiding judge. The use of these different questioning forms allows the attorney to go from the broad to the specific and then shift focus to another topic, depending upon the planned structure of the direct examination and the answers provided by the witness.

Open Questions:

Who . . .?

What . . .?

When . . .?

Where . . .?

Why . . .?

How . . .?

Most effective wide-open questions are used immediately following a Headline that has oriented the witness to the topic the advocate wishes to discuss. Wide-open questions normally direct the witness to a specific **time**, **place**, **person**, or **event** identified in an earlier question or Headline. Once the wide-open question orients the witness to the area the attorney is interested in talking about, the advocate then uses directive open questions to narrowly focus the topic the witness should address next. Directive open questions are normally coupled with a Headline so that the witness and fact-finder understand the scope and direction of the advocate's inquiry.

> **Wide-Open Questions:**
>
> *Describe for us . . .*
>
> *Explain . . .*
>
> *Tell us about . . .*

Directive open questions coupled with a Headline are an effective and capable way to orient the witness to a very specific issue while ensuring that the fact-finder and the judge understand exactly what you are discussing. They are often followed by open questions that allow the witness to further explain the specific issue identified through directive open questions.

> **Examples of Directive Open Questions Used With a *Headline:***
>
> - *I'd like to ask you about the letter you received that day.* What did you do with the letter?
> - *I want to ask you some questions about the store on the corner of Fifth and Madison.* Did you or didn't you go into the store?
> - *Let's now talk about the window of the store.* Could you see inside the store through the window?
>
> **A Follow-Up Wide-Open Question Would Be:**
>
> - *What did you see?*

Open questions identify relevant information about a specific **time**, **place**, **person**, or **event** that the advocate wants to explore further by allowing the witness to answer with more details. The structure of open questions allows for maximum explanation by the witness, opening the door for the witness to answer completely based upon her own knowledge and experience.

The most specific and controlled type of open-ended questions are probing and testing questions. Advocates use these to elicit the last few bits of relevant information. While narrowly constructed, they are still open questions and lead the witness to the specific fact you wish to discuss without suggesting the answer. These are focused questions beginning with a verb or other element that clarifies or explains an issue or point in the case. Lead the witness to a particular issue with these types of questions, but do not suggest the answer. The test for an appropriate probing or testing question is whether or not it focuses on a specific item requiring further inquiry to explain a relevant point for your case. Examples include: (1) *Did you . . .?*, (2) *What about . . .?*, (3) *How about . . .?*, and (4) *Did you consider . . .?*

After you have wrung every last bit of relevant information from the witness on a specific item, use coupling questions to emphasize the portions of the testimony that you want the jury to remember. Coupling questions also provide a flow and continuity to the direct examination. They allow the witness and the fact-finder to understand where the examination is going and to anticipate answers. It also mimics normal speech patterns, creating a sense of believability and credibility concerning the examination. A coupling question takes a word or words from the witness's answer and then uses it to connect or couple the prior answer to the current question.

This type of coupling arrangement allows the advocate to subtly underline the most important parts of a witness' testimony without shifting the focus away from the witness. It also uses repetition to teach the jurors the facts as related by the witness. Finally, when the words of an advocate mirror the testimony of credible witnesses it renders the advocate more credible in the eyes of the jury which is not a bad thing to be.

Coupling Questions:

Q: *Mr. Witness, I draw your attention to what happened immediately after the gun went off.* What did you see the defendant do next?

A: **I saw the defendant drop the gun to the floor and walk quickly towards the exit of the restaurant.**

Q: *After the defendant let his gun drop to the floor and he began to quickly walk towards the restaurant door,* what did you do?

Attorneys are not prohibited from using open questions during other portions of the trial. There is a distinct difference between being *allowed* to do something and it being a *good idea* to do it. More than one advocate has snatched defeat from the jaws of victory by asking the wrong open-ended question during cross examination. New advocates should concentrate on using open questions during direct examination and rarely, if ever, use them during cross examination. There are sound tactical and strategic reasons for adopting this strategy as a general rule.

B. The Law of Direct Examination

FRE 611 addresses witnesses. It establishes the manner and scope of witness testimony. The judge has a great deal of latitude when it comes to the form of questions posed by counsel. While FRE 611 provides guidelines and empowers the judge to enforce them, they are just that—guidelines. The most important paragraph is subsection (a). It is a clear and definitive statement that the judge is in control and advocates should conduct questioning within the court to assist in ascertaining truth, avoid wasting of time, and to protect witnesses from harassment or undue embarrassment. Advocates that understand the breadth of the judge's authority benefit when responding to objections in a manner that supports their position.

Example 1: Federal Rule of Evidence 611 (2004)

Article VI. Witnesses. Rule 611. Mode & Order of Interrogation & Presentation:

(a) Control by court. The court shall exercise reasonable control over the mode and order of interrogating witnesses and presenting evidence so as to (1) make the interrogation and presentation effective for the ascertainment of the truth, (2) avoid needless consumption of time, and (3) protect witnesses from harassment or undue embarrassment.

(b) Scope of cross-examination. Cross-examination should be limited to the subject matter of the direct examination and matters affecting the credibility of the witness. The court may, in the exercise of discretion, permit inquiry into additional matters as if on direct examination.

(c) Leading questions. Leading questions should not be used on the direct examination of a witness except as may be necessary to develop the witness' testimony. Ordinarily leading questions should be permitted on cross-examination. When a party calls a hostile witness, an adverse party, or a witness identified with an adverse party, interrogation may be by leading questions.

Both the Federal Rules of Civil Procedure and the Federal Rules of Criminal Procedure specify that the preferred means of testimony is in open court, unless otherwise required by statute in criminal cases, or at the discretion of the court and for good cause shown in civil cases. The stated preference is for in-court testimony, with a greater restriction upon that right in civil cases when the confrontation clause is not potentially at issue. The confrontation clause bars most, if not all contemporaneous transmissions of testimony in a criminal case. Advocates addressing the possibility of out-of-court testimony in a criminal case would do well to consider those cases that have attempted to work around the confrontation clause.

Examples of Procedural Rules:

Federal Rule of Criminal Procedure 26: "In every trial the testimony of witnesses must be taken in open court, unless otherwise provided by a statute or by rules adopted under 28 U.S.C §§ 2072—2077."

Federal Rule of Civil Procedure 43(a): "Form. In every trial, the testimony of witnesses shall be taken in open court, unless a federal law, these rules, the Federal Rules of Evidence, or other rules adopted by the Supreme Court provide otherwise. The court may, for good cause shown in compelling circumstances and upon appropriate safeguards, permit presentation of testimony in open court by contemporaneous transmission from a different location."

Most litigation in this area has involved sexual assault and child victims. This preference, if not requirement, for open court testimony ensures that direct examination is not only about the words that come from the witness, but the manner in which those words are spoken. This legal preference for in-court testimony emphasizes the importance of where the attorney stands, how the witness appears, and how their voices sound. The system understands that the jury measures credibility on substance, appearance, and delivery. The superior advocate will consider each of these issues when employing the skill, law, and art of direct examination.

Whenever witnesses testify and the testimony contains disputed facts, the primary issue the jury will face is who to believe. Most courts provide the jury with a set of instructions designed to assist them in sorting through issues of credibility. Understanding how the judge will inform the jury about credibility issues should assist you in structuring your direct examination. The superior advocate uses the information that will be provided in the jury instructions to structure her direct examinations in accordance with the basic principles the judge will use to assist the jury in deciding who to believe.

C. The Art of Direct Examination

1. *Organization*

Your case analysis develops a persuasive factual theory, a sound logical legal theory, and invokes a compelling moral theme. Your factual theory explains the undisputed evidence and the opponent's evidence, shows why the other side is wrong, and establishes the facts necessary to carry your case. It does this by bearing the burden of fairness and common sense. To be effective, the factual theory relies upon the everyday experiences of the jurors. The judge instructs jurors that they should use their common sense during deliberations. Use that instruction when shaping your persuasive factual theory. Once you have chosen a factual theory everything else you do at trial *must* support that theory.

Your legal theory applies the law to the factual theory, empowering the jury to decide in your favor. It gives the jury the legal means to decide the factual questions for your side. Think of your legal theory as the source of energy for your factual theory. It empowers the factual theory to move the jury based upon your moral theme.

A good moral theme creates emotional force. It invokes a sense within the jury of the innate "tightness" of your position. Effectively developed, it also provides the structure to package and present your factual theory. The best moral themes demand that the jury perform some specific action to right the wrong that has been committed against your client. Identify that specific action for your closing argument. It also exists beneath the surface of the entire trial. Call it to the attention of the jurors when appropriate. When done correctly the moral theme rises from the depths like a great beast, savaging the momentum and presentation of your opponent. The factual theory, when combined with the legal theory, provides the jury the tools to right the wrong expressed in your moral theme. An effective direct examination of a witness will contribute to one or more, and hopefully all three, of these areas.

Planning & Presenting Direct Examination:

- Chronological examination
- The development of cause and effect
- Topical examination by subject matter

You must plan each witness's testimony to include background information, substantive testimony, and an appropriate ending point. The fact-finder should feel as though they are listening in on a conversation that focuses the witness on providing relevant and admissible information in an interesting and believable manner—one that also supports your theme and theory. Background information questions introduce the witness to the jury and explain the relevancy of their testimony. Spend sufficient time to ensure that the introduction of the witness and development of her background contribute to your moral theme, factual theory, or legal theory without wasting time.

You may have several discrete sections of substantive testimony for each witness, depending upon how they support your theme and theory. Different options exist for presenting substantive blocks regardless of the structure you choose. Prudent opportunities for blocks of narrative must exist within each section. Appropriate ways to incorporate a narrative include conducting a chronological examination, use of cause and effect, and performing a topical examination by subject matter.

Make certain your direct examination ends on a question that focuses the jury on your theme or theory and is one that is not subject to suppression by a timely objection. It should also be a point that the opposing side cannot successfully attack through cross examination.

2. *Physical Presence*

After deciding the organization of your direct, consider your location in the courtroom. In the beginning of this chapter we talked about how the focus during direct examination is on the witness and not the attorney. One way to increase the focus on your witness is to position yourself, when allowed by the court, in a location that forces your witness to look at the jury.

By taking a stand at the end of the jury box, you force your witness to speak loudly enough so that you may hear her, also ensuring that the jury can, too, without ever having to tell the witness to speak up. In addition, you provide the witness with her best opportunity to look the jury in the eye. Psychologically you have assumed a position as the "13th juror"—again, not a bad thing to be.

The more the jury views you as just another person trying to find the truth of this particular dispute, the more likely they are to trust you and, more importantly, to trust what you are saying. Positioning yourself in the courtroom is a step in the right direction, particularly during direct when the focus should be on your witness. By the same token, consider using what are normally considered cross examination positions in the courtroom when impeaching your own witness to focus the jury on what you are saying instead of what your witness is communicating.

By changing her location an advocate can assume a position in the courtroom that focuses attention on her. It is impossible to successfully ignore an advocate who has taken a position of strength in the center of the courtroom. Use this technique to shift focus, break the monotony of a direct examination, or to focus the jury on the words coming from you. Do not overuse this position, but have it in your kit to use at the appropriate time.

When deciding when to move, make certain that your assumption of a new location is tied to a topic in your direct examination that will benefit from this shift in focus. Over time you will develop "comfort zones"—positions from which you will prefer to address certain issues within a particular trial. When done appropriately, returning to that spot in the courtroom during your closing argument will bring the jury back to the testimony given at that time. This can greatly increase the jury's memory of the testimony by providing them with a visual clue that ties into the words and demeanor of the witness. Let us move on now to the words used during direct examination.

3. Language

Words are the tools of your trade; choose them wisely. Whenever possible, use short, plain, concise words. The larger and more complex the word the more likely that its use is tied to an argument the advocate wants to make or an evidentiary objection they are attempting to avoid. One syllable words are best. "Car" is better than "vehicle," and much better than "motor vehicle." It suggests a picture to the jury and is the language of everyday life. "Vehicle" and "motor vehicle" are cop-speak that most jurors normally hear on TV. They have no place in your courtroom vocabulary.

Word Choice:

assist	help
indicate	said
inquire	ask
locate	find
observe	see
premises	place
prior	before
proceed	go
profession	job
reside	live
residence	home
subsequent	after
utilize	use
vehicle	car

You cannot allow language to obliterate your own human condition. If you want the jury to trust you then you must talk to them the way you would in a bar, not the way you would if you were learning how to become an FBI agent at Quantico.

Always use the short, common words of everyday speech, preferably those that suggest mental pictures. These words increase the jury's understanding of the witness's testimony and allow for clearer communication by the witness. Action verbs and a commitment to avoiding the passive voice will help you avoid sounding like a lawyer.

There is a *play* of sound in conversation that should be repeated in direct examination. Like *water* running over a brook.

Some advocates fear using simple words. They are afraid their use will remove persuasion from their voice and keep them from swaying the jury with the strength of their position. Nothing could be further from the truth. You must speak the language of your audience. Failure to use words that help create a mental picture can destroy the meaning of an otherwise generally accepted and clearly understood position. These words create wonderful visual images. In a classic example of this concept, George Orwell satirized academic scholarship by providing an academic translation of an earlier work, followed by the original text.

Orwell's Translation:	**The Original Text:**
Objective consideration of contemporary phenomenon compels the conclusion that success or failure in competitive activity exhibits no tendency to be commensurate with innate capacity, but that a considerable element of the unpredictable must invariably be taken into account.	I returned, and saw under the sun, that the race *is* not to the swift, nor the battle to the strong, neither yet bread to the wise, nor yet riches to men of understanding, nor yet favor to men of skill; but that time and chance happeneth to them all.

The difference is striking. The power of the original, along with its poetry and motion, is lost in the use of the large, nebulous words by Orwell. Keep it simple, and you will communicate your thoughts clearly.

Along with the use of simple words that create mental pictures, eliminate unnecessary words, redundancies, and doublespeak. Don't say "emergency situation," say "emergency." Have "innovations," not "new innovations." Doublespeak words deceive, distort, misrepresent, and confuse. Juries hate them, and opposing counsel love to point out their qualities.

uncontrolled contact with the ground	airplane crash
diagnostic misadventure	malpractice
negative patient care outcome	patient died
non-decision making status	unconscious
extra-pair copulation	adultery
grain consuming animal units	livestock

Finally, rid your vocabulary of clichés that have lost their power amid the clutter of colloquial speech. Words clutter if they do not contribute to the narrative's persuasiveness, supply a reason for how someone acted, make an important fact more or less likely, impact witness credibility, believability, or reliability, or enhance your moral theme.

Consider the following example of a bad questioning technique on direct that does not use simple words:

> Questioner: *When he departed the area, had you also departed, or embarked upon leaving, or had she, if she had expressed a desire to do so and been capable at that time, if given that she were not otherwise constrained by attendant circumstances, gone also, would he, then, assuming he displayed an awareness of that fact, have brought, you, meaning therewith you and she, along with him, in the car, to the bar?*
>
> Opposing Counsel: *Objection your honor. I have no idea what counsel was asking, and I'm not sure he does either!*

Look at how well these simple questions work instead:

> Questioner: ***Where*** *were you going that evening?*
>
> Questioner: ***Who*** *was with you in the car?*
>
> Questioner: ***When*** *did you get to the bar?*
>
> Questioner: ***What*** *was the first thing you did when you got to the bar?*
>
> Questioner: ***Why*** *did you do that?*

Avoid these pitfalls by using literary forms that enhance information retention in direct examinations. These forms include repetition, parallelism, and the Rule of Threes. Repetition comes from our oral storytelling tradition and is likely the first way that we each were taught by our parents. Parallelism takes facts that are logically parallel and places them alongside each other to show their relationship, connection, or contrast. Use parallel questions to bring out parallel facts, or the lack of parallel facts, to support or contradicting persuasive factual or legal theories. The Rule of Threes presents ideas in a structure that implies a sense of completeness, significance, and believability. This rule applies to words, sentences, and paragraphs. Look again at this last paragraph to see the Rule of Threes in action.

As advocates, we often fear appearing stupid. We try to wrap ourselves in officious-sounding words to avoid the appearance of a lack of knowledge. It does not work. We all have within us the ability to formulate dumb questions and your use of large specious words will not eradicate your ability to appear stupid. However, practice can minimize this fear by exposing our stupidity to ourselves before we share it with others. For this very reason, I strongly suggest you practice your questions aloud.

* * *

E. Direct Examination Checklist

The following checklist summarizes the information presented on direct examination. You should use it as a starting point in developing your own questioning skills. This checklist is not "Holy Writ" and is merely the soil in which you should plant the seeds of your own creativity.

I. Direct Examination Overview:

a. It is all about asking questions that the jury wants to know the answer to so that they can decide the issues in the case.

b. When we mimic conversational tones during direct examination we create interest and anticipation in the jury.

II. Seven Steps to Superior Direct Examination:

a. Start and end direct preparation with case analysis.

b. Organize logically. Be brief, but sufficient.

c. Simple language—vary pace with tone, body position, movement.

d. Exhibits—use them.

e. Use headlines, orientations, transitions, and coupling questions.

f. Set the scene though background, descriptive words, action words.

g. Listen to your witness—build your next question on their response. Remember to ask the questions you planted in the juror's mind during voir dire and opening statement.

III. Identifying Topics for Direct Examination:

a. List all factual theories for the witness with supporting facts. Potential sources include;

   i. Documents authored by the witness

   ii. Documents associated with the witness

   iii. Other exhibits associated with the witness

   iv. Other witnesses

   v. The witness

b. Decide whether to avoid any factual theories for the witness based upon your case analysis—create a final list of topics addressing the best and worst facts for each witness.

c. Organize the presentation order for each topic in direct examination. Methods include:

   i. Time lines or chronologies.

   ii. Presentation must make logical sense to a first-time listener.

   iii. Organize to maximize persuasion.

IV. Good Direct Examination Techniques:

a. Form of the Question on Direct

   i. Wide-open questions

   ii. Directive questions

   iii. Open questions

   iv. Probing or testing questions

   v. Coupling questions

b. Planning and Presenting the Direct Examination

   i. Chronological examination.

   ii. The development of cause and effect.

   iii. Topical examination by subject matter.

c. Organization

   i. Headlines

   ii. Accredit the witness

   iii. No compound questions

   iv. Looping

   v. Limit use of notes

vi. Go from general to specific

vii. Brevity is your friend

viii. Exhibits are your friend

ix. Build direct around key facts

d. Physicality

i. Make eye contact

ii. Gesture appropriately

iii. Relax

iv. Posture

v. Listen

vi. React to the witness

vii. Do not talk over the witness

viii. Body position matters

e. Language

i. Emphasis where needed

ii. Paint pictures with words

iii. Use normal language

iv. Delete filler words

v. Conversational tone

vi. Let the silence work for you

vii. Voice inflection persuades

viii. Less is usually more

F. Conclusion

The fundamental tenets of direct examination serve as the backdrop for our discussion of proper cross examination techniques. They lurk in the background, ready for us to bring them out when they complement and strengthen the purpose of our cross. When you understand the relative strength and weakness of the questioning techniques for both disciplines you will be well on your way to mastering the questioning of any witness. Let us move on to the fundamentals of cross examination.

Relevant Rules

1. Evidentiary Rule Matrix

Table 1 serves as a starting point for additional inquiry into the relationships between specific tasks on direct examination and the rules of evidence. Your case analysis should assist you in identifying when these particular issues will arise. You should use the table to review your knowledge of the evidentiary rules so that you can include that in your legal theory of the case.

Issues Arising During Direct Examination	**Applicable Federal Rule of Evidence**
Character traits of the victim or accused	404(a), 404(b) & 405
Character of a witness for truthfulness	608
Out-of-court statements offered for the truth of the matter asserted therein (hearsay)	801–807
Offering evidence of other crimes, wrongs and & acts (*Chapter 10*)	404(b)
Prior convictions of a witness (*Chapter 10*)	609
Legal relevancy: Is the probative value substantially outweighed by the danger of unfair prejudice?	403
Are the questions logically relevant?	401 & 402
Competency of a witness	610
Personal knowledge of the witness	602
Questioning witnesses	611 & 614

Table 1: Potential Evidentiary Rules Applicable During Direct Examination

2. *Professional Responsibility Rule Matrix*

Table 2 serves as a starting point for additional inquiry into the potential professional responsibility issues implicated during direct examination. Counsel must ensure that they do not cross certain lines when investigating cases, preparing witnesses, and controlling direct testimony. Pay particular attention to your jurisdiction's interpretation and application of the Candor Towards the Tribunal standard found in Rule 3.3. A thorough grasp of these issues will assist you in avoiding perjury and improper conduct. You should use the table to review your knowledge of the ethical rules so that you can include that in your planning for your direct.

Issues Arising During Direct Examination	Applicable Rule of Professional Responsibility
(a)(1)–(3): A lawyer must not offer false evidence.	Rule 3.3: Candor Toward the Tribunal
(e): A lawyer must not "allude to any matter that [she] does not reasonably believe is relevant or that will not be supported by admissible evidence. . . ." She must neither "assert personal knowledge of facts in issue . . ." nor "state a personal opinion as to the justness of a cause, the credibility of a witness, the culpability of a civil litigant or the guilt or innocence of an accused."	Rule 3.4: Fairness to Opposing Party & Counsel
(a): A lawyer must not illegally "seek to influence a judge, juror, prospective juror or other official." (d): A lawyer must not intentionally disrupt the court and must conduct herself with respect for the court.	Rule 3.5: Impartiality & Decorum of the Tribunal
(a): A lawyer must not attempt to be an advocate and witness in the same trial (with some limited exceptions).	Rule 3.7: Lawyer As Witness

Table 2: The Most Prevalent Professional Conduct Rules During Direct Examination

. . .

POST-CLASS REFLECTION MEMO

Draft and submit a memo in response to the question below:

- How will you take the lessons you have learned in class today and apply them to your work in representing clinic clients?

HANDOUT

Choice #1: How can I design my questions to maximize the effectiveness of witness testimony?

1. Are my questions leading?
2. Are my questions otherwise objectionable?
3. Am I structuring my questions to retain control of the story?

Choice #2: How can I simplify the story so it is most likely to be understood?

Choice #3: What principle works best to organize the witness's testimony?

1. Should I develop a line of background questions?
2. Have I ensured that the fact finder can easily follow the chain of events?
3. Have I thought through how the organizational structure relates the story's dramatic impact?

Choice #4: How can I most effectively set the scene?

1. What aspects of the scene help clarify the events for the fact finder?
2. Are aspects of the setting critical to my theory or to the law that controls this case?

Choice #5: How can I maximize the vividness and drama of the story?

1. Have I provided a clear picture of what happened in each incident?
2. Am I listening to the witness's answers?
3. Have I established all necessary legal elements to support my case-in-chief?
4. Have I considered how to effectively vary the pace of the examination?
5. Have I made strong strategic choices about when to use exhibits, so they best enhance the story?

Choice #6: What opportunities exist to bolster the witness's credibility?

1. Have I considered the impact of the witness's demeanor?
2. Have I considered volunteering weaknesses?
3. Have I introduced my witness in a way that enhances his or her credibility?

4. Have my questions enhanced my witness's testimony and made my client's version credible?

CHAPTER 11

CROSS EXAMINATION

LEARNING GOALS

The learning goals for this class include helping you to:

- Understand the strategic impact of structure, topic, or chapter selection, and question form
- Understand the lawyer's role in shaping the testimony of opposition witnesses
- Think strategically about the relationships between cross examination and other aspects of casework, including case theory, fact investigation, direct examination, and closing argument
- Achieve clarity on the importance of preparation

DESCRIPTION OF CLASS

During this class, we will discuss the art of cross examination, to help you prepare for drafting and performing cross examinations of witnesses in your clinic cases. Students will then observe an incident and use it as the basis for developing their own lines of cross examination questions to perform and critique with the class.

READING ASSIGNMENT

Charles H. Rose III, *Cross Examination, in* FUNDAMENTAL TRIAL ADVOCACY (2d ed. 2011).

READING

Charles H. Rose III
Cross Examination
FUNDAMENTAL TRIAL ADVOCACY
(2nd ed. 2011)[1]

. . .

A. What is Cross Examination?

Cross examination is the most misunderstood subject taught in trial advocacy. Historically, most who professed to know something about how to conduct cross examination surrounded the task with mystic discussions concerning its difficulty, the dangers witnesses present and how it can only be learned through repetition. Their war stories focused on the ability of the attorney to humiliate and dominate the witness or sometimes, even worse, of the witness destroying the attorney. Advocates attempting to learn cross examination came away from these presentations with a sense that maybe the best thing to do was to just not do anything, or as little as possible—perhaps as a last resort they might attack and destroy the witness, establishing domination and preeminence in the courtroom.

> Cross examination is a skill that is *easily learned* and *readily applied* . . . Everything is designed to make your case look better and your opponent's case look worse.

I could not disagree more with this historical approach to teaching cross examination. Cross examination is a skill easily learned and readily applied in most situations. That learning process must be guided by some fundamental concepts if it is to be effective. These concepts are based upon a common sense approach to the purposes behind questioning the witness that is grounded in superior case analysis. Cross examination is just one more skill at the advocate's disposal designed to accomplish a purpose identified based upon the themes and theories of the case.

It really doesn't matter if you call it an art or a science—what does matter is the development of a working logical construct, and that is what

---

1 Some footnotes and illustrations have been omitted or realigned. Unless otherwise specifically indicated, all professional conduct rules referenced are taken from the Delaware Supreme Court's professional responsibility rules. Those rules are almost identical to the model rules promulgated by the American Bar Association and are public domain documents.

we will focus on in this chapter. When we are done you will have all of the tools necessary to conduct effective, efficient and persuasive cross examinations. In order to do this we will identify why we cross, how we cross, and when we cross.

Many advocates approach cross examination with awe, fear, and trepidation. They have seen the television shows where the witness breaks down and admits to committing the crime and realize in the pit of their stomach that juries have been conditioned to expect great things from cross examination. They fear they are not up to the task and wonder how in the world they can ever adequately represent their client while employing all of the possibilities that cross examination is supposed to offer. They have read the writings of legal experts describing cross examination as a difficult art that most will never master, and even worse, they believe what they have read.

These advocates often respond by embarking on a cross examination that reiterates the direct examination and then descends into a slash and burn campaign designed to destroy the credibility of the witness. This usually backfires, damaging the credibility of the advocate—not the witness. Poorly done cross examinations are devastating to the advocate who performs them. Despite what many others have written, cross examination is actually a readily developed skill that lies within the abilities of any competent trial lawyer. What is required is preparation, attention to detail and a commitment to approaching cross examination through the lens of your case theme and theory. Advocates who plan cross examination with these concepts in mind are well along the way to mastering the art of cross examination. Everything is designed to make your case look better and your opponent's case worse; keep that in mind as you prepare cross and you will have an attainable goal. Consider the words of those who have gone before:

> *"[Cross examination is] the greatest legal engine ever invented for the discovery of truth."*
>
> *"Cross examination is the principal means by which the believability of a witness and the truth of his testimony are tested."*
>
> *"The age-old tool for ferreting out truth in the trial process is the right to cross examination. For two centuries past, the policy of the Anglo American system of evidence has been to regard the necessity of testing by cross examination as a vital feature of the law."*

Now that we know what the expectations are, let us begin to develop the tools every advocate needs to produce first-rate cross examinations.

B. The Skill of Cross Examination

1. *Why Cross Examine a Witness*

Your goals during cross examination are to: (1) control the witness, (2) establish facts that build to a theme and theory, and (3) establish facts that build up the credibility of your witnesses and diminish the credibility of your opponent's witnesses, including the witness being cross examined. In order to accomplish this you must know more than the witness does. That is only accomplished by a thorough, complete, and continuing case analysis. When preparing specifically for cross examination your first step is to identify and list the legal issues in the case that work with your case theme and theory. If you cannot do this, it is a red flag indicating that the theme and theory you have chosen does not fit the available facts. You must adapt your theme and theory to one that is supported by the facts. While doing this keep in mind the seven steps to creating a successful cross examination.

> Advocates are *not only allowed, but encouraged* to ask leading or closed questions during cross examination.

2. *Preparing for Cross Examination*

Once you have identified the legal issues you must determine which of them represent the "hard questions of fact" the jury must decide. These questions should be framed in the language of common sense and everyday life. Your job as an advocate is to translate the legal issues into a persuasive form for the jury. Brainstorm the good facts and bad facts associated with the witness from all available sources of information. For each good and bad fact you must identify a readily available witness, document, or exhibit that supports the existence of that fact. For each witness you must list the good and bad facts with the location of the documentation that supports the fact in question. Done properly this will create a matrix that you can use to easily and quickly retrieve the evidence supporting each identified fact when necessary during cross examination. ***This is a crucial point in the cross examination preparation process.*** If you don't take the time to properly analyze the legal issues and facts that support them in light of your case theme and theory you are guaranteeing an ineffective and possibly self-destructive cross examination. You cannot arrive at a destination if you have not chosen one. Failure to properly analyze the case is a failure to choose a destination. If you do not, your opponent will—and I guarantee that you will *not* enjoy the ride to that location.

Seven Steps to a Superior Cross Examination:

- Start and end preparation with case analysis
- Every section has a clearly defined purpose tied to theme, theory, or credibility
- CONTROL THE WITNESS!
- Organize the cross to accomplish your goals – not your opponent's
- Details give control
- Impeachment must matter
- Use the witness's own words

Once you have compared the identified "hard questions of fact for the jury" with your list of good and bad facts for the witness you should choose the best points and worst points for each hard question of fact. You must then organize each of these clusters of good and bad facts into different sections of your cross examination. Applying the Rule of Threes to this process will organize your good and bad facts for maximum efficiency and persuasive power during the actual cross examination. After you have identified these facts you must cross reference them with the legal theory, factual theory, and moral theme you developed during your case analysis.

Primary Goals of Cross Examination

- Control the witness
- Establish facts that bolster your theme and theory; and
- Establish facts that build up the credibility of your witnesses and diminish the credibility of your opponent's witnesses

Look to see if any of these potential good or bad facts contradict your theme and theory, are of minimal persuasive value, or are too dangerous to use during cross examination. Remember to always follow the first rule of trial advocacy—do nothing that is not in accordance with your case theme and theory. If the best facts for the witnesses support your theme and theory and do not contradict your version of the facts you should identify them as potential topic headlines for your cross examination outline. Make certain that you do not organize your cross examination in the same chronological fashion that opposing counsel used on direct examination. The witness has practiced their direct and just delivered testimony. If you choose to use the same structure that the witness is familiar with you are increasing their sense of comfort and control—two feelings that you rarely, if ever, want to engender in an adverse witness.

After identifying the topic headlines for your cross, you must employ advocacy techniques that maximize the persuasive impact of the answers to the questions you will ask. To draw out those best facts: (1) cluster together all of the facts that enhance and support the topic, (2) lay out the facts one question at a time leading up to your final point, and (3) identify similar facts based upon your knowledge of human nature that support your final topic. Ask questions about those similar facts before making your final point.

Each of these techniques is designed to create tension by building suspense and sparking the interest of the jury, while suggesting the answer that everyone expects is coming. There is nothing wrong with that expectation. If your case analysis was sufficient to the task, the story that you told in opening statement and developed through the testimony of your witnesses on direct examination has already laid a trail of bread crumbs leading to this moment in the cross examination of the witness. When you do this, make certain that you have the available resources to impeach the witness if they stray from the good or bad facts that you previously identified through your case analysis. ***This point is crucial. If the witness challenges you, and the law allows you to respond to that challenge—you must.*** Failure to do so empowers the witness, weakens your theme and theory of the case, and calls into question your credibility as an advocate in the eyes of the fact finder.

Maximize the Persuasive Impact of Answers on Cross:

- Cluster together all of the facts that enhance and support the topic
- Lay out the facts one question at a time leading up to your final point, and
- Identify similar facts based upon your knowledge of human nature and then using them to make your final point.

Consider the worst point identified by your case analysis; you must determine how you are going to handle it. Can you put it into context in a way that neutralizes the point or explain it in a fashion that helps your theme and theory? If so, you should include it in your cross and turn it to your advantage. If you can't put it into context or explain it then do not touch it in cross examination. The law of direct, cross, and re-direct will not allow the opposing side to use it again on redirect if you leave it alone during cross. If it is not beneficial to your case it is bad enough that the jury heard it once, don't make the mistake of replowing ground that hurts you and then allowing the other side to cover it yet again on redirect.

If you are going to go after a "worst point" on cross, make certain that you have a connection that is worthwhile to your theme and theory and strike that connection hard during your closing argument. If it does not meet the test of what you will say in closing then ***do not use it,*** even if you can explain it or put it in context. If you decide to go after one of these worst points on cross you should approach it by identifying a cluster of questions that you can ask to minimize, place in context, or explain the worst fact. This places the worst point in the best light possible as it relates to your theme and theory. To increase the persuasive nature of this type of cross examination you should break down the questions as simply as possible into one-fact increments. This way you will control the witness and lead the jury to the conclusion that you want them to make about this particular issue. It is imperative that you have the supporting points to control the witness if they attempt to wander during your one-fact build up.

After identifying the hard facts you must next organize the topics you need to cover in cross examination. The arrangement of topics must be effective and persuasive. Each topic either relates to a point in your favor or diminishes the opponent's position. The order of presentation is dictated by the impact you believe the witness should have. Determine if this particular witness has non-controverted facts that support your theme and theory. If you have identified good facts that help, get them out of the witness quickly before you have to challenge and control the witness. Once you are forced to exert control over this witness through the use of pointed questions that may call for an impeachment that attacks the witness's character, you will never be able to go back and effectively get out the good facts that are not in controversy. A smooth cross examination can flow from the direct into the cross in a nonconfrontational manner—forcing the witness to agree with facts that help your case. Don't be the bad guy until the witness gives you a reason to be. When they later refuse to agree on facts that are in controversy, their disagreement and unwillingness to go your way will be emphasized for the jury. If you then have a set of facts to support your theory as to why they refuse to admit the truth as you see it, you can very successfully diminish the witness's credibility as to their entire testimony. Because cross is of an adverse witness, you may have to be creative to stay focused. You must stay organized, but let your cross be fluid to persuasively communicate the facts you want the jury to hear.

Starting the Cross:

Begin your cross exam with non-threatening or uncontroverted fact questions that support your theme and theory to keep the same momentum as on direct.

Remember that your primary goals during cross examination are to: (1) control the witness, (2) establish facts that bolster your theme and theory, and (3) establish facts that build up the credibility of your witnesses and diminish the credibility of your opponent's witnesses, including the witness being cross examined. One of the best ways to accomplish these goals is to begin the cross examination with a series of non-threatening questions. Set a professional and businesslike tone with short, leading questions. Keep it to one fact per question. This gets the witness in a rhythm. They become used to answering "yes", "no", or some other short answer. This subconsciously conditions the witness to answer your questions without conflict. Make that first topic an easy one and it will give you witness control. This is a great place in the cross examination to identify those uncontroverted facts that this witness must admit to that support your case.

After you have identified how you will establish control of the witness next consider how to organize the rest of the cross. Whatever you choose, ***do not commit the cardinal sin of rehashing the direct examination by chronologically covering the same testimony that the jury just heard***. If you do the jury will hear it three times, once on direct, once on cross and then again on redirect. Any doubts they may have had about the veracity of the witness's version of events will be wiped away by this reverse use of the rule of threes. This is a common mistake made by most advocates. If the witness has practiced the direct so that they were fully prepared, why in the world would you think that asking them about it a second time would produce a result appreciably different from the direct? It will not, and you will look ineffective while your client's cause suffers.

Reasons for Cross Examination:

- To elicit facts supporting your legal theory, factual theory or moral theme.
- To expose facts or bias that weakens your opponent's legal theory, factual theory or moral theme.
- To establish the credibility of your own witnesses or attack the credibility of opposing witnesses (when required by your legal theory, factual theory or moral theme).

Use the doctrine of primacy and recency to place your strongest points where the jury will be sure to notice them. This doctrine, when used in conjunction with a cross examination that is organized around substantive sections, each with a purpose and a connection to other sections, is very effective in producing witness control and a persuasive presentation of your case. If you decide to address weaker points during the cross examination, strengthen them by sandwiching them between strong points.

When attempting to cross effectively on these weak points, it helps to use the same words in your questions that are found in the previous statements of the witness. This narrowly defines the inquiry, and will prevent the witness from running for cover or explaining away the issue. This is particularly important when attempting to cross on a "weak point" that has the potential to hurt your case. You will only be able to effectively accomplish this if you prepare adequately. Using the witness's precise words is a way to establish control and credibility. It puts the witness between a rock and a hard place—they either admit that you are correct or appear to prevaricate just because they do not want to admit the truth of what they said earlier. Either way, you win.

3. *Questioning Techniques*

A closed-ended question is designed to identify the witness's knowledge of the facts or to challenge their credibility. The structure of a closed-ended question ensures that the witness can only respond with one possible truthful answer already known to the advocate posing the question. A variety of techniques are available to formulate closed/leading questions. They include: (1) telling the witness instead of asking, (2) using taglines to force agreement by the witness, and (3) asking one fact questions.

Two "styles" of phraseology are normally used when performing cross examination. The first is a leading question with a "tag" on the end of it. An example would be "You own a baseball bat, *don't you?"* The "tag" is "don't you?" and takes many forms (e.g., "*didn't you?*", "*isn't it true?*", etc.). The other style is to drop the tag entirely. A leading question can still be asked with identical language without the tag. When you do this properly, there is a much greater emphasis on voice inflection. For example, "You own a baseball bat." Make this declarative sentence a leading question by placing the inflection on the word "bat."

Examples Using Taglines On Cross:

"You got out of your car, didn't you?"

"You closed the car door, correct?"

"Isn't it true that you walked across the sidewalk?"

Because leading questions are not truly inquisitive, voice inflection makes the critical difference. This is especially true with non-tag, leading questions. Thus, the question "You own a baseball bat" can be leading or non-leading. If the inflection drops when saying "bat," it is leading. As discussed above, the falling inflection of the questioner does not reflect doubt or true inquisitiveness. If, however, your inflection rises on the word "bat," it demonstrates the questioner is uncertain or at least inviting an explanation. A good cross-examination question marries proper form with tailored inflection. This skill comes with practice and is both fundamental and crucial.

Examples Telling the Witness Instead of Asking:

"You got out of your car."

"You closed the car door."

"You walked across the sidewalk."

When you make statements on cross examination that requires agreement or disagreement by the witness, you establish a high degree of control and accuracy. The absence of taglines allows you to state the issue as though it is a fact that merely requires agreement or disagreement. This can be somewhat frightening and awkward the first few times you try it. Some witnesses will stare at you blankly while others will ask, "Was that a question?" Do not allow this attempt at manipulation to work. Confidently look the witness in the eye and state your fact again, waiting in the silence for their response. They will respond—they have to. Count on that and use it to your benefit. Make certain that their response is in words and not through some sort of head gesture. The record of trial will not include head movement or grunts that may or may not indicate agreement or disagreement with your stated position. When witnesses try to avoid answering through noncommittal sounds or body movements, call them on it. Inform them that it is important that they speak clearly for the benefit of the court reporter and then make sure they do.

Each of these questioning techniques requires agreement or disagreement by the witness. The difference between them is marked. First, your voice rises when you use a tagline. The rising inflection can indicate that you have some doubts as to the veracity of your position. It may invite the witness to challenge your position or imply to the jury that you really are not sure if the question you are asking is correct. Second, the use of taglines can sometimes become an annoying habit. Jurors begin to listen for the taglines and keep count of how many times you may use the phrase during a given cross examination. Avoid anything that draws their attention away from the substantive issues you are raising. Since the purpose of your cross is to support your case theme and theory or to attack witness credibility, it is always substantive. Otherwise you should not be doing it. Finally, the choice of whether or not to use taglines is one of style and demeanor. Make certain that you experiment with both and then choose one that works for you.

Remember to ask one-fact questions. Examples of one-fact questions can be found throughout this chapter. Their use allows the advocate to control the witness and focus the inquiry so that it is understood by the jury. It becomes very difficult for a witness to prevaricate when only one factual issue is posed in the question. One-fact questions are the building blocks that allow you to make your ultimate conclusion to the jury during closing argument when the witness is not there to argue about it.

Closed and leading questions are normally used during cross examination of adverse witnesses, when laying a foundation for the admissibility of evidence through any witness, or when the witness's demeanor or nature requires closed or leading questions in order to assist the fact-finder in getting to the testimony of the witness. This usually occurs when the witness has diminished communication ability due to their age or status as a victim of a violent crime. Always keep in mind that these closed/leading questions are used to control witnesses, showcase the advocate, and to lay foundations for the admissibility of evidence. The focus for leading questions is on the advocate, not the witness. Closed questions allow the advocate to probe for logical weaknesses or fallacies in the witness's testimony, while also providing a vehicle to test the credibility of the witness through the crucible of cross examination.

. . .

D. The Art of Cross Examination

1. *Fundamental Precepts*

While every cross examination is unique, there are certain fundamental precepts that counsel should always consider when preparing cross examinations. Some of these are part of the historical development of our collective advocacy consciousness and are grounded in two seminal works—*THE ART OF CROSS EXAMINATION* written by Francis L. Wellman and a lecture given by one of the best CLE presenters that has ever taught—Professor Irving Younger. The more relevant and useful ideas can be found in Terry MacCarthy's work, as well as the text by Larry Posner and Roger Dodd. Wellman's book is an excellent read for historical reasons, but is otherwise of little practical use. Younger's lectures on cross examination have been affectionately referred to as the new testament of cross examination by an expert in the field. While there is a lot of good thought in Professor Younger's ideas, they are somewhat dated now. They sound good in the classroom but don't work quite so well in the courtroom. Nonetheless a text on cross examination that does not at least pay homage to the spirit behind his approach would be sadly lacking. Several of the techniques discussed below can be traced to each of the great minds I have just mentioned. They include:

(a) "Cross-examination is a commando raid, not the invasion of Europe!"

The idea behind this shibboleth is to limit the number of points sought from each witness in order to maximize the effectiveness of those points that you do make. It serves as a screen to force advocates to truly consider the quality of what they are asking and the answers they expect to get.

In theory too much information from one witness obscures the facts from the testimony that may very well address your "hard questions of fact" for the jury. Trying to cross a witness on every fact reduces the impact of the cross and runs the danger of boring the fact-finder. When you limit the issues addressed with a particular witness to the important information germane to that witness you tell a better story. This is good as a general rule, but sometimes you can cluster important points with more than one witness, teaching through repetition. Terry MacCarthy points out that when the only thing you have is a large number of small issues, then the sheer number of points you are making on cross examination is best supported by a long and detailed inquiry into each small inconsistency. Terry refers to this in his famous impeachment "fishing lecture" as catching a mess of small fish.

When trying to decide how much detail to enter into with each witness consider using the rule of threes, parallelism and the theory of primacy and recency when to decide what to ask, what not to ask, and when to ask it with each witness. You cannot do this effectively without proper case analysis.

(b) Use Primacy and Recency

It is a well-established theory of persuasion that people tend to remember the first thing you present and the last thing you present. Advocates who use this to their advantage make their strongest points at the beginning and end of the cross, sandwiching the less important or controversial issues of fact in the middle of the presentation where they can get credit for addressing them but the potential damage that might happen if the inquiry goes badly is much less.

Advocates using this approach begin and end the cross of the witness with a point that strongly supports their theory of the case. It must also be a hook that the witness cannot remove themselves from with sufficient wriggling. Judge Jeanne Jordan teaches that you should begin and end your cross examination with an unassailable point on an island of safety. When making these choices advocates should consider whether the need to initially establish control through questioning on uncontroverted facts is sufficiently important to put up front in the cross, even if it is not the most important point from a case theory perspective.

(c) Avoid the Ultimate Question!

The idea of avoiding the ultimate question can be traced back, at least in the modern era, to Professor Younger's lectures on cross. His thought process was that cross examination is an art that is just too difficult and the dangers of asking the ultimate question were not worth the potential damage. He often argued that more than one advocate snatched defeat from the jaws of victory by ruining a successful cross-exam when they erroneously believed that the witness would admit the critical and ultimate fact at issue. He would tell the stories focusing on how the witness would skewer the advocate with the answer that destroyed the inference made during the cross examination.

Now it is true that the witness may be able to do that. It is also true that you can prevent them from doing that during cross examination by not asking the ultimate question. As a general rule it is a very good basic technique to not push the envelope. Like every good basic rule there is an exception and a problem with it—in this case it is called redirect. When you don't deal with the ultimate question head on you have just laid out the scope and purpose of the redirect. The redirect often begins like this:

C: Mr. Witness, on cross examination the defense counsel asked you a series of questions about X, but he didn't ask you why X happened. Would you like an opportunity to explain X, placing it in context?

W: Absolutely.

C: Why did X happen?

W: Blah, blah, blah, blah blah.

By the time the witness is through on redirect much of the damage of the cross examination has been repaired, if the jury even remembers what your point might have been to begin with. We will visit the issue of dealing with the ultimate question during our chapter on advanced cross examination.

That being said, you should not reach for the Perry Mason moment and fall flat on your face. AVOID this temptation. If you cannot effectively deal with the witness's response to the ultimate question during cross, the safer course is to save the ultimate question for closing argument. There you can argue the inference without giving the witness a chance to explain it away. Do not be greedy: if you bite off more than you can chew you might develop a terminal case of indigestion!

(d) Single-Fact Questions—No Expansive Narratives

Questions should be short, single-fact, and leading. Lead the witness, and the jury, to a desired response. Do not allow the witness to give expansive narratives. There is seldom a place for "How" or "Why" or "Tell the court" lines of questioning. When you ask that question you are effectively turning over control to the witness. If you have hurt them or insulted them during the cross they are waiting for the chance to get even; don't give it to them.

(e) Vary Your Questioning Techniques!

As discussed previously, you can judiciously use taglines to direct the questioning, but prefacing every question with "isn't it true?" or ending every question with "wouldn't you agree?" can be very distracting. When used sparingly, taglines may help maintain control of the witness, the flow of cross examination and the topics discussed. The key word here is "sparingly." On balance, taglines are a crutch and one only uses a crutch when one needs to use it. In court that should rarely be the case.

(f) Do Not Play with Fire

Normally you should not ask questions to which you do not know the answer. Doing so places you in a position where you are at the mercy of a witness that has been called by the opposing side and is normally not inclined to assist you in your case. On rare occasions it may be necessary to ask the question for which you do not know the answer. If the worst possible answer to the question you are posing will leave you in a position that is not any worse than your current one then take the plunge. Sometimes the practice of law requires you at times to ask questions for which you do not know the answer. The proper methodology is to limit those instances, and proceed carefully when you must go fishing for information.

(g) Develop a Toolbox of Control Techniques

Canned responses that allow you to control hostile witnesses, are as simple as, "perhaps you didn't hear my question," "so the answer is yes," "maybe you could answer my question this time," "my question was . . . ", "I appreciate that you needed to say that, now could you please answer the question that I asked" and the time honored classic, "so we can agree that. . . ." However, using these control techniques too liberally can also be distracting. Use them strategically to control an adverse witness. Never ask the judge to help you control the witness; when you do, you have just admitted to the entire room that you need assistance. Only do this when the witness's demeanor and actions have clearly established that they are not being reasonable or fair. Seek the judge's assistance only as a last resort.

Finally, the words of Winston Churchill are applicable here. You control the cross. Metaphorically, you have the ability to destroy the credibility of the witness; there is no need to be rude while doing so. The jury remembers and will not forgive you for doing so, unless the witness was so rude that the jury would like to do it for you. When faced with that situation, "cry havoc and release the dogs of war!"

2. *Combining Skill with Art—Effective Crosses*

Cross examination is a goal-oriented process designed to accomplish one or more of three primary purposes; (1) introducing a new fact to the jury, (2) weakening or highlighting a fact that has already been introduced, or (3) weakening or strengthening the credibility of a witness. A well-done cross examination consists of *selective* attacks on specific areas of the witness's testimony. Do not retell the whole thing again through cross examination. In order to accomplish these goals you should always apply these three primary rules during cross examination.

The best way to ensure that you only address one fact with each question is to break your questions down into their smallest parts. Simple questions do not leave the witness with any option other than to answer or be obstructive. Either decision by the witness will be to your benefit. Simplicity destroys witness escape routes, builds precision, and ensures control by the advocate. This basic premise must be followed. One-fact questions are the gold standard for cross examination. When creating these questions use descriptive words that create a picture in the jury's mind. Consider the following workman-like approach to this task:

Initial Question: You saw a woman lying in a parking lot?

A better arrangement of short, one-fact questions using simple leading questions, descriptive statements, adding one new fact at a time would be:

You saw a woman hit by a car?

She was struck by a green Jeep?

The woman was lying on the asphalt?

In the parking lot?

Her blood covered the asphalt immediately around her?

There is no reason to make cross examination more difficult than it needs to be. Use leading questions on cross-examination. Leading questions give you control. They are questions that *declare* the answer. The best leading questions are short declarative statements of fact—with a question mark at the end. Look at the difference between these examples:

Good: Do you like to drink?

Better: You like to drink?

Best: You drink? *Followed by:* You like it?

Using a logical progression to reach a specific goal on cross examination is the best construct for educating the jury. It allows you to forecast issues, foreshadow potential answers and create a sense of tension and finality as you lead them to the one unalterable conclusion posited by your logically-progressing, one-fact leading questions. In the eyes of others, a logical questioning progression makes the goal of the questions appear logically true. It also greatly reduces the witness's ability to evade. Finally, it allows you to penalize the witness through sarcasm, impeachment and lack of credibility when they try to evade the logical progression of your questions.

An excellent way to create logical progression is to view your cross examination as a series of staircases, each with their own landing. Each one is a *controlled* inquiry into a specific area. Each one is a series of questions that leads you up the staircase to an established *goal question* that serves as the landing. The final question and answer advances your theory of the case one goal at a time. Each question is a step-up the staircase towards a location that everyone can see, but no one can avoid without being either false or rude.

In order to create functional paths towards your goal question you must review your materials to see how many different ways you can prove the goal question, and then select the witness or witnesses that you should cross examine on that particular goal. When creating these lines of inquiry, first move backwards in the sequence of questions until you reach a general point where the witness must agree with the question posed. From that starting point, draft a series of questions leading to the goal. Those questions should be general initially, becoming increasingly specific in nature, right up to the goal question.

The progression creates context and makes the goal fact more persuasive. By using a series of questions, you support the goal fact with as much detail and supporting facts as you can to ensure the goal fact is believed and understood. Single questions on a goal fact sacrifice the opportunity to surround the goal question with other questions that establish its veracity.

The Truck Was Blue?

You saw the color of the truck?

The sun was shining?

It was around 3 pm?

Five feet from you?

The truck drove past you?

You were standing on the corner?

You can also get the same information out with one question:

Q: The truck was blue?

A: Yes.

This single-fact leading question does an adequate job of getting the information out, but it lacks emphasis. The use of simple, directed, supporting, facts changes the entire tenor of the goal question and the impact it will have on the jury. Consider how such a progression would look as part of a trial transcript:

Q: You were standing on the corner?

A: *Yes.*
Q: The truck drove past you?
A: *Yes.*
Q: The truck drove within five feet of you:
A: *Around 5 feet.*
Q: It was about 3:00 PM?
A: *Around that, yes.*
Q: You got a good look at the truck?
A: *Well yes, it was only a few feet from me.*
Q: You are certain of its color?
A: *Yes.*

Goal question: The truck was blue?

. . .

F. Cross Examination Checklist

The following checklist summarizes the information presented throughout this chapter on cross examination. You should use it as a starting point in developing your own questioning skills. This checklist is not "Holy Writ" and is merely the soil in which you should plant the seeds of your own creativity.

I. Seven Steps to Superior Cross Examinations:

   a. Start and end preparation with case analysis.

   b. Every section has a clearly defined purpose tied to theme, theory or credibility.

   c. CONTROL THE WITNESS.

   d. Details give control.

   e. Organize the cross to accomplish your goals—not your opponent's.

   f. Impeachment must matter.

   g. Use the witness's own words.

II. Primary Goals of Cross Examination:

   a. Control the witness.

   b. Establish facts that bolster your theme and theory.

   c. Establish facts that build up the credibility of your witnesses and diminish the credibility of your opponent's witnesses.

III. Maximize the Persuasive Impact of Answers on Cross:

a. Cluster together all of the facts that enhance and support the topic.

b. Lay out the facts one question at a time leading up to your final point.

c. Identify similar facts based upon your knowledge of human nature and then using them to make your final point.

IV. Why Cross?

a. To elicit facts supporting your legal theory, factual theory or moral theme.

b. To expose facts or bias that weakens your opponent's legal theory, factual theory or moral theme.

c. To establish the credibility of your own witnesses or attack the credibility of opposing witnesses (when required by your legal theory, factual theory or moral theme).

V. Fundamental Precepts of Cross:

a. It is a commando raid, not an invasion.

b. Use primacy and recency.

c. Avoid the ultimate question.

d. One fact questions.

e. Vary questioning techniques.

f. Do not play with fire.

g. Develop control techniques.

VI. Cross Examination Sequencing:

a. Do not use chronological order in confrontational cross examinations.

b. Avoid chronological order in informational cross examinations.

c. Lay your theme early and often.

d. Close cross examination with a theme vignette.

e. When attacking credibility, attack in the first vignette.

f. Show bias, interest, or motive early in the cross examination.

g. End with a power vignette.

h. Develop risky areas only after establishing control of the witness through safe vignettes.

i. Never lead or end with a risky vignette.

j. If you have more than one impeachment vignette, use the cleanest first.

k. Disperse impeachment vignettes throughout the cross examination.

l. When expecting a 'no' answer to one goal question, precede that chapter with a sure 'yes' answer.

m. Bundle vignettes that need to be done together in order to complete a coherent picture of a single event.

n. Prepared vignettes countering the power of the opponent's case are best performed in the middle of cross examination.

G. Conclusion

Now that we have discussed both the fundamental tenets of direct and cross examination we can move on and develop some additional skills that are specific to certain situations in either direct or cross. Those skills will then serve as the starting point for our development of advanced examination skills.

* * *

Relevant Rules

1. *Evidentiary Rule Matrix*

Table 1 serves as a starting point for additional inquiry into the relationships between specific tasks on cross examination and the rules of evidence. Your case analysis should assist you in identifying when these particular issues will arise. You should use the table to review your knowledge of the evidentiary rule so that you can include that in your legal theory of the case. Particular attention should be paid to understanding the fundamental rules concerning impeachment and their interactions with the other rules of evidence.

Issue Arising During Cross Examination	Applicable Federal Rule of Evidence
Character traits of the victim or accused	404(a), 404(b), 405
Character of a witness for truthfulness	608
Out of court statements offered for the truth of	801–807

Issue Arising During Cross Examination	Applicable Federal Rule of Evidence
the matter asserted therein (hearsay)	
Offering evidence of other crimes, wrongs & acts (*see Chapter 10*)	404(b)
Prior convictions of a witness (*see Chapter 10*)	609
Legal relevancy—Is the probative value substantially outweighed by the danger of unfair prejudice et al.	403
Are the questions logically relevant	401, 402
Competency of a witness	610
Personal knowledge of the witness	602
Questioning witnesses	611, 614

Table 1: Potential Evidentiary Rules Applicable During Cross Examination

2. *Professional Responsibility Rule Matrix*

Table 2 serves as a starting point for additional inquiry into the potential professional responsibility issues implicated during cross examination. Counsel must ensure that they do not cross certain lines when investigating cases, preparing witnesses and performing cross. The same issues exist when listening to an opposing counsel's cross examination. You must pay particular attention to your jurisdiction's interpretation and application of the fairness towards opposing counsel rule found in Rule 3.4. A thorough grasp of these issues will assist you in determining whether your conduct and that of your opponent's raises any ethical issues. Your case analysis should help in identifying when these particular issues will arise. You should use the table to review your knowledge of the ethical rules so that you can include them when planning cross examinations.

Issue Arising During Cross Examination	Applicable Rule of Professional Responsibility
(a)(1–3) A lawyer must not offer false evidence.	Rule 3.3: Candor Toward the Tribunal

Issue Arising During Cross Examination	Applicable Rule of Professional Responsibility
(e) A lawyer must not allude to any matter that she does not reasonably believe is relevant or that will not be supported by admissible evidence. She must not assert personal knowledge of facts in issue and never state a personal opinion as to justness of a cause, the credibility of a witness, the culpability of a civil litigant or the guilt or innocence of the defendant.	Rule 3.4: Fairness to Opposing Party and Counsel
(a) A lawyer must not illegally seek to influence a judge, juror, prospective juror or other official. (d) A lawyer must not intentionally disrupt the court and must conduct herself with respect for the court.	Rule 3.5: Impartiality and Decorum of the Tribunal
(a) A lawyer must not attempt to be an advocate and witness in the same trial (with some limited exceptions).	Rule 3.7: Lawyer as Witness

Table 2: The Most Prevalent Professional Conduct Rules During Cross Examination

---

POST-CLASS REFLECTION MEMO

Draft and submit a memo in response to the questions below:

- How will you take the lessons you've learned in class today and apply them to your work in representing clinic clients?
- How will your insights about connections between cross, case theory, and fact investigation affect your casework over the next several days or weeks?
- How will you take the lessons you've learned in class today and apply them to your work in representing clinic clients?
- How will your insights about connections between cross, case theory, and fact investigation affect your casework over the next several days or weeks?

CHAPTER 12

ADMISSION OF EXHIBITS INTO EVIDENCE

LEARNING GOALS

The learning goals for this class include helping you to:

- Understand the legal factors that control the admission of exhibits into evidence
- Understand the strategic importance of exhibits
- Understand the technique for the admission of exhibits into evidence

DESCRIPTION OF CLASS

In this class, we will discuss the kinds of exhibits that can be useful in our clinic cases and why judges and juries find exhibits valuable. Once we identify the exhibits we might use in our cases, we will discuss the strategic choices that arise when lawyers consider whether to use an exhibit and determine what law controls its admission into evidence. Finally, we will practice the examination techniques needed to secure the admission of an exhibit into evidence so that you will understand how to gain the admission of exhibits in your clinic cases. The readings will help you determine the laws governing the admission of various exhibits and will suggest techniques to secure their admission.

ASSIGNMENT IN PREPARATION FOR CLASS

Introducing Exhibits into Evidence: Problem Sets

Domestic Violence or Civil Clinic

For this class, you will be assigned in small groups to one of the following problems, each of which requires you to work through all of the steps necessary to admit an exhibit into evidence. Clinic faculty will distribute the exhibits to each team in advance of class. For each exercise, team members will need to role-play the appropriate foundation witness (or witnesses), as well as the attorney conducting the examination of that witness. The examination should be developed collaboratively by the entire team.

The examining attorney should pose all appropriate questions to the witness to ensure that the exhibit is admitted into evidence, including developing a brief amount of background information to demonstrate the exhibit's relevance. To introduce your exhibit into evidence, you will need to cover all of the steps set out in the reading materials, think carefully about what questions to ask and why you will ask them, and practice the exercise in advance so that it goes smoothly in class. If your exhibit can be photocopied, please bring a sufficient number of copies to class so that everyone can review it. While you should follow evidence law faithfully, feel free to be creative and have fun as you develop the facts of your direct examination.

During the in-class exercise, all students who are not engaged in a role-play will be expected to participate by making appropriate objections. As a result, it is important to prepare to respond to all possible objections that may arise in your role-play.

> **Problem 1: Tangible Object.** This team is responsible for introducing a tangible object—a rock—into evidence. You can assume the red mark on the rock is blood from the scene of an assault. Create the facts that would make the admission of a rock relevant to your case, and then ask all questions necessary to ensure the admission of the rock into evidence.
>
> **Problem 2: Tape Recording.** This team is responsible for introducing a tape recording into evidence. Create the facts that would make the admission of the recording relevant to your case, and then ask all questions necessary to ensure the admission of the recording into evidence.
>
> **Problem 3: Business Record.** This team is responsible for introducing a business record into evidence. Introducing a business record into evidence requires two witnesses: one witness who can testify about why the record is relevant; and one witness who can act as a custodian of records for the business that created the exhibit. Create a direct examination for each witness.
>
> **Problem 4: Prior Conviction.** This team is responsible for introducing the judicial order related to a prior conviction into evidence. For this exercise, assume that the defendant has been convicted of a criminal offense. You represent the plaintiff, and you intend to impeach the defendant's credibility with this prior

conviction. Start with a brief cross-examination in which the defendant denies being convicted of a crime. Next, fast-forward to your rebuttal case, and try to impeach the defendant's credibility by introducing the exhibit into evidence.

Problem 5: Photograph. This team is responsible for admitting a photograph into evidence. Create the facts that would make the admission of the photograph relevant to your case, and then proceed with a full set of questions to ensure the admissibility of the photograph into evidence.

Problem 6: Diagram. This team is responsible for admitting a diagram, made to scale, into evidence. Create the facts that would make the admission of the diagram relevant to your case, and then proceed with a full set of questions to ensure the admissibility of the diagram into evidence.

Problem 7: Telephone Records. This team is responsible for introducing phone records into evidence. Create facts that would make the admission of a phone bill relevant to your case, and then proceed with a full set of questions to ensure the admissibility of the phone record into evidence.

Problem 8: Email Message/Texts. This team is responsible for introducing either an email message or a text message on a phone. You have a smartphone with email and text capacity. Create facts that would make the admission of the message relevant to your case, and then proceed with a full set of questions to ensure the admissibility of the message into evidence.

Criminal or Juvenile Delinquency Defense Clinic

For this class, you will be assigned in teams to one of the following problems, each of which requires you to work through all of the steps and related questions necessary to plan and prepare for the admission of a particular exhibit into evidence. For each exercise, team members will need to role-play the appropriate foundation witness (or witnesses), as well as the attorney conducting the examination of that witness. The examination should be developed collaboratively by the team.

The examining attorney should pose all appropriate questions to the witness to ensure that the exhibit is admitted into evidence, including developing a brief amount of background information to demonstrate the exhibit's legal relevance. To introduce your exhibit into evidence, you will need to cover all of the steps set out in the reading materials, think carefully about what questions to ask and why you will ask them, and practice the exercise in advance so that it goes smoothly in class.

Problem 1 asks you to prepare the exhibit yourself. Other exhibits will be distributed by the clinic faculty in class. The clinic faculty will play the role of witness, as well as judge.

During the exercise, all students not conducting the examination will be permitted to object to the admission of the exhibit. Thus, you should all be prepared to respond to all possible objections that might arise during your role-play.

Factual Background

The following excerpt from a police form provides the basic factual background for this problem set. Defendant Michael Wright has been charged with evading arrest, possession of narcotics, and failure to stop for a stop sign. Defendant Timothy Wright has been charged with unlawful possession of a firearm.

POLICE REPORT

> I, the undersigned police officer, Officer Mark Martin, was in my car on Thomas Street, at the intersection of Thomas and 13th Streets, when I observed a Chevrolet Impala heading north on 13th Street. The car passed through a stop sign and turned left onto Thomas Street. The vehicle was occupied by suspect 1, Timothy Wright, who was seated in the front passenger seat. A second suspect, Michael Wright, was operating the vehicle. The car bore the license tag number GLW 716. I observed that the driver's side rear vent window was broken, so I called into the dispatcher and initiated a license plate check. It was revealed that the car was not stolen.
>
> I followed the vehicle and activated my squad car emergency lights to conduct a traffic stop for running a stop sign. At that time, the vehicle failed to stop or pull over to the curb. The vehicle approached police officer William Randolph, who was standing outside his police vehicle at 14th and Thomas Streets. Officer Randolph directed the vehicle to pull over. The vehicle failed to pull over on Thomas Street and turned right onto 14th Street. As it reached 14th and Upton Streets, I pulled alongside the vehicle and ordered the driver to pull over to the curb and stop, which he did. I exited my vehicle and approached the driver's side front door. At that time, I observed that the steering column was broken. I asked the occupants to step out of the car. Officer Randolph took custody of the defendants while I searched the car. The search revealed a 9 mm Luger pistol under the front passenger seat, and a bag of white rock substance later tested to be cocaine under the front driver's seat. Subsequent to the

arrests, the Crime Scene Investigation Unit took possession of the car and processed it for investigation purposes.

Problem 1: Diagram

1A Assume you are the prosecutor and want Officer Martin to draw a map of the scene of the chase on a chart during the direct examination at trial. Prepare a direct examination that permits the officer to use a map that he draws while testifying about the chase.

1B Assume you are the prosecutor and want Martin to testify using a map that was prepared by a law clerk in advance of the trial. Which witness would you call to authenticate the map? Prepare the map and prepare the direct examination that authenticates the prepared map.

Problem 2: Photographs

There are two photographs available for use by counsel. They are marked on the back Exhibit #1 and Exhibit #2, respectively. Exhibit #1 shows the broken steering column of the car with wires hanging, as viewed from the driver's window. It was taken by Officer Edison, who was called to the scene by the arresting officer. Officer Martin completed the police report excerpted above. Exhibit #2 shows the steering column from the passenger window showing an intact ignition switch. It was taken by a defense investigator who accompanied the defense attorney to Nick's Garage, at 2001 14th Street, where the police had towed the car and where it had been left for repair by the car's owner, Jonah Simmons.

2A Which witness would the prosecutor call to authenticate photo #1? Prepare the direct examination needed to introduce the photos into evidence.

2B Which witnesses could and would the defense attorney call to authenticate Exhibit #2? Prepare the direct examination(s) needed to introduce the photograph into evidence.

Problem 3: Weapon

3A Assume Officer Martin recovered the pistol, test fired it, stored it in the evidence locker, and brought it to court. Assume the chain of custody for the gun is directly from Officer Martin to the court. Prepare the prosecutor's direct examination of Officer Martin to admit the evidence.

3B Assume that Officer Martin gave the weapon to Officer Randolph, who test fired it and then gave it to Officer Wells, who stored it in a police evidence locker. Officer Martin then brought the weapon to court. Who would the prosecutor need to call to authenticate the weapon? Prepare the direct examination of all of the officers that the prosecutor would need to call to authenticate the weapon that was found in the car so that it can be moved it into evidence.

Problem 4: Business Record

Assume the prosecutor wants to prove that the white substance found in the car was an illegal narcotic. The chain of custody for the substance goes from Officer Martin to Officer Randolph, who placed the substance in a sealed envelope and then placed the envelope in a police evidence locker for testing by chemist Dawn Jones. The prosecutor seeks to admit the substance by introducing the official business records of the chemistry lab. The prosecutor wishes to call a records administrator to introduce the business records.

4A Are there issues beyond the normal authentication, relevance, privilege, and hearsay requirements that affect the admissibility of the drugs if you use a records administrator instead of Chemist Dawn Jones? What are they?

4B Assume Dawn Jones will testify. You seek both her live testimony and the admission of the lab records concerning this case. Prepare the direct examination of Dawn Jones and any other witnesses you will need to admit the evidence as a business records exception to the hearsay rule.

READING ASSIGNMENT

1. Federal Rules of Evidence 401–403; 801, 803, 804; 901, 902; 1001–1007; Admission of Exhibits: "Selected Federal Rules of Evidence" https://georgetown.box.com/s/5oyn7vibchc1nwkzewqt or comparable local rules of evidence.
2. Charles H. Rose III, *Exhibits, in* FUNDAMENTAL TRIAL ADVOCACY (2d. ed. 2011).

READINGS

Federal Rules of Evidence

Admission of Exhibits: "Selected Federal Rules of Evidence" https://georgetown.box.com/s/5oyn7vibchc1nwkzewqt

The Federal Rules of Evidence are the accepted evidentiary rules for authentication, relevance, best evidence, and hearsay and its exceptions. Your familiarity with these rules will depend on whether you have taken an Evidence course prior to enrolling in the clinic. If your state has not adopted the Federal Rules of Evidence, find the state rule analog to the relevant Federal Rule.

Charles H. Rose III
Exhibits
FUNDAMENTAL TRIAL ADVOCACY (2nd ed. 2011)[1]

. . .

A. The Skill of Exhibits

. . .

Advocates engage in the art of persuasion. What, how, and where they say and do something matters.

. . .

This chapter focuses on how advocates use exhibits to maximize the impact of a witness's testimony. The purpose of the exhibit is to persuade. When used properly exhibits increase the credibility of the advocate's theme and theory by providing information to visual learners through a medium from which they find it easier to learn. Exhibits also reinforce spoken testimony.

When used improperly, or not at all, exhibits represent lost opportunities. As an advocate in the courtroom few things are more enjoyable than seeing your opponent's exhibits sitting there out of the sight of the jury, unused and unappreciated. This often happens because the advocate did not understand the law behind exhibits, the skill needed

---

[1] Some footnotes and illustrations have been omitted or realigned. Unless otherwise specifically indicated, all professional conduct rules referenced are taken from the Delaware Supreme Court's professional responsibility rules. Those rules are almost identical to the model rules promulgated by the American Bar Association and are public domain documents.

to admit them, and the proper art in using them. When confronted with the perceived difficulties attached to their use many advocates simply turn away and leave them at counsel's table. When we are done with this chapter you will be the master of the exhibit—not your opponent, not the witness, and certainly not the judge.

Seven Fundamental Principles When Dealing with Exhibits

- Use them—Opening, direct, cross, and closing
- Know the type of exhibit you have and the limitations on their use
- Identify your foundational requirements early and have them on hand in the courtroom for reference
- Practice, practice, practice
- Script foundations for persuasive impact as well as legal requirements
- Do not be afraid to voir dire
- BARPH when necessary

In order to properly admit and use exhibits you must first be able to place the exhibit into its proper evidentiary category. This is necessary to lay a proper foundation, showing the court that the item is what it claims to be and that we can rely upon its authenticity and relevancy. Evidence offered at trial falls into three evidentiary categories: (1) testimonial, (2) demonstrative, and (3) real. Real evidence can be further divided into two sub-categories: (1) fungible and (2) non-fungible. Properly identifying the nature of the evidence is the first step in determining the foundational requirements for admissibility. The required foundation questions depend on the type of evidence offered and the purpose of the offered evidence. Categorizing the evidence is the single most important step in this process. Each type of evidence must be properly authenticated and admitted through the testimony of a sponsoring witness.

Three Categories of Exhibits

- Testimonial
- Demonstrative
- Real evidence
  - Fungible
  - Non-fungible

Foundational requirements are derived from the evidentiary rules addressing each particular type of evidence. The foundation must be "laid" through the questions of the offering counsel and the responses of the witness. An improper foundation will prompt an objection and may prevent the offered evidence from being accepted by the court. The type of evidentiary objections that must be overcome are derived from the nature of the evidence counsel is seeking to admit, the foundational questions asked, and the responses received. Finally, sometimes evidence may fall into more than one category. Counsel must properly offer the evidence to ensure that they can use it for their intended purpose. This becomes important during jury deliberations since most jurisdictions do not allow demonstrative evidence back into the jury deliberation room.

Attorneys are required to ask foundational questions in order to establish the admissibility of evidence. These foundational questions are derived from the common law, evidentiary law, and local court practices. They serve as a short cut for answering challenges to a piece of evidence based upon potential objections. Foundational questions normally deal with best evidence issues, authenticity, relevancy, personal knowledge, and hearsay. "The requirement of authentication or identification as a condition precedent to admissibility is satisfied by evidence sufficient to support a finding that the matter in question is what its proponent claims." FRE 901 addresses authentication. For example, only a witness with personal knowledge of the scene may authenticate a diagram. They must be able to testify that the diagram is a "fair and accurate" depiction of the scene in question. The proponent of the diagram should ensure that the witness also explains labels and other markings present on the diagram prior to admitting it and using it.

Regardless of the type of proffered evidence it is the judge who determines the sufficiency of the authentication. That issue is a question of fact under Federal Rule of Evidence 104(a). In addition to the authentication requirement, the proponent of demonstrative evidence must be prepared to respond to other evidentiary objections raised by opposing counsel that may bar the admissibility of the evidence. An easy acronym to use when addressing possible evidentiary objections to exhibits is BARPH. Counsel should always lay all foundational elements when dealing with exhibits. These foundational questions can be used to not only authenticate the evidence, but to persuade the jury that the evidence is worthy of consideration.

Easy Guide to Courtroom Objections (BARPH):

B – est Evidence

A – uthentication

R – elevance

P – ersonal Knowledge

H – earsay

Let us use our earlier example of a diagram to discuss how you would admit it. First the diagram must be shown to the sponsoring witness, giving them the opportunity to examine it. Next you should ask the witness if the diagram is a "fair and accurate" depiction of the scene at that time. Unless exact distances are crucial the diagram need not be to scale, although this is a common objection that you will have to deal with if you have not created a diagram that is to scale. The lack of scale may be established on either direct or cross-examination. If the diagram is drawn to scale, it should be noted on the record and the scale clearly shown on the diagram.

Foundation Elements for Diagrams

- The diagram depicts a certain area or object;
- The witness is familiar with that area or object;
- The witness explains the basis for his knowledge of the area or object;
- The witness affirms the accuracy of the diagram.

Once you have established that the diagram is relevant and authentic you offer it into evidence. You must then use it in the testimony of the witness and publish it to the jury. Publication may be accomplished in a variety of ways. You can provide copies to the jury, blow the exhibit up so that everyone may see it or place it in a location where the jury is able to reference as the witness testifies. There is room for creative advocacy during publication. Advocates should make certain that the jury can see the exhibit, that the witness has access to it and that the judge can see it. Opposing counsel should request permission of the judge to move around the courtroom so that they may also observe the use of the diagram.

Using Exhibits at Trial:

- Introduce the exhibit.
- Lay the foundation for admission.
- Authenticate the exhibit.
- Offer into evidence.
- Have witness mark the exhibit as needed.
- Publish the exhibit to the jury.

The following questions normally meet the foundational requirement for various types of exhibits. Each jurisdiction may modify or rearrange these foundational questions, but they serve as a competent and thorough basis from which to begin. As you read them carefully note the specific differences for each type of exhibit. The foundational requirements vary because the evidentiary rules necessary to authenticate the evidence and establish its relevancy are influenced by the physical nature of the offered exhibit.

A photograph is authenticated by a witness who attests that the photograph accurately and fairly depicts the scene in question. There is no need to address the mechanics of exposing or developing the film or the working condition of the camera. Also, it is important to note that a photograph does not need to be authenticated by the photographer, but must be authenticated by a witness with personal knowledge of the scene depicted in the photograph.

Foundational Elements for Photographs

- The witness is familiar with the object or scene;
- The witness explains the basis for his familiarity with the object or scene;
- The witness recognizes the object or scene in the photograph;
- The witness testifies the photograph is a "fair," "accurate," "true," or "correct" depiction of the object or scene at the relevant time.

Non-fungible evidence is evidence having a unique characteristic that allows it to be identified by individuals who have personal knowledge of that unique characteristic. The nature of the unique characteristic is not identified by the rules of evidence, but in practice it is a relatively common sense rule. The person who initially takes custody of the evidence has the opportunity to observe the evidence carefully. They look for indications of uniqueness. Such indications might include a serial number on a weapon, a nick in a particular location on the blade of a knife, the nature of a scratch or disfiguring mark on the piece of evidence.

Additionally, relatively common items can be given unique characteristics by the individual taking them into custody. The classic example of this is when the police officer places her initials on the butt of a weapon seized at the crime scene. Conversely, fungible evidence is evidence that does not have a unique characteristic rendering it readily identifiable. Fungible evidence requires additional foundational steps before it can be admitted, usually involving some type of chain-of-custody. Examples of non-fungible evidence include a gun with a serial number or other unique items seized for their evidentiary value.

Foundational Elements for Non-Fungible Evidence

- The object has a unique characteristic;
- The witness observed the characteristic on a previous occasion;
- The witness identifies the exhibit presented as the object;
- The witness rests the identification on his present recognition of the characteristic; and
- To the best of the witness's knowledge, the exhibit is in the same condition as it was when the witness initially saw or received the object.

Foundation 3 - Non-Fungible Evidence

Sometimes a non-fungible piece of evidence also contains fungible evidence. Consider the scenario of a bloody knife seized at the crime scene. The knife will have some unique characteristic that will allow the police officer testifying at trial to properly identify it—the blood does not. If the police intend to test the blood for DNA identification they must safeguard that blood from the moment it is taken into custody. Certain procedures must be followed to ensure that the fungible blood is what it purports to be—blood taken from the knife found at the scene of the crime. These are referred to as chain-of-custody documents. Before the court would allow a witness to testify as to the nature of that blood the judge must be satisfied that the blood has not been adulterated either intentionally or unintentionally. That concern does not exist as to the knife because it has unique characteristics making it an identifiable non-fungible piece of evidence—you can mark it in a manner that lets you ensure it is controlled. But, while you cannot mark the blood in order to ensure it remains in the state that it was when collected, but you can create both procedures that safeguard the fungible evidence and documents that verify those procedures.

Because the blood does not have unique characteristics a court will be concerned with the chain-of-custody documents that establish that the blood has not been tampered with. The offering party must lay the foundation for the chain-of-custody documents first, admitting them subject to a relevancy connection to the case.

Elements of the Foundation of Fungible Evidence

- The witness is familiar with the item of evidence;
- The witness acquired this familiarity by obtaining the item;
- The witness uniquely marked the item of evidence to enable him to identify it later;
- The witness properly safeguarded the item while it was in his possession to prevent the evidence from being lost or altered;
- The witness ultimately disposed of the item (retention, destruction, or transfer to another individual);
- To the best of his knowledge, the witness can positively identify the item of evidence as that which he previously had custody over; and
- That the item of evidence is in the same condition as it was when he had custody previously.

Foundation 4 - Fungible evidence & Non-fungible evidence

Fungible evidence has the potential to be easily modified, adulterated, or replaced by people having access to it. In order to guarantee its relevance and authenticity, fungible evidence must be carefully guarded to prevent contamination or destruction. As part of the process in laying the foundation for the admissibility of fungible evidence the offering party must first establish that the fungible evidence has been properly safeguarded against potential contamination. Chain-of-custody procedures accomplish this purpose. To admit fungible evidence, the chain-of-custody documents relating to the evidence must be offered and admitted before the fungible evidence itself can be offered and admitted.

Establishing a proper chain-of custody for fungible evidence is a condition precedent to its admissibility. This is a precise and important skill that a competent trial attorney must master. Improperly authenticated evidence may result in crucial evidence being excluded that could deal a fatal blow to your case. While this skill is important, it is relatively easy to master. All that is required is attention to the local rules of court, an understanding of how the rules of evidence impact foundational questions, and a commitment to preparation that includes taking examples of foundational requirements for your intended exhibits into court with you and having them readily available if you run into difficulties.

Foundational Elements for Chain-of-Custody Documents

- The witness has personal knowledge of the business' filing or records system;
- The witness removed the record (chain-of-custody document) in question from a certain file;
- It was a proper file or entry;
- The witness recognizes the exhibit as the record (chain-of-custody document) he removed from the file;
- The witness specifies the basis on which he recognized the exhibit.

Foundation 5 - Chain-of-Custody Documents

Once counsel establishes the authenticity of a business record they must next establish that the contents of the chain-of-custody document are admissible as an exception to the hearsay rule, usually under the business records exception found in FRE 803(6). After lying the foundations for the fungible evidence and the chain-of-custody documents counsel can then move to admit both into evidence.

Foundational Elements for Chain-of-Custody Documents (Hearsay Exception)

- Document prepared by a person having a relationship with the agency preparing the document;
- The person had a duty to record the information on the document;
- The person had personal knowledge of the facts or events recorded in the document;
- The document was prepared contemporaneously with the event(s);
- It was a routine practice of the business to prepare such document;
- The document was reduced to written form; and
- The document was prepared in the regular course of business.

Foundation 6 - Laying a Foundation for a Chain-of-Custody Document (Hearsay Exception)

Let us now consider how other rules of evidence and the procedures involved in admitting exhibits create additional legal issues and advocacy opportunities.

B. The Law of Exhibits—Voir Dire & Objections

When an exhibit is offered into evidence opposing counsel must decide whether or not to object. In your initial thought process you should consider how allowing this evidence to be admitted will affect your chosen theme and theory. If it doesn't hurt let it in, especially if you have found a way to make it work to your advantage. If it does hurt, opposing counsel may: (1) voir dire on the exhibit, (2) object as to the foundation, or (3) object based upon BARPH.

Easy Guide to Courtroom Objections (BARPH)

B – est Evidence

A – uthentication

R – elevance

P – ersonal Knowledge

H – earsay

Opposing counsel may request to voir dire the witness on the exhibit for the purposes of developing an objection to the exhibit's admissibility. This voir dire about an exhibit is a cross-examination of the witness that is limited in scope to questions addressing only the potential admissibility of the exhibit. Questions concerning the weight that the evidence might be given are outside the scope of the voir dire and should instead be asked during normal cross examination of the witness. Since voir dire on an exhibit occurs during the direct examination of a witness by opposing counsel, judges are careful to restrict the scope of voir dire on exhibits. Save your questions designed to attack the weight that the exhibit should be given for your cross examination.

A common objection often made during the voir dire is that it is "outside the scope of the direct." When a judge sustains this objection you can be confident that she perceives that you are asking questions about weight and not admissibility. Another common objection is "Your honor that goes to weight, and not admissibility." That is another way of saying "outside the scope" that is accepted in most jurisdictions. Normally, questions asked during voir dire on the exhibit will not be allowed during cross, but creative counsel can easily tie what was earlier an admissibility issue to a greater weight issue later. If counsel chooses to not request voir dire on an exhibit then they must either agree to its admission or object.

When counsel stands and says: "Objection, insufficient foundation," the judge must either rule on the objection, or respond to the objecting counsel by asking how the foundation is insufficient. If the court sustains the objection without an explanation, the proponent of the exhibit may inquire for the reasons for the ruling under the rules of evidence. When the objection is other than foundational the counsel opposing admissibility should stand and say "Objection," and then give a BRIEF statement of the grounds for the objection without testifying through the use of a rambling objection that is really designed to make arguments to the jury. The judge will either rule on the objection or ask the proponent of the exhibit how they respond to opposing counsel's objection. If the court sustains the objection, the proponent is not barred from continuing to attempt to lay an adequate foundation to get the exhibit into evidence.

C. The Art of Exhibits

1. *Persuasive Use of Exhibits*

Although foundations for a diagram are relatively easy to establish, the effective use of diagrams and other exhibits as persuasive tools depends upon how well you prepare for, and practice, their use. In this day and age one technique to consider is using the highest-quality possible computer-generated graphics. We live in the video age and slick presentations are now expected on cell phones, let alone by attorneys in court. The routine use of computer-generated products has created high expectations for all graphic products among our community. You should strive to meet or exceed those expectations in order to increase the effectiveness of your exhibits.

A shabby diagram may well be interpreted as an indication that your case or investigation is also less than average, especially if your opposing counsel has chosen the high-tech route. A powerful diagram will continue selling your case long after the witness has left the stand. Diagrams should appear in opening statements, be used by witnesses during testimony, and referred to during closing arguments. In jurisdictions that allow demonstrative evidence into the jury room, exhibits will continue to speak until the case is decided, long after counsel's final closing exhortations have faded from the courtroom and the minds of the jurors.

Regardless of the type of diagram, demonstrative aid, or exhibit you are using, its presentation must be fluid. This requires a commitment to practicing with the exhibit, both alone and with the witness that will authenticate it. Different courtrooms are going to require different types of demonstrative evidence to be truly effective. Take the time to learn what delivery systems will be available in court. Once you have found the one that works best for you create your exhibits, practice, modify, and then practice some more until you and the witness are comfortable in the type, manner, and effectiveness of the presentation. Position the exhibit and your witness so that the jury and the judge can see the exhibit and you are able to use it effectively.

One collateral benefit of diagrams and other demonstrative evidence is they permit you to have the witness testify more than once about issues related to the diagram. First, have the witness tell the story during direct examination without the assistance of a diagram or other demonstrative aid. Next, lay the foundation for the exhibit, being careful to explain through your foundational questions how the use of the exhibit will further develop the witness's testimony. The witness will necessarily relate elements of their previous testimony a second time while laying the foundation for the exhibit and explaining its relevance. Finally, have the witness develop their testimony in greater detail, relying upon and using the exhibit to explain what happened. While you may run the danger of a cumulative objection, proper organization of questions should overcome and even prevent this problem.

Remember to always inform the judge when you intend to use demonstrative evidence and be sure to give her an opportunity, along with opposing counsel, to view the demonstrative aids you intend to use. Judges hate surprises. You should never hide demonstrative aids or exhibits until the last minute in a futile attempt to surprise the opposing side; the surprise may be your own when the judge sustains the objection and does not allow you to use them.

2. Admitting Exhibits

There are a variety of ways to approach admitting exhibits at trial, most of which are either derived from the customary practices of the particular local jurisdiction or promulgated in the local rules of court. Advocates must also take the time to ascertain the particular local rules that are "unwritten" when preparing exhibits. Customs of the court are just that—customs. An advocate should not refrain from approaching the court and requesting that they be allowed to use an exhibit in a particular fashion.

These issues are normally addressed during pretrial conferences with the court or by the experience of doing it wrong and being reprimanded. While both methods are effective, the former is much more enjoyable than the latter. There are no surprises when it comes to exhibits so there is no valid reason for counsel to attempt exhibit by ambush. Show them to the judge and opposing counsel. Address any concerns about their relevancy and authenticity and then use them—often.

The Following Steps Serve as an Excellent Set of General Guidelines for Dealing with Admitting Exhibits at Trial:

- Have the exhibit *marked* by the court reporter
- Show exhibit to *opposing counsel* for inspection and objection
- Ask the judge's *permission* to approach the witness
- Show the exhibit to the *witness*
- **Lay *foundation* for the exhibit**—Focus on relevancy, authenticity and reliability
- *Offer* exhibit into evidence: "I offer what has been marked as prosecution exhibit 1 for ID into evidence as prosecution exhibit 1."

Advocates following these steps will ensure that the exhibit is not only admitted, but used in a persuasive fashion. These fundamental steps serve as the guideline for properly handling the exhibit in a manner that removes potential objections, ensures that proper foundations are laid; and allows the jury to focus on the viability of the exhibit.

This list should be copied by the advocate and placed prominently in their trial notebooks for continued use. Once the advocate is familiar with the list the only portion that changes is the fifth step, and that particular section changes based upon the nature of the exhibit proffered. This text contains sample foundation questions for the most common forms of exhibits admitted at trial. Now, let us look at some examples to see this list in action.

3. Sample Foundations

The following two examples show how to employ the techniques discussed in this chapter. Note the degree of control and direction that the advocate has over their witness even though this is direct examination. You are able to sprinkle a certain number of leading questions during direct examination when you are laying a foundation for the admissibility of an exhibit. When used artfully these leading questions reinforce control, establish pace and let the witness know with little to no uncertainty the direction that the advocate wishes to take.

Q: Mr. Witness, WHERE did the robbery occur?

A: At the ATM machine located in the grocery store parking lot across from the Mini-Mall on State Street.

Q: Please look at the diagram located on the easel to your left, marked Prosecution Exhibit 1 for identification. Do you recognize it?

A: Yes.

Q: WHAT is it?

A: *It is a diagram of the area around the ATM machine where I was robbed.*

Q: HOW do you recognize it?

A: *I've lived in this neighborhood for fifteen years and have done most of my ATM banking through that machine for the last eight years. I am very familiar with that area.*

Q: HOW often do you use this ATM?

A: *I used it about three times a week for the last eight years before the robbery. Since the robbery I haven't been able to go back to that spot.*

Q: Is this diagram a fair and accurate representation of the area around the ATM?

A: *Yes, it looks good to me.*

This completes the foundation of an unmarked diagram. If the diagram has been pre-marked by counsel, it is now necessary to have the witness explain the labels that have been superimposed on various objects on the diagram. That explanation could go as follows:

Q: Mr. Witness, HOW did you get to the ATM on the night of the robbery?

A: *I drove my car there.*

Q: WHERE did you park your car when you got there?

A: *In the grocery store parking lot on State Street, about 40 feet from the ATM Machine.*

Q: Is the position of your parked car shown on this diagram, P.E. 1 for ID?

A: *Yes, it is shown as a car with the word "Car" next to it on the diagram.*

Q: HOW is the ATM machine marked on the diagram?

A: *There is a picture of a building with the letters "ATM" next to it.*

Q: You testified earlier that it was dark outside when you arrived at the ATM. Was the area around the ATM also dark?

A: *No. It was lit fairly well by the streetlight located about fifteen feet from the ATM.*

Q: Please point out the location of the street lamp for the jury.

A: *Okay. There is a picture of a street lamp which is labeled "Light" on the diagram.*

Q: Mr. Witness, what happened after you arrived at the ATM?

A: *Well my friend stayed in the car and I went to the machine to withdraw some cash. As I was entering my PIN number, a man in a ski mask came around the side of the machine and pointed a gun at me. He said that he would kill me if I didn't give him all my money.*

Q: [To the Judge] Your honor, request permission to have the witness approach the diagram.

J: Go ahead.

Q: Using the blue marker, please place an "X" where you were standing when the masked man approached you.

A: *All right.*

Q: The witness marked P.E. 1 for ID, as directed. Now using the red marker, draw an arrow to indicate the approach used by the gunman before he robbed you.

A: *Right here.*

Q: [To the Judge] The witness marked P.E. 1 for ID with a red arrow as directed.

Counsel may offer the diagram into evidence at this time or any time before passing the witness. The diagram may not be further marked after it is admitted. Opposing counsel may ask that the judge instruct the jury that the diagram is not to scale.

(b) Sample Photograph Foundation

Q: Mr. Witness, where do you work?

A: *I work at the grocery store on State Street across from the Mini-Mall.*

Q. [To the Judge] I am showing opposing counsel what has previously been marked as Prosecution Exhibit-1 for Identification. (*Show it to opposing counsel.*) Your Honor, may I approach the witness? [Most jurisdictions require counsel to do this when initially approaching each witness, but you usually only need to ask once per witness.]

J: You may approach the witness counsel.

Q: I now hand you P.E.-1 for Identification. What is it?

A: *It is a picture of the ATM Machine located in our grocery store parking lot.*

Q: How do you recognize it?

A: *I have worked at that store as the assistant manager in charge of the night shift for the last twelve years. I was there when it was installed and have used it many times. I took this picture of the machine at the request of the store owner about 6 months ago. We were worried about the safety of our customers when they used it.*

Q: From what angle was this photograph taken?

A: The picture is slightly left of center from the front of the ATM machine where customers use it.

Q: Does this photo fairly and accurately depict the ATM Machine as it appeared six months ago?

A: Absolutely.

Q: Your Honor, I offer P.E.-1 for Identification into evidence as P.E.-1.

These two examples are excellent starting points for developing your own techniques when laying foundations for admitting exhibits. Remember to review the foundational requirements that may be unique to your particular jurisdiction when preparing for trial. Place scripts within your trial notebook that allow you to quickly and efficiently ask the appropriate foundational questions when you come to that point in your direct examination.

If the judge sustains an objection do not allow it to fluster you. Simply regroup and go through your foundational questions again. If the judge sustains another foundational objection it sometimes helps to show the judge that you are actually reading the foundational questions from an approved example in your jurisdiction. You have the ability to take the drudgery that is sometimes associated with laying foundations for exhibits and turn it into yet another opportunity for persuasive advocacy.

. . .

E. Exhibit Checklist

The following checklist summarizes the information presented throughout this chapter on exhibits. You should use it as a starting point in developing your own questioning skills. This checklist is not "Holy Writ" and is merely the soil in which you should plant the seeds of your own creativity.

I. Seven Fundamental Principles Dealing with Exhibits:

  a. Use them. Opening, direct, cross, and closing.
  b. Know the type of exhibit you have and the limitations on their use.
  c. Identify your foundational requirements early and have them on hand in the courtroom for reference.
  d. Practice, practice, practice.
  e. Script foundations for persuasive impact and legal requirements.
  f. Do not be afraid to voir dire.
  g. BARPH when necessary.

II. Types of Exhibits:

  a. Testimonial

  b. Demonstrative

  c. Real evidence

    i. Physical evidence / tangible objects

    ii. Pictures

    iii. Diagrams, maps, models

    iv. Witness demonstrations

    v. Film recordings / computer simulations

III. Common Courtroom Objections (BARPH):

  a. **B** – est Evidence

  b. **A** – uthentication

  c. **R** – elevance

  d. **P** – ersonal Knowledge

  e. **H** – earsay

IV. Admitting Exhibits at Trial:

  a. Have the exhibit *marked*

  b. Show exhibit to *opponent*

  c. Ask Judge's *permission* to approach the witness

  d. Show the exhibit to the *witness*

  e. **Lay *foundation***

    i. Only bedrock requirement is that the evidence supports a finding that the thing is what it purports to be.

    ii. Authentication = more defined relevancy process

    iii. Foundation = evidence supporting a finding that the exhibit is "what its proponent claims."

    iv. *Authentication* deals only with the foundation required for admitting evidence

    v. *Adequacy* of that foundation is determined by the trial judge—screening function only under 104(b)

  f. *Offer* exhibit into evidence

V. Publish the Exhibit to the Jury:

  a. Documents: enough photocopies for everyone!

b. Charts

c. Diagrams

d. PowerPoint

e. Use the exhibit to illustrate, show your point

F. Conclusion

Proper use of exhibits is a fundamental skill for both cross and direct examination. Applying the skills discussed in this chapter, in concert with our earlier discussions about direct and cross examination, will empower you to competently deal with a tremendous component of persuasion at trial—visuals. It also serves as the third component in our basic understanding of witness testimony.

. . .

Relevant Rules

1. Evidentiary Rule Matrix

Table 1 serves as a starting point for additional inquiry into the relationships between specific tasks dealing with exhibits and the rules of evidence. Your case analysis should assist you in identifying when these particular issues will arise. You should use the table to review your knowledge of the evidentiary rule so that you can include that in your legal theory of the case. Particular attention should be paid to understanding the fundamental rules concerning impeachment and their interactions with the other rules of evidence.

Issues Arising Dealing with Exhibits	Applicable Federal Rule of Evidence
Authentication and identification rules	901–902
Best evidence rules	1001–1004
Business records	803(6)
Contents of writings, recordings and photographs	1001–1008
Documents and instruments	901–902
Public records	803(8)
Real and demonstrative evidence	901

Table 1: Potential Evidentiary Rules Applicable to Exhibits

2. *Professional Responsibility Rule Matrix*

Table 2 serves as a starting point for additional inquiry into the potential professional responsibility issues that are implicated when exhibits are involved. Counsel must ensure that they do not cross certain lines when investigating cases, preparing witnesses and controlling direct testimony. The same issues also exist when listening to an opposing counsel's direct examination. You must pay particular attention to your jurisdiction's interpretation and application of the candor towards the tribunal standard found in Rule 3.3. A thorough grasp of these issues will assist you in avoiding perjury and improper conduct. Your case analysis should help in identifying when these particular issues will arise. You should use the table to review your knowledge of the ethical rules so that you can include them in your planning for your use of exhibits.

Issues Arising Dealing with Exhibits	**Applicable Rule of Professional Responsibility**
(a)(1–3) A lawyer must not offer false evidence.	Rule 3.3: Candor Toward the Tribunal
(e) A lawyer must not allude to any matter that she does not reasonably believe is relevant or that will not be supported by admissible evidence. She must not assert personal knowledge of facts in issue and never state a personal opinion as to justness of a cause, the credibility of a witness, the culpability of a civil litigant or the guilt or innocence of the defendant.	Rule 3.4: Fairness to Opposing Party and Counsel
(a) A lawyer must not illegally seek to influence a judge, juror, prospective juror or other official. (d) A lawyer must not intentionally disrupt the court and must conduct herself with respect for the court.	Rule 3.5: Impartiality and Decorum of the Tribunal
(a) A lawyer must not attempt to be an advocate and witness in the same trial (with some limited exceptions).	Rule 3.7: Lawyer as Witness

Table 2: The Most Prevalent Professional Conduct Rules to Exhibits

. . .

POST-CLASS REFLECTION MEMO

Draft and submit a memo in response to the question below:

- How will you take the lessons you have learned in class today and apply them to the cases on which you are working?

CHAPTER 13

MAKING OBJECTIONS

LEARNING GOALS

The learning goals for this class include helping you to:

- Understand the laws of evidence that control objections
- Think strategically about how objections may impede a witness's testimony
- Understand the technique for making objections and rephrasing questions to overcome objections
- Understand that objections and responses to them can be planned in advance.
- Understand the interconnected nature of evidentiary issues in a hearing

---

DESCRIPTION OF CLASS

We will discuss what kind of objections can arise in our clinic cases and determine what law controls the court's ruling. We will explore why planning to make objections during trial and designing questions that avoid objections by the opposition are essential. Once we identify the kinds of objections that might arise during a trial, we will discuss the strategic choices that arise when lawyers consider whether to pose or forego an objection to a question. Finally, we will practice the ways objections are made and defended during the opposition's case and the way to respond to an objection to a question as you present evidence in your clinic cases.

The readings will help you determine the law that governs the various kinds of objections that are common in our cases and will suggest techniques to make and support your objections and to respond to an objection to one of your questions.

ASSIGNMENT IN PREPARATION FOR CLASS

In this class, we will focus on the process of posing, defending, and responding to objections to witness testimony at trial. To prepare, review the Fact Scenario below. The scenario is based on allegations that your client, Catherine Jones, neglected her father, Thomas Black. The opposing attorney is putting on his case-in-chief, and has called Officer Reynolds, the police officer who discovered the elderly Mr. Black wandering in the street, to the stand.

In role as the attorney for Ms. Jones, try to anticipate the questions the opposing lawyer might ask of the witness, as well as the testimony the witness might provide. Consider how you would attempt to limit the testimony offered by the witness, by posing objections based on hearsay, relevance, privilege, or any other appropriate ground.

In class, the teacher will conduct a direct examination of Officer Reynolds. As the witness testifies, each student will take turns being "on call" to serve as counsel for Ms. Jones. When you are on call, listen carefully to the testimony. If you hear an objectionable question or an objectionable answer, stand and object to the question or move to strike the witness's answer. All objections must be supported by appropriate legal authority. Because many objections posed at trial are not totally clear cut, you will be expected to offer compelling arguments to convince the court to sustain the objections you pose. Simply making the objection alone will not be sufficient; the judge will expect a reasoned argument.

In addition, at various points in class you may be called upon to serve as co-counsel for the opposing side. Therefore, you also will need to be prepared to defend against any objections another student might pose. Again, you will need to provide appropriate legal support for your position.

Fact Scenario

Client Information

You have been appointed to represent Catherine Jones at a trial that is scheduled today. Ms. Jones is accused of neglecting her father, Thomas Black, on January 10 of this year. Mr. Black and Ms. Jones both reside at 11720 Worth Court in Smallville.

Summary of the Police Report

On January 10 of this year, Officer Reynolds was dispatched to the area of 19213 Johnsbury Lane to investigate a report about an elderly man wandering around outside, disoriented, and not wearing a coat. Officer Reynolds found a disoriented white male with grey hair, identified as Thomas Black, age 72, walking down the street and looking extremely cold. He weighed 135 pounds and stood 5'8" in height. He was wearing a red shirt, light jacket, thin green pants, and tennis shoes without socks. He had no gloves. When approached, Black immediately said, "I'm cold," and repeated that statement several times. The temperature outside was in the single digits and snow was predicted that day. A passerby approached Officer Reynolds during the investigation and reported that Mr. Black had been seen in the area for at least one hour prior to being stopped by Officer Reynolds. When asked where he lived, Mr. Black said "McDonald's and Wendy's." His nose was running and his face appeared frozen. Mr. Black asked for a tissue. His health and life were definitely in immediate danger due to exposure to the cold.

Officer Reynolds discovered that Mr. Black resided at 11720 Worth Court. He took him to that residence to return him to his home. When the officer pulled up in front of the residence, Mr. Black stated, "Catherine kicked me out. She doesn't want me here anymore." He also stated that "Pete tapes the refrigerator closed and takes my socks and cuts holes in them." Mr. Black also said that "Pete is fat because he eats all the food."

Mr. Black also appeared to be in fear of Pete. He repeated several times "Pete's mean, Pete's mean." We later determined that "Pete" is Peter Jones, Mr. Black's son-in-law.

When Officer Reynolds went to knock on the door of the house he found a note tacked to the door saying:

> Dear Police—If you knock on this door concerning Thomas Black, you will be doing it for nothing other than to wake us up and have us swear your asses out and he will still be out there with you. So thank you for not knocking. Signed, Peter and Catherine.

The note was taken for handwriting analysis. Subsequent analysis demonstrated that the note could have been written by either Catherine or Pete. While in the house, Office Reynolds found some notes that Ms. Jones said she wrote. The handwriting looked the same.

Officer Reynolds knocked on the door and was threatened and cussed out by a man who identified himself as Peter Jones. Officer Reynolds tried to get Mr. Jones to talk about letting Mr. Black come inside but Jones kept cussing loudly. He was hard to understand because he had food in his mouth. Jones said his wife told him that she was tired of taking care of Black. Officer Reynolds heard an adult female voice from upstairs telling Jones to ignore the police.

Investigation revealed that Catherine Jones is the daughter of Thomas Black, and that she was at home on the evening of January 10 of this year. Black had previously been living at the Millwood Nursing Home until he was removed from the home by his daughter. Since then, he has been living in the Jones's house. Social workers within the County Department of Social Services verified that Catherine Jones had removed her father from the nursing home after a dispute with Black's doctors. Social Worker Bonnie Cohen, of the Department of Social Services, was interviewed. Social Worker Cohen is also Catherine Jones's social worker, and has spoken to her on a number of occasions concerning the potential neglect of Mr. Black and to provide counseling and assistance. Based on the interview with Cohen, Officer Reynolds believes there is a pattern of neglect, that Mr. Black has been abused, and that he is in danger of continued abuse.

Applicable Law

Civil or Domestic Violence Clinic

This lawsuit is based on the allegation that your client has neglected an elderly person. The relevant statute reads: "Neglect means the intentional failure to provide necessary assistance and resources for the physical needs of a vulnerable adult, including food, clothing, toileting, essential medical treatment, shelter, or supervision. A care giver, parent, or other person who has permanent or temporary care or responsibility for the supervision of a vulnerable adult, or any household member or family member who causes abuse or neglect of a vulnerable adult is subject to an injunction to cease such neglect or abuse, liable for any and all financial damage caused to the neglected person, and is subject to a civil penalty equal to the cost of remedying any medical care required for the abused and neglected person.

Criminal Defense or Juvenile Delinquency Clinic

The offense alleged is the neglect of elderly persons. The relevant statute reads: "Neglect means the intentional failure to provide necessary assistance and resources for the physical needs of the vulnerable adult, including food, clothing, toileting, essential medical treatment, shelter, or supervision. A care giver, a parent, or other person who has permanent or temporary care or responsibility for the supervision of a vulnerable adult, or any household member or family member who causes abuse or neglect of a vulnerable adult is guilty of a felony and upon conviction is subject to a fine not exceeding $5,000 or imprisonment for not more than five years, or both.

READING ASSIGNMENT

1. Federal Rules of Evidence 401, 402, 501, 602, 701, 702, 801, 802, 803; Making Objections: "Selected Federal Rules of Evidence" https://georgetown.box.com/s/5oyn7vibchc1nwkzewqt or comparable local rules of evidence.
2. Charles H. Rose III, *Objections, in* FUNDAMENTAL TRIAL ADVOCACY (2d ed. 2011).
3. Charles H. Rose III, *Common Objections, in* FUNDAMENTAL TRIAL ADVOCACY (2d ed. 2011).

READINGS

Federal Rules of Evidence

Making Objections: "Selected Federal Rules of Evidence" https://georgetown.box.com/s/5oyn7vibchc1nwkzewqt

The Federal Rules of Evidence are the accepted evidentiary rules for authentication, relevance, best evidence, and hearsay and its exceptions. Your familiarity with these rules will depend on whether you have taken an Evidence course prior to enrolling in the clinic. If your state has not adopted the Federal Rules of Evidence, find the state rule analog to the relevant Federal Rule.

Charles H. Rose III
Objections
FUNDAMENTAL TRIAL ADVOCACY (2nd ed. 2011)[1]

. . .

A. How to Object

Objections are an area of trial advocacy where the advocate must develop an ability to act instinctually in response to the violation of an evidentiary rule. In order to develop this skill the advocate must learn the key phrases or situations that foreshadow a violation of an evidentiary

1 Some footnotes and illustrations have been omitted or realigned. Unless otherwise specifically indicated, all professional conduct rules referenced are taken from the Delaware Supreme Court's professional responsibility rules. Those rules are almost identical to the model rules promulgated by the American Bar Association and are public domain documents.

rule and the moments in trial where they are most likely to occur. Most new advocates list objections as one of the areas of trial practice with which they are least comfortable. This discomfort comes from the fast-paced nature of objections during the trial and the lack of connectivity between evidentiary law and trial skills when the advocate first learned evidence and trial advocacy. Fortunately, both of these issues can be overcome through practice and study.

Type of Objections:

- Form
- Substance

The first step along the path to mastering objections is to identify objectionable questions and evidence in the context of the moment in trial where they are going to arise. This process begins during case analysis and continues throughout the trial. The advocate should review all prior statements of the noticed witness, identify the potential fungible and non-fungible evidence that the witness may be used to admit and review carefully any interview notes. This review process should focus on potential evidentiary issues that may occur. Counsel should note those issues, forecast how opposing counsel may object, and then identify their potential response to counsel's objection.

Once you learn how to do this, it is simply a matter of then deciding whether the question is objectionable and whether it is to your advantage to object. Case analysis should assist you in determining when you want to fight over an objectionable piece of evidence or testimony and when letting it go will help your case. You should always evaluate the situation before deciding whether or not to object. Ask yourself if the evidence is probably going to come in anyway? For example, if the objection is strictly to a lack of proper foundation, your objection will merely allow opposing counsel to fix the problem, making additional advocacy points while doing so. If that is the case why object? You may wind up keying jury members to the importance of evidence upon which you would rather they not focus.

Identifying, Planning & Preparing for Objections:

- Review all prior statements
- Identify the potential fungible and non-fungible evidence
- Review witness interview notes
- Identify potential evidentiary issues
- Forecast opposing counsel's objection
- Identify appropriate evidentiary response
- Forecast opposing counsel's response
- Plan you final response

The ability to make and respond to objections is a key skill for the advocate. To properly exercise this skill you must not only understand the rules of evidence, but also have a system that allows you to recall needed information amidst the heat of trial. This is an advocacy skill that is reactionary in most situations, in that you are responding to the actions of opposing counsel. You can plan for that reaction, using the actions described above as a checklist. It is a skill that develops through practice. A list of common objections and the corresponding rules of evidence in your trial notebook will help you prepare to properly execute this skill.

. . .

Practice with the rules is another step toward competency in the area of trial advocacy. You should not despair; making good objections is a skill you can develop. Given that most evidentiary rulings by the court are reviewed at the appellate level under an abuse of discretion standard, this is an important skill to have so you may win this battle at trial.

B. The Skill of Objections

Objections are both strategic and tactical. A thorough case analysis and preparation of your direct and cross examinations will alert you to possible objections from opposing counsel, as well as arm you with objections to make when opposing counsel is examining a witness. These objections are planned in depth and fall into the strategic category. Others arise in the heat of the moment and more fairly can be said to fall into the tactical category of objections. Sometimes something will simply not sound right and you will be on your feet objecting while still formulating the specific basis for your objection.

How to Object:

- Stand up
- Say: "Objection, your honor, the question is" (leading, improper, argumentative, etc.)
- Grab your objection reference guide in case the judge wants further information
- Listen to the judge or your opponent and prepare to respond

One aspect of objecting that you may consider is whether an objection will cause your opponent to lose momentum or get flustered. While it is improper to make an objection solely to disrupt your opponent, it is proper to object whenever you have a good faith basis. Be cautious in this area. Tactical objections may work against you by making you appear overly contentious to the jury. It may also annoy the judge. Consider the judge to be a sleeping lion: if you are going to poke it with a stick, make sure it is on an issue that matters and the reaction that you get is not too severe.

The mechanics of making an objection depend upon your local jurisdiction and the preferences of the trial judge. Some judges will require you to state the basis and the applicable rule of evidence. Others only need to hear the word "objection," and they will start to interrogate opposing counsel. Be aware, especially as defense counsel, that appellate courts will often find waiver of an issue if the objection is not sufficiently specific. This may sometimes require a citation to relevant case law. Some judges will try to get counsel to agree or simply will listen to evidentiary arguments and never actually rule. Advocates must be prepared to force the issue of a final ruling when that happens. Waiver occurs in some jurisdictions if the objection is not renewed each time the disputed evidence or testimony is offered. Conversely, you can request that the judge note your continuing objection to evidence of the same type. When in doubt—object!

When you hear an objection you should think about what you just said and why it may be objectionable. Reasons might include: (1) how the question was phrased (leading, argumentative, vague, ambiguous, compound); (2) what you were asking the witness (answered a question that you already asked, gave a conclusion or opinion that is improper, answered with hearsay, gave a narrative response, disclosed privileged information); or perhaps (3) you have gotten ahead of yourself (assuming a fact not in evidence, incomplete or improper foundation, bolstering a witness before credibility is attacked). Wait to hear what the judge says. He may overrule the objection outright. If he invites a response, state your position. If the problem is a matter of phrasing or you tried to enter evidence before the foundation was complete, ask for leave to rephrase the question or to complete the foundation. If you do not understand the objection, but the point that you were attempting to make was critical, ask the judge for clarification before responding.

Responding to Objections:

- Stop talking and listen to the judge.
- Do not immediately concede or offer to rephrase.
- Be prepared to answer the judge's concerns.
- Do not be argumentative in front of the jury.
- Answer the judge, not opposing counsel.

C. The Art of Objections

Whenever opposing counsel violates the rules of evidence as to either the form of the question or the nature of the evidence they are attempting to admit, you must decide whether or not to object. You should consider whether the theme and theory you identified through case analysis will be aided by your objection. It is also appropriate to use objections to assist you in preventing your opponent from furthering their theme and theory. If either of these two predicate possibilities exist then it may be appropriate to object.

On the other hand, if it does not hurt your case, consider passing on the potential objection, especially if you have found a way to make the objectionable issue work to your advantage. If you are not sure, but it simply does not sound right when you hear it, then consider using BARPH.

Easy Guide to Courtroom Objections (BARPH)

B – est Evidence

A – uthentication

R – elevance

P – ersonal Knowledge

H – earsay

An alternative to BARPH is to structure your objections for maximum persuasion. The judge is your target, so stop and think for a moment of how the objections might appear from the judge's perspective. We will use something as simple as a letter that talks about the lack of character of the accused for our example. Let us say that the letter was written by the alleged victim in a homicide case. The defense counsel who is trying to keep this evidence out has a variety of objections potentially available. The order in which she chooses to raise these objections is crucial. Consider the following:

Prosecutor (P): *Ma'am I hand you what has been marked as PE-1 for ID. Do you recognize it?*

Witness (W): *Yes.*

P: *What is it?*

W: *It is a letter written by my dear sweet murdered daughter. She was talking about her sorry husband in it.*

Defense (D): [To the Judge] *Objection, this violates 403. May I be heard?*

Judge (J): *Briefly counsel*

D: *Your honor this note has a high probability of unfairly prejudicing my client. Any probative value is substantially outweighed by the danger of unfair prejudice.*

J: *Overruled. You may proceed, State.*

P: *I offer PE-1 for ID into evidence as PE-1.*

J: *Admitted as marked.*

Consider what would have happened if the young defense counsel had planned her objections to create a greater degree of concern about the ultimate substantial danger of unfair prejudice. In order to accomplish this she needs to stack and arrange her objections so that she gets the judge's attention. It might go like this:

Prosecutor (P): *Ma'am I hand you what has been marked as PE-1 for ID. Do you recognize it?*

Witness (W): *Yes.*

P: *What is it?*

W: *It is a letter written by my dear sweet murdered daughter. She was talking about her sorry husband in it.*

Defense (D): [To the Judge] *Objection, may I be heard?*

Judge (J): *Briefly counsel. Basis?*

D: *Your honor counsel has not laid a proper foundation.*

J: *Overruled. You may proceed, State.*

D: *Objection, best evidence rule.*

J: *Explain.*

D: *Your honor this letter is a copy of an original that is not available for comparison.*

J: *I'm going to overrule that objection as well. You may proceed, State.*

D: *Objection—authentication. May I be heard?*

J: *All right counsel.*

D: *Your honor the state has not properly authenticated this letter to show that it was in fact written by the alleged victim. We would request they do so before you admit it.*

J: *Okay. Lay a foundation, State.*

P: [State lays a foundation] *I offer. . .*

D: *Objection, authentication and hearsay.*

J: *Counsel, I am overruling the authentication objection. State, how do you respond to the hearsay objection?*

P: *Your honor it is a dying declaration.*

D: *Your honor, how can a letter be a dying declaration? The state has not laid sufficient foundation to support that hearsay exception.*

J: *I disagree, counsel. Objection as to hearsay is overruled.*

D: *Objection, impermissible character evidence.*

J: *Counsel this getting old. How is this letter impermissible character evidence?*

D: *It relates alleged prior misconduct by my client that the jury could improperly consider.*

J: *How do you respond, State?*

P: *Your honor, we offer it under the 404(b) exception and request a limiting instruction to the jury as to its permissible use under 105.*

J: *Based upon that offer I overrule the objection.*

D: *Your honor, may I be heard?*

J: *Extremely briefly counsel.*

D: *Your honor, we have established concerns with admitting this letter that include foundation, authentication, hearsay and impermissible character evidence. Although you have overruled each of these objections their cumulative effect is to point out quite clearly the substantial danger of unfair prejudice to my client if this letter is admitted. We request you exclude it under 403.*

J: [rubbing his eyes] *Counsel, I'll consider your objection over lunch. We are in recess.*

The defense counsel in this second example may very well lose the 403 objection, but they have made an excellent record. They have also raised so many concerns that the judge may decide to exclude this piece of evidence. This technique is useful when you want to send the signal to the judge that this particular issue is important and worthy of careful consideration. This approach will only work if you save it for the right moment. If you throw every objection available out indiscriminately then the judge will eventually tune you out.

When Arranging or Stacking Objections You Should Consider:

- Logical relevance, FRE 401
- Authentication, FRE 900
- Foundation, FRE 900
- Hearsay *when applicable*, FRE 800
- Character *when applicable*, FRE 400
- Opinion *when applicable*, FRE 700
- Legal relevance, FRE 403

Another danger exists if you have a judge that either prefers or requires that you state every relevant objection to a piece of evidence when raising an objection about that evidence. Advocates must know the local court's preference on this issue. While the preference of the judge is not dispositive on whether or not you raise all issues at one time, it may be that you need to do so to get the judge's attention. When that is the case you still stack your objections, but you just make a complete stack at one time.

Regardless of whether you are BARPHing or stacking, you should stand and say "objection" and then briefly state the basis for your concern. You should focus on the judge and her reactions, never looking at opposing counsel. The judge will either rule on your objection outright or ask opposing counsel to respond. Listen carefully both to what opposing counsel says and the judge's response. If opposing counsel cannot give the judge a valid basis to overrule the objection then you should remain silent. Do not snatch defeat from the jaws of victory when objecting by talking too much. If you lose the objection you can make an offer of proof, and, when necessary, refer back to that objection when attempting to admit or suppress other evidence.

In addition to dealing with objections off the cuff, the superior advocate will plan for potential objections in depth on those important, if not dispositive, legal and factual issues identified during case analysis. This is accomplished by: (1) identifying potentially objectionable issues through case analysis; (2) researching the basis and strength of your objection (with favorable case law identified and prepared); (3) analyzing potential responses by opposing counsel; and then (4) preparing your counter-response.

This type of in-depth planning creates the sense on the part of the judge that you know what you are talking about. They will take you seriously because their primary concern is protecting the record. When you can get inside of the decision-making loop the judge uses to protect the record you are well on your way to winning the evidentiary battle over objections.

D. The Law of Objections

There are two general types of trial objections, form and substance. "Objections to Form" attack the way counsel *asked* the question. FRE 611(a) and (c) empowers the trial court to control the mode and order of interrogation and to limit the use of leading questions. "Objections to Substance" attack the admissibility of the testimony elicited. All of these objections are derived directly from the law of evidence. The most common objections are outlined below with the form of the objection, an explanation of the basis for the objection, possible responses to the objection by a trial judge or by opposing counsel and, where applicable, more recent federal decisions addressing the objection.

1. Objections to Form

Advocates often identify objections to form based upon "feel." They listen for questions that are either not properly formed or are not sufficiently focused based upon the rules of evidence and norms of practice in their jurisdiction. Proper considerations of the basic questioning techniques discussed in Chapter 3 can assist advocates in avoiding objections to the form of their own questions. They also serve as a good starting point when listening for questions that are objections to form. A nice place to begin is with the concept that bad questions are objectionable.

Ambiguous, Confusing or Unintelligible Question—FRE 611(a)

Objection: *The question is ambiguous/confusing/unintelligible.*

Response: *I will rephrase.*

Explanation: A question is ambiguous if it may be interpreted in several ways, or if it is so vague or unclear that it may confuse the jury, judge, or the witness.

Argumentative Question—FRE 611(a)

Objection: *The question is argumentative.*

Response: *Rephrase the question.*

Explanation: A question is argumentative if it is an attempt to make an argument to the jury, to summarize, draw inferences from, or comment on the evidence, or to ask the witness to testify as to his own credibility. A question can also be argumentative if it is unduly hostile or sarcastic.

Asked and Answered or Unduly Repetitious—FRE 403, 611(a)

Objection: *The witness has already answered the question.*

Response: *The witness has not yet answered this particular question.*

Explanation: Repetitious questions are unlikely to elicit additional evidence of probative value. *See U.S. v. Collins,* 996 F.2d 950, 952 (8th Cir. 1993), cert. denied, 510 U.S. 956 (1993) (objection to question posed during re-direct examination on basis that it had been asked and answered on direct examination sustained).

Assumes Facts Not in Evidence—FRE 601, 611(a)

Objection: *Assumes facts not in evidence.*

Responses: *(1) The existence of this fact may be inferred from evidence which has been admitted; (2) if permitted to answer the fact will be in evidence; or (3) the fact will be proved during the testimony of Witness X. We will "tie it up" later.*

Explanation: A question that assumes facts not yet in evidence effectively allows counsel to testify as to those facts without personal knowledge.

Multifarious; Compound Question—FRE 611(a)

Objection: *Compound Question.*

Response: *I will rephrase the question.*

Explanation: A question combining more than one inquiry is likely to be confusing and misleading to both the witness and the fact-finder.

Harassing the Witness—FRE 403, 611(a)(3)

Objection: *Harassing the witness.*

Response: *I will rephrase the question.*

Explanation: A question that is asked to harass or embarrass a witness, for example, a question that unnecessarily delves into a witness's personal life, is impermissible.

Leading Question—FRE 611(c)

Objection: *Leading.*

Responses: *(1) The question is not a leading question simply because it elicits a yes or no answer. It is generally to elicit preliminary or background information from a witness through leading questions, (2) the witness is an adverse party, or the witness is hostile, (3) leading questions are allowed of one's own witnesses on cross examination if the witness is called by the adverse party, or (4) I'll rephrase the question.*

Explanation: A leading question is one that suggests to the witness the answer desired by the examiner. Leading questions are generally impermissible on direct examination.

Calls for Narrative Answer—FRE 403, 611(a)

Objection: *I object. The question calls for narrative testimony and deprives us of an Objection: Calls for a narrative. Counsel is trying to admit inadmissible evidence.*

Response: *I will rephrase the question.*

Explanation: Narrative, unspecific, or long "rambling" answers are not per se objectionable, but are likely to contain hearsay or other inadmissible evidence to which counsel is deprived of an opportunity to objcct. *Scc U.S. v. Plcss,* 982 F.2d 1118, 1123 (7th Cir. 1992) ("there is nothing particular, unusual, or incorrect, in a procedure of letting a witness relate pertinent information in a narrative form as long as it stays within the bounds of pertinence and materiality").

Mischaracterizes or Misquotes the Witness or Prior Evidence—FRE 611(a).

Objection: *I object. The question mischaracterizes, misstates, or misquotes the prior testimony. . .*

Response: *I'll rephrase the question.*

Explanation: Questions that misquote previous testimony or evidence are likely to mislead or confuse the jury.

---

2. *Objections to Substance*

Objections as to substance address evidentiary issues dealing with the portions of the Federal Rules of Evidence dealing with admitting or excluding evidence. These include questions of character, authenticity, credibility, relevancy, impeachment and hearsay. These are the types of objections that have a greater potential impact upon those issues in controversy that must be proven at trial. These are the types of objections that are not waived if you were to fail to make them during a deposition. New advocates should think of them as being objections that have more potential for a prejudicial impact if they are not properly raised and addressed.

Lack of Authentication—FRE 901, 902

Objection: *I object. The evidence has not been properly authenticated.*

Response: *The item is sufficiently authenticated by* _______ *(a method listed in Rule 901(b)).*

Examples of sufficient authentication include:

- Testimony of a witness with knowledge.
- Non-expert opinion on the genuineness of handwriting.
- Comparison by trier-of-fact or expert witness to authenticated specimens.
- Distinctive characteristics of the item offered.
- Voice identification by opinion based upon hearing the voice under circumstances connecting it with the alleged speaker.
- Public records or reports.
- The item is self-authenticating under FRE 902.

Examples of self-authenticating evidence under FRE 902 include:

- Domestic public documents under seal.
- Domestic public documents not under seal if officer certifies that the signature is genuine.
- Foreign public documents.
- Certified copies or public records.
- Official publications.

- Newspapers and periodicals.
- Acknowledged or notarized documents.
- Commercial paper and related documents.

Explanation: Authentication is not satisfied if insufficient evidence has been offered to support a finding that the matter in question is what its proponent claims is it. *See U.S. v. McGlory,* 968 F.2d 309, 328–29 (3d Cir. 1992), cert. denied, 507 U.S. 962 (1993) (to show authenticity there must be a prima facie showing of authenticity to the court; the jury will ultimately determine the authenticity of the evidence).

Best Evidence Not Offered—FRE 1001, 1002, 1003, 1004

Objection: *I object. The evidence is not the best evidence.*

Response: *The evidence qualifies as an original or as a duplicate.*

Explanation: The best evidence rule requires the original writing, recording, or photograph to prove the content of the writing, recording, or photograph. FRE 1001 defines original and duplicate. An "original" is the writing or recording itself, any counterpart intended to have the same effect, the negative or print therefrom if the evidence is a photograph, and any printout or other output shown to accurately reflect the data of an original that is stored in a computer.

A "duplicate" is a counterpart produced by the same impression as the original, or from the same matrix, or by means of photography, including enlargements and miniatures, or by mechanical or electronic re-recording, or by chemical reproduction, or by other equivalent techniques. Duplicates are admissible to the same extent as originals.

Response: *The rule is inapplicable because the proponent is not seeking to prove the content of the item.*

Response: *The original is not obtainable and secondary evidence is therefore admissible.*

Explanation: Secondary evidence is admissible if the original has been lost or destroyed except for when the loss or destruction was done in bad faith by the proponent. Other examples for when secondary evidence is admissible from FRE 1004 include: (1) the original is unobtainable by any available judicial process or procedure, (2) the original is under the control of the opponent and the opponent does not produce the original when put on notice that it will be subject of proof at a hearing, (3) the item is offered for a collateral purpose. *See U.S. v. Haddock* 956 F.2d 1534, 1545 (10th Cir. 1992), cert. denied, 506 U.S. 828 ("due to modern and accurate reproduction techniques, duplicates and originals should normally be treated interchangeably").

Improper Use of Character Evidence—FRE 404, 405, 608

Objection: *I object. The question calls for inadmissible character evidence.*

Response: *The person's character trait is "in issue."*

Explanation: A person's character is "in issue" when it is an element of a charge, claim, or defense. For example, in a claim of negligent entrustment, the trait of incompetence of the person to whom the defendant entrusted the dangerous instrumentality to is an element of the claim and is "in issue." Proof of character may then be made by opinion or reputation testimony, or by evidence of specific instances of conduct. Character evidence is generally inadmissible to show that a person acted in conformity with that character on a particular occasion. Character evidence may be proved only by reputation or opinion testimony, not by specific acts, except where a trait of the person's character is "in issue," or for the purpose of impeachment or rehabilitation on cross examination.

Objection: *I object. Evidence of specific acts is impermissible to prove character.*

Response: *The character evidence is offered for the purpose of impeachment or rehabilitation on cross-examination and is therefore admissible under FRE 608.*

Explanation: A witness that has testified as to the character of a person may be asked on cross examination about specific acts of that person in the form of "have you heard?" or "do you know?" questions to test the factual basis of their testimony on direct examination. A witness may always be asked on cross examination about specific instances of his or her own conduct that are probative of untruthfulness. Counsel must have a good faith basis for making the inquiry (FRE 608).

Objection: *I object. The question calls for inadmissible character evidence.*

Response: *The person's character trait is "in issue" because it is an element of a charge, claim, or defense.*

Explanation: The specific act is offered to prove something other than character. Evidence of other crimes, wrongs, or acts may be admissible to prove motive, opportunity, intent, preparation, plan, knowledge, identity, or absence of mistake or accident (FRE 404(b)). *See US. v. Roberts,* 887 F.2d 534 (5th Cir. 1989) (character trait was in issue on a question of whether defendant formed the requisite intent, and evidence of personality traits was therefore properly admitted); *U.S. v. McGuiness,* 764 F. Supp. 888 (S.D.N.Y. 1991) (evidence of defendant's previous refusal to accept bribes not admissible to prove character of defendant and action in conformity with that character); *U.S. v. Nazarenus,* 983 F.2d 1480 (8th Cir. 1993) (extrinsic evidence of defendant's driving habits inadmissible to impeach defendant as specific acts may not be proved by extrinsic evidence for the purpose of attacking or supporting the witness's credibility) (FRE 608(b)).

Bolstering the Credibility of a Witness—FRE 607, 608, 801(d)(1)(B)

Objection: *I object. Counsel is bolstering the witness.*

Response: *The witness's credibility has been attacked and this evidence is proper rehabilitation.*

Explanation: FRE 608(a) permits evidence of a witness's character for truthfulness only after the witness's character for truthfulness has been attacked. Bolstering refers to a proponent's attempt to offer otherwise inadmissible character evidence solely to enhance his witness's credibility when the witness has not yet been impeached. *See U.S. v. Hedgcorth,* 873 F.2d 1307, 1313–1314 (9th Cir. 1989), cert. denied, 493 US. 857 (1989) (testimony as to defendant's character for truthfulness properly excluded where government had not attacked defendant's character for truthfulness).

Impeachment on a Collateral Matter—FRE 403, 608

Objection: *I object. Extrinsic evidence of specific instances is inadmissible to impeach a witness on collateral matters.*

Responses: *(1) The extrinsic evidence is independently relevant to a substantive issue in the case, (2) the evidence is offered to prove bias, which is not a collateral matter, or (3) evidence of specific acts of a witness are admissible when offered to prove something other than a witness's untrustworthy character.*

Explanation: This objection arises most commonly when a party seeks to impeach a witness by introducing extrinsic evidence that contradicts an answer given by the witness. *See U.S. v. Abel,* 469 U.S. 45 (1984) (bias is not collateral); *Foster v. General Motors Corp.,* 20 F.3d 838, 839 (8th Cir. 1994) (evidence relevant to a material issue is admissible).

Conclusion of Law or Ultimate Issue—FRE 701, 702, 704

Objection: *I object. The witness is testifying to an ultimate issue.*

Response: *The expert or lay witness has knowledge or expertise of the matter, and the evidence is helpful. An adequate foundation has been laid.*

Explanation: Testimony phrased in conclusory terms is less helpful than testimony that provides information to the jury so that it may draw its own conclusions. Conclusions of law are generally inadmissible. Lay or expert witness testimony must be based on the lay witness's perception or must be within the scope of the expertise of an expert witness, and must be helpful to the fact finder. Opinions on an ultimate issue are generally admissible (FRE 704). *See U.S. v. Lockett,* 919 F.2d 585, 590 (9th Cir. 1990) (expert opinions about guilt or innocence inadmissible); *Kostelecky v. NL Acme Tool/NL Industries, Inc.,* 837 F.2d 828, 830 (8th Cir. 1988) ("evidence that merely tells the jury what result to reach is not sufficiently helpful to the trier of fact to be admissible").

Cross Examination beyond the Scope of Direct—FRE 611(b)

Objection: *I object. The question asked goes beyond the scope of the matters raised on direct.*

Response: *The question is permissible because the subject matter of direct includes all inferences and implications arising from direct.*

Explanation: Cross examination that raises subjects not raised on direct is generally inadmissible.

Cumulative—FRE 403

Objection: *I object. The evidence is cumulative.*

Response: *A party has a right to present a persuasive case and the cumulative evidence concept should not interfere with that right.*

Explanation: If the evidence is needlessly cumulative or repetitious, it may be excluded. *See Davis v. Mason County,* 927 F.2d 1473 (9th Cir. 1991), cert. denied, 502 U.S. 899 (1991) (testimony of expert witness properly excluded on ground that two other experts had testified on the same topic).

Hearsay—FRE 801, 802, 803, 804

Objection: *I object. The question calls for hearsay.*

Responses: *(1) The statement is not hearsay because it is not offered to prove the truth of the matter asserted, (2) the statement is not hearsay under the rules. . . (3) I am offering it for a non-hearsay purpose, or (4) the statement is hearsay, but is specifically exempted by the rules. . .*

Explanation: Hearsay is inadmissible unless it falls within an established exception. Key exceptions, as listed in FRE 801, 803 and 804, include:

- Prior statements by witness
- Admissions by party-opponent offered against party-opponent
- Present sense impressions
- Excited utterances
- Statement of the declarant's then existing state of mind
- Statements for the purpose of medical diagnosis or treatment
- Recorded recollections
- Records of regularly conducted activity
- Public records and reports
- Learned treatises
- Former testimony of unavailable declarant
- Statement under belief of impending death where the declarant is unavailable
- Statement against interest of an unavailable declarant

Impermissible Hypothetical Question—FRE 705

Objection: *I object Counsel is posing a hypothetical question that contains facts not in evidence.*

Response: *A hypothetical question need not refer to all of the relevant facts in evidence. The witness is an expert witness, and an expert may base an opinion on facts that are not admitted into evidence, as long as they are the type reasonably relied upon by experts in forming opinions on the subject.*

Explanation: A hypothetical question is inadmissible if it contains facts that are not already in evidence, that will not be introduced before the close of evidence, or that are not reasonably drawn from such facts. *See Toucet v. Maritime Overseas Corp.,* 991 F.2d 5, 10 (1st Cir. 1993) (a hypothetical question should include only those facts suggested by the evidence).

Witness is Incompetent or Lacks Personal Knowledge—FRE 601–606

Objection: *I object. The witness is incompetent or lacks sufficient capacity to testify, or no showing has been made that the witness has personal knowledge about this matter.*

Responses: *(1) Rule 601 abolishes objections to a witness's competence, (2) The witness is competent under state law, (3) A personal assertion by the witness is sufficient to show personal knowledge, (4) I will ask additional questions sufficient to lay the foundation to establish personal knowledge.*

Explanation: All persons are presumed competent to testify except as otherwise provided in the rules. However, incompetence of a witness may be the basis for an objection in two situations: where state law supplies the rule of decision with respect to an element of a claim or defense, and the witness is incompetent under state law; or where insufficient evidence has been introduced to support a finding that the witness has personal knowledge of the matter. *See U.S. v. Phibbs,* 999 F.2d 1053 (6th Cir. 1993) (admission of testimony from witness with history of mental problems was not error as all persons are presumed competent to testify); *Kemp v. Balboa,* 23 F.3d 211 (8th Cir. 1994) (nurse not allowed to testify because she lacked personal knowledge as to the facts stated in medical records which she had not prepared).

Misleading—FRE 403

Objection: *I object. The evidence will mislead the jury. Or, if a bench trial: I object, the evidence is misleading.*

Response: *The probative value of the evidence outweighs the danger of misleading the jury or the court.*

Explanation: The danger of misleading the jury usually refers to the possibility that the jury will attach undue weight to the evidence. If the probative value of the evidence is substantially outweighed by the danger of misleading the jury, the evidence may be excluded. *See Rogers v. Raymark Indus.,* 922 F.2d 1426 (9th Cir. 1991) (evidence of observations taken at defendant's asbestos plant was properly excluded because plaintiff's complaint was based on activities at a different plant and there was no evidence of similarity among the plants).

Prejudicial Effect Outweighs Probative Value—FRE 403

Objection: *I object. The probative value of this evidence is outweighed by the danger of unfair prejudice.*

Response: *All probative evidence is prejudicial. The rule does not afford protection from evidence that is merely detrimental to a party's case. In this instance the probative value of the evidence outweighs the danger of unfair prejudice.*

Explanation: Evidence is unfairly prejudicial if it suggests a decision on an improper basis, most commonly an emotional basis. If the probative value of the evidence is substantially outweighed by the danger of unfair prejudice, the evidence may be excluded. *See U.S. v. Skillman,* 922 F.2d 1370, 1374 (9th Cir. 1990), cert. dism'd, 502 U.S. 922 (1991) (rule only protects against evidence that is unfairly prejudicial).

Confusion of the Issues—FRE 403

Objection: *I object. The evidence will confuse the issues.*

Response: *The probative value of the evidence outweighs the risk of confusion.*

Explanation: Evidence is confusing if it tends to distract the jury from the proper issues of the trial. If the probative value of evidence is outweighed by the danger of confusion, it may be excluded. See *Ramos-Melendez v. Valdejully,* 960 F.2d 4, 6 (1st Cir. 1992) (evidence of other suits properly excluded as distracting the jury from the issues at hand).

Privilege—FRE 501

Objection: *I object. The question calls for privileged information.*

Response: *The privilege asserted is not one created by constitution, court, or state rule, or one recognized by common law. The communication at issue is not privileged.*

Explanation: Privileged information based on the attorney-client privilege, doctor patient privilege, spousal privilege, and other privileges recognized by Common or statutory law is inadmissible. Privilege law is generally governed by the principles of common law as interpreted by the United States courts, but in civil actions, state privilege law applies with respect to an element of a claim or defense as to which state substantive law governs.

The privilege has been waived. *See U.S. v. Moscony,* 927 F.2d 742, 751 (3d Cir. 1991), cert. denied, 501 U.S. 1211 (1991) (although Congress did not enact the Supreme Court's proposed privilege rules which discussed individual privileges, courts often refer to those rules for guidance).

Speculation—FRE 602, 701, 702

Objection: *I object. The question calls for the witness to speculate.*

Response: *I will rephrase the question to establish the witness's personal knowledge or basis for the witness's statement.*

Explanation: A question which asks a witness to speculate as to what occurred or what caused an event may conflict with the requirement that a witness have personal knowledge of a matter testified to, or in the case of an expert witness, may be an impermissible attempt to elicit an opinion beyond the scope of the witness's expertise.

. . .

Charles H. Rose III
Common Objections
FUNDAMENTAL TRIAL ADVOCACY 503 (2nd ed. 2011)

The following list of common objections is provided in alphabetical order. You should use this list to assist you in identifying the source of objections raised by others when you are not familiar with the rule that forms the basis for the objection.[2]

AMBIGUOUS: Confusing question in that it is capable of being understood in more than one sense. FRE 611(a).

ARGUMENTATIVE: (a) Counsel's question is really argument to the jury in the guise of a question. Example: counsel summarizes facts, states conclusion, and demands witness agree with conclusion. (b) Excessive quibbling with witness. FRE 611(a).

ASKED AND ANSWERED: Unfair to allow counsel to emphasize evidence through repetition. An especially useful objection during re-direct examination; greater leeway on cross-exam, however, to test recollection. FRE 611(a).

ASSUMES A FACT NOT IN EVIDENCE: A fact not testified to is contained within the question. FRE 103(c) and 611(a).

AUTHENTICATION LACKING: Proof must be offered that the exhibit is in fact what it is claimed to be. FRE 901(a).

---

[2] These materials come from the excellent work of Professor Bill Eleazer and are used here with his permission. He has a wealth of extremely practical and useful materials that are available to anyone who goes into court. We require them for our students at Stetson and I offer them for your consideration.

BEST EVIDENCE RULE: If rule applies, original document must be offered or its absence accounted for. If contents of document are to be proved, rule usually applies. FRE 1002. *See also* 1003 and 1004.

BEYOND SCOPE (of direct, cross, etc.): Question unrelated to examination immediately preceding, or to credibility. Questioner should be required to call witness as own. FRE 611(b).

BOLSTERING: Improper to bolster the credibility of a witness before credibility is attacked. FRE 608(a).

COMPOUND: More than one question contained in the question asked by counsel. FRE 611(a).

CONCLUSION: Except for expert, witness must testify to facts within personal knowledge; conclusions are for the jury and counsel during closing argument. FRE 602 and 701.

CONFUSING: Unfamiliar words, disjointed phrases, or question confuses the evidence. FRE 611(a).

COUNSEL TESTIFYING: Counsel is making a statement instead of asking a question. FRE 603.

CUMULATIVE: The trial judge has discretion to control repetitive evidence. Repeated presentation of the same evidence by more exhibits or more witnesses is unfair, unnecessary and wastes time. FRE 102 and 611(a).

FOUNDATION LACKING: No proper foundation for testimony or exhibit. Ex: Offer of "recorded recollection" without showing memory failure; similar to objection for lack of authentication or personal knowledge. FRE 602 and 901(a).

HEARSAY: (answer)—Question did not call for hearsay, but witness gave it anyway. Move to strike and ask judge to instruct that response be disregarded. FRE 802.

HEARSAY: (question)—Answer would elicit hearsay, and no exception has been shown. FRE 802.

IMPEACHMENT BY PROPER MEANS: Methods of impeachment are limited and specific. FRE 607–610.

IMPROPER: When you are sure the question is improper, but cannot think of the correct basis for an objection, try, "Objection, Your Honor, improper question." The judge may know the proper basis and sustain your objection, and if judge asks for your specific basis, you have gained time to think of it. To be used very infrequently. FRE 103(c) and 611.

IMPROPER CHARACTERIZATION: The question or the response has characterized a person or conduct with unwarranted suggestive, argumentative, or impertinent language. Example: "He looked like a crook." FRE 404, 405, and 611(a).

INCOMPETENT WITNESS: Lack of qualification, such as oath or mental capacity. Also applies if the judge or juror is called as a witness. FRE 104(a), 603, 605, and 606.

IRRELEVANT: Would not tend to make any fact that is of consequence more probable or less probable. FRE 402.

LEADING: Form of question tends to suggest answer. Note: this is permitted, of course, on cross-examination. FRE 611(c).

MISQUOTING WITNESS (or MISSTATING EVIDENCE): Counsel's question misstates prior testimony of witness. Similar to objection based on assuming fact not in evidence. FRE 103(c).

NARRATIVE: Question is so broad or covers such a large time period it would allow witness to ramble and possibly present hearsay or irrelevant evidence. The judge has broad discretion in this matter. FRE 103(c) and 611(a).

OPINION: Lay opinion or inference that is beyond the scope permitted by FRE 701; personal knowledge lacking; or expert witness has not been qualified as such. FRE 602, 701, and 702.

PREJUDICE OUTWEIGHS PROBATIVE VALUE: Out of the jurors' hearing, argue that "the probative value of the evidence is substantially outweighed by its prejudicial effect." May apply to exhibits as well as testimony. Note: Don't let the jurors hear you say that the evidence is prejudicial. They may be impressed. FRE 403.

PRIVILEGED: Answer would violate valid privilege (lawyer-client, husband-wife, clergyman, etc.) FRE 501.

SPECULATION AND CONJECTURE: Question requires witness who lacks personal knowledge to guess. FRE 602.

UNRESPONSIVE: Answer includes testimony not called for by the question. Especially applicable to voluntary response by hostile witness. NOTE: an objection based solely on this ground is generally deemed appropriate only if made by the examining attorney; thus opposing counsel should state some additional basis for the objection. FRE 103(c) and 611(a).

POST-CLASS REFLECTION MEMO

Draft and submit a memo in response to the questions below:

- How will you take the lessons you have learned in class today and apply them to your current clinic cases?
- Think about your current clinic case(s). What information do you need to obtain from certain witnesses that will require advance planning to anticipate or avoid objections?
- Will you now feel more comfortable posing and responding to objections?
- What areas of evidence law might you need to research as part of that planning?
- What specific questions might you redraft based on the lessons you learned in class today?

CHAPTER 14

OPENING STATEMENTS AND CLOSING ARGUMENTS

LEARNING GOALS

The learning goals for this class include helping you to:

- Understand the variety of strategic goals that can be served through each of these litigation opportunities
- Think strategically about the relationships between openings and closings and other aspects of case work, including case theory, fact investigation, direct examination and cross-examination
- Take full advantage of the opportunity to be argument-driven (in opening statements)
- Take full advantage of the opportunity to develop a wide range of argument (in closing arguments)

DESCRIPTION OF CLASS

This topic will be covered in a series of two classes. The first class will be devoted primarily to a lecture about how to develop strong opening statements and closing arguments. The class will conclude with an exercise designed to create a case theory for both of the parties in the trial transcribed for the reading assignment. The second class will center on an exercise in which students will craft, deliver, and critique portions of an opening statement and closing argument, based on the facts in the assigned transcript.

ASSIGNMENT IN PREPARATION FOR CLASS

Domestic Violence or Plaintiff-Side Civil Clinic

Read the transcript of the *Jackson v. Doe* protection order hearing, paying careful attention to the factual details. In preparation for class, respond as extensively as possible to each of the items below.

Analyze the facts in preparation for closing argument by identifying the following:

- Each element of each legal claim asserted by the Petitioner
  - Facts that support each element
  - Facts that undermine each element
- Favorable and unfavorable inferences that could be drawn based on the record evidence
  - For the Petitioner
  - For the Respondent
- Facts that might cast either a positive or a negative light on the motives
  - Of the Petitioner
  - Of the Respondent
- Facts that support and facts that undermine the personal credibility
  - Of the Petitioner
  - Of the Respondent
- Facts that support and facts that undermine the overall logic, common sense, and believability of the story put forth
  - By the Petitioner
  - By the Respondent
- Each of the Petitioner's potential claims for relief
  - Facts that support each claim
  - Facts that undermine each claim

Unemployment Insurance Benefits or Defense-Side Civil Clinic

Read the transcript of the *Winsome Sports Club v. Shields* hearing, paying careful attention to the factual details. In preparation for class, respond as extensively as possible to each of the items below.

Analyze the facts in preparation for closing argument by identifying the following:

- Each element of each legal claim asserted
  - By the Employer (who bears the burden of proving that the Claimant does not qualify for an award of unemployment insurance benefits)
  - By the Claimant (who bears the burden of proving that the voluntary leaving was based on "good cause" and who must respond to the Employer's evidence of possible misconduct)
  - For each party's claim:
    - Identify the facts that support each element
    - Identify the facts that undermine each element
- Favorable and unfavorable inferences that could be drawn based on the record evidence
  - For the Claimant
  - For the Employer
- Facts that might cast either a positive or a negative light on the motives
  - Of the Claimant
  - Of the Employer
- Facts that support and facts that undermine the personal credibility
  - Of the Claimant
  - Of the Employer
- Facts that support and facts that undermine the overall logic, common sense, and believability of the story put forth
  - By the Claimant
  - By the Employer

Criminal Defense or Juvenile Delinquency Clinic

Read the transcript of the *State v. Doe* misdemeanor trial, paying careful attention to the factual details. In preparation for class, respond as extensively as possible to each of the items below.

Analyze the facts in preparation for closing argument by identifying the following:

- Each element of each legal claim asserted by the Government
    - Facts that support each element
    - Facts that undermine each element
- Favorable and unfavorable inferences that could be drawn based on the record evidence
    - For the Defendant
    - For the Government
- Facts that might cast either a positive or a negative light on the motives
    - Of the Defendant
    - Of the Complaining Witness
- Facts that support and facts that undermine the personal credibility
    - Of the Defendant
    - Of the Complaining Witness
- Facts that support and facts that undermine the overall logic, common sense, and believability of the story put forth
    - By the Defendant
    - By the Government
- Facts that support or undermine the government's burden of proof beyond a reasonable doubt
    - By the Defendant
    - By the Government

READING ASSIGNMENT

1. Charles H. Rose III, *Opening Statements, in* FUNDAMENTAL TRIAL ADVOCACY (2d ed. 2011).
2. Charles H. Rose III, *Closing Arguments, in* FUNDAMENTAL TRIAL ADVOCACY (2d ed. 2011).
3. Trial transcript and law:

   Domestic Violence or Plaintiff-Side Civil Clinic

   1. Transcript of Jackson v. Doe; and

2. Statutory provisions defining the elements of a civil protection order and the elements of assault.

Unemployment Insurance Benefits or Defense-Side Civil Clinic

1. Transcript of Winsome Sports Club v. Shields; and
2. Regulations governing voluntary leaving and entitlement to unemployment insurance benefits.

Criminal Defense or Juvenile Delinquency Clinic

1. Transcript of State v. Doe; and
2. Statutory provisions defining the elements of a civil protection order and the elements of assault.

READINGS

Charles H. Rose III
Opening Statements
FUNDAMENTAL TRIAL ADVOCACY (2nd ed. 2011)[1]

. . .

A. The Skill of Opening Statements

A young attorney stands before the jury, armed with nothing but a few facts that help, some facts that hurt, and the law. From those paltry tools, she is expected to fashion an introduction to her case that rings with truth, brings the jury to her side, and provides a roadmap to justice. A roadmap that not only helps the jury understand what happened, but why justice demands that the attorney's client prevails. This chapter will empower you to face that moment with confidence and a plan—a plan that highlights your facts, foreshadows the law, and establishes the sense of injustice that feeds your moral theme. Language is the tool of your craft. Use it.

---

1 Some footnotes and illustrations have been omitted or realigned. Unless otherwise specifically indicated, all professional conduct rules referenced are taken from the Delaware Supreme Court's professional responsibility rules. Those rules are almost identical to the model rules promulgated by the American Bar Association and are public domain documents.

Good Opening Statements:

- Tell the story
- Preview the law
- Ask the jury to right a wrong

The opening statement is the jury's first opportunity to hear your version of the case and you must make it count. Jurors are concerned with what happened, how it happened, and why it happened. Provide them with that information during your opening statement so they can begin to look for the solution to the issues that confront them.

Your opening statement to the jury is a promise about the case. When done properly it establishes your credibility as a viable guide during the trial. When done poorly it reflects on everything else that you do. Promise is a powerful word, but appropriate in this instance. Jurors take your comments about the case as promises made to them. You fail to keep these promises at your own peril. You pick the jury during voir dire, but during opening statement is when they begin to pick an attorney. When appearing before jurors, it is a good idea to adopt an old adage passed down through the enlisted ranks of most militaries: "Look good when they are looking at you, and never forget—they are looking at you all the time." You are the first, last, and best witness for your case. Your credibility, fairness, and trustworthiness are always being weighed and measured by the jury. Aristotle referred to this as the "character" portion of the art of rhetoric. You can increase the jury's belief in you by being what they are looking for—someone they can rely upon to help them in their charged task. If you lose your integrity in their eyes, you are done. This selfish incentive should be sufficient to help you follow those ethical standards espoused by the bar and expected by the rest of the nation.

Seven Steps to a Superior Opening Statement:

- Use primacy and recency
- Tell the story
- Create structure
- Focus the jury
- Use appropriate tone & pace
- Preview the law
- Set the hook for closing arguments

The opening statement is your first and best opportunity to influence the jury's decision-making process. Except for those jurisdictions that allow attorneys to conduct voir dire, this is your first chance to be in charge. You should use the theme and theory identified in your case analysis to choose the most persuasive story of the facts to give the jury a framework on which they can organize the evidence as it is received during the case-in-chief. It is much easier to persuade someone to adopt a particular position than to persuade them to change their mind after they have already adopted another way of thinking about things. Use the opening statement as an opportunity to prevent jurors from deciding to view the case in a way that is unfavorable for your client. Given these factors and the way jurors operate, counsel for the plaintiff or prosecution should ***never*** waive the opening statement, and a defense counsel should ***rarely,*** if ever, reserve the opening statement to the beginning of the defense's case. Possibly in instances where the criminal defense attorney is basing her entire case on the manner in which the prosecution proceeds, reserving opening may be appropriate. In those rare instances the defense is essentially choosing to allow the theme and theory of the case to develop based upon the prosecution's witnesses and mistakes. This happens in reasonable doubt cases, but it is dangerous territory for the new advocate and is best entered only after careful consultation with more experienced trial advocates. Like most rules, exceptions exist, but they are rare.

Examples of One-Liners that Grab the Jury's Attention:

- If doesn't fit, you must acquit.
- Where's the beef?
- Wrong place, wrong time, wrong attitude.
- The line between love and hate is thin, and the defendant crossed over that line.
- If she couldn't have him, no one would. . . .
- Swan's don't swim in the sewer . . .

Your objectives during the opening statement must include planting and cultivating the seeds of your theme and theory. The opening statement explains the factual and legal theory of your case in light of the selected theme that creates a sense of moral injustice for your client. Moral injustice is the wrong that the jury can only right by deciding in your favor. To accomplish these objectives a good opening statement may use a variety of devices to place the issue in context. These devices include rhetorical questions, a "one-liner" of what the case is about (often referred to as a grabber or hook), and a story structure that leads the jury to the question that is central to the advocate's case.

The theme grabs the emotions of the jury and relies upon their past human experiences and the shared humanity of the group to make an argument that sways the jury to see the case in a light most favorable to your client. Emotion by itself, however, is not effective in the legal arena. In order to be truly effective it must be coupled with a logical theory of the facts that is consistent with the legal theory of the case. The opening statement explains the relationship between the facts, the legal theory, and the moral theme with an overview of potential admissible evidence. The best vehicle to accomplish these tasks in the opening statement is the grand storytelling tradition of humanity. Centuries ago we crouched around fires and told tales of how we caught the bison. Now we sit around the flame of the television set and watch stories from all over the world. The methodologies found in the old oral traditions coupled with the organizational and thematic constructs of current entertainment vehicles such as TV and movies create a synergy that maximizes persuasiveness. Let us now identify the substantive pieces and procedural steps required when creating a superior opening statement.

B. The Law of Opening Statements

1. *Rules of Evidence and Procedure*

Unlike other portions of trial, opening statements are not governed by the rules of evidence. In most jurisdictions the applicable law is either procedural or case law and varies substantively from state to state, as well as within the federal court system. A review of the relevant law establishes certain fundamental concepts that advocates rely upon as a baseline when creating effective, passionate, and persuasive openings.

Seven Basic Legal Principles of Opening Statements:

- The judge sets the guidelines.
- Do not argue—tell the story.
- Do not vouch for the credibility of witnesses.
- No personal opinions—lawyers are advocates, not witnesses.
- Do not mention evidence excluded during pretrial proceedings.

- Do not refer to evidence in opening if there is no good faith basis to believe it will be admitted.
- Never violate the "golden rule" by asking the jurors to place themselves in a party's shoes.

These acceptable opening statement persuasion techniques focus the jury in a way that brings them to your side by communicating your factual theory, previewing your legal theory, and establishing your moral theme. You have an ethical duty to your client to summon sufficient moral courage to make the opening that must be made. As long as you know where the land mines are in your particular jurisdiction that you should not step on, you are free to be creative. A good starting point is to identify the local rules of court and review the relevant case law in the jurisdiction in which you practice.

Judges have discretion in controlling the manner and substance of opening statements; they also instruct the jury about opening statements by letting them know what they mean and how to weigh them. You must review the standard jury instructions in your jurisdiction so that you know what the judge will tell the jury about openings. You should then use that as you fashion the most persuasive presentation you can summon. Instructions are one of the most readily available resources for an advocate. They represent the opinions and actions of the bench within that jurisdiction and often provide the structure that the judge relies upon to identify and solve issues that have been dealt with by other judges. They also serve as a repository for the culture of a particular bar, capturing the daily practice of the attorneys who appear using those instructions. *If you remember nothing else from this text, remember to review the instructions where you practice.* It is time well spent.

The seven basic legal principles for opening statements serve as an excellent starting point as you develop your understanding of how the law impacts openings. In most instances they should keep you out of trouble with the judge. They apply in most, if not all, jurisdictions. The court expects advocates to make powerful and persuasive opening statements that relay the facts, establish moral themes, and forecast legal issues. Beyond that there is relatively little uniformity with the exception of exhibits. Most jurisdictions let you use them—both tangible objects and documents—during opening if they have been either pre-admitted or there is a good faith basis to believe you will be able to admit them at trial.

. . .

C. The Art of Opening Statements

1. *Structuring the Opening Statement*

As we begin to discuss how to structure an opening statement, we would do well to consider the words of Associate Supreme Court Justice Joseph Story:

Be brief, be pointed; let your matter stand

Lucid in order, solid, and at hand;

Spend not your words on trifles, but condense;

Strike with the mass of thought, not drops of sense;

Press to the close with vigor, once begun,

And leave, (how hard the task!) leave off, when done. . . .

Victory in law is gain'd as battles fought,

Not by the numbers, but the forces brought.

This advice, poetic as it may seem by today's standards, is nonetheless as appropriate today as it was in 1831.

A superior opening statement contains cohesive and complementary legal and factual theories as well as morally appropriate themes. While legal or factual theories do not win cases by themselves, their absence can undermine an otherwise powerful moral theme. The theme provides the moral force behind the decision-making process of the jury. It is the moral imperative that empowers the jury to emotionally accept and apply the facts and law, ultimately giving the victory to one side.

The opening statement begins with a thematic statement setting the stage for the story about to be told. These are often referred to as "hooks" or "grabbers" by trial attorneys. Thematic statements connect the jury to the timeless human themes present in this particular trial. Instead of beginning with "Once upon a time, in a kingdom by the sea, lived a sad and lonely princess . . ." opening statements might start instead with "Abandoned and abused by a family that did not love her, Jessica took the only steps she could towards freedom—steps that placed her in direct confrontation with the state. The state arrayed its overwhelming might against this young woman, and wonder of wonders—she fought back." A superior opening statement has a line in it that captures the essence of your theme and ties it to your legal and factual theory. We teach advocates to place that line in a spot that makes certain the jury remembers it. One way to do this is through the doctrine of primacy and recency. We know that people usually are focused on our presentation at the beginning and the end. They cue in from an attention standpoint at those points. Advocates should use that knowledge to ensure that they give the jury something worth paying attention to during the time when they are focused.

One-Liners & Grabbers:

- If doesn't fit, you must acquit.
- Where's the beef?
- Wrong place, wrong time, wrong attitude.
- The line between love and hate is thin, and the defendant crossed over that line.
- If she couldn't have him, no one would. . . .
- Swan's don't swim in the sewer . . .
- They did nothing. . . .
- Desperate, distraught & devastated . . .

People remember what they hear first and last. Placing a thematic statement at the beginning and end of your opening statement is an organizational construct often referred to as "bookending." This provides structure to the opening. You should bookend your opening statement to quickly capture and present your theme and theory of the case to the jury. The story that you tell between those bookends forecasts the evidence that supports your position and will have persuasive power. As the jury listens, your story is tied directly to the wrong that you are asking the jury to make right. The moral force of your position will complement and buttress your evidence, creating acceptance by the jury, or at least a willingness to potentially accept your version of the facts. This technique also relies upon communication theories of primacy and recency.

Consider carefully the first words out of your mouth. You will never have more undivided attention from a jury than when you first approach them to begin your opening statement. Stand silently before them. Take advantage of that moment in time to ring the bell of truth through an appropriately crafted beginning. A proper theme and theory will resonate through the opening, be supported by the testimony of witnesses during the case-in-chief, and be expounded upon in closing argument. People remember the first thing and the last thing you say. Make yours count.

Though they should never be read, an opening statement must be well planned while still appearing to be extemporaneous. Outline your thoughts before you begin to practice your opening. By the time you prepare your opening you should have already identified the substance of your closing, interviewed witnesses, and ordered their testimony based upon the relative strength of their facts for your side and for your theme and theory. The opening statement is the preview of your case that makes the jury want to watch the rest of your movie and root for your hero or heroine. Do not make the mistake that many poor movies make of promising more than they can deliver. Audiences know when the best part of the movie is found in the previews. If that is happening in your case, you are guaranteeing that the jury will think the lawyer who gave the opening statement is a great orator. You are also ensuring they will not like the rest of the movie. While jurors cannot walk out in the middle of the trial, they do get to vote. Remember this, and only promise a portion of what you think you will be able to deliver during trial. While less is more, make certain that the less you deliver is coherent, both thematically and theoretically.

Paint an active picture for the jury through the use of words, pictures, and exhibits. Tell them the story of what happened without ever using the word "story." Ensure that your presentation has a clear beginning, middle, and end. When possible, use the narrative style in the present tense to ensure believability, simplicity, and movement towards persuasion. Some structures include using a chronological story line, flashbacks, and parallelism. Strive for that sense of transparency that removes the storyteller from the process, allowing the tale to stand upon its own merits. When you have identified the right theme in accordance with your legal and factual theory, it will strike a chord with those who hear it. Making a connection with a jury member during opening statement is the beginning process in creating in that juror an advocate for your client in the deliberation room where the true final arguments are made.

2. *Delivering the Opening Statement*

"A lawyer and an actor are akin. It is true I have no mask, I have no set lines, I have no black cloth and I have no floodlights to bring illusion; but out of the miseries and the joys and the strivings and experiences of men, I must create an atmosphere of living reality so that it may be felt and understood by others, for that is advocacy."

SIR EDWARD MARSHALL HALL, K.C., famous English barrister

You set the stage for communication between yourself and the jury during every moment you are in the courtroom. The opening statement is a golden opportunity—you will never have the same degree of focus from the jury as you do in those first few precious moments when words have not yet been spoken. The canvas is blank. The colors with which you choose to paint are yours. The palette from which you may select includes eye contact, body movement, word choice, and delivery. It is that first opportunity in the trial where the preliminaries have been dispensed with and it is time to get down to business. You must feel enthusiasm for your case. That does not mean cheerleading or table pounding, but it does mean caring—and believing—strongly about the case and the position you are advocating. This care and belief is reflected throughout the opening statement and the trial, by the words you choose and the manner in which you deliver them. You will achieve this degree of care and belief only when you are truly comfortable in your place in the process.

Preparation, preparation, and more preparation will bring comfort. Gerry Spence says "Prepare, prepare, prepare, and win." Truer words have rarely been spoken about trial practice. Command of the trial arena comes from developing the ability to communicate through the spoken word as viewed through your knowledge of, and comfort with, the factual and legal issues present in your case, and that comfort is the child of hard work.

(a) Beginning the Opening

All eyes in the courtroom should be on you when your opening statement begins. Getting them there, and then keeping the jurors engaged and keeping them that way, is a necessary skill you must develop. There are several things you can do to increase dramatic tension and focus the jury on your message. The first is to truly connect with your audience. You may create those connections with words, movements, and eye contact. It begins with the judge looking at you and asking if you are prepared to proceed. Stand up, look the judge in the eye, and say something like, "Yes, Your Honor, the state/defense/plaintiff/defendant is prepared to make an opening statement."

Beginning the Opening:

Acknowledge the court

- Assume the position
- Breathe
- Eye contact
- Let the jury give you permission to begin
- Catch their attention immediately:
    - Grabber
    - One-Liner
    - Storytelling

The judge will then give you leave to proceed. Take a breath. Acknowledge the presence of the judge and opposing counsel in the courtroom, and then walk comfortably to a spot centered on the jury, but far enough away from them that you are not intruding into their personal space.

Stop. Plant both of your feet firmly on the ground and then look at your jurors. Eye contact is extremely important. It creates a connection between you and the jurors, opening a channel for communication that cannot be completely duplicated through alternative means. Nonetheless, some very successful communication specialists recommend looking at the forehead of the jurors, focusing on their nose or picking a spot above them and focusing on that spot when you speak to them to avoid the dangers of direct contact. This idea comes from public speaking courses in school that teach students who are afraid to make eye contact to compensate with such techniques.

Some of you are unable to make direct eye contact and this technique is a sufficiently successful option for those of you who become paralyzed by the fear of looking jurors in the eye. However, think about the thought process behind this type of advice. While it may work fine for public speaking situations with a large audience, in front of jury it is a poorer choice because it reflects fear—fear of connecting with others. It is a crutch designed to allow you to "get through" the opening statement, but it sends the wrong message to the jury and is an admission to yourself that you are not completely comfortable with the process.

More importantly, why should you be afraid to look the people who will decide the case in the eye? By the time openings begin, these people are not strangers. If you are not hiding facts or law from the jury then you have no external reason to fear them. The fear that you are feeling must come from within you and that is why you are afraid or uncomfortable with making eye contact. Give yourself permission to connect with this jury. If you stop and think, you should realize that you already know a great deal about the people you are facing. You have read their questionnaires, asked them questions in open court, and chosen who will remain. Now is not the time to be afraid to extend to them the gift of trust.

Truthfully, you have to do it anyway. Regardless of how afraid you may be, the jurors are still going to decide this case. Overcome that fear and meet them eye-to-eye during your opening. Allow yourself this small gift of trust. Your eyes are the easiest and most accepted way of connecting with another person—do it. If you are not ready, then do not take this step, but at some point you should step off into this area of trust. Doing so can transform your attitudes about advocacy.

The longer you are silent at the beginning of an opening statement, the greater the tension within the room It will seem like forever to you, but not to others.

. . .

Center yourself on the jury, but not so close that you invade their personal space. Most experts advise that you should never touch the railing in front of the jury. Many jurisdictions specifically prevent you from coming too close to the jury, but some do allow it. In those jurisdictions you should be careful to experiment in practice before attempting this technique.

In any event, at all times during the opening statement you should be mindful of your size and the subordinate position of the jury by their being seated and therefore smaller than you. Find a comfortable position from which you can survey and connect with the entire jury. Make eye contact and include them all in your opening statement. If you are too close you not only make them uncomfortable, but you lose the ability to connect with those that may not be completely on your side. Frankly, you want this set of people as comfortable with you as possible, and you need to take the time to find what works for you in the moments of opening statement.

(b) Using Body Language

Your physical presence in the courtroom is part of your persuasive ability. There is a need for you to fill the space without filling it with words and this is best accomplished by your body language and presence. Presence is attitude, body language is physicality. While the concept of body language may mean different things to different people, we are concerned here with the art of persuasion. You cannot persuade someone if they don't believe what you are saying. Your body language must create a sense of credibility, of believability, in you. You are the first, last, and best witness for your case. Let us consider body language purely from the standpoint of how it opens, or closes off, communication.

Once you have taken your position and used that moment of silence to draw the jury's attention to you, allow your hands to drop to your sides, exposing your body to the members of the jury. By letting your hands drop you are sending a message to the jury that you are not defensive and that you trust them not to hurt you. This position will make you feel exposed, but in actuality it is a position of power because there is no impediment between you and the jury. Try this exercise; take a podium and place it between yourself and your audience. You feel safe behind that podium—protected and invulnerable. You are also cut off from those that you are speaking to by that object. Now step out from the behind the podium and face your audience with nothing between but open space and your words. Feel the difference? That feeling is what is accomplished by standing in front of a jury with your hands at your sides; you are both vulnerable and powerful at the same time. In that situation all you have is your case, your voice, and your body. Use all three to make the best impression possible.

The issue of what to do with the podium in the courtroom is one of the eternal conundrums that advocacy professors continually quibble over. Some have a personal preference for its removal, often citing to the rationale similar to that mentioned in the preceding paragraph. Others are devoted to its use, and suggest that it serves as an anchor to which the advocate can tie themselves, creating security in an insecure situation. Still others suggest that perhaps it would be best to experiment with it, without it, and somewhere around it. The best advice is to use it as a tool when it increases your persuasive power and ignore it when it does not. Every moment that you are worrying about the podium is a moment when you are not focused on the story of your case, and the story is what always matters.

After you have acknowledged the presence of the jury through your body language and eye contact, you can begin to speak. Hit them immediately with a statement that captures your theme and theory. It can be something as simple as a one-word statement like, "Accountability," "Credibility," "Gold-digger," "Rage," or "Greed." Find short pithy statements that capture the essence of what you want to say without adopting some cliché. The classic example in recent history is "If it doesn't fit, you must acquit." Be creative. You know your case better than anyone else at this point and make sure that knowledge and preparation is reflected in the theme found in the beginning of the opening statement.

After you have begun you should allow your hands to move in concert with your words. Avoid haphazard movement, but use it when necessary to make a point. Every movement should be choreographed to bring a point home. Like your words, movement in the courtroom has persuasive power. Understand this and use it. Do not allow your nervous energy to leak out through various bodily tics and random movements that creates the perception that you might be one or two tacos short of a combination platter.

(c) Verbal Keys

There are several generally accepted verbal keys that you should have in your kit. One is tone of voice. Make certain that your tone matches the case you are trying. Outrage is good, but save it for the lying witness. The jury should be relatively neutral at this point so, do not scare them over to the other side. Be persuasive without arguing through word choice, body movement, and voice inflection. Your language should be clear, concise, dynamic, and positive with a definite preference for the present tense as you tell the story of what you believe happened.

Use Appropriate Language:

✓ Present tense

✓ Clear

✓ Concise

✓ Dynamic

✓ Positive

✓ Tone of voice

✓ Modulation

Overly emotional presentations or theatrics should be avoided. They will not persuade anyone at this point and call into question your believability as well as expose your bias for your client. Strive for a conversational tone that accurately reflects the subject you are discussing. Talk *with* the jury instead of *at* them.

Jurors will summon mental images of people, places, facts, objects, and locations from the words you speak. Choose your words carefully, with a full and complete understanding of the possible connotations they may hold for the jury. While the terms "billiards parlor" and "pool hall" both describe a place where a game is played, they create very different images about that place. The billiards parlor is filled with well-heeled individuals who drink expensive whiskey and talk about their stock investments. The guys in the pool hall are crouched under a cheap stained-glass florescent lamp, counting the beer stain circles on the pool table railing.

Gripping and persuasive language does not have to be flamboyant, but it should capture an image for the listener. Don't strain to be a poet or a troubadour. Capture the truth simply, using language that the jurors will accept, understand, and interpret in a way you can influence and predict. Avoid legal jargon and cop-speak. You do not want to remind the jury that you are a professional doing your job. You want them to see you as a fellow human being helping them to discover the truth.

(d) Dangers of Improper Argument

Little is gained by attempting to "stretch the envelope" of opening statement into the realm of argument as it is normally defined. To a certain extent the entire opening is argument in that it is designed to lead the jury and prepare them to make conclusions. It is not, however, argument in the classic sense; in that you do not provide the jury with conclusions during the opening statement. Instead, save the conclusions for closing argument after you have prepared the jury through your case-in-chief to accept them. From a common-sense perspective that makes sense. You cannot expect jurors to accept your conclusions during opening statements when they have not yet been exposed to the facts and the law. You have spent a great deal of time immersed in the facts and the law during your case preparation and analysis. Do not attempt to drown your jurors with a fire hose of conclusions based upon your preparation. Give them time to accept your facts and the law, and they will conclude on their own that you are right.

A well-prepared and well-delivered opening is in and of itself persuasive. When the statements made during opening cannot be tied to a fact that a witness will disclose through testimony, then you are not making an opening statement—you are arguing. Comments on the credibility, believability, or reliability of the expected evidence are not a forecasting of what the evidence will be, but a comment on its validity. Once you start sliding down the slippery slope towards argument you lose the jury. This reminds them that you are doing a job for someone you represent, when you should be helping them sort through a complex issue to ascertain the truth. You become a lawyer and someone who cannot be trusted.

Why sacrifice your credibility for a few glorious moments of argumentative prose? Save it for the closing, when being argumentative is what you are supposed to do. In opening, only discuss what the evidence will show. There is no swifter way to lose credibility—and to play into the hands of an alert opponent—than to promise something in an opening and not deliver. This invites your opponent to flog you during their closing with not delivering on your promise. A good advocate watches for this mistake and makes the opponent pay, and pay, and pay.

By the same token, you should not waste this precious opportunity. Do not talk about the function of an opening statement, how it is not evidence, etc. It sounds defensive, juries don't care, and it invites them to ignore you. This is the judge's job—why should you do it for her? Worry about doing yours and let her do hers. You are the advocate, so advocate. By beginning with a civics lesson during the opening statement, you are simply throat-clearing and buying time because you are not prepared to deliver a cogent theme and theory. It is wasted time and space. This does not mean you should not mention legal concepts when appropriate, but you should do so in a manner that makes sense, advances the theme and theory of your case, and does not waste the time of the jury.

The other side will hammer at your weaknesses. When you have a particularly strong part to your case, for example an extremely sympathetic victim or an informant with a checkered past, it is difficult to over-sell those positions of strength. Remember the purposes of your planned impeachments. If you have one planned during the case that will be particularly persuasive, forecast that impeachment in your opening. Give the jury a taste of what is to come, much like a good movie trailer.

On the other hand, do not forget to compensate for your weaknesses when appropriate. Volunteer and account for some of those significant weaknesses, just not all of them. Address the obvious weaknesses in your case, such as compromises made by the victim, errors in lab results, admissions by the opposing party or "bad witnesses" that are impeachable under Federal Rules of Evidence 404(b), 405(a), 608, 609, 613, or 801(b). Expose these weaknesses when your theme and theory require it, but do so with a plan. This will establish candor and show a sense of balance while furthering your goal of getting the jury to pick you as the voice of reason. Where possible and practicable, couple admissions of weakness with a compensating fact that diminishes the damage and gives the jury a better context in which to place the weakness, hopefully in a fashion that supports your case theme and theory.

When considering what to do with exhibits during opening, remember these words of William Shakespeare from *THE RAPE OF LUCRECE:* "To see sad sights moves more than [to] hear them told." ***If you are going to take the jury's time to admit evidence during the course of the trial, then refer to it and use it during the opening statement.*** Giving notice to opposing counsel of your intent to use exhibits and providing them an opportunity to object during a pretrial hearing to that use are hurdles you should easily overcome if the evidence is to be admitted at trial.

You can also handle those issues through pretrial admissibility. If it is important enough to admit the exhibits, then it is important enough to use them. From your opponent's perspective, the best exhibits are those that are admitted but never used. Begin using those exhibits in the opening statement and continue to do so throughout the trial. If you do, the jury will see them at opening, anticipate them during direct and cross examinations, and listen to what you think about them during your closing argument. Finally, in the deliberation room, the jurors will hold those exhibits in their hands and remember and adopt your words when discussing their impact on the case.

A proper voir dire will identify certain jurors you believe will be receptive to the factual theory, legal theory, or moral theme of your case. The advocate plants information about these issues into receptive jurors by discussing them during voir dire. You should use your body language, eye contact, and inflection to accomplish this goal. When done correctly, the juror takes ownership of those facts and runs with them, making your arguments for you during deliberations. The jury is there to do a job—to ascertain the truth. They are judging you to try and determine if they can rely upon you and the evidence you produce to assist them in finding out what happened. The verbal and nonverbal clues you send to them go a long way toward helping the jury make that decision. In Chapter 5 we will look at direct examination, which provides the building blocks from which you create your factual theory, legal theory, and moral theme.

. . .

E. Opening Statement Checklist

The following checklist summarizes the chapter on opening statements. You should use it as a starting point in developing your own opening skills. This checklist is not "Holy Writ" and is merely the soil in which you should plant the seeds of your own creativity.

I. Effective Opening Statements:

- a. Thematic Statement
  - i. Grabber
  - ii. One-Liner
  - iii. Hook
- b. Primacy and Recency
  - i. Bookend the theme front and back
  - ii. Most important information up front
  - iii. Weaknesses fronted during the middle
- c. Tell the Story
  - i. Use structure
  - ii. Present tense verbs
  - iii. Appropriate language
- d. Preview the Law
  - i. Give them a taste
  - ii. Identify how the law is important for this case
  - iii. Use the instructions you know will be coming
- e. Set the Hook for Closing Argument

II. Basic Legal Principles of Opening Statements

- a. Judge is in charge
- b. Do not waste time arguing, tell the story!
- c. Do not vouch for witness credibility
- d. No personal opinions
- e. If evidence is excluded do not mention it

f. Do not mention evidence if you have no good faith basis to believe it will be admitted

g. Do not violate the "Golden Rule" argument

III. The Art of Opening Statements

a. Structuring

i. Cohesive and complementary legal and factual themes

ii. Powerful moral theme

iii. Thematic statement

iv. Bookending

v. Focus on the story

vi. Preview the Law

vii. End on a reminder of what is coming in Closing (thematic bookending)

b. Delivering

i. First impression

ii. Beginning the Opening

1. Acknowledge the court
2. Assume the position
3. Breathe
4. Eye contact
5. Jury gives you permission to begin
6. Start strong!

iii. Body Language

1. Fill the space quietly
2. Command the room
3. Start from a still position
4. Movement follows the words
5. Podium – BAD
6. Eye contact – GOOD

iv. Verbal Keys

1. Present tense verbs
2. Clear language
3. Concise

4. Dynamic language
5. Positive approach
6. Tone
7. Modulation

v. Dangers of Improper Argument

1. Do not stretch the envelope
2. Persuasion comes from structure, not argument
3. Civics lesson waste time
4. No throat clearing
5. Do not spend time on your weaknesses

F. Conclusion

Now that we have developed the core set of skills necessary to make effective and persuasive promises to the jury during opening statement we will move on to a discussion of how to keep that promise through the testimony of witnesses during direct examination. If you cannot fulfill the promise made in opening then all of your words are hot air, signifying nothing.

Relevant Rules

1. Evidentiary Rule Matrix

Table 1 serves as a starting point for additional inquiry into the relationships between specific tasks during opening statement and the rules of evidence. Your case analysis should assist you in identifying when these particular issues will arise. You should use the table to review your knowledge of the evidentiary rules so that you can include that in your legal theory of the case. Your understanding of these rules and their impact on the admissibility of evidence will assist you in determining which facts you can rely upon with confidence during your opening statement. This knowledge is crucial if you wish to prevent over promising during opening statements. A faulty understanding of these rules will cause you to promise jurors facts the judge will not allow your witnesses to deliver.

Issues Arising During Opening Statements	Applicable Federal Rule of Evidence
Character of a witness for truthfulness	608
Out of court statements offered for the truth of	801–807

Issues Arising During Opening Statements	Applicable Federal Rule of Evidence
the matter asserted therein (hearsay)	
Offering evidence of other crimes, wrongs and acts (*see Chapter 10*)	404(b)
Prior convictions of a witness (*see Chapter 10*)	609
Legal relevancy: Is the probative value substantially outweighed by the danger of unfair prejudice?	403
Are the questions logically relevant	401 & 402
Competency of a witness	610
Personal knowledge of the witness	602

Table 1: Potential Evidentiary Rules Applicable During Opening Statements

2. *Professional Responsibility Rule Matrix*

Table 2 serves as a starting point for additional inquiry into the potential professional responsibility issues that are implicated during opening statements. These rules for the most part reflect goals of civility and integrity. Counsel must ensure that they do not cross certain lines delivering opening statements. You should pay particular attention to Rule 3.5, Impartiality and Decorum of the Tribunal. If you internalize now the normative practices embodied in these rules you will be taking the first steps towards not only being an effective advocate, but an excellent colleague and credit to our profession.

Issues Arising During Opening Statements—Rule Section & Summary	Applicable Rule of Professional Responsibility
(a)(1)–(-3): A lawyer must not offer false evidence.	Rule 3.3: Candor Toward the Tribunal
(e): A lawyer must not "allude to any matter that [she] does not reasonably believe is relevant or that will not be supported by admissible evidence . . ." She must not "assert personal knowledge of facts in issue . . . or "state a personal opinion as to the justness of a cause, the credibility of a witness, the culpability of a civil litigant or the	Rule 3.4: Fairness to Opposing Party & Counsel

Issues Arising During Opening Statements—Rule Section & Summary	Applicable Rule of Professional Responsibility
guilt or innocence of an accused."	
(a): A lawyer must not illegally "seek to influence a judge, juror, prospective juror or other official." (d): A lawyer must not intentionally disrupt the court and must conduct herself with respect for the court.	Rule 3.5: Impartiality & Decorum of the Tribunal

Table 2: The Most Prevalent Professional Conduct Rules During Opening Statement

. . .

Charles H. Rose III
Closing Arguments
FUNDAMENTAL TRIAL ADVOCACY (2nd ed. 2011)[2]

. . .

A. Introduction

The entire weight of a trial—the testimony, the exhibits, the legal arguments, rests upon your shoulders when you begin to close. The eyes of your client or the needs of the people you represent are focused on your words. This is the point where the jury hopes for guidance, clarity and justice. If you have properly analyzed and prepared your case the majority of what you have planned to talk about is present in the courtroom. Now is the time when you pull from the testimony the facts you need and juxtapose them with what the law requires or allows. Properly done the jury hears you argue in closing for what you previewed during opening statements and provided as evidence during the testimony of witnesses. We will discuss the art of presentation during closing arguments later in this chapter, but before you can focus on the performance you must have properly laid the foundations for success.

---

[2] Some footnotes and illustrations have been omitted or realigned. Unless otherwise specifically indicated, all professional conduct rules referenced are taken from the Delaware Supreme Court's professional responsibility rules. Those rules are almost identical to the model rules promulgated by the American Bar Association and are public domain documents.

The Rule of Threes:

- Tell them what you are going to tell them (opening statement)
- Tell them (case-in-chief)
- Tell them what you told them and why it means you win (closing argument)

. . .

[C]losing arguments drive the entire trial process, serving as the destination that the trial has been pointed towards. Every action taken during opening statements, motions arguments, jury instruction conferences, direct examinations, and cross examinations have been designed to maximize the persuasive power of your legal, factual, and moral position as expressed during closing argument.

During case analysis you identified what you needed to say and how you wanted to say it by applying the three primary steps of case analysis. You then developed the theories and themes to assist you in bringing the jury to the point where they would believe, accept and internalize your position. The goal was to empower the jury to argue for you in the deliberation room where all true final arguments are made. Now that it is time to create the final closing argument you should discover that the argument exists as an independent entity—a creation of your case analysis and preparation. The work you did up front pays off during closing arguments in that you know what you are going to talk about: the question is how.

Closing arguments must contain the words empowering the jury to decide the case in your favor. It melds the facts and the law of the case, casting them in a moral light. A good closing argument demands that the jury do nothing other than what you ask. If you have properly identified the legal issues, factual issues, and picked the right theme and theory, the closing argument comes as an organic expression of what you have shown to be true during the trial.

The Three Primary Steps in Case Analysis:

- Identify and analyze the legal issues.
- Identify and analyze the factual issues.
- Develop a moral theme and legal theory.

If that is not the case you will struggle to find a closing argument that makes sense and fits the facts and law as admitted to the jury and ruled upon by the court. There is great danger in choosing a closing argument that is not grounded in the facts and law as perceived by the jury. You may sound like the second coming of Gerry Spence delivering it, but the jury will be left cold in the end, and will turn to the side of the advocate whose argument makes the most sense, both rationally and emotionally.

There are certain organizational techniques that you must employ, but they are "much ado about nothing" without your internal understanding of what your position truly is and how your argument must flow from there. The jury will know if you are not genuine, and will distrust you. Do not make this mistake. If you have not found the center of your position within your case you will not find the superior closing argument. If you cannot see yourself standing before the jury in that moment, with those words, then you have not done your job during case analysis and you are not yet ready to close.

B. The Skill of Closing Arguments

1. Case Analysis

Closing argument is the destination where you expected to take the jury through the course of the trial. It is imperative that you identify your closing argument's legal theories, factual theories and moral themes during case analysis. This must be done before you begin with any other portion of your case. It must also be continuously revisited as you prepare for trial. Use the expected closing argument as a sanity check on your case. If you find yourself straying from your original destination make certain that you ask yourself why.

If you cannot answer the "why" question you are in definite danger of losing. Most cases are lost through a lack of organization and cohesive presentation. The dangers of losing focus are particularly high when the closing argument shifts based upon the presentation during the case.

Seven Fundamental Steps to a Superior Closing Argument:

- Case Analysis, first, last, always (opening).
- Grabber, one-liner, hook (moral).
- Argue! Use the law and evidence to create inferences supporting your theme and theory.
  - Answer the questions in the jury's mind.
  - Beware the burden of boredom.

- Uses appropriate rhetorical devices.
  - Primacy & recency.
  - Rule of threes.
  - Parallelism.
  - Analogies & inferences.
- Engage multiple senses.
- Meet the burden of common sense (facts).
- Instructions are your friend (law).
- Tell the jury what you want them to do, what the evidence demands

Do not allow the opposing side to determine your destination because you did not take the time to do so during your case analysis. You must know where you are going in order to get there. ***Go back now and retrieve the list of questions that you recorded the first time you read through the case file. Has your case analysis answered them?*** Did the legal theory and moral theme that you chose adequately allow you to address the issues that you believe are in the jury's mind through the testimony of witnesses during the case-in-chief? Have you clearly identified the relevant instructions you expect the judge to give after closing argument? Only when you can answer these questions are you prepared to begin crafting your closing argument. As you begin, keep in mind the application of the rule of threes that you utilized during opening statement, direct examinations, and cross examinations. Do not abandon the use of this powerful advocacy tool during closing arguments.

Your closing argument should use primacy and recency by beginning with a high impact point. The jurors are tired from sitting through a contested trial and you want this opportunity to focus them on what really matters. Normally this point should hit on your moral theme from the opening statement, capturing the essence of why an injustice will be done if your side does not win. It should capture the jury's attention, challenge their perceptions and by its very existence argue continually for your side, long after you have concluded. You want that initial impact to resonate in the jury deliberation room where the true final arguments are made.

2. Argue

Make sure that you ARGUE! Tell the jurors why your side should win using the facts, the law, and all reasonable inferences from the evidence. Use your knowledge of the case, as presented at trial, to connect through logical inferences disparate portions of your case. Place the issues in context during argument so the jurors can draw the appropriate inferences from the evidence, the law own personal knowledge. It can be done through sarcasm, common sense observations or humor. The important point is that now is the time to connect what is known with what is not known in light of the experiences and knowledge of the jury. They must rely upon their common sense and understanding of human nature to sort through all of the trial testimony. Use those facts to fashion a closing argument that echoes their own experiences. It gives your interpretation credibility, and creates synergy for your side. At the same time, you need to trust the jury. Now is not the time to rehash the evidence ("Agent Charles told you. . . . "). Avoid clichés, or use them with a novel twist. The first word of your argument should directly and powerfully relate to why your side wins.

Do not be afraid to show enthusiasm for your case. This does not necessarily mean cheerleading or table pounding like a caricature of a bad TV lawyer, but it does mean caring—or seeming to care—strongly about the case and the position you are advocating. Enthusiasm can be reflected in a number of ways, most obviously in inflection and word choice, but also your command of the courtroom, presentation of a case, and unapologetic advocacy for your client. If you do not care enough about this case to get excited and energized, how can you expect the jury to care?

During the opening statement a member of your team should have taken careful notes about the promises made by opposing counsel. If they have not kept those promises then during your closing argument you should hold the other side's opening against them. Listen carefully during your opponent's opening and remind the jury, in your closing, of promises made in the opening that your opponent did not keep. When those promises show an attempt to hide the ball or manipulate the process, drive that home and use it to attack the credibility of opposing counsel's case (but not necessarily the credibility of opposing counsel themselves). Sometimes you win merely by the other side losing. You should wield exhibits in the courtroom early and often. If they were worth admitting into evidence, they're worth reinforcing at every opportunity. Blow them up, put them on PowerPoint slides, use the document camera. Do whatever it takes to engage multiple senses of the jury during your argument.

Never state your personal opinions. "I think the defendant . . ." Of course you think: you're an advocate! You need not even (and should not) say "the defense believes" or "it is the government position." Sometimes this is spillover from the opening statement, after which counsel may become too cautious about arguing. Assertions made during argument in a closing need no preface or attribution; they call it argument for that reason and it is total advocacy. What you think or believe is not important or relevant. What the evidence demands, what common sense shows and what a basic understanding of human nature requires is where you should spend your time. It gives you the most bang for your buck and drives home the mission of argument, which is to persuade.

Do not give a civics lesson. Every second spent talking about the function of a closing argument sounds defensive and condescending. You will lose your audience. It invites the jury to ignore you, and the judge is going to tell the jury what the purpose and limitations of a closing argument are anyway. Giving the civics lesson is almost like saying, "Well I've got to stand up and argue now, but please feel free to ignore anything I say." If you start off that way rest assured, they will ignore you. This is not to say that you should not mention legal concepts when a case turns on a significant legal point, just do it when it makes sense. Expect the jury to understand your well-planned, lucid explanation of the law and to appreciate it, when it is relevant to their job.

The Do's of Closing Argument:

- Deal candidly with your weaknesses.
- Be confident in arguing your position.
- Maintain eye contact, but not so much to make jurors uncomfortable.
- Structure your argument – don't simply re-hash the facts.
- Draw on the jury's common sense.
- Use visual aids or physical evidence from the trial.
- Address the standard of proof.
- (Prosecution) Use rebuttal argument to hammer home your strongest points, how you refuted the defense's contentions, and remain positive in your case!

The other side will hammer at your weaknesses; when you have a particularly strong part to your case (extremely sympathetic victim, registered source with checkered past), you can hardly over-sell it, highlight those strengths. Remember the rule of threes and primacy/recency when you are determining how to emphasize your strengths and compensate for your weaknesses during closing. You should take the time during your closing argument to account for significant weaknesses, but not for every weakness. You have to decide which are important and which will slip by your opponent. The obvious weaknesses of your case—perhaps compromises made by your victim, lab errors, and admissions by your client—need to be addressed by you, but do so with a plan. It gives you an opportunity to establish candor and credibility with the jury and suggests a sense of balance. However you should couple the admission with a compensating fact that diminishes the damage and gives the jury an "out" or better context in which to place the weakness so that it has less of an impact on your case. Just as primacy and recency work for your strongest points, common sense should tell you to sandwich weaker points in the middle of your argument.

Counsel should know all or virtually all of the instructions the judge will use in a given case. Part of your analysis and preparation is the identification of probable instructions and the request for specific instructions. When you discuss them with the jury there is no need to preface that discussion with "the judge will instruct you" because (a) she might not, and may choose this opportunity to point that out, and (b) better that you steal the language of the instruction, so that when the judge utters it, she appears to be affirming your wisdom.

Do Nots of Closing Argument:

- Misstate the evidence or the law.
- Argue facts not in evidence.
- State your personal belief in the justice of your cause.
- Personally vouch for the credibility of a witness.
- Comment on the accused's exercise of a fundamental right (prosecution).
- Make personal attacks on opposing counsel.

Advocates usually are given liberal rein to argue inferences from the evidence and matters outside of the evidence that are part of generally accepted knowledge. Counsel must be careful, however, only to rely on evidence that has been properly admitted for an appropriate purpose. Care must be taken to ensure that evidence that is admitted by the court with a limiting instruction is not used to argue a point for which it has not been allowed. One example would be to take evidence of a prior inconsistent statement that was admitted for the limited purpose of attacking a witness's credibility and then arguing the facts within that statement to prove an element or to disprove an element of an offense or cause of action. The extra burden on defense counsel is to abide by the ethical rule that forbids calling the attention of the jury to the absence of evidence when in fact that evidence was suppressed.

C. The Law of Closing Arguments

Most legal issues regarding closing arguments revolve around the problems dealing with the effects of impermissible argument. A review of the case law dealing with what constitutes impermissible argument provides us with some broad legal principles that advocates can rely upon in setting the limits as to what is appropriate argument in most jurisdictions. Advocates who find themselves in a position where they wish to push the boundaries of permissible argument would do well to take the time to review the case law in their jurisdiction regarding these suggested legal principles.

Legal Principles for a Proper Closing Argument:

- You are confined to the record. If evidence is not admitted you cannot argue it.
- The trial court has supervisory authority over the scope and direction of closing argument, but should give deference to counsel unless the law is misstated.
- Prosecutors cannot argue merely to inflame or arouse passions—the courts will consider whether a substantial right of the accused was violated when reviewing this issue.
- Advocates cannot intentionally misstate evidence or attempt to lead the jury to draw improper inferences from admitted evidence.
- Personal beliefs and opinions of counsel are forbidden.
- Reasonable inferences are permissible and expected.
- It is improper to refer to evidence which was either successfully objected to as to admissibility, stricken from the record, or otherwise excluded.

The development of the case law concerning closing arguments has generally taken two paths. The first path is an analysis of whether or not the conduct of the advocate making the argument was not ethical. The courts often refer to rules of professional conduct and the American Bar Association guidelines for prosecution and defense conduct concerning closing arguments when trying to make this decision. Once a determination has been made as to whether or not the advocate violated ethical norms (at this point the advocate often has a bar related issue), the next question is whether or not that violation resulted in the loss of a substantial right of a party, usually the accused. If so then relief may be provided by the court.

D. The Art of Closing Arguments

Legal and factual theories are the application of the relevant law to the specific facts of your case. They form the basis for the legal or procedural reasons that you win. Theory is how the jury is empowered by the law to decide the case in your favor. Moral theme, on the other hand, is the emotional reason you should win. It is why the jury wants to decide the case your way. You must weave these three facets together when creating superior closing arguments. This is not a magic act, a play, or a movie. You have just guided the jury on a long journey. It may have been dangerous, it may have been boring, but it must have been important. Closing argument reminds the jury why the journey of the trial was important, and explains what the journey signifies in a way that they can accept, understand as true, and take action upon.

Themes are as varied as the people, places and situations they capture and represent. Theme provides the moral force that brings the case to life. A good theme not only gets the jury on your side, it creates a feeling of comfort within them about deciding things your way. If you cannot find a theme within your case that will resonate with the jury, try to determine what sense of injustice exists. Is there a wrong that has been committed against your client that will get the jury to decide the case for you? Examples of such themes include the government rushing to judgment because your client is a member of a minority, the innocent person wronged by circumstance, and someone else did it. Other examples include the destruction of a way of life or the health of an individual through the greed of a soulless corporation. The storylines are as varied and complex as the tales of humanity that surround us each day. If you watch television, go to the movies, or read fiction they are there for each of us to find and use.

Make sure that you start strong and end strong. This is classic primacy and recency; people remember what they hear first and last. Think hard about the first words out of your mouth as well as your closing lines; an ideal closing argument should appear spontaneous, but should not actually be spontaneous. Not only must you be able to start and end strong, you also have to create a sense of the humanity of your client. Sometimes this requires you to humanize them in the eyes of the jury. Part of this is terminology, but it should be more than calling the defendant by name if you are defense counsel or "the defendant" if the government's. Counsel should paint pictures of victims or the defendant by placing them in scenarios and filling in human details that bring them to life; jurors will remember these facts and it will help you get past the temptation to look at the case as (merely) a contest between lawyers.

Argue! The only purpose in getting out of your chair is to persuade the jury to do something. Every sentence in the argument, every word choice, every decision of what evidence to highlight, ignore, or explain away, every decision of what to talk about in what sequence should move the jury or judge toward that end. You will know you are arguing when you:

- **Draw conclusions and make inferences based upon the available evidence.** The admitted evidence will always support any number of interpretations, from the plausible to the fanciful—argue yours. If you cannot say it with a straight face how can the jury believe it?
- **Comment on witness demeanor.** Do not underestimate the extent to which judgments about credibility are based on effect, how a witness looks and sounds. Pounce on this. It is how we judge the credibility of other people whom we meet in life. Jurors do the same thing.
- **Apply law (including instructions) to the facts.** It is not appellate argument but neither is it a plebiscite. Assume that juries try to analyze the case in light of the law; make it easier for them.
- **Refute the opponent's case.** This is most critical for the defense in its lone closing argument. Skilled prosecution/plaintiff's counsel will often give a "minimalist" closing argument and save their strongest arguments for rebuttal, the one argument of the day to which the defense does not get to reply.

. . .

G. Closing Argument Checklist

The following checklist summarizes the information presented throughout this chapter on closing arguments. You should use it as a starting point in developing your own questioning skills. This checklist is not "Holy Writ" and is merely the soil in which you should plant the seeds of your own creativity.

I. Use the Rule of Threes:

  a. Tell them what you are going to tell them.

  b. Tell them.

  c. Tell them what you told them and why it means you win.

II. Remember the Three Primary Steps of Case Analysis:

  a. Identify and analyze the legal issues.

  b. Identify and analyze the factual issues.

c. Develop a moral theme and legal theory.

III. Use the Seven Steps to Superior Closing Arguments:

a. Case Analysis, first, last, always (opening).

b. Grabber, one-liner, hook (moral).

c. Argue! Use the law and evidence to create inferences supporting your theme and theory.

i. Answer the questions in the jury's mind.

ii. Beware the burden of boredom.

d. Uses appropriate rhetorical devices.

i. Primacy & recency.

ii. Rule of threes.

iii. Parallelism.

iv. Analogies & inferences.

v. Engage multiple senses.

e. Meet the burden of common sense (facts).

f. Instructions are your friend (law).

g. Tell the jury what you want them to do (what the evidence demands).

IV. The Do's of Closing Argument:

a. Be confident in arguing your position.

b. Maintain eye contact, but not so much to make jurors uncomfortable.

c. Structure your argument—don't simply re-hash the facts.

d. Draw on the jury's common sense.

e. Use visual aids or physical evidence from the trial.

f. Address the standard of proof.

g. (Prosecution) Use rebuttal argument to hammer home your strongest points, how you refuted the defense's contentions, and remain positive in your case!

V. The Do Nots of Closing Argument:

a. Misstate the evidence or the law.

b. Argue facts not in evidence.

c. State your personal belief in the justice of your cause.

d. Personally vouch for the credibility of a witness.

e. Comment on the accused's exercise of a fundamental right (prosecution).

f. Make personal attacks on opposing counsel.

VI. Legal Principles for a Proper Closing Argument:

a. You are confined to the record. If evidence is not admitted you cannot argue it.

b. The trial court has supervisory authority over the scope and direction of closing argument, but should give deference to counsel unless the law is misstated.

c. Prosecutors cannot argue merely to inflame or arouse passions. The courts will consider whether a substantial right of the accused was violated when reviewing this issue.

d. Advocates cannot intentionally misstate evidence or attempt to lead the jury to draw improper inferences from admitted evidence.

e. Personal beliefs and opinions of counsel are forbidden.

f. Reasonable inferences are permissible and expected.

g. It is improper to refer to evidence which was either successfully objected to as to admissibility, stricken from the record, or otherwise excluded.

H. Conclusion

Applying the lessons of this chapter will assist you greatly persuading the jury to follow your line of reasoning at the close of the trial. If you properly identify your closing arguments' legal theories, factual theories and moral themes during case analysis you will be able to answer the why question that is always present in the minds of the jury. Remember, you must not allow the opposing side to determine your destination during closing argument.

If you do not take the time to sort it out using the tools provided in this chapter you are at the mercy of the opposing counsel who does. That is not a place that anyone wants to be. Let us turn out attention now to jury selection. Once we have identified how we expect the case to proceed from opening through closing we must identify those jurors who cannot serve in a fair and impartial manner. Jury selection is the vehicle for this process.

Relevant Rules

1. Evidentiary Rule Matrix

Table 1 serves as a starting point for additional inquiry into the potential evidentiary pitfalls advocates should be aware of as they prepare and deliver their own closing arguments. The same issues also exist when listening to an opposing counsel's closing argument. A thorough grasp of these issues will assist you in avoiding objections when you are performing and identifying them when others are closing. Your case analysis should assist you in identifying when these particular issues will arise. You should use the table to review your knowledge of the procedural rules so that you can include that in your planning for your closing argument.

Issues Arising During Closing Arguments	Applicable Federal Rules of Evidence
Properly address evidence admitted with a limiting instruction	105(b)
Out-of-court statements offered for the truth of the matter asserted therein (hearsay)	801–807
Properly arguing evidence of other crimes, wrongs & acts (Chapter 10)	404(b)
Legal relevancy—is the probative value substantially outweighed by the danger of unfair prejudice, et al.	403
Are the questions logically relevant	401, 402

Table 1: Potential Evidentiary Rules Applicable During Closing Arguments

2. Professional Responsibility Rule Matrix

Table 2 serves as a starting point for additional inquiry into the potential professional responsibility issues that are implicated during closing arguments. Counsel, particularly prosecutors, must ensure that they do not cross certain lines when arguing during closing. The same issues also exist when listening to an opposing counsel's closing argument. A thorough grasp of these issues will assist you in avoiding improper argument and identifying the improper argument of others. Your case analysis should assist you in identifying when these particular issues will arise. You should use the table to review your knowledge of the procedural rules so that you can include that in your planning for your closing argument.

Issues Arising During Closing Arguments	Applicable Rule of Professional Responsibility
(a)(1–3) A lawyer must not offer false evidence.	**Rule 3.3 Candor Toward the Tribunal**
(e) A lawyer must not allude to any matter that she does not reasonably believe is relevant or that will not be supported by admissible evidence. She must not assert personal knowledge of facts in issue and never state a personal opinion as to justness of a cause, the credibility of a witness, the culpability of a civil litigant or the guilt or innocence of the defendant.	**Rule 3.4 Fairness to Opposing Party and Counsel**
(a) A lawyer must not illegally seek to influence a judge, juror, prospective juror or other official. (d) A lawyer must not intentionally disrupt the court and must conduct herself with respect for the court.	**Rule 3.5 Impartiality and Decorum of the Tribunal**

Table 2: The Most Prevalent Professional Conduct Rules During Closing Arguments

. . .

Law and Transcripts

Domestic Violence or Plaintiff-Side Civil Clinic: Law and Transcript

1. Statutory Provisions Defining the Elements of a Protection Order Statute and Elements of Assault

Smallville Code Ann., Section 16–1005(a): If, after hearing, a judicial officer finds that a preponderance of the evidence supports the conclusion that the respondent has committed a criminal offense (as defined in Section 16–1005(b)) against the petitioner, the judicial officer may issue a protection order that:

1. Directs the respondent to refrain from committing criminal offenses against the petitioner;

2. Requires the respondent to stay away from or have no contact with the petitioner;
3. Requires the respondent to participate in appropriate counseling programs;
   (a) Directs the respondent to relinquish possession of personal property owned jointly by the parties or owned by the petitioner individually; and
   (b) Directs the respondent to perform or refrain from other actions that may be appropriate to the effective resolution of the matter.

Smallville Code Ann., Section 16–1005(b): The elements of the criminal offense of assault are as follows:

1. An attempt, with force or violence, to injure another;
2. Apparent present ability to injure; and
3. General intent to perform the acts that constitute the assault.

2. Transcript of Jackson v. Doe

DISTRICT COURT
FOR THE DISTRICT OF SMALLVILLE

RUTH JACKSON, Docket Number: 1234-56

Petitioner

vs.

MICHAEL DOE,

Respondent.

The above-entitled action came on for a hearing before the Honorable JANE SMITH, Judge, in Courtroom Number 113, commencing at 10:20 a.m.

APPEARANCES:

On Behalf of the Petitioner:

RINA ROTHMAN, Certified Student Attorney

SARAH STONE, Certified Student Attorney

JENNIFER BLACK, Esquire, Supervising Attorney

On Behalf of the Respondent:

SAMANTHA SMITH, Esquire.

Deposition Services, Inc.

4321 Executive Boulevard

Smallville, USA

DEPUTY CLERK: Ruth Jackson versus Michael Doe, Case No. 1234-56.

MS. ROTHMAN: Rina Rothman, certified student attorney, for the petitioner.

THE COURT: Good morning.

MS. STONE: Good morning, Your Honor, Sarah Stone, certified student attorney, for the petitioner.

THE COURT: Good morning.

MS. BLACK: Good morning, Your Honor, Jennifer Black, supervising attorney.

THE COURT: Good morning. Ma'am, state your name please.

MS. JACKSON: Ruth Jackson.

MS. SMITH: Samantha Smith, representing Mr. Michael Doe.

THE COURT: Sir, state your name please.

MR. DOE: Michael Doe.

MS. STONE: Thank you, Your Honor. I'd like to waive my opening statement. I request permission to call Ruth Jackson to the stand.

THE COURT: Yes, let me just ask, for planning purposes, how many witnesses do you intend to call?

MS. STONE: Two, Your Honor.

THE COURT: Including your client, or --

MS. STONE: Including our client.

THE COURT: Alright. Alright, call your two witnesses.

MS. ROTHMAN: Petitioner calls Ruth Jackson to the stand.

THE COURT: Ma'am, come to the witness stand. Come around this way. Remain standing and raise your right hand, please.

Thereupon,

RUTH JACKSON

having been called as a witness for and on behalf of the petitioner, and having been first duly sworn by the Court, was examined and testified as follows:

THE COURT: You may be seated. Thank you. If there are individuals in the courtroom who've been told that you may be or will be witnesses in this case, I'm going to ask you to leave the courtroom right now and have a seat right outside, and when it's time for your testimony you'll be called in. Is there any witness in the courtroom now? Ms. Smith, do you have any witnesses other than Mr. Doe?

MS. SMITH: Only Mr. Doe, Your Honor.

THE COURT: All right. And are your witnesses in the courtroom? Is your other witness in the courtroom?

MS. STONE: No, Your Honor.

THE COURT: All right. Counsel, you may inquire.

MS. ROTHMAN: Thank you, Your Honor.

DIRECT EXAMINATION

BY MS. STONE:

Q Good afternoon, Ms. Jackson. Please state and spell your full name for the record.

A Ruth JACKSON, R-U-T-H, J-A-C-K-S-O-N.

Q Where are you currently living, Ms. Jackson?

A I'd rather not say at this time.

Q Why not?

A Because I don't want Michael Doe to know where I'm staying at.

Q What is your relationship to the respondent, Michael Doe?

A We were engaged to be married.

Q Why are you living at your current undisclosed location?

A Because there was violence and I left out.

Q Ms. Jackson, where did you go to college?

A Smallville University.

Q What did you study there?

A Education.

Q What do you do in your free time?

A I have a friend that I teach for – I teach him English and he teaches me French.

Q Ms. Jackson, how long were you engaged to be married to the respondent?

A Two and a half years.

Q And how long were you romantically involved with the respondent?

A Three years.

Q Are you currently romantically involved with the respondent?

A No.

Q Ms. Jackson, where were you living until August 25th?

A In the home of Michael Doe and his parents.

Q At what address?

A 6789 70th Street, in Smallville.

Q How long did you live there?

A For two and a half years.

Q Why did you move in with the respondent?

A To see how things would work as far as us getting married and getting our own place.

Q How was your relationship after you moved in with him?

A It was very good.

Q When did it stop being good?

A In May.

Q What happened in May?

A He admitted to me that he had cheated on me with one of my girlfriends.

Q In May of what year?

A Of this past year.

Q How did you feel when the respondent told you he had cheated on you?

A Hurt and very upset.

Q How was your relationship with the respondent after he told you this?

A I didn't have any more trust in him.

Q How did the respondent act after he told you this?

A I don't know—he started sleeping somewhere else, only coming back to the house once every week or two.

Q How often was he sleeping at the house before he told you that he had cheated on you?

A Regularly.

Q Ms. Jackson, let me direct your attention to July 7 of this year. Where were you that night?

A At home in bed asleep.

Q At what address?

A 6789 70th Street.

Q What time did you go to sleep?

A About 9:00.

Q Was anyone else in the bedroom when you went to sleep?

A No.

Q What time did you wake up?

A About 1:00 in the morning.

Q Why did you wake up?

A Michael Doe woke me up.

Q How did he wake you up?

A He came into the room loud. He was stumbling around, like he does when he's been drinking.

Q What made you think that he was drinking?

A I could smell the liquor on him, and his speech was slurred.

Q What was the respondent doing?

A He was standing over me fussing.

Q What was he fussing about?

A About something someone had said.

Q What did you do when you woke up?

A I sat up on the side of the bed.

Q What was the respondent's demeanor like when he woke you up?

A He was angry.

Q How did you know that he was angry?

A The tone of his voice was really harsh.

Q What did the respondent do when you woke up?

A He looked at me with a really mean face and said something terrible.

Q What did he say?

A He said, Ruth, you are going to get it. I mean it this time, you will really get it bad.

Q What did you understand this to mean?

A That he was going to hurt me badly.

Q Why did you believe he meant that?

A Because he was really mad and when he spoke he had his fist balled up.

Q What did the respondent do next?

A He stormed out of the room.

Q Ms. Jackson, how did you feel after this incident?

A Scared.

Q Why were you scared?

A Because I was pretty sure he was going to hurt me.

Q Let me direct your attention to August 25th of this year. Where were you that night?

A Sleeping in my bed.

Q At what address?

A 6789 70th Street, in Smallville.

Q What time did you wake up?

A About 1:00 or 1:30 a.m.

Q Why did you wake up?

A Because Michael Doe entered the room.

Q Where was the respondent when he entered the room?

A Standing at the foot of the bed.

Q What was his demeanor like?

A He was real drunk and angry.

Q What did the respondent do when he entered the room?

A He grabbed for my pocketbook.

Q What did he say?

A He was asking something about a credit card.

Q What did you say when the respondent asked about the credit card?

MS. SMITH: Objection, hearsay.

THE COURT: Overruled. Counsel has laid the foundation for an excited utterance.

A I told him I didn't know what he was talking about and to put my pocketbook back where it was.

Q What did the respondent do when you told him to put the pocketbook back?

A He said he paid for the pocketbook, he could do what he wanted to with it.

Q How did you feel when you saw the respondent going through your pocketbook?

A Upset, like he was intruding on my privacy.

Q What did the respondent do with your pocketbook?

A He was going through it, and I went to reach for it. He told me that he bought it, he would tear it up. He started tearing the straps off.

Q How did you react when he started tearing the straps off your pocketbook?

A I reached for it to get it back.

Q Where were you, in relation to the respondent, at this point?

A Standing up right near him.

Q What did the respondent do when you reached for the pocketbook?

A He grabbed me by my arm, pushed me up against the closet door.

Q How hard did the respondent push you?

A He pushed me hard enough where I ended up with a bruise on my elbow.

Q What did you do after the respondent pushed you against the door?

A I grabbed my pocketbook, put it back on the bed behind me.

Q What did the respondent do next?

A He grabbed me by my arm and pushed me on the bed.

Q What position was your body in when it landed on the bed?

A My feet were on the floor.

Q What part of your body did you land on?

A On my back.

Q What did the respondent do after he pushed you onto the bed?

A He sat on top of me.

Q What part of your body did he sit on?

A He sat on my chest.

Q Which direction was he facing when he sat on your chest?

A His face was facing my face.

Q Did you try to push the respondent off of your chest?

A No.

Q Why not?

A Because he was too heavy.

Q How much does the respondent weigh?

A I guess about 190.

Q How did it feel when the respondent sat on you?

A I couldn't breathe.

Q Why couldn't you breathe?

A I have asthma.

Q How long have you had asthma?

A All my life.

Q How do you treat your asthma?

A I have inhalers.

Q Have you ever had an asthma attack in front of the respondent before?

A Yes.

Q How did you feel, emotionally, while the respondent was sitting on our chest?

A Scared.

Q Why were you scared?

A Because I didn't know what he was going to do, and I couldn't breathe.

Q What else did the respondent do while he was sitting on you?

A He put his hand around my throat.

Q Which hand?

A His right hand.

Q What did he do with the hand that was around your throat?

A Well he squeezed hard enough that I had a bruise on my neck.

Q What did the respondent do with his other hand?

A He hit me with it.

Q How did the respondent hit you?

A With his open hand.

Q Where did he slap you?

A On my head.

Q What part of your head?

A My forehead.

Q What did your forehead look like after the respondent hit you?

A I had a scratch on it.

Q How long was the scratch?

A About an inch.

Q What was the respondent saying as he hit you?

A I can't remember.

Q How did you feel as the respondent was doing these things to you?

A Scared. I was trying to push him off of me.

Q What happened to respondent when you tried to push him off of you?

A I ended up scratching him on the back of his neck.

Q What did the respondent do next?

A He jumped up and said that he was bleeding.

Q What did you do after the respondent got off of you?

A I reached for my cell phone.

Q Why did you reach for your cell phone?

A To call 9-1-1.

Q What did the respondent do when you reached for your cell phone?

A Grabbed my cell phone away from me and threw it on the floor.

Q What happened to the cell phone when he threw it on the floor?

A It broke in pieces.

Q What did you do after the respondent threw your phone on the floor?

A I picked the pieces up and went out the door.

Q What did you do when you went out the door?

A I went upstairs to the bathroom, put my phone back together, and called 9-1-1

Q About what time was it when you called 9-1-1?

A About 1:30 or 2:00.

Q What was the respondent doing as you were calling 9-1-1?

A I don't know. I know a few minutes later he came up and knocked on the bathroom door.

Q How did you react when the respondent came upstairs?

A Well, when he knocked on the bathroom door and told me to open the door, I opened the door and I had 9-1-1 on the phone. I went back downstairs.

Q When did the police arrive?

A About five minutes later.

Q What time did the police leave?

A I really don't know what time it was when they left.

Q What did the police do right before they left?

A They handcuffed Michael Doe.

MS. STONE: Let the record reflect that I'm showing Exhibits 1-A and 1-B for identification to Respondent's counsel.

MS. STONE: Your Honor, may I approach the witness?

(MS. STONE laid the proper foundation for admission of the photographs.)

MS. STONE: Your Honor, I'm offering Petitioner's Exhibits 1-A and 1-B into evidence.

THE COURT: Any objection, Ms. Smith?

MS. SMITH: No, Your Honor.

THE COURT: I'll accept them.

(Petitioner's Exhibit Nos. 1-A and 1-B were admitted into evidence.)

BY MS. STONE:

Q What does the photograph marked Petitioner's Exhibit 1-A show?

A A picture of my throat.

Q What does your throat look like?

A Swollen.

Q Please point to where it's swollen.

A Around in here.

MS. STONE: Let the record reflect the petitioner is pointing to the center of the throat.

THE COURT: Could you ask her to mark on it so that the respondent sees where she's indicating?

BY MS. STONE:

Q Would you mark where on the throat it's swollen?

MS. STONE: For the record, she's marking in blue pen.

BY MS. STONE:

Q What does the photograph marked Petitioner's Exhibit 1-B show?

A A picture of my forehead.

Q What does your forehead look like in the picture?

A There's a scratch on it.

Q Where is the scratch?

A On my left-hand side.

Q How big is the scratch?

A About an inch.

MS. STONE: Your Honor, may I have permission to approach the Clerk to hand him the photographs?

THE COURT: Yes. But before you do that, if you could just show what you had her mark to the respondent's counsel.

BY MS. STONE:

Q Ms. Jackson, would you like the Court to order the respondent not to assault or threaten you?

A Yes.

Q Would you like the Court to order the respondent to stay away from you and your home?

A Yes.

Q Would you like the Court to order the respondent not to contact you by phone, in writing, or in any other manner?

A Yes.

Q Would you like the Court to order the respondent to return or reimburse you for personal items of yours that he has kept from you?

A Yes.

Q Where were your personal items when you left the respondent's house on August 25?

A I had packed them in a bag and left them in the room. When I went back to get my items my bags had been, they had been messed up.

Q When did you go to pick up your bags?

A A few days later.

Q Where are the bags now?

A At a friend of mine's.

Q Were all of the items in the bags when you picked them up?

A No.

Q What items were missing?

A I'm missing a winter coat and a pair of Nike tennis shoes.

Q How much did the coat cost?

A $70.

Q How much did the tennis shoes cost?

A $120.

Q Who paid for these items?

A My mother paid for the coat and the boots. The other items I paid for myself.

Q And how do you know how much the items cost that your mother paid for?

A Because I was with my mother when she bought them.

Q Where were these items when you last saw them?

A In my bag that I had packed.

Q How did you know that the bags had been gone through?

A Because the bags had been changed. The things I had packed were in different bags, that were different colors, from the ones I had them in.

Q Where are the personal items that are not in the bags?

A I don't know.

Q Ms. Jackson, do you have another warm coat for the winter?

A No.

Q And Ms. Jackson, would you like the court to order the respondent to enroll in and complete alcohol counseling?

A Yes.

Q Why are you requesting this relief?

A He gets drunk all the time and when he's drunk, he gets angry.

Q How frequently does the respondent get drunk?

A At least a few times a week.

Q Ms. Jackson, is there anything else you would like the court to do for you?

A Yes, I would like the judge to order Michael Doe to pay for self defense classes for me.

Q Why do you need this relief?

A Because I am really scared now that he attacked me and need to feel safer.

Q Ms. Jackson, how do you feel around the respondent?

A Scared.

Q Why are you scared?

A Because I don't know what he might do to me.

MS. STONE: No further questions. Thank you, Ms. Jackson.

THE COURT: Ms. Smith, do you have any cross examination?
MS. SMITH: Yes.

Q You lived with Mr. Doe for two years?

A Yes.

Q You lived with Mr. Doe's parents?

A Yes.

Q You spent time with Mr. Doe's family?

A Yes.

Q You ate dinner together?

A Yes.

Q You watched television together?

A Yes .

Q Mr. Doe's parent's run a church in their home?

A Yes.

Q Mr. Doe's parents are pastors?

A Yes.

Q You attended this church with them?

A Yes.

Q You were treated as one of the family?

A Yes.

Q But you and Mr. Doe are no longer dating?

A No – we're not.

Q And you're not living in the house anymore?

A No.

Q Ms. Jackson, your mother lives in southern Virginia?

A Yes.

Q Your mother lives in a retirement community?

A Yes.

Q You don't want to live with her?

A No.

Q You are not close to your brothers?

A Not really.

Q You moved out of Mr. Doe's house on August 25?

A Yes.

Q You moved out because Mr. Doe told you to leave?

MS. STONE: Objection, the question calls for hearsay

MS. SMITH: This statement comes in as non-hearsay—we are introducing it not to prove the matter asserted but rather to show the impact it had on the listener.

THE COURT: Overruled.

A Yes.

Q This scared you?

A No, it didn't scare me.

Q You had been living there for two years?

A Yes.

Q And now you had to leave?

A Yes.

Q You went to file for a protection order the day Mr. Doe told you to leave?

A No.

Q There were advocates who help you move into a free room at a shelter when you filed for the protection order?

A Yes.

Q Ms. Jackson, you have asthma?

A Yes.

Q You have had asthma your entire life?

A Yes.

Q You need an inhaler when you are struggling breathing?

A Yes.

Q You carry this inhaler with you everywhere you go?

A Yes.

Q Asthma medication is expensive?

A Yes—I think so.

Q You are unemployed?

A Yes.

Q And you do not have health insurance?

A No.

Q Mr. Doe's sister works in a pharmacy?

A Yes.

Q And you get your asthma medication from her?

A Yes.

Q You only have one inhaler left?

A Right.

Q You have only had a job off and on for the past 2 years?
A Yes.
Q You have a cell phone?
A Yes.
Q But Mr. Doe pays the bill?
A Yes.
Q You don't receive food stamps?
A No.
Q Mr. Doe used to buy your food?
A Yes.
Q Mr. Doe bought your clothes?
A Yes.
Q Mr. Doe owns the home you lived in?
A Yes.
Q Mr. Doe no longer pays for your food, clothing, and housing?
A No.
Q You owe Mr. Doe money?
A Yes.
Q You have taken his credit cards before?
A Only when he gives them to me.
Q You have spent Mr. Doe's money without his permission?
A No. He always tells me I can use the money.
Q You testified that Mr. Doe was dating other women?
A Yes.
Q One was named Monica?
A Yes.
Q Monica was a friend of yours?
A Yes.
Q Mr. Doe started dating her in May?
A Yes.
Q Mr. Doe is now dating someone new?
A Yes.

Q Her name is Jackie?

A Yes.

Q You testified that Mr. Doe told you that he was cheating?

A Yes.

Q You have known about these other relationships for the past several months?

A Yes.

Q Mr. Doe doesn't sleep at home that often?

A No.

Q In fact, Mr. Doe has stayed away for weeks at a time?

A Yes.

Q But you continued to live at the house?

A Yes.

Q You thought you and Mr. Doe had an exclusive relationship?

A Yes.

Q You agreed only to date each other?

A Yes.

Q You were living together?

A Yes.

Q You were engaged to be married?

A Yes.

Q You would not have cheated on him?

A No.

Q It wouldn't have been right?

A No

Q Mr. Doe had no right to date other women?

A Right.

Q And especially, he had no right to do it publicly, so other people would know about it?

A Right.

Q It was disrespectful?

A Right.

Q It made you look bad?

A I don't think so.
Q You allege that two weeks ago Mr. Doe threw you on the bed?
A Yes
Q You allege that he choked you?
A Yes.
Q The police report says that you scratched Mr. Doe?
A I guess.
Q You did scratch Mr. Doe?
A Yes.
Q You scratched him on his neck?
A Yes.
Q You scratched him hard?
A I don't think so.
Q You scratched him so hard he bled?
A I didn't really notice.
Q He was still bleeding when the police arrived 20 minutes later?
A I'm not sure about that.
Q Ms. Jackson, you're 5' 8" tall?
A Yes.
Q Mr. Doe is only 5' 6"?
A That sounds right.
Q After Mr. Doe allegedly choked you, you got up?
A Yes.
Q And you went upstairs to call the police?
A Yes.
Q You didn't run upstairs?
A No. I can't run with my asthma.
Q So you walked?
A Yes.
Q You went upstairs to the bathroom?
A Yes.
Q Then you called the police?

A I sure did.

Q Mr. Doe was right outside the bathroom when you called?

A Yes.

Q After you called, you came out of the bathroom?

A Yes.

Q The police were not there yet.

A Right, but I needed to gather my things.

Q Later, you called the police again?

A Well, I . . . right.

Q You told them not to come?

MS. STONE: Objection, hearsay.

MS. SMITH: Statement of a party opponent, your honor.

THE COURT: Overruled.

A Yes, that's right, but only because I realized that I could just leave without their help.

Q Let me go back to the asthma for a moment. Asthma interferes with your ability to breath?

A Yes.

Q And when you lose your breath, you need your inhaler?

A Yes.

Q You use your inhaler several times a day?

A Yes.

Q You have lost your breath from walking too fast?

A Yes.

Q You have lost your breath even when you are walking slow?

A Yes.

Q You have lost your breath walking up and downstairs?

A Yes.

Q You have lost your breath when you get really excited about something?

A Yes.

Q You lose your breath when you get scared or spooked?

A Yes.

Q You also can lose your breath when you get upset?

A Yes.

MS. SMITH: No further questions.

THE COURT: Very well. All right, ma'am, you may step down. Ms. Stone, call your next witness.

MS. STONE: He's right outside now. Thank you, Your Honor.

THE COURT: Sir, come to the witness stand please.

Thereupon,

DETECTIVE JOHN JONES

having been called as a witness for and on behalf of the petitioner, and having been first duly sworn by the Deputy Clerk, was examined and testified as follows:

DEPUTY CLERK: Thank you, you may be seated.

DIRECT EXAMINATION

BY MS. STONE:

Q Please state your name for the record.

A Yes, ma'am, my name is John Jones.

Q Mr. Jones, please state your occupation.

A My duty assignment is an investigator assigned to the Domestic Violence Unit, working for the Smallville Police Department for the past 8 years.

Q Detective Jones, directing your attention to August 25 of this year, where were you at around 1:00 in the morning?

A I was dispatched to the home of Ms. Ruth Jackson.

Q When you arrived on the scene, did you see Ms. Jackson?

A Yes.

Q How would you describe her appearance?

A She seemed scared and upset, crying. I noticed she had an abrasion – a scratch on her forehead. I also observed that she had a swollen neck.

Q Thank you.

MS. STONE: Your Honor, I have no further questions.

THE COURT: Ms. Rothman, any questions for this officer?

MS. ROTHMAN: No, Your Honor.

THE COURT: You may step down, sir.

THE WITNESS: Thank you, ma'am.

(Witness excused.)

THE COURT: All right, do you all have another witness?

MS. STONE: Your Honor, we have no further witnesses. The petitioner rests.

Thereupon,

MICHAEL DOE

having been called as a witness for and on behalf of the respondent, and having been first duly sworn by the Deputy Clerk, was examined and testified as follows:

MS. SMITH: State your name please, sir.

MR. DOE: Mr. Michael Doe.

Q What do you do for a living, sir?

A I am a contractor for the ABC Corporation.

Q What do you do for them?

A I work on the computer system.

Q What is your educational background?

A I got a degree from State University and computer certificate from State Tech.

Q What is the nature of your relationship with the Petitioner?

A Well, I met her several years ago. She was homeless. She was very nice person. Friends with my parents. We dated and I told her she could stay with us.

Q Were you ever engaged?

A No. Never. Ruth kept asking if we could get married, but no, I didn't think we had much of a relationship. I was just trying help her out.

Q Drawing your attention to July 7 of this year, did you see Petitioner that night?

A Absolutely. She was at home when I got home from work. She was sleeping.

Q How did you react when you saw her?

A I just quietly getting my things from the room, taking them upstairs to go sleep. I hadn't been sleeping in the room for a while—our romantic relationship had pretty much ended.

Q Did Petitioner remain asleep?

A No, she woke up, started asking me questions.

Q What type of questions?

A She had heard that I was dating a friend of hers. She flew into blind rage. She was very jealous. Screaming terrible things about "the bitches" I was seeing. She spat at me, said she would kill me.

Q How did you feel when she said that?

A Really scared. I didn't know what she might do. She was really not herself.

Q So what did you do?

A I called the police and told them what was happening.

Q Did they come?

A They never showed up. I don't know why.

MS. SMITH: I have a recording of the 911 tape here and petitioner's counsel has stipulated to the authenticity of the tape, if I could just play it for the court?

THE COURT: Very well, admitted. You can play the recording.

(Respondent's Exhibit No. 1 was admitted into evidence and the recording was played.)

BY MS. SMITH:

Q Turning your attention to August 25 of this year, what was the status of your relationship at that point?

A Oh, really bad. I had had enough of her. I had told her that she would have to leave.

Q When did you tell her that?

A Oh, a lot. But when I got back from work that night I told her that again. I told her it was over.

Q Well, let's go back. What did you find out that night?

A Okay. August 25th—Well, August 25th I got off from work, okay, and before I came in the room I went upstairs to my mother and my father. So then my mother told me something about my credit card. So I went down in the room to check my paperwork. I saw another charge I didn't recognize on my credit card. So I called the 1-800 number. And I called the 1-800 number and they told me, "You are above your limit." I say, "Okay, thank you." Then I came back to her in the room.

MS. STONE: Objection your honor, hearsay as to the statements of the credit card operator and Respondent's statements.

THE COURT: Excuse me, sir. I'm going to accept not for the truth of the matter, but for the effect on the listener.

MS. STONE: Thank you, Your Honor.

THE COURT: Overruled.

BY MS. SMITH:

Q Who did you come back to?

A To Ruth. I checked with Ruth, "Do you have any business with using my credit card? Did you use my credit card?" She told me, "No." I said, "Are you sure? Well I called and the people told me, say, I went over my limit, and you are the only person who has my key and everything. So why are you trying to deny this?" Then I called back again for the second time.

Q You called back where?

A I called the credit card company for the second time. And they told me that the person charged the credit card—my credit card with big charges the last few days.

Q Continue.

A Okay. And I came back to her in the room. I said, "Oh, Ruth, somebody used my credit card, and because you the only person got access to all my things in the room." She said, "I know nothing about a credit card."

MS. STONE: Objection your honor. A standing objection to Respondent's statements as hearsay.

THE COURT: Overruled. I will admit them for effect on the listener.

BY MS. SMITH:

Q What else did Petitioner say at this point?

A So she said, "Maybe it's one of your women using your credit card." I said, "How sure are you that one of my women is using my credit card? Who are my women?"

Q What did you do at this point?

A Before I went to take the key from the, from the nightstand, she was behind me, and she hit me on my neck. I said, "Ruth, why'd you hit me on my neck? I didn't do anything wrong to you. I took you in for two years and seven months, and you pay nothing to me and I take care of you. But now it's time for you to move out. It's over."

Q How did she react?

A Right away she said that she would call the police. So I left her in the room and she said she was calling the police. I said, "Okay, call the police." And I went upstairs. So right away the police knocked, they never asked me any questions, they put cuffs on my hands, and they sent me in the car. So I was there in the car, they asked her to explain what happened, but never asked me, and then they took me to the police station.

Q I'm sorry, you were in the police car and then what did the officers do?

A And then the police were in the house, okay? Then one officer told the other officer, "Okay, take him to the station." That's all that happened.

Q Did you sustain any injuries?

A She scraped me. I think the police have the picture of that scrape on my shoulder.

Q Is there any other testimony that you care to give?

A No, no, I don't have any testimony to, to say anything. I was just trying to ask her if she used my credit card. But when I was putting my hand out to take my key and go upstairs, she thought I was taking her bag. She just took that bag and she hit me on my shoulder. But I never said anything to her.

Q And Mr. Doe, do you have anything to say about this property she says you took? The Nike shoes, or her coat?

A I don't know what she's talking about. I don't know about her stuff.

Q Mr. Doe, are there other people who live in your house?

A My parents.

MS. SMITH: Thank you. No further questions.

THE COURT: All right, then I'm going to allow the lawyer for the petitioner to ask you questions.

MR. DOE: Okay.

CROSS-EXAMINATION

BY MS. STONE:

Q Mr. Doe, Ms. Jackson has asthma?

A I don't know.

Q She had asthma the entire time you were dating?

A I don't know nothing about she had asthma, no.

Q You've seen her using her inhaler?

A No.

Q You weigh more than Ms. Jackson.

A She weighs more than me.

Q You heard Ms. Jackson testify about an incident that occurred on August 25 of this year?

A Yes, I heard what she said.

Q You came home that night?

A I came home from work, uh huh.

Q You came home, and you went downstairs?

A I went upstairs first.

Q You went downstairs after?

A Yeah, I went downstairs.

Q You went into your bedroom?

A I went into my bedroom, yes.

Q Ms. Jackson was in bed?

A She was in bed.

Q You were worried about your credit cards?

A I—say that again.

Q You were worried about your credit cards?

A No, I was not worried about my credit card. But I was asking her about my credit card, I was not worried.

Q You thought that Ms. Jackson had your credit card?

A She—I asked her if she used my credit card.

Q You picked up Ms. Jackson's pocketbook?

A No.

Q You were looking for your credit cards?

A I put my credit card on the nightstand, on the dresser. That where I put all my stuff, on the dresser. Okay, so I was trying to find out about my card, and my mother asked me to do something for her that night. So I told her, I say, okay, the next day I would do it, but immediately I called to the credit company and the credit company said you're over your limit. And I said, "What, over my limit?" And I never hardly—I never use that credit card.

Q You thought that Ms. Jackson had used your credit cards then?

A Huh?

Q You thought that Ms. Jackson had used your credit cards?

A I called the credit company and they say somebody in the house used it, and she has all my keys to my room.

Q So you thought Ms. Jackson had used your credit cards?

A Sure.

Q And you were upset?

A No, I was not upset. I was not upset.

Q Ms. Jackson called the police that night?

A She called the police on me that night. I said, "Why are you calling the police?"

Q The police arrested you that night?

A The police arrested me because she called the police and she was screaming, crying.

MS. STONE: Thank you, no further questions.

THE COURT: Counsel, any redirect?

MS. SMITH: Mr. Doe, is there anything else you want to add?

MR. DOE: Okay. Particularly about saying that I should keep far from her. She needs to keep far from me too. I need protection too.

THE COURT: All right. Does the petitioner have any rebuttal testimony to present?

MS. STONE: No, Your Honor.

THE COURT: Do you have any closing remarks?

MS. STONE: Yes, Your Honor.

Digitally signed by April Downes

ELECTRONIC CERTIFICATE

I, April Downes, transcriber, do hereby certify that I have transcribed the proceedings had and the testimony adduced in the case of RUTH JACKSON vs. MICHAEL DOE, Docket No. 1234-56.

I further certify that the foregoing pages constitute the official transcript of said proceedings as transcribed from audio recording to the best of my ability. In witness whereof, I have hereto subscribed my name.

April Downes

Transcriber

Unemployment Insurance Benefits or Defense-Side Civil Clinic: Law and Transcript

1. Statutory Provisions Defining the Elements of Administrative Appeal of Denial of Unemployment Insurance Benefits Based on "Voluntary Quit"

Smallville Code Ann., Sections 311.0–311.7, states as follows:

311.0 Following an initial determination that an employee does not qualify for unemployment insurance benefits, an employee is entitled to a de novo review in the Office of Administrative Hearings. At this proceeding, the employer bears the burden of proving that the employee ("claimant") does not qualify. The employer must satisfy the following elements, as defined in the subsequent statutory sections:

(1) The claimant has engaged in misconduct at work;

(2) The claimant quit the job (as opposed to being fired); and

(3) The decision to quit was voluntary.

If the employer successfully proves these elements, the burden of proof shifts to the employee, who must prove that the "voluntary leaving" was based on good cause, as defined in Sections 311.4 – 311.7, below.

311.1 Pursuant to § 10(a) of the Act, the Director of the Department of Employment Services shall disqualify for benefits any individual who left his or her most recent work voluntarily, without good cause connected with the work.

311.2 In determining whether a leaving disqualifies an individual for benefits, it shall appear from the circumstances of a particular case that the leaving was voluntary in fact, within the ordinary meaning of the word "voluntary."

311.3 A leaving shall be presumed to be involuntary unless:

(1) the claimant acknowledges that the leaving was voluntary; or

(2) the employer presents evidence sufficient to support a finding by the Director that the leaving was voluntary.

311.4 If it is established that a leaving was voluntary, the claimant shall have the responsibility of presenting evidence sufficient to support a finding by the Director of good cause, connected with the work, for the voluntary leaving.

311.5 The circumstances which constitute good cause connected with the work shall be determined by the Director based upon the facts in each case. The test shall be, "what would a reasonable and prudent person in the labor market do in the same circumstances?"

311.6 The following shall *not* constitute good cause connected with the work for voluntary leaving:

(a) Refusal to obey reasonable employer rules;

(b) Minor reduction in wages;

(c) Transfer from one type of work to another which is reasonable and necessary;

(e) General dissatisfaction with work; and

(f) Personal or domestic responsibilities.

311.7 Reasons considered to be good cause connected with the work for voluntary leaving include, but are not limited to, the following:

(a) Racial discrimination or harassment;

(b) Sexual discrimination or harassment;

(c) Failure to provide remuneration for employee services; and

(d) Transportation problems arising from the relocation of the employer, a change in the primary work site, or transfer of the employee to a different work site; provided, that adequate, economical, and reasonably distanced transportation facilities are not available.

2. Transcript of Winsome Sports Center v. Shield

DISTRICT COURT
FOR THE DISTRICT OF SMALLVILLE

WINSOME SPORTS CENTER, Docket Number: 1234-56

Employer,

vs.

DOROTHY SHIELDS,

Claimant.

The above-entitled action came on for a hearing before the Honorable JANE SMITH, Judge, in Courtroom Number 113, commencing at 10:20 a.m.

APPEARANCES:

On Behalf of the Employer:

RINA ROTHMAN, Certified Student Attorney

JOAN WHITE, Supervising Attorney

On Behalf of the Claimant:

SARAH STONE, Certified Student Attorney

JENNIFER BLACK, Supervising Attorney

DEPUTY CLERK: Winsome Sports Center versus Dorothy Shields, Case No. 1234-56.

MS. ROTHMAN: Rina Rothman, certified student attorney, representing Winsome Sports Center.

THE COURT: Good morning.

MS. WHITE: Joan White, Your Honor, supervising attorney.

MS. STONE: Sarah Stone, certified student attorney, for the Claimant. Dorothy Shields.

THE COURT: Good morning.

MS. BLACK: Good morning, Your Honor, Jennifer Black, supervising attorney.

THE COURT: Good morning. Ma'am, state your name please.

MS. SHIELDS: Dorothy SHIELDS.

MS. ROTHMAN: Thank you, Your Honor. I'd like to waive my opening statement. I request permission to call my first witness to the stand.

THE COURT: Yes, let me just ask, for planning purposes, how many witnesses do you intend to call?

MS. ROTHMAN: One, Your Honor.

MS. STONE: Two, Your Honor, including our client.

THE COURT: Alright. Alright, Employers may call their first witness.

MS. ROTHMAN: Petitioner calls Edward WINSOME to the stand.

THE COURT: Sir, come to the witness stand. Come around this way. Remain standing and raise your right hand, please.

Thereupon,

EDWARD WINSOME

having been called as a witness for and on behalf of the petitioner, and having been first duly sworn by the Court, was examined and testified as follows:

THE COURT: You may be seated. Thank you. If there are individuals in the courtroom who've been told that you may be or will be witnesses in this case, I'm going to ask you to leave the courtroom right now and have a seat right outside, and when it's time for your testimony you'll be called in. Is there any witness in the courtroom now? Ms. Stone, is your second witness in the courtroom?

MS. STONE: No, Your Honor.

THE COURT: All right. Counsel, you may inquire.

MS. ROTHMAN: Thank you, Your Honor.

DIRECT EXAMINATION

BY MS. ROTHMAN:

Q Thank you, your honor. Mr. Winsome, could you state your name and occupation for the record?

A My name is Edward Winsome. I am the owner and manager of Winsome Sports Club at 734 Dale Ave. here in the city.

Q How long have you been the manager there?

A A little over 12 years. I founded the company almost 13 years ago.

Q Do you know Ms. Shields?

A Yes, I hired her as an employee three years ago, on September 22.

Q What position was Ms. Shields hired for?

A Personal trainer, at the club.

Q Could you please describe your experience with Dorothy Shields as an employee in your company?

A She came in like any new trainer and I set her up with some walk-ins to get her client base up. She was actually really good with the ladies and, pretty soon, she had a lot of clients, all women. But after around two years, she started having problems. Like attitude problems. She was talking down the Club to her customers.

Q How long did Ms. Shields work with the company?

A Almost three years. Her employment ended two months ago, just short of three years.

Q How did her employment end?

A I guess she sort of quit. She just stopped coming in at some point, so I fired her.

Q When was the last day Ms. Shields showed up to work?

A It was August 27.

Q Did she say anything when she left that day?

A She said she couldn't live on the amount of money she was making.

Q When personal trainers are not working with clients, what are their duties at Winsome Sports Center?

A Helping clients generally, helping around the club, cleaning up, stuff like that.

Q What is the pay structure at WSC?

A It's an hourly wage—$8/hour. And then if you're a personal trainer, you get a portion of the hourly rate that the client pays on top of the hourly wage.

Q How was Ms. Shields as an employee at WSC?

A She was an okay worker at first, you know, she was enthusiastic and worked hard and so on. And she started to get some personal training clients of her own.

Q Did there come a time when things did not go so well with Ms. Shields at the club?

A About two years in, things started to go a bit downhill. She started complaining to clients, kind of badmouthing WSC, and a lot of her clients went to a rival club. We put some write ups in her file about it.

Q Did Ms. Shields appear to you to be content in her job?

A At first she seemed alright. But then she got really surly.

Q What happened to her business at that point?

A Her performance really deteriorated too, so she lost a lot of her training clients, and she was kind of slacking around the club in general.

Q Do you have a customer complaint system at WSC?

A Yes, any customer complaints are sent to me, I investigate, talk to the employee, put the complaint in the employee's personnel file, and discipline the employee if appropriate.

Q Did you receive any complaints about Ms. Shields during the time period we've been discussing?

A Yes, I got a few complaints about her.

Q What was the nature of these complaints?

A People complained about her attitude, said she was complaining about the club.

Q Were any of these complaints submitted to her employment file?

A Yes. I have reviewed her file and there are several complaints and a letter to the file that was shared with Ms. Shields. Her initials appear at the bottom of the letter, indicating that she read it.

Q Mr. Winsome, I am showing you what has been previously admitted as Employer's Exhibit #1. Please read the letter aloud.

A "Letter to file, from lead personal trainer. I had a conversation with Ms. Jones about Dorothy Shields today and she said that Dorothy was complaining about the club and the way it treated her. I believe Dorothy is talking down the club to clients and generally being insubordinate. Spoke with Dorothy who acknowledged this complaint."

Q Did any of Ms. Shields' clients ever leave the club?

A Yes.

Q Did you speak with them about their departure?

A Yes. I spoke to two clients about four months before Ms. Shields left the club. They told me that Dorothy had complained about how she was getting paid, and that they had decided to go to a rival club, Fit and Trim. I spoke with Ms. Shields and told her that she should stop being insubordinate.

Q What impact did this have on Ms. Shields' employment at WSC?

A Well, not having so many training clients meant that Dorothy wasn't making as much money, see, because you get $8 an hour, but then on top of that you get a cut from personal training fees. So I guess Dorothy decided the job wasn't worth it, and so she left.

Q No further questions.

THE COURT: Ms. Stone, do you have any cross examination?

MS. STONE: Yes, Your Honor.

Q Mr. Winsome, personal trainers get a portion of the hourly rate for individual clients, correct?

A Yes. Based on their expertise, they get a percentage.

Q And after the trainer gets eight or more new clients, that rate is 60% of what the client pays, correct?

A For some trainers, they get 60%, others get less.

Q At the time Ms. Shields worked for you, you had eight personal trainers at WSC, seven men and one woman, correct?

A Yes.

Q And all seven of those men received 60% of the fees generated by their personal training clients?

A Yes, all seven have been with the club for several years and they all have excellent employment record.

Q At the time Ms. Shields' worked for you, she received a 50% cut of the fees paid by her personal training customers, right?

A Yes, but that was because she was insubordinate.

Q No further questions.

MS. ROTHMAN: No redirect, Your Honor. We have no further witnesses, and we rest.

THE COURT: Very well. All right, sir, you may step down.

Thereupon,

DOROTHY SHIELDS

having been called as a witness for and on behalf of the Claimant, and having been first duly sworn by the Deputy Clerk, was examined and testified as follows:

MS. STONE: Please state your name for the record.

MS. SHIELDS: Ms. Dorothy Shields.

Q Ms. Shields, you live at 4435 Watson Avenue, correct?

A Yes.

Q Did you ever work at Winsome Sports Club?

A Yes, I started on September 22, three years ago. I worked there until August 27th of this year.

Q Why did you leave WSC?

A I left because they were discriminating against me by paying me less than the male trainers and I just couldn't make ends meet. When I complained, they assigned me terrible duties.

Q How were you paid at WSC?

A It was $8/hour, and then I also got a cut of the fees paid by my personal training clients. The clients were charged $80/hour and I got $40 out of that fee.

Q What was your relationship like with your boss, Mr. Winsome?

A I guess it was okay for a while. Until I figured out I was getting screwed and started asking him about it. Then he and the other employees started treating me badly.

Q How many clients did you have at the peak of your time at WSC?

A I had about 25 clients who worked just with me. So things were pretty active for about two years, until around last February. That's when I learned about the pay differential.

Q And how much money were you making at that time?

A The most was probably about $1,200/week. That was my training fee and hourly wage combined for a total of about 40 hours per week.

Q Were you satisfied with this pay structure?

A I was, until I found out that I was making less than the guys.

Q How did you discover that you were being paid less?

A One of my friends, Chuck, told me.

Q What did he tell you?

MS. ROTHMAN: Objection, calls for hearsay.

MS. STONE: Your Honor, I am not offering this for the truth of the matter asserted, but for its effect on the hearer.

THE COURT: As you know, counsel, hearsay is admissible in this administrative hearing, so I will allow the testimony.

A Chuck told me in February that he got 60% of his client's fees. I only got 50%. He also told me that he knew all of the other guys were getting 60%, because he had seen their checks.

Q What did you do when you learned that you were being paid less?

A I went to Mr. Winsome and told him I expected to get paid the same as the guys. He told me I did not deserve to get as much as they did, because I was late for work sometimes. But I wasn't late any more than the guys were, and I never came late for a client appointment. Besides, I had more clients than almost all of the guys.

Q Did the information about pay differences affect your work?

A No. I continued to work as hard as I always did but the clients I had worked with for a while could tell that I was upset.

Q Did you discuss your concerns about your pay with your clients?

A No, well, I never raised it, but a couple of them asked me why I seemed less happy, and I told them what I had found out.

Q Did those clients do anything about it?

A One of them went to Mr. Winsome to complain. That resulted in the write up that Mr. Winsome brought to court. He got it all wrong. The client was criticizing him for being a sexist, not me for being disgruntled. I only signed the write up to get him off my back.

Q Did your clients do anything else?

A Well, I think they told some of my other clients about it and they all were upset on my behalf. They all ended their memberships at WSC, and moved their business to Fit and Trim. One of them called to tell me that Fit and Trim would hire me, but I had signed a non-compete agreement with WSC. I know they thought they were helping me, but I lost about 13 of my clients, and my income was cut in half.

Q Did you ever learn why your clients left Winsome Sports?

A I don't know for sure. I think it was because they found out how unfairly I was being treated. And because a better place, Fit and Trim, opened up nearby.

Q What happened at WSC after your clients left?

A I was really demoralized and I hated the place. I guess the rest of my clients could pick up on that and a couple asked for a different trainer and the rest went away, maybe to Fit and Trim, I don't know.

Q What happened next?

A Basically, WSC stuck it to me. They wouldn't give me more training clients and they basically made me function as a housekeeper. Mr. Winsome started assigning me really bad tasks, like cleaning the toilets and wiping down the machines after each person worked out. This started around March and went on until I left at the end of August.

Q Were these tasks that the other personal trainers also were expected to do?

A I never saw any of them do this kind of scut work.

Q Did WSC give you any walk-ins to build your client base back up?

A No, they gave all the walk-ins to the new trainers and the overflow to the other guys and didn't give me any. They told me I had to build my client base back up myself.

Q How much money were you making then?

A Not enough to survive, just $8.00 an hour.

Q What happened at the end of August?

A I just couldn't take it anymore. I didn't want to spend my life cleaning toilets, working for a sexist pig and making next to nothing. I left one day and did not go back. They didn't even call to check on me. I think they were glad I left.

Q No further questions.

THE COURT: Cross examination?

MS. ROTHMAN: Yes.

Q Ms. Shields, when you were hired at Winsome Sports, you knew that the base pay was $8.00 per hour, right?

A Yes.

Q And you knew that anything you earned over that was entirely in your hands—that if you got clients, you were able to earn more, right?

A Well, yes.

Q Ms. Shields, you were unhappy about the fact that your friend Chuck made more money than you did, weren't you?

A Of course.

Q Your disappointment about that affected your energy level with your clients, right?

A Well, it wasn't right to pay me less.

Q Ms. Shields, on August 22, you came in to work, collected your paycheck and left WSC with the intention of never coming back, right?

A Yes. Like I said, I couldn't take it any more.

Q No one told you to leave, did they?

A No.

Q When personal trainers are not working with clients, they are expected to pick up around the club, right?

A Yes, but. . . .

Q They are getting paid for that time and are expected to actually work and not sit around?

A Yes.

Q When asked, you told your clients that you thought WSC was mistreating you?

A I sure did. It was the truth.

Q You told Ms. Haftley and Ms. O'Sullivan, two of your clients at WSC, that Mr. Winsome was a sexist?

A I told them about the pay differential. They could come to their own conclusions.

Q Ms. Shields, did you or did you not say to Ms. Haftley and Ms. O'Sullivan that "Ed Winsome is a sexist pig. He pays me less than the guys and when I asked him about it he just smiled. This place sucks."

A I don't remember saying the part about "This place sucks."

MS. ROTHMAN: No further questions.

MS. STONE: No redirect. The defense now calls Chuck Jones as a witness.

Thereupon,

CHUCK JONES

having been called as a witness for and on behalf of the Claimant, and having been first duly sworn by the Deputy Clerk, was examined and testified as follows:

MS. STONE: Please state your name and address for the record.

A My name is Chuck Jones and I live at 1514 Stafford Street.

Q Where do you currently work, Mr. Jones?

A I work at Winsome Sports Club as a personal trainer.

Q How long have you worked at WSC, Mr. Jones?

A About four years.

Q Do you know Dorothy Shields?

A Yes, we used to work together at WSC.

Q What is your pay structure at WSC, Mr. Jones?

A I make $8.00 per hour and I get a 60% cut of personal training fees for the clients I assist.

Q Are you aware of how much Ms. Shields made as a personal trainer at WSC?

A She showed me one of her paystubs. She made $8.00 per hour and a percentage of her client fees. I think she got 50% of the client fees.

Q Do you know why she made a lower percentage of the client fees than you did?

A I just figured that the clients she signed up had some deal and therefore paid less, so Dorothy got less.

Q How many other personal trainers do you work with at WSC?

A There are six total now. When Dorothy was there, there were seven.

Q What are the genders of the WSC trainers?

A All six of us are men, but I think we are hiring a woman next week.

Q Do you know what the percentage cut of the personal training fees that the other trainers get?

A I think they get what I get but I can't be sure of that. The club is always cutting deals with clients and taking it out of our hides.

Q What kind of deals?

A Like offering free personal training as an incentive...which means we don't get anything but the $8.00 an hour. Things like that.

Q Did you tell Ms. Shields that all of the guys were getting a 60% cut?

A I think I only said that I thought they were. It was a bit surprising that she was getting only 50%. Since I started bringing in clients, I have always gotten 60%.

Q How would you describe Ms. Shields as a personal trainer?

A She was good. The women clients really liked her. She was really thoughtful about putting together personalized workout plans, and she got lots of clients, pretty fast.

Q Do you know what happened that caused those clients to leave WSC?

A Well, Dorothy became pretty unhappy, and that was hard on her clients, I guess.

Q Do you know why she was unhappy?

A Sure, I think she felt like she was being unfairly treated by Mr. Winsome.

Q No further questions.

THE COURT: Cross examination, Ms. Rothman?

MS. ROTHMAN: Yes, Your Honor.

Q Mr. Jones, when you are not working with clients at the club, your duties include cleaning the bathrooms and wiping down the machines, right?

A Yes.

Q Did you ever overhear Ms. Shields disparaging WSC?

A I'm not sure what you mean. Dorothy was pretty chummy with her clients. I may have heard her talking about unfairness on a few occasions, but I'm not sure.

Q No further questions.

MS. STONE: Redirect, Your Honor?

THE COURT: You may proceed, counsel.

Q Mr. Jones, you are currently employed by Winsome Sports Club, right?

A I sure am.

Q And Mr. Winsome here is your boss, right?

A Yes.

Q No further questions.

THE COURT: All right. Does the Employer have any rebuttal testimony to present?

MS. ROTHMAN: No, Your Honor.

Digitally signed by April Downes

ELECTRONIC CERTIFICATE

I, April Downes, transcriber, do hereby certify that I have transcribed the proceedings had and the testimony adduced in the case of WINSOME SPORTS CLUB vs. DOROTHY SHIELDS, Docket No. 1234-56.

I further certify that the foregoing pages constitute the official transcript of said proceedings as transcribed from audio recording to the best of my ability. In witness whereof, I have hereto subscribed my name.

April Downes

Transcriber

Criminal Defense or Juvenile Delinquency Clinic: Law and Transcript

1. Statutory Provisions Defining the Elements of Assault

Smallville Code Ann., Section 16-1005(b): The elements of the criminal offense of assault are as follows:

1. An attempt, with force or violence, to injure another;
2. Apparent present ability to injure; and
3. General intent to perform the acts that constitute the assault.

2. Transcript of State v. Doe

DISTRICT COURT
FOR THE DISTRICT OF SMALLVILLE

STATE OF SMALLVILLE

Docket Number: 1234-56

vs.

MICHAEL DOE,

Defendant.

The above-entitled action came on for a hearing before the Honorable JANE ROTHMAN, Judge, in Courtroom Number 113, commencing at 10:20 a.m.

APPEARANCES:

On Behalf of the Government:

SARAH STONE, Certified Student Attorney

JENNIFER BLACK, Esquire, Supervising Attorney

On Behalf of the Defendant:

RINA ROTHMAN, Certified Student Attorney

JOAN WHITE, Assistant District Attorney and Supervising Attorney.

Deposition Services, Inc.

4321 Executive Boulevard

Smallville, US

DEPUTY CLERK: State versus Michael Doe, Case No. 1234-56.

MS. STONE: Good morning, Your Honor, Sarah Stone, certified student attorney, for the Government.

THE COURT: Good morning.

MS. BLACK: Good morning, Your Honor, Jennifer Black, District Attorney's Office and supervising attorney.

MS. ROTHMAN: Rina Rothman, certified student attorney, for the defendant, Michael Doe.

THE COURT: Good morning.

MS. WHITE: Joan White, supervising attorney.

THE COURT: Sir, state your name please.

MR. DOE: Michael Doe.

MS. STONE: Thank you, Your Honor, I'd like to waive my opening statement. I request permission to call Ruth Jackson to the stand for the Government.

THE COURT: Yes, let me just ask, for planning purposes, how many witnesses you intend to call?

MS. STONE: Two, Your Honor.

THE COURT: Alright. Alright, call your first witness.

MS. ROTHMAN: The Government calls Ruth Jackson to the stand.

THE COURT: Ma'am, come to the witness stand. Come around this way. Remain standing and raise your right hand, please.

Thereupon,

RUTH JACKSON

having been called as a witness for and on behalf of the government, and having been first duly sworn by the Court, was examined and testified as follows:

THE COURT: You may be seated. Thank you. If there are individuals in the courtroom who've been told that you may be or will be witnesses in this case, I'm going to ask you to leave the courtroom right now and have a seat right outside, and when it's time for your testimony you'll be called in. Is there any witness in the courtroom now? Ms. Rothman, do you have any witnesses other than Mr. Doe?

MS. ROTHMAN: Only Mr. Doe, Your Honor.

THE COURT: All right. And are your witnesses in the courtroom? Is your other witness in the courtroom?

MS. STONE: No, Your Honor.

THE COURT: All right. Counsel, you may inquire.

MS. ROTHMAN: Thank you, Your Honor.

DIRECT EXAMINATION

BY MS. STONE:

Q Good afternoon, Ms. Jackson. Please state and spell your full name for the record.

A Ruth JACKSON, R-U-T-H, J-A-C-K-S-O-N.

Q Where are you currently living, Ms. Jackson?

A I'd rather not say at this time.

Q Why not?

A Because I don't want Michael Doe to know where I'm staying at.

Q What is your relationship to the defendant, Michael Doe?

A We were engaged to be married.

Q Why are you living at your current undisclosed location?

A Because there was violence and I left out.

Q Ms. Jackson, where did you go to college?

A Smallville University.

Q What did you study there?

A Education.

Q What do you do in your free time?

A I have a friend that I teach for— teach him English and he teaches me French.

Q Ms. Jackson, how long were you engaged to be married to the defendant?

A Two and a half years.

Q And how long were you romantically involved with the defendant?

A Three years.

Q Are you currently romantically involved with the defendant?

A No.

Q Ms. Jackson, where were you living until August 25th?

A In the home of Michael Doe and his parents.

Q At what address?

A 6789 70th Street, in Smallville.

Q How long did you live there?

A For two and a half years.

Q Why did you move in with the defendant?

A To see how things would work as far as us getting married and getting our own place.

Q How was your relationship after you moved in with him?

A It was very good.

Q When did it stop being good?

A In May.

Q What happened in May?

A He admitted to me that he had cheated on me with one of my girlfriends.

Q In May of what year?

A Of this past year.

Q How did you feel when the defendant told you he had cheated on you?

A Hurt and very upset.

Q How was your relationship with the defendant after he told you this?

A I didn't have any more trust in him.

Q How did the defendant act after he told you this?

A I don't know – he started sleeping somewhere else, only coming back to the house once every week or two.

Q How often was he sleeping at the house before he told you that he had cheated on you?

A Regularly.

Q Ms. Jackson, let me direct your attention to July 7 of this year. Where were you that night?

A At home in bed asleep.

Q At what address?

A 6789 70th Street.

Q What time did you go to sleep?

A About 9:00.

Q Was anyone else in the bedroom when you went to sleep?

A No.

Q What time did you wake up?

A About 1:00 in the morning.

Q Why did you wake up?

A Michael Doe woke me up.

Q How did he wake you up?

A He came into the room loud. He was stumbling around, like he does when he's been drinking.

Q What made you think that he was drinking?

A I could smell the liquor on him, and his speech was slurred.

Q What was the defendant doing?

A He was standing over me fussing.

Q What was he fussing about?

A About something someone had said.

Q What did you do when you woke up?

A I sat up on the side of the bed.

Q What was the defendant's demeanor like when he woke you up?

A He was angry.

Q How did you know that he was angry?

A The tone of his voice was really harsh.

Q What did the defendant do when you woke up?

A He looked at me with a really mean face and said something terrible.

Q What did he say?

A He said, Ruth, you are going to get it. I mean it this time, you will really get it bad.

Q What did you understand this to mean?

A That he was going to hurt me badly.

Q Why did you believe he meant that?

A Because he was really mad and when he spoke he had his fist balled up.

Q What did the defendant do next?

A He stormed out of the room.

Q Ms. Jackson, how did you feel after this incident?

A Scared.

Q Why were you scared?

A Because I was pretty sure he was going to hurt me.

Q Let me direct your attention to August 25th of this year. Where were you that night?

A Sleeping in my bed.

Q At what address?

A 6789 70th Street, in Smallville.

Q What time did you wake up?

A About 1:00 or 1:30 a.m.

Q Why did you wake up?

A Because Michael Doe entered the room.

Q Where was the defendant when he entered the room?

A Standing at the foot of the bed.

Q What was his demeanor like?

A He was real drunk and angry.

Q What did the defendant do when he entered the room?

A He grabbed for my pocketbook.

Q What did he say?

A He was asking something about a credit card.

Q What did you say when the defendant asked about the credit card?

MS. ROTHMAN: Objection, hearsay.

THE COURT: Overruled. Counsel has laid the foundation for an excited utterance.

A I told him I didn't know what he was talking about and to put my pocketbook back where it was.

Q What did the defendant do when you told him to put the pocketbook back?

A He said he paid for the pocketbook, he could do what he wanted to with it.

Q How did you feel when you saw the defendant going through your pocketbook?

A Upset, like he was intruding on my privacy.

Q What did the defendant do with your pocketbook?

A He was going through it, and I went to reach for it. He told me that he bought it, he would tear it up. He started tearing the straps off.

Q How did you react when he started tearing the straps off your pocketbook?

A I reached for it to get it back.

Q Where were you, in relation to the defendant, at this point?

A Standing up right near him.

Q What did the defendant do when you reached for the pocketbook?

A He grabbed me by my arm, pushed me up against the closet door.

Q How hard did the defendant push you?

A He pushed me hard enough where I ended up with a bruise on my elbow.

Q What did you do after the defendant pushed you against the door?

A I grabbed my pocketbook, put it back on the bed behind me.

Q What did the defendant do next?

A He grabbed me by my arm and pushed me on the bed.

Q What position was your body in when it landed on the bed?

A My feet were on the floor.

Q What part of your body did you land on?

A On my back.

Q What did the defendant do after he pushed you onto the bed?

A He sat on top of me.

Q What part of your body did he sit on?

A He sat on my chest.

Q Which direction was he facing when he sat on your chest?

A His face was facing my face.

Q Did you try to push the defendant off of your chest?

A No.

Q Why not?

A Because he was too heavy.

Q How much does the defendant weigh?

A I guess about 190.

Q How did it feel when the defendant sat on you?

A I couldn't breathe.

Q Why couldn't you breathe?

A I have asthma.

Q How long have you had asthma?

A All my life.

Q How do you treat your asthma?

A I have inhalers.

Q Have you ever had an asthma attack in front of the defendant before?

A Yes.

Q How did you feel, emotionally, while the defendant was sitting on your chest?

A Scared.

Q Why were you scared?

A Because I didn't know what he was going to do, and I couldn't breathe.

Q What else did the defendant do while he was sitting on you?

A He put his hand around my throat.

Q Which hand?

A His right hand.

Q What did he do with the hand that was around your throat?

A Well he squeezed hard enough that I had a bruise on my neck.
Q What did the defendant do with his other hand?
A He hit me with it.
Q How did the defendant hit you?
A With his open hand.
Q Where did he slap you?
A On my head.
Q What part of your head?
A My forehead.
Q What did your forehead look like after the defendant hit you?
A I had a scratch on it.
Q How long was the scratch?
A About an inch.
Q What was the defendant saying as he hit you?
A I can't remember.
Q How did you feel as the defendant was doing these things to you?
A Scared. I was trying to push him off of me.
Q What happened to defendant when you tried to push him off of you?
A I ended up scratching him on the back of his neck.
Q What did the defendant do next?
A He jumped up and said that he was bleeding.
Q What did you do after the defendant got off of you?
A I reached for my cell phone.
Q Why did you reach for your cell phone?
A To call 9-1-1.
Q What did the defendant do when you reached for your cell phone?
A Grabbed my cell phone away from me and threw it on the floor.
Q What happened to the cell phone when he threw it on the floor?
A It broke in pieces.
Q What did you do after the defendant threw your phone on the floor?
A I picked the pieces up and went out the door.
Q What did you do when you went out the door?

A I went upstairs to the bathroom, put my phone back together, and called 9-1-1.

Q About what time was it when you called 9-1-1?

A About 1:30 or 2:00.

Q What was the defendant doing as you were calling 9-1-1?

A I don't know. I know a few minutes later he came up and knocked on the bathroom door.

Q How did you react when the defendant came upstairs?

A Well, when he knocked on the bathroom door and told me to open the door, I opened the door and I had 9-1-1 on the phone. I went back downstairs.

Q When did the police arrive?

A About five minutes later.

Q What time did the police leave?

A I really don't know what time it was when they left.

Q What did the police do right before they left?

A They handcuffed Michael Doe.

MS. STONE: Let the record reflect that I'm showing Government Exhibits 1-A and 1-B for to Defendant's counsel.

MS. STONE: Your Honor, may I approach the witness?

(Ms. Stone laid the proper foundation for admission of photographs into evidence.)

MS. STONE: Your Honor, I'm offering Government's Exhibits 1-A and 1-B into evidence.

THE COURT: Any objection, Ms. Rothman?

MS. ROTHMAN: No, Your Honor.

THE COURT: I'll accept them.

(Government's Exhibit Nos. 1-A and 1-B were admitted into evidence.)

BY MS. STONE:

Q What does the photograph marked Government's Exhibit 1-A show?

A A picture of my throat.

Q What does your throat look like?

A Swollen.

Q Please point to where it's swollen.

A Around in here.

MS. STONE: Let the record reflect the witness is pointing to the center of the throat.

THE COURT: Could you ask her to mark on it so that the defendant sees where she's indicating?

BY MS. STONE:

Q Would you mark where on the throat it's swollen?

MS. STONE: For the record, she's marking in blue pen.

BY MS. STONE:

Q What does the photograph marked Government's Exhibit 1-B show?

A A picture of my forehead.

Q What does your forehead look like in the picture?

A There's a scratch on it.

Q Where is the scratch?

A On my left-hand side.

Q How big is the scratch?

A About an inch.

MS. STONE: Your Honor, may I have permission to approach the Clerk to hand him the photographs?

THE COURT: Yes. But before you do that, if you could just show what you had her mark to the defendant's counsel.

MS. STONE: No further questions. Thank you, Ms. Jackson.

THE COURT: Ms. Rothman, do you have any cross examination?

MS. ROTHMAN: Yes.

Q You lived with Mr. Doe for two years?

A Yes.

Q You lived with Mr. Doe's parents?

A Yes.

Q You spent time with Mr. Doe's family?

A Yes.

Q You ate dinner together?

A Yes.

Q You watched television together?

A Yes .

Q Mr. Doe's parent's run a church in their home?

A Yes.

Q Mr. Doe's parents are pastors?

A Yes.

Q You attended this church with them?

A Yes.

Q You were treated as one of the family?

A Yes.

Q But you and Mr. Doe are no longer dating?

A No – we're not.

Q And you're not living in the house anymore?

A No.

Q Ms. Jackson, your mother lives in southern Virginia?

A Yes.

Q Your mother lives in a retirement community?

A Yes.

Q You don't want to live with her?

A No.

Q You are not close to your brothers?

A Not really.

Q You moved out of Mr. Doe's house on August 25?

A Yes.

Q You moved out because Mr. Doe told you to leave?

MS. STONE: Objection, the question calls for hearsay

MS. ROTHMAN: This statement comes in as non-hearsay – we are introducing it not to prove the matter asserted but rather to show the impact it had on the listener.

THE COURT: Overruled.

A Yes.

Q This scared you?

A No, it didn't scare me.

Q You had been living there for two years?

A Yes.

Q And now you had to leave?

A Yes.

Q You went to file for a protection order the day Mr. Doe told you to leave?

A No.

Q There were advocates who help you move into a free room at a shelter when you filed for the protection order?

A Yes.

Q Ms. Jackson, you have asthma?

A Yes.

Q You have had asthma your entire life?

A Yes.

Q You need an inhaler when you are struggling breathing?

A Yes.

Q You carry this inhaler with you everywhere you go?

A Yes.

Q Asthma medication is expensive?

A Yes—I think so.

Q You are unemployed?

A Yes.

Q And you do not have health insurance?

A No.
Q Mr. Doe's sister works in a pharmacy?
A Yes.
Q And you get your asthma medication from her?
A Yes.
Q You only have one inhaler left?
A Right.
Q You have only had a job off and on for the past two years?
A Yes.
Q You have a cell phone?
A Yes.
Q But Mr. Doe pays the bill?
A Yes.
Q You don't receive food stamps?
A No.
Q Mr. Doe used to buy your food?
A Yes.
Q Mr. Doe bought your clothes?
A Yes.
Q Mr. Doe owns the home you lived in?
A Yes.
Q Mr. Doe no longer pays for your food, clothing, and housing?
A No.
Q You owe Mr. Doe money?
A Yes.
Q You have taken his credit cards before?
A Only when he gives them to me.
Q You have spent Mr. Doe's money without his permission?
A No. He always tells me I can use the money.
Q You testified that Mr. Doe was dating other women?
A Yes.
Q One was named Monica?

A Yes.

Q Monica was a friend of yours?

A Yes.

Q Mr. Doe started dating her in May?

A Yes.

Q Mr. Doe is now dating someone new?

A Yes.

Q Her name is Jackie?

A Yes.

Q You testified that Mr. Doe told you that he was cheating?

A Yes.

Q You have known about these other relationships for the past several months?

A Yes.

Q Mr. Doe doesn't sleep at home that often?

A No.

Q In fact, Mr. Doe has stayed away for weeks at a time?

A Yes.

Q But you continued to live at the house?

A Yes.

Q You thought you and Mr. Doe had an exclusive relationship?

A Yes.

Q You agreed only to date each other?

A Yes.

Q You were living together?

A Yes.

Q You were engaged to be married?

A Yes.

Q You would not have cheated on him?

A No.

Q It wouldn't have been right?

A No

Q Mr. Doe had no right to date other women?

A Right.

Q And especially, he had no right to do it publicly, so other people would know about it?

A Right.

Q It was disrespectful?

A Right.

Q It made you look bad?

A I don't think so.

Q You allege that two weeks ago Mr. Doe threw you on the bed?

A Yes

Q You allege that he choked you?

A Yes.

Q The police report says that you scratched Mr. Doe?

A I guess.

Q You did scratch Mr. Doe?

A Yes.

Q You scratched him on his neck?

A Yes.

Q You scratched him hard?

A I don't think so.

Q You scratched him so hard he bled?

A I didn't really notice.

Q He was still bleeding when the police arrived 20 minutes later?

A I'm not sure about that.

Q Ms. Jackson, you're 5' 8" tall?

A Yes.

Q Mr. Doe is only 5' 6"?

A That sounds right.

Q After Mr. Doe allegedly choked you, you got up?

A Yes.

Q And you went upstairs to call the police?

A Yes.

Q You didn't run upstairs?

A No. I can't run with my asthma.

Q So you walked?

A Yes.

Q You went upstairs to the bathroom?

A Yes.

Q Then you called the police?

A I sure did.

Q Mr. Doe was right outside the bathroom when you called?

A Yes.

Q After you called, you came out of the bathroom?

A Yes.

Q The police were not there yet.

A Right, but I needed to gather my things.

Q Later, you called the police again?

A Well, I ... right.

Q You told them not to come?

MS. STONE: Objection, hearsay.

MS. ROTHMAN: Only to show the witness' state of mind, your honor.

THE COURT: Overruled.

A Yes, that's right, but only because I realized that I could just leave without their help.

Q Let me go back to the asthma for a moment. Asthma interferes with your ability to breath?

A Yes.

Q And when you lose your breath, you need your inhaler?

A Yes.

Q You use your inhaler several times a day?

A Yes.

Q You have lost your breath from walking too fast?

A Yes.

Q You have lost your breath even when you are walking slow?

A Yes.

Q You have lost your breath walking up and downstairs?

A Yes.

Q You have lost your breath when you get really excited about something?

A Yes.

Q You lose your breath when you get scared or spooked?

A Yes.

Q You also can lose your breath when you get upset?

A Yes.

MS. ROTHMAN: No further questions.

THE COURT: Very well. All right, ma'am, you may step down. Ms. Stone, call your next witness.

MS. STONE: He's right outside now. Thank you, Your Honor.

THE COURT: Sir, come to the witness stand please.

Thereupon,

DETECTIVE JOHN JONES

having been called as a witness for and on behalf of the petitioner, and having been first duly sworn by the Deputy Clerk, was examined and testified as follows:

DEPUTY CLERK: Thank you, you may be seated.

DIRECT EXAMINATION

BY MS. STONE:

Q Please state your name for the record.

A Yes, ma'am, my name is John Jones.

Q Mr. Jones, please state your occupation.

A My duty assignment is an investigator assigned to the Domestic Violence Unit, working for the Smallville Police Department for the past 8 years.

Q Detective Jones, directing your attention to August 25 of this year, where were you at around 1:00 in the morning?

A I was dispatched to the home of Ms. Ruth Jackson.

Q When you arrived on the scene, did you see Ms. Jackson?

A Yes.

Q How would you describe her appearance?

A She seemed scared and upset, crying. I noticed she had an abrasion – a scratch on her forehead. I also observed that she had a swollen neck.

Q Thank you.

MS. STONE: Your Honor, I have no further questions.

THE COURT: Ms. Rothman, any questions for this officer?

MS. ROTHMAN: No, Your Honor.

THE COURT: You may step down, sir.

THE WITNESS: Thank you, ma'am.

(Witness excused.)

THE COURT: All right, do you all have another witness?

MS. STONE: Your Honor, we have no further witnesses. The petitioner rests.

Thereupon,

MICHAEL DOE

having been called as a witness for and on behalf of the defendant, and having been first duly sworn by the Deputy Clerk, was examined and testified as follows:

MS. ROTHMAN: State your name please, sir.

MR. DOE: Mr. Michael Doe.

Q What do you do for a living, sir?

A I am a contractor for the ABC Corporation.

Q What do you do for them?

A I work on the computer system.

Q What is your educational background?

A I got a degree from State University and computer certificate from State Tech.

Q What is the nature of your relationship with Ms. Jackson?

A Well, I met her several years ago. She was homeless. She was very nice person. Friends with my parents. We dated and I told her she could stay with us.

Q Were you ever engaged?

A No. Never. Ruth kept asking if we could get married, but no, I didn't think we had much of a relationship. I was just trying help her out.

Q Drawing your attention to July 7 of this year, did you see Ms. Jackson that night?

A Absolutely. She was at home when I got home from work. She was sleeping.

Q How did you react when you saw her?

A I just quietly getting my things from the room, taking them upstairs to go sleep. I hadn't been sleeping in the room for a while—our romantic relationship had pretty much ended.

Q Did Ms. Jackson remain asleep?

A No, she woke up, started asking me questions.

Q What type of questions?

A She had heard that I was dating a friend of hers. She flew into blind rage. She was very jealous. Screaming terrible things about "the bitches" I was seeing. She spat at me, said she would kill me.

Q How did you feel when she said that?

A Really scared. I didn't know what she might do. She was really not herself.

Q So what did you do?

A I called the police and told them what was happening.

Q Did they come?

A They never showed up. I don't know why.

MS. ROTHMAN: I have a recording of the 911 tape here and petitioner's counsel has stipulated to the authenticity of the tape, if I could just play it for the court?

THE COURT: Very well, admitted. You can play the recording.

(Defense Exhibit No. 1 was admitted into evidence and the recording was played.)

BY MS. ROTHMAN:

Q Turning your attention to August 25 of this year, what was the status of your relationship at that point?

A Oh, really bad. I had had enough of her. I had told her that she would have to leave.

Q When did you tell her that?

A Oh, a lot. But when I got back from work that night I told her that again. I told her it was over.

Q Well, let's go back. What did you find out that night?

A Okay. August 25th—Well, August 25th I got off from work, okay, and before I came in the room I went upstairs to my mother and my father. So then my mother told me something about my credit card. So I went down in the room to check my paperwork. I saw another charge I didn't recognize on my credit card. So I called the 1-800 number. And I called the 1-800 number and they told me, "You are above your limit." I say, "Okay, thank you." Then I came back to her in the room.

MS. STONE: Objection your honor, hearsay as to the statements of the credit card operator and Defendant's statements.

THE COURT: I'm going to accept not for the truth of the matter, but for the effect on the listener.

MS. STONE: Thank you, Your Honor.

THE COURT: Overruled.

BY MS. ROTHMAN:

Q Who did you come back to?

A To Ruth. I checked with Ruth, "Do you have any business with using my credit card? Did you use my credit card?" She told me, "No." I said, "Are you sure? Well I called and the people told me, say, I went over my limit, and you are the only person who has my key and everything. So why are you trying to deny this?" Then I called back again for the second time.

Q You called back where?

A I called the credit card company for the second time. And they told me that the person charged the credit card—my credit card with big charges the last few days.

Q Continue.

A Okay. And I came back to her in the room. I said, "Oh, Ruth, somebody used my credit card, and because you the only person got access to all my things in the room." She said, "I know nothing about a credit card."

MS. STONE: Objection your honor. A standing objection to Defendant's statements as hearsay.

THE COURT: Overruled. I will admit them for effect on the listener.

BY MS. ROTHMAN:

Q What else did Ms. Jackson say at this point?

A So she said, "Maybe it's one of your women using your credit card." I said, "How sure are you that one of my women is using my credit card? Who are my women?"

Q What did you do at this point?

A Before I went to take the key from the, from the nightstand, she was behind me, and she hit me on my neck. I said, "Ruth, why'd you hit me on my neck? I didn't do anything wrong to you. I took you in for two years and seven months, and you pay nothing to me and I take care of you. But now it's time for you to move out. It's over."

Q How did she react?

A Right away she said that she would call the police. So I left her in the room and she said she was calling the police. I said, "Okay, call the police." And I went upstairs. So right away the police knocked, they never asked me any questions, they put cuffs on my hands, and they sent me in the car. So I was there in the car, they asked her to explain what happened, but never asked me, and then they took me to the police station.

Q I'm sorry, you were in the police car and then what did the officers do?

A And then the police were in the house, okay? Then one officer told the other officer, "Okay, take him to the station." That's all that happened.

Q Did you sustain any injuries?

A She scraped me. I think the police have the picture of that scrape on my shoulder.

Q Is there any other testimony that you care to give?

A No, no, I don't have any testimony to, to say anything. I was just trying to ask her if she used my credit card. But when I was putting my hand out to take my key and go upstairs, she thought I was taking her bag. She just took that bag and she hit me on my shoulder. But I never said anything to her.

Q And Mr. Doe, do you have anything to say about this property she says you took? The Nike shoes, or her coat?

A I don't know what she's talking about. I don't know about her stuff.

Q Mr. Doe, are there other people who live in your house?

A My parents.

MS. ROTHMAN: Thank you. No further questions.

THE COURT: All right, then I'm going to allow the lawyer for the government to ask you questions.

MR. DOE: Okay.

CROSS-EXAMINATION

BY MS. STONE:

Q Mr. Doe, Ms. Jackson has asthma?

A I don't know.

Q She had asthma the entire time you were dating?

A I don't know nothing about she had asthma, no.

Q You've seen her using her inhaler?

A No.

Q You weigh more than Ms. Jackson.

A She weighs more than me.

Q You heard Ms. Jackson testify about an incident that occurred on August 25 of this year?

A Yes, I heard what she said.

Q You came home that night?

A I came home from work, uh huh.

Q You came home, and you went downstairs?

A I went upstairs first.

Q You went downstairs after?

A Yeah, I went downstairs.

Q You went into your bedroom?

A I went into my bedroom, yes.

Q Ms. Jackson was in bed?

A She was in bed.

Q You were worried about your credit cards?

A I—say that again.

Q You were worried about your credit cards?

A No, I was not worried about my credit card. But I was asking her about my credit card, I was not worried.

Q You thought that Ms. Jackson had your credit card?

A She—I asked her if she used my credit card.

Q You picked up Ms. Jackson's pocketbook?

A No.

Q You were looking for your credit cards?

A I put my credit card on the nightstand, on the dresser. That where I put all my stuff, on the dresser. Okay, so I was trying to find out about my card, and my mother asked me to do something for her that night. So I told her, I say, okay, the next day I would do it, but immediately I called to the credit company and the credit company said you're over your limit. And I said, "What, over my limit?" And I never hardly—I never use that credit card.

Q You thought that Ms. Jackson had used your credit cards then?

A Huh?

Q You thought that Ms. Jackson had used your credit cards?

A I called the credit company and they say somebody in the house used it, and she has all my keys to my room.

Q So you thought Ms. Jackson had used your credit cards?

A Sure.

Q And you were upset?

A No, I was not upset. I was not upset.

Q Ms. Jackson called the police that night?

A She called the police on me that night. I said, "Why are you calling the police?"

Q The police arrested you that night?

A The police arrested me because she called the police and she was screaming, crying.

MS. STONE: Thank you, no further questions.

THE COURT: Counsel, any redirect?

MS. ROTHMAN: Mr. Doe, is there anything else you want to add to your testimony?

MR. DOE: Okay. Particularly about saying that I should keep far from her. She needs to keep far from me too. I need protection too.

THE COURT: All right. Does the petitioner have any rebuttal testimony to present?

MS. STONE: No, Your Honor.

THE COURT: Do you have any closing remarks?

MS. STONE: Yes, Your Honor.

Digitally signed by April Downes

ELECTRONIC CERTIFICATE

I, April Downes, transcriber, do hereby certify that I have transcribed the proceedings had and the testimony adduced in the case of STATE vs. MICHAEL DOE, Docket No. 1234-56.

I further certify that the foregoing pages constitute the official transcript of said proceedings as transcribed from audio recording to the best of my ability. In witness whereof, I have hereto subscribed my name.

April Downes

Transcriber

POST-CLASS REFLECTION MEMO

Draft and submit a memo in response to the questions below:

- How will you take the lessons you have learned in class today and apply them to your current work in representing clinic clients?
- How will the insights you have gained about connections between crafting an opening statement or a closing argument and the process of developing direct and cross-examinations, case theory, and fact investigation concretely affect your casework over the next several days or weeks?

HANDOUTS

Domestic Violence or Plaintiff-Side Civil Clinic

Group 1

Opening: Develop the petitioner's opening statement.

Consider:

- Style as well as substance
- Integrating the theory of the case
- Providing a framework for the evidence
- Avoiding impermissible argument, but stringing facts together so that your statements are argument-driven
- Highlighting powerful factual details
- Using storytelling techniques
- Depicting your client as sympathetic and credible
- Dealing with any weaknesses' in the client's case

- What evidence might you wish to avoid mentioning
- Providing information about the requested relief

Group 2

Closing: Apply the law to the facts and argue that the petitioner has met her burden of proof for each element of the alleged assault.

Consider:

- Style as well as substance
- Accuracy in stating the legal elements of the petitioner's claim and applicable burden of proof
- Drawing on all possible sources to adduce evidence to support each element of the claim
- Going beyond the record facts and drawing inferences to support your arguments
- Anticipating the respondent's arguments

In addition:

As you develop your argument, note any areas where more fact investigation or direct or cross-examination questioning would have been useful to strengthen your argument.

Group 3

Closing: Argue that the petitioner is more credible, and that her story is more persuasive based on logic and common sense, than that of the respondent.

Consider:

- Style as well as substance
- Supporting the petitioner's credibility
- Drawing on all relevant sources of record evidence
- Going beyond the record facts and drawing inferences to support your arguments
- Anticipating the respondent's likely arguments
- Challenging the credibility of the respondent
- Using logic and common sense to support the petitioner's credibility and undermine that of the respondent

In addition:

As you develop your argument, note any areas where more fact investigation or direct or cross-examination questioning would have been useful to strengthen your argument.

Group 4

Closing: Develop arguments in support of the petitioner's and against the respondent's competing theories of the case.

Consider:

- Style as well as substance
- Supporting your client's theory of the case
- Drawing on all relevant sources of record evidence
- Going beyond the record facts and drawing inferences to support your arguments
- Undermining the respondent's theory of the case

In addition:

As you develop your argument, note any areas where more fact investigation or direct or cross-examination questioning would have been useful to strengthen your argument.

Group 5

Closing: Argue that petitioner is entitled to each for of relief she seeks, making separate arguments for each separate form of relief.

Consider:

- Style as well as substance
- Supporting each form of relief the petitioner is seeking, drawing on all relevant sources of record evidence
- Going beyond the record facts and drawing inferences to support your arguments
- Anticipating the respondent's arguments against each form of relief sought

In addition:

As you develop your argument, note any areas where more fact investigation or direct or cross-examination questioning would have been useful to strengthen your argument.

Unemployment Insurance Benefits or Defense-Side Civil Clinic

Group 1

Opening: Develop the claimant's opening statement.

Consider:

- Style as well as substance
- Integrating the theory of the case
- Providing a framework for the evidence
- Avoiding impermissible argument, but stringing facts together so that your statements are argument-driven
- Highlighting powerful factual details
- Using storytelling techniques
- Depicting your client as sympathetic and credible
- Dealing with any weaknesses' in the client's case
- What evidence might you wish to avoid mentioning
- Meeting the applicable burden of proof, and/or avoiding taking on the other side's burden of proof
- Providing information about the requested relief

Group 2

Closing: Apply the law to the facts and argue that the employer has failed to meet its burden of proof for as many elements of the claim as possible.

Consider:

- Style as well as substance
- Accuracy in stating the legal elements of the employer's case and applicable burden of proof
- Drawing on all possible sources to adduce evidence to undermine each element of the employer's case
- Going beyond the record facts and drawing inferences to support your arguments
- Anticipating the employer's arguments

In addition:

As you develop your argument, note any areas where more fact investigation or direct or cross-examination questioning would have been useful to strengthen your argument.

Group 3

Closing: Apply the law to the facts and argue that the claimant has successfully met her burden of proof for the relevant portion of the claim.

Consider:

- Style as well as substance
- Accuracy in stating the legal elements for which the claimant has the burden of proof
- Drawing on all possible sources to adduce evidence to support each element of the claimant's burden
- Going beyond the record facts and drawing inferences to support your arguments
- Anticipating the employer's arguments

In addition:

As you develop your argument, note any areas where more fact investigation or direct or cross-examination questioning would have been useful to strengthen your argument.

Group 4

Closing: Argue that the claimant is more credible, and that her story is more persuasive based on logic and common sense, than that of the employer.

Consider:

- Style as well as substance
- Supporting the claimant's credibility
- Drawing on all relevant sources of record evidence
- Going beyond the record facts and drawing inferences to support your arguments
- Anticipating the employer's likely arguments
- Using logic and common sense to support the claimant's credibility and undermine that of the employer

In addition:

As you develop your argument, note any areas where more fact investigation or direct or cross-examination questioning would have been useful to strengthen your argument.

Group 5

Closing: Develop arguments in support of the claimant's and against the employer's competing theories of the case.

Consider:

- Style as well as substance
- Supporting your client's theory of the case
- Drawing on all relevant sources of record evidence
- Going beyond the record facts and drawing inferences to support your arguments
- Undermining the plaintiff's theory of the case

In addition:

As you develop your argument, note any areas where more fact investigation or direct or cross-examination questioning would have been useful to strengthen your argument.

Criminal Defense or Juvenile Delinquency Clinic

Group 1

Opening: Develop the defendant's opening statement.

Consider:

- Style as well as substance
- Integrating the theory of the case
- Providing a framework for the evidence
- Avoiding impermissible argument, but stringing facts together so that your statements are argument-driven
- Highlighting powerful factual details
- Using storytelling techniques
- Depicting your client as sympathetic and credible
- Dealing with any weaknesses' in the client's case
- What evidence might you wish to avoid mentioning
- Meeting the applicable burden of proof, and/or avoiding taking on the other side's burden of proof
- Providing information about the requested relief

Group 2

Closing: Apply the law to the facts and argue that the government has failed to meet its burden of proof for as many elements of the alleged assault as possible.

Consider:

- Style as well as substance
- Accuracy in stating the legal elements of the government's case and applicable burden of proof
- Awareness of affirmative defenses
- Drawing on all possible sources to adduce evidence to undermine each element of the government's case
- Going beyond the record facts and drawing inferences to support your arguments
- Anticipating the government's arguments

In addition:

As you develop your argument, note any areas where more fact investigation or direct or cross-examination questioning would have been useful to strengthen your argument.

Group 3

Closing: Argue that the defendant is more credible, and that his story is more persuasive based on logic and common sense, than that of the government.

Consider:

- Style as well as substance
- Supporting the defendant's or other witness's credibility
- Drawing on all relevant sources of record evidence
- Going beyond the record facts and drawing inferences to support your arguments
- Anticipating the government's likely arguments
- Challenging the credibility of the government's witnesses
- Using logic and common sense to support the defendant's credibility and undermine that of the government witnesses

In addition:

As you develop your argument, note any areas where more fact investigation or direct or cross-examination questioning would have been useful to strengthen your argument.

Group 4

Closing: Develop arguments in support of the defendant's and against the government's competing theories of the case.

Consider:

- Style as well as substance
- Supporting your client's theory of the case
- Drawing on all relevant sources of record evidence
- Going beyond the record facts and drawing inferences to support your arguments
- Undermining the government's theory of the case

In addition:

As you develop your argument, note any areas where more fact investigation or direct or cross-examination questioning would have been useful to strengthen your argument.

Group 5

Closing: Argue that defendant is entitled to a not guilty verdict.

Consider:

- Style as well as substance
- Emphasizing the fact that the government, not the defendant, bears the burden proof
- Emphasizing the high standard of proof beyond a reasonable doubt.
- Supporting your client's theory of the case
- Drawing on all relevant sources of record evidence
- Going beyond the record facts and drawing inferences to support your arguments

Undermining the government's theory of the case and their claim to have met their burden of proof.

CHAPTER 15

CONDUCTING AND CLOSING NEGOTIATIONS

LEARNING GOALS

The learning goals for this class include helping you to:

- Identify areas of mutual interest among parties and stakeholders
- Develop an appreciation for the importance of planning and prioritization
- Disaggregate the lawyer's own needs from those of the client, and ensure that the client's interests control
- Think creatively about the scope of potential solutions within legal as well as extra-legal frameworks
- Develop an awareness of the importance of process, clarity, and closure
- Develop effective interpersonal skills

DESCRIPTION OF CLASS

This class begins with a brief lecture, designed to introduce you to key negotiation concepts, techniques, and terminology. We will then do a simulated negotiation exercise, with some students in role as lawyers for each side of a legal issue, and others in role as negotiation observers. The simulated negotiation proceeds in the following stages: (1) negotiating an oral agreement; (2) reducing the agreement to writing; (3) discussing feedback provided by the student observers; and (4) exploring the difference between reaching an oral versus a written agreement.

ASSIGNMENT IN PREPARATION FOR CLASS

Your teacher will be giving you a role assignment and material that you will use during the negotiation. You are expected to do this exercise independently; you should not share your work with other students.

Assignment for Negotiating Attorneys in Prepared Factual Scenarios

Review the negotiation General Facts and your client's Secret Instructions.

1. Draft a statement of the problem that is the subject of negotiation.
   - How might you want to frame this negotiation? What problem do you see as the subject here?
   - Is your "opponent" likely to share that problem definition?
   - Why or why not?
   - Is there a way to frame the problem that might be agreeable to both?
     - What would that look like?
2. In drafting the statement, identify the common ground or shared interests among the parties.
   - How might these common interests guide the negotiation?
     - What might you say to establish an initial focus on common interests?

Assignment for Negotiating Attorneys Using Own Facts

Review the description of the issue to be negotiated. If you have questions about the objective of the negotiation, you and your opposing negotiator should ask for clarification from your supervisor. Once you have obtained clarification, do the following independently:

1. Draft a statement of the problem that is the subject of negotiation.
   - How might you want to frame this negotiation? What problem do you see as the subject here?
   - Is your "opponent" likely to share that problem definition?

- Why or why not?
- Is there a way to frame the problem that might be agreeable to both?
    - o What would that look like?

2. In drafting the statement, identify the common ground or shared interests among the parties.
    - How might these common interests guide the negotiation?
        - o What might you say to establish an initial focus on common interests?

Assignment for Negotiation Observers

Assignment Based on Factual Scenarios in This Chapter

Review the Handout for Negotiation Observers, and think through what you might look for as you observe the upcoming negotiation. In addition, review the General Instructions and Secret Instructions for both sides, and consider each of the questions posed below:

- Identify the common ground or shared interests between the parties.
- How might these common interests guide the negotiation? How might the negotiators establish an initial focus on common interests?
- What problem do you see as the subject here? How might the parties want to frame this negotiation?

Assignment Based on Students' Own Cases or Projects

Review the Handout for Negotiation Observers, and think through what you might look for as you observe the upcoming negotiation. In addition, review the description of the issue and objective of the negotiation that has been given to the negotiating parties. Recognizing that you may not have full information about this case or project, consider each of the questions posed below:

- Given the nature of the issue, can you identify any potential common ground or shared interests between the parties?
- How might these common interests guide the negotiation? How might the negotiators establish an initial focus on common interests?

- What problem do you see as the subject here? How might the parties want to frame this negotiation?

READING ASSIGNMENT

1. Daniel L. Shapiro, *A Lawyer's Guide to Emotion: Four 'Laws' to Effective Practice*, DISPUTE RESOLUTION MAGAZINE 3 (Winter 2001).
2. Danny Ertel, *Getting Past Yes: Negotiating as if Implementation Mattered*, HARVARD BUSINESS REVIEW 454 (Nov. 1, 2004).
3. Jayne Seminare Docherty, *Culture and Negotiation: Symmetrical Anthropology for Negotiators*, 87 MARQUETTE L. REV. 711 (2004).
4. Carrie Menkel-Meadow, *When Winning Isn't Everything: The Lawyer As Problem Solver*, 28 HOFSTRA L. REV. 905 (2000).

READINGS

Daniel L. Shapiro
A Negotiator's Guide to Emotion: Four 'Laws' to Effective Practice
DISPUTE RESOLUTION MAGAZINE 3 (Winter 2001)*

Freud tells the story of a professor who encounters some troubles while giving a lecture in a large hall. A student in the second row chats incessantly and shuffles his feet through-out the lecture, completely distracting the otherwise attentive class. After several unsuccessful attempts to quiet the student, the professor announces that he cannot continue with the lecture. At that point, three brawny, dedicated classmates stand up and, after a short struggle, carry the interrupter outside the classroom doors. They lodge chairs against the doors to prevent the interrupter from reentering. In an act of bitter and reckless retaliation, the expelled student shouts and bangs on the doors with his fists, interfering with the lecture even more than his bad behavior had before.

The moral: Just because we exclude something does not mean that it no longer affects us.

This moral is important for negotiators to keep in mind. Many negotiators intensely focus on substantive matters, considering the

* Endnotes omitted.

potential costs and benefits of one proposal over another, this concession over that one. We presume that substantive gains represent the essence of good negotiation and that our singular attention on substantive matters is rationally a wise maneuver that will maximize our negotiation success.

Yet we often forget that the person on the other side of the table (or in the second row of the class) is more than a robot or rock-hard adversary interested only in tangible matters. He or she gets angry and sad, annoyed or enthusiastic, and wants to preserve a particular image, social identity and reputation. Wittingly or unwittingly, the other party holds a personal, emotional stake in the interaction. We forget that our behavior, too, is in large part the result of the pushes and pulls of our own emotions. In essence, matter isn't the only matter that matters in negotiation.

The role of an effective negotiator includes elements of both a physicist and a psychotherapist because virtually all negotiations involve both substantive and emotional issues. Physicists focus on matter—the raw material out there in the real world—to understand and better deal with the physical, "objective" world. Analogously, one dimension of the negotiation process relates to the "physics of negotiation"—identification of key substantive issues under dispute, and exploration and strategic planning of how to create value and divvy up substantive items to optimize parties' satisfaction levels.

In contrast, psychotherapists focus on relationships—intangible, interpersonal bonds—to help people understand and better deal with the emotional, "subjective" terrain of interactions. Analogously, a second dimension of the negotiation process deals with the "metaphysics of negotiation"—the experience and back-and-forth volleying of emotions during negotiation.

While physics is the study of the "objective" world, metaphysics is the study of what is outside of objective experience—namely, emotion and other affective experiences. The metaphysics of negotiation describes the fact that within every negotiation, our conversations reflect not only substantive issues, but also intangible emotional and identity issues.

There are patterns to our interactions beyond the dollars and sense of substantive negotiation. Emotions thrive in negotiations—they push us, pull us, and influence our decision to negotiate longer or agree now, to push the other side harder or storm out of the room this moment. If we can understand the workings of the emotional world, we can better manage, control and deal productively within it.

Just as Newton observed laws in the physical universe, there are similar "laws" that affect our dealings with emotions in negotiation. In this article, I present a sampling of the "metaphysics of negotiation": four laws of emotion pertinent to effective negotiation. These laws are not absolutes. Rather, they are empirical regularities—patterns—that more often than not accurately describe things that happen. I've developed these laws to help negotiators deal effectively with emotions within the negotiation process.

#1: The Law of Perpetual Emotion

Emotions are a constant stream within us, just as rivers and streams flow with an endless deliverance of water. We constantly respond emotionally to the environment surrounding us and to our own thoughts, feelings and behaviors. We react emotionally when other negotiators arrive late, smirk at our idea, raise their voices, appreciate our ideas or listen closely. We also react emotionally when *we* question the truth of the other's statement, worry about how we are going to close me meeting in time to pick up the kids at school, and so on.

During negotiation, we are personally *affected* in many different kinds of ways. In other words, we experience a whole range of *affective currents*—including impulses, emotions, moods and attitudes:

- *Impulses.* Impulses are intense desires to do a particular behavior *now*—spontaneously and without much thought about potential consequences. We sometimes feel the short-lived urgency of impulses, such as when a burst of energy tempts us to storm out of the negotiation room or yell at a subordinate's sloppy work.

- *Emotions.* We often feel the more generalized pushes of emotions, our short-lived reactions to the feelings, thoughts and behaviors of ourselves or others. Whereas impulses propel us to do a particular *behavior* now (e.g., to yell at the other party in response to his inconsiderateness), emotions motivate us toward general *kinds* of behavior (e.g., to hurt the other party *in some manner* for his inconsiderateness). Emotions usually last for a few minutes, as compared to the more punctuated urges of impulses and the more enduring experience of moods.

The Four 'Laws' of Emotion

- **The Law of Perpetual Emotion:**

We always experience emotions of some sort.

- **The Law of Emotional Complexity:**

Emotions rarely come alone; they travel in groups.

- **The Law of Variable Expression:**

Appearances may not reveal feelings.

- **The Law of Diagnostic Clarity:**

Every emotion has a cause, and a function.

- *Moods.* We experience moods as long-term, dull aches or highs. Moods are low-intensity emotional states, background music to our thoughts and actions. We wake up on Monday morning in a bad mood, and it sticks with us throughout the day's negotiation like a faithful companion.

- *Attitudes.* We hold attitudes, positive or negative opinions of people. We often hold varying attitudes of the various individuals involved in the negotiation.

These four types of affective currents frequently interact with one another. Consider the experience of a young jazz singer negotiating for compensation for performance at a popular music hall. She drove to the meeting feeling general excitement about the upcoming negotiation (a good mood). The hall owner quickly expressed interest in having the singer perform, and they negotiated monetary compensation. After 15 minutes, she agreed to $200, a price the owner suggested was standard for a music hall the size of his. Throughout the negotiation, she felt a kinship with the owner (an attitude), and thus trusted his suggested price. She left the negotiation invigorated (an emotion), called a fellow musician with the good news, and learned that $200 is significantly below market standard for someone with her talent.

The singer felt hurt and deceived (emotions). She imagined herself rampaging back into the music hall and yelling at the owner (an impulse). Without a moment's thought, she picked up the phone, called the owner and cursed at him for his apparent act of deception (impulsive behavior). "I thought you were an honest guy!" she shouted (attitude shift). The owner retorted that his price was fair and angrily revoked his offer for her to perform. The singer was crushed, and the rest of her day was ruined (mood change). The singer's affective currents—her emotions, moods, impulses, and attitudes—led her down a dismal path leading to the loss of a desirable opportunity.

Advice for dealing with 'perpetual emotion'

a. Monitor the affective currents of the interaction. Awareness of the emotional terrain is critical to negotiation success. Awareness of your emotions (and theirs) increases the effectiveness and sustainability of your decisions and relationships.

You can monitor the emotional climate of your negotiation interactions by becoming aware of each of the affective currents:

- *Impulses:* Do you or the other party have the urge to do a particular behavior, such as to storm out of the room or yell at the other?
- *Emotions:* What emotions are you feeling now? What is the other party feeling?
- *Mood:* How positive or negative is your mood right now? How about his or hers?
- *Attitude:* What is your attitude toward the other party (collegial, adversarial, apathetic)? What's your best guess about his or her attitude toward you?

b. Use an incremental approach. Gradually work on trying to become more aware of the affective currents within your interactions. Don't immediately think of yourself as an emotionally omniscient negotiator—you will set yourself up for failure, as every interaction is filled with a complexity of affective currents. Instead, work on gradually developing skill in monitoring affective currents.

c. Go to the balcony. Emotions often are hard to see at ground level. After negotiating an agreement for four months, you may still have unaddressed concerns, yet may feel pressure to sign the agreement upon hearing the impatient goading of the other party. How do you make sense of complicated situations like this? Go to the balcony. Step back from the situation at hand and imagine that you are watching the negotiation on a stage—with you in the balcony of the theatre. Observe the interaction and try to make sense of what the various parties are feeling and why.

#2: The Law of Emotional Complexity

During conflict situations, we often see the emotional terrain as having only one dimension—I am angry, she is angry, and that is that. Anger is our stereotypic interpretation of why people act the way they do in conflict. He's just angry; she's just acting out her pent-up rage.

Attributing only anger to someone else's behavior is the easy way out. In reality, disputants experience a variety of complex emotions, including shame, envy, indignation, enthusiasm, frustration, joy, happiness, bitterness, embarrassment, excitement, disgust, hope and curiosity.

Thus, Law # 2 is the "Law of Emotional Complexity." The point of this law is that we are complicated emotional reactors. During conflict and negotiation, we experience a variety of emotions, often at the same point in time.

Consider the negotiator who proposes a creative idea, only to have the idea shot down by the 10 others sitting at the table. Numerous emotions stir through him simultaneously. He feels proud of his idea, angry at the lack of collegial support, embarrassed that the idea was not embraced, and frustrated by the slow turn of events within the negotiation.

Advice for dealing with 'emotional complexity'

a. Complexify the seemingly straightforward. Think of the emotional world as multi-dimensional, not one-dimensional. In conflict situations, don't fall prey to the trap of assuming that you and others are simply angry.

Brainstorm emotions that you or the other side might be experiencing but that, unlike the salient ferocity of anger, are not immediately evident. Make a list of emotions in your schedule book and refer to it before, during and after negotiations to reflect upon the emotional terrain of the interaction.

Two neighbors, who had been long-time friends, disputed the boundary of their property. Each claimed the property line was 10 feet onto the "other's" property. They called in a mediator to help them resolve the dispute. Upon talking with the disputants, the mediator soon realized that a substantive agreement on the boundary line was the least of the neighbors' concerns. Because neither family had plans to move for years and years to come, the mediator realized that they especially needed to mend their broken relationship with one another. The mediator facilitated an emotion-focused discussion that uncovered a world of emotional complexity beneath the seemingly simple surface dispute. The neighbors talked not only about their anger toward one another, but also about the shame of engaging in such an explosive dispute with an old friend, the embarrassment of having the larger community find out about their dispute, the distrust that escalated from day to day, and the fear that the other neighbor would behave irrationally, such as by breaking a window. Once the neighbors explored these sensitive subjects, the relationship began to mend, and the property issue in effect resolved itself.

You need to hold a mirror up to yourself, too, and to complexify your own emotional landscape. You walk into a negotiation and think, "I'm a little nervous about today's meeting." That's a valid description of your emotional experience, but it's also pretty flat. How can you broaden your personal awareness? Consider additional emotions that you may be experiencing, such as hope ("I hope I do well in this important negotiation"), fear ("I'm fearful that I won't be able to meet the expectations of my boss") and excitement ("I'm excited to negotiate with their legal counsel, who used to be a law school classmate of mine").

b. Realize that there is probably more going on than you think. The other side often has hidden emotional fears and hopes. Because of this element of the unknown, be careful not to draw negative character attributions too quickly. The person who is repeatedly late to your negotiations may be disrespectful or may be dealing with the trauma and confusion of having a recently hospitalized child. Who knows?

Similarly, you are not always aware of all the issues and factors affecting *you*. On a personal level, what fears and wishes of yours manifest within the negotiation? Do you want to be perceived as competent, intelligent, sociable or likeable? What image of yourself do you want to convey to the other, and what image do you suspect he or she wants to convey?

Four Steps for improving Your Emotional Awareness

1. *Identify low-risk interactions* in which to practice becoming aware of affective currents. Low-risk interactions are those in which your job, marriage and the like do not depend upon the success of the negotiation. You might identify as your interactions low-intensity conflicts with your spouse, colleagues, friends, or children.

2. For a week, *monitor your own emotions* during the low-risk interactions. Become aware of your mood, emotions, attitude toward the other and any impulses you experience. During the interactions, what emotions do you experience? What kind of mood are you in before, during and after the interaction? What impulses do you feel? How does your attitude toward the other party change, if at all?

After each interaction, reflect upon your affective currents and write down your thoughts and feelings in a journal or in your schedule book. Reflecting on your affective currents in a journal can help you to organize and understand the interaction from a different perspective. The act of reflection in itself will aid you in developing increased proficiency at recognizing affective currents, because through reflection you will have to dissect the interaction moment-by-moment.

3. For the following week, *monitor the affective currents of both you AND the other party.* Again, after the interactions, reflect and write down your observations in a journal.

4. After the second week, *try out your developing skills of awareness in higher-risk situations,* such as in negotiations you take part in at work. Continue your journal entries.

Consider these personal issues before negotiating and be sensitive to their existence during the negotiation. If feeling intelligent is very important to you, you will be more sensitive to any perceived slight against your intellect. In advance of the negotiation, consider how you will deal with such slights. Will you verbalize your feeling? Will you talk yourself out of feeling upset? Or will you hold the slight as an irreparable mark against the individual who apparently insulted you? Some advanced thinking on how to deal with personal sensitivities can smooth a potentially bumpy negotiation.

#3: The Law of Variable Expression

The "Law of Variable Expression" states that our emotional expressions are not always an accurate depiction of our internal emotional state, and vice versa. In other words, our insides don't always match our outsides. Picture the guards at Buckingham Palace with their stern faces, steadfast eyes and stolid stand. No matter how hard we try to make them laugh, cry or grimace, they stand motionless and ostensibly emotionless.

The mismatch between our insides and outsides can be deliberate or unintentional.

Deliberate mismatching. Sometimes we have an emotion pitted in our gut, and yet we mask its expression deliberately. We may subdue the expression of the emotion, such as when we come home from work after a bad day, our spouse asks how the day went, and we say "fine" to avoid broaching the details of the day at that moment.

Or we may exaggerate the expression of the emotion. A colleague takes your stapler day after day and doesn't return it. Finally, you storm over to his desk, shouting and waving your hands, yelling and hollering for him never to do that again! Meanwhile, you are fully aware that your display of anger is a major exaggeration of the anger you feel internally; you just want the colleague to get the point that you do not appreciate routine fetching of your stapler.

Unintentional mismatching. Emotions often slip out unintentionally, causing us to furrow our eyebrows in frustration, look down in shame, or shake with excitement. In some interactions, we express our emotions minimally, but they represent important emotional messages. Suppose we ask the other side what they think about the current proposal. Although they say, "It's pretty good," we can see by their facial expressions of disgust and annoyance that they are far from agreeing with any proposal put on the table. In other interactions, we express our emotions a lot, but they hold little emotional importance. We all know of a colleague or two who overreacts to important and unimportant issues with equal, overbearing intensity.

Advice for dealing with 'variable expression'

a. Don't assume how others feel. Because insides and outsides don't always match, it's not always a safe bet to assume how others feel just from what they tell you or how they express their ideas. Develop ideas about their emotional state only after gathering information from multiple sources, including their body posture, tone of voice and facial expressions. Another important source of information is their self-reports about how they feel. Simply ask them questions such as, "How do you feel about the proposal as it stands?"

b. When you ask how they feel, make sure you get a "feeling" answer. Often, when you ask others how they feel about an idea, they respond descriptively about the idea. Consider the following dialogue between two colleagues who work closely together on negotiation projects:

Mort: "How'd you feel about the meeting?"

Jen: "I thought that most of the people in the meeting found our presentation helpful."

In this dialogue, Jen does not respond directly to Mort's question. Instead of responding about how she *personally* feels about the meeting, she describes her general "thought" of the meeting. This information paints Jen as an observer of the meeting rather than as an active, involved subject. While these thoughts provide Mort with valuable perspective, they do not give him insight into her personal evaluation of the meeting. Compare the previous dialogue with this one:

Mort: "How'd you feel about the meeting?"

Jen: "I was surprised that most of the people found our meeting helpful. Going into the meeting, I was worried that the boss was going to shoot our ideas down. I'm relieved that he didn't."

Notice the qualitative difference between the two dialogues. In the second set, a much richer picture of the negotiation emerges, in which Jen reflects on some of her emotional experiences, including surprise, worry and relief.

This emotional information improves negotiation effectiveness. It enhances the coordination of the teamwork between negotiators. Because Jen and Mort negotiate as a team, their emotional revelations help each of them to understand and predict the other's behavior in particular situations. Future negotiations will run more smoothly because they will each have a better "sense" of the other's sensitivities and emotional inclinations. For example, Mort now understands that one of Jen's sensitivities concerns the boss's reactions to their ideas; he can use this information to support Jen in their future endeavors.

The emotional information also provides parties with qualitative data about the success of the negotiation process. What are the concerns of the various individuals involved in your negotiation? To what degree do you *feel* that those concerns have been addressed? By discussing with others emotional reactions about your negotiation, you can learn a lot about the delicate, subtle issues hidden within a seemingly straightforward interaction.

c. *Check the emotional temperature.* In many conflicts, it is difficult to determine just how upset or tense disputants feel. One simple tool is to take the emotional temperature of the room. If mediating, ask disputants to rate how tense or upset they feel on a scale from 1 to 10, 1 being "not at all upset" and 10 being "extremely upset." Even if you are negotiating rather than mediating, you can take the temperature. Give the other party your temperature, and ask them if they would share theirs.

Taking the temperature is a helpful diagnostic tool. For starters, it allows you to discover when things are too hot to handle. If your temperature is a boiling nine and theirs is, too, a break may be in order. Physiologically, breaks can do wonders, because the body system in charge of dealing with stress has time to cool down. Without time for decompression (i.e., typically about 15 or so minutes), your anger and other "hot" emotions can ignite much more quickly. Remember, too, that some types of breaks are better than others: Breaks usually are counterproductive when you use them to develop additional arguments about why *you* are right and *they* are wrong. Make sure that if you take a break, you use your time to problem solve, to put things into perspective, or to distract yourself from the heated issues by watching television, reading or doing an unrelated task. Second, taking the temperature allows you to find out the other's emotional state. A surprising amount of the time, people inaccurately assess others' feelings. As the Law of Variable Expression suggests, people are quite good at hiding their true emotional states and they are not the best at detecting others' "true" emotional states. Taking the temperature can help you overcome this detection hurdle.

#4: The Law of Diagnostic Clarity

"My own brain is to me the most unaccountable of machinery—always buzzing, humming, soaring roaring diving, and then buried in mud. And why? What's this passion for?"

—Virginia Woolf

Psychologists often recommend that to cope with a particularly strong emotion, such as anger, we should ask ourselves why we feel that way: What's the diagnosis? What few psychologists realize, though, is that the question has two potential types of answers, each of which is important to evaluate.

First, we need to understand the *cause* of our emotion—why the emotion arose in the first place. Did someone insult us, ignore us or excite us? Did the other party give us no eye contact? Are we still holding onto frustrations from our quarrel with our spouse last night? The cause of the emotion represents the sources of influence that prompted our current emotional experience.

Second, it's helpful to understand the *function* of our emotion. For what purpose are we experiencing the emotion? What benefits might the emotion provide us? Consider former president Clinton's anger at the Wye River Summit, where he mediated between PLO President Arafat and Israeli Prime Minister Netanyahu. During segments of the meeting, Netanyahu allegedly acted abrasively toward Arafat, providing the *cause* of Clinton's anger: Clinton had hoped that the participants would treat one another with continuous respect. Yet the anger had quite a different *function.* It sent a message to Netanyahu that disrespectful behavior would not be tolerated. Following Clinton's expressions of anger, the negotiation proceeded much more efficiently.

Advice for dealing with 'diagnostic clarity'

a. Learn from your emotional signals. Distressing emotions signal that things are not going as well as you wish. Your personal or professional goals are not being reached, or significant obstacles lie in your way. Specific issues call for your attention, and your emotions signal which issues.

b. Identify potential causes of emotion. In a negotiation, once you identify problematic emotions being experienced, consider potential causes of the emotions. For example, at the Wye Summit, Clinton allegedly noticed that Netanyahu's abrasive behavior engendered problematic emotions in Arafat.

Causes of problematic emotions often relate to:

- not enough decision-making leverage,
- perceived lack of respect,
- not enough room to speak your mind, and
- not feeling appreciated.

'To some extent, it is wise for negotiators to focus on substantive issues—how to shuffle, expand or divide the pot of gold sparkling in the center of the negotiation table. However, negotiations are more effective when we also recognize, understand, and deal effectively with emotions, ours and theirs.'

c. Address the hypothesized causes. After you identify potential causes of problematic emotions, work to address them. For example, in response to Netanyahu's abrasive behavior at the Wye Summit, Clinton allegedly expressed to Netanyahu that disrespectful behavior would not be tolerated at the negotiating table. By enforcing ground rules of respect, Clinton attempted to address underlying causes of friction between Netanyahu and Arafat, with the goal of reestablishing a collegial working relationship between the leaders in conflict.

d. Identify potential functions of emotion. Recognize the functions of your emotion and deal with them constructively. Consider guilt. When you do something that goes against your internal moral standards, you feel guilty. A function of guilt is to motivate you to rectify your wrongdoing. Suppose, for example, that a negotiation doesn't go your way, you get frustrated and you insult the other side. On reflection, you realize that the insult was not appropriate and you feel guilty. Your guilt functions to prompt an apology.

In essence, you want to look beneath others' expressed emotion at the message the emotion represents. When they are excited, why are they excited? What is the source and function of the emotion? When they are angry, what message are they trying to send you? Like former president Clinton, are they trying to express that a particular behavior will not be tolerated at the mediation table? Or are they expressing that they are frustrated with the length of the mediation? What else might the anger functionally represent?

Likewise, look beneath your own emotional experiences at the message the emotion represents. What message is your own anger, excitement or shame trying to express? How might you use that message toward constructive ends?

A mindful focus

Negotiations often do not go as well as we would like. As diligently as we may try, we still experience stalemates, we still get angry and distrustful, and we still leave potential joint gains on the table untapped. To some extent, it is wise for negotiators to focus on substantive issues—on how to shuffle, expand or divide the pot of gold sparkling in the center of the negotiation table. However, negotiations are more effective when we also recognize, understand and deal effectively with emotions, ours and theirs.

Each of these "laws" I have offered in this article leads to prescriptive insights on how to deal with emotions. If we understand the workings of the emotional terrain, we can better manage, control, and deal effectively within it. A mindful focus on the emotional terrain can lead us to improved substantive outcomes and stronger, more sustainable relationships.

Danny Ertel
Getting Past Yes: Negotiating as if Implementation Mattered
HARVARD BUSINESS REVIEW 454 (Nov. 1, 2004)*

The Idea in Brief

Why do so many deals that looked great on paper end up in tatters? Negotiators on both sides probably focused too much on closing the deals and squeezing the best terms out of one another—and not enough on implementation. Bargainers with this **deal-maker mind-set** never ask how—or whether—their agreement will work *in practice*. Once implementation begins, surprises and disappointments crop up—often torpedoing the deal.

How to avoid this scenario? Bargain using an **Implementation mind-set.** Define negotiation not as closing the deal but as setting the stage for a successful long-term relationship. Brainstorm and discuss problems you might encounter 12 months down the road. Help the other party think through the agreement's practical implications, so your counterparts won't promise something they can't deliver. Ensure that both sides' stakeholders support the deal. And communicate a consistent message about the deal's terms and spirit to both parties' implementation teams.

* Endnotes omitted.

Deals negotiated from an implementation mind-set don't "sizzle" like those struck by bargainers practicing brinksmanship. But as companies like HP Services and Procter & Gamble have discovered, a deal's real value comes not from a signature on a document but from the real work performed long after the ink has dried.

The Idea in Practice

To adopt an implementation mind-set, apply these practices *before* inking a deal:

Start with the End in Mind

Imagine that it's a year into implementation of your deal. Ask:

- **Is the deal working?** What metrics are you using to measure its success?
- **What has gone wrong so far?** What have you done to put things back on course? What signals suggest trouble ahead?
- **What capabilities are needed to accomplish the deal's objectives?** What skills do your implementation teams need? Who has tried to block implementation, and how have you responded?

By answering these questions now, you avoid being blindsided by surprises during implementation.

Help the Other Party Prepare

Coming to the table prepared to negotiate a workable deal isn't enough—your *counterpart* must also prepare. Before negotiations begin, encourage the other party to consult with their internal stakeholders throughout the bargaining process. Explain who you think the key players are, who should be involved early on, and what key questions about implementation you're asking yourself.

Treat Alignment as a Shared Responsibility

Jointly address how you'll build broad support for the deal's implementation. Identify both parties' stakeholders—those who will make decisions, affect the deal's success through action or inaction, hold critical budgets, or possess crucial information. Map how and when different stakeholders' input will be solicited. Ask who needs to know what in order to support the deal and carry out their part of its implementation.

Send One Message

Ensure that each team responsible for implementing the deal understands what the agreement is meant to accomplish. Communicate *one* message to them about the terms of the deal, the spirit in which it was negotiated, and the trade-offs that were made to craft the final contract.

- **Example**

  During IBM Global Services' "joint handoff meetings," the company's negotiators *and* their counterparts brief implementation teams on what's in the contract, what's different or nonstandard, and what the deal's ultimate intent is.

Manage Negotiation Like a Business Process

Establish a disciplined process for negotiation preparation in your company. Provide training in collaborative negotiation tools and techniques for negotiators *and* implementers. Use post-negotiation reviews to capture learning. And reward individuals for the delivered success of the deals they negotiated—not for how those deals look on paper.

In July 1998, AT&T and BT announced a new 50/50 joint venture that promised to bring global interconnectivity to multinational customers. Concert, as the venture was called, was launched with great fanfare and even greater expectations: The $10 billion start-up would pool assets, talent, and relationships and was expected to log $1 billion in profits from day one. Just three years later, Concert was out of business. It had laid off 2,300 employees, announced $7 billion in charges, and returned its infrastructure assets to the parent companies. To be sure, the weak market played a role in Concert's demise, but the way the deal was put together certainly hammered a few nails into the coffin.

For example, AT&T's deal makers scored what they probably considered a valuable win when they negotiated a way for AT&T Solutions to retain key multinational customers for itself. As a result, AT&T and BT ended up in direct competition for business—exactly what the Concert venture was supposed to help prevent. For its part, BT seemingly outnegotiated AT&T by refusing to contribute to AT&T's purchase of the IBM Global Network. That move saved BT money, but it muddied Concert's strategy, leaving the start-up to contend with overlapping products. In 2000, Concert announced a complex new arrangement that was supposed to clarify its strategy, but many questions about account ownership, revenue recognition, and competing offerings went unanswered. Ultimately, the two parent companies pulled the plug on the venture.

Concert is hardly the only alliance that began with a signed contract and a champagne toast but ended in bitter disappointment. Examples abound of deals that look terrific on paper but never materialize into effective, value-creating endeavors. And it's not just alliances that can go bad during implementation. Misfortune can befall a whole range of agreements that involve two or more parties—mergers, acquisitions, outsourcing contracts, even internal projects that require the cooperation of more than one department. Although the problem often masquerades as one of execution, its roots are anchored in the deal's inception, when negotiators act as if their main objective were to sign the deal. To be successful, negotiators must recognize that signing a contract is just the beginning of the process of creating value.

During the past 20 years, I've analyzed or assisted in hundreds of complex negotiations, both through my research at the Harvard Negotiation Project and through my consulting practice. And I've seen countless deals that were signed with optimism fall apart during implementation, despite the care and creativity with which their terms were crafted. The crux of the problem is that the very person everyone thinks is central to the deal—the negotiator—is often the one who undermines the partnership's ability to succeed. The real challenge lies not in hammering out little victories on the way to signing on the dotted line but in designing a deal that works in practice.

The Danger of Deal Makers

It's easy to see where the deal maker mind-set comes from. The media glorifies big-name deal makers like Donald Trump, Michael Ovitz, and Bruce Wasserstein. Books like *You Can Negotiate Anything, Trump: The Art of the Deal,* and even my own partners' *Getting to Yes* all position the end of the negotiation as the destination. And most companies evaluate and compensate negotiators based on the size of the deals they're signing.

But what kind of behavior does this approach create? People who view the contract as the conclusion and see themselves as solely responsible for getting there behave very differently from those who see the agreement as just the beginning and believe their role is to ensure that the parties involved actually realize the value they are trying to create. These two camps have conflicting opinions about the use of surprise and the sharing of information. They also differ in how much attention they pay to whether the parties' commitments are realistic, whether their stakeholders are sufficiently aligned, and whether those who must implement the deal can establish a suitable working relationship with one another. (For a comparison of how different mind-sets affect negotiation behaviors, see the figure 1 "Deal-Minded Negotiators versus Implementation-Minded Negotiators.")

This isn't to say deal makers are sleazy, dishonest or unethical. Being a deal maker means being a good closer. The deal maker mind-set is the ideal approach in certain circumstances. For example, when negotiating the sale of an asset in which title will simply be transferred and the parties will have little or no need to work together, getting the signatures on the page really does define success.

But frequently a signed contract represents a commitment to work together to create value. When that's the case, the manner in which the parties "get to yes" matters a great deal. Unfortunately, many organizations structure their negotiation teams and manage the flow of information in ways that actually hurt a deal's chances of being implemented well.

An organization that embraces the deal maker approach, for instance, tends to structure its business development teams in a way that drives an ever growing stream of new deals. These dedicated teams, responsible for keeping negotiations on track and getting deals done, build tactical expertise, acquire knowledge of useful contract terms, and go on to sign more deals. But they also become detached from implementation and are likely to focus more on the agreement than on its business impact. Just think about the language deal-making teams use ("closing" a deal, putting a deal "to bed") and how their performance is measured and rewarded (in terms of the number and size of deals closed and the time required to close them). These teams want to sign a piece of paper and book the expected value; they couldn't care less about launching a relationship.

The much talked about Business Affairs engine at AOL under David Colburn is one extreme example. The group became so focused on doing deals—the larger and more lopsided the better—that it lost sight of the need to have its business partners actually remain in business or to have its deals produce more than paper value. In 2002, following internal investigations and probes by the SEC and the Department of Justice, AOL Time Warner concluded it needed to restate financial results to account for the real value (or lack thereof) created by some of those deals.

The deal maker mentality also fosters the take-no-prisoners attitude common in procurement organizations. The aim: Squeeze your counterpart for the best possible deal you can get. Instead of focusing on deal volume, as business development engines do, these groups concentrate on how many concessions they can get. The desire to win outweighs the costs of signing a deal that cannot work in practice because the supplier will never be able to make enough money.

Think about how companies handle negotiations with outsourcing providers. Few organizations contract out enough of their work to have as much expertise as the providers themselves in negotiating deal structures, terms and conditions, metrics, pricing, and the like, so they frequently engage a third-party adviser to help level the playing field as they select an outsourcer and hammer out a contract. Some advisers actually trumpet their role in commoditizing the providers' solutions so they can create "apples to apples" comparison charts, engender competitive bidding, and drive down prices. To maximize competitive tension, they exert tight control, blocking virtually all communications between would-be customers and service providers. That means the outsourcers have almost no opportunity to design solutions tailored to the customer's unique business drivers.

The results are fairly predictable. The deal structure that both customer and provider teams are left to implement is the one that was easiest to compare with other bids, not the one that would have created the most value. Worse yet, when the negotiators on each side exit the process, the people responsible for making the deal work are virtual strangers and lack a nuanced understanding of why issues were handled the way they were. Furthermore, neither side has earned the trust of its partner during negotiations. The hard feelings created by the hired guns can linger for years.

The fact is, organizations that depend on negotiations for growth can't afford to abdicate management responsibility for the process. It would be foolhardy to leave negotiations entirely up to the individual wits and skills of those sitting at the table on any given day. That's why some corporations have taken steps to make negotiation an organizational competence. They have made the process more structured by, for instance, applying Six Sigma discipline or a community of practice principles to improve outcomes and learn from past experiences.

Sarbanes-Oxley and an emphasis on greater management accountability will only reinforce this trend. As more companies (and their auditors) recognize the need to move to a controls-based approach for their deal-making processes—be they in sales, sourcing, or business development—they will need to implement metrics, tools, and process disciplines that preserve creativity and let managers truly manage negotiators. How they do so, and how they define the role of the negotiator, will determine whether deals end up creating or destroying value.

Negotiating for Implementation

Making the leap to an implementation mindset requires five shifts.

1. Start with the End in Mind

For the involved parties to reap the benefits outlined in the agreement, goodwill and collaboration are needed during implementation. That's why negotiation teams should carry out a simple "benefit of hindsight" exercise as part of their preparation.

> Imagine that it is 12 months into the deal, and ask yourself:
>
> *Is the deal working?* What metrics are we using? If quantitative metrics are too hard to define, what other indications of success can we use?
>
> *What has gone wrong so far?* What have we done to put things back on course? What were some early warning signals that the deal may not meet its objectives?
>
> *What capabilities are necessary to accomplish our objectives?* What processes and tools must be in place? What skills must the implementation teams have? What attitudes or assumptions are required of those who must implement the deal? Who has tried to block implementation, and how have we responded?

If negotiators are required to answer those kinds of questions before the deal is finalized, they cannot help but behave differently. For example, if the negotiators of the Concert joint venture had followed that line of questioning before closing the deal, they might have asked themselves, "What good is winning the right to keep customers out of the deal if doing so leads to competition between the alliance's parents? And if we have to take that risk, can we put in mechanisms now to help mitigate it?" Raising those tough questions probably wouldn't have made a negotiator popular, but it might have led to different terms in the deal and certainly to different processes and metrics in the implementation plan.

Most organizations with experience in negotiating complex deals know that some terms have a tendency to come back and bite them during implementation. For example, in 50/50 ventures, the partner with greater leverage often secures the right to break ties if the new venture's steering committee should ever come to an impasse on an issue. In practice, though, that means executives from the dominant party who go into negotiations to resolve such impasses don't really have to engage with the other side. At the end of the day, they know they can simply impose their decision. But when that happens, the relationship is frequently broken beyond repair.

Tom Finn, vice president of strategic planning and alliances at Procter & Gamble Pharmaceuticals, has made it his mission to incorporate tough lessons like that into the negotiation process itself. Although Finn's alliance management responsibilities technically don't start until after a deal has been negotiated by the P&G Pharmaceuticals business development organization, Finn jumps into the negotiation process to ensure negotiators do not bargain for terms that will cause trouble down the road. "It's not just a matter of a win-win philosophy," he says. "It's about incorporating our alliance managers' hard-won experience with terms that cause implementation problems and not letting those terms into our deals."

Finn and his team avoid things like step-down royalties and unequal profit splits with 50/50 expense sharing, to name just a few. "It's important that the partners be provided [with] incentives to do the right thing," Finn says. "When those incentives shift, you tend to end up [with] difficulties." Step-down royalties, for instance, are a common structure in the industry. They're predicated on the assumption that a brand is made or lost in the first three years, so that thereafter, payments to the originator should go down. But P&G Pharmaceuticals believes it is important to provide incentives to the partner to continue to work hard over time. As for concerns about overpaying for the licensed compound in the latter years of the contract, Finn asserts that "leaving some money on the table is OK if you realize that the most expensive deal is one that fails."

2. Help Them Prepare, Too

If implementation is the name of the game, then coming to the table well prepared is necessary—but not sufficient. Your counterpart must also be prepared to negotiate a workable deal. Some negotiators believe they can gain advantage by surprising the other side. But surprise confers advantage only because the counterpart has failed to think through all the implications of a proposal and might mistakenly commit to something it wouldn't have if it had been better prepared. While that kind of an advantage might pay off in a simple buy-sell transaction, it fails miserably—for both sides—in any situation that requires a long-term working relationship.

That's why it's in your best interest to engage with your counterpart before negotiations start. Encourage the other party to do its homework and consult with its internal stakeholders before and throughout the negotiation process. Let the team know who you think the key players are, who should be involved early on, how you hope to build implementation planning into the negotiation process, and what key questions you are asking yourself.

Take the example of Equitas, a major reinsurer in the London market. When preparing for commutations negotiations—whereby two reinsurers settle their mutual book of business—the company sends its counterpart a thorough kickoff package, which is used as the agenda for the negotiation launch meeting. This "commutations action pack" describes how the reinsurer's own commutations department is organized, what its preferred approach to a commutations negotiation is, and what stages it follows. It also includes a suggested approach to policy reconciliation and due diligence and explains what data the reinsurer has available—even acknowledging its imperfections and gaps. The package describes critical issues for the reinsurer and provides sample agreements and memorandums for various stages of the process.

The kickoff meeting thus offers a structured environment in which the parties can educate each other on their decision-making processes and their expectations for the deal. The language of the commutations action pack and the collaborative spirit of the kickoff meeting are designed to help the parties get to know each other and settle on a way of working together before they start making the difficult trade-offs that will be required of them. By establishing an agreed-upon process for how and when to communicate with brokers about the deal, the two sides are better able to manage the tension between the need to include stakeholders who are critical to implementation and the need to maintain confidentiality before the deal is signed.

Aventis Pharma is another example of how measured disclosure of background and other information can pave the way to smoother negotiations and stronger implementation. Like many of its peers, the British pharmaceutical giant wants potential biotech partners to see it as a partner of choice and value a relationship with the company for more than the size of the royalty check involved. To that end, Aventis has developed and piloted a "negotiation launch" process, which it describes as a meeting during which parties about to enter into formal negotiations plan together for those negotiations. Such collaboration allows both sides to identify potential issues and set up an agreed upon process and time line. The company asserts that while "formally launching negotiations with a counterpart may seem unorthodox to some," the entire negotiation process runs more efficiently and effectively when partners "take the time to discuss how they will negotiate before beginning."

3. Treat Alignment as a Shared Responsibility

If their interests are not aligned, and they cannot deliver fully, that's not just their problem—it's your problem, too.

Unfortunately, deal makers often rely on secrecy to achieve their goals (after all, a stakeholder who doesn't know about a deal can't object). But leaving internal stakeholders in the dark about a potential deal can have negative consequences. Individuals and departments that will be directly affected don't have a chance to weigh in with suggestions to mitigate risks or improve the outcome. And people with relevant information about the deal don't share it, because they have no idea it's needed. Instead, the typical reaction managers have when confronted late in the game with news of a deal that will affect their department is "Not with my FTEs, you don't."

Turning a blind eye to likely alignment problems on the other side of the table is one of the leading reasons alliances break down and one of the major sources of conflict in outsourcing deals. Many companies, for instance, have outsourced some of their human resource or finance and accounting processes. Service providers, for their part, often move labor-intensive processes to Web-based self-service systems to gain process efficiencies. If users find the new self-service system frustrating or intimidating, though, they make repeated (and expensive) calls to service centers or fax in handwritten forms. As a result, processing costs jump from pennies per transaction to tens of dollars per transaction.

But during the initial negotiation, buyers routinely fail to disclose just how undisciplined their processes are and how resistant to change their cultures might be. After all, they think, those problems will be the provider's headache once the deal is signed. Meanwhile, to make requested price concessions, providers often drop line items from their proposals intended to educate employees and support the new process. In exchange for such concessions, with a wink and a nod, negotiators assure the provider that the buyers will dedicate internal resources to change-management and communication efforts. No one asks whether business unit managers support the deal or whether function leaders are prepared to make the transition from managing the actual work to managing the relationship with an external provider. Everyone simply agrees, the deal is signed, and the frustration begins.

As managers and employees work around the new self-service system, the provider's costs increase, the service levels fall (because the provider was not staffed for the high level of calls and faxes), and customer satisfaction plummets. Finger-pointing ensues, which must then be addressed through expensive additions to the contract, costly modifications to processes and technology, and additional burdens on a communication and change effort already laden with baggage from the initial failure.

Building alignment is among negotiators' least favorite activities. The deal makers often feel as if they are wasting precious time "negotiating internally" instead of working their magic on the other side. But without acceptance of the deal by those who are essential to its implementation (or who can place obstacles in the way), proceeding with the deal is even more wasteful. Alignment is a classic "pay me now or pay me later" problem. To understand whether the deal will work in practice, the negotiation process must encompass not only subject matter experts or those with bargaining authority but also those who will actually have to take critical actions or refrain from pursuing conflicting avenues later.

Because significant deals often require both parties to preserve some degree of confidentiality, the matter of involving the right stakeholders at the right time is more effectively addressed jointly than unilaterally. With an understanding of who the different stakeholders are—including those who have necessary information, those who hold critical budgets, those who manage important third-party relationships, and so on—a joint communications subteam can then map how, when, and with whom different inputs will be solicited and different categories of information might be shared. For example, some stakeholders may need to know that the negotiations are taking place but not the identity of the counterpart. Others may need only to be aware that the organization is seeking to form a partnership so they can prepare for the potential effects of an eventual deal. And while some must remain in the dark, suitable proxies should be identified to ensure that their perspectives (and the roles they will play during implementation) are considered at the table.

4. Send One Message

Complex deals require the participation of many people during implementation, so once the agreement is in place, it's essential that the team that created it get everyone up to speed on the terms of the deal, on the mind-set under which it was negotiated, and on the trade-offs that were made in crafting the final contract. When each implementation team is given the contract in a vacuum and then is left to interpret it separately, each develops a different picture of what the deal is meant to accomplish, of the negotiators' intentions, and of what wasn't actually written in the document but each had imagined would be true in practice.

"If your objective is to have a deal you can implement, then you want the actual people who will be there, after the negotiators move on, up front and listening to the dialogue and the give-and-take during the negotiation so they understand how you got to the agreed solution," says Steve Fenn, vice president for retail industry and former VP for global business development at IBM Global Services. "But we can't always have the delivery executive at the table, and our customer doesn't always know who from their side is going to be around to lead the relationship." To address this challenge, Fenn uses joint hand-off meetings, at which he and his counterpart brief both sides of the delivery equation. "We tell them what's in the contract, what is different or nonstandard, what the schedules cover. But more important, we clarify the intent of the deal: Here's what we had difficulty with, and here's what we ended up with and why. We don't try to reinterpret the language of the contract but [we do try] to discuss openly the spirit of the contract." These meetings are usually attended by the individual who developed the statement of work, the person who priced the deal, the contracts and negotiation lead, and occasionally legal counsel. This team briefs the project executive in charge of the implementation effort and the executive's direct reports. Participation on the customer side varies, because the early days in an outsourcing relationship are often hectic and full of turnover. But Fenn works with the project executive and the sales team to identify the key customer representatives who should be invited to the hand-off briefing.

Negotiators who know they have to brief the implementation team with their counterparts after the deal is signed will approach the entire negotiation differently. They'll start asking the sort of tough questions at the negotiating table that they imagine they'll have to field during the postdeal briefings. And as they think about how they will explain the deal to the delivery team, they will begin to marshal defensible precedents, norms, industry practices, and objective criteria. Such standards of legitimacy strengthen the relationship because they emphasize persuasion rather than coercion. Ultimately, this practice makes a deal more viable because attention shifts from the individual negotiators and their personalities toward the merits of the arrangement.

5. Manage Negotiation Like a Business Process

Negotiating as if implementation mattered isn't a simple task. You must worry about the costs and challenges of execution rather than just getting the other side to say yes. You must carry out all the internal consultations necessary to build alignment. And you must make sure your counterparts are as prepared as you are. Each of these actions can feel like a big time sink. Deal makers don't want to spend time negotiating with their own people to build alignment or risk having their counterparts pull out once they know all the details. If a company wants its negotiators to sign deals that create real value, though, it has to weed out that deal maker mentality from its ranks. Fortunately, it can be done with simple processes and controls. (For an example of how HP Services structures its negotiation process, see the sidebar "Negotiating Credibility.")

More and more outsourcing and procurement firms are adopting a disciplined negotiation preparation process. Some even require a manager to review the output of that process before authorizing the negotiator to proceed with the deal. KLA-Tencor, a semi-conductor production equipment maker, uses the electronic tools available through its supplier-management Web site for this purpose, for example. Its managers can capture valuable information about negotiators' practices, including the issues they are coming up against, the options they are proposing, the standards of legitimacy they are relying on, and the walkaway alternatives they are considering. Coupled with simple postnegotiation reviews, this information can yield powerful organizational insights.

Preparing for successful implementation is hard work, and it has a lot less sizzle than the brinksmanship characteristic of the negotiation process itself. To overcome the natural tendency to ignore feasibility questions, it's important for management to send a clear message about the value of postdeal implementation. It must reward individuals, at least in part, based on the delivered success of the deals they negotiate, not on how those deals look on paper. This practice is fairly standard among outsourcing service providers; it's one that should be adopted more broadly.

Negotiating Credibility

HP Services is growing in a highly competitive market, and its success is partly due to its approach to negotiating large outsourcing transactions. In a maturing market, where top tier providers can demonstrate comparable capabilities and where price variations inevitably diminish after companies bid against one another time and time again, a provider's ability to manage a relationship and build trust are key differentiators. The negotiation and the set of interactions leading up to it give the customer a first taste of what it will be like to solve problems with the provider during the life of the contract. "Decisions made by clients regarding selection have as much to do with the company they want to do business with as with price, capability, and reliability," acknowledges Steve Huhn, HP Services' vice president of strategic outsourcing. "Negotiating these kinds of deals requires being honest, open, and credible. Integrity is critical to our credibility."

Huhn's team of negotiators uses a well-structured process designed to make sure that the philosophy of integrity is pervasive throughout the negotiation and not just a function of who happens to be at the table on any given day. It begins with the formation of a negotiation team. Because transition in complex outsourcing transactions represents a period of high vulnerability, it is important to involve implementation staff early on; that way, any commitments made can be validated by those who will be responsible for keeping them. A typical negotiation team consists of a business leader, or pursuit lead, who is usually responsible for developing the business and structuring the transaction; a contract specialist, who brings experience with outsourcing contract terms and conditions; and the proposed client manager, who will be responsible for delivery.

Negotiation leads work with a high degree of autonomy. Huhn believes that a negotiator without authority is little more than a messenger, and messengers are unlikely to earn trust or build working relationships with counterparts. At HP, negotiators earn that autonomy by preparing extensively with templates and by reviewing key deal parameters with management. A negotiator's mandate does not just cover price: It also encompasses margins, cash flow, and ROI at different times in the life of the contract; the treatment of transferred employees; the ways various kinds of risk will be allocated; and how the relationship will be governed. All these interests must be addressed—both in preparation and at the negotiation table.

HP's outsourcing negotiators are subject to informal reviews with full-time deal coaches as well as formal milestone reviews. The reviews, which are designed to get key stakeholders committed to implementation, happen before the formal proposal is delivered and before the deal is signed.

The pursuit team leaders aren't finished once the agreement is signed. In fact, they retain responsibility during the transition phase and are considered "liable" for the deal's performance during the next 18 to 24 months. That means negotiators can't simply jump to the next alluring deal. On the contrary, they have a vested interest in making sure the closed deal actually meets its targets.

Improving the implementability of deals is not just about layering controls or capturing data. After all, a manager's strength has much to do with the skills she chooses to build and reward and the example she sets with her own questions and actions. In the health care arena, where payer-provider contentions are legion, forward-thinking payers and innovative providers are among those trying to change the dynamics of deals and develop agreements that work better. Blue Cross and Blue Shield of Florida, for example, has been working to institutionalize an approach to payer-provider negotiations that strengthens the working relationship and supports implementation. Training in collaborative negotiation tools and techniques has been rolled down from the senior executives to the negotiators to the support and analysis teams. Even more important, those who manage relationships with providers and are responsible for implementing the agreements are given the same training and tools. In other words, the entire process of putting the deal together, making it work, and feeding the lessons learned through implementation back into the negotiation process has been tightly integrated.

. . .

Most competitive runners will tell you that if you train to get to the finish line, you will lose the race. To win, you have to envision your goal as just beyond the finish line so you will blow right past it at full speed. The same is true for a negotiator. If signing the document is your ultimate goal, you will fall short of a winning deal.

The product of a negotiation isn't a document; it's the value produced once the parties have done what they agreed to do. Negotiators who understand that prepare differently than deal makers do. They don't ask, "What might they be willing to accept?" but rather, "How do we create value together?" They also negotiate differently, recognizing that value comes not from a signature but from real work performed long after the ink has dried.

Jayne Seminare Docherty
Culture and Negotiation: Symmetrical Anthropology for Negotiators
87 MARQUETTE L. REV. 711 (2004)*

> To try to learn a culture from lists of traits and custom is akin to trying to learn English by memorizing the OED [Oxford English Dictionary]: all vocabulary, no grammar. This method is particularly ill suited if what one is trying to master in another culture is a dynamic process to begin with—a process such as negotiation.

I. INTRODUCTION

At least in the academic community, with a few notable exceptions, the debate of the 1980s over whether conflict resolution practitioners—including negotiators—need to pay attention to culture seems to have been won by those who answered, "Yes, culture matters." Culture is now given at least a brief mention in most negotiation textbooks. Unfortunately, many people try to approach the problem of culture and negotiation by talking about culture as a list of traits or a catalogue of admonishments about what not to do when negotiating with a person from culture X. As Kevin Avruch notes, this is not an adequate approach to understanding culture in the context of negotiation. This paper examines three ways of thinking about culture in negotiation, each more sophisticated and complete than the previous method, and concludes with some suggestions for how to teach reflective practitioners of negotiation cultural competency skills.

One commonly used heuristic device for thinking about culture is the iceberg. This model begins with the empirical observation that cultures differ in terms of normative behaviors and other traits, but assumes that these are like the tip of an iceberg. There is much more to culture under the surface of what we can readily observe. Above the surface we find behaviors, artifacts and institutions. Just below the surface we find norms, beliefs, values and attitudes. A sensitive observer can "uncover" these and become more knowledgeable about a culture. The deepest level is all but invisible even to members of a cultural group. It contains the deepest assumptions about the world, the sense-making and meaning-making schemas and symbols, the beliefs about what is real in the world, and beliefs about how individuals experience the world. This is a useful model, but it is also misleading. It does not reflect the dynamic quality of cultures, which are far from frozen. It also implies that all of the individuals in a given iceberg (culture) share that culture evenly; this is never the case.

---

* Footnotes omitted.

II. LOOKING AT THE TIP OF THE ICEBERG

Unfortunately, some negotiation texts—particularly but not exclusively popular books on negotiation—focus almost entirely on the part of the iceberg visible above the surface. In these texts, cultures are presented as lists of do's and don'ts. These lists are rooted in stereotypes and are of dubious value. Teaching negotiators about culture in this manner is of limited value and might actually be dangerous in some settings.

Furthermore, this approach contains a number of faulty assumptions about human beings and about culture. Lists of do's and don'ts: Do not offer your left hand to an Arab; learn how to deeply bow to a Japanese negotiator; understand the protocols for offering refreshment to a Turkish counterpart; treat culture as a superficial overlay that covers a universal human nature or perhaps a universal human culture; deep down, where it counts, all persons are fundamentally the same when it comes to reasoning, emotionality, needs, and desires. This confusion arises because there is a generic human culture, "a species-specific attribute of Homo sapiens, an adaptive feature of our kind on this planet for at least a million years or so." But there are also local cultures—"those complex systems of meanings created, shared, and transmitted (socially inherited) by individuals in particular social groups." It is local cultures that can create problems in a negotiation.

III. LEARNING PATTERNS OF CULTURE

A more sophisticated approach to culture in negotiation involves identifying patterns or types of cultures by studying a large group of cultures. Instead of getting inside of a specific culture to understand it, this approach stands outside of cultures and looks for patterns or cultural styles. These are often presented as a list of dichotomous characteristics including: high context/low context; individualism/collectivism; and egalitarian/hierarchical. A high-context culture often relies on indirect communication, because the participants are expected to understand the complex meaning of relatively small non-verbal gestures. A low-context culture will tend to rely on direct statements and formal, clear ratification of written negotiated agreements. Negotiators from individualist cultures may worry less about preserving relationships than negotiators from collectivist cultures. And, negotiators from egalitarian cultures are likely to be less concerned about issues of rank and privilege than negotiators from hierarchical cultures. . . .

The goal in identifying types of cultures or developing cultural profiles is to alert negotiators to communication patterns and to provide cautionary advice about how to communicate in a particular cultural context or with someone from a particular culture. This way of thinking about culture is more useful for negotiators than lists of traits as long as they recognize the following: these dichotomies are actually continua; within cultures, changes in context (e.g., family versus business setting) will lead people to locate in different places along the continua; there are subcultural variations within any culture; and not all individuals carry their culture in exactly the same way. . . .

IV. SYMMETRICAL ANTHROPOLOGY

The most complete and sophisticated way of thinking about culture and negotiation requires that we greatly enrich our definition of culture. Avruch offers the following definition: "For our purposes, *culture* refers to the socially transmitted values, beliefs and symbols that are more or less shared by members of a social group, and by means of which members interpret and make meaningful their experience and behavior (including the behavior of 'others')," He also points out that this definition includes a number of assumptions. First, individuals belong to multiple groups and therefore carry multiple cultures. The implication is that an encounter between two individuals is likely to be a *multicultural* encounter since each participant can draw on more than one culture to make sense of the situation. This includes negotiation encounters. Second, it is important to understand the institutions and mechanisms that transmit culture. Third, culture is almost never perfectly shared by all members of a community or group. Individuals have the capacity to selectively adopt and adapt their multiple cultures, so you cannot assume that a person from culture X will do Y. Each party can draw from, adapt, and modify a multifaceted set of cultural norms and rules; therefore every intercultural encounter is a complex improvisational experience.

It is critically important to remember that our own cultures are largely invisible to us; they are simply our "common sense" understandings of the world. Hence, "conflict is, at essence, the construction of a special type of reality. Most of the time we assume and take for granted that we share a single reality with others, but we do not." We see culture when we are forced to recognize that not everyone experiences and lives in the world the way we do. Perhaps we experience "language shock" when we recognize that someone may be speaking the same language, but we are not sure they live on the same planet we do. Or, we may encounter someone whose "moral order"—their "pattern of . . . compulsions and permissions to act in certain ways and [their] prohibitions against acting in other ways"—differs from our own. In negotiations, these moments of shock and surprise may occur around issues of risk because risk is very much a cultural construct. We may also experience surprise when people use the same language, even the same metaphors, but we discover that their shared language is actually covering over profound differences in their sense of reality. What *we* assume is negotiable may not be negotiable to another person and vice versa.

As negotiators, the recognition that we have a culture too reshapes the reality within which we work. We are forced to grapple with the fact that the very domain of our work—social conflict—is culturally constructed.

> Culture frames the context in which conflict occurs. It does this partly by specifying what manners of things are subjects for competition or objects of dispute, often by postulating their high value and relative (or absolute) scarcity: honor here, purity there, capital and profits somewhere else. It does so by stipulating rules, sometimes precise, usually less so, for how contests should be pursued, including when they begin and how to end them.

. . . Culture frames our responses to conflict by giving us cognitive and affective frameworks for interpreting the behavior and motives of others and ourselves. Most negotiation models assume that "each individual human being pursues his or her personal values and self-interest, typically in the context of—and against others—rationally pursuing their own self-interest and their personal values." But this is not the only way to think about human beings and their motives. Some cultures may assume that human beings are inherently relational beings who seek to preserve their relationships even if it "costs" them something. Or a culture may assert that protecting traditions is the most important imperative for all members of the community.

When we encounter cultural differences about when and how to negotiate, we can focus on what the other person is doing "wrong" compared to us. This approach does, in fact, appear in many negotiation books and articles. If we look closely, we can see that the implicit, sometimes explicit, question is "how do we get the X (fill in the name of another culture of group) to negotiate 'properly'?" Most commonly, this appears in the form of a question about how we get these other people to negotiate "rationally," with no recognition that rationality is culturally constructed.

Or, instead of focusing on what is wrong with the other culture, we can become adept at a form of "symmetrical anthropology" that is "capable of confronting not beliefs that do not touch us directly—we are always critical enough of them—but the true knowledge to which we adhere totally." We can subject our own culture(s) to the same scrutiny we apply to the culture(s) of others. That means we will need to become critically aware of our own assumptions about negotiation. What does it mean to say "get beneath positions to interests?" Does everyone share the assumptions about human nature and social relationships on which this approach to finding a "win-win" solution rests?

V. TEACHING CULTURAL SKILLS TO NEGOTIATORS

So, how do negotiators learn to become "symmetrical anthropologists" in cross cultural settings? How do they learn to read the culture of their interlocutors and heighten their awareness of their own culture? First, they broaden their expectations about negotiation behavior. They do not always assume the other party is a cost-benefit calculator who is motivated only, or even primarily, by self-interest. They recognize that the reasons individuals choose one action over another are complex and that they are shaped by context. In a car dealership, I might be a rational actor trying to maximize my own benefit. But in a divorce, I might be operating with much more complicated motives and much different sets of moral imperatives and prohibitions.

Having widened their set of expectations about human motivations, negotiators need some "quick and dirty" methods for exploring the motivations of other parties in a negotiation. Obviously, it is impossible to explain these tools in detail in this paper. What follows is a short discussion of some ways of listening for culture while negotiating.

One way into culture is through worldviews, or more accurately, through the worldviewing process that every human being engages in every day. "[*W*]*orldview* denotes a *concept* that attempts to articulate the consequences of human activities that are individual as well as collective, psychological as well as social. . . . Worldviewing is a universal activity, even though worldviews differ significantly from one community to another." Our own worldviewing (and our own worldviews) are largely invisible to us unless we bump up against a worldview other than our own or we confront a new experience for which we do not have easy answers. Every individual and every society engages in worldviewing—which is not a conscious, rational, intellectual activity, but a largely unconscious process of ordering the world and giving it meaning. A useful way to think about and get hold of a worldview (our own or someone else's) is to think of people as answering the following five questions at an unconscious level as they move through their daily lives:

- What is real?
- How is the real organized?
- What is valuable about those things (or people or institutions or traditions, etc.) that are real?
- How do we know about what is real?
- How should I (or we) act (or not act)?

People are not able to answer these questions directly, but their answers "leak out" in their language, in their actions, and in their institutions—in their culture. So, if we hold these questions in mind while we are listening to a party in a conflict tell his story, we can learn to hear his worldview. From that we know what matters to him, what he thinks he can and cannot do, what he values, and what kinds of knowledge he will accept or reject. These are all factors that will motivate him in a conflict.

Taking this perspective seriously, we see that in a multi-party conflict over the management of fragile rangelands in the Southwest, a rancher who says, "My grandfather managed for beef, my father managed for grass (beef is a byproduct of grass), and I am trying to manage for ecosystem health" is telling us that, in his family, worldviews about ranching have shifted considerably in three generations—at least in some ways. Like his grandfather, he still values being a cowboy; but his sense of how the terrain on which he ranches is organized and his responsibility for that terrain differ from his grandfather's, Associated with these different ways of thinking about ranching (and the identity of a rancher) is a pattern of compulsions and permissions about how a rancher should and should not act.

As negotiators, mediators, or facilitators, when we hear what sounds like a significant and important indicator of a party's worldview (cultural assumptions), we can gently probe for clarification. In the case above, we might probe a little more on what it means to manage a ranch for ecosystem health. We will want to be particularly attentive to places the rancher says, "I must do or I should do X" or "I can't do or I mustn't do Y." This pattern of compulsions and permissions and prohibitions will reveal possible sticking points for the negotiation and/or possible points for an integrative agreement.

Metaphors are another window onto culture. "Metaphors link two concepts together by employing familiar entities or systems to give shape to unfamiliar entities or systems. By drawing an analogy between the (relatively) known and the (relatively) unknown, metaphors guide perception, action, and reasoning." It makes a difference whether we call the forest a farm or a wilderness. We will advocate for different policies and take different actions depending on which metaphor we validate. When someone uses a metaphor—particularly if it resonates with others or it brings a negative response from others—we can gently probe for more information. Metaphor interviewing—taking someone's own metaphor or a metaphor used by another party and asking the interviewee to expand on the metaphor—elicits stories that are rich in worldviewing information.

Metaphors can be used in conflict resolution to help parties explore creative options in a non-threatening way. For example, with a church that is experiencing conflict between the older, long-standing members and the younger new members, do we continue doing what we have always done or do we try new things? Here, the metaphor of renovating a house can be helpful. A facilitator can acknowledge that the older members feel like the newer members have "brought in a wrecking ball and want to tear the whole house down," but perhaps the newer members just want to put on an addition or do some remodeling so everyone can fit in the house. If this metaphor resonates with the parties, people will start "chaining on" the remodeling metaphor by playing with it. The church community can have a "playful" and less threatening conversation about their needs by thinking about what they need in their home—not just physical space, but activities and programs and services.

Metaphors can also be dangerous in conflict resolution agreements. Parties may agree on a metaphor, but interpret it very differently. A four year dialogue process on managing forest lands can produce a report and recommendations that are rich in metaphorical language—"a healthy forest and a healthy economy go hand in hand" and "our future depends on good stewardship"—and when the parties try to implement the proposals, they discover they are still deeply entrenched in conflict. Why did this happen? Because they did not take time to discover whether they meant the same thing by a healthy forest! Furthermore, the stewardship metaphor in environmental conflicts frequently covers over profound worldview (cultural) differences.

Social scripts are also a window into culture. A script is "a commonly assumed temporal ordering for some kind of event, for example, 'a meal in a restaurant', 'trip to the beach.' " Formal education is a widely shared life experience, but the script for "participating in a class" varies considerably depending on cultural context. As an undergraduate I enrolled in many small classes. The script for attending class involved rigorous preparation before class, vigorous discussion and debate during the class, and a sense of intellectual equality—ideas were judged on their merit, not on whether they came from the professor or the students. When I went to Scotland for graduate school, I discovered that the script for attending class involved sitting quietly and taking notes while the professor lectured. Years later, when teaching in South Carolina in a conflict resolution program, I created a script for attending class that required active participation in a wide variety of activities including discussions, role plays, listening to and responding to short lectures, group work, and brainstorming. . . .

Every culture, and every individual, carries a script—or more likely a set of scripts—for negotiation. We may see one script applying to family negotiations and another script applying to business negotiations.

Whatever script or scripts we have to work with creates a range of choices for our own actions and a set of expectations about the other party's behaviors. It is precisely when these scripts clash that we think there is a "cultural issue" or a "cultural problem" in a negotiation. The good thing about scripts is that they can be flexible. We can improvise new scripts, and in fact, we do that when we try to find ways to negotiate in cross-cultural settings. Or, at least we do that if we do not treat culture asymmetrically by assuming the real problem is to get the other person to take a "proper" role in our script.

One of the most obvious places that culture can be seen in a conflict resolution process, including negotiation, is when we have a problem with framing and reframing the problem, the process, or both. Negotiators can become more culturally adept by learning how to see frames and work with them.

VI. CONCLUSION

Since the big battles of the 1980s over whether culture was a significant factor at all in negotiation and conflict resolution practice, we have seen an increasing awareness of the importance of culture in negotiation. Concepts of culture being taught in negotiation courses have become richer and more complex. However, we have not yet integrated the richest understanding of culture into our curricula or our practice. There is much work to be done on this pressing issue.

Carrie Menkel-Meadow
When Winning Isn't Everything: The Lawyer as Problem Solver
28 HOFSTRA L.REV. 905 (2000)*

. . . Today I want to address the question of what the modern lawyer needs to *know* and what the modern lawyer must know how to *do* to be good at what he or she does, to be helpful to clients, to lead a fulfilling life, and hopefully, to leave the world a better place than he or she first found it. . . .

I will explore the goals and means of effective negotiation, because, as lawyers, we accomplish things only by working with clients, legislators, policy makers, judges, administrative officials, other lawyers, and other people's clients—a process we need to pay more attention to in our teaching, learning, and self-evaluation. I also want to talk about problem solving as a legal goal that is different from "winning" (it can be both more and less than winning, but is often different). This is a focus on

* Footnotes omitted.

different substantive outcomes for the cases, matters, problems, and transactions on which we work.

I do not mean "win-win" negotiations either, for that is often a misnomer in legal negotiations. It is rare in legal negotiations or in life that everyone can win something. But problem solving negotiation means that the parties can do better than they might otherwise do, especially if they are employing an unnecessarily unproductive adversarial approach.

Consider a case or matter you are working on, or . . . a case you have just studied for class. What are the conceptual frames or assumptions you bring to work on the case—what are the clients' or parties' goals, what are the lawyers' goals, and what are the system's concerns with respect to the matter? Then, consider what strategies or behaviors are conjured up by trying to achieve these goals. In the legal system as lawyers know it, most of them, especially after three years of law school training, adopt what the economists would call certain "default," or what I would call "reflexive," mind-sets. If it is a "case," lawyers must be seeking to "win" something from the other side, ask the court to interpret a statute, or rule, or the facts in their favor, or, in a transaction, they hope to "get the better deal." These mind-sets, which can be labeled together as "maximizing individual or client gain," produce certain assumptions of scarcity or at least zero-sum games of limited resources which, in turn, produce either binary or polarized solutions (court judgments or I win-you lose) or split the difference compromises. Lawyers hope to win, yet they know they could lose—in fact, if they do not go to trial, the most common result in our legal system will be some sort of monetary valuation of a case and some compromise value. (In one shot, two person pricing problems, like car or home buying, they can predict that the final price will be close to the mid-point of the first offers).

These assumptions of goals and outcomes lead, too often, to behaviors that I have labeled the "culture of adversarialism," with an emphasis on argument, debate, threats, hidden information, deception, lies, persuasion, declarations, and toughness. These behaviors, in turn, often escalate and lead to the most common results of adversarial bargaining—stalemate or mindless mid-point compromise. Even a "win" will be a loss if the other side is so beaten down or regretful that it will resist complying with a negotiated agreement. Consider the many examples from Twentieth Century international relations and war.

Even "wins" in the legal system often represent "imprecise" justice. The law all too often deals in binary on/off positions. There is contract or no contract, negligence or no negligence, and guilt or innocence with very few "mediated" substantive choices—comparative negligence in torts, material breach, promissory estoppel or quantum meruit in contracts, or "not proven" in Scottish criminal law as a few examples. Yet, on/off decisions these days seldom reflect the complex reality of post-modern life and lawsuits with multiple parties and issues, complex causation chains and liability and responsibility, and situations where two "rights" or claims for justice may stand in equipoise on opposite sides of a case (for example, free speech and regulation against hate speech and child custody cases).

The forces which produce this thinking are many and complex and I do not mean to simplify them. They are epistemological—many believe the truth is learned better by having two sides square off and "fight" each other (an evolutionary move forward from trial by ordeal or battle). Many believe that clear rules are necessary to guide society and that disputes belong to the polity and not to the disputants once they enter the public courthouse. They are structural—our litigation system most often consists of two sides (plaintiff and defendant), even when modern day problems are more likely to be multi-party and multi-issue. Judges have "limited remedial imaginations," meaning that by law they can only order certain things—past-oriented verdicts for one side or another, guilt or innocence, or injunctions and monetary damages. Juries may nullify or compromise, but they also have limited remedies or solutions at their disposal. The jurisdiction of courts to craft remedies and solve problems is limited—by legal principles and by procedure. And, the forces of adversarial thinking are behavioral—the structures and frames of thinking about the legal system have together created a system of adversarialism that leads us to argue in oppositional modes, to see black or white, to resist nuance and complexity, and at worst, to be uncivil to each other.

To develop another mind-set or *reflective* approach to legal problem solving requires, therefore, both conceptual or structural change and behavioral and processual change in how we conceive of legal problems. . . . Effective legal problem solvers must learn to *think* differently before they learn to *act* differently. This is the *science* and the *art* of negotiation.

. . . [R]eturn to the case or matter I asked you to think about a few moments ago. Imagine that in addition to the commonly "briefed" questions students pose today in the "IRAC" mode (issue, ruling/reasons, analysis/arguments, conclusions), we also considered the following questions:

1. What brings these parties/clients to a lawyer? What are they trying to accomplish?

2. What are their underlying needs or interests (as they experience them)? As the lawyer will translate them or frame them as "legal problems?"

3. What are the likely/possible needs/interests/concerns of the other parties involved in the matter/case or transaction? (Of the adversaries or third parties affected by the matter?)

4. What is really at stake in the dispute or transaction? (What is the "res" of the dispute—scarce commodities, divisible items (money), reputation, on-going business relations, legal principles, harms or hurts not easily compensable by our legal system?)

5. What are the legal, social, economic, political, psychological, moral, ethical and organizational issues, benefits, and risks implicated in the matter?

6. How might the process chosen to resolve these issues affect them?

7. How will or do the parties feel about the resolutions/solutions/outcomes that are produced?

8. What outcomes are produced by what processes?

Structures do just that—they structure thinking. Litigation begets win/lose; some think mediation begets "split the difference" or compromise. Triadic decision making produces a ruling from above. Dyadic negotiation produces, at least in theory, control by the parties or their agents.

Adding these questions to the more conventional questions asked about legal cases broadens our notions of what is relevant to consider, as it broadens the possibilities of choices that we should consider. Instead of "maximizing individual gain," we can be focused on "solving the problem," "creating the transaction," "planning for the future," "improving relationships," and perhaps even seeking "joint gain" and "achieving justice." Thus, a good legal problem solver needs a greater repertoire of intellectual choices or "tropes" as well as a much broader and deeper set of behaviors. . . . [T]ake a minute to contrast the problem solving mode with the more conventional legal mind-set.

I do not mean to overly polarize these models . . . but a problem solving approach to legal issues does suggest other goals (joint-gain, acknowledging that the other party is part of the problem to be solved), which should produce different behaviors and different outcomes. Problem solving does not mean cooperation (cooperation must be earned—we do not simply give in to the other side) or unnecessary compromise. When my brother and I fought over the last piece of chocolate cake, my mother made the mistake of all reasonable mothers—she cut the cake in half and told us to share. This was unnecessary—if she had asked us what our interests were, she would have learned that I like icing and my brother likes cake—a simple "horizontal" cut, rather than a vertical one, would have made us both 100% happy (rather than the 50% compromise)—in economic terms, a "Pareto optimal" solution. Problems like these have become the staple of game theorists and mathematicians as well as city planners and military strategists, and jurisprudes and philosophers. Thus, problem solvers need to seek information, first from clients and then from the other people in the legal matter. At a behavioral level, lawyers need to learn to ask more questions, rather than to make so many declarative statements and arguments (seeking to persuade before one really knows what the other side values and will find persuasive). A good problem solver "collaborates" or "coordinates" with the other side—testing information he or she already has in order to find out what the parties need and want, learning whether the other side can be trusted to collaborate, and then exercising the creativity that is so seldom taught and learned in lawyering.

And now . . . it is time for your to work. . . . [L]et me illustrate what I think good legal negotiators and problem solvers need—more training, teaching, and thought about creativity and problem solving. Legal analysis is a necessary, but not sufficient, condition of good problem solving.

Try to solve the following problems:

Draw three rows of three equally spaced dots:

• • •

• • •

• • •

1) Connect the dots with four straight lines without taking the pen off the page.

2) Now connect the dots with three lines.

3) Now connect the dots with one straight line.

4) Now take a piece of paper from your notebooks—put your entire body through that piece of paper.

Solutions? What is learned? Ideal problem solvers must:

1) Think out of the box (the legal box of precedent—the way things are usually done). To connect the dots, one must transgress the perceived limitations of a "box" created by the four corners of the dots.

2) Reframe (without violating) the instructions. What are the definitions of the concepts we are working with? What are "dots," what are "lines"?

3) Reconstituting the material (or altering the "res") with which we are dealing—transform the paper, transform the relationship, and

transform the transaction into something else closer to what the parties want.

4) Learn something about our thinking processes. How did you approach this problem? By looking at someone else's work (cheating, "borrowing," or translating from others, from book or precedent)? Thinking about the words and how they can be stretched? Fighting the hypo? Thinking out of the box? Remembering the solution to the problem when your child showed it to you? (Can you replicate the solutions if you "knew" the solution? Problem solving includes execution and implementation, as well as analytic understanding.)

All of these answers will tell a problem solver something about their thinking processes. Now ask others how they attempted to solve the problems. Were the problem solving approaches similar? Different? This will explain what happens when different negotiation styles meet up to try to solve a problem. It also illustrates that often "two heads are better than one"—different approaches to problems may lead to more, or different, solutions.

Those who study thinking processes—cognitive and social psychologists and decision scientists—have produced empirical studies and helpful information about how individuals and groups make decisions, judgments, and draw conclusions—all of which affect the ability to negotiate with others and solve problems. For years, the stated problem in cognitive psychology was to consider why human beings departed from "rational" choices. Psychologists have learned that human beings are subject to many "heuristic biases," some of which especially affect legal negotiators.

Reactive devaluation—a subset of "attribution theory"—occurs when someone on the other side suggests something and one cannot hear it (or "process" it) simply because it comes from the other side, (Reactive devaluation is one reason to use a mediator. A mediator presents suggestions and ideas in a more "neutral" format so that both sides can consider the merits of an idea, without the emotional rejection or attachment to a particular side.) Individuals often give too much credit to the first thing they hear (primacy) or the most recent thing they hear (recency) which is why attorneys care about the order of opening and closing arguments . . . when one has just a few minutes to get out his or her case (such as in a too short court-annexed mediation or arbitration statement). Individuals make different choices to avoid losing what they already have, rather than risking for gain something they do not have yet (the difference between loss and risk aversion) and each individual differs in how he or she values these things.

Despite all the efforts to study departures from "rational" thinking . . . there is now some strong empirical evidence that some decision makers do not use legalistic and rational "decision-trees" with choices and pros and cons. . . . Instead, many decision makers, particularly those with "professional expertise," use more intuitive or experience based "naturalistic" types of decision processes, called "pattern recognition primed reasoning," in which situations are "sized up" from past experiences and a solution is chosen and used until it does not work and a new solution emerges and is tried. This is creativity in context and it is what is needed, among other things, to solve problems and to think "out of the box" for so many of the complex and difficult problems the legal system currently faces. . . .

A good problem solver must take the problem, transaction, or matter presented by the client, analyze what the problem or situation requires, and then use creative abilities to solve, resolve, arrange, structure, or transform the situation so it is made better for the client, not worse. To do this, the lawyer must also take account of the other side, not as someone to be "bested" or beaten, but as someone with needs, interests, and goals as well. How can both or all parties (including the state and the defendant in a criminal case, the plaintiff-victim and the tortfeasor, the breaching contractors, buyer-sellers, the regulated and private industry, and the many responsible parties in a clean-up site in an environmental case) attempt to structure their negotiations so that they learn what they want to do and what they can do?

Here, the important observation of social psychologist George Homans is significant: people often have complementary interests. Individuals do not always value things exactly the same way. . . . By having many issues and many different preferences, individuals actually increase the possibility of reaching an agreement, whether it is settling a case or arranging a transaction. It may be useful if judges and litigators narrow the issues for trial, but it is detrimental to the settlement process to narrow issues. The more issues, the more likely trades or "log-rolls," as the legislators call them, will be possible. Therefore, seeing many issues and parties and all organizational needs and preferences is essential to good problem solving.

Before one starts to compete with the other side, it is useful to see if the pie for which one is fighting can be expanded, before one divides it, if one must. This is what negotiation theorists call "expanding the pie" or "value creation," before one gets to the nasty "value claiming" or pie-dividing stages. . . . So, one should always ask the journalist's basic questions of every matter: 1) WHAT (What is at stake? What is the "res" of the dispute? Can it be changed, expanded or traded?); 2) WHEN (Must one resolve this now? Are installments possible? Are there any tax consequences or contingency agreements? What risk allocation and sharing is involved?); 3) WHERE (Where can something be moved or transferred? Can a change of forum or process be effected?); 4) WHO (Who are all the relevant parties here? Can one add some people or entities with resources and the power to do things?); 5) HOW (What means may be used to solve the problem: money, land, or an apology?); and finally; 6) WHY (Why are the parties here? What are the underlying reasons, motivations, or interests in this matter? Can one reconstruct the reasons for being here and look for new ways to resolve the issues?). Answering these questions often, not always, provides new insights and new resources for solving problems.

One still needs law and a lot of other knowledge to solve problems and structure transactions. . . . "[P]attern recognition" helps those with experience quickly analyze and diagnose a problem and select a single solution, which is abandoned if it does not work. Lawyers need life experiences and they need to be generalists who can recognize many different kinds of patterns. Specialization may be increasing because of a perception or belief that individuals can only recognize a limited number of "patterns" in their experiences. I want to suggest that good legal problem solving, however, also requires the cross-fertilization of solving problems across fields. Individuals develop creativity by translating from one realm to another—transfers of assets lead us to see the possibilities of transfers of people—to new uses, to more satisfying jobs, to removing difficult personalities from each other. The cost sharing of clean-up sites in environmental law is related to market share settlement grids in mass torts. The "structured settlement" or annuity in tort can work in installment payments for other damages or employment settlements. What I like most about being a mediator in a wide variety of fields is learning how one industry or one substantive field "solves" its risks and contingency problems and seeing how that solution can be adapted to other fields. So, in this sense, problem solving is analytic, rigorous, intellectual, interdisciplinary, and certainly more than doctrinal learning. Lawyers must learn to think of themselves in terms of experts in problem solving who draw on a wide range of disciplines. Lawyers are intelligent; they work with words and concepts ("linguistic intelligence"). They must learn to be facile with more systems of thought, as well as with the experiences on the ground, such as the experiences of the people they serve.

Finally . . . [we need to recognize] that professionals solve human and legal problems by working with others. The emphasis on argument, debate, issue spotting, moot courts, and trials does, I think, encourage a culture of acrimony, or as author Deborah Tannen calls it, "The Argument Culture." As problem solvers, lawyers must learn to be more effective interpersonally. . . . One begins, of course, with one's client. Clients often have good ideas about what they want to achieve. I begin every client interview with the question: "How would you like this to turn out?" Often the lawyer may have to redirect the client to what is legally possible, but a good possible solution or suggestion that is new or different might come from one's client, or, surprisingly, the client on the "other side." . . .

Training in questioning and active listening serves lawyers, not just as trial advocates, but as mediators and as representatives in mediation or other ADR settings where all kinds of facts may be important beyond what is legally discoverable or admissible. I call these "settlement facts," which include such items as the feelings of the parties, financial information, plans for product development, expansion, down-sizing, human resource realignments, land development, acquisitions, and other things which are relevant to the parties' intentions about their dealings with each other and conflicts or transactions that may be bigger than the concretized disputes before them.

Thus, learning to speak clearly and to listen "heedfully" are essential interpersonal skills for the lawyer. . . . Studies of effective decision makers suggest that people who can "see the invisible," "hear the silences," and "read other people's minds," develop a sense of the relationship of the past and future to the present and the other party's desires to the achievement of their goals. Consider the famous brainteaser about finding a common location to meet a friend or significant other when one is lost in a large public place—the development of empathy—true knowledge of the other side of the problem. This kind of "intuitive" or "gestalt" knowledge is actually experience-based and can be learned, or at least reflected upon and systematized.

What was the last problem you solved? . . . What did you use to do it? Logistics or "forward-thinking" (arranging children, transportation, or meeting the family's competing needs regarding a vacation)? Asking a friend for advice? . . . Translating from another domain or solution? Using an analogy or metaphor? This attention to the *je ne sais quoi* part of human decision making, as well as different forms of cognition and knowledge, is important in legal problem solving. Some lawyers suffer from what decision scientists call "hyperrationality" and are surprised when the other side does not respond to "clear and rational arguments" or "the numbers." Other things, such as values and emotions—fear, altruism, vengeance, need for certainty—often motivate parties—and prevent consideration of otherwise rational "solutions."

. . . In the vastly changing multi-cultural and international context in which lawyers do their work, processes like negotiation, mediation, consensus building, and other forms of facilitated communication will be essential to bridge the language, cultural, and legal divides of the parties to any dispute or transaction. To negotiate or mediate is to use communication to achieve results for groups of people who cannot do it alone. Lawyers have an opportunity to serve as leaders of a hybridized "bridge" discipline, which can, on its good days, speak to different kinds of people. To the extent that traditional lawyers speak only the adversarial language of litigation and winning, they will be used narrowly for only one function, trial work, when that function is increasingly wasteful and inefficient, as well as emotionally draining, on most, if not all, of the players. . . . To the extent that processes like negotiation and mediation open up broader passages of communication and allow more creative forms of thought than the boilerplate of form contracts or the bargains extracted "in the shadow of the law," legal work, for both lawyer and clients, will be improved as more creative forms of problem solving are pursued. . . .

[T]here is nothing like the "rush" of helping a person, of really solving a problem. How much sweeter than the temporary victory of a lawsuit, so often followed by resentment, enforcement problems, and the economic and psychological costs to the body and soul of clients and lawyers. Imagine if lawyers were not only the protectors of rights, but also the architects and engineers of justice and the satisfaction of human needs. . . . Try one final thought experiment: consider one intractable problem that you face in your cases, your work life, your family, an institution you are a member of, and consider how thinking out of the box, or employing a different process for resolving it might give you some new insight or some new way to think about being a problem solving lawyer. There are enough human problems to go around; what is needed are more problem solvers who care, not just about winning, but about really solving the problems.

POST-CLASS REFLECTION MEMO

Draft and submit a memo in response to the questions below:

- How did your pre-negotiation planning affect the conduct of the negotiation?
- Think about your client's interests and your own preferences with regard to settlement or negotiated outcome. As a lawyer, how can you ensure that you are clearly focused on your client's interests? What can you do if your client's interests seem at odds with what you, personally, believe is the best outcome?
- What are the most important insights you take away from the negotiation exercise?

- How do those insights translate into your work on your current clinic cases or projects?

HANDOUT FOR NEGOTIATION OBSERVERS

- Was the bargaining engaged in by the parties primarily positional or interest-based (hard or soft) bargaining?
- Did one or both parties make an attempt to identify or highlight common ground?
  - Examples?
- Did one or both parties pose questions that sought information?
  - Examples?
- Did the parties' disclose or ask each other for their BATNAs?
  - How did they use that information in the negotiation?
- Did one or both parties seek justification from the other for any positions taken?
  - Examples?
- Did you discern an overall strategy employed by one or both sides?
  - Examples?
- How did each side handle concessions?
  - Examples?
- Did one or both sides make efforts at trust building?
  - Examples?
- Did one or both sides mention the consequences of failing to come to an agreement?
  - Examples?

CHAPTER 16

PRESENTATION SKILLS

LEARNING GOALS

The learning goals for this class include helping you to:

- Create an opportunity to distill your ideas into a clear concise presentation
- Appreciate the need to be goal directed in presentations
- Develop the ability to articulate your goals to an audience
- Develop appreciation for different approaches to oral presentations, and to choose among them in planning a presentation
- Adapt presentations to audience needs and appreciate the importance of that adaptation
- Enhance collaboration around oral presentations
- Explore different models of oral presentation, from structure and form to speaking style and body language
- Develop skills/approaches to create effective presentations

---

DESCRIPTION OF CLASS

This class on presentation skills is designed to develop your ability to distill ideas, communicate with clarity and variety with an awareness of the audience and do it within a very short time. You will prepare an 8 minute presentation with an audience in mind before class, using whatever visual aids you and your team choose. In class, your team will do your presentation to the group, as will the other teams. After each presentation, the class will provide feedback focused on several areas including areas your team identifies.

ASSIGNMENT IN PREPARATION FOR CLASS

Your teacher will divide you into teams. Please work with your team and prepare the following:

Transactional and Project-Based Clinics

- An 8-minute presentation about your work in the clinic, with particular attention to:
  - Goals
  - Audience
  - Outcomes
  - Criteria for assessing whether these goals and outcomes have been met
  - Key steps you will take to achieve these goals and outcomes

Litigation Clinics

- An 8-minute presentation about your work in the clinic, with particular attention to:
  - Goals
  - Audience
  - Next steps

Transactional and Project-Based Clinics

Each presentation group will be assigned a different target audience. You will be assigned to one of the groups below by a separate memo.

- **Group One:** A community group, of which your client is a member, interested in one of the issues that is the subject of your work
- **Group Two:** The governing board of the your client organization or a legislative committee concerned about one of the issue(s) that is the subject matter of your work
- **Group Three:** A potential funder for your client organization or an organization that works on one of the issues that may ultimately benefit your client
- **Group Four:** A potential community partner for the organization with which you are seeking to collaborate

Litigation Clinics

Each presentation group will be assigned a different target audience. You will be assigned to one of the groups below by a separate memo.

- **Group One:** A community group concerned about the subject matter of your client representation work wants to be educated about how a lawyer thinks through putting on an effective case
- **Group Two:** The State Judicial Training Committee wants to drop a brief segment into the judicial training on the legal and social issues that clients like yours face when appearing in court.
- **Group Three:** A legislator has approached the clinic and requests a presentation to her staff about a single legal or policy change that might improve access to justice for our clients
- **Group Four:** The clinic has just learned that the law school is considering cutting back on clinical legal education and the dean has asked that you meet with him and the senior administrators and present about why clinic is a valuable educational experience.

Each group is responsible for preparing their presentation in advance of class. In addition, each team should prepare a handout identifying three aspects of the presentation about which feedback would be particularly useful. The issues should be identified through short and focused questions. Bring a copy of the handout for each member of the class. When you present, two class members will be assigned to focus only on providing a critique. The rest of the class will play the role of the audience to whom the presentation is addressed.

NOTE: Each presentation must be no more than 8 minutes long. (They will be timed.)

If you have any audiovisual needs, please let the clinic administrator know as soon as possible.

After each presentation, we will:

- Have a fellow clinic student or students summarize their understanding, based on the presentation, of whether the team did the following:
  - Tailored the presentation for the audience
  - Addressed an identifiable issue in the presentation
  - Where appropriate, discussed
    - The potential outcomes of the work
    - The steps you will take to achieve these outcomes
    - The criteria for success of your work

- Offer general feedback about the effectiveness and clarity of your presentation.

READING ASSIGNMENT

1. David Dempsey, *Breaking Your Speaking Template,* LEGALLY SPEAKING: 40 POWERFUL PRESENTATION PRINCIPLES LAWYERS NEED TO KNOW 3 (2009).
2. Presentation Skills: Andrew Dlugan, *25 Public Speaking Skills Every Speaker Must Have,* SIX MINUTES (Sept. 6, 2013), https://georgetown.box.com/s/5oyn7vibchc1nwkzewqt.
3. Presentation Skills: Marjorie Brady, *Presentation Power: Four Ways to Persuade,* SIX MINUTES (Jan. 9, 2011), https://georgetown.box.com/s/5oyn7vibchc1nwkzewqt.
4. Two creative models for oral presentations:
   A. Presentation Skills: Dick Hart, *Identity 2.0,* SIX MINUTES (2005), https://georgetown.box.com/s/5oyn7vibchc1nwkzewqt
   B. Presentation Skills: Brene Brown, *The Power of Vulnerability*, TED: IDEAS WORTH SPREADING (Dec. 2010), https://georgetown.box.com/s/5oyn7vibchc1nwkzewqt

---

READING

David Dempsey
Breaking Your Speaking Template
LEGALLY SPEAKING: 40 POWERFUL PRESENTATION PRINCIPLES LAWYERS NEED TO KNOW 3 (2009)

PRINCIPLE 1

Break Your Speaking Template

Practicing law is immensely challenging. Most lawyers are stretched to capacity, and we have neither the time nor the inclination to add tasks to our crammed agendas. All of us would acknowledge the importance of communicating persuasively, but our immediate demands take priority. So rather than making the effort to improve our vital communication skills, we either avoid opportunities to speak, or we rely on our comfortable, and usually ineffective, presentation patterns. We create excuses for not making time to enhance our speaking skills:

- "What I do works, so why bother?"
- "I am better than most of the attorneys I hear speak."
- "How I make the record is irrelevant as long as I make it."
- "What I say is most important, not how I say it."

Do any of these sound familiar?

WHY YOU MUST ENHANCE YOUR COMMUNICATION SKILLS

If you want to truly excel when you speak, you must break your speaking template—your method of communication that you have relied on for years. There are several valid reasons that you must—not should, *must*—learn to speak with power, passion, and persuasion, not occasionally, but *every* time you speak, to every audience, every client, every judge, every jury, and every organization.

First, speaking is unavoidable for lawyers, so we should do so in the most compelling and persuasive way possible. We should strive to make a lasting, favorable impression every time we speak. The principles outlined in this book will give you a decided advantage in making that type of impact.

Second, mediocre speaking should be completely unacceptable to every attorney. Just enough should never be enough. Every time you step into the arena to speak, reflect on why you chose this profession and the idealistic standards you had in law school. Are you willing to compromise those standards by just getting by? To excel in this profession, your standards must be anything but standard.

Finally, the competition in the legal field intensifies every day. As the starting salaries for associates have soared to levels few ever imagined, applications for law school have likewise skyrocketed. The legal market has become saturated with talented attorneys vying for a limited amount of legal work. In this increasingly competitive marketplace, attorneys will not be able to conduct business as usual to retain existing clients and obtain new clients. Are you prepared for that challenge?

. . . Those who master the skills of communicating with conviction will have an enormous advantage in the marketplace, in the courtroom, in the classroom, and in their practices. It may be threatening to drag your deficient communication skills into the harsh glare of the sunlight, but the most significant step will surely be the first—a willingness to break your speaking template, to challenge yourself, and to raise your standards. Those who are prepared to do that will excel. Your greatest risk? Not taking one. . . .

COMMON SPEAKING SHORTCOMINGS

Attorneys often see themselves as skillful communicators when the truth is that they are proficient in the exact set of skills they learned in law school: analyzing and dissecting legal problems, negotiating compromises, and drafting documents. Law school does very little, however, to prepare attorneys to speak persuasively, cogently, and decisively. We are taught legalistic language that we use to construct complicated and confusing sentences that often baffle our target audience. Rather than asking, "How fast were you going?"—a direct, easily understood question—we ask, "At what rate of velocity were you operating your vehicle?" This convoluted communication frustrates our listeners. When we speak, we assume an "attorney's veneer." We use complex terms and sound aloof. We hardly seem like real people.

Sometimes our communication is simply unintelligible, such as the following attorney's argument in a zoning dispute: "In cases where land is taken for public purposes for legal lots of record, at the time of such taking in such a manner as to reduce yards previously provided in relation to a portion of a structure below yard requirements generally applicable within the district, the portion of the structure involved shall be construed nonconforming." Hearing this, the conscientious jurors valiantly attempted to suppress their bewilderment and laughter. They failed.

The most difficult hurdle to overcome for attorneys is to recognize that we are, as a group, ineffective communicators. Many attorneys talk *at* the audience, heaving words and thoughts at it. They seldom talk *to* the audience. They delude themselves into thinking that the jurors or audience members will patiently sort through a blizzard of information and decipher their messages. They are sadly mistaken.

When some attorneys see and hear a recording of their presentations, it is often a shocking revelation. They are mortified. Sometimes, however, an attorney will view a videotape of a perfectly abysmal presentation he has made with no comprehension of just how ineffective he was. At the conclusion of such a presentation, I will ask for the attorney's self-evaluation. I am surprised to hear a reply like, "I thought that it was pretty good. Next time, though, I will wear my red power tie."

No tie, no suit, no complete makeover will enhance that type of presentation. The message was convoluted and the audience dazed. Why can't attorneys see this? Several potential explanations exist for this apparent disconnect with reality. Perhaps the speakers have never seen a truly powerful presentation, and thus they have no basis to form a valid comparison. Maybe they evaluate their performance in comparison to that of other attorneys, in which event it might indeed be "pretty good." Perhaps they are in complete denial, or possibly, attorneys are incapable of setting their egos aside and objectively evaluating their performances. Usually all of these factors contribute to the problem. Some of the best and brightest attorneys I have worked with have been some of the worst communicators.

What steps should you take to improve your communication skills? The first step on the journey to becoming a truly effective speaker is to admit that your speaking skills are deficient. You should seek blunt and honest feedback on your presentations. You should weigh the feedback openly, and be willing to apply the suggestions. You should critically analyze your presentations. Most importantly, you should park your ego at the door if you are serious about converting the intangible concept of powerful communication into reality.

Effective speaking is a learned craft, a skill that must be constantly honed and practiced. The journey can be arduous, but the rewards are immense.

PRINCIPLE 6

Analyze Your Audience Before You Speak

Most members of your audience are juggling enormous personal and professional demands on their time. While they are listening to you, they are simultaneously thinking about a variety of issues: Will they get their children to soccer practice on time? Will the rush-hour traffic be horrendous? Will the Gleason case settle? Will they be able to escape for a long weekend? Your audience members may be compelled to attend your presentation, but no one can make them listen. It is up to you, the speaker, to make the audience members or jurors *choose* to listen.

Audience members and jurors are giving you their most precious commodity-their time. They will resent it if you waste their time by rambling in a disorganized fashion, by failing to prepare, or by flouting time constraints for the presentation. A speaker who commits any of those transgressions sends a clear message to everyone listening: "I did not respect you enough to prepare for this presentation." Conversely, audience members and jurors will give their undivided attention to any speaker who quickly demonstrates: "I am prepared, I have an important message for you, I respect your time, and you will benefit by listening to me."

WHY YOU MUST KNOW YOUR AUDIENCE

A speaker should know as much as possible about the audience members before speaking: What are their preconceptions about you and your topic?

What is their level of understanding? What do they want to know? What do they need to know? Without this understanding, you are laboring under the misconception that the same message delivered in the same manner is right for every audience.

For example, suppose you are advocating a zoning variance on behalf of your developer client at a neighborhood planning meeting. Your client needs the variance to begin construction of a shopping center. You have researched this issue, and you have concluded that your client is legally entitled to develop this land in the manner requested. Nevertheless, your client has no desire to engage in a protracted legal dispute or a battle in the court of public opinion with the proactive neighborhood group; he would prefer to resolve this amicably and build goodwill with the neighbors.

In making your presentation to the neighborhood group, rather than studying and understanding the audience's preconceptions, you rely on your powers of persuasion and the strength of your legal arguments. You know very little about the audience, and you chose not to research it. From the outset of your presentation, you are met with open hostility from the audience members. They shake their heads in disagreement; they sit, jaws locked, arms folded and rigid; they glare at you. You wonder why your logic and the overwhelming facts have not swayed them.

If you had analyzed the audience members beforehand, you might have known that they felt betrayed by previous misrepresentations from other developers and their counsel. You might have also known that it was one or two instigators from the neighborhood who were fanning the flames of discontent. No amount of logic or legal theories would have worked with this audience, but that is information you needed to discover before the presentation, not during or after it. Once you are in the midst of the maelstrom, with the audience's hostility swirling all around you, it is too late.

If you had studied this audience's history with developers, you would have been in a position to tailor your presentation to carefully address their concerns and perhaps defuse or neutralize some of the hostility. Your presentation based on law and logic might have been entirely appropriate in court, and it might have swayed a judge or jury, but it was wholly inappropriate for this defensive and emotional audience.

Excellent trial attorneys identify the characteristics of ideal jury members before the trial. They exhaustively profile the jury, often having trial experts and psychologists assist them in preparing for their *voir dire*. They attempt to garner as much information as possible about the jury panel in order to eliminate jurors who do not fit their profile. This detailed preparation provides them with a distinct advantage.

In the same manner, if you carefully prepare for a presentation by understanding as much as possible about the audience members, you have a distinct advantage. You are leaving little to chance because you are able to tailor your remarks to the interests of the audience members, and you can anticipate and defuse objections. That significantly enhances the likelihood of delivering a successful presentation.

AUDIENCE PROFILING QUESTIONS

What should you know about the members of the audience? Begin by answering demographic, philosophical, and psychological questions such as the following:

- What is the average age of the audience members? You will need to elaborate on a topic focusing on a historical event that occurred before the audience members were born, or one involving pop culture issues that might be lost on senior citizens. Without further explanation, your point will be lost.
- What is the ethnicity of the audience? Do the audience members share a collective heritage and a sense of ethnic pride? Do they share customs, characteristics, language, and history?
- What is the general education level of the audience members? Will they understand the legal or technical terminology you will be using?
- What is the economic status of the audience members? Are they living in poverty, comfort, or luxury? Audience members will be far more receptive to a message that demonstrates an understanding of and sensitivity to their economic conditions.
- What group affiliations do the audience members have, such as fan clubs, university alumni clubs, political parties, fraternities, civic organizations, professional associations, and similar organizations? Members of the Sierra Club will react far differently to a presentation involving expanding oil exploration in wilderness regions than a group of business executives.
- What are the values, beliefs, and attitudes of the audience members? Are they consistent with your message, or will your speech challenge their shared values and beliefs?
- What are the real-life experiences and concerns of the audience members? What keeps them awake at night?

- Is the audience familiar with your topic and the issues you will be addressing, or are they hearing the concepts for the first time? This will affect the topic you select and the amount of detail you include in the presentation.
- What is the audience's attitude toward you and your topic? Will the audience members listen to you with preconceptions or rigidly formed opinions? Are you entering a political quagmire? Do members of the audience have a hidden agenda?
- Are the audience members there voluntarily, because they are genuinely interested in your topic, or are they a captive audience (such as jurors) who may be required against their will to be present?
- Will your message offend anyone in the audience because of its controversial, religious, or political content?
- What do the audience members expect to hear? What do they want to hear? What do they need to hear?
- Has this audience heard other presentations on your topic that either supported or contradicted your position? Does your presentation offer a new perspective?
- What is the size of the audience? The dynamics of speaking at an intimate gathering are different than speaking to a large audience.

Once you have all of this information, you are better prepared to decide what is important to the audience members, and what issues you should address. More importantly, you are able to tailor your remarks in a manner that will result in a far more effective presentation. Does that mean that you should not address controversial issues or only speak to friendly audiences? No, but it does mean that you must be well prepared, that you must anticipate the audience's reactions, and that you must take appropriate steps to prepare your presentation with the potential risks and benefits in mind. For instance, it would be counterproductive and insulting to your listeners if you discussed the nuances of an esoteric legal theory and addressed concepts that the audience members would not understand. While you might feel that you were impressing the audience with your expertise, the audience members would most likely become resentful toward you, if they continued to listen.

I once heard a dreadful presentation by a young attorney from a government agency in which he droned on for 30 minutes (which seemed like an eternity to every unfortunate soul in the audience) about the proper way to complete a 25-page government procurement proposal. The speech was riddled with detailed terminology and acronyms understandable only to government employees. His audience was comprised of young, ambitious Internet executives who had neither the interest nor the inclination to listen to him talk about something that they would in all likelihood, never use in their professions. The speaker had asked none of the audience assessment questions outlined above before robotically plowing ahead with his speech. He knew nothing, or cared nothing, about his audience and it showed. It was an enlightening lesson on the importance of knowing and understanding your audience from the outset.

It is time consuming to answer these profiling questions, but the advantages you gain and the pitfalls you avoid with this knowledge will greatly benefit you. It is also far more likely that a message tailored to the audience will resonate with them. You may get lucky and simply guess right. But, if you simply make assumptions about your audience, the likelihood that you are guessing incorrectly is excellent.

PRINCIPLE 10

Organize for Impact

One of the few absolutes in the communication process is that every presentation must be clearly organized. No matter how interesting or entertaining the speaker, if the presentation is disorganized, it is far less likely to be successful, memorable, or persuasive.

For any variety of reasons—lack of time, lack of experience, or simple lack of preparation—many presentations by attorneys are disorganized and ineffective. For example, during a jury trial involving complex, technical issues, one attorney was both inexperienced and unprepared to present his case in a compelling manner. Ironically, he knew the facts and the law better than anyone in that courtroom, but his inability to present his arguments or the facts in a coherent fashion undermined his case. He launched into his opening statement while shuffling documents and repeatedly apologizing for his lack of organization. There was confusion where there should have been focus. You could see the bewildered looks on the faces of the jurors as they struggled to understand the vast amount of information he heaped upon them. The frustrated jury quickly stopped listening. The results were awful for his client, excellent for mine.

NINE METHODS FOR ORGANIZING A PRESENTATION

You can use numerous templates to organize your presentations. Set forth below are nine proven methods.

1. Tell Them, Tell Them, Tell Them

This method has been drummed into your head since you were a child. The opening tells the audience what you will tell them, the body of the presentation tells them, and the closing tells what you have told them. It is a simple and very effective method to give your presentation structure.

2. Topical

Topical organization is based on specific points broken down into key ideas. For example, if you are attempting to recover damages on a claim of negligence, you would address, under the general topic of damages, the specific types of damages: Compensatory, pain and suffering, and punitive. This method of organization is particularly effective to break down complex topics into understandable segments.

3. Problem/Solution

First, you present a problem followed by the solution you advocate. This is very useful for attorneys since they are typically dealing with legal problems that need to be resolved. For instance, you might explain the problem to the jury: "My client was injured by the negligence of Mr. Walters, who was driving 30 miles per hour over the speed limit and lost control of his car before it slammed into my client's car." Then you would offer the solution: "Ladies and gentlemen of the jury, my client has incurred medical expenses, lost wages, and rental costs in the amount of $49,177, and endured pain and suffering for which he should be compensated in the amount of $250,000."

4. Spatial

Attorneys can utilize spatial organization to show proximity or function. For instance, in a product liability lawsuit, an attorney might use a model to demonstrate how a steering wheel cable was designed to function, how parts of the steering wheel assembly function together, and how the assembly failed during certain maneuvers.

5. Cause and Effect

In this organizational template, you demonstrate that the effect flowed from the cause. For instance, an attorney might demonstrate that his client's paralysis was caused by the adverse interaction of the medicines prescribed by the defendant, a careless physician. Trial lawyers, in particular, tend to organize and think in this pattern, and it is a method that a jury or judge can readily follow: "Dr. Browne's negligence in prescribing a dosage of medication for Ms. Hargrove's pain, that clearly exceeded the pharmaceutical company's recommended dosage, caused my client to experience kidney failure and partial paralysis."

6. Advantages Versus Disadvantages

Objectively laying out the pros and cons, the arguments for and against a respective issue, enhances a speaker's credibility and provides a balanced perspective. After outlining the advantages and disadvantages of the respective positions, a speaker will defend one position or the other. This pattern of organization permits a speaker to frame the argument in his or her favor before it is addressed by an opponent.

7. Acronyms

Using the first letters of key words to guide your audience through a presentation is an effective way both for the speaker to organize the speech and for the audience members to recall the points. Professional speakers often use this technique. For example, professional speaker and coach David Greenberg encourages speakers to use his *PIE* technique to organize their speeches: *P,* state your point; *I,* illustrate your point; and *E,* emphasize the point's connection to the audience.

8. Sequential Pattern

Often told in the form of a story from start to finish, a sequential pattern is easy for your audience to follow since this is the way we generally communicate: "On Tuesday, December 23, 2008, two days before Christmas, Mr. Smith received a telephone call from his nephew Jason telling him that his flight would be arriving on Thursday, Christmas morning. Mr. Smith picked Jason up at the airport on Christmas, and they spent the next four days catching up on years of lost memories. On Monday, December 29, Mr. Smith drove his nephew to the airport. . . ." Chronological order, or reverse chronological order in some instances, is easy for your audience to follow. This method is particularly effective since you can signal in the presentation when transitions have been made from point to point.

9. Numbering/Grouping the Points

It is easier for audience members or jurors to follow along if they know the points a speaker is attempting to make. A speaker might say, for example, "There are four reasons this proposition should be rejected—first, the cost; second, the safety issues; third, the inherent unreliability of this solution; and finally, the better alternatives. Let's begin with reason one, the cost. . . ." This method is not only an easy way to organize your points, but it also provides signposts throughout a presentation to signal to your audience where you are.

LIMIT YOUR POINTS

An essential aspect of organizing any presentation is distilling your message to its essence. One attorney running for a local office began a speech by stating, "There are 20 reasons why I deserve your vote." The audience laughed awkwardly, no doubt convinced that he was simply engaging in hyperbole. He was not.

Thirty minutes into the presentation, after he had covered the fifth point, it was obvious that he fully intended to cover all 20 points in excruciating detail. He lost the audience that day, and he ultimately lost the election, no doubt because the voters feared that they would have to listen to another one of his speeches.

Many lawyers have problems distilling their messages to the essential points. Walk into any courtroom, in any city, on any day, and observe lawyers questioning a witness, addressing the court, or making an opening statement or closing argument. Invariably, you will see them covering dozens of points in a hazy fashion rather than making three points clearly. As a general rule, remember that it is always better to make three or four points that stick with the audience rather than a dozen cursory points that are soon forgotten. If you fail to limit your points, you risk that the listeners will retain none of the points.

FOUR KEYS TO MAKING YOUR POINTS

There are no concrete rules on how many points you should include in a presentation. You must consider factors such as the amount of time you have to address the audience, the relative importance of each of the points you wish to make, and the audience's interest level and knowledge of your topic. Clearly, 20 points is far too many because an audience is unable to remain focused for the time it would take to properly develop each of those points. Here are four guidelines:

1. Identify the Essential Points

If winning your case depends on establishing only five critical points, and you will lose your case if you fail to establish any one of them, those five points comprise the essence of your case. Your constant focus should be on how you can clearly make those points. Anything else is superfluous and should be eliminated.

2. Do Not Overwhelm the Audience with Information

Just because you know every detail about the topic you are addressing does not mean that the audience needs or wants to know everything. Most likely, they do not. Moreover, you will leave only hazy impressions if you overwhelm your listeners with too many points.

3. Limit the Points to the Time Allowed

The time constraints may limit your points (principle 30). If you have 30 minutes for your opening statement, for instance, you probably can make no more than four or five points. Any more and the jury will be lost. Too often, attorneys try to make every point they would like to make by simply talking faster. This is seldom effective. Distill your case to its essence.

4. Categorize Your Points

It will be much easier for your audience to understand and retain your message if you compartmentalize the points. In other words, rather than stating that you have eight points you would like to make, try dividing them up in a way that will be easier for your audience to assimilate: "First, I will share three reasons why you should vote no on the amendment. Second, I will propose an alternative plan, and discuss three reasons why that plan is far superior to that under consideration today. Finally, I will explain the two immediate benefits of accepting and adopting my plan today."

It is essential that you organize your presentation to maximize its impact. Make your points vivid and easy for the audience to understand. Moreover, make only those points that are essential to your purpose. Do this and you are much more likely to make a lasting impression.

POST-CLASS REFLECTION MEMO

Draft and submit a memo in response to the questions below:

- What insights do you have about your collaboration efforts in putting the presentation together and presenting it?
- How might your presentation have changed had you been assigned another audience?
- What facts and ideas emerged when you were forced to reduce the case or project to eight minutes? How does that affect the way you think about your case?
- Did you discover any gaps in knowledge or understanding when planning this presentation that suggest further fact investigation?

HANDOUTS FOR USE IN CLASS

Project Plan Presentations: General Listener Feedback

Project: ______________________

- What are the goals of this presentation?
    - Who is the audience?
- What collaboration choices did the team appear to make to achieve their presentation goals?
- Has the presentation convinced you of the value of the goals. Why?

- Do you know what your next steps are after this presentation?
- What choices did this team make in the way they presented their plan? What worked? What would you change? Be specific about the choices you see being made and the techniques of presentation used.

Assigned Listener Feedback Form

- Summarize your understanding, based on the presentation, of the following:
    - Who the audience was
        - How specifically you were able to discern the audience?
    - The issue addressed by the presentation
        - Can you state the issue in one sentence?
    - The potential outcomes of the work
        - Do these outcomes seem doable?
    - The steps you will take to achieve these outcomes
        - What steps have been taken and what steps are yet to come?
    - The criteria for success of the work
        - How will they know if they have achieved the outcome sought?
- Offer general feedback about the effectiveness and clarity of the presentation.

CHAPTER 17

WRITING

LEARNING GOALS

The learning goals for this class include helping you to:

- Appreciate the importance of clarity in writing and develop a practice of simplification
- Recognize that "legal" writing extends well beyond briefs and memoranda and includes even the simplest email
- Understand that being a lawyer means being a "professional" writer
- Develop strategies for overcoming resistance to committing ideas to paper and for developing confidence in writing
- Understand that written communication involves strategic thinking that requires analysis of the pros and cons of various approaches
- Understand the importance of audience in the writing process
- Understand all aspects of writing from the minute to the substantial, but also appreciate the need for a holistic structure for the writing
- Appreciate the importance of summarizing accurately and efficiently
- Appreciate the importance of openness to revision as well as peer and supervisor critique to perfecting writing projects

---

DESCRIPTION OF CLASS

This class is designed to help you develop strategies for writing by offering a structure that can assist in enhancing your legal writing in virtually any context. The structure breaks writing down into four stages: (1) Idea Generation, (2) Topic Sentences, (3) Drafting, and (4) Reviewing.

Within those stages are a number of considerations including understanding your audience and your client's goals and purpose, as well as awareness of the importance of proper grammar, tone, and word choice. During the class, you will draft an important email using those stages while being attentive to the writing choices you are making. We will then engage in self, peer and group critique to explore ways that we can improve our writing.

ASSIGNMENT IN PREPARATION FOR CLASS

Read the following letter, and then edit it. Hand in your revised version prior to class. Although this assignment will not be used in class, you should submit it in advance and expect feedback on your work within the next week.

Dear Congressman Berl,

I believe emergency healthcare should be a right for all people including myself, my family, my friends, even you, although I know that you probably have already made sure that you have emergency healthcare even if the American people do not. I know that the Congress is considering alot of bills, including ones that have to do with health care. You vote on bills all the time. I want you to vote in favor of one that is of great importance to the people of this country. It is H-695, The Emergency Health Care Insurance Act. It is sponsored by many congressmen, but not you, I see. My partner is very sick and we cannot afford the necessary medicine and surgeries that will keep her alive. I am at wit's end and my minister said that I should write to you. I live in your district. I voted for you. The bill will come before your committee, and I know that you are Chair, in the next week. I hope you make sure that it gets voted for. I have heard that this law is really just a subset of the Affordable Care Act and needs this little bit of law to make it work.

Thank you.

As you edit, consider the following issues:

- What is the goal of the letter?
    - How is that goal supported by the writing?
    - What facts are material to that goal?

- What action does the writer want the recipient to take?
  - How does the writing affect the likelihood that the recipient will act accordingly?
- Who is the audience?
  - How did consideration of the audience affect your rewrite of the letter?
- What is the most strategically appropriate tone?
  - Why?
- Once you have finished rewriting, evaluate your newly drafted letter:
  - Have you used active voice?
  - Have you eliminate any legalese?
  - Have you used a clear, easy-to-follow sentence structure?
  - Does each sentence flow logically from the one before?
  - Does your letter advance its goal?
  - If not, how could it be rewritten again to do so?

IN-CLASS EXERCISE

Civil Clinic

Your client has a condition that was only diagnosable by the use of a special test. The reliability of the test is critical to the case. You need an expert to provide an affidavit stating that the test used to diagnose this particular medical condition is reliable and generally used by physicians in the field. Someone told you that there is an expert in this field who lives nearby and who has done pro bono work in the past. The person knows his name, but does not know how to reach him by phone or in person. You have discovered an email address and nothing else. There is some real time pressure here, because you need an expert affidavit before next week, when you will be having a settlement conference with the opposing party.

Domestic Violence Clinic

Your client's hearing for a protection order is set for next week, and you know there will be a serious fight about custody of the children. You know that your client's son has talked to his teacher about the violence at home, and that the teacher has observed the effects of the violence on the child. You believe that the teacher's testimony is key to obtaining a judicial order for supervised visitation, which your client believes is critical to protect her son from physical and emotional harm. The only contact information you have for the teacher is an email address. The teacher's name is so common that it is impossible to find a phone number, and the school will not cooperate. The school has a policy that teachers are discouraged from getting involved in custody disputes, and the hearing will be held during the day, so the teacher could be required to take time off in order to testify.

Criminal Defense Clinic or Juvenile Delinquency Clinic

Your client, a young black man, is accused of shoplifting at a local department store. He was stopped at the front of the store and accused of stealing. When stopped, he was wearing a pair of shorts with the tags still attached. The store detective seemed to be following him around the store, and when your client decided to leave, the detective grabbed him and took him to the back room. There, the detective and a store manager examined his pants, saw the tags, and immediately called the police. He was charged with shoplifting. Your client says that he came into the store wearing the pants, and that he had the tags still attached because that is cool. He says that before he went into the store, he was playing basketball with some guys, and he knows one of them because they go to the same school. He thinks this guy might be able to provide useful testimony, because during the game, one guy kept calling your client "Tags," and the group teased him about wearing pants with the tags still attached. The game ended right before he went to the department store. Your client tried to approach this guy at school, but the guy said he did not want to get involved. Your client thinks that if you contacted the guy, he might be willing to testify. The only contact information he has is the boy's email address.

Transactional or Project-Based Clinic

Your client is trying to get a non-profit up and running. It is an organization that provides immigration assistance for people with HIV. Your client has identified several potential seed-money grants available through the city government. The grant application requires that another non-profit in the community dealing with similar issues write a letter of support, outlining why your client's organization would be a good addition to the range of services currently offered. There are two other organizations that deal with these issues. One is a long-standing immigrants' rights legal service provider, and another is a full-service case-management provider for people with HIV. Your client is concerned that the immigrants' rights provider believes that they can handle the immigration law needs of people with HIV without additional assistance, because they do not believe the population is large. Your client says that in fact, the population is larger than they think; many of those in this group do not wish to identify themselves because they are undocumented. The other organization is fairly new, and your client fears they may be applying for the same grant to expand this aspect of their services. The grant deadline is next week, and the only initial communication either organization will accept is an email. Choose one of the organizations and write an email requesting their support for your client.

READING ASSIGNMENT

1. James McElhaney, *More Than Just Words: This Is What It Really Means to Talk Like a Lawyer,* ABA JOURNAL LAW NEWS NOW (Jan. 1, 2012), http://www.abajournal.com/magazine/article/more_than_just_words_this_is_what_it_really_means_to_talk_like_a_lawyer/.
2. Wayne C. Booth, Gregory G. Colomb & Joseph M. Williams, *Making Good Arguments: An Overview, in* THE CRAFT OF RESEARCH 108 (2008).
3. Miriam Kass, *The Ba Theory of Persuasive Writing,* LITIGATION 47 (1985–1986.)
3. Bryan Garner, HBR GUIDE TO BETTER BUSINESS WRITING 3 (2013).

READINGS

McElhaney on Litigation
More Than Just Words
ABA JOURNAL LAW NEWS NOW (Jan. 1, 2012)

It was humiliating. The young lawyer had put in more than a hundred hours on the brief. He had a novel interpretation of the appliance safety act that he was urging his firm to adopt in an important case. One of his memos had caught the attention of their client's chief counsel, who suggested a strategy conference to discuss the young lawyer's position.

The young lawyer knew he would have to talk about some of his ideas, but he wasn't ready for what happened. "All right," said the general counsel. "Let's say that Mr. Baker and I are the court of appeals. We want to hear your argument. How are you going to convince us that for 60 years our reasoning has been wrong?"

The young lawyer was caught off guard. He floundered around for almost half an hour, hopping from one point to another, never really making a coherent statement. He was frankly relieved when the general counsel shifted his attention back to Mr. Baker and left him out of the discussion for a while. But by the end of the meeting, he could see that they had decided not to risk using his argument.

The ride back to the firm's office was the worst part of it. Mr. Baker wanted to talk about the dynamics of what had happened.

"Maxwell caught you by surprise, didn't he?" Baker said. "I should have told you that's what he does. I still like your idea, but we may have to wait for a client who is more willing to take a chance."

The young lawyer didn't say anything.

"But you still got a lot out of that meeting, didn't you?" said Baker.

"What do you mean?" said the young lawyer.

"You learned something a lot of lawyers never understand," said Baker. "A lawyer is a professional speaker. You talk for a living. Every time you say something as a lawyer, you are making a professional presentation.

"It doesn't matter whether you're in trial, arguing to an appellate court, talking to a client or giving a CLE lecture. There are some basic rules for any kind of speech that you should follow if you're going to be an effective advocate."

That young lawyer was Angus. And now, 25 years later, he was making those same points to Beth Golden. I was there when Angus talked to Beth, and here are my notes.

BOND WITH YOUR AUDIENCE

Even the simple "May it please the court" is an instinctive recognition that pleasing your audience is the key to persuading it.

And there are all kinds of bonds that tie speakers to audiences—some simple and appealing, others base, even ignoble. The psychology of the bond lies in our most primitive past. Should the cavemen gathered around the communal fire even listen to this stranger from another clan? Any lawyer who has been subjected to "home cooking" has felt the power of "the cave." It can be overcome, but it takes a lot of work.

Fortunately, there are other bonds that can tie a lawyer to the audience. One of the strongest bonds a lawyer can draw on is the very reason for everyone being in court in the first place: to right a wrong.

ACCEPT RESPONSIBILITY

You didn't design the courtroom, the bench, the jury box or the lectern. You have only a limited responsibility for who is in the jury box, and even less for who is on the bench. You have only a little control over when you start to speak and how much time you have.

The same things are true in all kinds of other settings in which you must speak as a lawyer.

But whatever the surroundings, whoever the audience, whatever your goal and however long you have, you are the one responsible for effective communication. It is your job to make yourself understood—not your audience's job to try to understand you.

Accepting responsibility for communication means a number of things—all of them important:

• Focus on your audience. Watch their faces for signs of understanding or confusion. Respond to the signals they send you. Even on very formal occasions, your job is to get ideas across, not to perform an idle litany.

• Don't complain about the adversities you face, such as the surrounding noise, the lateness of the hour, the fact that you were deprived of some of your time to speak, or that you only had a short time to prepare. It's up to you to overcome these obstacles, not to blame them.

• Respect your audience. Treat them as equals. Let them understand that getting your ideas across to them is the most important task you have.

CREATE A PERCEPTION OF CREDIBILITY

One of the reasons lawyers try so hard to sound like lawyers is that we suppose it gives us the trappings of credibility. If we know the magic words, we must know what we're talking about.

But the problem is that the rest of the world didn't learn our new vocabulary with us, so sounding like a lawyer is usually a self-defeating effort. You should choose other ways to look like you know what you're talking about.

One of the best ways is to make sure that what you say is true. Talk only about what you know. Whenever you try to fake it, little verbal and nonverbal clues will give you away.

Show that you have prepared for your presentation. Sharing a few bits of interesting information or using a pertinent quotation not only grabs your audience's attention but also says you have done your homework.

Use audible and visible organization. It validates what you're saying by showing that you are not simply winging it. If you announce at the beginning of your presentation that you have three main points and then call them out as you come to them, everyone will know that you have thought through what you're saying.

Of course, there are lots of ways to shoot yourself in the foot (or some more painful place). You can show that you don't know the facts or don't understand the law. Even showing dislike for the topic can be disastrous.

HAVE SOMETHING TO SAY

There was a psychology course that I always wanted to take when I was a college undergraduate, but somehow I never got around to it. Early every fall, students in the class would accost people walking through the student union and ask them to participate in an experiment. They would ask you to study the contents of a cigar box for 15 or 20 seconds. The box would have a number of ordinary objects scattered around the bottom and glued in place.

After the time was up and the box was closed, you would be asked to recite what you had seen in the box. It was fascinating how easy it was to forget objects you had just seen—even those you had consciously noted and decided you were going to remember.

But if you linked the objects together in a story, a theme or even a fanciful chain of absurd cause and effect, then your memory was vastly improved.

The point is simple: Never make a random cigar box presentation. Even organization is not enough. You need a point of view, a story with an object, a theme. You need to have something to say.

SHOW, DON'T TELL

If a point is worth making, it is worth illustrating.

Good examples—apt analogies—are more precious than rubies. They have the power to persuade because they make the audience think your point through for themselves. So when they reach their conclusion, it is their idea—not yours.

But just as an apt analogy is a powerful argument, so is one that turns around on you. That means you must be careful about picking your analogies. Test them ahead of time.

KEEP IT SIMPLE

The art of simplicity is not only knowing how everything fits together, but also knowing what can safely be discarded. And this is where lawyers have trouble.

Probably our most rigorous training as lawyers is in spotting exceptions to general propositions. So as soon as we make a simple declarative sentence, we start thinking of the situations in which it does not apply. Inevitably, we start talking about those exceptions. Or even worse, we start talking about why we are not talking about the exceptions.

Stop it.

Forget the exceptions unless they are directly relevant to what you are doing. Your function is not to cover everything; it is to make a focused presentation.

MAKE A MEMORY

Usually your goal is not to impress your audience with what a fine speaker you are, but rather to persuade.

And that means the memories you create should be vivid word pictures—sometimes even uncomfortably vivid word pictures—that will argue your case for you.

In classical times, it was said that when Athenian statesman Demosthenes spoke, people would say, "What a wonderful speaker." But when Roman leader Cato the Elder spoke, the people would rise up and shout, "On to Carthage!"

STOP

When you are done, stop. Afterthoughts, recapitulations, repetitive exhortations and the dismal trailing off by the speaker who is not certain he has finished cost more than whatever they could possibly add to a presentation.

It's much better to leave your audience thinking they want more than knowing they have heard too much.

Jim McElhaney is the Baker and Hostetler Distinguished Scholar in Trial Practice at Case Western Reserve University School of Law in Cleveland and the Joseph C. Hutcheson Distinguished Lecturer in Trial Advocacy at South Texas College of Law in Houston.

Wayne C. Booth, Gregory G. Colomb, & Joseph M. Williams
Making Good Arguments
THE CRAFT OF RESEARCH 108 (2008)

You can't wait to plan an argument supporting the answer to your question until you have every last bit of data. In the first place, you'll never get them all. But more important, you can't know what data you need until you sketch the argument they fit into. Only after you sort your data into the elements of an argument that answers your readers' predictable questions can you see what research you still have to do. But more than that, when you plan your argument early, you grasp your material better and avoid wasted effort, especially return trips to the library.

7.1 ARGUMENT AS A CONVERSATION WITH READERS

In a research report, you make a *claim,* back it with *reasons,* support them with *evidence, acknowledge* and *respond* to other views, and sometimes explain your *principles* of reasoning. There's nothing arcane in any of that, because you do it in every conversation that inquires thoughtfully into an unsettled issue:

A: I hear last semester was a little rocky. How do you think this term will go? [*A poses a problem that interests her, put in the form of a question.*]

B: Better, I hope. [*B makes a claim that answers the question.*]

A: Why is that? [*A asks for a reason to believe B's claim.*]

B: I'll finally be taking courses in my major. [*B offers a reason.*]

A: Why will that make a difference? [*A doesn't see how B's reason is relevant to his claim that he will do better.*]

B: When I take courses I'm interested in, I work harder. [*B offers a general principle that relates his reason to his claim.*]

A: What courses? [*A asks for evidence to back up B's reason.*]

B: History of architecture, introduction to design. [*B offers specific instances on which he based his reason.*]

A: But what about that calculus course you have to take again? [*A offers a point that contradicts B's reason.*]

B: I know I had to drop it last time, but I found a really good tutor. [*B acknowledges A's objection and responds to it.*]

A: But won't you be taking five courses? [*A raises another reservation.*]

B: I know. It won't be easy. [*B concedes a point he cannot refute.*]

A: Will you pull up your GPA? [*A asks about the limits of B's claim.*]

B: I should. I'm hoping for a 3.0, as long as I don't have to get a part-time job. [*B limits the scope of his claim and adds a condition.*]

If you can imagine yourself in that conversation, as *either* A or B, you'll find nothing strange about assembling the argument of a research report, because every argument, research or not, is built out of the answers to five questions in that conversation, questions that you must ask yourself on your readers' behalf:

1. What is my **claim**?
2. What **reasons** support my claim?
3. What **evidence** supports my reasons?
4. Do I **acknowledge** alternatives/complications/objections, and how do I **respond**?
5. What **principle** makes my reasons *relevant* to my claim? (We call this principle a **warrant**.)

CLARIFYING SOME TERMS

So far, we've used two terms to name the sentence that sums up the results of your research. In the context of questions, we called it your *answer*. In the context of problems, we called it your solution. Now in the context of an argument, we'll call it your *claim,*

- A *claim* is a sentence that asserts something that may be true or false and so needs support: *The world is warming up.*
- The *main claim* of a report is the sentence (or more) that the whole report supports (some call this sentence your *thesis*). If you wrote a report to prove that the world is warming up, the sentence stating that would be your main claim.
- A *reason* is a sentence supporting a claim, main or not.

These terms can be confusing, because a reason is also a (sub)claim that can be supported by more reasons. What we call it depends on its context. For example:

> TV can have harmful psychological effects on children*main claim* because when they are constantly exposed to violent images, they come to think violence is natural.*claim/reason 1 supporting main claim* Those exposed to lots of such visual entertainment tend to adopt the values of what they see.*claim/reason 2 supporting reason 1*

Reasons support main claims, but "lower" reasons can support "higher reasons."

7.2 SUPPORTING YOUR CLAIM

At the core of every research report is the answer to your research question, the solution to your problem—your main claim. You have to back up that claim with two kinds of support: reasons and evidence.

7.2.1 Base Claims on Reasons

> The first kind of support, a reason, is a statement that gives your readers cause to accept your claim. We often join a reason to a claim with *because:*

The emancipation of Russian peasants was an empty gesture*claim* because it did not improve the material quality of their daily lives.*reason*

TV violence can have harmful psychological effects on children*claim* because their constant exposure to violent images makes them think that violence is natural.*reason*

You usually need more than one reason to support a contestable claim, and in a detailed argument, each reason will usually be a separate sentence.

7.2.2 Base Reasons on Evidence

The second kind of support is the evidence on which you base your reasons. Now the distinction between reasons and evidence can seem just a matter of semantics, and in some contexts the words do seem interchangeable:

You have to base your claim on good reasons.

You have to base your claim on good evidence.

But they are not synonyms, and distinguishing them is crucial in making sound arguments. Compare these two sentences:

What evidence do you base your reason on?

What reason do you base your evidence on?

That second sentence seems odd: we don't base evidence on reasons; we base reasons on evidence.

There are other differences:

- We think up reasons by the action of our mind.
- We have to search for evidence "out there" in the "hard" reality of the world, then make it available for everyone to see.

It makes no sense to ask, *Where do I go to see your reasons?* It does make sense to ask, *Where do I go to see your evidence?* For example, we can't see TV naturalizing violence for children, but we could see a child answer the question: *Do you think that fighting on TV is real?* In principle, *evidence* is what you and your readers can see, touch, taste, smell, or hear (or is accepted by everyone as a remembered fact—the sun came up yesterday morning). That oversimplifies the idea of "evidence from out there," but it illustrates the difference between evidence and reasons.

In casual conversation, we usually support a claim with just a reason:

> We should leave.*claim* It looks like rain.*reason*

Few ask, *What's your evidence that it looks like rain?* But when you address serious issues, readers expect you to base each reason on its own foundation of evidence, because careful readers don't accept reasons at face value. They ask for the evidence, the data, the facts on which you base those reasons:

> TV violence can have harmful psychological effects on children*claim 1* because those exposed to lots of TV tend to adopt the values of what they see.*reason 1 supporting claim 1/claim 2* Constant exposure to violent images makes them unable to distinguish fantasy from reality.*reason 2 supporting reason 1 and claim 2* Smith (1997) found that children ages 5–7 who watched more than three hours of violent television a day were 25 percent more likely to say that what they saw on television was "really happening."*evidence supporting reason 2*

With reasons and evidence, we have the core of a research argument:

> CLAIM *because of* REASON *based on* EVIDENCE

To offer a complete argument, however, you must add at least one more element and often a second: you must acknowledge other points of view and offer what we call *warrants,* which show how a reason is *relevant* to a claim.

7.3 ACKNOWLEDGING AND RESPONDING TO ANTICIPATED QUESTIONS AND OBJECTIONS

A responsible researcher supports a claim with reasons based on evidence. But unless your readers think exactly as you do (unlikely, given the fact that you have to make an argument in the first place), they may draw a different conclusion or even think of evidence you haven't. No thoughtful reader will accept your claim based solely on *your* views: you must also address theirs.

Careful readers will question *every* part of your argument, so you must anticipate as many of their questions as you can, and then acknowledge and respond to the most important ones. For example, when readers consider the claim that children exposed to violent TV adopt its values, they might wonder whether children are drawn to TV violence because they are *already* inclined to violence. If you think readers might ask that question, you would be wise to acknowledge and respond to it:

> TV violence can have harmful psychological effects on children*claim 1* because those exposed to lots of it tend to adopt the values of what they see.*reason 1 supporting claim 1/claim 2* Their constant exposure to violent images makes them unable to distinguish fantasy from reality.*reason 2 supporting reason 1 and claim 2* Smith (1997) found that children ages 5–7 who watched more than three hours of violent television a day were 25 percent more likely to say that most of what they saw on television was "really happening."*evidence supporting reason 2* **Of course, some children who watch more violent entertainment might already be attracted to violence.***acknowledment* **But Jones (1999) found that children with no predisposition to violence were as attracted to violent images as those with a violent history.** *response*

The challenge all researchers face, however, is not just responding to readers' questions, alternatives, and objections, but imagining them in the first placc. (In chapter 10 we'll discuss the questions and objections you should expect.)

Since no research argument is complete without them, we add acknowledgment/responses to our diagram to show that they relate to all the other parts of an argument:

CLAIM	REASON	EVIDENCE
I claim that . . .	because of these reasons . . .	which I base on this evidence . . .

I acknowledge these questions, objections, and alternatives, and I respond to them with these arguments. . . .

7.4 WARRANTING THE RELEVANCE OF YOUR REASONS

Even when your readers agree that a reason is true, they may still object that it's not *relevant* to your claim. It's what most of us would say to this little argument:

> We should leave*claim* because 2 + 2 = 4 *reason*

Most of us think, *I don't get it. What's the connection?*

This is where the logic of an argument can get difficult to understand. For example, suppose you offer this less bizarre argument:

> We are facing significantly higher health care costs in Europe and North America*claim* because global warming is

> moving the line of extended hard freezes steadily northward.*reason*

Readers might accept the *truth* of that reason, but question its *relevance* to the claim, asking:

> What do higher health costs have to do with hard freezes? I don't see the connection.

To answer, you must offer a *general* principle that justifies relating your *particular* reason to your *particular* claim:

> When an area has fewer hard freezes, it must pay more to combat new diseases carried by subtropical insects no longer killed by those freezes.

Like all warrants, that one says that if a general circumstance exists (an area has fewer hard freezes), then we can infer a general consequence (that area will have higher costs to combat new diseases). The logic behind all warrants is that if a generalization is true, then so must be specific instances of it.

But for that logic to work, readers must agree with four things. Two are easy to understand:

1. The warrant is true: fewer hard freezes in fact mean higher medical costs.
2. The reason is true: hard freezes in fact are moving north.

The next two are more difficult:

3. The specific circumstance in the reason qualifies as a *plausible instance* of the general circumstance in the warrant.
4. The specific consequence in the claim qualifies as a *plausible instance* of the general consequence in the warrant.

We can illustrate that logic like this:

This General Circumstance	*predictably leads to*	**This General Consequence**
When an area has few hard freezes,		it will pay more to combat diseases carried by subtropical insects no longer killed by hard freezes.

This is a good instance of this.		**This is a good instance of this.**

Global warming is moving the line of extended hard freezes steadily north.*reason*	*so*	We are facing significantly higher health care costs.*claim*
This Specific Circumstance	*lets us infer*	**This Specific Consequence**

As we'll see, it's not easy to decide when you even need a warrant. Experienced researchers state them only when they think readers might question whether a reason is relevant to their claim! If you think they will see its relevance, you don't need a warrant. But if they might not, you must add a warrant to justify the connection, usually before you make it:

> **When an area has fewer hard freezes, it can expect higher medical costs to cope with diseases carried by subtropical insects that do not survive freezes.***warrant* Europe and North America must thus expect higher health care costs*main claim* because global warming is moving the line of extended hard freezes steadily north.*reason* In the last one hundred years, the line of hard freezes lasting more than two weeks has moved north at the rate of roughly . . .*evidence*

We can add warrants to our diagram to show that they connect a claim and its supporting reason:

WARRANT

The principle that lets me connect my reason and claim is . . .

CLAIM *because of* REASON *based on* EVIDENCE

ACKNOWLEDGMENT AND RESPONSE

(We know this matter of warrants is not easy to grasp; we explain it again in more detail in chapter II.)

7.5 BUILDING A COMPLEX ARGUMENT OUT OF SIMPLE ONES

Those five elements constitute the core of a "basic" argument. But arguments in research reports are more complex.

- We almost always support a claim with two or more reasons, each of which must be supported by its own evidence and perhaps justified by its own warrant.
- Since readers think of many alternatives and objections to any complex argument, careful researchers typically have to respond to more than one or two of them.

Moreover, each element of an argument may itself have to be treated as a subclaim, supported by its own argument:

- Each response to an objection may need reasons and evidence to support it.
- If your readers doubt the truth of a warrant, you may have to treat it as a subclaim and support it with its own argument, including reasons, evidence, and perhaps even its own warrant with its own acknowledgments and responses.

Only the evidence "stands alone," but even then you must explain where you got it and maybe why you think it's reliable, and that may require yet another argument.

And finally, most arguments include background, definitions, explanations of issues that readers might not understand, and so on. If, for example, you were making an argument about the relationship between inflation and money supply to readers not familiar with economic theory, you would have to explain how economists define "money." Serious arguments are complex constructions. Chapters 8–11 explain them in detail.

7.6 CREATING AN ETHOS BY THICKENING YOUR ARGUMENT

This process of "thickening" an argument is one way that writers earn the confidence of their readers. Readers judge your arguments not just by the facts you offer, but by how well you anticipate their questions and concerns. In so doing, they also judge the quality of your mind, even your implied character, traditionally called your *ethos.* Do you seem to be the sort of person who considers issues from all sides, who supports claims with evidence that readers accept, and who thoughtfully considers other points of view? Or do you seem to be someone who sees only what matters to her and dismisses or even ignores the views of others?

When you acknowledge other views and explain your principles of reasoning in warrants, you give readers good reason to work *with* you in developing and testing new ideas. In the long run, the ethos you project in individual arguments hardens into your reputation, something every researcher must care about, because your reputation is the tacit sixth element in every argument you write. It answers the unspoken question, *Can I trust you?* That answer must be *Yes.*

COGNITIVE OVERLOAD: SOME REASSURING WORDS

It's at about this point that many students new to research begin to feel overwhelmed. If so, your anxieties have less to do with your intelligence than with inexperience. One of us was explaining to teachers of legal writing how being a novice makes many first-year law students feel like incompetent writers. At the end of the talk, one woman reported that she had been a professor of anthropology whose published work was praised for the clarity of her writing. Then she switched careers and went to law school. She said that during her first six months, she wrote so incoherently that she feared she was suffering from a degenerative brain disease. Of course, she was not: she was going through a kind of temporary aphasia that afflicts most of us when we try to write about matters we do not entirely understand for an audience we understand even less. She was relieved to find that the better she understood the law, the better she wrote about it.

If you feel overwhelmed you can take comfort in that story, as did one reader who e-mailed us this:

In *Craft of Research* you write about a woman who switched from anthropology to law and suddenly found herself unable to write clearly. After being an assistant professor of graphic design for five years, I recently switched to anthropology and suddenly found that writing anthropology papers is like pulling teeth. I thought to myself that I might have a degenerative brain disorder! I laughed out loud when I read about the anthropologist who switched to law. It made me feel a bit better.

QUICK TIP: *A Common Mistake—Falling Back on What You Know*

Arguments fail for many reasons, but inexperienced researchers often stumble when they rely too much on what feels familiar and fall back on kinds of argument they already know. If you learned in a first-year writing class to take a personal stand and search for evidence in your own experience, do not assume that you can do the same in fields that emphasize "objective data," such as sociology or experimental psychology. On the other hand, if as a psychology or biology major you learned to gather hard data and subject them to statistical analysis, do not assume that you can do the same in art history. This does not mean that what you learn in one class is useless in another. All fields share the elements of argument we describe here. But you have to learn what's distinctive in the way a field handles those elements and be flexible enough to adapt, trusting the skills you've learned.

You may oversimplify in a different way after you learn your field's typical problems, methods, schools of thought, and standard forms of argument. When some new researchers succeed with one kind of argument, they keep making it. They fail to see that their field, like every other, has a second kind of complexity: competing methodologies, competing solutions, competing goals and objectives—all marks of a lively field of inquiry. So when you learn to make one kind of argument, don't assume that you can apply it to every new claim. Seek out alternative methods, formulate not only multiple solutions but multiple ways of supporting them, ask whether others would approach your problem differently.

If you are new to your topic or to your field, you'll need ways to manage the complexity of new ideas and new ways of thinking. We discuss many of them in this book. But guard against the easy but risky way: uncritically imposing a familiar method on a new problem. The more you learn, the more you'll recognize that while things are not as blindingly complex as you first feared, neither are they as simple as you then hoped.

Miriam Kass
The Ba Theory of Persuasive Writing
12 LITIGATION 47 (1985–1986)

Persuasion is making someone feel your idea is right.

Feel.

Know from the gut and the heart, not just the brain. The idea should feel like an old shoe, a threadbare teddy, the shredded satin edging of a cherished baby blanket—the Ba you used to curl up with, to rub on your cheek, to clutch as you sucked your tender puckered thumb. Persuasion is making someone feel your idea is fundamentally, yea, primordially, right.

This is the Ba Theory of persuasive writing, based on the observation that we spend our lives trying to feel good (winning trials, drinking Scotch, running to keep fit, and so forth), that we experienced some of our best feelings in the nursery, and that most of us would like to recapture that early contentment if we could do it without feeling foolish. (If you are the macho type, pretend you are reading this for a friend.) The Ba Theory says, make the reader curl up contentedly with your ideas by getting rid of bad writing habits that make the reader grouchy, then enrich your writing to make your idea feel good.

The big bad habit is writing so your idea is hard to follow. Struggle is distracting, frustrating, and tiring. It makes the reader want to run away and hide. Your ideas, through your words, should flow into the reader's mind without resistance or self-consciousness.

Think of the reader's mind as a small container. Do not fill it with dead words, bloated sentences, or other garbage that makes reading feel like eating boney fish or fat meat. Garbage hogs the space and wastes the mind's energies cleaning house. Adopt the marketing strategy of Mark Twain:

> I never write 'metropolis' for seven cents when I can get the same price for 'city.'

Do not use a long word when a short one will do. Short words are not only easier to read, they are also more likely to be of Anglo-Saxon, rather than Latin, origin and to have a dependable salt-of-the-earth quality.

We will use this sample sentence to illustrate several points:

> Through the utilization of budgetary manipulations, a conspiracy with regard to the lease transaction was implemented by Defendants whereby expenses received treatment as capital investments.

Here is one way to trim it:

Defendants conspired to budget the lease expenses as capital investments.

Most of the big words cut out of the sample sentence are of Latin origin, sometimes through French. Is the idea to revert to the English language before the Norman conquest? No, English is rich because it is so inclusive. There is no denying the beauty of English used to its fullest. If you are Shakespeare or Faulkner, stop reading this, and go for it in your own style. But if you are an ordinary person trying to persuade ordinary people, read on, and be prepared, not for memorizing rules, but for developing a sense of what writing feels good and why.

Imagine yourself surveying a battlefield. Bodies are everywhere, some alive, some dead, some salvageable with proper treatment. Your job is triage. You must bypass the corpses, get them out of the picture, and devote yourself to life. Every word is a body. Ask yourself about each, "Is it alive?" If it is barely alive, ask if it is worth saving.

Dead Words

Does the "very" in "It was a very hot day" make the day feel hotter? Hmmm. How about those high-falutin' transitions:

It may be recalled that. . . .

In this regard, it is interesting to point out the fact that. . . .

To Michaelangelo, every piece of marble had a form hidden in it. He had only to chisel through to reveal a Pieta or a Moses. So it is with verbs hidden in and weighted down by noun forms like these:

negotiation

administration

documentation

utilization

transmittal

"Mr. Jones had the company's authorization" is correct, but "The company authorized Mr. Jones" is better. "They made a determination of" is correct, but "They determined" is better. Notice how many such words are in the sample sentence.

Whether a word is dead depends mainly on what it is doing in a sentence. Some words are dead because they are redundant. If every word cost you a dollar, which ones would you use? Surely not the italicized words in these phrases:

ask *the question whether*

advance planning

consensus *of opinion*

Some dead words are prepositions leading other dead words or phrases. Look at the sample sentence and see how many nouns with good verbs hidden in them are used as objects of prepositions. Prepositions should alert you to search for corpses, which also abound in these kinds of fancy phrases lawyers use when they could use one word:

in the event of (if)

in order to (to)

for the purpose of (for)

for the reason that (because)

at this point in time (now)

with regard to (about)

Have you ever noticed what new awareness does for you on any subject? Say you decide to have your yard landscaped. Suddenly you "see" colors and shapes of leaves, heights of bushes, effects of monkey grass along the sidewalk. Awareness works the same for everything from cars to gender roles. Something must first make you notice. Then you will see more and more refinements. So it is for writing.

How many times have you been told to avoid passive construction? Passive construction bloats sentences with dead words, especially those marbled verbs and excess prepositions. See how much garbage the sample sentence's passivity creates.

Passive construction backs ideas timidly into the reader's mind. Passivity is not merely a writing problem. It is a responsibility problem. Will the real subject of the sample sentence please stand up? The word "by" in a passive sentence often precedes and announces the real subject. "Defendants," not the "conspiracy," were the bad actors in the sample sentence. Put them where they belong and see how fast editing goes.

A sentence often feels passive when its verb is a form of "to be." Being is a passive thing to do. Being is nice for philosophers to speculate about, but it does not exactly sit up and sing. "The day was hot and humid" is not as active as "The day steamed." Instead of telling what, make the reader feel how. The following sentence combines a passive verb ("exists") in the main clause with another weak form, a conditional verb ("would preclude"), in a dependent clause:

> There exists no issue of material fact which would preclude the granting of this summary judgment.

Make the same point actively in fewer than half the words:

> No material fact issue prevents summary judgment.

Do not use conditional forms like "would" and "could" unless you really mean to speak conditionally, as in, "Mr. Jones would pay his debts, but he has no money."

Sometimes you will purposely weaken a point. "Intentionally untruthful testimony" is a lie. If there is a reason not to come out and say "lie," fine. Otherwise, be courageous and say what you mean. And when you do use a strong word, do not take the wind out of it with a timid modifier:

> somewhat terrified
>
> a bit malicious
>
> rather dishonest

The result is absurd, like being slightly pregnant.

Think about what it is like to start watching a movie that is half over. You may get the general idea, but you have to guess what happened before you came in. Then you can hang around and see the first part to find out if you guessed right. Trying to figure out what you should already know wastes mental energy, which should be spent understanding an idea.

There is an order that ordinarily makes sense for storytelling:

> Once upon a time, there was a boy. He was a mean boy. He played a dirty trick on his brother. He told their mother his brother had a ride home from school when he didn't. So his brother waited outside the school for his mother, who never came.

The story is easy to follow because each sentence supplies the information necessary to understand the next. The sample sentence does it backwards. It starts describing the conspiracy before it tells that there is a conspiracy and tells that there is a conspiracy before it tells who is responsible. The reader's mind wastes energy holding unrelated facts until it gets the basic who and what that make it all fit. That is fine if the purpose is to hide the ball, to create tension or suspense, but not if the purpose is to make the reader relax and curl up with your idea.

Short Sentences

Although it is easier to keep your ideas straight with short sentences than with long ones, logical unfolding is not necessarily related to the length of a sentence. The first four sentences in the mean boy story also unfold logically as one sentence:

> The mean boy played a dirty trick on his brother by telling their mother the brother had a ride home from school when he did not.

It is easier to write short sentences and turn them into a longer one than to write a long, convoluted sentence and break it into short ones in logical sequence. Whenever you write a long sentence, however, be sure you have not so separated the subject and the verb that the reader forgets who before learning what.

Although construction, not length, determines whether a sentence is easy to read, a good rule of thumb is to average about 20 words to a sentence. Some long sentences, well constructed, are interesting. Some very short ones are powerful as karate chops.

Varying sentence length purposely for effect goes beyond avoiding bad habits. It goes to stage two of the Ba Theory. Having assured that your reader will not develop a tummy ache or be seized with an impulse to run and hide, you can concentrate on rockabye good feelings to make the reader want to snuggle closer to your idea.

Serve with Spice

Legal writing tends to be bland. You have an edge if you can serve your idea with spice. Remember the old metaphors and similes from freshman English? They not only surprise, they clarify, by casting ideas in concrete and familiar forms. They tell little stories that are fun.

See how a simile conveys the impact of a transaction that dictated the parties' positions in a future plan of reorganization:

> In short, the parties to the PSA transaction were like actors given their lines to be recited on cue. When faced with a formal reorganization plan, they were bound to perform the roles assigned to them in the PSA transaction.

And notice how you can ridicule the attempt to stretch a case too far: Compare the parties to "Cinderella's stepsisters, pinching and straining to claim a glass slipper that does not fit." The stepsister simile evokes all the connotations of the Cinderella story—not only that the slipper did not fit the stepsisters but that they knew it was not theirs. Besides being ugly and clumsy, they were cynical, deceptive, and comical.

An analogy is sometimes a most powerful argument:

> The Union's argument that the [stock purchase program] equals a plan of reorganization not only lacks support, it lacks logic: They say restructuring of debtor's equity is an essential element of a plan; therefore, all restructuring of equity must signify a plan. The fallacy: All apple pies contain apples; therefore, all apples must be in apple pies.

In addition to the apple pie analogy, the paragraph makes its point by parallelism. Parallelism may also be used within sentences or paragraphs and often provides rhythm and repetition like this:

> The DC 10–30 lease transaction has nothing in common with the PSA transaction and the *Braniff* decision. It conditions nothing on a plan of reorganization. It dictates no voting for a future plan. It requires no release of claims against any party. It alters no priority. It evades no disclosures. It leaves inviolate those "hurdles erected in Chapter 11" to be scaled in a future reorganization plan.

Parallelism makes a sentence or paragraph easier to understand by exploiting the mind's natural comfort in order and predictability. It emphasizes similar relationships.

The DC 10–30 paragraph combines parallelism with contrast by negation. By saying what the proposed transaction does not do, it highlights what the transaction does do. It outlines the picture, clarifying what is in and what is out.

In another example of parallel construction, Bill Pannill of Houston, Texas (former Editor-in-Chief of LITIGATION), combined simile, parallelism, and negation by contrast to emphasize the hypertechnicality of the court's decision in a will case:

> Making a will is not playing a game or assembling a puzzle. It is not running an obstacle course. It is the final solemn act of a lifetime. It is an act of supreme importance to the dying.

The paragraph also persuades by shifting from the abstract to the human. The following sentence humanizes still further by painting a picture:

> The decision of the Court in this case is wrong. It is wrong as a matter of statutory interpretation and application. It is wrong as a matter of justice. It is also wrong because the respondent has been deprived of her right to an appellate ruling on her Point No. 3 in the Court of Appeals. If a woman can walk into a bank carrying a will prepared by a lawyer, sign the will in a ceremony attended by her lawyer and two other witnesses, have two witnesses subscribe under her signature and yet fail to make a will, the law does not make sense.

Nothing feels better than to be on the side of justice and morality. But justice and morality have meaning only for people. Humanize your position to dramatize its significance.

Saying point blank that something is right or wrong can be persuasive, but the statement must be well supported or it will ring dogmatic.

Irony, another powerful technique, must be used with care or it will sound sophomoric. When it is directed toward the opponent rather than the argument, it may appear mean or petty. The analogy is to cross-examination in trial, where you must damage a witness's credibility before you go in for the kill, or the jury may identify with the witness instead of you.

To be persuasive, you must establish your own credibility. Trial lawyers know that once a witness's credibility is undermined, it is hard to salvage. The same rule applies to writers. . . . Cite cases incorrectly, and you will deprive yourself, not only of case support, but of credibility. Grammar or spelling errors may also undermine your credibility.

If a cited case is helpful to you, but its language is not well focused for your purposes, paraphrase with more helpful words. But stretch the point beyond reasonable recognition, and you impeach your credibility for all other cases you discuss or cite.

Admitting or giving away a point you have probably lost anyway may enhance credibility, as you know from this kind of jury argument:

> Yes, Mr. Brimble did drink too much before he drove that night. He knows he has a drinking problem. He is not proud of it, and he is not asking you to excuse it. But the fact that he passed out at the stop sign did not give Beulah Bistro the right to ram the back of his pickup.

'Fessing up also works in writing:

> True, Dr. Pangloss did not introduce evidence that Mr. Rambo intended to waive his right to notice. Dr. Pangloss does not rely on the waiver defense. He does rely on estoppel.

To find a good giveaway, make a list starting with your strongest points and graduating to your weakest. Then consider whether you have a point so weak you may gain more by giving it away than by asserting it.

Your strongest-to-weakest list should also dictate the order in which you present your ideas. Use your strongest shots to bias the reader's evaluation of successively weaker points.

Journalists call writing from most to least important the "inverted pyramid." Editors, who may have to cut the story under deadline pressure, can begin at the end and cut paragraph after paragraph, yet leave a story that stands on its own. Especially in a long writing, where the reader's lapsing attention may in effect cut your story, get your best licks in at the beginning.

Now take that principle a step further. You remember your first day of school, first boss, first teacher, first trial. Because your reader is likely to remember best what you say first, begin your writing by summarizing your position in its most compelling light. Transcend technicalities and say exactly what you want your reader to conclude.

The language quoted below is from a response to an appeal challenging Continental Airlines' authority to expand its operation by leasing two aircraft. In a preliminary statement, counsel touted Continental's success under Chapter 11 and stressed that the airline industry is extremely competitive and that Continental has obtained its financial results, not by shrinking from the competition, but by challenging it vigorously in the marketplace.

> The Institutional Creditors . . . want to treat Continental's bankruptcy like the liquidation of the corner grocery store. Their constricted approach misses the point of Chapter 11 not merely to keep the debtor from dying, but to restore it to health and vigor.

Do Not Appear Defensive

The preliminary statement sets the mood for an offensive argument. The challenge of responding to a writing—to an appellant's brief, for example—is not to appear defensive. To avoid sounding defensive, do not repeat your opponent's position followed by your response. Repetition reinforces. Assert your idea positively, negating your opponent's by implication.

Do not be controlled by your opponent's overall organization. A logical order for your opponent may make sense for you, too, or it may put you on the defensive when you need not be. It may be better to stress a different order of importance, so that you need not respond dutifully to each point raised against you. Better yet, develop an argument that will subsume several of your opponent's points and cast them in a light favorable to you.

Headings and subheadings also help to focus the issues on your terms. Depending on the nature, complexity, and length of your writing, use them to assert your points in positive words. Headings should be short and easy to read. Like newspaper headlines, they oversimplify. Use that fact to your advantage. In a brief, headings and subheadings together form an assertive outline and table of contents. Repeating an idea in a table of contents, headings, and text creates familiarity and comfort. It reinforces.

Headings and subheadings do double duty. In addition to pointing the reader in the right direction, they require white space, and white space is restful. Reading is, after all, a visually aesthetic experience. The eyes see patterns on paper before the brain recognizes meaning.

A gray page is deadly. Paragraph indentations on a page promise a breath of air after submersion in an idea. White space lets you relax your focus as though you were gazing at the horizon. Leave good size margins and extra space between sections of your writing. Center quotes or lists.

The eye seeks variety, though not busy-ness. Underlinings, italics, and all capital letters vary the appearance of writing. They are refreshing in small doses but tiring in many single-spaced lines.

Change the scenery and rest the mind with pictures, plats, graphs, flowcharts, lists, or diagrams. Consider not only what already is, but what could be, in visual form. For example, a complex real estate transaction is clarified by a picture showing the flow of deeds and lien documents.

Footnotes interrupt the flow of argument, especially in the middle of a sentence or paragraph. Use them only if they are worth the interruption, and try to put them where there is a natural break or at the end of your writing.

The end of this writing has come, though there is no end of guidelines for persuasive writing, each with its elaborations and exceptions. Do not try to memorize rules. Instead, recall that the reader is a human being who wants first not to have an unpleasant reading experience and second to have a pleasant one. Writing your way into the nursery is hard labor, but better hard writing than hard reading.

Brian Garner
HBR GUIDE TO BETTER BUSINESS WRITING 3
Harvard Business Press (2013)

Know Why You're Writing

Many people begin writing before they know what they're trying to accomplish. As a result, their readers don't know where to focus their attention or what they're supposed to do with the message. So much depends on your *purpose* in writing that you must fix it firmly in your mind. What do you want the outcome to be? Do you want to persuade someone to sign a franchise contract, for instance? Or to stop using your trademark without permission? Or to come to a company reception?

Say clearly and convincingly what the issue is and what you want to accomplish. With every sentence, ask yourself whether you're advancing the cause. That will help you find the best words to get your message across.

Form follows function

Say your firm rents space in an office building that has thoroughly renovated the entrance and the entire first floor. Your general counsel has alerted you that the landlord has violated the Americans with Disabilities Act (ADA). For example, there are no wheelchair-access ramps or automatic doors. You've decided to write to the landlord. But *why* are you writing? The answer to that question determines much of what you'll say and *all* of the tone that you'll use. Consider three versions of the letter you might write:

Version #1

You're good friends with the landlord, but you think that the law should be followed for the good of your employees and your customers. Purpose: to gather more information. Tone: friendly.

Dear Ann:

The new foyer looks fantastic. What a great way for us and others in the building to greet customers and other visitors. Thank you for undertaking the renovations.

Could it be that the work isn't finished? No accommodations have yet been made for wheelchair accessibility—as required by law. Perhaps I'm jumping the gun, and that part of the work just hasn't begun? Please let me know.

Let's get together for lunch soon.

All the best,

Version #2

You're on good terms with the landlord, but on principle, you don't like being in a building that isn't ADA-compliant. You have a disabled employee on staff, and you want the situation righted. Purpose: to correct the oversight. Tone: more urgent.

Dear Ann:

Here at Bergson Company, we were delighted when you renovated the first floor and made it so much more inviting to both tenants and visitors. We are troubled, however, by the lack of wheelchair-access ramps and automatic doors for handicapped employees and customers, both of which are required by state and federal law. Perhaps you're still planning that part of the renovations. If so, please advise.

If this was a mere oversight, can you assure us that construction on ramps and automatic doors will begin within 60 days? Otherwise, as we understand it, we may be obliged to report the violation to the Vermont Buildings Commission. Without the fixes, you may be subject to some hefty fines—but we feel certain that you have every intention of complying with the law.

Sincerely,

Version #3

You've had repeated problems with the landlord, and you have found a better rental property elsewhere for your company. Purpose: to terminate your lease. Tone: firm, but without burning bridges.

Dear Ms. Reynolds:

Four weeks ago you finished renovating the first floor of our building. Did you not seek legal counsel? You have violated the Americans with Disabilities Act—as well as state law—by failing to provide a wheelchair-access ramp and automatic doors for handicapped visitors and employees. Because four weeks have elapsed since you completed the work, we are entitled under state law to terminate our lease. This letter will serve as our 30 days' notice.

Although we have no doubt that your oversight was a good-faith error, we hope that you understand why we can't stay in the building and have made plans to go elsewhere.

We hope to remain on friendly terms during and after the move.

Sincerely,

These three letters are quite different because you are writing them to accomplish different things. Focus on the reaction you're trying to elicit from the reader. You want results. Yet notice how even the sternest letter—Version 3—maintains a civil tone to foster goodwill. No hostility is necessary.

Recap

- Consider your purpose and your audience *before* you begin writing, and let these guide both what you say and how you say it.
- Plainly state the issue you're addressing and what you hope to achieve.
- Keep your goal in mind: Don't undermine your efforts with a hostile or inappropriate tone.

Understand Your Readers

Communication is a two-way exercise. Without knowing something about your readers—and about psychology in general, for that matter—you'll rarely get your ideas across. What are their goals and priorities? What pressures do they face? What motivates them?

Respect readers' time constraints

The most important things to realize about all business audiences are these:

- Your readers are busy—*very* busy.
- They have little if any sense of duty to read what you put before them.
- If you don't get to your point pretty quickly, they'll ignore you—just as you tend to ignore long, rambling messages when you receive them.
- At the slightest need to struggle to understand you, they'll stop trying—and think less of you.
- If they don't buy your message, you may as well have stayed in bed that day.

Each of these universal tendencies becomes magnified as you ascend the ranks of an organization. Your job as a writer, then, is to:

- Prove quickly that you have something valuable to say—valuable to *your readers,* not just to you.
- Waste no time in saying it.
- Write with such clarity and efficiency that reading your material is easy—even enjoyable.
- Use a tone that makes you likable, so that your readers will want to spend time with you and your message.

Do these things and you'll develop a larger reservoir of goodwill. You'll not only have a genuinely competitive edge, but you'll also save time and money.

Tailor your message

If you're writing a memo to colleagues, for example, consider where they sit in the organization and what they're expected to contribute to its success. Or if you're responding to a client's request for proposal, address every need outlined in the RFP—but also think about the client's industry, company size, and culture. Your tone will change depending on your recipients, and so will your content. You'll highlight the things they care about most—the ever-important "what's in it for them."

Connect with particular readers to connect with large audiences

It's challenging to write for a large, diverse group of readers, especially if you don't know them. But you can make it easier by focusing on some specific person you know. In his preface to the U.S. Securities and Exchange Commission's *Plain English Handbook,* Warren Buffett suggests grounding your prose by having a particular reader in mind:

> When writing Berkshire Hathaway's annual report, I pretend that I'm talking to my sisters. I have no trouble picturing them: Though highly intelligent, they are not experts in accounting or finance. They will understand plain English, but jargon may puzzle them. My goal is simply to give them the information I would wish them to supply me if our positions were reversed. To succeed, I don't need to be Shakespeare; I must, though, have a sincere desire to inform.

If you focus on a smart nonspecialist who's actually in your audience—or, like Buffett, imagine that you're writing for a relative or a friend—you'll strike a balance between sophistication and accessibility. Your writing will be more appealing and more persuasive.

Your readers may have little or no prior knowledge about the facts or analysis you're disclosing. But assume that they're intelligent people. They'll be able to follow you if you give them the information they need, and they won't be bamboozled by empty, airy talk.

NOT THIS:	**BUT THIS:**
We aspire to be a partner primarily concerned with providing our clients the maximal acquisition of future profits and assets and focus mainly on clients with complex and multi-product needs, large and midsized corporate entities, individual or multiple entrepreneurial agents, and profit-maximizing institutional clients. By listening attentively to their needs and offering them paramount solutions, we empower those who wish to gain access to our services with the optimal set of decisions in their possible action portfolio given the economic climate at the time of the advice as well as the fiscal constraints that you are subject to. Against the backdrop of	We're a client-focused firm dedicated to making sure you get the most out of our services. Our client base includes individual entrepreneurs, midsized companies, and large corporations. If you decide to do business with us, we'll give you financial advice that is in tune with the current economy and with what you can afford to invest. For years, we've consistently received the highest possible industry ratings, and we have won the coveted Claiborne Award for exceptional client satisfaction 17 of our 37 years in business. We hope to have the opportunity to work with you in

NOT THIS:	BUT THIS:
significant changes within our industry, we strive to ensure that we consistently help our clients realize their goals and thrive, and we continue to strengthen the coverage of our key clients by process-dedicated teams of senior executives who can deliver and utilize our integrated business model. On the back of a strong capital position and high levels of client satisfaction and brand recognition, we have achieved significant gains in market share. We hope that you have a favorable impression of our company's quantitative and qualitative attributes and will be inclined to utilize our services as you embark on your financial endeavors.	your financial endeavors.

Recap

- Understand that your readers have no time to waste: Get to the point quickly and clearly to ensure that your message gets read.
- Use a tone appropriate for your audience.
- Emphasize the items most important to your readers. If they can easily see how your message is relevant to them, they will be more likely to read it and respond.
- Choose an intelligent, nonspecialist member of your audience to write for—or invent one—and focus on writing for that person. Your message will be more accessible and persuasive to all your readers as a result.

Divide the Writing Process into Four Separate Tasks

Do you feel anxious every time you sit down to write? Your main difficulty is probably figuring out how to begin. Don't try to picture the completed piece before you've gathered and organized your material. It's much too soon to think about the final, polished product—and you will just make the challenge ahead of you seem overwhelming. The worry can take more out of you than the actual writing.

Instead, break up your work. Think of writing not as one huge task but as a series of smaller tasks. The poet, writer, and teacher Betty Sue Flowers has envisioned them as belonging to different characters in your brain: MACJ.[1] That stands for Madman-Architect-Carpenter-Judge, representing the phases that a writer must go through:

- **The Madman** gathers material and generates ideas.
- **The Architect** organizes information by drawing up an outline, however simple.
- **The Carpenter** puts your thoughts into words, laying out sentences and paragraphs by following the Architect's plan.
- **The Judge** is your quality-control character, polishing the expression throughout—everything from tightening language to correcting grammar and punctuation.

You'll be most efficient if you carry out these tasks pretty much in this order. Sure, you'll do some looping back. For example, you may need to draft more material after you've identified holes to fill. But do your best to compartmentalize the discrete tasks and address them in order.

Get *the Madman started*

Accept your good ideas gratefully whenever they come. But if you're methodical about brainstorming at the beginning of the process, you'll find that more and more of your good ideas will come to you early—and you'll largely prevent the problem of finally thinking of your best point after you've finished and distributed your document.

Get your material from memory, from research, from observation, from conversations with colleagues and others, and from reasoning, speculation, and imagination. The problem you're trying to solve may seem intractable, and you may struggle to find a good approach. (How on earth will you persuade the folks in finance to approve your budget request when they're turning down requests left and right? How will you get the executive board to adopt a new mind-set about a proposed merger?) Don't get hung up on the size of the challenge. Gathering ideas and facts up front will help you push through and defuse anxiety about the writing.

How do you keep track of all this preliminary material? In the old days, people used index cards. (I wrote my first several books that way.) But today the easiest way is to create a rough spreadsheet that contains the following:

- Labels indicating the points you're trying to support.

---

[1] Betty S. Flowers, "Madman, Architect, Carpenter, Judge: Roles and the Writing Process," *Proceedings of the Conference of College Teachers of English* 44 (1979): 7–10.

- The data, facts, and opinions you're recording under each point—taking care to put direct quotes within quotation marks.
- Your sources. Include the title and page number if citing a book or an article, the URL if citing an online source. (When writing a formal document, such as a report, see *The Chicago Manual of Style* for information on proper sourcing.)

As you're taking notes, distinguish facts from opinions. Be sure to give credit where it's due. You'll run aground if you claim others' assertions as your own, because you'll probably be unable to back them up convincingly. Worse, you'll be guilty of plagiarism.

This groundwork will save you loads of time when you're drafting and will help you create a well-supported, persuasive document.

Let the Architect take the lead

You may feel frustrated at first as you're groping for a way to organize your document. If a sensible approach doesn't come to mind after you've done your research and scouted for ideas, you may need to do more hunting and gathering. You want to arrive at the point of writing down three sentences—complete propositions—that convey your ideas. Then arrange them in the most logical order from the reader's point of view (see chapter 4), That's your bare-bones outline, which is all you typically need before you start drafting.

Give the Carpenter a tight schedule

The key to writing a sound first draft is to write as swiftly as you can (you'll read more about this in chapter 5). Later, you'll make corrections. But for now, don't slow yourself down to perfect your wording. If you do, you'll invite writer's block. Lock the Judge away at this stage, and try to write in a headlong rush.

Call in the Judge

Once you've got it all down, it's time for deliberation—weighing your words, filling in gaps, amplifying here and curtailing there. Make several sweeps, checking for one thing at a time: the accuracy of your citations, the tone, the quality of your transitions, and so on. (For an editorial checklist, see chapter 6.) If you try to do many things at once, you won't be doing any of them superbly. So leave plenty of time for multiple rounds of editing—at least as much time as you spent researching and writing. You'll ferret out more problems, and you'll find better fixes for them.

Recap

- Approach a writing project as a series of manageable tasks using the MACJ method.

- Use the Madman to gather research and other material for the project, diligently keeping track of quotations and sources. And allow more of your best ideas to come early by methodically brainstorming at the beginning of the process.
- As the Architect, organize the Madman's raw material into a sensible outline. Distill your ideas into three main propositions.
- In the Carpenter phase, write as quickly as possible—without worrying about perfecting your prose.
- Finally, assume the role of the Judge to edit polish, and improve the piece. Do this in several distinct passes, each time focusing on only one element of your writing.

POST-CLASS REFLECTION MEMO

Draft and submit a memo in response to the questions below:

- Think about sharing your work with other students. How did you experience giving and being critiqued?
- How did your work change after the critique?

CHAPTER 18

ESTABLISHING PROFESSIONAL BOUNDARIES

LEARNING GOALS

The learning goals for this class include helping you to:

- Identify, anticipate, and plan the situations in which professional boundary issues may arise
- Understand the complexities involved and potential for individual differences in defining where an individual lawyer may draw the line on a boundary issue
- Identify and fully explore potential constraints imposed by the Rules of Professional Conduct
- Understand the long-term implications of short-term choices

DESCRIPTION OF CLASS

In class, we will explore some of the challenges inherent in establishing professional boundaries with our clients. We will consider several different scenarios, each of which focuses on a different boundary scenario that frequently arises in clinic cases, and brainstorm a range of possible responses.

ASSIGNMENT IN PREPARATION FOR CLASS

Reflect on one or two challenging experiences you have had in establishing an interpersonal boundary with someone—a family member, a friend, an intimate partner, someone at work. Consider the following questions, and jot down notes to bring to class (the notes are to help guide your thinking, and will not be distributed):

Identify and describe the situation in which you felt you needed to draw a boundary. (It does not matter whether or not you ultimately did so, or did so successfully; just think of a situation where you felt that a boundary was needed.)

- What options were available to you in this situation?
  - What were the pros and cons of each option?
- Did you ultimately decide to draw a boundary in this situation?
  - If so, how did you do it, in terms of words and/or actions?
  - If not, why not?
- How did your decision affect your relationship with the other person?
- When you reflect on this boundary-drawing experience, what connections do you see with places where you have (or would expect to) draw boundaries with a client?
- How does your decision about where to draw boundaries relate to your vision of yourself as a lawyer?
  - About the relationships you want to have with clients in the clinic and in your future professional life?

READING ASSIGNMENT

1. Jane Aiken & Stephen Wizner, *Law as Social Work*, 11 WASH. U. J. L. & POL'CY 63 (2003).
2. Establishing Professional Boundaries: "Model Rules of Professional Conduct, " (https://georgetown.box.com/s/5oyn7vibchc1nwkzewqt.

   NOTE: Lawyers often assume that the *Rules of Professional Conduct* provide concrete guidance about the appropriate boundaries of an attorney-client relationship. In fact, they offer precious little help in this area. To prepare for class, skim the *Rules* to gain familiarity about the few places where they address any aspect of the boundaries that attorneys are required to set when defining the scope and substance of their relationships with clients.

READING

Jane Aiken and Stephen Wizner
Law as Social Work
11 WASH. U. J. L. & POL'CY 63 (2003)[1]

"THIS ISN'T LAW, IT'S SOCIAL WORK"

In our work as lawyers for low income clients and as clinical teachers, we are sometimes told by our professional counterparts in private practice—especially those who work in large corporate firms—that what we do "isn't law, it's social work." Similarly, our students sometimes complain that the work they do on behalf of low income clients "isn't law, it's social work."

In the past we have tended to respond to this "social worker" charge defensively. We insisted that what we . . . do *is* "law," that it is really no different from what private practitioners do for their paying clients, and that in many ways it is even more legally complex and sophisticated than much of what private lawyers do.

While this response is superficially true, on a deeper level it tends to obscure an important dimension of our work as . . . lawyers. . . . Our work does have an important social function. At its best, law is more than a business or trade by which lawyers use their education, training, professional license to earn a comfortable living by pursuing and protecting the personal—and typically, economic—interests of the clients who retain them, whoever those clients might be.

We have come to realize that our defensive response to the accusation that what we do is social work is the wrong response. What we should be saying is: "You're right. What *we* do *is* social work, and that is why it is so challenging and so important." As poor people's lawyers and as clinical teachers we should embrace and celebrate the truth of the claim that what we do is indeed social work.

Of course, simply saying that our practice of law is, or ought to be, "social work," is something of a play on words. There are significant differences in the professional education, training, expertise, practice, and professional ethics of lawyers and social workers. While we do not wish to ignore or minimize these differences, we do want to argue that there is much in social work education, ethics, and practice that can and should be adopted by lawyers. These qualities are especially important for those who represent, and those who teach others to represent, both low income and disadvantaged clients.

---

[1] Footnotes omitted.

THE ETHICAL WORDS OF LAWYERS AND SOCIAL WORKERS

It is commonly accepted that the professional expertise of lawyers is limited to "legal" issues: those involving the identification, interpretation, and application of relevant legal rules and concepts. Lawyers provide legal advice, counsel, representation, and advocacy to and on behalf of individual clients in private legal settings and public legal arenas. Pursuing social justice is not an explicit goal of the legal profession.

If lawyers think about social justice at all, they will see it as emerging from counseling and advocacy by individual lawyers on behalf of individual clients within the adversary system. Most lawyers do not view the pursuit of social justice as an obligation or function of their professional work.

The closest that lawyers' ethical rules come to articulating a social role for lawyers is found in the non-mandatory Preamble and pro bono provision of the Rules of Professional Conduct. The Preamble serves as a general introduction to the rules and as an overview of lawyers' professional responsibilities. It makes reference to "the legal profession's ideals of public service." However, it neither spells out what these ideals are, nor imposes any particular professional obligation that lawyers must perform. Similarly, the ethical rule regarding pro bono representation of those who are unable to afford legal services reads as an aspiration or recommendation, not an enforceable ethical duty.

In contrast to the generally accepted, narrowly legal and individualistic professional role of lawyers, social workers have adopted a broad, flexible, and multi-faceted professional role. This role not only focuses on the individual client, but also on the client's family and community, including the social, economic, racial, ethnic, and religious factors affecting the client's life. In addition, social justice is an explicit ethical norm of the social work profession, not only in process, but also as a substantive outcome.

The term "social work" often connotes a profession composed of caseworkers employed by public or private non-profit agencies whose work is limited to counseling and assisting primarily poor individuals and families to solve immediate "social work" problems. This role is similar to the narrow and individualistic role of lawyers with respect to legal problems. Yet the profession itself defines a much broader role for social workers, in that it encompasses not only individual casework, but also group work, community organizing, and social reform. The pursuit of social and economic justice and reform are as central to the professional obligations of social workers, as is the problem solving for individual clients and the empowerment of individuals, groups, and communities.

The Code of Ethics that guides the professional practice of social workers sets forth the pursuit of social justice as a "core value":

> *Social Workers challenge social injustice.*
>
> Social workers pursue social change, particularly with and on behalf of vulnerable and oppressed individuals and groups of people. Social workers' social change efforts are focused primarily on issues of poverty, unemployment, discrimination, and other forms of social injustice. These activities seek to promote sensitivity to and knowledge about oppression and cultural and ethnic diversity. Social workers strive to ensure access to needed information, services, and resources; equality of opportunity; and meaningful participation in decision making for all people.

In their education and training, social workers learn skills that are invaluable in their professional relationships with clients. Their clients include the poor, immigrants, children, the elderly, and individuals with serious illnesses, or those with physical, mental, or emotional disabilities. These skills include empathic interviewing, listening, and counseling; cross-cultural awareness and sensitivity; identification of the causes of clients' problems; assisting clients to formulate goals and strategies for achieving them; crisis intervention; group work; and community organizing.

Social workers employ a systems theory approach in their work, which means that they consider all aspects of a client's life and that they view clients in their social environment. Social workers consider not only the immediate problem faced by a client (as a lawyer might do), but also the "system" within which the client exists. In particular, social workers consider family, community, and other social and economic forces that affect the client, such as poverty, discrimination, and educational and employment opportunities.

Except in law school clinical programs, lawyers typically do not receive instruction in the skills of interacting with clients, particularly those from different economic, social, racial, ethnic, or religious backgrounds. There is no professional expectation or ethical rule that requires a lawyer to learn these professional skills, other than the general rule requiring lawyers to be "competent."

In contrast, one ethical principle of the social work Code of Ethics provides that "[s]ocial workers respect the inherent dignity and worth of the person." The Code further expounds on this principle by stating that:

> Social workers treat each person in a caring and respectful fashion, mindful of individual differences and cultural and ethnic diversity. Social workers promote clients' socially responsible self-determination. Social workers seek to enhance clients' capacity and opportunity to change and to address their own needs. . . .

As lawyers for low income clients and as clinical teachers, these social work ethical principles are ones that we can not only accept, but should embrace wholeheartedly. They are entirely consistent with what we see as effective lawyering on behalf of low income and disadvantaged clients. . . .

At their best, social workers have both the passion and ambition to serve the poor and oppressed, to use their professional skills to struggle against injustice, to help strengthen groups and communities, and to imagine better worlds and engage in social action to try to realize them.

Of course not all, or even most, social workers are motivated by such moral passion and ambition. Nor do they conduct their professional lives in a manner that reflects a commitment to social justice. Likewise, most lawyers do not and will not do so. Viewing and teaching law as "social work," in the aspirational sense of that term, would provide a good theoretical and practical model for us to follow. Social workers and lawyers, at their best, not only provide caring support and advocacy for the poor and powerless but contribute their professional knowledge and skills to the struggle against social injustice and economic exploitation. In function, they work for social change.

The social work profession manages to train its professionals with little of the disengagement that [some find] in legal education. Rarely, if ever, is the social worker challenged with a statement of, "that's not social work, that's law." Service to clients and the pursuit of justice are professional values that lawyers and social workers hold in common. Nevertheless, there are differences between law and social work that influence the differing experiences of law students and candidates for social work degrees. Legal training has little to do with fostering a passion for social justice. The law school curriculum is designed to neutralize that passion by imposing a rigor of thought that divorces law students from their feelings and morality. The law student is taught to be a dispassionate evaluator of both the client's case and the law governing it. By contrast, social work programs are apprentice based and require substantial hours in the field, by working with clients. All of this work with clients requires students to learn much more about their own values, beliefs, prejudices, and how they influence their interactions with clients. The ethical standards of social work mandate that social workers develop cultural competence, as well as a knowledge of social diversity and oppression as a prerequisite for practicing social work. The closest educational opportunity in a law school setting for this is within a clinical program.

In contrast to the typical educational experience of a law student, a social work student has had hundreds of hours of supervised clinical experience by the time he completes a graduate social work program. He has had to confront his own personal background and experience, and must evaluate their effect on his ability to interact with clients. He has learned that in order to serve clients well, it is most often necessary to view the larger picture. This results from seeing enough institutional problems to learn that there are systemic and structural roots to most client problems. Indeed, he is likely to have taken courses that help him identify the ways in which political, social, and economic forces create and sustain many problems of the poor. He may even have thought about ways in which he can contribute to collective efforts to remedy some of the problems of the poor and to empower disadvantaged individuals and communities.

We believe that teaching law students about the role of lawyers in challenging injustice and working for social change is an appropriate—indeed, obligatory—concern of legal education. Social justice education has the potential for inspiring students of law to engage in committed social work on behalf of the disadvantaged and powerless.

We are not saying that all lawyers can or should be social workers. We are only saying that social work skills and values, and the social work commitment to social and economic justice, should be part of the lawyer's repertoire of skills, values, and commitments. Further, the professional and social role of lawyers should be broadened to incorporate a social work dimension.

In arguing that lawyers should see themselves not only as legal technicians, but also as social workers, we are not unmindful of certain significant differences in the ethical obligations of lawyers and social workers, such as those obligations pertaining to confidentiality and mandatory reporting. As important as those differences may be, we want to emphasize the commonalities between law and social work practice, especially on behalf of socially and economically disadvantaged clients.

When social workers learn the law that governs the areas of their practice, and act as advocates on behalf of their clients, no one claims that what they are doing is "law, not social work." Rather, they are seen as broadening their knowledge and skills in order to be better social workers. That is what we aspire to for lawyers. We wish to help lawyers develop their "social work" knowledge and skills, and adopt social work values, in order to become better lawyers.

THE LAWYER AS SOCIAL WORKER

The lawyer we envision, one who manifests the characteristics of the lawyer as social worker . . . is competent within the field of law in which she practices and possesses a high level of specialized knowledge and skill. She has chosen her field of practice because she sees it as instrumental in achieving justice for her clients. She demonstrates a passion for her work and a dedication to excellence. She spends time with her clients, listening empathically to their accounts of the problems they face. She strives to understand the context in which the problems arose, and assists her clients to decide upon realistic goals and the best methods of achieving them. She recognizes that though adversarial litigation may be available, in many cases, it might not be in the clients' best interest.

The lawyer we envision attempts to grapple with the multitude of issues that the client might be facing. She attempts to look for root problems and solutions, and serves her clients holistically. She develops cultural competence and respect for difference. She seeks to understand the nature of social diversity and oppression with respect to race, ethnicity, national origin, color, sex, sexual orientation, age, marital status, political belief, religion and mental or physical disability. She is aware of the ways in which her own experience affects her perceptions of the client, the client's problem, and the possible solutions.

She makes efforts to empower the client by promoting the client's socially responsible self-determination. She treats each client with dignity, and in a caring and mindful fashion. She takes her role as a counselor seriously, which is to help each client clarify his or her goals for the short run and the long term. She considers the impact of the law on the client and the client's community when determining what might be a good legal outcome. She notes common patterns and seeks legal law reforms that might address on a systemic level the individual problems that clients bring to her.

She recognizes the connections between her personal choices and her clients' choices or lack of choices. She makes efforts to lend her privilege to more vulnerable individuals and groups. She engages in social and political action to ensure that all people have access to the resources, employment, services, and opportunities that they require to meet their basic human needs and to develop their potential.

The lawyer as social worker recognizes that all problems arise within a community and that even those problems that appear purely individual have a basis within that community. The problem may arise as a result of the community. For example, a disabled child may be having difficulty obtaining special education assistance because there are no advocacy organizations to ensure that children with special needs are accommodated. The problems that individual clients encounter certainly have an impact on the community, and the lawyer as social worker is sensitive to those effects. While helping a parent negotiate the intricacies of the special education laws and bureaucracy, the lawyer may think about policy initiatives that could provide broader help to other parents, who may not be able to obtain a lawyer. The lawyer may assist in bringing together the parents of children who are victimized by a school's zero-tolerance policies, and she may assist them in identifying legal, social, economic, and political interventions. The lawyer as social worker might offer training in lay advocacy and education about parents' and children's rights.

The lawyer as social worker spends a good deal of time with the client, and also in the community to gain insight into the context in which problems may arise. She establishes a trusting relationship with her clients by being reliable, following problems through completion, being a good listener, and being committed to client empowerment She is attentive to the many constituencies within the community that work toward that community's goals. She provides assistance to community groups, but may also facilitate links between individual clients and those proactive organizations. For example, a client who seeks an order of protection might be interested in organizations challenging welfare to work, in child care cooperatives, and in community economic development organizations that might provide her with employment. A client with an eviction problem might be interested in joining a tenant union, assisting in community economic development, and in groups advocating for affordable housing.

Social work identifies client empowerment and client investment in problem solving as one of the primary goals of the social worker/client relationship. There is no reason why this should not also be true of the lawyer/client relationship. The lawyer recognizes that unless the client is a partner in problem solving, the best that the lawyer can do is obtain a "legal solution" to a narrowly defined problem, a problem often defined by the lawyer as being limited to the solutions provided within existing law. Such a response may isolate the client and insulate the problem from its context. It may thus imply that the legal problem is idiosyncratic, and will dissuade engagement in the larger dialogue about justice.

The lawyer as social worker who works with groups recognizes that she is merely a resource, not the director of the activity. Once again, client empowerment is the goal and the use of coalition as a powerful tool. The lawyer assists the group in gaining access to courts and legislatures, in drafting legislative materials, and in researching available options. The lawyer can also facilitate the growth of the organization by referring potential clients to the group. The lawyer can offer insights into what kinds of class actions or legislative changes are necessary to meet the needs of the group.

POST-CLASS REFLECTION MEMO

Draft and submit a memo in response to the questions below:

- How will your insights about establishing professional boundaries affect your casework over the next several days or weeks?
- What concrete actions will you take based on these insights?

CHAPTER 19

CONDUCTING ROUNDS

LEARNING GOALS

The learning goals for this class include helping you to:

- Learn how to effectively reflect on and learn deeper lessons from your experience
- Understand and adopt a systematic method of reflection and learning that you can use effectively throughout your professional lives
- Surface common challenges that arise across different lawyering contexts
- Shift toward independent ownership of the learning and lawyering experience
- See that even at the outset of your careers you have much to teach and to learn from each other
- Understand the importance of a full exploration of the facts at an early stage of the problem-solving process
- Share the knowledge, experience, and challenges faced by all participants in the clinic, and thus enhance the learning of the entire group

DESCRIPTION OF CLASS

In class, we will discuss challenges that have arisen in your clinic client representation this semester. The discussion will be structured to best ensure that we are able to fully explore each factual situation presented, offer a variety of diagnoses, brainstorm multiple possible solutions, and check in with the presenter to ensure that the discussion has been a useful one.

ASSIGNMENT IN PREPARATION FOR CLASS

This class will be a "rounds" session. To prepare, please identify a challenge that has arisen in connection with your client, case, or project. You may be asked to serve as facilitator of a rounds discussion with your clinic colleagues. The most useful challenges for rounds discussions tend to be those where you perceived the choices available to you as significantly difficult or risky, and where the issues are either still pending or where the resolution was, in your view, less than successful. The challenge should be one for which you believe that your own thinking might benefit from group input. Once you have a challenge in mind, please describe it in as much detail as possible to provide a concrete sense of the issue as you experienced it. Please address the following topics:

- What is the context of the lawyering challenge you would like to discuss? What background information should the group have about the case, the client, the other participants, and the larger context, so that we can understand the issues raised?
- What is your diagnosis of the lawyering challenge, both in terms of the issue itself as well as its underlying causes (e.g., if the issue involves a client who has not provided specific, detailed information about important facts, what is your theory of what happened and why it happened in this particular instance, with this particular client)?
- How does your diagnosis relate to the lawyering approach you have used or intend to use?
- Why did you choose or why are you considering choosing to approach the issue as you did?
- Why did this issue feel so challenging?

Although it will not be possible for everyone to present their identified challenge, you will all have the opportunity to actively participate in the rounds led by your colleagues, as well as other opportunities to lead a rounds session later in the semester.

POST-CLASS REFLECTION MEMO

Draft and submit a memo in response to the question below:

- Name one specific way you will you use the lessons you have learned in this class to change or improve your clinic casework.

HANDOUT FOR CONDUCTING ROUNDS

Stages of Rounds Guide

1. Fact Gathering
2. Problem Diagnosis
3. Question Flooding
4. Problem Solving
5. Check-In
6. Reflection

CHAPTER 20

TARGETED LAWYERING ROUNDS

Includes Class Plans for:

Professional Ethics
Issues of Difference
Challenging Assumptions
Critical Reflections on System Change
Lawyering Performance Rounds

ROUNDS ON PROFESSIONAL ETHICS

LEARNING GOALS

The learning goals for this class include helping you to:

- Consider the *Model Rules of Professional Conduct* in a real-life client representation context
- Identify and fully explore potential behavioral constraints imposed by the *Rules*
- Critically examine the practical realities and the politics of the *Rules* as a system for ensuring appropriate professional behavior
- Make connections between the operation of the *Rules* and the availability of justice

ASSIGNMENT IN PREPARATION FOR CLASS

Please submit a memo that responds to the following questions:

- Identify one or more of the [state] *Rules of Professional Conduct* which has been brought to life through your experience representing clients. Describe how this has occurred.
- Did this experience lead you to understand the *Rule(s)* differently than you did when you examined them in a classroom or in any other more theoretical context?
- How has this experience affected your perceptions about the lawyer's professional role?
- How has this experience shaped your understanding of the norms of the legal profession?
- How has this experience made you think differently about how you, as an individual, feel both ease and tension with these norms?
- What implications do these reflections have in terms of broader social justice issues?

POST-CLASS REFLECTION MEMO

Draft and submit a memo in response to the questions below:

- Name one specific way you will you use the lessons you have learned in this class to change or improve your clinic casework.
- What concrete steps will you take to implement this change?

ROUNDS ON DIFFERENCE

LEARNING GOALS

The learning goals for this class include helping you to:

- Identify differences between yourself and your clients
- Consider how those differences can affect the lawyering process
- Develop strategies for dealing with differences in productive ways

---

ASSIGNMENT IN PREPARATION FOR CLASS

Please submit a memo that responds to the following questions:

- Identify a fundamental difference between you and at least one of your clients (for example, this could include race, gender, or class).
- How did this difference affect your relationship with your client, explicitly and/or implicitly?
- How did this difference affect your lawyering?
- What, if anything, surprised you about this experience of difference?
- Did you and your client discuss this difference?
    - Why or why not?
    - If your answer is yes, what worked about the conversation?
    - What didn't work?
- What strategies or methods do these reflections inspire you to consider as you look toward representing clients in the future?

POST-CLASS REFLECTION MEMO

Draft and submit a memo in response to the questions below:

- Name one specific way you will you use the lessons you have learned in this class to change or improve your clinic casework.
- What concrete steps will you take to implement this change?

ROUNDS ON CHALLENGING ASSUMPTIONS

LEARNING GOALS

The learning goals for this class include helping you to:

- Identify the deeply-rooted schema, or assumptions about meaning, which each of us instinctively use as lenses for interpreting new experiences

- Surface ways in which these schema can interfere with full, particularized understanding of new experiences
- Understand the potential negative impact of assumptions on high-quality lawyering
- Develop strategies for pushing past assumptions in your professional life.

ASSIGNMENT IN PREPARATION FOR CLASS

Please submit a memo that responds to the questions stated below:

- Identify an assumption you have made during your clinic experience. The assumption could be about our clients (or a particular client), a category of system actors you have encountered, the justice system as a whole, the role of lawyers in society, or anything else, but it must be something that you believed, but that was not based on actual facts or extensive experience.
- Examine the assumption you have identified. What was its source?
  - Something about your life experience?
  - Lack of life experience?
  - The media?
  - Anything else?
- How has this assumption affected your lawyering in general?
- How has this assumption played out in a concrete way in your clinic experience?
- What strategies or methods do these reflections inspire you to consider as you look toward representing clients in the future?

POST-CLASS REFLECTION MEMO

Draft and submit a memo in response to the questions below:

- Name one specific way you will you use the lessons you have learned in this class to change or improve your clinic casework.

- What concrete steps will you take to implement this change?

ROUNDS ON CRITICAL REFLECTION AND SYSTEM CHANGE

LEARNING GOALS

The learning goals for this class include helping you to:

- Adopt a big-picture, constructively critical perspective about the lawyering process and the legal system in which you have been steeped during clinic
- Make connections between smaller scale experiences with client representation and larger-scale, systemic problems
- Understand the lawyering role in multiple dimensions, including direct representation and work toward system change
- Realize the power inherent in a law degree for contributing to high-impact social change

---

ASSIGNMENT IN PREPARATION FOR CLASS

Take some time to think broadly about your experiences with client representation. Submit a memo that responds to the following questions:

- Identify and describe in detail a systemic challenge you have encountered during clinic. The challenge you focus on should be one for which you believe group discussion would be useful to deepening your own understanding of and insight into the problem. You can choose anything at all—issues related to attorney-client relationships and boundaries; the work/art of collaboration; the process of shifting roles from student to professional attorney; the justice/injustice of the legal system; etc.
- What is it that is troubling you?
    - Why did this issue feel so challenging?
    - What was it that really got to you about the problem you have identified?

- In what context did this issue arise for you during your clinic experience?
    - What background information should your clinic colleagues have so that we can fully understand the issues raised?
- What is your diagnosis of the underlying causes of the problem?
    - In other words, what is your theory of why this is happening?
- In light of your diagnosis, what approach or approaches might you or your colleagues use to alleviate or resolve this problem?
- How does your proposed solution relate to your diagnosis?

POST-CLASS REFLECTION MEMO

Draft and submit a memo in response to the questions below:

- Name one specific way you will you use the lessons you have learned in this class to change or improve your clinic casework.
- What concrete steps will you take to implement this change?

LAWYERING PERFORMANCE ROUNDS: CROSS EXAMINATION

LEARNING GOALS

The learning goals for this class include helping you to:

- Learn how to effectively reflect on and learn deeper lessons from your experience
- Understand and adopt a systematic method of reflection and learning that you can use effectively throughout your professional life
- Surface common challenges that arise across different lawyering contexts

- Shift toward independent ownership of learning and lawyering experience
- See that even at the outset of your careers, you have much to teach and learn from each other
- Share the knowledge, experience, and challenges faced by all participants in the clinic, and thus enhance the learning of the entire group

---

ASSIGNMENT IN PREPARATION FOR CLASS

Assign each student who is working on a cross examination in an actual clinic case to present the cross in the rounds session. Ask the students to prepare a brief presentation for their colleagues on the following issues:

- What are the facts of the case (in brief)?
- What is the case theory?
- What are the major strengths and weaknesses (factual and legal) of the case?
- Introduce the class to the witness being cross-examined.
- What role does the witness play?
- What are your goals in the cross examination?
- What particular challenges are you facing, where your colleagues' input would be most helpful?

POST-CLASS REFLECTION MEMO

Draft and submit a memo in response to the questions below:

- Name one specific way you will you use the lessons you have learned in this class to change or improve your clinic casework.
- What concrete steps will you take to implement this change?

CHAPTER 21

EXPLORING JUSTICE

LEARNING GOALS

The learning goals for this class include helping you to:

- Make connections between particular experiences with client representation and the more general systemic issues of justice
- Recognize that the concept of justice can have varied meanings, depending in part on context and perspective
- Develop an understanding of how lawyers make choices that can have an impact on the use of the justice system to remedy social problems

---

DESCRIPTION OF CLASS

This class is designed to create an opportunity for you to reflect on your semester and engage in a focused conversation about justice: How should we define it? What role should our concept of justice play in what we call the "justice system?" How have our conceptions of justice changed over time? What is the nature and scope of each lawyer's responsibility to make justice happen? The class will begin by thinking about the many meanings of justice. We will then look at the challenges our clients face and how we might use the legal system to correct injustice. Finally, we will discuss how a commitment to justice is likely to influence our professional lives.

ASSIGNMENT IN PREPARATION FOR CLASS

In class, we will reflect on our experiences in the semester thus far and how they relate to broad questions of working to promote justice. Before class, please think about the following questions:

1. What does "justice" mean to you?

2. Take a moment to reflect on your client representation experiences in clinic.

   - What insights have those experiences given you into the justice system?
     - How effective is the justice system for our clients?
     - How well does it meet our clients' needs?
   - What other social problems have affected your client or had an impact on your ability to achieve justice for your client?
   - How might your client answer the question "what does justice mean to you?"

READING ASSIGNMENT

1. Statistics on Inequality:

   "Exploring Justice: Inequality Is . . ." https://georgetown.box.com/s/5oyn 7vibchc1nwkzewqt

   "Exploring Justice: Understanding Inequality with Data." https:// georgetown.box.com/s/5oyn7vibchc1nwkzewqt

2. William Quigley, Revolutionary Lawyering: Addressing The Root Causes of Poverty and Wealth, 20 WASH. U. J.L. & POL'Y 101 (2006).

3. Jane Harris Aiken, Striving to Teach "Justice, Fairness, and Morality," 4 CLIN. L. REV. 1 (1997).

4. *Model Rules of Professional Conduct, Public Service*, Rule 6.1 Voluntary Pro Bono Publico Service and commentary, "Exploring Justice: Rule 6.1 and Commentary." https://georgetown.box.com/s/5oyn 7vibchc1nwkzewqt.

READINGS

William Quigley
Revolutionary Lawyering: Addressing the Root Causes of Poverty and Wealth
20 WASH. U. J.L. & POL'Y 101 (2006)

INTRODUCTION

There are more than enough lawyers in this world defending the way things are. Plenty of lawyers protect and guide people and institutions engaged in the injustices of our social, economic and political systems, which are steeped in racism, militarism and materialism. They are plentiful and well-compensated. We need no more of them.

Poverty, wealth, racism, materialism and militarism cannot be changed by aiming at small revisions or modest reforms. If we are going to transform our world, we need lawyers willing to work with others to dismantle and radically restructure our current legally protected systems. We need revolutionaries. Martin Luther King, Jr.'s, call for a radical revolution of values can be the basis for revolutionary lawyering.

Lawyers can be revolutionaries. Martin Luther King called each of us to join together to undergo a radical revolution of values and to conquer racism, materialism, and militarism.[32] He did not say his call extended to everyone except lawyers. He also did not call us to merely reform racism, materialism and militarism. Revolutionaries are called not just to test the limits of the current legal system or to reform the current law, but also to join in the destruction of unjust structures and systems and to tear them up by their roots. We are called to replace them with new systems based on fairness and justice.[33]

It is true that lawyers are rarely revolutionaries. In fact, the idea may seem like an oxymoron (like corporate ethics), but some people are, and others can be, revolutionary lawyers. Our profession is, at the core of its practice, the primary profession world-wide that protects and defends the machines, computers, profit motives and property rights so rightly condemned by Dr. King.[34] We use our training, wealth, and position in society to facilitate commerce without conscience, to accumulate wealth without responsibility, and to serve the needs of corporations over and above the rights and needs of people. Yet still, some lawyers can be revolutionaries.

Part I of this Article highlights some of the most glaring details about poverty, wealth and the working poor and provides some facts about

---

[32] *Id.*

[33] *Id.*

[34] *Id.*

racism, materialism and militarism, both nationally and internationally. The briefest look at who is rich and who is poor, and the reasons behind such status, demonstrates the continued accuracy of Dr. King's prophetic description of why a radical revolution of values is needed, now even more than when he first spoke these words. Part II of this Article discusses some areas of the law that need radical change, law that needs to be torn up by its roots and replaced. Part III reflects on how lawyers who want to be revolutionaries can do so. The Article concludes with signs of hope and a charge to lawyers to consider joining the radical revolution of Dr. King.

I. POVERTY, WEALTH, THE WORKING POOR, RACISM, MATERIALISM, AND MILITARISM

Hope has two beautiful daughters: anger and courage; anger at the way things are, and courage to change them.

—Augustine of Hippo[35]

One of my friends, who has gone to federal prison twice for protesting U.S. training of military human rights abusers, is also a counselor for incest survivors. She told me that in her experience, there are only three ways to deal with evil. The first is to fight evil with evil. The second is to say that there is nothing I can do and turn away. The third is to look at evil head-on and try to meet it with love.[36]

In order to address poverty, wealth and the working poor, we must first look at these phenomena head-on, even if it angers us. We must face the way things actually are in our nation and in our world. Then we must have the courage to change them.

This section begins with a Social Justice Quiz to reveal some facts about poverty, wealth and the working poor in light of racism, materialism and militarism. The answers to these questions are in the footnotes.

A. *Social Justice Quiz*

1. In 1968, the minimum wage was $1.60 per hour.[37] How much would the minimum wage be today if it had kept pace with inflation?[38]

---

[35] David Krieger, *Rising to the Challenge of Peace,* WAGING PEACE, Nov. 25, 2003, http://www.wagingpeace.org/articles/2003/11/25_krieger_challenge-peace.htm.

[36] Interview with Judy Bierbaum, School of Americas Watch, Columbus, Ga. (Jan. 22, 2004).

[37] Paul K. Sonn, *Citywide Minimum Wage Laws: A New Policy Tool for Local Governments,* ECON. POL'Y BRIEF (Brennan Ctr. for Justice, New York, N.Y.), June 2005, at 6 n.2, *available at* http://www.brennancenter.org/programs/downloads/minimumwage-policybrief.pdf.

[38] *Id.* at 1.

2. In 1965, CEOs of major companies made twenty-four times more money than the average worker.[39] In 2003, CEOs earned how much more than the average worker?[40]

3. The nation has 3066 counties.[41] In how many of them can someone who works full-time and earns the federal minimum wage afford to pay rent and utilities on a one-bedroom apartment?[42]

4. How much must the typical U.S. worker earn per hour to rent a two-bedroom apartment if that worker dedicates thirty percent of his income, as suggested, to rent and utilities?[43]

5. How many people in the United States earn poverty-level wages of less than $8.19 per hour?[44]

6. To what are the combined populations of Alabama, Arkansas, Iowa, Kansas, Kentucky, Maine, Minnesota, Mississippi, Nebraska, North Dakota, Oregon, South Dakota and Tennessee equivalent?[45]

7. What do you get when you add to the last figure the populations of Delaware, Hawaii, Montana, New Hampshire, New Mexico, Rhode Island, Vermont, West Virginia and Wyoming?[46]

8. "In 2001, the average financial wealth for black households was only about 12% of the average for white households."[47] What was the median financial wealth for blacks?[48]

9. In the entire twenty-eight year history of the Berlin Wall, 287 people perished trying to cross it. In the ten years since the Clinton administration implemented the current U.S. border strategy with Mexico, how many people have died trying to cross?[49]

---

39 ECON. POLICY INST., STATE OF WORKING AMERICA 2004/2005: WAGES 2, *available at* http://www.epinet.org/books/swa2004/news/swafacts_wages.pdf.

40 *Id.*

41 *Study Finds Housing Costs Outpace Incomes of the Working Poor*, N.Y. TIMES, Dec. 25, 2004, at A21.

42 In only *four* of the nation's 3066 counties can someone who works full-time and earns the federal minimum wage afford to pay rent and utilities on a one-bedroom apartment. *Id.*

43 The typical U.S. worker must earn $15.37 per hour in order to dedicate thirty percent of their income to housing costs. *Id.*

44 More than thirty million workers in 1999. William P. Quigley, ENDING POVERTY AS WE KNOW IT: GUARANTEEING A RIGHT TO A JOB AT A LIVING WAGE 24 (2003).

45 The number of people in the United States living below the official poverty line. *Id.* at 23–24.

46 The total number of people below 125% of the official poverty line—the combined populations of twenty-two states. *Id.*

47 Econ. Policy Inst., STATE OF WORKING AMERICA 2004/2005: MINORITIES 2, *available at* http://www.epinet.org/books/swa2004/news/swafacts_minorities.pdf.

48 $1100, less than three percent of the corresponding figure for whites. *Id.*

49 Almost ten times as many—more than 2500 people—have died trying to cross. Marc Cooper, *On the Border of Hypocrisy,* L.A. WEEKLY, Dec. 5, 2003, *available at* http://www.commondreams.org/scriptfiles/views03/1204-10.htm.

10. Where does the U.S. rank worldwide in the imprisonment of its citizens?[50]

11. In 2004, what was the direct reported U.S. military budget?[51]

12. In 2004, the U.S. military budget was how many times larger than the Chinese military budget, the second largest spender?[52]

13. How many times larger is the U.S. military budget than the combined spending of the "rogue states" of Cuba, Iran, Iraq, Libya, North Korea, Sudan, and Syria?[53] The U.S. military budget is larger than how many of the next largest countries' budgets combined?[54]

14. The difference in income per capita between the richest nation and the poorest nation in 1750 was about five to one. What is it today?[55]

15. Of the 6.2 billion people in the world today, how many live on less than $1 per day?[56] How many live on less than $2 per day?[57] The richest 1% in the world receive as much income as what percentage of the poorest?[58]

16. The U.S. Congress under President Bush has been more generous in helping poor countries than under President Clinton.[59] In 2003, the United States increased official development assistance to poor countries by one-fifth.[60] Where does the U.S. contribution rank among the top twenty-two countries in proportion to our economy?[61]

---

[50] First. In 2004, the United States imprisoned over 700 persons per 100,000. Russia was second with 534. SENTENCING PROJECT, FACTS ABOUT PRISONS AND PRISONERS (2005), *available at* www.sentencingproject.org/pdfs/1035.pdf.

[51] In 2004, the direct reported U.S. military budget was over $399 billion, or $12,000 per second. *See* Anup Shah, High Military Expenditure in Some Places, http://www.globalissues.org/geopolitics/armstrade/spending.asp (last visited Feb. 5, 2006).

[52] Eight times larger. *Id.*

[53] The U.S. military budget was more than thirty times as large as the combined spending of these seven "rogue states." *Id.* Even if you add China and Russia's military spending to that of the seven potential enemies, all nine nations together spent $134.2 billion, thirty-four percent of the U.S. military budget. *Id.*

[54] The U.S. military budget is more than the combined spending of the next twenty-three nations. *Id.*

[55] Today, the difference between the richest nation, Switzerland, and the poorest nation, Mozambique, is about 400 to 1. David S. Landes, THE WEALTH AND POVERTY OF NATIONS: WHY SOME ARE SO RICH AND SOME SO POOR, at xx (1st ed. 1998).

[56] Of the 6.2 billion people in the world today, 1.2 billion live on less than $1 per day. UNITED NATIONS DEV. PROGRAMME, HUMAN DEVELOPMENT REPORT 2002: DEEPENING DEMOCRACY IN A FRAGMENTED WORLD 17 (Stephanie Flanders & Bruce Ross-Larson eds., 2002), *available at* http://hdr.undp.org/reports/global/2002/en/pdf/front.pdf.

[57] 2.8 billion people live on less than $2 per day. *Id.*

[58] The richest 1% in the world receives as much income as the poorest 57% combined. *Id.* at 19.

[59] Nicholas D. Kristof, Op-Ed., *Land of Penny Pinchers*, N.Y. TIMES, Jan. 1, 2005, at A23.

[60] *Id.*

[61] Last. *Id.*

17. Americans on average give how much per day in government assistance to poor countries?[62]

18. Americans on average spend how much on soft drinks each day?[63]

* * * *

These eighteen questions and their answers illustrate that poverty, racism, materialism and militarism have flourished, while working people, human rights, and human dignity have been downsized. There are an unlimited number of additional facts showing that despite incredible world-wide wealth, there are millions of working poor people in deep poverty in this country, and billions more throughout the world.

B. *Growing Economic Inequality in the U.S.*

Growing economic inequality in the U.S. is not some socialist-spun critique. Work and poverty walk hand-in-hand.[64] According to a recent twenty-seven city survey of hunger and homelessness by the U.S. Conference of Mayors, thirty-four percent of the adults requesting emergency food assistance were employed.[65] Even bastions of unrestrained capitalism such as the *Wall Street Journal* and *The Economist* note the growing income gap in the United States.

The *Wall Street Journal* recently published a series on the lack of social mobility in the United States.[66] It reported:

> Escalators of social mobility haven't compensated for the growing distance between economic cellar and penthouse; America has become more unequal in the past 35 years, but it's no more common for people to rise from poverty to prosperity or to fall from wealth to the middle class. Researchers find less intergenerational mobility in the U.S. than academics believed a couple of decades ago. And available evidence suggests that an

---

[62] Americans, on average, give fifteen cents per day in government aid to poor countries. *Id.*

[63] Sixty cents. *Id.*

[64] *See generally* Stephanie Luce, FIGHTING FOR A LIVING WAGE (2004); QUIGLEY, *supra* note 14; Jerold L. Waltman, THE CASE FOR THE LIVING WAGE (2004).

[65] Press Release, U.S. Conference of Mayors, Hunger, Homelessness Still on the Rise in Major U.S. Cities 2 (Dec. 14, 2004), *available at* http://usmayors.org/uscm/news/press_releases/documents/hunger_121404.pdf.

"The president and other political leaders should be focused on rewarding work with living wages, not accepting that 34 percent of adults needing food are employed." Claire McKeever, *Am Working and Hungry,* SOJOURNERS, June 2005, at 10 (quoting Yonce Shelton, public policy director for Call to Renewal in Washington, D.C.).

[66] Bob Davis, *Lagging Behind the Wealthy, Many Use Debt to Catch Up,* WALL ST. J., May 17, 2005; Robert Frank, *Rich vs. Richer: In Palm Beach, The Old Money Isn't Having a Ball,* WALL ST. J., May 20, 2005; David Wessell, *As Rich-Poor Gap Widens in the U.S., Class Mobility Stalls,* WALL ST. J., May 13, 2005; David Wessell, *How Parents, Genes and Success Intersect,* WALL ST. J., May 26, 2005.

> American's economic fate is more closely tied to his or her parents than a continental European's.[67]

The Economist agreed:

> There is little doubt that the American social ladder is getting higher. In 1980–2002 the share of total income earned by the top 0.1% of earners more than doubled. But there is also growing evidence that the ladder is getting stickier: that intergenerational mobility is no longer increasing, as it did during the long post-war boom, and may well be decreasing.[68]

The *New York Times* began this analysis with a series on class in the United States.[69] Bob Hebert summarized "The Mobility Myth":

> Consider, for example, two separate eras in the lifetime of the baby-boom generation. For every additional dollar earned by the bottom 90 percent of the population between 1950 and 1970, those in the top 0.01 percent earned an additional $162. That gap has since skyrocketed. For every additional dollar earned by the bottom 90 percent between 1990 and 2002 . . . each taxpayer in that top bracket brought in an extra $18,000.
>
> It's like chasing a speedboat with a rowboat. Put the myth of the American Dream aside. The bottom line is that it's becoming increasingly difficult for working Americans to move up in class. The rich are freezing nearly everybody else in place, and sprinting off with the nation's bounty.[70]

Likewise, the enduring effects and practices of racism are part of the institutional structure of this country and of many parts of the world. In this country:

> If you lined up all African-American families by the amount of assets they owned minus their debts and then looked at the family in the middle, that median family in 2001 had a net worth of $10,700 (excluding the value of automobiles). Line up all whites, and *that* median family had a net worth of $106,400, almost 10 times more. Less than half of African-American families own their own home, while three out of four white families do. Latinos are even less wealthy: the median Latino

---

[67] *See* Wessell, *How Parents, Genes and Success Intersect, supra* note 36.

[68] *Minding About the Gap*, ECONOMIST, June 15, 2005.

[69] Anthony DePalma, *15 Years on the Bottom Rung,* N.Y. TIMES, May 26, 2005; Timothy Egan, *No Degree, and No Way Back to the Middle,* N.Y. TIMES, May 24, 2005; Bob Hebert, *The Mobility Myth,* N.Y. TIMES, June 6, 2005; David Leonhardt, *The College Dropout Boom,* N.Y. TIMES, May 24, 2005; Tamar Lewin, *A Marriage of Equals,* N.Y. TIMES, May 19, 2005; Janny Scott & David Leonhardt, *Class in America: Shadowy Lines that Still Divide,* N.Y. TIMES, May 15, 2005.

[70] Hebert, *supra* note 39.

family in 2001 had only $3000 in assets, and less than half own their own homes.[71]

No one seriously contests the disparities among whites, African-Americans and Latinos in the United States. While some suggest that these disparities are behind us, it is difficult to take those arguments as anything other than evidence of continuing racism.

The racial wealth gap is not only real, but it is also understandable and predictable when one considers decades of government policies that directly, openly, and systematically discriminated against people on the basis of race. Native Americans, Latinos, African-Americans and Asians were consciously excluded by both law and practice from many government wealth-building opportunities.[72] Similar gaps exist in employment, with more than one in ten African-Americans unemployed—more than twice the rate for whites.[73] Moreover, there is evidence that this racial employment gap is increasing.[74] Racism, militarism and materialism are flourishing in the U.S.

C. World Economic Injustice

There is enough food to feed everyone in the world.[75] Yet the United Nations announced that the number of hungry people in the world is increasing.[76] There are approximately 798 million people world-wide who are chronically hungry—one out of every seven persons, and more people than the total population of Latin America and sub-Saharan Africa combined.[77] Other reports predict that the number of hungry people is even higher.[78]

---

[71] Meizhu Lui, DOUBLY DIVIDED: THE RACIAL WEALTH GAP 42 (2004), http://www.racialwealthdivide.org/documents/doublydivided.pdf.

[72] Randall L. Kennedy, *Racial Critiques of Legal Academia,* 102 HARV. L. REV. 1745 (1989); James A. Kushner, *Apartheid in America,* 22 HOW. L.J. 547 (1979); Martha Mahoney, *Law and Racial Geography: Public Housing and the Economy in New Orleans*, 42 STAN. L. REV. 1251 (1990); John A. Powell, *Opportunity-Based Housing,* 12 A.B.A. J. AFFORDABLE HOUSING & COMMUNITY DEV. L. 188 (2003); Florence Wagman Roisman, *Sustainable Development in Suburbs and Their Cities: The Environmental and Financial Imperatives of Racial, Ethnic, and Economic Inclusion,* 3 WIDENER L. SYMP. J. 87 (1998); Lee Payne, *FDNY Puts out No Welcome Mat for Blacks,* NEWSDAY, Jan. 27, 2002, at B6.

[73] Dena Libner, *Unequal Recovery: Unemployment Rates Show African Americans Losing Ground While Whites Regain Their Footing,* DOLLARS & SENSE, May-June 2005, at 31, *available at* http://www.allbusiness.com/periodicals/article/496969-1.html.

[74] *Id.* at 30–31.

[75] The Food and Agricultural Organization (FAO) of the United Nations noted in a 1998 report that "[i]f the available food was distributed according to need, it would be sufficient to feed everyone in the world." *See* FAO, Map Shows the Food Supply Gap Between Rich and Poor Countries, http://www.fao.org/NEWS/1998/981204-e.htm (last visited Feb. 12, 2006).

[76] Robert F. Drinan, *Report Shows World Hunger Increasing,* NAT'L CATHOLIC REP., Apr. 2, 2004, at 17.

[77] *Id.*

[78] *Hunger Costs Millions of Lives and Billions of Dollars—FAO Hunger Report,* FAO NEWSROOM, Dec. 8, 2004, http://www.fao.org/newsroom/en/news/2004/51809/index.html (estimating that there are 852 million hungry people world-wide).

Over eleven million children under the age of five die each year from preventable diseases like diarrhea, respiratory illnesses, measles and malaria.[79] In 2000, it was estimated that sixty percent of those deaths were associated with undernutrition.[80] Indeed, diarrhea is a major killer of young children, and the risk of death from this infectious disease is nine times higher for children who are significantly underweight;[81] in the 1990s it killed more children than the total people lost to armed conflict since the Second World War.[82] In sub-Saharan Africa alone, 4.8 million children under the age of five die each year—nine children per minute.[83]

Over 14,000 children die each day from malnutrition and hunger in a world that has enough food? And another 17,000 children die each day from diseases that are preventable? Over 30,000 children each day needlessly die of poverty and unjustly distributed resources.[84] There is food available in the countries where poor people are starving, but it is not freely distributed. In Niger, for example, the U.N. World Food Programme explains that "interfering with the free market could disrupt Niger's development out of poverty."[85]

While there may be conflicting evidence on whether the world is growing more or less unequal as a whole, there is little argument that the distance between those at the very top and those at the very bottom continues to grow dramatically.[86] "The top one-tenth of U.S. Citizens now receive a total income equal to that of the poorest 2.2 billion people in the rest of the world."[87]

To repair this inequality, a radical revolution is needed. Laws that create and support these unjust systems are one of the places to start.

---

[79] FAO, THE STATE OF FOOD INSECURITY IN THE WORLD: 2002, at 6, *available at* http://www.fao.org/docrep/005/y7352e/y7352e00.htm.

[80] *Id.* at 7.

[81] *Id.* at 6.

[82] UNITED NATIONS DEV. PROGRAMME, HUMAN DEVELOPMENT REPORT 2003, at 9, *available at* http://hdr.undp.org/reports/global/2003/pdf/hdr03_frontmatter.pdf.

[83] UNITED NATIONS DEV. PROGRAMME, SUB-SAHARAN AFRICA—THE HUMAN COSTS OF THE 2015 "BUSINESS-AS-USUAL" SCENARIO 1 (2005), *available at* http://hdr.undp.org/docs/events/Berlin/Background_paper.pdf.

[84] *See supra* notes 45–52 and accompanying text.

[85] Jeevan Vasagar, *Plenty of Food—Yet the Poor Are Starving,* GUARDIAN (London), Aug. 1, 2005, at 1.

[86] *Rich and Poor in the Global Economy: Interview with Bob Sutcliffe,* DOLLARS & SENSE, Mar.–Apr. 2005, at 13.

[87] *Id.* Sutcliffe explains the differing indications of inequality:

> Over the last 25 years, you find that the bottom half of world earners seems to have gained something in relation to the top half (so, in this sense, there is less inequality), but the bottom 10% have lost seriously in comparison with the top 10% (thus, more inequality), and the bottom 1% have lost enormously in relation to the top 1% (much more inequality). None of these measures is a single true measure of inequality; they are all part of a complex structure of inequalities, some of which can lessen as part of the same overall process in which others increase.

Id.

II. LAW NEEDS REVOLUTIONARY CHANGE

There is a large and tragic divide between what is legal and what is just. This part of the Article will discuss some areas of the law that need radical change—old law that needs to be torn up by its roots and replaced with new law. It is important, but ultimately insufficient, to insist only on the right of every person to a job and living wages as a means of addressing poverty, wealth and the working poor.[88] The root causes that support and underpin the current unjust systems must instead be identified and dismantled.

It is impossible to build a better house unless one plans to change the foundation. There is not space here to catalogue all the areas of the law that need radical change, but I will briefly analyze several in which change such as that called for by Dr. King can address root causes of poverty, wealth and the working poor.[89] Before looking at these areas of the law in critical and creative ways, we must start by opening and freeing our minds.[90]

A. *The Traditional Role of Lawyers in Supporting the Status Quo*

Freeing our minds requires us to face the role that lawyers really play in our world. As Louis Brandeis said in 1905: "Instead of holding a position of independence between the wealthy and the people . . . able lawyers have . . . neglected their obligation to use their powers for the protection of the people."[91]

Lawyers have lost their way.[92] We only rarely suggest that our profession is one of justice, because we know it is one of law. We no longer worry whether people admire us, as long as they fear us. Some wanted to

---

88 Quigley, *supra* note 14, at 100–36.

89 *See* King, Jr., *supra* note 1. Obviously, these categories could be more extensively analyzed than they are in this Article. However, they are worth mentioning, even briefly, in order to provoke further discussion and action.

90 I recently saw a message about this spray-painted on a railroad car: "You can't escape from prison if you cannot see the bars." One activist told me that "those who want a revolution must realize that those who do not want change have very effectively set up camps of the status quo in our imaginations, so that we cannot even think change is possible." Conversation with Karl Meyer, 2002.

91 Louis D. Brandeis, *The Opportunity in the Law,* 39 AM. L. REV. 555, 559 (1905).

92 *See generally* Anthony T. Kronman, THE LOST LAWYER: FAILING IDEALS OF THE LEGAL PROFESSION (1993) (arguing that the emptiness of the legal profession has lost the ideal of the lawyer-statesman, replaced by the soulless reality of the large urban law firm business); SOL M. Linowitz & Martin Mayer, THE BETRAYED PROFESSION: LAWYERING AT THE END OF THE TWENTIETH CENTURY (1994) (asserting that lawyering as a profession has been abandoned and is now a well-paid business that pays lip service, if that, to the ideals of the past); Deborah L. Rhode, IN THE INTEREST OF JUSTICE (2000) (arguing that the pursuit of money, power and prestige at the expense of the public good removes the legal profession from its connection with justice and meaning); Jean Stefancic & Richard Delgado, HOW LAWYERS LOSE THEIR WAY: A PROFESSION FAILS ITS CREATIVE MINDS (2005) (arguing that the internalized formalism of legal education and relentless pursuit of billable hours beyond real creative and critical analysis of justice ruins the lives of lawyers).

be lawyers to help change the world and believed in our country and in our system, but are now lost.

Our profession now follows the cruel definition of justice outlined by Thrasymachus in Plato's *The Republic*.[93] This sweeping discussion of justice is framed as a dialogue between Socrates and a number of thinkers. One of the most cited passages from *The Republic* is the speech by Thrasymachus.[94] This young man articulates a definition of justice that Plato and Socrates dispute, but the speech outlines what has become the current perspective on justice. Thrasymachus, while arguing with Socrates about what justice really is, says:

> I say that justice or right is simply what is in the interest of the stronger party. . . . Each type of government enacts laws that are in its own interest, a democracy democratic laws, a tyranny tyrannical ones and so on; and in enacting these laws they make it quite plain that what is "right" for their subjects is what is in the interest of themselves, the rulers, and if anyone deviates from this he is punished as a lawbreaker and "wrongdoer." That is what I mean when I say that "right" is the same thing in all states, namely the interest of the established government; and government is the strongest element in each state, and so if we argue correctly we see that "right" is always the same, the interest of the stronger party.[95]

The majority of the legal profession has chosen to adopt Thrasymachus' definition as its workplan for law and justice. The profession works for the interests of the strongest, the richest, and the most powerful. In assisting the rich and powerful, lawyers are but well-fed Doberman Pinschers, protecting the grand homes and institutions of those in control.[96] However, lawyers do not merely protect the powerful; they also enable them.

Lawyers can be and often are destructive of real justice.[97] Lawyers draft justifications for torture.[98] Lawyers draft defenses for tobacco and other toxic poisoning.[99] Lawyers help protect corporations as they engage

---

[93] Plato, THE REPUBLIC 77–78 (Henry Desmond Pritchard Lee trans., 2d rev. ed. Penguin Books 1974).

[94] *Id.*

[95] *Id.*

[96] I had a disappointing conversation with a bright young American student in Haiti who was deeply interested in human rights. He wondered whether he could do more as a lawyer or a doctor. He decided to go into medicine because, he said, "What can lawyers really do? Doctors can at least help people directly in a concrete way. Lawyers . . . what can they actually do?"

[97] *See* David Cay Johnston, PERFECTLY LEGAL: THE COVERT CAMPAIGN TO RIG OUR TAX SYSTEM TO BENEFIT THE SUPER RICH—AND CHEAT EVERYBODY ELSE (2003).

[98] Julie Angell, *Ethics, Torture, and Marginal Memoranda at the DOJ Office of Legal Counsel,* 18 GEO. J. LEGAL ETHICS 557, 557–59 (2005).

[99] Richard A. Daynard, *Lawyer Management of Systems of Evil: The Case of the Tobacco Industry,* 5 ROGER WILLIAMS U. L. REV. 117 (1999).

in fraud and deceit. Will history impose on today's lawyers the same criticisms that it imposed on the lawyers of slave-owners? How will it judge lawyers for the employers of child laborers, or the lawyers for big corporate trusts? What about the lawyers of Nazi Germany? What about the lawyers who prosecuted Susan B. Anthony, Martin Luther King, Jr., Gandhi, or Nelson Mandela? The lawyers who justify the expansion of nuclear weapons? The lawyers who assist in implementing the death penalty? What about the lawyers who defended segregation? Or redlining? Or who lobby against increases in the minimum wage or health insurance?[100]

Those who proclaim their neutrality despite their work for the powerful must realize that neutrality is no excuse. As Archbishop Desmond Tutu explained: "When the elephant has his foot on the tail of the mouse, and you say you are neutral, the mouse will not appreciate your neutrality."[101] Professors Shaffer and Rodes have likewise observed that "[i]f we set out to deal evenhandedly between rich and poor, we will inevitably end up favoring the rich. If we set out to do no more than justice requires, we will end up doing less."[102]

Current professional responsibility courses do not address justice or fundamental inequality and the lawyer's role in fashioning and maintaining that inequality. Instead, the courses are rather like learning the rules in a driver license manual in order to pass the test.[103]

Older lawyers are jaded and many young lawyers are just plain lost. We must undergo, as Dr. King suggested, a radical revolution of our values. For those who want to engage in another type of lawyering, radical change is possible.

B. Radical Change is Possible

We have been taught to believe that radical change is impossible, or at least very, very dangerous. People exploring the possibility for serious change must constantly contend with false messages: "This is the best we can do;" "We live in the most generous and best nation in the history of the world;" "Unrestrained capitalism is the ultimate and only way of solving all our problems;" "Our problems are too big for anyone to handle;" "Go slowly;" "Just look out for number one;" "Do not be a radical;" "Do not be a revolutionary;" and most importantly, "Be afraid, be *very* afraid, of terrorists, illegal immigrants, black men, pushy women, of

[100] For a discussion of lawyers' roles in some of these areas, see Symposium, *Lawyer Collaboration with Systems of Evil,* 5 ROGER WILLIAMS U. L. REV. 19 (1999).

[101] William Sloane Coffin, A PASSION FOR THE POSSIBLE: A MESSAGE TO U.S. CHURCHES 36 (1st ed. 1993).

[102] Thomas L. Shaffer & Robert E. Rodes, Jr., *A Christian Theology for Roman Catholic Law Schools,* 14 U. DAYTON L. REV. 5, 17 (1988).

[103] Thomas L. Shaffer, The Private Practice of Law as the Practice of Social Justice: Hoffman, Field and Brandeis (unpublished manuscript, on file with author).

people who are trying to take advantage of us, of international cooperation, of accountability, and most of all, of big change."

Professor Robert E. Rodes, Jr., elegantly describes the message that radical change in law is dangerous and bad as "a pervasive set of assumptions introduced into the law by false consciousness. These are the assumptions that stand in the way of imposing accountability on the ruling class and making effective use of law for human ends."[104]

Rodes explains four sets of defective assumptions in support of the status quo: (1) the values behind current law are the most important ones for the law to implement; (2) the legal system is basically good and the cost of change will outweigh any benefits; (3) nothing can really be done for those who are left out of current legal arrangements—their situation is an unfortunate but inevitable consequence of this "basically beneficent system;" (4) the political power of those who are left out of this system must be limited or they are likely to upset it, because they cannot understand how good the system really is, how inevitable their suffering is, or how fruitless and counterproductive change will be.[105]

Despite these significant obstacles to radical change in law, history shows that all good ideas for revolutionary change are at first shocking, then resisted, then understood, then enacted, and then described as inevitable. Indeed, as Gandhi said: "First they ignore you, then they ridicule you, then they fight you, then you win."[106] Cautioned by Gandhi, let us now turn to several areas of the law that need radical change.[107]

1. Taking Human Rights Seriously

Taking human rights seriously starts with the simple, yet revolutionary, statement that every single person in the world has inherent and equal dignity and is an equal member of the human family.

> Whereas recognition of the inherent dignity and of the equal and inalienable rights of all members of the human family is the foundation of freedom, justice and peace in the world . . .
>
> . . . .
>
> Whereas the peoples of the United Nations have in the Charter reaffirmed their faith in fundamental human rights, in the dignity and worth of the human person and in the equal

---

[104] Robert E. Rodes, JR., PILGRIM LAW 108 (1998).

[105] *Id.*

[106] Quote DB, Mahatma Gandhi, http://www.quotedb.com/quotes/2776 (last visited Feb. 12, 2006).

[107] Every one of these areas of law is immersed in issues of race, gender, class and sexual identity. These areas are toxins which permeate every institution and person in our society. They are injustices in themselves and they also increase the effects of other kinds of injustices. Unlike a bunch of weeds, they cannot just be pulled out, for they are now in the very earth itself. Challenging these must be a part of every effort to radically restructure our lives. They are a part of every issue we face and a part of how we face ourselves.

> rights of men and women and have determined to promote social progress and better standards of life in larger freedom.
>
> . . . .
>
> All human beings are born free and equal in dignity and rights. They are endowed with reason and conscience and should act toward one another in a spirit of brotherhood.[108]

This is the foundation of the United Nations' Universal Declaration of Human Rights.[109] Moreover, the principles expressed above form the foundation of most world religions.[110] However, our world and our country do not take human rights nearly seriously enough.[111]

The United States acknowledges, to some degree, those procedural and political rights that are incorporated in our Constitution, but repeatedly refuses to take seriously other social, cultural, economic and political human rights.[112] U.S. Supreme Court Justice Ruth Bader Ginsburg acknowledged that "since the United Nations' 1948 adoption of the Universal Declaration of Human Rights, the U.S. Supreme Court has mentioned that basic international Declaration a spare six times—and only twice in a majority decision."[113] However, the U.S. Supreme Court

---

[108] Universal Declaration of Human Rights, G.A. Res. 217A, at pmbl. & art. 1, U.N. GAOR, 3d Sess., 1st plen. mtg., U.N. Doc A/810 (Dec. 12, 1948).

[109] *Id.*

> Article 3. Everyone has the right to life, liberty and security of person.
>
> . . . .
>
> Article 6. Everyone has the right to recognition everywhere as a person before the law.
>
> Article 7. All are equal before the law and are entitled without any discrimination to equal protection of the law.
>
> . . . .
>
> Article 22. Everyone, as a member of society, has the right to social security and is entitled to realization, through national effort and international co-operation and in accordance with the organization and resources of each State, of the economic, social and cultural rights indispensable for his dignity and the free development of his personality.
>
> . . . .
>
> Article 28. Everyone is entitled to a social and international order in which the rights and freedoms set forth in this Declaration can be fully realized.

Id.

[110] *See* Robert Traer, FAITH IN HUMAN RIGHTS: SUPPORT IN RELIGIOUS TRADITIONS FOR A GLOBAL STRUGGLE (1991). Traer cites many examples of religious support for basic human rights, including liberal Protestants, *id.* at 19; Roman Catholics, *id.* at 33; conservative Protestants, *id.* at 49; Jews, *id.* at 99; Muslims, *id.* at 111; and Hindus and Buddhists, *id.* at 129.

[111] For examples, see Jeanne M. Woods & Hope Lewis, HUMAN RIGHTS AND THE GLOBAL MARKETPLACE 3–40 (2005).

[112] "The United States has been also been characterized as a scofflaw for its refusal to abide by those international documents and U.N. resolutions related to human rights to which it has previously agreed." Deborah M. Weissman, *The Human Rights Dilemma: Rethinking the Humanitarian Project,* 35 COLUM. HUM. RTS. L. REV. 259, 313 (2004).

[113] Ruth Bader Ginsburg, *Looking Beyond Our Borders: The Value of a Comparative Perspective in Constitutional Adjudication,* 40 IDAHO L. REV. 1, 8 (2003) (citing Knight v. Florida, 528 U.S. 990, 996 (1999) (Breyer, J., dissenting); Dandridge v. Williams, 397 U.S. 471, 521 n.14

has taken increasing notice of international human rights and practices in deciding recent cases, and many members of the Supreme Court have written and spoken about the need to look to international law in interpreting U.S. law.[114]

In a 2005 case outlawing the imposition of the death penalty upon juveniles, Justice Kennedy observed "the stark reality that the United States is the only country in the world that continues to give official sanction to the juvenile death penalty."[115] Writing for the Court in *Lawrence v. Texas,* Justice Kennedy made a point of citing a 1981 decision of the European Court of Human Rights, now authoritative in forty-five countries, as part of its decision to protect consensual sex between people of the same gender.[116] In a 2003 case upholding academic affirmative

---

(1970) (Marshall, J., dissenting); Zemel v. Rusk, 381 U.S. 1, 4, 15 n.13 (1965); Kennedy v. Mendoza-Martinez, 372 U.S. 144, 161 n.16 (1963); Int'l Ass'n of Machinists v. Street, 367 U.S. 740, 776 (1961) (Douglas, J., concurring); Am. Fed'n of Labor v. Am. Sash & Door Co, 335 U.S. 538, 550 n.5 (1949) (Frankfurter, J, concurring)).

114 Justice Ginsburg advocated in 2003 for courts to look beyond our borders at international law treaties and the experiences of other nations. *See* Ginsburg, *supra* note 83.

Justice Breyer has also advocated for a greater focus on international law in the U.S. courts. *See* Justice Stephen Breyer, Address at the American Society of International Law 97th Annual Meeting: The Supreme Court and the New International Law (Apr. 4, 2003) (transcript available at http://www.humanrightsfirst.org/us_law/inthecourts/Supreme_Court_New_Interl_Law_Just_Breyer.pdf).

Justice Rehnquist wrote:

> For nearly a century and a half, courts in the United States exercising the power of judicial review [for constitutionality] had no precedents to look to save their own, because our courts alone exercised this sort of authority. When many new constitutional courts were created after the Second World War, these courts naturally looked to decisions of the Supreme Court of the United States, among other sources, for developing their own law. But now that constitutional law is solidly grounded in so many countries, it is time that the United States courts begin looking to the decisions of other constitutional courts to aid in their own deliberative process.

William H. Rehnquist, *Constitutional Courts—Comparative Remarks, in* GERMANY AND ITS BASIC LAW: PAST, PRESENT, AND FUTURE—A GERMAN-AMERICAN SYMPOSIUM 411, 412 (Paul Kirchhof & Donald P. Kommers eds., 1993); *see also* Washington v. Glucksberg, 521 U.S. 702, 710 n.8, 718 n.16 (1997) (Rehnquist, C.J.) (referring to a decision of the Supreme Court of Canada that upheld a ban on assisted suicide, and observing that "in almost every western democracy[,] it is a crime to assist a suicide").

In a 2003 speech at the Southern Center for International Studies, Justice O'Connor discussed the concept of "transjudicialism," and advocated a more robust use of international law by American courts. *See* Justice Sandra Day O'Connor, Remarks at the Southern Center for International Studies (Oct. 28, 2003) (transcript available at http://www.humanrightsfirst.org/us_law/inthecourts/SOUTHERN_CENTER_INTERNATIONAL_STUDIES_Justice_O%27Connor.pdf).

In another forum, Justice O'Connor said: "While ultimately we must bear responsibility for interpreting our own laws, there is much to learn from other distinguished jurists who have given thought to the same difficult issues that we face here." Justice Sandra Day O'Connor, Keynote Address Before the 96th Annual Meeting of the American Society of International Law (Mar. 16, 2002), *in* 96 AM. SOC'Y INT'L L. PROC. 348, 350 (2002).

115 Roper v. Simmons, 543 U.S. 551, 574–75 (2005). The majority opinion goes on at some length to review international human rights treaties and the practices of other countries. *Id.* at 575–78.

116 Lawrence v. Texas, 539 U.S. 558, 573 (2003) (citing Dugeon v. United Kingdom, 45 Eur. Ct. H.R. 52 (1981)).

action, Justice Ginsburg, in a concurrence joined by Justice Breyer, pointed out the importance of the International Convention on the Elimination of All Forms of Racial Discrimination, ratified by the United States in 1994.[117] Justice Ginsburg also noted the importance of the 1979 Convention on the Elimination of All Forms of Discrimination Against Women, which the United States has not ratified.[118] In a 2002 decision invalidating the death penalty for mentally disabled offenders, Justice Stevens noted that "within the world community, the imposition of the death penalty for crimes committed by mentally retarded offenders is overwhelmingly disapproved."[119] The Supreme Court's acknowledgment of international human rights is a step in the right direction, but more is needed.

To radically change our world, we must start by taking human rights much more seriously.[120] We must respect the promise of all human rights—personal, civil, political, social, economic and cultural—in our laws. These promises are an overlooked part of U.S. history.[121] Perhaps one of the reasons that few people in power seem to take human rights seriously is because these rights have implications.[122] Certainly, being equal members of the same family has implications.

I was with a group of people recently, and one person told me that her sister had won the lottery—nearly twenty million dollars. But the sister refused to share any of her winnings with her family members. Everyone in the group was horrified and ashamed. How could this be? The first people you share with are your sisters and brothers!

Well, some in our world have won a different kind of lottery, and also refuse to share with their sisters and brothers. Most who have won this lottery—based in large part on where they were born, the color of their skin, their gender, their parent's income, and their opportunity for education—do not even think they "won," but instead think they "earned"

---

[117] Grutter v. Bollinger, 539 U.S. 306, 344 (2003) (Ginsburg, J., concurring).

[118] *Id.*

[119] Atkins v Virginia, 536 U.S. 304, 316 17 n.21 (2002). The *Atkins* court also noted the earlier decision of *Thompson v. Oklahoma,* in which the Court agreed that it was worthwhile to consider the views of "respected professional organizations, by other nations that share our Anglo-American heritage and by leading members of the Western European community." *Id.* (quoting Thompson v. Oklahoma, 487 U.S. 815, 830–31 n.31 (1988)).

[120] *See* Alan Jenkins & Larry Cox, *Bringing Human Rights Home,* THE NATION, June 27, 2005, http://www.thenation.com/doc/20050627/cox.

[121] *See* Cass R. Sunstein, THE SECOND BILL OF RIGHTS: FDR'S UNFINISHED REVOLUTION & WHY WE NEED IT MORE THAN EVER (2004). Sunstein's book addresses one of our nation's best kept secrets—President Franklin D. Roosevelt's proposed Second Bill of Rights. In January, 1944, Roosevelt asked the nation to include a new set of rights for all citizens that included a right to a job that earned a living wage, a right to decent housing, a right to adequate medical care, and a right to a good education. *Id.* at ix. This book is a very welcome addition to the dialogue about human rights. *See also* CHALLENGING U.S. HUMAN RIGHTS VIOLATIONS SINCE 9/11 (Ann Fagan Ginger ed., 2005).

[122] *See infra* Part II.B.2.

their prize![123] Anyone who believes they earned their own fortune by hard work should consider what they would have achieved had they been borne in Sri Lanka or Haiti.[124]

Each person counts as much as everyone else. This is a radical thought with even more radical consequences. If everyone is inherently equal, they do not have to earn their equality, but are entitled to equality in the same way as everyone else simply by the fact that they are human. If everyone is equal and we are all members of the same human family, what does it mean that some are so well off, while tens of thousands of others die in poverty each day? What does it mean to take human rights seriously in a world in which over 30,000 children die each day of hunger and preventable diseases, while the average U.S. citizen contributes just pennies a day through taxes for world poverty relief—less than they spend on soft drinks each day?[125]

Part of taking human rights seriously is taking the idea of common good seriously.[126] Human rights include not only the right to human

---

[123] Listen to Bill Gates, Sr.:

> Individual effort is indispensable to wealth building. But success is not entirely the result of individual brains and effort. Success is a product of having been born in this country, a place where education and research are subsidized, where there is an orderly market, where the private sector reaps enormous benefits from public investment. For someone to assert that he or she has grown wealthy in America without the benefit of substantial public investment is pure hubris.

William H. Gates, Sr. & Chuck Collins, WEALTH AND OUR COMMONWEALTH 122 (2002).

[124] Newsflash to those who think they earned their place in this world through individual hard work. The working poor of the world work harder than anyone else. Many of the working poor in the United States work several jobs to make ends meet. One out of every four workers earns less than poverty level wages, even under the artificially low U.S. poverty guidelines. *See* QUIGLEY, *supra* note 14, at 77.

Worldwide, many of the working poor start each day not knowing where their food will come from for the next day—they work very, very hard to survive. They live each day in the ultimate survivor reality. Recall that of the 6.2 billion people in the world today, one of every five people, a total of 1.2 billion, live on less than $1 per day. *See* HUMAN DEVELOPMENT REPORT 2002, *supra* note 26, at 5.

[125] *See* Kristof, *supra* note 29.

[126] *See* Universal Declaration of Human Rights, *supra* note 78.

> Article 29. (1) Everyone has duties to the community in which alone the free and full development of his personality is possible. (2) In the exercise of his rights and freedoms, everyone shall be subject only to such limitations as are determined by law solely for the purpose of securing due recognition and respect for the rights and freedoms of others and of meeting the just requirements of morality, public order and the general welfare in a democratic society.

Id.; see also Pope John XXIII, *Pacem in Terris* ¶ 60–61, *reprinted in* CATHOLIC SOCIAL THOUGHT: THE DOCUMENTARY HERITAGE 141 (David J. O'Brien & Thomas A. Shannon eds., 1992).

> It is agreed that in our time the common good is chiefly guaranteed when personal rights and duties are maintained. The chief concern of civil authorities must therefore be to ensure that these rights are acknowledged, respected, coordinated with other rights, defended and promoted, so that in this way each one may more easily carry out his duties. For "to safeguard the inviolable rights of the human person, and to facilitate the fulfillment of his duties, should be the chief duty of every public authority."

dignity and equality, but also a full range of economic, social, civil and political rights.[127] We must insist that the Universal Declaration of Human Rights be recognized and implemented as a starting point for the rights of all persons.[128] These rights must be implemented in the social and international order.[129]

Taking human rights seriously expands the idea of solidarity beyond national borders, and the quest for respect, justice and human dignity beyond individual laws. Many revolutionaries, including Malcolm X, have promoted this idea.[130] In its essence, taking human rights seriously means putting people at the center of all policy decisions and treating every single person with the dignity and respect they deserve. Taking human rights seriously means a fundamental change in the approach to law in the world and in this country. It is a step that must be taken if we are to work towards justice and the revolution of values.

2. Human Rights Trump Privilege and Property Rights

(1) The needs of the poor take priority over the wants of the rich;
(2) The freedom of the dominated takes priority over the liberty of

---

> This means that, if any government does not acknowledge the rights of man or violates them, it not only fails in its duty, but its orders completely lack juridical force.

Id. (internal citations omitted).

[127] For an excellent overview, see Woods & Lewis, *supra* note 81.

The 1981 *African Charter on Human and Peoples' Rights* explicitly recognizes the need for these rights to be inter-related:

> [I]t is henceforth essential to pay a particular attention to the right to development and that civil and political rights cannot be dissociated from economic, social and cultural rights in their conception as well as universality and that the satisfaction of economic, social and cultural rights is a guarantee for the enjoyment of civil and political rights. . . .

Org. of African Unity [OAU], *African (Banjul) Charter on Human and Peoples' Rights,* at 2, OAU Doc. CAB/LEG/67/3rev.5 (June 27, 1981).

[128] These rights include: adequate food; jobs; living wages; healthcare; shelter; and free quality education, including higher education. *See* Universal Declaration of Human Rights, *supra* note 78, arts. 22–26.

[129] "Everyone is entitled to a social and international order in which the rights and freedoms set forth in this Declaration can be fully realized." *Id.* art. 28.

[130]

> Malcolm X continually warned Black America that we should expand our horizons beyond civil rights. Civil rights, he emphasized, set our struggle for freedom solely within the context of the United States. Human rights, on the other hand, situated our struggle internationally, and alongside the struggles against colonialism and foreign domination that were taking place in Africa, Asia, the Caribbean and Latin America.
>
> . . . .
>
> Malcolm helped us to better understand that our problem was not a law or set of laws.

Bill Fletcher, Jr., *Malcolm at 80,* TRANSAFRICA FORUM NEWSLETTER (TransAfrica Forum, Wash. D.C.), May 19, 2005, *available at* http://www.transafricaforum.org/Malcolmat80.html.

> *the powerful; (3) The participation of marginalized groups takes priority over the preservation of an order which excludes them.*
>
> —David Hollenbach[131]

If the basic human rights of all are not met, as they cannot be when one in five people in the world lives on less than one dollar per day,[132] then true human rights policy cannot honor the privileges of those who have profited by current laws and institutions. True human rights policy must anticipate the inevitable conflict between rights. When there are conflicts, they must be resolved by a hierarchy of values. Current arrangements privilege many, but, in the revolution of values, must yield.[133]

In a new justice-based value system, people must be valued more than property. Human rights must be valued more than property rights. Minimum standards of living must be valued more than the privileges that come from being well-off. Basic freedom for all must be valued more than the privileged liberty of accumulated political, social and economic power. Finally, the goal of increasing the political, social, and economic power of those who are left out of current arrangements must be valued more than the preservation of the existing order that created and maintains unjust privileges.[134]

This principle of prioritizing human rights creates conflict because it essentially turns current practice upside down. It looks at the world from the perspective of the working poor, the powerless, and the left-out, and makes a conscious decision to make radical changes to that world. No current rules, laws, or institutions are more important than justice and equality. Prioritizing human rights will free advocates from being bound by the privileges conferred by an unjust system. However, undoing unjust privilege to reorder the world will not occur without serious conflict and resistance from those who benefit from current inequities.[135]

> To imagine a world in which each and every individual is treated with respect and dignity, receives equal protection, enjoys

---

[131] David Hollenbach, CLAIMS IN CONFLICT: RETRIEVING AND RENEWING THE CATHOLIC HUMAN RIGHTS TRADITION 204 (1979).

[132] Of the 6.2 billion people in the world today, one of every five people on earth, a total of 1.2 billion, live on less than $1 per day. HUMAN DEVELOPMENT REPORT 2002, *supra* note 26, at 5; *cf.* Universal Declaration of Human Rights, *supra* note 78.

[133] Current arrangements are more similar to what Dr. King described: "When machines and computers, profit motives and property rights are considered more important than people, the giant triplets of racism, materialism, and militarism are incapable of being conquered." King, Jr., *supra* note 1.

[134] Hollenbach, *supra* note 101, at 203–07.

[135] *Id.* at 204–05 ("Conflict between the needs of some and the wants of others, both within nations and across national boundaries, is one of the predominant characteristics of contemporary society. An adequate human rights policy cannot avoid this conflict if it is to be responsive to the actual situation.").

> freedom, and is accorded social justice is to threaten virtually any tradition or practice based on privilege and hierarchy, birth or wealth, exclusivity, and prejudice. The reason is not difficult to explain, for as one experienced observer notes succinctly: "The struggle for human rights has always been and always will be a struggle against authority." Visions of human rights, by their nature, defy the legitimacy and threaten the existence of all forms of political, economic, social, or cultural despotism, tyranny, dictatorship, oligarchy, or authoritarian control. . . . They are thus capable of presenting a potent focus and a resounding rallying cry for those who want change.[136]

Visions of human rights have always presented a profound threat to special privilege. They still do. From the perspective of those at the top (those who thrive under current laws and policies), there does not seem to be much need for radical reform. Indeed, radical reform may even appear unjust to those who stand to lose their comforting privileges. However, when examined from the underside, the need for dramatic change is evident.

A radical revolution of values prizes the perspective of those at the margins. Why? Because it is in listening to and standing with the victims of injustice that the need for critical thinking and action becomes clear. Liberation theology calls this the "preferential option for the poor."[137] Those without property, wealth, food, and basic human rights are the members of our human family who show us the injustices of our world and the directions needed for the revolution.[138]

---

[136] Paul Gordon Lauren, THE EVOLUTION OF INTERNATIONAL HUMAN RIGHTS 283 (2d ed. 2003).

[137] Rodes, Jr., *supra* note 74, at 96. Other scholars discuss how this preferential option must be aimed at structural changes:

> [T]he fact that there are poor in North America and in other parts of the world is not an accident. It is the explicit outcome, the necessary result, of the way we have structured society politically, economically, and culturally. Inequitable concentration of wealth, income and power lead [sic] to tax laws, employment policies, welfare programs, housing plans and other policies and structures which directly and adversely affect the poor. Therefore the option for the poor will never be satisfied with responses only of charity. There must also be a commitment to justice, to structural change.

Peter J. Henriot, OPTING FOR THE POOR: THE CHALLENGE FOR THE TWENTY-FIRST CENTURY (2004).

[138] The Jewish and Christian scriptures demand constant attention to the needs of the poor, the widow, the orphan, the refugee, and the worker. While these teachings have frequently been ignored by the practices of organized religion, the principles remain vigorous.

The most searing criticism by the prophets of Israel was reserved for people and institutions that failed to listen to the cries of the poor and who built up their own comfort and power at the expense of the common good. *See* Abraham J. Heschel, THE PROPHETS 5 (1962). "Prophecy is the voice that God has lent to silent agony, a voice to the plundered poor, to the profaned riches of the world." *Id; see also* Clodovis Boff & George V. Pixley, THE BIBLE, THE CHURCH, AND THE POOR (Paul Burns trans., 1989).

Radical change requires more than traditional reforms that try to solve problems without upsetting current power relationships. It is not possible to bring about justice without radical change, and radical change is not possible without reducing the power, influence and comfort of those who have more than their fair share of the world's resources.

It is essential to apply these principles with an international perspective.[139] We are citizens of the world, and we must protect our global common good in order to survive. Our sisters and brothers are not just those in our families, our communities, or our nations—they are across the world. A strategy that does not acknowledge our inter-connectedness and interdependence can never be the basis for true change.

Thus, human rights necessary for survival must trump property rights. Likewise, human rights to basic needs and participation must trump the privileges accumulated by those who benefit from an unjust system. This will upset those at the top who enjoy these privileges, but this is a predictable result in a world that needs revolutionary change.

3. Re-defining Property

We must lay hold of the fact that economic laws are not made by nature. They are made by human beings.

—President Franklin Delano Roosevelt[140]

Support of private ownership does not mean that anyone has the right to unlimited accumulation of wealth. "Private property does not constitute for anyone an absolute or unconditional right. No one is justified in keeping for his exclusive use what he does not need, when others lack necessities."[141]

Any reason worthy of the name must therefore come to the conclusion that all economic structures, institutions, and actions must be reconstructed according to the logic of the survival of all.[142]

In looking at poverty, wealth, and the working poor, we must look at wealth, as well as poverty, in a radical new way. As such, the right to property must be re-defined. Property rights must always be subordinate

---

[139] *See* Fletcher, Jr., *supra* note 100 (discussing the importance of Malcolm X and the need for a global connection to struggling people).

[140] President Franklin Delano Roosevelt, Nomination Address Before the Democratic National Convention ¶ 54 (July 2, 1932), *available at* http://newdeal.feri.org/speeches/1932b.htm.

[141] Pastoral Letter from U.S. Catholic Bishops on Catholic Social Teaching and the U.S. Economy: Economic Justice for All, ¶ 115, 35 (1986), http://www.osjspm.org/cst/eja.htm (internal citations omitted).

[142] Ulrich Duchrow & Franz J. Hinkelammert, PROPERTY FOR PEOPLE, NOT FOR PROFIT: ALTERNATIVES TO THE GLOBAL TYRANNY OF CAPITAL 159 (Elaine Griffiths et al. trans., 2004).

to justice and peoples' rights to basic survival. This is an explicit part of the revolution of values that Dr. King sought.[143]

Undeniably, there is value in private property. Owning your own home is generally understood as a right that is in the interest of society and of the common good. But what about the situation in which people with property rights have excessive amounts of resources, while billions of others live on a dollar per day?[144] What about the previously mentioned fact that "[t]he top one-tenth of U.S. Citizens now receive a total income equal to that of the poorest 2.2 billion people in the rest of the world"?[145] It is apparent that a few hold a large and inordinate share of the world's resources, while others have a grossly inadequate share. If private property is a valued common good, should not everyone have access to it?

It is at this point, where massive scarcity and excess co-exist, that the human rights of justice and equality are openly violated. If it is true that no current rules, laws, arrangements or institutions are more important than justice and equality, then it is time to change the rules; it is time to re-define property rights.

In *The Second Treatise of Civil Government,* John Locke described the right to private property in a manner that clearly limits that right to those situations in which the conversion of common property to private property does not harm the common good, and in which it leaves sufficient amounts in common for others.[146] Others have argued that making common property private is only legitimate when it actually provides a positive benefit to the common good.[147] Likewise, some have stated that private property operates under a "social mortgage," meaning that the right to private property is subject to the more fundamental principle that the goods of the world are meant for all persons.[148]

---

[143] *See* King, Jr., *supra* note 1.

[144] For a great place to start the discussion on re-imagining property, see Joseph William Singer, *Property, in* THE POLITICS OF LAW: A PROGRESSIVE CRITIQUE 240, 240–58 (David Kairys ed., 3d ed. 1998).

[145] *See Rich and Poor in the Global Economy, supra* note 56, at 13.

[146] JOHN LOCKE, THE SECOND TREATISE OF CIVIL GOVERNMENT AND A LETTER CONCERNING TOLERANCE 15 (J.W. Gough ed., Blackwell Oxford 1946) (1690).

> Sec. 27. Though the earth, and all inferior creatures, be common to all men, yet every man has a property in his own person: this no body has any right to but himself. The labour of his body, and the work of his hands, we may say, are properly his. Whatsoever then he removes out of the state that nature hath provided, and left it in, he hath mixed his labour with, and joined to it something that is his own, and thereby makes it his property. It being by him removed from the common state nature hath placed it in, it hath by this labour something annexed to it, that excludes the common right of other men: for this labour being the unquestionable property of the labourer, no man but he can have a right to what that is once joined to, at least where there is enough, and as good, left in common for others.

Id.

[147] *See* Jeffrey Riedinger, *Property Rights and Democracy: Philosophical and Economic Considerations,* 22 CAP. U. L. REV. 893, 895–909 (1993).

148

Earlier thinkers, like Ambrose and Augustine in the 300s, took a sharper view of the obligation to return private property to the common good. Ambrose stated:

> Not from your own do you bestow upon the poor man, but you make return from what is his. For what has been given as common for the use of all, you appropriate to yourself alone. The earth belongs to all, not to the rich; but fewer are they who do not use what belongs to all than those who do. Therefore, you are paying a debt, you are not bestowing what is not due.[149]

Augustine was even more pointed: "Take what suffices; other things, superfluous things, are the necessities of others. The superfluous things of the wealthy are the necessities of the poor. When superfluous things are possessed, others' property is possessed."[150]

Thus, private property should be a protected right to the extent that it provides to a person and their family the right to live in basic human decency and to pursue their rightful place consistent with the common good. However, when a person or entity claims property in excess of what is necessary for basic human survival, and when there are people who need these same basic elements, then it is time to re-define the laws of property to share the earth's resources in a manner more consistent with justice, equality and the shared human dignity of all. If there are people in desperate need while others enjoy excess, then justice dictates that the excess is no longer their private property. To the extent that people possess what is not theirs, it is theft.

Such a re-definition of property is a basic ideal of the push for a just living wage, both world-wide and in this country. Does a person, corporation, or business have a right to take home a profit if they have not paid their taxes? Do they have a right to take home a profit if they have not paid their creditors? If the answer is no, then why should they be allowed to take home a profit if they do not pay a living wage to their workers? Paying a just wage is a fundamental element of any business that employs people. If a business cannot pay a just and living wage to its employees, why does the community need that business? As one Republican U.S. Senator, who was a great friend of business, argued, the

---

> It is necessary to state once more the characteristic principle of Christian social doctrine: the goods of this world are *originally meant for all.* The right to private property is *valid and necessary,* but it does not nullify the validity of this principle. Private property, in fact, is under a "social mortgage," which means that it has an intrinsically social function, based upon and justified precisely by the principle of the universal destination of goods.

Pope John Paul II, *On Social Concern* ¶ 42, *reprinted in* CATHOLIC SOCIAL THOUGHT, *supra* note 96, at 393, 426.

[149] Charles Avila, OWNERSHIP: EARLY CHRISTIAN TEACHING 66 (1983).

[150] *Id.* at 113.

right to a living wage is more important than the right to operate a business.[151]

Thus, at the point of excess, private property ceases to be a right, and the social mortgage can be exercised by proper authority to provide for the basic unmet needs of others. At this point, excess individual wealth actually belongs to the poor. If excessive wealth can be the solution to life-threatening poverty, then it should be.

Re-thinking property should also consider the push for privatization—making formerly public assets and services private. There is considerable movement towards privatizing formerly public works and institutions, such as water, health, sanitation, education, roads, and security. This movement will inevitably privilege those with economic resources to the disadvantage of those without.

Privatization must be radically questioned, with the burden of persuasion on those who seek it.[152] Privatization must be challenged, particularly when it seeks to privatize essential services and resources.[153] Even advocates of privatization are reluctant to take such action without considerable public planning, participation and accountability.[154] Indeed, privatization must be accompanied by public participation and transparent decision-making. Moreover, there must be clear, prompt, and acceptable methods of reversing privatization efforts without damaging community resources in cases in which it is not in the common good. Re-defining property rights is another step towards justice.

---

[151] During a debate in the 1930s about enacting a minimum wage, Senator William E. Borah of Idaho had the following exchange with other Senators:

> MR. BORAH. "I look upon a minimum wage such as will afford a decent living as a part of a sound national policy. I would abolish a wage scale below a decent standard living just as I would abolish slavery. If it disturbed business, it would be the price we must pay for good citizens. . . . I take the position that a man who employs another must pay him sufficient to enable the one employed to live."
>
> MR. PEPPER. "What if he cannot afford to pay it?"
>
> MR. BORAH. "If he cannot afford to pay it, then he should close up the business. No business has a right to coin the very lifeblood of workmen into dollars and cents.
>
> . . . .
>
> I insist that American industry can pay its employees enough to enable them to live."
>
> MR. ELLENDER. "Without exception?"
>
> MR. BORAH. "Yes; without exception. If it cannot do so, let it close up. . . . I am opposed to peon labor, whether it is employed by one man or another. I start with the proposition that the right to live is higher than the right to own a business."

81 CONG. REC. 7775, 7795–96 (1937).

[152] *See* Duchrow & Hinkelammert, *supra* note 112 ("The currently fashionable ideology of privatization must be questioned radically.").

[153] A great story about the successful efforts to resist privatization can be found in Oscar Olivera & Tom Lewis, COCHABAMBA!: WATER WAR IN BOLIVIA (2004).

[154] Joseph E. Stiglitz, GLOBALIZATION AND ITS DISCONTENTS 54–59 (1st ed. 2002).

4. Democratizing Corporations

Democratizing economics is no more unlikely a task than democratizing government—in a sense it's only finishing the task. It won't happen overnight, but it's a good bet it will happen. Major system-wide change is possible. It happened when the monarchy fell, and it can happen again. The lesson of history is clear: democracy always wins in the end.

—Marjorie Kelly[155]

The leading lawyers of the United States have been engaged mainly in supporting the claims of the corporations; often in endeavoring to evade or nullify the extremely crude laws by which legislators sought to regulate the power or curb the excesses of corporations.

—Louis Brandeis[156]

To address the root causes of wealth and poverty, we must look at democratizing the main form of world economic power: the corporation. If we expect to bring about justice in our world, corporations cannot be allowed to focus exclusively on "machines and computers, profit motives and property rights" any more than people can.[157] Law and lawyers have played a fundamental role in the growing problem of the corporation, and there must be a radical change in both.

It is essential that corporations be brought under democratic control and regulated for the purposes of the community and justice. In order to do so, fundamental changes must be made. Revolutionary thought must be directed toward re-asserting democratic control over all elements of corporations, eliminating corporate personhood, and phasing out socially unnecessary corporations.

It is time to recall the words of Justice Marshall, who wrote that a corporation "is an artificial being, invisible, intangible, and existing only in contemplation of law. Being the mere creature of law, it possesses only those properties which the charter of its creation confers upon it, either expressly, or as incidental to its very existence."[158] It is time to reassert the democratic control of people over corporations.

---

[155] Robert Hinkley, *Toppling the Corporate Aristocracy,* COMMON DREAMS NEWSLETTER (Common Dreams, Portland, Me.), Apr. 19, 2002, ¶ 34, http://www.commondreams.org/views 02/0419-09.htm (interviewing Marjorie Kelly).

[156] Brandeis, *supra* note 61, at 560.

[157] King, Jr., *supra* note 1.

[158] Trustees of Dartmouth College v. Woodward, 17 U.S. (4 Wheat.) 518, 636 (1819).

Massive corporate layoffs, environmental disasters, financial fraud and collapse are common topics in the news.[159] In three polls taken between 1996 and 2000, *Business Week* magazine found that between 71% and 82% of those polled agreed with the statement that "business has gained too much power over too many aspects of [American] lives."[160]

Most of the analysis of the essential problems of corporations has not occurred in legal circles, but there are many "extra legal critiques."[161] Lawyers need to listen and take leads from these critiques, and ultimately help translate them into change.

There have always been corporate critics in the legal community, and work on these issues continues.[162] There is a growing group of progressive corporate legal scholars who are trying to find ways to make fundamental changes in corporate law and governance to eliminate corporate political activities, limit corporate personhood, change the responsibilities of directors, reform limited liability and treat all large corporations as quasi-public entities subject to increased social control.[163]

There are also a number of recent books documenting extensive corporate problems and calling for significant change in the status and regulation of corporations.[164] These books suggest a range of reforms to

---

159 *See, e.g., Corporate Execs in Season,* PITTSBURGH TRIB. REV., July 21, 2005, *available at* http://pittsburghlive.com/x/tribune-review/s_355533.html (noting over 400 cases of criminal fraud being pursued against corporate executives); Rex Nutting, *Layoffs Surge to 17-Month High,* MARKETWATCH, July 6, 2005, at 1, *available at* http://www.marketwatch.com/News/Story/Story.aspx?guid=#5E273562"1479"43BB"AA67"F00966B7BF96'&sideid=google (noting that over 110,000 people were laid off by automotive and retail corporations in June, 2005, a dramatic increase).

160 Aaron Bernstein, *Too Much Corporate Power?,* BUS. WK. ONLINE, Sept. 11, 2000, http://www.businessweek.com/2000/00_37/b3698001.htm.

161 Kellye Y. Testy, *Capitalism and Freedom—For Whom?: Feminist Legal Theory and Progressive Corporate Law,* 67 LAW & CONTEMP. PROBS. 87, 88–89 (2004).

The leading think tank for dramatic change in corporations is the Program on Corporations, Law and Democracy. For information on this group, see http://www.poclad.org/index.cfm (last visited Feb. 12, 2006).

162 *See, e.g.,* CA. Harwell Wells, *The Cycles of Corporate Social Responsibility: An Historical Retrospective for the Twenty-First Century,* 51 U. KAN. L. REV. 77 (2002).

163 Testy, *supra* note 131, at 88, 105–08; *see also* Douglas M. Branson, *Corporate Social Responsibility Redux,* 76 TUL. L. REV. 1207, 1212–16 (2002); Ronnie Cohen, *Feminist Thought and Corporate Law,* 2 AM. U. J. GENDER & L. 1 (1994); Thomas Linzey, *Killing Goliath: Defending Our Sovereignty and Environmental Sustainability Through Corporate Charter Revocation in Pennsylvania and Delaware,* 6 DICK. J. ENVTL. L. & POL'Y 31 (1997); Lawrence E. Mitchell & Theresa A. Gabaldon, *If I Only Had a Heart: Or, How Can We Identify a Corporate Morality,* 76 TUL. L. REV. 1645 (2002); Kellye Y. Testy, *Linking Progressive Corporate Law with Progressive Social Movements,* 76 TUL. L. REV. 1227 (2002).

164 Joel Bakan, THE CORPORATION: THE PATHOLOGICAL PURSUIT OF PROFIT AND POWER (2004); Dan Butts, HOW CORPORATIONS HURT US ALL: SAVING OUR RIGHTS, DEMOCRACY, INSTITUTIONS, AND OUR FUTURE (2003); DEFYING CORPORATIONS, DEFINING DEMOCRACY (Dean Ritz ed., 2001); Charles Derber, REGIME CHANGE BEGINS AT HOME: FREEING AMERICA FROM CORPORATE RULE (2004); George Draffan, THE ELITE CONSENSUS: WHEN CORPORATIONS WIELD THE CONSTITUTION (2003); William Greider, ONE WORLD, READY OR NOT: THE MANIC LOGIC OF GLOBAL CAPITALISM (1997); Thom Hartmann, UNEQUAL PROTECTION: THE RISE OF CORPORATE DOMINANCE AND THE THEFT OF HUMAN RIGHTS (2002); MARJORIE KELLY, THE DIVINE RIGHT OF CAPITAL: DETHRONING THE CORPORATE ARISTOCRACY 147–49 (2001); David C. Korten, THE POST-

make large corporations more ethical and accountable to society, including:

- A Constitutional amendment declaring that corporations are not natural persons and are not entitled to constitutional rights;
- Granting states the power to revoke corporate charters based on immoral conduct negatively impacting the community (e.g., mass layoffs, pollution, plant relocation);
- Requiring corporations to allow employees to vote on parity with shareholders and to serve on the board of directors;
- Requiring corporations to make environmental and social disclosures in addition to their financial disclosures;
- Allowing directors to focus on the long-term health of the corporation by granting five-year terms for directors and by issuing annual earnings reports (instead of quarterly);
- *Requiring* (rather than merely *permitting*) directors to take account of so-called *stake*holders in addition to *stock*holders; and
- Amending the accounting rules and/or tax codes to reflect the contributions of workers as an "asset" and to provide incentives for socially responsible corporations.[165]

The efforts to rein in and reform corporations are very important and should be supported. However, even more fundamental change is needed to address the roles of corporate participation and leadership in creating and maintaining global injustice. Corporate personhood itself must be eliminated.[166] Unfortunately, current law grants corporations constitutional rights that make it exceedingly difficult for democracy to rein them in—rights that the corporations have exercised strenuously.[167]

The historical basis for corporate constitutional rights is weak. The Fourteenth Amendment was passed in 1868 to ensure that all citizens of the United States, particularly people of color, had full rights. Nothing was ever said about granting constitutional rights to corporations. But in 1886, the Supreme Court, in *Santa Clara County v. Southern Pacific*

CORPORATE WORLD: LIFE AFTER CAPITALISM (1999); Lawrence E. Mitchell, CORPORATE IRRESPONSIBILITY: AMERICA'S NEWEST EXPORT 97 (2001).

[165] Douglas Litowitz, *Are Corporations Evil?*, 58 U. MIAMI L. REV. 811, 821–22 (2004).

[166] For much more on this topic, see William Quigley, *Catholic Social Thought and the Amorality of Large Corporations: Time to Abolish Corporate Personhood,* 5 LOY. J. PUB. INT. L. 109 (2004).

[167] *See* Richard L. Grossman, *Wresting Governing Authority from the Corporate Class,* 1 SEATTLE J. SOC. JUST. 147 (2002); Robert L. Kerr, *Subordinating the Economic to the Political: The Evolution of the Corporate Speech Doctrine,* 10 COMM. L. & POL'Y 63 (2005).

Railroad,[168] granted corporations legal personhood under an unprecedented interpretation of the Fourteenth Amendment.[169] Ten years later, the Supreme Court, in *Plessy v. Ferguson,* approved "separate but equal" racial segregation.[170] Thus, the Supreme Court interpreted the Fourteenth Amendment, explicitly passed to assist former slaves, to give full rights to corporations, while denying these rights to the exact people who were intended to receive its protection. The irony was that "[i]n less than 30 years, African Americans had effectively lost their legal personhood rights while corporations had acquired them."[171]

Inspiration for reversing corporate personhood can be found in a powerful dissent by Justice Hugo Black in *Connecticut General Life Insurance Company v. Johnson.*[172] Justice Black pointed out that the protections of the Fourteenth Amendment, which was established to protect black citizens, instead had been used mostly to protect corporations. "[O]f the cases in this Court in which the Fourteenth Amendment was applied during the first fifty years after its adoption, less than one-half of one per cent invoked it in protection of the negro race, and more than fifty per cent asked that its benefits be extended to corporations."[173]

Organizations such as the National Lawyers Guild, the Green Party, the Women's International League for Peace and Freedom, and Reclaim Democracy have initiated campaigns to abolish corporate personhood.[174] Lawyers must join those efforts and help reduce constitutional rights of artificial business entities, while creating more opportunities for the human rights of people.[175]

A final suggestion to reverse corporate dominance and democratize corporations is to literally cut them down to size—to dramatically cut back on large corporations. A major problem in asserting democratic control over corporations is their massive size. Major transnational corporations financially dwarf the countries in which they operate, and are effectively unaccountable to the people they impact. For example,

---

168 118 U.S. 394 (1886).

169 Writing about the case sixty years later, Justice William O. Douglas stated: "There was no history, logic or reason given to support that view." *See* Richard Grossman & Frank T. Adams, *Taking Care of Business, in* DEFYING CORPORATIONS, DEFINING DEMOCRACY, *supra* note 134, at 59, 68 (internal citations omitted).

170 163 U.S. 537, 550–52 (1896).

171 Molly Morgan & Jan Edwards, *Abolish Corporate Personhood,* 59 GUILD PRAC. 209, 211 (2002).

172 303 U.S. 77, 83–90 (Black, J., dissenting).

173 *Id.* at 90.

174 *See* Quigley, *supra* note 14, at 128–29.

175 *See* Kimberly French, *Taking on the System,* UU WORLD, May-June 2003, *available at* http://www.uuworld.org/2003/03/feature1d.html; Tom Stites, *How Corporations Became 'Persons',* UU WORLD, May-June 2003, *available at* http://www.uuworld.org/2003/03/feature1a.html; David Wolman & Heather Wax, *Fighting City Hall,* UU WORLD, May-June 2003, *available at* http://www.uuworld.org/2003/03/feature1b.html.

Fortune magazine's Global 500 rankings for 2005 lists Wal-Mart as the world's biggest corporation with revenues of over $287 billion, making it larger than the economies of more than 133 countries.[176] Even the 100th largest corporation, Time Warner, with revenues of over $42 billion, is larger than the economies of eighty-nine countries.[177] People in these large institutions often do not see themselves as having any social accountability.[178] Given the size disparities between corporations and many countries, much less between corporations and local communities, how can there be a realistic expectation that individuals can hold corporations accountable?

The problem of democratizing large corporations is one that can be addressed by progressively eliminating the largest ones that society determines it does not need.[179] There is a historical basis for citizens to re-assert control over growing and powerful business interests by breaking them into smaller entities that can be regulated by the people.[180] The key question is the public good, and we should determine the ways in which large corporations contribute to or harm the public good. Some large corporations might actually be in society's interest, while others certainly are not. There is no reason that a progressive, phased-in cap on corporate size cannot be implemented,[181] with the burden on large corporations to persuade the public to which they are theoretically responsible that they should not be broken into smaller units with more accountability, transparency, and democratic control.

---

[176] *The 2005 Global 500,* FORTUNE, *available at* http://money.cnn.com/magazines/fortune/fortune500/; Nationmaster.com, Map & Graph: Countries by Economy, http://www.nationmaster.com/graph-T/eco_gdp_ppp&int=-1 (last visited Feb. 21, 2006) (providing a listing of the gross domestic product of each of the world's countries, compiled from a CIA databook).

[177] *See The 2005 Global 500, supra* note 146.

[178] *See* Litowitz, *supra* note 135, at 832–41. Litowitz summarizes the positions of both critics and proponents of corporations, but suggests that each side overlooks the ethical problems of people desperate for work in large institutions.

[179]

> I have one idea that is more radical, but still simple: A phased-in size cap for corporations. The cap would limit the revenues, assets and number of employees of any one corporation, and be lowered each year; and no individual or group of individuals would be allowed to beneficially own or control more than *one* corporation. The complexities of beneficial ownership and control have already been worked out in most Western nations' tax codes. The use of multiple corporations serves no social or business purpose other than to evade taxes, obscure the true ownership of "anonymous" corporations and evade legal responsibility and liability for corporate wrongdoing. Spinning off businesses from those that exceed the size cap would not be hard to do, and would democratize corporations and make them more manageable and resilient, and redistribute wealth equitably and painlessly. I truly believe that most of the emergent evils of corporations are more a function of their sheer staggering size than their profit motivation.

How to Save the World, Undermining Corporatism: Some Old and New Ideas, http://blogs.salon.com/0002007/categories/politicsEconomics/2004/07/08.html (July 8, 2004, 13:56).

[180] Marjorie E. Kornhauser, *Corporate Regulation and the Origins of the Corporate Income Tax,* 66 IND. L.J. 53 (1990).

[181] *See* How to Save the World, *supra* note 149.

These are not prescriptions for a transition to a state-run market, but rather a plan to exert democratic control over economic systems that impact the daily lives of people and contribute in a powerful way to the current challenges of poverty and wealth.[182] Will corporations and their lawyers resist efforts to democratize? Of course they will. Is that any reason not to do it? Of course not. It is time to re-assert democratic control over corporations.

5. Demilitarizing and Reversing the Arms Race

> *Every gun that is made, every warship launched, every rocket fired signifies, in the final sense, a theft from those who hunger and are not fed, those who are cold and are not clothed. This world in arms is not spending money alone. It is spending the sweat of its laborers, the genius of its scientists, the hopes of its children. . . . This is not a way of life at all, in any true sense. Under the cloud of threatening war, it is humanity hanging from a cross of iron.*
>
> —Dwight D. Eisenhower[183]

The United States has achieved unprecedented world military domination and clearly intends to maintain it.[184] The United States remains the only nation to have used nuclear weapons on civilian populations—actions that certainly would be considered war crimes had the United States lost that war.[185] As Martin Luther King, Jr., pointed out, militarism is one of the evils that must be addressed to bring about a world based on justice.[186]

---

[182] For other ideas about progressive challenges to economics as usual, see Robin Hahnel, ECONOMIC JUSTICE AND DEMOCRACY: FROM COMPETITION TO COOPERATION (2005).

[183] Dwight D. Eisenhower, Address Before the American Society of Newspaper Editors: The Chance for Peace (Apr. 16, 1953), *available at* http://www.quotedb.com/speeches/chance-for-peace).

[184] THE NATIONAL SECURITY STRATEGY OF THE UNITED STATES OF AMERICA 1 (2002), *available at* http://www.whitehouse.gov/nsc/nss.html [hereinafter NATIONAL SECURITY STRATEGY]; *see also* Thomas Donnelly, THE PROJECT FOR THE NEW AMERICAN CENTURY, REBUILDING AMERICA'S DEFENSES: STRATEGY, FORCES AND RESOURCES FOR A NEW CENTURY (2000), *available at* http://www.newamericancentury.org/RebuildingAmericasDefenses.pdf.

> The U.S. is the world's only superpower, combining pre-eminent military power, global technological leadership, and the world's largest economy. . . . At present the United States faces no global rival. America's grand strategy should aim to preserve and extend this advantageous position as far into the future as possible. . . . Preserving the desirable strategic situation in which the United States now finds itself requires a globally preeminent military capability both today and in the future.

Id. at i.

[185] Marcella David, *Grotius Repudiated: The American Objections to the International Criminal Court and the Commitment to International Law,* 20 MICH. J. INT'L L. 337, 348–49 (1999).

[186] *See* King, Jr., *supra* note 1.

U.S. military dominance has come about at an unimaginable financial, physical, and moral cost to the well-being of the world and of the nation itself. Obviously, the costs include draining resources away from opportunities to address poverty. In addition to the waste of resources, there remains a justice question—under what theory of human rights, justice or dignity can the United States stake its claim to world military dominance and unilateral military and nuclear action? Under what theory of human dignity and justice does the United States justify huge stockpiles of nuclear weapons and the right to use them again? The law and lawyers are often involved in justifying and assisting our world military dominance. Justice must work to radically undermine and root out the current legal practices that allow the leaders of one nation a unilateral right to invade and destroy the people of another by preemptive conventional or nuclear actions. Otherwise, there can be no realistic expectation that human dignity will be respected, or that the inequalities that result in poverty will be fundamentally addressed at any time.

The United States' global military dominance is breathtaking.[187] Military spending in the United States, totaling over $450 billion, represents 47% of all the money spent on militaries in the entire world.[188] This is more than the combined military budgets of the United Kingdom, France, Japan, China, Germany, Italy, Russia, Saudi Arabia, South Korea, India, Israel, Canada, Turkey and Australia—the next fifteen countries combined.[189] The United States recently criticized China for increasing its military budget, while maintaining one of its own that is seven to eighteen times larger.[190] The U.S. military budget is more than thirty times as large as the combined spending of the seven "rogue states" (Cuba, Iran, Iraq, Libya, North Korea, Sudan and Syria).[191]

The United States maintains a world-wide military presence.[192] The U.S. Department of Defense admits to having 725 military bases in thirty-eight countries outside of the United States,[193] in addition to the

---

[187] Andrew J. Bacevich, THE NEW AMERICAN MILITARISM: HOW AMERICANS ARE SEDUCED BY WAR (2005). Bacevich, a West Point graduate and Vietnam veteran, describes a country that is moving beyond a militarized society into a society where civilians assume a permanent military outlook on the world. *Id.* at 1–3.

[188] Stockholm Int'l Peace Inst., The 15 Major Spenders in 2004, http://www.sipri.org/contents/milap/milex/mex_major_spenders.pdf (last visited Feb. 21, 2006).

[189] *Id.*

[190] *China's Armed Forces: Casus Belli,* ECONOMIST, June 11, 2005, at 1–2, *available at* 2005 WL 9244442.

[191] The U.S. military budget is greater than the combined spending of the next thirteen nations. *See supra* note 21.

[192] *See* Chalmers Johnson, THE SORROWS OF EMPIRE: MILITARY, SECRECY, AND THE END OF THE REPUBLIC 154 (1st ed. 2004). In September, 2001, the United States deployed 254,788 military personnel in 153 countries. *Id.*

[193] *Id.* (quoting the Department of Defense report titled *Worldwide Manpower Distribution by Geographical Area*).

969 military bases within the United States.[194] The United States trains about 100,000 foreign soldiers each year,[195] and is by far the biggest seller of weapons—in only four years, from 1997 to 2001, we exported over $44 billion worth of arms.[196] Since World War II, the United States has launched over fifty military and CIA interventions in nations around the world, not counting the latest invasion of Iraq.[197]

Nuclear weapons provide several specific challenges: staggering costs, current perils, and the fundamental question of their legitimacy. The cost to the United States of building and maintaining nuclear weapons has been documented at more than $5.5 trillion from 1940 to 1996.[198] What is $5.5 trillion? The amount spent on nuclear weapons alone "exceeds the combined total over the same period of federal spending on education, training, employment, and social services; on agriculture; on natural resources and the environment; on general science and space research; on community and regional development, including disaster relief; on law enforcement; and on energy production and regulation."[199]

The United States is the only nation to have used nuclear weapons on civilians, certainly a crime against humanity.[200] Tens of thousands were killed in these nuclear strikes.[201] In Hiroshima, it is estimated that 45,000 died the first day and 19,000 more died within four months; in Nagasaki, an estimated 22,000 people died the first day and approximately 17,000 others died within four months.[202] The use or potential use of nuclear weapons is generally considered to be illegal. The International Court of Justice (ICJ) issued an opinion on July 8, 1996, stating that "[t]he threat or use of nuclear weapons would generally be contrary to the rules of international law applicable in armed conflict, and in particular the principles and rules of humanitarian law."[203] The court

---

[194] Tony Judt, *The New World Order,* N.Y. REV. BOOKS, July 14, 2005, at 5.

[195] Johnson, *supra* note 162, at 132.

[196] *Id.* at 133.

[197] William Blum, KILLING HOPE: U.S. MILITARY AND CIA INTERVENTIONS SINCE WORLD WAR II (2d ed. 2004).

[198] *See* Stephen I. Schwartz, *Check, Please!*, BULL. ATOMIC SCIENTISTS, Sept.-Oct. 1998, at 34–35, *available at* http://www.thebulletin.org/article.php?art_ofn=so98schwartz_025.

[199] *Id.*

[200] David, *supra* note 155, at 348–49.

[201] Jefferson D. Reynolds, *Collateral Damage on the 21st Century Battlefield,* 56 A.F. L. REV. 1, 14–15 (2005).

[202] URANIUM INFORMATION CENTRE, NUCLEAR ISSUES BRIEFING PAPER NO. 29, HIROSHIMA, NAGASAKI, AND SUBSEQUENT WEAPONS TESTING 2 (2004), *available at* http://www.uic.com.au/nip29.htm.

For photos documenting some of the devastation of Hiroshima and Nagasaki, see A Photo-Essay on the Bombing of Hiroshima and Nagasaki (unpublished manuscript), http://www.english.uiuc.edu/maps/poets/g_l/levine/bombing.htm (last visited Feb. 21, 2006).

[203] Advisory Opinion on Legality of the Threat or Use of Nuclear Weapons, 1996 I.C.J. 226, ¶ 105(2)E [hereinafter I.C.J. Advisory Opinion]. This part of the opinion was decided by a vote of seven to seven and went on to say:

went on to conclude unanimously that "[t]here exists an obligation to pursue in good faith and bring to a conclusion negotiations leading to nuclear disarmament in all its aspects under strict and effective international control."[204]

Yet, the United States continues to stockpile and maintain at readiness thousands of nuclear weapons. The United States retains over 10,000 nuclear weapons, over 5000 of which are currently operational.[205] The annual cost of maintaining the nuclear weapons program was estimated in 1998 at $35 billion.[206]

The United States makes explicit its willingness to take preemptive military action when it thinks that it or "[its] allies and friends" are faced with danger.[207] The invasion of Iraq shows the willingness of the United States to take action based on the flimsiest of frauds in order to exercise military power for political means.[208] Under what concept of human dignity and justice can the United States claim the right to be the world's biggest military power for now and the future?

Radical change is needed. Laws that justify the creation, presence and deployment of nuclear weapons must be discarded. Laws that justify and support spending on military dominance must likewise be destroyed. Lawyers must work with others to reverse the direction of these policies, or else there may be nothing left for anyone to defend. We must demilitarize and reverse the arms race in order to redirect resources to people, instead of to perpetual, preemptive, and possibly world-ending wars.

6. Other Areas

There are many other areas of law that need revolutionary change. These areas, including immigration policy, prison reform, education, and reparations, are noted briefly here.

> However, in view of the current state of international law, and of the elements of fact at its disposal, the Court cannot conclude definitively whether the threat or use of nuclear weapons would be lawful or unlawful in an extreme circumstance of self-defense, in which the very survival of a State would be at stake.

Id.; see also Francis A. Boyle, THE CRIMINALITY OF NUCLEAR DETERRENCE (2002); John Burroughs, THE (IL)LEGALITY OF THREAT OR USE OF NUCLEAR WEAPONS 21–22 (1997); NUCLEAR WEAPONS ARE ILLEGAL: THE HISTORIC OPINION OF THE WORLD COURT AND HOW IT WILL BE ENFORCED (Ann Fagan Ginger ed., 1998).

204 I.C.J. Advisory Opinion, *supra* note 173, ¶ 105(2)F.

205 Robert S. Norris & Hans M. Kristensen, *U.S. Nuclear Forces, 2005,* BULL. ATOMIC SCIENTISTS, Jan.-Feb. 2005, at 73–75, *available at* http://www.thebulletin.org/article_nn.php?art_ofn=jf06norris.

206 Brookings Inst., 50 Facts About U.S. Nuclear Weapons, Fact 50, http://www.brook.edu/FP/PROJECTS/NUCWCOST/50.HTM (last visited Feb. 21, 2006).

207 NATIONAL SECURITY STRATEGY, *supra* note 154, at 14.

208 Robert M. Lawrence, *The Preventive/Preemptive War Doctrine Cannot Justify the Iraq War,* 33 DENV. J. INT'L L. & POL'Y 16 (2004).

First, justice demands that we scrap current immigration laws and most proposed reforms, and recognize that no person is illegal. It is a strange version of justice that gives nearly global freedom of movement to money and companies, but refuses it to people.[209] Current globalization is based on the free movement of capital and goods. Wal-Mart, Toyota, GM, Citibank, and other corporations are allowed to set up shop anywhere and move freely between countries with ease.[210] People, however, are not nearly as free to migrate.[211] National borders should be secondary to the pursuit of human rights. Artificial boundaries between nations cannot be considered legal or just reasons for excluding people from pursuing the conditions necessary for human dignity.[212] This is yet another area in which non-lawyers have taken leadership action.[213] How can anyone be illegal if we are all, according to the Universal Declaration of Human

---

209

> The major forces behind the drive for increased globalization are the transnational corporations whose logic requires the free movement of capital, goods and skilled peoples across borders. This free movement succeeds best when national sovereignty is replaced by the "supra-sovereignty" of international agencies like the WTO, the IMF and NAFTA. The rules imposed by these international organizations are designed to give priority to the needs of capital.

A CD Focus on Sovereignty in Canada, CANADIAN DIMENSION, July 1, 2002, *available at* 2002 WL 7241846.

210 *Id.*

211 Duchrow & Hinkelammert, *supra* note 112, at 146.

212 I ask my students: "What justice-based reason gives children born five miles north of the Rio Grande unlimited economic and educational possibility, while children born five miles south have geographically and legally imposed limits on their human potential?"

The myth that the United States welcomes all comers conflicts with actual practice. This myth is based on real proclamations of principle, such as that of George Washington, who stated that "[t]he bosom of America is open to receive not only the Opulent and respectable Stranger, but the oppressed and persecuted of all Nations And Religions." RESPECTFULLY QUOTED: A DICTIONARY OF QUOTATIONS 169 (Suzy Platt ed., 1989), *available at* http://www.bartleby.com/73/884.html. And who can forget the welcome of the Statue of Liberty: "Give me your tired, your poor, Your huddled masses yearning to breathe free, The wretched refuse of your teeming shore. Send these, the homeless, tempest-tost to me. I lift my lamp beside the golden door!" *Id.* at http://www.bartleby.com/66/39/35139.html (quoting Emma Lazarus).

Yet the practice is quite different. Bill Ong Hing writes:

> There have always been two Americas. Both begin with the understanding that America is a land of immigrants. One America has embraced the notion of welcoming newcomers from different parts of the world. . . . The other America has remained largely mired in a Eurocentric (originally *western* Eurocentric) vision of America that idealized the *true* American as white, Anglo-Saxon, English-speaking and Christian.

Bill Ong Hing, DEFINING AMERICA THROUGH IMMIGRATION POLICY 5 (2004). For a historical perspective on immigration, see Gerald L. Neuman, *The Lost Century of American Immigration Law (1776–1875),* 93 COLUM. L. REV. 1833, 1846–59 (1993); *see also* Seyla Benhabib, THE RIGHTS OF OTHERS: ALIENS, RESIDENTS AND CITIZENS (2004) (advocating for porous, but not absolutely open, national boundaries that would allow refugees and asylum seekers).

213 "No Human is Illegal" was the theme of the 2003 Immigrant Workers Freedom Ride. There are many groups trying to dismantle immigration policies that discriminate based on race, gender and politics. *See* No One Is Illegal, http://noii.trick.ca/HomePage (last visited Feb. 21, 2006); No One Is Illegal-Toronto, http://sanspapier.revolt.org/ (last visited Feb. 21, 2006; *see also* No Border, Welcome!, http://www.noborder.org (last visited May 14, 2006).

Rights, sisters and brothers?[214] No one is illegal and the law must be fundamentally changed to reflect this principle.[215]

Second, the prison system in the United States is shameful and must be abolished;[216] not just reformed, but abolished.[217] People serious about justice must insist on radical change and demand a process of reparation and reconciliation based on the human rights of all, rather than based on retribution and vengeance.[218] Our prison system is the end result of a profoundly dysfunctional, racist, and anti-poor process almost satirically termed the criminal justice system.[219] Society certainly can and should protect itself from the people who endanger it, but prisons are not the answer.[220] Forcibly detaining people in inhumane conditions does not

---

[214] Universal Declaration of Human Rights, *supra* note 78, at art. 1.

[215] Virginie Guiraudon, Book Review, *No One Is Illegal: Asylum and Immigration Control Past and Present,* 17 J. REFUGEE STUD. 142 (2004); *see also* Anthony Gregory, *In Defense of Open Immigration,* FREEDOM DAILY, Oct. 2004, *available at* http://www.fff.org/freedom/fd0410e.asp.

[216] *See supra* note 20 (noting that the United States ranks first worldwide in the imprisonment of its citizens, with over 700 persons per 100,000 in prison).

What can the United States learn from the following nations that put so few people in prison? Japan—45 per 100,000; Australia—110; Canada—105; Finland—50; France—80; Italy 95; Ireland—80; Sweden—65; and Iceland—30. Peter Wagner & Brigette Sarabi, THE PRISON INDEX: TAKING THE PULSE OF THE CRIME CONTROL INDUSTRY 40–41 (2003).

[217] Again, non-lawyers are taking the lead in this area. Look particularly at the group Critical Resistance, http://www.criticalresistance.org (last visited Feb. 21, 2006); *see also* Angela Y. Davis, ARE PRISONS OBSOLETE? (2003); THE CASE FOR PENAL ABOLITION (W. Gordon West & Ruth Morris eds., 2000).

A good source on prison reform is Michael Jacobson, DOWNSIZING PRISONS: HOW TO REDUCE CRIME AND END MASS INCARCERATION (2005). Jacobson's story is interesting in part because he ran much of the New York City penal system for years. For a good summary of the different approaches to prison, reform and abolition, see Vanessa Huang, *Two Million Imprisoned=Too Many,* ALTERNET, Aug. 4, 2005, http://www.alternet.org/story/23889/.

[218] DAVIS, *supra* note 187, at 107. Interestingly, the U.S. Catholic Bishops agree with Professor Davis. While not calling for absolute abolition, the U.S. Catholic bishops clearly indicated the need for a transformation of the current system in a 2000 statement. U.S. CONFERENCE OF CATHOLIC BISHOPS, RESPONSIBILITY, REHABILITATION, AND RESTORATION: A CATHOLIC PERSPECTIVE ON CRIME AND CRIMINAL JUSTICE (2000), *available at* http://www.usccb.org/sdwp/criminal.htm. As a result of this analysis, the Catholic bishops concluded that the criminal justice system must change from a punitive and retributive one to one that emphasizes restorative justice and insists that punishment have a constructive and rehabilitative purpose. *Id.* at 13–19.

For more on Catholic social thought and offenders, see William P. Quigley, *Prison Work, Wages, and Catholic Social Thought,* 44 SANTA CLARA L. REV. 1159, 1167–75 (2004); *see also* Alvin J. Bronstein & Jenni Gainsborough, *Using International Human Rights Laws and Standards for U.S. Prison Reform,* 24 PACE L. REV. 811 (2004).

[219] Tara Herivel & Paul Wright, PRISON NATION: THE WAREHOUSING OF AMERICA'S POOR (2003) (demonstrating clear connections between poverty and prisons, race and prisons, and private profit and prisons).

For an excellent short examination of some of the major flaws in the criminal law system, see David Cole, *Two Systems of Criminal Justice, in* THE POLITICS OF LAW, *supra* note 114, at 41; *see also* Katherine Beckett & Theodore Sasson, THE POLITICS OF INJUSTICE: CRIME AND PUNISHMENT IN AMERICA (2000); John Irwin & James Austin, IT'S ABOUT TIME: AMERICA'S IMPRISONMENT BINGE (1994).

[220] The discussion about alternatives to prison must start with the premise that there is not a single solution. Prison is used now as the final answer to crime and social protection, but many other options are available. Imagining and working toward a world without prisons means addressing underlying causes of crime, as well as coming up with creative responses to failure.

further the common good. Moreover, the system ensnares far more than just the criminally dangerous. "Jails and prisons have become, in effect, the country's front-line mental health providers."[221] If we created a decent mental health care system, ten to twenty percent of the current jail and prison population could be released.[222] If currently illegal drugs were decriminalized, twenty-five percent of people in jail could be released.[223] The American prison system demands radical change.

Tragically, the U.S. and many other countries have failed to provide an adequate education to the people who need it most.[224] Worse, many have grown discouraged and have lost the impetus to imagine and work for radical change.[225] The right to adequate education must be dramatically re-imagined and re-invigorated, both in the United States and globally.[226] Given the new demands of work, this right must include a right to free higher public education.[227]

The abolition movement is not looking for a magic prison substitute, such as placing everyone under house arrest or electronic monitoring, but a true radical transformation which will address the dignities of the victim and of society, as well as the dignity of the offender, in a just way. *See* DAVIS, *supra* note 187, at 105–15.

The movement to abolish prisons seeks to progressively replace them and the rest of the present criminal justice system with various models of restorative justice. *See* THE CASE FOR PENAL ABOLITION, *supra* note 187, at sec. IV; *see also* Jim Holt, *Decarcerate?*, N.Y. TIMES MAG., Aug. 15, 2004, at 20–21.

[221] HUMAN RIGHTS WATCH, ILL-EQUIPPED: U.S. PRISONS AND OFFENDERS WITH MENTAL ILLNESS 16 (2003), *available at* http://www.hrw.org/reports/2003/usa1003/.

[222] "Somewhere between two and three hundred thousand men and women in U.S. prisons suffer from mental disorders, including such serious illnesses as schizophrenia, bipolar disorder, and major depression." *Id.* at 1.

[223] About 25% of the two million people who are behind bars are there for drug offenses—not violent or other offenses indirectly connected to criminalized drugs, but drug offenses themselves. Walter Cronkite, *Prisons Needlessly Overpopulated with Drug Offenders,* CENTRE DAILY TIMES, Aug. 6, 2004, *available at* http://www.mapinc.org/tlcnews/v04/n1118/a03.htm?155; *see also* Bureau of Justice Statistics, Prison Statistics: Summary Findings, http://www.ojp.usdoj.gov/bjs/prisons.htm (last visited Feb. 21, 2006). "Between 1995 and 2001, the increasing number of violent offenders accounted for 63% of the total growth of the State prison population; 15% of the total growth was attributable to the increasing number of drug offenders." *Id.*

[224] In the United States, the failure to provide an adequate education to those who most need it is the result of many factors, including the historical legacies of racial discrimination in housing, transportation and employment; systematic withdrawal of public support during integration; and the prevalence of low-wage work.

[225] Witness the unfortunate movement toward using high-stakes tests as an indicator of individual educational progress and achievement. *See* William P. Quigley, *Due Process Rights of Grade School Students Subjected to High-Stakes Testing,* 10 B.U. PUB. INT. L.J. 284 (2001).

[226] Eric Berger, *The Right to Education Under the South African Constitution,* 103 COLUM. L. REV. 614 (2003); Sumi Cho, *From Massive Resistance, to Passive Resistance, to Righteous Resistance: Understanding the Culture Wars from* Brown *to* Grutter, 7 U. PA. J. CONST. L. 809 (2005); James A. Gross, *A Human Rights Perspective on U.S. Education: Only Some Children Matter,* 50 CATH. U. L. REV. 919 (2001); C. Raj Kumar, *International Human Rights Perspectives on the Fundamental Right to Education—Integration of Human Rights and Human Development in the Indian Constitution,* 12 TUL. J. INT'L & COMP. L. 237 (2004).

[227] Mark Dudzic & Adolph Reed Jr., *Free Higher Ed!*, NATION, Feb. 23, 2004, *available at* 2004 WLNR 17889313.

> Make every public institution of higher education free for all who meet the admissions standards. No means testing, no service or work requirements, no minimum or

Finally, victimized peoples and nations deserve reparations to counterbalance the continuing effects of injustice.[228] Theologian Walter Brueggeman states that the definition of justice is to "sort out what belongs to whom, and to return it to them."[229] Reparations should be made to people who have been subjected to injustices by governments or corporations.[230] Reparations should also be made internationally where appropriate.[231] Reparations often address core issues of racism—social structures that perpetuate the advantages compiled over hundreds of years of privilege.[232]

These areas of law are but a few of those that support current systems of racism, militarism and materialism, and that must be radically changed. While nearly every area of the law is in need of radical change, lawyers must become revolutionaries for that change to occur.

III. BECOMING A REVOLUTIONARY LAWYER

> *It is not enough merely to call for freedom, democracy, and human rights. There has to be a determination to persevere in the struggle, to make sacrifices in the name of enduring truths, to*

> maximum ages. Just make it free for all. Free higher education is a simple idea that has a profound resonance with the shared values of the American people. Recent polls have shown that more than 80 percent agree that a college diploma is essential to success. Seventy percent think higher education is being priced beyond the income of the average family.

Id.

[228] Mari Matsuda, *Looking to the Bottom: Critical Legal Studies and Reparations,* 22 HARV. C.R.-C.L. L. REV. 323, 381–83 (1987).

[229] Walter Brueggemann et al., TO ACT JUSTLY, LOVE TENDERLY, WALK HUMBLY: AN AGENDA FOR MINISTERS 5 (1997).

[230] A variety of groups are deserving beneficiaries of reparations. For material on indigenous Australians, see Michael Legg, *Indigenous Australians and International Law: Racial Discrimination, Genocide and Reparations*, 20 BERKELEY. J. INT'L L. 387 (2002).

For information on African-Americans, see Jeremy Levitt, *Black African Reparations,* 25 S.U. L. REV. 1 (1997); Kyle D. Logue, *Reparations as Redistribution,* 84 B.U. L. REV. 1319 (2004); Alfreda Robinson, *Corporate Social Responsibility and African American Reparations*, 55 RUTGERS L. REV. 309 (2003); Edieth Y. Wu, *Reparations to African-Americans,* 3 CONN. PUB. INT. L.J. 403 (2004).

For reparations material on Mexican-Americans, see Jon Michael Haynes, What is It About Saying We're Sorry? New Federal Legislation and the Forgotten Promises of the Treaty of Guadalupe Hidalgo, 3 SCHOLAR 231 (2001).

For material on reparations for Japanese-Americans and Holocaust survivors, see Alfred L. Brophy, *Some Conceptual and Legal Problems in Reparations for Slavery,* 58 N.Y.U. ANN. SURV. AM. L. 497, 499–500 (2003).

On reparations and Haitian-Americans, see Malissia Lennox, Note, *Refugees, Racism, and Reparations: A Critique of the United States' Haitian Immigration Policy*, 45 STAN. L. REV. 687 (1993).

[231] *See* Libby Adler & Peer Zumbansen, *The Forgetfulness of Noblesse: A Critique of the German Foundation Law Compensating Slave and Forced Laborers of the Third Reich,* 39 HARV. J. ON LEGIS. 1 (2002); Peter G. Fischer, *The Victims' Trust Fund of the International Criminal Court—Formation of a Functional Reparations Scheme,* 17 EMORY INT'L L. REV. 187, 192–204 (2003).

[232] *See* Christian Sundquist, *Critical Praxis, Spirit Healing, and Community Activism: Preserving a Subversive Dialogue on Reparations,* 58 N.Y.U. ANN. SURV. AM. L. 659 (2003).

> *resist the corrupting influences of desire, ill will, ignorance, and fear. Saints, it has been said, are the sinners who go on trying . . . It is his capacity for self-improvement and self-redemption that which most distinguishes man from the mere brute. At the root of human responsibility is the concept of perfection, the urge to achieve it, the intelligence to find a path towards it, and the will to follow that path . . . It is man's vision of a world fit for rational, civilized humanity which leads him to dare and to suffer to build societies free from want and fear.*
>
> —Aung San Suu Kyi[233]

The world does not need more lawyers that support the status quo. We need revolutionaries.[234] Over the years, I have listened to hundreds, maybe thousands, of people who are actively working to make radical changes in the world. From those conversations, I have distilled a few principles regarding what I term "reflective activism," and I will share these here.

It is my observation that some people interested in radical change are not activists, but hyper-activists. Hyper-activists want radical change now, and will work like crazy to achieve it. When it does not come immediately, or within two or three years, they become burned out and give up.. Those that practice reflective activism remain committed and active agents of social change over the long haul. Revolutionaries must be committed to the long haul, and what follows are my thoughts about how best to do that.

These are not specific instructions, or a cookbook for radical action, but rather reflections on remaining committed to radical change. Revolutionary change is not the sprint of a specific campaign, but a marathon of life work. What is needed is not a map of where to go, because the destination continually changes, but rather a compass that will help orient us toward the goals we seek in our journey. These principles can help orient us toward a lifetime of acting as revolutionaries, and help us deal with the joys and defeats that are inevitable in such a journey.

Becoming a revolutionary lawyer first involves "un-learning" most of what we were taught in law school and what we have learned in the practice of law. We must change teachers and skills, but, most of all, we must change our minds and hearts. We must be humble and admit what

---

[233] Lauren, *supra* note 106.

[234] Many lawyers have been called revolutionaries, including Mahatma Gandhi, Nelson Mandela, many signers of the Declaration of Independence, and Thurgood Marshall. *But see* Richard Delgado & Jean Stefancic, FAILED REVOLUTIONS: SOCIAL REFORM AND THE LIMITS OF LEGAL IMAGINATION (1994).

we do not know. We must learn from our "clients" and be willing to be uncomfortable.

A. *Solidarity*

If there is a first principle of radical change, it is the principle of solidarity.[235] Radical change only comes about by working *with* people; it is never the result of working *for* people.[236] Liberation is never something that people do *for* others, but something that people achieve *with* others. This is best summed up by the quote: "If you have come to help me, you are wasting your time. . . . But if you have come because your liberation is bound up with mine, then let us work together."[237]

Working in solidarity means that we must constantly challenge racism, paternalism, patriarchy, homophobia, classism, nationalism and all of the other violent divisions hard-wired into our selves and our systems. Those systems of division were set up and are maintained to keep us from being in solidarity with others struggling for justice.[238] We must make common cause with others to identify and overcome those divisions. Solidarity also means no borders; globalized liberation is the goal.[239]

People should never expect to achieve revolutionary change alone, but only by organizing with others to confront injustice and to create new ways of living.[240] Solidarity also means that unless each of us realizes that we directly and personally benefit from actions for change, we will not have enough reason to keep working for justice.[241] Moreover, solidarity

---

235

> Solidarity requires that one enter into the situation of those with whom one is solidary [sic]; it is a radical posture. If what characterizes the oppressed is their subordination to the consciousness of the master, as Hegel affirms, true solidarity with the oppressed means fighting at their side to transform the objective reality which has made them these "beings for another."

Paulo Freire, PEDAGOGY OF THE OPPRESSED 34 (Myra Bergman Ramos trans., 1970).

236 "Political action on the side of the oppressed must be pedagogical action in the authentic sense of the word, and, therefore, action *with* the oppressed." *Id.* at 53.

237 University of the Poor, Welcome Letter, http://www.universityofthepoor.org/schools/social/welcome.html (last visited Feb. 21, 2006) (quoting Lilla Watson, an aboriginal artist and social worker).

238 Betsy Leondar-Wright, CLASS MATTERS: CROSS-CLASS ALLIANCE BUILDING FOR MIDDLE-CLASS ACTIVISTS (2005) (addressing class, race, gender, sexual orientation and other divisions in the effort to bring about radical change).

239 Jeremy Brecher et al., GLOBALIZATION FROM BELOW: THE POWER OF SOLIDARITY (2000); GLOBALIZE LIBERATION: HOW TO UPROOT THE SYSTEM AND BUILD A BETTER WORLD (David Solnit ed., 2004).

240 William P. Quigley, *Reflections of Community Organizers: Lawyering for Empowerment of Community Organizers,* 21 OHIO N.U. L. REV. 455, 456 (1994) ("Community organizing is *the* essential element of empowering organizational advocacy."); *see also* Kimberly A. Bobo et al., ORGANIZING FOR SOCIAL CHANGE (3d ed. 2001); Derek Denckla & Matthew Diller, COMMUNITY LAWYERING: THEORY AND PRACTICE (2000); Bill Moyer, DOING DEMOCRACY: THE MAP MODEL FOR ORGANIZING SOCIAL MOVEMENTS (2001); Randy Shaw, *Lawyers: Allies or Obstacles to Social Change?, in* THE ACTIVIST'S HANDBOOK: A PRIMER 185, 185–211 (updated ed. 2001).

241 "It is only the oppressed who, by freeing themselves, can free their oppressors." Freire, *supra* note 205, at 42.

also returns us to the first principle of the 1948 *Universal Declaration of Human Rights,* that all people are sisters and brothers and have an inherent right to human rights and dignity.[242] This simple statement has truly revolutionary implications. Solidarity is our first principle.

B. Seek out and Treasure Hope, Joy and Love

> *The dominant tendencies of our day are unregulated global capitalism, racial balkanization, social breakdown, and individual depression. Hope enacts the stance of the participant who actively struggles against the evidence in order to change the deadly tides of wealth inequality, group xenophobia, and personal despair. Only a new wave of vision, courage and hope can keep us sane—and preserve the decency and dignity requisite to revitalize our organizational energy for the work to be done. To live is to wrestle with despair yet never allow despair to have the last word.*
>
> —Cornel West[243]

No one can sustain the long haul of a life dedicated to revolutionary change without hope, joy and love. If your life and work do not involve generous doses of real hope, joy and love, then you must make radical changes before you can join with others in changing our world.

Some may think that a high priority on love is inconsistent with revolutionary change, but they are mistaken. Love is one of the most radical forces for change.[244] I am talking here about real love, not Hallmark-card love—love that energizes people to undertake actions that otherwise seem impossible; love that is willing to sacrifice for others; love that can triumph over the most challenging obstacles; love that accepts our mistakes and those of others and goes forward anyway.[245]

---

[242] *See* Universal Declaration of Human Rights, *supra* note 78. "Whereas recognition of the inherent dignity and of the equal and inalienable rights of all members of the human family is the foundation for freedom, justice and peace in the world. . . ." *Id.* at pmbl.

[243] Cornel West, *Prisoners of Hope, in* THE IMPOSSIBLE WILL TAKE A LITTLE WHILE: A CITIZEN'S GUIDE TO HOPE IN A TIME OF FEAR 293, 296–97 (Paul Rogat Loeb ed., 2004).

[244] The revolutionary Che Guavara stated:

> Let me say, with the risk of appearing ridiculous, that the true revolutionary is guided by strong feelings of love. It is impossible to think of an authentic revolutionary without this quality . . . One must have a large dose of humanity, a large dose of a sense of justice and truth, to avoid falling into extremes, into cold intellectualism, into isolation from the masses. Every day we must struggle so that this love of living humanity is transformed into concrete facts, into acts that will serve as an example.

Ernesto Che Guevara, MAN AND SOCIALISM IN CUBA 43 (1967).

[245] One of my favorite quotes about love is taken from Dostoevsky and was a favorite of Dorothy Day's, a radical Catholic who helped start the Catholic Worker Movement. The quote is:

> Love in action is a harsh and dreadful thing compared with love in dreams. Love in dreams is greedy for immediate action, rapidly performed and in the sight of all. Men will even give their lives if only the ordeal does not last long but is soon over, with all

Joy is also fundamental. Justice work cannot be only rock-breaking toil. There is wonderful joy in the shared struggles for peace and justice. There is joy in solidarity. And, in truth, there is much joy in the shared companionship and humor that are essential parts of every campaign for radical change.[246]

Hope is likewise essential. So many people are unable to join actions challenging injustice because they are paralyzed by a sense of futility and despair—exactly what the powerful want. Hope offers opportunity. But hope, as noted above, is not the same as optimism. Hope is the conviction that if people created the injustices imposed on us, then the dreams of our sisters and brothers and of ourselves can be realized if and when enough people join together to work for change. Hope recognizes that the history of justice is built on the work of others who we will never know, but who share in the unexpected advances toward justice.[247]

> looking on and applauding as though on the stage. But active love is labor and fortitude, and for some people too, perhaps, a complete science. But I predict that just when you see with horror that in spite of all your efforts you are getting farther from your goal instead of nearer to it—at that very moment I predict that you will reach it and behold clearly the miraculous power of the Lord who has been all the time loving and mysteriously guiding you.

Fyodor Dostoevsky, THE BROTHERS KARAMAZOV 49–50 (Constance Garnett trans., Ralph Matlaw ed., W.W. Norton & Co. 1976) (1879).

246

> It is hard to sustain ourselves in difficult work if the only reward is the possibility that somewhere down the line our work may have some positive effect, though we may be long dead. That's a lot to ask of people. We all want more than that out of life. We want joy and love. At least every now and then, we want to have a good time, including a good time while engaged in our work. No political movement can sustain itself indefinitely without understanding that, not just because people need—and have a right—to be happy, but because if there is no joy in it, then movements are more likely to be dangerous. The joy—the celebration of being human and being alive in connection with others—is what fuels the drive for change.
>
> People find joy in many different ways. As many people over the years have pointed out, one source of joy is in the struggle. I have spent a lot of time in the past few years doing political work, and some of that work isn't terribly fun. Collating photocopies for a meeting for a progressive political cause isn't any more fun than collating photocopies for a meeting for a corporate employer. But it is different in some ways: It puts you in contact with like-minded people. It sparks conversation. It creates space in which you can think and feel your way through difficult questions. It's a great place to laugh as you staple. It provides the context for connections that go beyond superficial acquaintanceships.

Robert Jensen, *Citizens of the Empire: Real Hope is Radical,* THINKING PEACE, http://www.thinkingpeace.com/Lib/lib023.html.

247 *Id.*

> The hope comes not from some delusional state, but from what I would argue is a sensible assessment of the situation. Cynicism might be an appropriate reaction to injustice that can't be changed. Hope is an appropriate response to a task that, while difficult, is imaginable. And once I could understand the structural forces that produced injustice, I could imagine what a world without those forces—and hence without the injustice—might look like. And I could imagine what activities and actions and ideas it would take to get us there. And I could look around, look back into history and realize that many people have understood this and that I hadn't stumbled onto a new idea.

We cannot give what we do not have. If we want a world that is more loving, more joyful, and more hopeful, then we must first have those qualities in abundance in our own lives. If we do not have them, we must seek them out, find them, and integrate them into our lives. Justice-seekers are sometimes dismissed as fanatical, scary people, and, truthfully, some of us are like that some of the time. That is called burnout, and it is a part of most people's jobs. However, if you are dedicated to helping bring about revolutionary change and you are regularly burning out, you must make a change—either a change in what you are doing or a change in yourself.[248]

C. *Overcome Fear*

There is a popular bumper sticker that says "No Fear." For purposes of revolutionary change, that phrase is mistaken. There is plenty to be fearful of. Fear is a technique of control often used by those in power to scare people away from thinking about and acting for fundamental change.[249] Courage is not having no fear, but rather facing our fears, overcoming them, and taking action despite them.[250]

A willingness to be uncomfortable is part of the challenge of being a revolutionary. I am uncomfortable when in new places, with new people, with challenging ideas and when called to new ways of living and acting.

Id.

248

> If you find yourself blowing up at people, getting irritated over the littlest problem, or not enjoying your work, you need to review your work habits. If you are working excessive hours, you will become less effective in the time you do work and will begin thinking of yourself as a martyr (and everyone will avoid you). The social change movement of the 2000s does not need more martyrs. It needs effective, well-balanced organizers who are building power by involving people in winning real victories.

BOBO, *supra* note 210, at 340–41.

[249] *See Fascism,* THE COLUMBIA ENCYCLOPEDIA (6th ed. 2000), *available at* http://www.bartleby.com/65/fa/fascism.html.

> The growth of democratic ideology and popular participation in politics in the nineteenth century was terrifying to some conservative elements in European society, and fascism grew out of the attempt to counter it by forming mass parties based largely on the middle classes and the petty bourgeoisie, exploiting their fear of political domination by the lower classes. Forerunners of fascism, such as Georges Boulanger in France and Adolf Stöker and Karl Lueger in Germany and Austria, played on people's fears of revolution with its subsequent chaos, anarchy, and general insecurity in their efforts to gain political power. They appealed to nationalist sentiments and prejudices, exploited anti-Semitism, and portrayed themselves as champions of law, order, Christian morality, and the sanctity of private property.

Id.

[250] "The brave man is not he who feels no fear, For that were stupid and irrational; But he, whose noble soul its fears subdues, And bravely dares the danger nature shrinks from." Joanna Baillie, *Basil: A Tragedy, in* 1 THE COMPLETE POETICAL WORKS OF JOANNA BAILLIE 39 (1832), *available at* http://www.bartleby.com/73/353.html.

We must be willing to push the envelope and to go to new places, both personally and professionally.[251]

We must also prepare to be criticized.[252] If you take any action, much less challenge the status quo, many people will not like it. As Dom Helder Camara said: "When you speak about the poor, you are a holy person; if you speak about the root causes of poverty, you are a communist."[253] Those who profit from current arrangements will criticize and attack.[254] If you cannot take conflict and criticism, you cannot be in this struggle.[255] Moreover, it is important to actually listen to criticism, because some of it is accurate and can help adjust our actions to achieve our goals.

D. Continually Engage in Critical Re-education

To live a life of radical change, we must continually and critically re-educate ourselves. Conventional education is not about independent or critical thinking. Rather, it reinforces the idea that there is nothing

---

[251] Marc Galanter, *A Vocation for Law? American Jewish Lawyers and Their Antecedents,* 26 FORDHAM URB. L.J. 1125, 1131 (1999). "As modern readers, we tend to respond to the prophets' elevated universal morality and admire their courage, while filtering out their group-centered and god-centered revivalism and retaining a 'thin residue of ethical monotheism, cultic criticism and social justice.' " *Id.*

[252]

> It is not the critic who counts; not the man who points out how the strong man stumbles, or where the doer of deeds could have done them better. The credit belongs to the man who is actually in the arena, whose face is marred by dust and sweat and blood; who strives valiantly; who errs and comes short again and again, because there is no effort without error and shortcoming; but who does actually strive to do the deeds; who knows the great enthusiasms, the great devotions; and spends himself in a worthy cause; who at best knows in the end the triumph of high achievement, and who at the worst, if he fails, at least fails while daring greatly, so that his place shall never be with those cold and timid souls who know neither victory nor defeat.

Theodore Roosevelt, Speech Given at the Sorbonne, Paris, France: Citizenship in a Republic (Apr. 23, 1910), *reprinted in* 13 THE WORKS OF THEODORE ROOSEVELT 510 (1926), *available at* http://www.bartleby.com/73/10.html.

[253] This quote is attributed to Dom Helder Camara in Fred Kammer, DOING FAITHJUSTICE: AN INTRODUCTION TO CATHOLIC SOCIAL THOUGHT 156 (1991). For background on Camara, see Beatriz Lecumberri, *Brazil's Helder Camara, Champion of Poor, Dies at 90,* AGENCE FRANCE PRESSE, Aug. 28, 1999.

[254] Men in authority will always think that criticism of their policies is dangerous. They will always equate their policies with patriotism, and find criticism subversive. Henry Steele Commager, FREEDOM AND ORDER: A COMMENTARY ON THE AMERICAN POLITICAL SCENE (1966).

[255]

> If there is no struggle there is no progress. Those who profess to favor freedom and yet deprecate agitation, are men who want crops without plowing up the ground, they want rain without thunder and lightning. They want the ocean without the awful roar of its many waters. This struggle may be a moral one, or it may be a physical one, and it may be both moral and physical, but it must be a struggle. Power concedes nothing without a demand. It never did and it never will.

Frederick Douglass, Speech Delivered at Canandaigua, New York: West India Emancipation (Aug. 4, 1857), *reprinted in* 2 THE LIFE AND WRITINGS OF FREDERICK DOUGLASS 437 (Philip S. Foner ed., 1950), *available at* http://www.bartleby.com/73/443.html.

anyone can do to change this best of all possible worlds.[256] Part of the challenge of revolutionary thought is revolutionary re-education.

Independent and critical thinking is our job.[257] If we fail to do our job, no one will educate us about alternatives to the status quo, and no one will insist that we learn about alternative views. For example, corporate mainstream media has little interest in telling the truth about justice or in showing justice-based alternatives.[258] If all we do is read or watch mainstream news, we are not likely to hear very much about justice. We will, however, hear a lot about driving cars, drinking beer and staying slim.[259]

The Internet provides many opportunities for re-education, but it is up to us to seek them out and critically analyze them.[260] There are also social justice films and documentaries that can help.[261] Biographies of revolutionaries are often a great inspiration and can assist in real education.[262] Likewise, we should discover the real histories of social justice and revolutionary movements—these can be both inspiring and comforting as we realize the humanity of the organizing efforts involved.[263] It is no excuse to say that we are too busy engaging in social

[256] *See* FREIRE, *supra* note 205. Paulo Freire spends quite a bit of time discussing the failings of conventional education. It is the "banking" concept of education, where "knowledge is a gift bestowed by those who consider themselves knowledgeable upon those whom they consider to know nothing. Projecting an absolute ignorance on others, a characteristic of the ideology of oppression, negates education and knowledge as processes of inquiry." *Id.* at 58. Freire goes on to state that "[t]he more completely [the students] accept the passive role imposed on them, the more they tend simply to adapt to the world as it is." *Id.* at 60.

[257] *See* RETHINKING GLOBALIZATION: TEACHING FOR JUSTICE IN AN UNJUST WORLD (Bill Bigelow & Bob Peterson eds., 2002). The book is accessible and includes many thought-provoking stories, cartoons and examples. My favorite is a cartoon of a small fish being pursued by a medium fish who is being pursued by a large fish. The small fish says, "There is no justice in this world!" The medium size fish says, "Sometimes there is justice in this world." And the big fish says, "The world is just!" *Id.* at 73.

[258] For example, consider the lack of mainstream coverage of a memo contradicting the U.S. version of how the invasion of Iraq came to be. *See* David Michael Green, *Downing Street: A Dead-End in American Media,* IN THESE TIMES, July 13, 2005, http://www.inthesetimes.com/site/main/article/2252.

For other examples, see Eric Alterman, *Lying Liars & the Presidents Who Employ Them,* NATION, July 18, 2005, http://www.thenation.com/doc/20050718/alterman; John Nichols & Robert W. McChesney, *FCC: It Could Get Worse,* NATION, Feb. 21, 2005, http://www.thenation.com/doc/20050221/nichols.

[259] Read Jean Kilbourne, CAN'T BUY MY LOVE: HOW ADVERTISING CHANGES THE WAY WE THINK AND FEEL (1st Touchstone ed. 1999). Then watch television and think about what mass media actually sells us—women as objects, corruption of relationships, addiction, and violence. There is nothing about radical change—unless it is the new "American Revolution," brought to us by Chevrolet.

[260] *See, e.g.,* Alternative Media Watch, http://www.zmag.org/altmediawatch.htm (last visited Feb. 21, 2006).

[261] For some suggestions, see BLUEPRINT FOR SOC. JUST., Apr.-May 2005, *available at* http://www.loyno.edu/twomey/blueprint/vol_lviii/No-08_AprMay_2005.pdf.

[262] As one wise student advised me: "Listen to the elders of other movements." *See* Robert Shetterly, AMERICANS WHO TELL THE TRUTH (1st ed. 2005) (discussing numerous and diverse U.S. citizens from whom we could profitably learn).

[263] This author has enjoyed learning from: Taylor Branch, PARTING THE WATERS: AMERICA IN THE KING YEARS, 1954–63 (1988); Taylor Branch, PILLAR OF FIRE: AMERICA IN THE KING

justice or revolutionary activity, because re-education will help ensure that the activities we engage in are just.

E. Community and Family Support

A radical friend of mine, Daniel Berrigan, was asked, "Who are your heroes?" He replied, "I don't believe in heroes, I believe in community."[264] There is no such thing as the solo revolutionary or solo activist. Anyone trying to live this life must have a supportive community.[265] For many, this will be family; for others, it will be close friends. These communities often change over time, but to engage in a life working with others for radical change, we must constantly create and engage in communities.

Families, life partners and close friends are important for the long haul. If the person closest to you does not share your values, you are in deep trouble. If all of your friends only watch SportsCenter or recreationally shop, you are in trouble. You must expand your circle and add some new friends. True justice-seeking friends and families not only support us, but also pull us into justice work.

We can only swim against the stream for so long if we try to do it alone. Psychologists have proven that it is extremely difficult for a person alone to resist even clearly unreasonable commands of authority.[266] The presence of even one person who dissents from an incorrect majority view will greatly enhance the ability of others to stand up for what they believe is correct.[267] The ability of one lone person to dissent against the

---

YEARS, 1963–65 (1998); Adam Hochschild, BURY THE CHAINS: PROPHETS AND REBELS IN THE FIGHT TO FREE AN EMPIRE'S SLAVES (2005); Paul Gordon Lauren, THE EVOLUTION OF INTERNATIONAL HUMAN RIGHTS: VISIONS SEEN (2d ed. 2003); NONVIOLENT SOCIAL MOVEMENTS: A GEOGRAPHICAL PERSPECTIVE (Stephen Zunes et al. eds., 1999); Linda Rabben, FIERCE LEGION OF FRIENDS: A HISTORY OF HUMAN RIGHTS CAMPAIGNS AND CAMPAIGNERS (2002).

See also the analysis of the civil rights movement, the anti-nuclear energy movement, the gay and lesbian movement, and the globalization movement in MOYER, *supra* note 210.

[264] Panel with Daniel Berrigan at Loyola University New Orleans Institute for Ministry (Jan. 17, 1998).

[265] "We all need personal support networks, families and close friends, who can share our joys and sorrows. Developing close relationships requires time. . . . Strong relationships provide organizers with a base of support for sustaining themselves for the long haul and assistance in developing self-confidence." BOBO, *supra* note 210, at 341.

[266] *See* Ric Simmons, *Not "Voluntary" But Still Reasonable: A New Paradigm for Understanding the Consent Searches Doctrine,* 80 IND. L.J. 773 (2005) (describing the Milgram experiments). Professor Stanley Milgram conducted a series of experiments in the 1960s in which he asked volunteers to administer increasingly strong electric shocks to people who failed to answer questions correctly. Though the subjects evidenced incredible pain, apparently even fatal shocks continued to be given by person after person who followed authority and did as ordered. *Id.* at 802–04.

[267] *See* Kenneth B. Davis, Jr., *Structural Bias, Special Litigation Committees, and the Vagaries of Director Independence,* 90 IOWA L. REV. 1305, 1318 (2005).

> When asked to compare the length of a series of lines, subjects were induced to give clearly incorrect responses after a number of other perceived subjects (actually confederates of the experimenter) had done the same. When, on the other hand, a second unwary subject was added to the experiment or one of the confederates was instructed to give the correct answer, the level of conformity declined significantly.

conventional wisdom and to work for justice is more than most of us can handle, but with allies, our abilities and our opportunities expand dramatically.

F. The Preferential Option for the Poor and Powerless

> *Whenever you are in doubt, or when the self becomes too much with you, apply the following test. Recall the face of the poorest and the weakest person whom you have seen, and ask yourself if the next step you contemplate is going to be of any use to that person. Will that person gain anything by it? Will it restore that person to a control over his or her own life and destiny? In other words, will it lead to freedom for the hungry and spiritually starving millions? Then you will find your doubts and your self melting away.*
>
> —Mahatma Gandhi[268]

Liberation theology has given the community seeking radical change a wonderful gift by emphasizing a principle called the "preferential option for the poor."[269] This is not a new thought, as the above Gandhi quote and many biblical verses attest, but it is a new description of an important way of thinking and acting. Advocates of liberation theology define all poverty as oppression, and call for all who seek to change the world to adopt a "preferential option for the poor."[270]

This justice perspective demands that we turn our world view upside down and look at fairness from the point of view of those billions who live at the base of the mountain. From the top, things look natural and

---

Id. (describing the Solomon Asch study).

268 Mohandes Gandhi (Aug. 1947), *in* MOHANDAS GANDHI: ESSENTIAL WRITINGS 190–91 (John Dear ed., 2002).

269 The "preferential option for the poor" has been described as a challenge "to create conditions for marginalized voices to be heard, to defend the defenseless, and to assess lifestyles, policies and social institutions in terms of their impact on the poor . . . to strengthen the whole community by assisting those who are most vulnerable." Univ. of Notre Dame, Ctr. for Social Concerns, An Introduction to the Principles of Catholic Social Thought, http://centerforsocialconcerns.nd.edu/mission/cst/cst4.shtml (last visited Feb. 21, 2006).

270 "So first we need to have direct knowledge of the reality of oppression/liberation through objective engagement in solidarity with the poor. This pre-theological stage really means conversion of life, and this involves a 'class conversion,' in the sense of leading to effective solidarity with the oppressed and their liberation." Leonard Boff & Clodovis Boff, INTRODUCING LIBERATION THEOLOGY 23 (1987); *see also* Gerald West, *The Bible and the Poor: A New Way of Doing Theology*, *in* THE CAMBRIDGE COMPANION TO LIBERATION THEOLOGY 131 (Christopher Rowland ed., 1999).

> In other words, theologies of liberation require that we not only make "an option for the poor," but that we also accept the epistemological paradigm shift in which the poor and marginalized are seen as the primary dialogue partners of theology. Theology begins with the reality, experience, needs, interests, questions, and resources of the poor and marginalized.

Id. For more on this topic, see Henriot, *supra* note 107.

inevitable. From the bottom, however, who would not question the inequality? Looking from the bottom, we easily see the racism, militarism and excessive materialism of those who are perched comfortably at the top.

Since we in the United States live at the top of the mountain, we are not naturally in a position to understand the perspective of those at the bottom. Therefore, we must continually re-educate ourselves about justice and injustice. The conventional wisdom from the top is that "we are doing all we can," "things are much better than they used to be," and "don't worry about it; someone else is working on this right now." True re-education is our job. A preferential option for the poor insists that we vigorously challenge the current social, economic, military and religious arrangements that teach us these false truths.[271]

It is incumbent upon us to seek out the voices of the poor and listen to them. The media is not going to do that for us. The view of the United States from Haiti, Sri Lanka, South Africa, or China looks quite different than the view from Washington, D.C. Likewise, the view of the United States from the perspective of inner-city underemployed or unemployed workers and their families, or from those in prisons or domestic violence shelters, is quite different than views from other perspectives.

> [A]n option for the poor is not primarily the choice of a less-affluent life-style by individuals or groups. It is a commitment to resist the structural injustice which marks our world. The person who makes such an option is undertaking to work to change the unjust economic, social and political structures which determine how power and resources are shared out in the world. . . . An "option for the poor" . . . means a series of choices, personal or communal, made by individuals, by communities, or even by corporate entities. . . . It is the choice to disentangle themselves from serving the interests of those at the "top" of society and to begin instead to come into solidarity with those at or near the bottom.[272]

Turn the world upside down and look at it from the perspective of workers, the poor and the international community. The rich and powerful think the current system works fine most of the time. Billions of others do not agree. We must engage in solidarity with those others to participate in the radical transformation that our world needs.

---

[271] William P. Quigley, *Seven Principles for Catholic Law Schools Serious About a Preferential Option for the Poor,* 1 U. ST. THOMAS L.J. 128, 129 (2003).

[272] Donal Dorr, OPTION FOR THE POOR: A HUNDRED YEARS OF VATICAN SOCIAL TEACHING 3, 4 (rev. ed. 1992).

G. *Do Not Accept Reality-Particularly for the Future*

> *Somewhere deep inside us we seem to know that we are destined for something better than strife. Now and again we catch a glimpse of the better thing for which we are meant—for example, when we work together to counter the effects of natural disasters and the world is galvanized by a spirit of compassion and an amazing outpouring of generosity; when for a little while we are bound together by bonds of a caring humanity . . . . when we sign charters on the rights of children and of women; when we seek to ban the use of antipersonnel land mines; when we agree as one to outlaw torture and racism. Then we experience fleetingly that we are made for community, for family, that we are in a network of interdependence.*
>
> —Desmond Tutu[273]

If you work for radical change, people will frequently tell you that the future is already determined, and there is nothing anyone can do about it. Do not believe them. In the past, slavery was widespread and legal; women were prosecuted and jailed for voting; domestic violence was an acceptable part of relationships; child labor was legal; labor unions were outlawed; only white men with substantial property could vote; there was no minimum wage; and the disabled were told to stay at home and hide away, as were gays and lesbians.[274] Everyone who worked to bring about those changes was told repeatedly that it was useless to organize for justice, that the present was the best that could be done under the circumstances, and that the powerful would never allow change.

Refuse to accept the reality of those who think that our future is pre-determined by the powerful and will never change.[275] Certainly never accept our current reality as the inevitable future. Accept no limits. Never let anyone tell you what you can achieve or who you can become. Challenge injustice even if you do not know the solution. Do not accept false choices-demand a third way.[276] Our choice is not between living a life

---

[273] Desmond Tutu, *No Future Without Forgiveness, in* THE IMPOSSIBLE WILL TAKE A LITTLE WHILE, *supra* note 213, at 394–95.

[274] *See* THE TREE OF LIBERTY: A DOCUMENTARY HISTORY OF REBELLION AND POLITICAL CRIME IN AMERICA (Nicholas N. Kittrie & Eldon D. Wedlock, Jr., eds., 1986) (documenting the struggles for suffrage, freedom, and civil rights).

[275] "The secret weapon of Jesus and Gandhi, of Martin Luther King and Nelson Mandela, of Shirin Ebadi and Wangari Maathai, and of all great human rights activists, is simply the willingness to suffer loss after loss, again and again, until you win!" Letter from Fr. Gerard Jean-Juste to U.S. Ambassador to Haiti (Nov. 9, 2004), *available at* http://www.aristide.org/articles/LetterHaitianJail.htm.

[276] Jean Bertrand Aristide recalls asking a four-year-old girl named Florence if the pool in which she was going to swim for the first time was big or small. She answered, "It is beautiful." Later, when asked which she preferred, cola or rum, she responded firmly, "I prefer juice."

of justice and starving, or selling-out and prospering. Demand and create another livable option. Moreover, our choice is not between merely accepting the situation, or making superficial reforms. We can insist on a third way in order to create a just system. As Dorothy Day said: "Our problems stem from our acceptance of this filthy, rotten system."[277] Do not accept it, transform it!

H. *Create and Maintain an Interior Life*

> *Many people are aware of the world's suffering; their hearts are filled with compassion. They know what needs to be done, and they engage in political, social, and environmental work to try to change things. But after a period of intense involvement, they may become discouraged if they lack the strength needed to sustain a life of action. Real strength is not in power, money or weapons, but in deep, inner peace.*
>
> —Thich Nhat Hanh[278]

> *We cannot do anything for peace without ourselves being peace. If you cannot smile, you cannot help other people smile. If you are not peaceful, then you cannot contribute to the peace movement. We know that our situation is very dangerous. A nuclear war can happen at any moment. Practicing meditation is to practice awareness of what is going on. Therefore, if we are aware, if we know what is going on, we will be peace and make peace, so that the worst may not occur.*
>
> —Thich Nhat Hanh[279]

> *The insistence that the oppressed engage in reflection on their concrete situation is not a call to armchair revolution. On the contrary, reflection—true reflection—leads to action.*
>
> —Paulo Freire[280]

> When I presented two options, big or small, she created a third one. When I asked which she preferred, rum or cola, again Florence created a third choice. Florence is a child responding in a spontaneous way. But we adults thinking rationally—can't we do the same? When presented with only two options, we can create a third way.

Jean-Bertrand Aristide, EYES OF THE HEART: SEEKING A PATH FOR THE POOR IN THE AGE OF GLOBALIZATION 19–20 (2000).

[277] Jim Forest, *What I Learned About Justice from Dorothy Day,* SALT OF THE EARTH, 1996, *available at* http://salt.claretianpubs.org/issues/DorothyDay/learned.html.

[278] Thich Nhat Hanh, PEACE IS EVERY STEP: THE PATH OF MINDFULNESS IN EVERYDAY LIFE 99 (1991).

[279] Thich Nhat Hanh, *Being Peace, in* PEACE IS THE WAY: WRITINGS ON NONVIOLENCE FROM THE FELLOWSHIP OF RECONCILIATION 153, 156–57 (Walter Wink ed., 2000).

Have you ever seen a gerbil running furiously on a wire wheel? That gerbil illustrates the difference between action and progress. There is a tendency in working for change to get wrapped up in being active, even hyper-active, without actually making any progress.

One important way to recognize the difference between action and progress is to create and maintain an interior life of reflection. Some people call this meditation, while others call it reflection, prayer, or yoga. Whatever you call it, people who want to change the world must have this interior life. Nelson Mandela gave the following advice about reflection while in jail:

> You may find that the cell is an ideal place to get to know yourself, to search realistically and regularly the process of your own mind and feelings. In judging our progress as individuals we tend to focus on external factors such as one's social position, influence and popularity, wealth and standard of education . . . but internal factors may be even more crucial in assessing one's development as a human being: honesty, sincerity, simplicity, humility, purity, generosity, absence of vanity, readiness to serve your fellow men—qualities within the reach of every soul—are the foundations of one's spiritual life . . . At least if nothing else, the cell gives you the opportunity to look daily into your entire conduct to overcome the bad and develop whatever is good in you. Regular meditation, say of about fifteen minutes a day before you turn in, can be very fruitful in this regard. You may find it difficult at first to pinpoint the negative factors in your life, but the tenth attempt may reap rich rewards. Never forget that a saint is a sinner who keeps on trying.[281]

We must create inner peace in order to engage in purposeful action. Without inner peace and a true sense of direction, we spend much of our time reacting to outside influences and day-to-day distractions, instead of trying to achieve justice and peace. Life is hectic enough, and not dedicated to radical change. If we are going to find and build peace, love and understanding in this world, we must be prepared. A healthy interior life is part of our preparation to live as fully as we can each and every day.

I. Sustainable Living

> *[H]umanity's consumption and waste production today exceed the Earth's capacity to create new resources and absorb waste . . . We are, as a result, liquidating certain natural capital to support*

---

[280] *See* Freire, *supra* note 205, at 52.

[281] Nelson Mandela, MANDELA: AN ILLUSTRATED AUTOBIOGRAPHY (1st ed. 1996).

current resource use, thereby reducing the Earth's capacity to support future life.[282]

Sustainability is a revolutionary principle because it assumes that every person has a right to enough of the world's resources to survive, and that no person has a right to take more than his or her fair share. This is a profoundly un-American idea, and it challenges every person and institution in the United States.

The United States represents less than five percent of the population of the world.[283] According to the U.S. Geological Survey, the United States consumed approximately 39% of the world's oil production, 23% of the world's natural gas production, and 23% of the world's coal production in 1998.[284] Europe and Japan consume less than half as much energy per person as the United States.[285]

Does the rest of the world wake up each day and say, "Let's give the United States an extra large helping of energy today, tomorrow and every day?" No. The unequal global distribution of resources is a justice issue. We must acknowledge that the current wealth of the United States is built in part on structural injustices around the world. We must acknowledge that the United States takes precious non-renewable resources from others—either by direct force or by unequal bargaining power.

Recall that over one billion people in the world live on less than one dollar per day, and that over two billion people live on less than two dollars per day.[286] Consider these facts about U.S. standards of living: as of 2003, there were more private cars than licensed drivers, and gas-guzzling sport utility vehicles were among the best-selling vehicles; new houses were 38% larger in 2002 than in 1975, despite there being fewer people per household on average; an estimated 65% of U.S. adults are overweight or obese, leading to an annual loss of 300,000 lives and at

---

[282] Mathis Wackernagel et al., REDEFINING PROGRESS, ECOLOGICAL FOOTPRINT OF NATIONS, NOVEMBER 2002 UPDATE, at 8 (2002), *available at* http://www.rprogress.org/publications/ef1999.pdf. The Worldwatch Institute reports:

> Calculations show that the planet has available 1.9 hectares of biologically productive land per person to supply resources and absorb wastes—yet the average person on Earth already uses 2.3 hectares worth. These "ecological footprints" range from the 9.7 hectares claimed by the average American to the 0.47 hectares used by the average Mozambican.

Worldwatch Institute, The State of Consumption Today, http://www.worldwatch.org/press/news/2004/02/04 (last visited Feb. 21, 2006).

[283] Thomas M. McDevitt & Patricia M. Rowe, U.S. CENSUS BUREAU, THE UNITED STATES IN INTERNATIONAL CONTEXT: 2000, at 1 (2002), *available at* http://www.census.gov/prod/2002pubs/c2kbr01-11.pdf.

[284] U.S. Geological Survey, U.S. Energy and World Energy Production and Consumption Statistics, http://energy.cr.usgs.gov/energy/stats_ctry/Statl.html (last visited Feb. 21, 2006).

[285] Allen R. Myerson, *U.S. Splurging on Energy After Falling off Its Diet,* N.Y. TIMES WEB, Oct. 22, 1998, http://www.colorado.edu/Economics/morey/4545/auto/offdiet.html.

[286] *See* HUMAN DEVELOPMENT REPORT 2002, *supra* note 26.

least $117 billion in health care costs in 1999; in 2002, 61% of U.S. credit card users carried a monthly balance, averaging $12,000 at 16% interest, and amounting to approximately $1900 per year in finance charges—more than the average per capita income of at least thirty-five countries in purchasing power parity.[287]

Sustainability is a direct challenge to consumerism and materialism. We cannot live lives of affluence without profiting from an unjust distribution of resources. We as individuals and as institutions must change dramatically for a just distribution of global resources. This requires a transformation of personal, community, national and international standards and practices. We must look seriously at our lifestyles and institutions and radically modify them. True justice must address the local, national and global inequalities of poverty and wealth. The absence of sustainable living is another glaring example of why we must continually work for change.

J. Victory or Failure-Be Humble and Ready to Start over

Whether there is victory or failure (and the revolutionary will have plenty of both), we must learn from our experiences and be ever-ready to start over. When we fail, we must take time to heal our wounds and learn from that experience. When we succeed, we must celebrate with the community and savor the victory, so that it can sustain us in the struggles ahead. Being open to new ideas means that we must cultivate humility.[288] And, if you are like me, you have plenty to be humble about.

Finally, we must care for ourselves as well as the world and our community on this journey toward radical change. As the Buddha said: "You can search throughout the entire universe for someone who is more deserving of your love and affection than you are yourself, and that person is not to be found anywhere. You yourself, as much as anybody in the entire universe, deserve your love and affection."[289]

SIGNS OF HOPE AND CONCLUSION

> *I am convinced that if we are to get on the right side of the world revolution, we as a nation must undergo a radical revolution of values. We must rapidly begin the shift from a "thing-oriented" society to a "person-oriented" society. When machines and computers, profit motives and property rights are considered*

---

[287] *See* Worldwatch Institute, *supra* note 252. There are many ways to calculate how sustainable our individual lifestyles are. One of the most graphic is the ecological footprint. *See* Earth Day Footprint Quiz, http://www.earthday.org/footprint/index_reset.asp?pid=50077456 35675848 (last visited Feb. 21, 2006).

[288] Bill Quigley, *Ten Ideas for Social Justice Organizing After September 11,* BLUEPRINT FOR SOC. JUST., Nov. 2001, *available at* http://www.loyno.edu/twomey/blueprint/vol_lv/No-03_Nov_2001.html.

[289] Sharon Salzberg, LOVINGKINDNESS: THE REVOLUTIONARY ART OF HAPPINESS 25 (1st ed. 1995).

more important than people, the giant triplets of racism, materialism, and militarism are incapable of being conquered. A true revolution of values will soon cause us to question the fairness and justice of many of our past and present policies.

—Martin Luther King, Jr.[290]

This Article begins and ends with Dr. King's speech titled *Time to Break Silence.* It is time for lawyers to break silence and admit the profound changes that are necessary to bring about justice in this country and in this world. It is time for lawyers to switch sides and work for justice, instead of continuing to labor at the disposal of those who pay us well to defend the injustices of current systems and institutions.[291] Thankfully, there are signs of hope for the vision of Dr. Martin Luther King, Jr.

In the United States, a grassroots coalition of immigrant farm workers fighting for better wages recently won a huge upset victory over a transnational corporation. They did so by organizing community, college and church groups nationwide.[292] In fact, state and local authorities have passed over 130 living wage ordinances in order to diminish the gap between work and poverty.[293] Many other local and campus-based living wage campaigns have been initiated,[294] in addition to movements that seek to raise the integrity of work and working conditions.[295]

Respect in the United States for international human rights is beginning to grow, often led by local initiatives.[296] Major human rights

---

[290] *See* King, Jr., *supra* note 1.

[291] I must admit that some of these suggestions for radical change could be wrong. One never knows about the vitality of ideas until they are tested in action, but I am very confident that the problems identified here are real and demand radical revolutionary changes. Others may well have better ideas—indeed, I hope so.

[292] *See* Coalition of Immokalee Workers, http://www.ciw-online.org/news.html (last visited Feb. 21, 2006) (describing the coalition's boycott of Taco Bell).

[293] For examples of living-wage victories, see Living Wage Resource Center, Living Wage Successes, http://www.livingwagecampaign.org/index.php?id=1958 (last visited Feb. 21, 2006).

Florida recently voted overwhelmingly for a raise in its minimum wage and voted to index the raise to inflation, lifting the wages of over 850,000 workers. Tyler Hauck, *Florida's Low-Wage Workers Get a Pay Raise,* DOLLARS & SENSE, May-June 2005, at 7.

[294] ACORN's Living Wage Resource Center lists many local and university-based campaigns. *See* Living Wage Resource Center, Living Wage Campaigns Underway, http://www.livingwagecampaign.org/index.php?id=1960 (last visited Feb. 21, 2006).

[295] PHILOSOPHICAL AND SPIRITUAL PERSPECTIVES ON DECENT WORK (Dominique Peccoud ed., 2004) (collecting hope-filled perspectives from religious traditions such as Confucianism, Hindu, Buddhist, Islam, Jewish, Catholic, and Protestant).

[296] *See* U.S. Human Rights Network, www.ushrnetwork.org (last visited Feb. 21, 2006); Human Rights First, http://www.humanrightsfirst.org/index.html (last visited Feb. 21, 2006) (formerly Lawyers for Human Rights).

There have been many local efforts to adopt and enforce international human rights protections in various cities. Examples include Berkeley's efforts to prevent human rights violations since 9–11, El Paso's protection of immigrants, and San Francisco's protection of the rights of women. *See* Ann Fagan Ginger, *Report of 180 Types of U.S. Human Rights Violations* organizations have emphasized human rights violations in the United States, thereby helping to encourage dialogue on the issue.[297]

There are even signs of hope in law schools. Law schools have expanded clinical programs that directly introduce students to justice issues and often directly challenge assumptions.[298] New human rights programs (including clinical programs) teach the basics of human rights to the next generation of lawyers. Law schools realize the necessity of loan-forgiveness programs, which enable highly-indebted graduates to undertake social justice work.[299] This is how we will rediscover the essence of justice.

There are enough lawyers in this world defending the way things are. Plenty of lawyers protect unjust people and institutions in our social, economic and political systems. Plenty of lawyers work for structures that perpetuate and increase the racism, militarism and materialism in our world. These lawyers are plentiful and well-compensated. True structural and fundamental change will not come by aiming at small revisions or reforms. If we are going to transform our world, we need lawyers willing to work with others toward a radical revolution of our world. We need no more lawyers defending the status quo. We need revolutionaries.

Jane Aiken
Striving to Teach Justice, Fairness, and Morality
4 CLIN. L. REV. 1 (1997)

. . . Everything we do as law teachers suggests something about justice.[300] Recent studies of law schools are urging that we be more explicit about justice in legal education.[301] *The Report of the Task Force on*

Since 9/11, TRUTHOUT, July 8, 2005, http://www.truthout.org/docs_2005/070805P.shtml; Jenkins & Cox, *supra* note 90.

[297] Amnesty International and Human Rights Watch have started taking a much more aggressive stance for human rights monitoring in the United States. *See* Amnesty International's Human Rights Concerns, http://www.amnestyusa.org/countries/usa/index.do (last visited Feb. 21, 2006); Human Rights Watch, http://www.hrw.org/ (last visited Feb. 21, 2006).

[298] Fran Quigley, *Seizing the Disorienting Moment: Adult Learning Theory and the Teaching of Social Justice in Law School Clinics,* 2 CLINICAL L. REV. 37 (1995).

[299] *See, e.g.,* American Bar Association, Loan Repayment and Forgiveness Overview, http://www.abanet.org/legalservices/lrap/home.html (last visited Feb. 21, 2006).

[300] Justice in application is fundamentally a political phenomenon. *See* David Barnhizer, *The Justice Mission of American Law Schools*, 40 CLEV. ST. L. REV. 285, 293 (1992).

[301] *See* AMERICAN BAR ASSOCIATION SECTION OF LEGAL EDUCATION AND ADMISSIONS TO THE BAR, LEGAL EDUCATION AND PROFESSIONAL DEVELOPMENT—AN EDUCATIONAL CONTINUUM (REPORT OF THE TASK FORCE ON LAW SCHOOLS AND THE PROFESSION: NARROWING THE GAP) (1992) (hereinafter MACCRATE) and THE AMERICAN BAR ASSOCIATION, SECTION OF LEGAL EDUCATION AND ADMISSIONS TO THE BAR, PROFESSIONALISM COMMITTEE, TEACHING AND LEARNING PROFESSIONALISM (1996). The fact that these documents were produced by the ABA is significant because the ABA is the accrediting agency for law schools. Law schools must pay

Law Schools and the Profession: Narrowing the Gap (the MacCrate Report) exhorts us to use opportunities like this moment with the student not just to teach the law of health care powers of attorney but to raise those questions of justice, fairness, and morality that lurk just below the surface.[302] The MacCrate Report identifies four fundamental values of the profession:

1) provision of competent representation;

2) striving to promote justice, fairness and morality;

3) striving to improve the profession; and

4) professional self-development.

By far the most challenging value is the injunction to strive to promote justice, fairness, and morality. Arguably, the first value, the provision of competent representation, can be fostered by effective skills training. The third value, striving to improve the profession, can be fostered through active participation in the Bar. The fourth value, professional self-development, appears to be mainly concerned with effective Continuing Legal Education programs that enhance lawyers' ability to learn through experience. Yet methods of promoting the second value are not only less obvious than they are for the other three values, but also more difficult.[303] The MacCrate Report, although eloquent in its

---

attention to criticism of how they conduct their education of law students because it could have ramifications for continuing accreditation. Since the publication of the MacCrate Report, the ABA has refined accreditation standards to reflect many of the concerns raised by MacCrate. Furthermore, because law schools are increasingly looking to the Bar for funding for law school programs, lawyers' attitudes toward the effectiveness of legal education could have financial consequences. Law schools across the nation have created MacCrate task forces to begin the process of implementing its suggestions.

[302] MACCRATE, *supra* note 4, at 213. The MacCrate report, released in July 1992, has been the subject of much debate both within the ABA and the Academy. *See generally* Michael Norwood, *Legal Education: Past Developments, Present Status and Future Possibilities, Scenes from the Continuum: Sustaining the MacCrate Report's Vision of Law School Education into the Twenty-First Century,* 30 WAKE FOREST L. REV. 293 (1995); *Symposium on the MacCrate Report: Papers from the Midwest Clinical Teachers' Conference,* 1 CLIN. L. REV. 349 (1994); John J. Costonis, *The MacCrate Report: Of Loaves, Fishes, and the Future of American Legal Education,* 43 J. LEGAL EDUC. 157 (1993). Since the MacCrate Report's release, law schools have grappled with meeting the goals articulated in the report. Although the report is not designed to be prescriptive, it does identify a list of skills and values new lawyers should seek to acquire. There has been much written about the skills portion of the Statement of Skills and Values (SSV). Legal educators feel fairly confident that they know how to teach skills such as problem-solving, negotiation, counseling, and legal research. The only debate in this area is whether and how much the skills should be taught. But how does one promote justice, fairness, and morality? How does the law school participate in that endeavor through teaching?

[303] Educators have identified the questions that the issue of justice poses but have not outlined the ways in which those questions should be addressed in legal education. David Barnhizer identifies the following key questions that should be the focus of legal education:

1. What do we consider to be a just society?
2. What are the terms of such a society?
3. What kinds of behaviors tend toward facilitating the creation of such a society?
4. What behaviors undermine a society we consider just?

articulation of this value, only spends three pages discussing it. In its section on justice, fairness and morality, the report suggests three areas in which attorneys can promote this value in their daily practice. They are: 1) when the lawyer is making decisions for a client; 2) when counseling clients about decisions the client must make; and 3) by treating others with dignity and respect. In addition, members of the profession can strive to promote justice by ensuring that adequate legal services are provided for those who cannot afford to pay and working toward the enhancement of the law's ability to do justice.[304]

The MacCrate Report itself acknowledges that its inventory of skills and values is a "work in progress" and invites members of the legal community to expand and refine it.[305] This article responds to that invitation by suggesting ways in which we can teach future lawyers about how to promote justice in their daily practice. First, I discuss the ways in which legal education is presently failing in this endeavor. Next, I outline a learning theory that offers a model for teaching about justice through the systematic study of incidences of injustice. I then describe a clinical experience in which the students encountered injustice in the course of representing clients and analyze how and perhaps why that experience

---

5. How do we or ought we organize our political institutions so that they behave in a manner we consider just?
6. How do we or ought we ensure that our institutions are generative, adaptive, self-evaluative and regenerative?
7. What ideals are integral to a workable vision of the individual and social human committed to living a just life?
8. What can a law faculty, law schools, lawyers, judges and legislators do that helps American society address the awesome challenges it faces?

Barnhizer, *supra* note 3, at 322. These are questions rarely asked in a law school curriculum. Unmasking privilege is a prerequisite to being able to understand these questions and attempting to answer them. Otherwise, we are bound to reproduce power relations that undermine justice.

[304] The MacCrate Report specifically states:

Striving to Promote Justice, Fairness, and Morality

As a member of a profession that bears "special responsibili[ties] for the quality of justice," a lawyer should be committed to the values of:

2.1 *Promoting Justice, Fairness, and Morality in One's Own Daily Practice*, including:
   (a) To the extent required or permitted by the ethical rules of the profession, acting in conformance with considerations of justice, fairness, and morality when making decisions or acting on behalf of a client . . .;
   (b) To the extent required or permitted by the ethical rules of the profession, counseling clients to take considerations of justice, fairness and morality into account when the client makes decisions or engages in conduct that may have an adverse effect on other individuals or on society . . .;
   (c) Treating other people (including clients, other attorneys, and support personnel) with dignity and respect;

2.2 *Contributing to the Profession's Fulfillment of its Responsibilities to Ensure that Adequate legal Services Are Provided to Those Who Cannot Afford to Pay for Them;*

2.3 *Contributing to the Profession's Fulfillment of its Responsibilities to Enhance the Capacity of Law and Legal Institutions to Do Justice.*

MACCRATE, *supra* note 4, at 213.

[305] MACCRATE, *supra* note 4, at 123–24, 130–31.

affected the students' sense of justice. Finally, I look at ways in which the learning theory and the insights gained from this clinical experience can be used in other clinical courses as well as in traditional law school courses. I offer examples of methods that may make the MacCrate aspiration operational.

I. OUR FAILURE TO TEACH JUSTICE

The MacCrate Report suggests that legal education could be doing a better job of instilling the value of promoting justice, fairness, and morality. Legal education is failing both directly and indirectly. First, educators often act as if lawyers play no role in the achievement of justice. Consequently, legal educators neglect to address issues of justice when the opportunity arises. Second, in those circumstances in which justice is discussed, too often the message that students receive is that justice is merely the product of the application of neutral rules. We ignore the fact that the exercise of judgment, perhaps the most fundamental of legal skills, is inherently value laden.

We communicate a great deal about the (un)importance of justice when we do not focus on it explicitly. The professor who responds to the student concerned about fairness with questions that are limited to what "the law says" is communicating ideas about justice and morality. The failure to address the student's concerns may communicate that those concerns have no place in the practice of law. Legal education often ignores the significant role that lawyers play in shaping public policy.[306] It includes little or no discussion of the social consequences of a lawyer's acts and decisions not to act.[307] Yet, practicing lawyers make legally significant decisions on a daily basis, perhaps as much or more so than do judges, legislators and administrators.[308] Very few case books address

---

[306] *See, generally* Ian F. Haney Lopez, WHITE BY LAW: THE LEGAL CONSTRUCTION OF RACE (1996). It is not as if there were not a need for lawyers concerned with justice. In a national survey of people living at or below 125% of the poverty line, 80% of the legal problems were handled without the benefit of legal assistance. AMERICAN BAR ASSOCIATION CONSORTIUM ON LEGAL SERVICES AND THE PUBLIC, TWO NATIONWIDE SURVEYS: 1989 PILOT ASSESSMENTS OF THE UNMET LEGAL NEEDS OF THE POOR AND OF THE PUBLIC GENERALLY 37 (1989).

[307] Jerold S. Auerbach, *What Has The Teaching of Law To Do With Justice?,* 53 N.Y.U. L. REV. 457 (1978). If all I can do in law school is to teach students skills ungrounded in a sense of justice then at best there is no meaning to my work, and, at worst, I am contributing to the distress in the world. I am sending more people into the community armed with legal training but without a sense of responsibility for others or for the delivery of justice in our society.

[308] The need to make future lawyers aware of their responsibility toward the poor in this country becomes more crucial every day. State and federal legislatures are actively engaged in attacks on the poor and poor people's advocates. Congress has exacted deep cuts in funding and has created restrictions on the kinds of claims that can be brought by offices funded by the Legal Service Corporation. States are receiving waivers and are designing programs that significantly reduce public benefits and require the poor to jump over ever higher hurdles to maintain their meager benefits. Our students, however, are coming from backgrounds in which most are completely unaware of the needs of the poor. Income and wealth disparities in this country are greater than they have been in the last fifty years. *See Inequality: For Richer, For Poorer,* THE ECONOMIST, NOV. 5, 1994, at 19; *see also* Kevin P. Phillips, THE POLITICS OF RICH AND POOR: WEALTH AND THE AMERICAN ELECTORATE IN THE REAGAN AFTERMATH (1990).

issues of fairness, justice and morality.[309] When they do, many professors, intentionally or subconsciously, skip the cases or footnotes that focus on sexual harassment, sexual orientation, race and class issues, and the intricacies that arise due to the overlap of these characteristics.[310]

Focusing solely on "what the law says" also reinforces the idea that lawyers are legal technicians, that the practice of law is merely the exercise of applying fixed neutral rules to a given situation, that justice has no other content than the results that emanate from the application of these rules.[311] The pedagogical assumption within law schools is that our subject matter is innately neutral.[312] Law is merely a process and there is no common good, no common goals toward which everyone is collectively working.[313] Many of us urge students to approach the law with a studied detachment to rid themselves of the emotion and personal experiences that may color their approach to a problem.[314] Students learn quickly to search for the rule that will govern a given situation and take the passion out of the problem.[315] There is no room within this framework to examine how an individual learner's perspective affects his or her identification and assessment of the legal problem and choice of rule.[316] I have talked with professors who pride themselves on exams that if answered on the basis of the student's innate sense of justice, would

---

[309] *See, e.g.*, Ann Althouse, *The Lying Woman, The Devious Prostitute, and Other Stories from the Evidence Casebook*, 88 NW. U. L. REV. 914 (1994).

[310] *See* Leslie Bender, *Hidden Messages in the Required First-Year Law School Curriculum*, 40 CLEV. ST. L. REV. 387 (1992).

[311] This view assumes that the prevailing allocations of wealth and power are based on neutral principles and are acquired through pure merit.

[312] Even in our relationships with clients, the traditional image of the lawyer is that she can espouse any viewpoint of any client, that she is neutral as to political content. *See* Naomi R. Cahn, *Styles of Lawyering*, 43 HASTINGS L.J. 1039, 1063 (1992).

[313] These ideas are hardly unique to law. Lester C. Thurow describes this phenomenon in economics when he describes both democracy and capitalism as processes divorced from values:

> When anyone talks about societies being organic wholes, something more than the statistical summation of their individual members' wants and achievements, both capitalists and democrats assert that there is no such thing. In both, individual freedom dominates community obligations. All political or economic transactions are voluntary. If an individual does not want to vote, or buy something, that is his or her right. If citizens want to be greedy and vote their narrow self-interest at the expense of others, that is their right. In the most vigorous expression of capitalistic ethics, crime is simply another economic activity that happens to have a high price (jail) if one is caught. There is no social obligation to obey the law. There is nothing that one "ought" not to do. Duties and obligations do not exist. Only market transactions exist.

Lester C. Thurow, THE FUTURE OF CAPITALISM 159 (1996).

[314] Shauna Van Praagh, *Stories in Law School An Essay on Language, Participation, and the Power of Legal Education*, 2 COLUM. J. GENDER & L. 111 (1992). Perhaps one of the reasons for how little law schools examine oppression is the demographic composition of law school faculty.

[315] Nina J. Crimm, *A Study: Law School Student's Moral Perspectives In the Context of Advocacy and Decision-Making Roles*, 29 NEW ENG. L. REV. 1 (1994).

[316] Such a separation runs counter to the literature on adult learning and inhibits the learners' ability and openness to learning about justice and morality. *See* Carrie Menkel-Meadow, *Narrowing the Gap by Narrowing the Field: What's Missing from the MacCrate Report—Of Skills, Legal Science and Being a Human Being*, 69 WASH. L. REV. 621 (1994).

inevitably be answered "incorrectly."[317] Only that student who has successfully learned to leave her sense of compassion at the door will master this type of exam.[318] We are actively training students to divorce themselves from issues relating to justice, fairness and morality.[319]

Law schools often ignore the skill of exercising judgment and the enormous power with which lawyers are vested in the attorney/client relationship.[320] Lawyers' decisions, unlike those made by judges, legislators, and administrators, are not subject to any review by others. Making decisions for clients and counseling clients about the decisions they must make require lawyers to exercise judgment. MacCrate recognizes that this is where lawyers affect justice[321] since these decisions often reflect the value system of the lawyer.[322] Rarely do our students

---

[317] These exams assume that "thinking like a lawyer" means suppressing one's personal and political beliefs. For a thoughtful discussion of this attitude within the law school, see Angela P. Harris & Marjorie M. Shultz, *A(nother) Critique of Pure Reason: Toward Civic Virtue in Legal Education,* 45 STAN. L. REV. 1773 (1993).

[318] This has demonstrable effects on women students' ability to succeed in the traditional ways in law school. *See* Lani Guinier, Michelle Fine & Jane Balin, *Becoming Gentlemen: Women's Experience at One Ivy League Law School,* 143 U. PA. L. REV. 1 (1994).

[319] That separation from justice, reinforced daily in classes, only affirms privilege and perpetuates dominance. As an educator, I can only act ethically if I do not attempt to force my own perspective on the students but encourage learners to choose from a wide range of viewpoints. *See* Mezirow, *supra* note 2, at 225. Mezirow points out, however, that an educator is not bound to help a learner carry out actions that are in conflict with the educator's own code of ethics.

[320] *See* Tom Clark, *Teaching Professional Ethics,* 12 SAN DIEGO L. REV. 249 (1975); James R. Elkins, *The Pedagogy of Ethics,* 10 J. LEGAL PROF. 37 (1985); Anthony T. Kronman, *Living in the Law,* 54 U. CHI. L. REV. 835 (1987). There are many skills that are essential to effective lawyering. Obviously, it is not enough to understand privilege if one does not have the skills to put that knowledge into operation. Clinical legal education is one place in the law school curriculum where those skills are learned. As Norman Redlich points out, "[I]dealistic young men and women [are] leaving law school, intently anxious to deal with problems of poverty, discrimination, homelessness, or an inadequate education system, and [do] not possess the widest possible range of tools to make one's legal education effective." Norman Redlich, *Challenging Injustice: A Dedication to Bob McKay,* 40 CLEV. ST. L. REV. 347, 350 (1992).

[321] MACCRATE, *supra* note 4, at 213. The desire to promote justice is not a value that suddenly emerges upon admission to the Bar. *See* Jack Bass, UNLIKELY HEROES: THE DRAMATIC STORY OF THE SOUTHERN JUDGES OF THE FIFTH CIRCUIT WHO TRANSLATED THE SUPREME COURT'S BROWN DECISION INTO A REVOLUTION FOR EQUALITY (1981); Peter H. Irons, THE COURAGE OF THEIR CONVICTIONS (1988).

[322] The MacCrate Report identified the following fundamental skills: problem solving, legal analysis and reasoning, legal research, factual investigation, communication, counseling, negotiation, litigation and alternative dispute resolution procedures, organization and management of legal work, and recognizing and resolving ethical dilemmas. *Statement of Fundamental Lawyering Skills and Professional Values,* MACCRATE, *supra* note 4, at 15–84. The Report suggests that these skills are the foundation for effective, competent lawyering. The statement, however, also envisions the coexistence of fundamental professional values of justice, fairness, and morality. These qualities are hard to teach. Robert A. Solomon, *Teaching Morality,* 40 CLEV. ST. L. REV. 507 (1992). However, they are the backbone of judgment, which is perhaps *the* fundamental legal skill. In this article, I argue that we can teach students to exercise judgment so as to promote justice. In doing so, I recognize that formidable scholars have concluded that judgment is not a skill that is teachable. Immanuel Kant said that "judgment is a peculiar talent which can be practiced only, and cannot be taught. It is the specific quality of so-called mother-wit; and its lack no school can make good." Immanuel Kant, CRITIQUE OF PURE REASON *A133/B172 (Norman K. Smith trans., 1968). I am in agreement with David Luban and Michael Millemann, who specifically address this observation by Kant:

have the opportunity to discuss what kind of lawyer they want to be, what norms should control their behavior, and how they should relate to clients, adversaries, judges, support personnel, and other third parties.[323] Frequently the "values" portion of the law school curriculum is relegated to a two- or three-credit professional responsibility course.[324] In some cases, even these courses utterly fail to address the issue of justice, reducing value choices within the profession to the mere application of professional rules.[325] In those instances, there is frequently little or no discussion of the lawyer's responsibility to serve the public and to further the interests of justice, fairness, and morality.[326]

Justice, fairness, and morality are teachable, provided we offer the kinds of experiences that make compassionate insight possible.[327] Enhancing our students' awareness about justice, fairness, and morality also requires that we discuss those values more fully throughout the curriculum.[328] Discussion of justice is not sufficient. I suggest that the best way to teach about justice is to create opportunities for students to exercise judgment.[329] Through the examination of their judgment, we can

---

> We are inclined to deny Kant's implicit distinction between things that can be taught and things that can (only) be practiced—For the distinction overlooks the possibility that judgment can be taught through practice.

David Luban & Michael Millemann, *Good Judgment: Ethics Teaching in Dark Times,* 9 GEO. J. LEGAL ETHICS 31, 40 (1995).

[323] Roger C. Cramton & Susan P. Koniak, *Rule Story and Commitment in the Teaching of Legal Ethics,* 38 WM. & MARY L. REV. 145 (1996).

[324] *See id.*

[325] *See* Luban & Millemann, *supra* note 25.

[326] *See* Phoebe A. Haddon, *Education for a Public Calling in the 21st Century,* 69 WASH. L. REV. 573 (1994).

[327] Many scholars have argued that we should use legal education to teach our students about injustice and use clinics to pursue the goal of law reform. *See, e.g.,* Phyllis Goldfarb, *Beyond Cut Flowers: Developing a Clinical Perspective on Critical Legal Theory,* 43 HASTINGS L.J. 717 (1992); Carrie Menkel-Meadow, *Two Contradictory Criticisms of Clinical Education: Dilemmas and Directions in Lawyering Education,* 4 ANTIOCH L.J. 287 (1986); Abbe Smith, *Rosie O'Neil Goes to Law School The Clinical Education of the Sensitive New Age Public Defender,* 28 HARV. C.R.-C.L. L. REV. 1 (1993); Stephen Wizner & Dennis Curtis, *"Here's What We Do": Some Notes About Clinical Legal Education,* 29 CLEV. ST. L. REV. 673 (1980).

[328] *See generally* Thomas L. Shaffer & Robert F. Cochran, Jr., LAWYERS, CLIENTS, AND MORAL RESPONSIBILITY (1994); Burnelle W. Powell, *Lawyer Professionalism as Ordinary Morality,* 35 S. TEX. L. REV. 275 (1994): David A.J. Richards, *Moral Theory: The Development of Psychology of Ethical Autonomy and Professionalism,* 31 J. LEGAL EDUC. 359 (1981); Henry Rose, *Law Schools Should Be About Justice Too,* 40 CLEV. ST. L. REV. 443 (1992); Terrance Sandalow, *The Moral Responsibility of Law Schools,* 34 J. LEGAL EDUC. 163 (1984); Thomas Shaffer, *Moral Implications and Effects of Legal Education or: Brother Justinian Goes to Law School,* 34 J. LEGAL EDUC. 190 (1984); Michael I. Swygert, *Striving to Make Great Lawyers—Citizenship and Moral Responsibility: A Jurisprudence for Law Teaching,* 30 BOSTON COL. L. REV. 803 (1989). For a discussion of the problem of marginalizing professional responsibility within legal education and a proposed solution, *see* Deborah L. Rhode, PROFESSIONAL RESPONSIBILITY—ETHICS BY THE PERVASIVE METHOD (1994).

[329] For a discussion of this failure to teach our students to exercise judgment, see TEACHING AND LEARNING PROFESSIONALISM, *supra* note 4. We must attempt to enlarge students' thought so that they can recognize multiple points of view. This is hardly a new idea. Kant described it as *erweitcrer Denkkunstart.* Immanuel Kant, CRITIQUE OF JUDGMENT Sec. 40, at 137 (J.H. Bernard

increase our students' self-awareness and help them to develop a sense of justice.[330]

II. DEVELOPING A SENSE OF JUSTICE THROUGH DECONSTRUCTING POWER

Although the MacCrate Report identifies the need to do justice as a fundamental value of the profession,[331] the report does not define what it means by the term "justice." A jurisprudential treatment of the meaning of justice, fairness, and morality is well beyond this article, but justice—however one defines it—is about the exercise of power. In order to promote justice, one must be explicit about how power operates, particularly in its subtle and invisible manifestations. One way to approach learning about justice, fairness, and morality is to teach our students the ability to deconstruct power, to identify privilege, and to take responsibility for the ways in which the law confers dominance.[332] With that understanding, we can also learn to use our power and privilege in socially productive ways.[333]

There is an old Chinese proverb that says, "We see what is behind our eyes." In order to learn about how to promote justice, the learner must understand how power affects vision and values. The legal educator's role is to help students see how their experience affects their values and how these values affect their assessment of the law. We are essentially teaching our students the "skill" of compassion.[334] I define "compassion" as a sympathetic consciousness of others' distress with a desire to act to alleviate it. As this definition implies, compassion requires

---

trans., 1966). Of course, expanding one's mind is not sufficient in the exercise of judgment. For a thoughtful analysis of the limitations of Kant's view and an exploration of qualities necessary to teach in order to teach judgment, see Luban & Millemann, *supra* note 25.

[330] I believe that when people confront and understand their complicity in others' distress, they want to stop those acts that may contribute to that pain. Human beings do not want to feel morally responsible for the detrimental treatment of other human beings. This results in either a change in behavior or an attempt to distance themselves from responsibility and guilt. Our job as legal educators concerned about the public interest is to make the connections between the exercise of privilege and the reinforcement of hierarchy and to reduce our students' ability to ignore the role that they play in upholding unearned dominance in our society.

[331] MACCRATE, *supra* note 4, at 140. *See also* Solomon, *supra* note 25.

[332] Paul Tremblay argues that truly "rebellious lawyering" requires the lawyer to look toward long-term gains for the client rather than short-term solutions. This kind of lawyering seeks to empower the subordinated client. Paul R. Tremblay, *Rebellious Lawyering, Regnant Lawyering, and Street-Level Bureaucracy,* 43 HASTINGS L.J. 947, 951 (1992).

[333] This activity is not without costs. Often when people of privilege work to expose privilege and use it to assist others, they are discounted or treated with hostility. For example, white people who identify racism are often discounted as suffering from "terminal white guilt." Men who speak about sexism risk questions about their masculinity. These reactions only serve to expose the power and investment that those with privilege have in maintaining the status quo.

[334] The idea that one can strive for justice impliedly assumes that the law is not neutral. Mari J. Matsuda describes a perspective that is akin to one aspect of compassion, that of multiple consciousness. It is not the ability to see all points of view but rather "to see the world from the standpoint of the oppressed." Mari J. Matsuda, *When the First Quail Calls: Multiple Consciousness As Jurisprudential Method,* 14 WOMEN'S RTS. L. REP. 297 (1988).

action; it is not merely empathy. It requires more than the knowing nod and sympathetic gesture. A feeling of compassion causes a person to act because of a desire to alleviate the condition. The desire to "alleviate" another's distress, or to act affirmatively, is the essence of the concept. In the social justice context, the skill of compassion is the ability to appreciate that we operate with only a partial perspective and to recognize that many of us, law students and practicing attorneys, have privileges—most of them not earned through any personal effort on our part—which color our perceptions both of the client and the legal claim.

We often treat our vision as if it were not partial at all. We are not the objective actors applying neutral rules that the legal system assumes.[335] We can better promote justice if we understand how injustice depends on people's inability to examine how their own values may reinforce dominance.[336] One way to explore this is through an understanding of privilege.[337] The MacCrate Report suggests that this should be done on a personal level, uncovering privilege in our daily lives so that we can effectively participate in the process of social improvement.[338]

---

[335] Antonio Gramsci has described this phenomenon: "[T]he consciousness of what one really is [entails] 'knowing thyself' as a product of the historical process to date which has deposited in you an infinity of traces, without leaving an inventory." ANTONIO GRAMSCI, SELECTIONS FROM THE PRISON NOTEBOOKS 324 (Quintin Hoare & Geoffrey Nowell Smith eds. & trans., 1971).

[336] Stephen Ellmann describes this sensitivity as an aspect of empathetic lawyering. He says:

> Empathetic lawyering aspires to a vision of lawyers capable of overcoming their own limitations of perspective so as to see or feel the world as other persons do, despite the differences of race, gender, class, culture, or simply identity that divide us from each other. The experiences and perspectives of the powerful, however, are not the same as the powerless. To cross the gap—and to be perceived by one's client as having crossed it—the lawyer generally needs more than just intellectual curiosity. She needs some sympathetic identification with those with whom her experience might otherwise separate her.

Stephen Ellmann, *Empathy and Approval,* 43 HASTINGS L.J. 991, 1003 (1992). I believe that "sympathetic identification" is not sufficient to enable us to overcome our limitations in perspective. It is only when that identity allows us to see how our own privilege is paid off through other's pain that true change will occur.

[337] *See generally* Stephanie M. Wildman, PRIVILEGE REVEALED: HOW INVISIBLE PREFERENCE UNDERMINES AMERICA (1996). We must also appreciate the importance of constantly paying attention to context. As Jean Love points out:

> In one situation, I may play the role of the oppressed woman among men, for example. In another situation, I may play the oppressor—a white woman in a predominately white society, for example. At some point in time in our lives, we all experience both the roles of oppressor and oppressed. We all practice both domination and resistance. Different though our individual experiences may be, we all learn something about the impact of oppression upon both its victims and its perpetrators. This creates a capacity for shared understanding of oppression. If we choose to talk with each other about our experiences of the phenomenon of oppression, we will eventually create a common language for devising solutions about the problem of oppression.

Scott Brewer et. al., *Afterword: Symposium on the Renaissance of Pragmatism in American Legal Thought,* 63 S. CAL. L. REV. 1911, 1923 (1990).

[338] Section 2.1(c) of the MacCrate Report's Statement of Professional Values says that in order to achieve the value of striving to promote justice, fairness, and morality, a lawyer should

I use the term "privilege" to describe that "invisible package of unearned assets that I can count on cashing in each day, but about which I was 'meant' to remain oblivious."[339] It is conferred dominance.[340] It is the vehicle by which systems of power operate. Too often we focus on disadvantage as the sole result of power disparities rather than recognizing that there is a subtle system of privilege that necessarily follows systems of subordination.[341] We are taught to think of oppression as acts of cruelty by one group against another group or an individual.[342] We look for intentional acts [343] rather than "invisible systems" conferring dominance to particular groups.[344]

---

treat "other people . . . with dignity and respect." MACCRATE, *supra* note 4, at 213. The Commentary notes that:

> [T]his necessarily includes refraining from sexual harassment and any form of discrimination on the basis of gender, race, religion, ethnic origin, sexual orientation, age or disability in one's professional interactions with clients, witnesses, support staff, and other individuals.

Id. at 214.

[339] Peggy McIntosh, *Unpacking the Invisible Knapsack: White Privilege,* CREATION SPIRITUALITY 33 (Jan./Feb. 1992).

[340] The term "privilege" does not capture this concept fully. It is misleading because it implies something positive and always desired. I use it because I am unable to come up with a better word for the phenomenon. Peggy McIntosh is also troubled by the word. *See id.* The literature in this area adopted the term and so it has become imbued with particular meaning within critical legal theory. The term has taken on an overly rhetorical quality that often gives rise to a charge of being "P.C."; nevertheless, I believe that the term, if properly used, adds clarity to our understanding of how power functions in our society.

In this paper, I focus on race, sexuality, gender, and class privilege. One can easily identify other privileges (religion, ableness, etc.) and I would urge the reader to do so. I hope that my analysis is generalizable. I am concerned with conferred dominance in which the characteristics of the privileged group define the societal norm, allowing the privileged group to rely on its privilege and ignore oppression.

[341] *See* Stephanie M. Wildman, *Privilege and Liberalism in Legal Education: Teaching and Learning in a Diverse Environment,* 10 BERKELEY WOMEN'S L.J. 88 (1995); Stephanie M. Wildman & Adrienne D. Davis, *Language and Silence: Making Systems of Privilege Visible,* 35 SANTA CLARA L. REV. 881 (1995). Gregory Howard Williams describes his life as a child first treated as white and then as black. His story starkly shows the effect of privilege. GREGORY H. WILLIAMS, LIFE ON THE COLOR LINE: THE TRUE STORY OF A WHITE BOY WHO DISCOVERED HE WAS BLACK (1995).

[342] *See* Harlon L. Dalton, RACIAL HEALING: CONFRONTING THE FEAR BETWEEN BLACKS AND WHITES (1995). Dalton points out that racism often focuses on race-based animosity or disdain, but that such a definition is flawed because it is indifferent to questions of hierarchy and social structure; it applies with equal force to the fox and the hound. He explains that a second flaw is that we do not reach the behavior of people who have no malice in their hearts, but who still create and reproduce racial hierarchy. He embraces Wellman's idea that racism consists of "culturally acceptable beliefs that defend social advantages that are based on race." David T. Wellman, PORTRAITS OF WHITE RACISM 4 (1993). A definition that focuses on the search for acceptable ways of justifying racial hierarchy has many advantages. It gets us away from focusing on malice or ill will. It makes the racism charge less personally accusatory. It eliminates a ready escape hatch of being pure of heart. Such a definition also mirrors how people of color actually experience racism. Dalton suggests that people with white sheets are not the only ones holding us down. Racism can exist even when there is no discrimination and no prejudice; all it requires is the desire to preserve what one has and the capacity to form supporting attitudes and beliefs. DALTON, *supra* at 92–95.

[343] In fact, our jurisprudence has adopted this concept, as illustrated by the requirement that proof of a discriminatory intent is necessary to establish that a facially neutral law violates

Examples of "privilege" include a multitude of white skin privileges—for example, the ability to exist in the world without being labeled by race.[345] Therefore, we seldom assume that a white person possesses the

---

the Equal Protection Clause on the basis of race. Washington v. Davis, 426 U.S. 229 (1976). For criticisms of the intent requirement, *see, e.g.*, Barbara J. Flagg, *"Was Blind, But Now I See": White Race Consciousness and the Requirement of Discriminatory Intent,* 91 MICH. L. REV. 953, 958 (1993) (whites fail to recognize that facially neutral norms are transparent white norms that actively participate in the maintenance of racism); Kenneth Karst, *The Costs of Motive-Centered Inquiry,* 15 SAN DIEGO L. REV. 1163, 1165 (1978) (motive-centered doctrines place a practicably impossible burden on the wrong side because improper motives are easy to hide and result from the interaction of many motives and sometimes several decisionmakers); Charles R. Lawrence, III, *The Id, The Ego, and Equal Protection: Reckoning with Unconscious Racism,* 39 STAN. L. REV. 317, 323 (1987) (racial matters are influenced by factors that can be characterized as neither intentional nor unintentional, but unconscious racial motivations because of our cultural experiences); Donald Lively & Steven Plass, *Equal Protection: The Jurisprudence of Denial and Evasion,* 40 AM. U. L. REV. 1307 (1991) (intent inquiry avoids unsettling race questions and is the sophisticated grandchild of the separate but equal doctrine).

[344] McIntosh, *supra* note 42. This view of the world distracts people's attention from the larger historical and contemporary context in which oppression is practiced. As one friend puts it, we can ask the question "Are you a racist?," answer "No," and pass the lie detector test. This does not mean that we are not racist. *See* Ruth Frankenberg, WHITE WOMEN, RACE MATTERS: THE SOCIAL CONSTRUCTION OF WHITENESS 242 (1993). Frankenberg describes this phenomenon as "power-evasion." Moreover, we point to individual triumphs or advantage and use them to argue that systematic oppression does not exist Lawrence, *supra* note 46, at 321. Recent theorists have challenged the assimilationist approach to discrimination jurisprudence. *See, e.g.,* Kevin M. Fong, *Comment: Cultural Pluralism,* 13 HARV. C.R.-C.L. L. REV. 133 (1978); Gerald Torres, *Critical Race Theory: The Decline of the Universalist Ideal and the Hope of Plural Justice—Some Observations and Questions of an Emerging Phenomenon,* 75 MINN. L. REV. 993 (1991); Patricia J. Williams, Metro Broadcasting, Inc. v. FCC: *Regrouping in Singular Tones,* 104 HARV. L. REV. 525 (1990). As Adrienne Davis says:

> Domination, subordination, and privilege are like three heads of a hydra. Attacking the most visible heads, domination and subordination, trying bravely to chop them up into little pieces, will not kill the third head, privilege. Like a mythic multi-headed hydra, which will inevitably grow another head, if not all heads are slain, discrimination cannot be ended by focusing only on . . . subordination and domination.

Wildman & Davis, *supra* note 44, at 895.

[345] Barbara Flagg labels this the "transparency phenomenon," and defines it as "the fact that white people tend to be unconscious of whiteness as a distinct racial characteristic, and so tend to equate whiteness with racelessness." Barbara J. Flagg, *On Selecting Black Women as Paradigms for Race Discrimination Analyses,* 10 BERKELEY WOMEN'S L.J. 40, 40 (1995). She says: "White people externalize race. For most whites, most of the time, to think or speak about race is to speak about people of color, or perhaps, at times, to reflect on oneself (or other whites) in relation to people of color. But we do not tend to think of ourselves or our racial cohort as racially distinctive. Whites' 'consciousness' of whiteness is predominately unconsciousness of whiteness. We perceive and interact with other whites as individuals who have no significant racial characteristics. In the same vein, the white person is unlikely to see or describe himself in racial terms, perhaps in part because his white peers do not regard him as racially distinctive. Whiteness is a transparent quality when whites interact with whites in the absence of people of color. Whiteness attains opacity, becomes apparent to the white mind, only in relation to, and in contrast with, the 'color' of nonwhites." Flagg, *supra* note 46, at 970.

Sometimes the idea that only whites have no vested interest or no "race" has risen to the level of court challenges. Judge Constance Baker Motley of the United States District Court for the Southern District of New York was assigned to preside over a case in which the law firm of Sullivan and Cromwell was being sued by an applicant for an attorney position on the ground that she was discriminated against on the basis of her sex. Prior to trial, the lawyer representing the firm requested that Judge Motley disqualify herself from hearing the case because she was female and might not be able to deal with the sex discrimination claim in an unbiased manner. The attorney also noted that because Judge Motley was Black, she might have a heightened sensitivity to discrimination. Judge Motley denied the request, stating that "if [the] background

same characteristic observed in another white person.[346] Male gender privilege allows men to work without any concern by employers that they may be limited by child care responsibilities.[347] Class privilege allows us

---

or sex or race of each judge were, by definition, sufficient grounds for removal, no judge on this court could hear this case, or many others, by virtue of the fact that all of them were attorneys, of a sex, often with distinguished law firm or public service backgrounds." Blank v. Sullivan & Cromwell, 418 F. Supp. 1, 4 (S.D.N.Y. 1975). The lawyers viewed Judge Motley as having a vested interest yet did not realize that under their argument a judge who shared their characteristics would pose an unacceptable risk of bias against a female plaintiff. Other challenges that have assumed that the dominant perspective is no perspective include: Paschall v. Mayone, 454 F. Supp. 1289 (S.D.N.Y. 1978) (defendants in civil rights action requested that the trial judge disqualify himself because of his employment background, specifically his civil rights involvement); Menora v. Illinois High School, 527 F. Supp. 632 (N.D. Ill. 1981) (defendant requested judge recuse himself because he was of the same religious affiliation as the plaintiffs); Lindsey v. City of Beaufort, 911 F. Supp. 962 (D.S.C. 1995) (request by defendant that judge recuse himself because judge represented "black student activists" in similar civil rights case).

[346] As Mahoney says, " 'Race' as a social construction is not only produced by the persistence of 'old' attitudes or ignorance, but by social processes that directly reproduce poverty and segregation and then identify poverty and unemployment as features of blackness and inner-city space and, therefore identify stability, employment, and employability as features of whiteness." Martha R. Mahoney, *Segregation, Whiteness, and Transformation,* 143 U. PA. L. REV. 1659, 1675 (1995). The concept of race is complicated, as recent debate on multiracial identity indicates. *See* Bill O. Hing, *Beyond the Rhetoric of Assimilation and Cultural Pluralism: Addressing the Tension of Separtism and Conflict in an Immigration-Driven Multiracial Society,* 81 CAL. L. REV. 863 (1993).

Peggy McIntosh offers 46 examples of white skin privilege and notes that this is just the beginning of the list. Her list includes:

- I can, if I wish, arrange to be in the company of people of my race most of the time.
- I can avoid spending time with people whom I was trained to mistrust and who have learned to mistrust my kind or me.
- If I should need to move, I can be pretty sure of renting or purchasing a home in an area which I can afford and in which I would want to live.
- I can be reasonably sure that my neighbors in such a location will be neutral or pleasant to me.
- I can go shopping alone most of the time, fairly well assured that I will not be followed or harassed by store detectives.

McIntosh, *supra* note 42, at 34.

Too often we think of "discrimination" in broad terms, such as not being hired because of one's race. McIntosh's understanding of the daily effects of white privilege that have been granted merely by birth heightens white people's awareness of this limited understanding of the effect of race. *Id.*

[347] Other examples of male privilege include the ability to deal with others with relative assurance that the other person will not be condescending; to walk to one's car at night without fear of rape; never to think that a boss's interest in you may be merely to get you in bed; and to have others assume achievements are due to worth and not due to sexual favors or flirtatiousness. Catherine MacKinnon describes male privilege as follows:

> Men's physiology defines most sports, their health needs largely define insurance coverage, their socially designed biographies define workplace expectations and successful career patterns, their perspectives and concerns define quality of scholarship, their experiences and obsessions define merit, their military service defines citizenship, their presence defines family, their inability to get along with each other—their wars and rulerships—defines history, their image defines god, and their genitals define sex.

Catherine A. MacKinnon, TOWARD A FEMINIST THEORY OF THE STATE 224 (1989).

One can be denied some privilege, yet exercise others. Harlon Dalton describes his own experience of privilege:

to ignore others' lack of health care, shelter and public transportation.[348] Heterosexual privilege allows us to live without questions about why we live with our partner.[349] For each category, there are many associated privileges for individuals who possess the favored characteristic.[350] When

---

> White skin privilege is a birth right, a set of advantages one receives simply by being born with features that society values especially high. Although I can't claim skin privilege, I have a sense of what it must be like to possess it. I am, after all a beneficiary of male privilege. I didn't create it, I usually don't seek it out, and I am often made uncomfortable by it.

DALTON, supra note 45, at 110–11.

[348] For a comprehensive discussion of class privilege, see R. George Wright, DOES THE LAW MORALLY BIND THE POOR OR WHAT GOOD IS THE CONSTITUTION WHEN YOU CAN'T AFFORD A LOAF OF BREAD? (1996). bell hooks notes that our notions of class assume that it is merely a question of economic standing. In actuality, class determines values, standpoint and interests. Law schools assume that a student coming from a poor, working-class background is eager to shed that background and take on the dominant values. hooks notes that class status is never talked about in educational settings. She describes her own experience as a college student:

> During my college years, it was tacitly assumed that we all agreed that class should not be talked about, that there would be no critique of the bourgeois class biases shaping and informing pedagogical process (as well as social etiquette) in the classroom. Although no one ever directly stated the rules that would govern our conduct, it was taught by example and reinforced by a system of rewards. As silence and obedience to authority were most rewarded, students learned that this was the appropriate demeanor in the classroom. Loudness, anger, emotional outbursts, and even something as seemingly innocent as unrestrained laughter were deemed unacceptable, vulgar disruptions of classroom order. These traits were also associated with being a member of the lower classes. If one was not from a privileged group, adopting a demeanor similar to that group could help one advance. It is still necessary for students to assimilate bourgeois values in order to be deemed acceptable.

hooks, TEACHING, *supra* note 1, at 178.

[349] Other examples of heterosexual privilege that McIntosh identifies include:

- I have no difficulty finding neighborhoods where people approve of our household.
- Our children are given texts and classes that implicitly support our kind of family unit and do not turn them against my choice of domestic partnership.
- Most people I meet will see my marital arrangements as an asset to my life or as a favorable comment on my likability, my competence, or my mental health.
- I can talk about the social events of a weekend without fearing most listeners' reactions.

McIntosh, *supra* note 42, at 36.

Other examples that occur to me include:

- I do not have to attend firm or business functions alone because of fear of repercussions.
- I will not be prevented from making decisions for my partner if he is faced with a serious illness or death.
- I can purchase a life insurance policy with my partner as the beneficiary without any questions or suspicions. I will not have to provide a family member as the beneficiary and then be required to add my partner through a change of beneficiary form months later. I am certain that he will receive the money in the event of my death.
- I can purchase gifts for my partner without having to dodge questions.
- If I am fired from my job because of a specific characteristic that defines me, I will have legal recourse.

[350] As much as we need to learn from others who are "different" from us, there is always the risk that the focus on such difference will reinforce subordination. Brewer, *supra* note 40, at 1923. I am arguing for a two-sided analysis: First, we must try to learn from those we believe are

taken together, these privileges create the construct of oppression for those who have no access to those privileges.[351]

We do not experience the messages we receive culturally as explicit lessons.[352] Instead we perceive them merely as the way things are.[353] These privileges operate to oppress others, but, generally, when privilege is exercised, the person is unaware of the role such privilege plays in

---

"different" from us. Second, we must analyze why we perceive them as "different" and how that perception may reinforce existing power structures.

[351] Marilyn Frye offers an analogy that captures this phenomenon. She says:

> Consider a birdcage. If you look very closely at just one wire in the cage, you cannot see the other wires. If your conception of what is before you is determined in this myopic focus, you could look at that one wire, up and down the length of it, and be unable to see why a bird would not just fly around the wire at any time it wanted to go somewhere. Furthermore, even if, one day at a time, you myopically inspected each wire, you still could not see why a bird would have trouble going past the wires to get anywhere. There is no physical property of any one wire, *nothing* that the closest scrutiny could discover, that would reveal how a bird could be inhibited or harmed by it except in the most accidental way. It is only when you step back, stop looking at the wires one by one, microscopically, and take a macroscopic view of the whole cage, that you see why the bird does not go anywhere; and then you will see it in a moment It will require no great subtlety of mental powers. It is perfectly *obvious* that the bird is surrounded by a network of systematically related barriers, no one of which would be the least hindrance to its flight, but which, by their relations to each other, are as confining as the solid walls of a dungeon.

Marilyn Frye, THE POLITICS OF REALITY: ESSAYS ON FEMINIST THEORY (1983).

An important aspect of privilege is that it defines what is desirable. Deviations from that "norm" are less desirable. This reinforces the existing power structure. Barbara J. Flagg, *Fashioning a Title VII Remedy for Transparently White Subjective Decisionmaking,* 104 YALE L.J. 2009 (1995). Flagg identifies cases that demonstrate white skin privilege's effect on assessment of worth: Lasson v. Woodmen of the World Life Ins. Co., 741 F.2d 1241, 1243 (10th Cir. 1984), *cert. denied,* 471 U.S. 1099 (1985) (reviewing trial court's finding that Hispanic male was passed over for state manager position because white male chosen "had more management experience and . . . his personality and leadership skills made him a more desirable choice than plaintiff"); Clay v. Hyatt Regency Hotel, 724 F.2d 721, 722 (8th Cir. 1984) (reviewing trial court's conclusion that assertive black male "would not fit into defendant's organization as well as other applicants would"); Leisner v. New York Tel. Co., 358 F. Supp. 359, 365 (S.D.N.Y. 1973) (approving employer's decision not to promote based on the question: "Is this person going to be successful in our business?"). *See also* Cheshire Calhoun, *Sexuality Injustice,* 9 NOTRE DAME J.L. ETHICS & PUB. POL'Y 241 (1995).

[352] Jonathan Kozol describes the powerful messages that indigent children receive in school in SAVAGE INEQUALITIES: CHILDREN IN AMERICA'S SCHOOLS (1991). One compelling passage illustrates the point that these are not explicit lessons:

> In a somewhat mechanical way, the teacher lifts a picture book of Mother Goose and flips the pages as the children sit before her on the rug. "Mary had a little lamb, its fleece was white as snow . . . Old Mother Hubbard went to the cupboard to fetch the poor dog a bone . . . Jack and Jill went up the hill . . . This little piggy went to market . . ." The children recite the verses with her as she turns the pages on the book. She is not very warm or animated as she does it, but the children are obedient and seem to like the fun of knowing the words. The book looks worn and old, as if the teacher's used it for many years, and it shows no signs of adaptation to the race of the black children in the school. Mary is white. Jack is white. Jill is white. Little Jack Horner is white. Mother Goose is white. Only Mother Hubbard's dog is black. "Baa, Baa, black sheep," the teacher reads, "have you any wool?" The children answer: "Yessir, yessir, three bags full. One for the master . . ." The master is white. The sheep are black.

[353] For a discussion of the ways in which cultural messages are internalized and justified, see Lawrence, *supra* note 46.

perpetuating systematic oppression.[354] Most people simply live their lives trying not to act as conscious agents of oppression.[355]

Protection against seeing privilege is a necessary component and reinforcer of privilege itself.[356] The invisibility of privilege allows us to reinforce dominance without any moral accountability for our actions.[357] If we are to treat others with dignity and respect and to strive for justice and fairness within the legal system, we need to confront that unawareness.[358] It is the invisibility of privilege and its supposed inevitability that makes systemic change so difficult. Since the actors are unaware of their privilege, they fail to accept moral responsibility for their oppressive acts. As educators, we can help our students promote justice through unmasking privilege.

Unmasking privilege allows a person to challenge long-held assumptions and to develop a healthy skepticism about law's neutrality. Once we strip the facade of neutrality, helping our students to understand the ways in which privilege operates, then those students can never go back to innocent obliviousness. If we couple this with an understanding that one's exercise of privilege indirectly causes pain to others, then we can generalize the learning about privilege. This learning experience can be the catalyst for the student and teacher to continue to question the law's assumptions, to become more skilled at identifying privilege, and to become more attuned to the power dynamics that infect the attorney/client relationship and the client's claim.[359] Revealing

---

[354] Flagg, *supra* note 46, at 958.

[355] Iris M. Young, *Five Faces of Oppression, in* RETHINKING POWER 174 (Thomas Wartenberg ed., 1992).

[356] Mahoney, *supra* note 49, at 1665.

[357] *See* Amy H. Kastely, *Out of Whiteness: On Raced Codes and White Race Consciousness in Some Tort, Criminal and Contract Law,* 63 U. CIN. L. REV. 269 (1994).

[358] Frankenberg demonstrates how this can be transformative. She says:

> Attention to the construction of white "experience" is important, both to transform the meaning of whiteness and to transforming the relations of race in general. This is crucial in a social context in which the racial order is normalized and rationalized rather than upheld by coercion alone. Analyzing the connections between white daily lives and discursive orders may help make visible the processes by which the stability of whiteness—as location of privilege, as culturally normative space, and as standpoint, is secured and reproduced. In this context, reconceptualizing histories and refiguring racialized landscapes are political acts in themselves.

Frankenberg, supra note 47, at 242. *See also* Judith G. Greenberg, *Erasing Race From Legal Education,* 28 MICH. J.L. REF. 51 (1994).

[359] This requires those of us who take on this agenda to struggle with those issues ourselves, acknowledging, among other things, the deep effects of racism on American culture. *See* Patricia H. Colons, BLACK FEMINIST THOUGHT: KNOWLEDGE, CONSCIOUSNESS, AND THE POLITICS OF EMPOWERMENT (1991); W.E.B. DuBois, THE SOULS OF BLACK FOLK (1961); Henry L. Gates & Cornel West, THE FUTURE OF THE RACE (1996). We need to strive to confront the assumptions that poverty is the fault of the poor and that we are powerless to change the plight of poor people. *See* Christopher Jencks, RETHINKING SOCIAL POLICY: RACE, POVERTY, AND THE UNDERCLASS (1992). Our cultural experience necessarily colors our beliefs about those whom we perceive to be different from ourselves. *See* bell hooks, KILLING RAGE: ENDING RACISM (1995). Those beliefs deeply affect our ideas about our own power to effect change and influence our exercise of judgment.

privilege is a "transformative project."[360] If we can identify how privilege operates and identify points in which we can share our privilege, we can actually begin to fulfill MacCrate's injunction to "enhance the capacity of law and legal institutions to do justice."[361]

Power itself is not a negative.[362] It is how power is used that determines its moral status. We are educating students to exercise power as lawyers. For those of us who choose to raise issues of justice and morality, one question that MacCrate invites us to ask is whether we are going to use this power to reinforce and maintain coercive hierarchies.[363] It is through helping learners perceive "invisible" privilege that we can expect them to become accountable for their choices.[364]

Privilege is generally not something one can "give up." It comes with the characteristic. However, unearned, conferred power can be shared. If we assume that someone is more credible, for example, on the basis of the privilege associated with his or her skin color, then that person can exercise that privilege to benefit those disadvantaged in our society by

---

[360] The concept of "Transformative Project" is developed by Martha Mahoney. Mahoney, *supra* note 49.

[361] Section 2–3, Statement of Professional Values, MACCRATE, *supra* note 4, at 213.

[362] *But see* McIntosh, *supra* note 42, at 33.

[363] The MacCrate Report urges us to "act in conformance with considerations of justice, fairness, and morality when making decisions or acting on behalf of a client." MACCRATE, *supra* note 4, at 213. See hooks, TEACHING, *supra* note 1, at 188. Harlon Dalton describes the Race Game. His description gives insight into how power is used to determine moral status. The object of the Race Game is to ascend to the top of the social pecking order. It is similar to the children's game, King of the Hill, except that the Race Game is played in teams. Once one team makes it to the top, the goal is to keep the one below from climbing higher. Teams at the bottom have one goal—to climb higher and those in between are torn between maintaining their position with relation to those below and trying to climb higher still. Rules establish the racial pecking order and the way to prevail is to retain those rules. Usually the existing rules benefit the ones on top, who use the power of their position to keep them intact. Sometimes the rules cease to favor the status quo. When this happens it is in the interest of the King of the Hill to change the rules. Dalton provides an example in the admission to elite colleges. Admittance was once based on a broad range of aptitude so long as entrants came from the proper social stratum. People of color, Jews and White Christian commoners were excluded. Over time, various forces compelled elite colleges to become egalitarian and as they became academically (as opposed to socially) exclusive, they began to rely on standardized test scores even though tests tend to screen out a disproportionate number of African Americans, Latinos, and Native Americans. As the scores of Asian-Americans soared, many of the same schools suddenly began to look beyond numbers and to take into account activities that reflect creativity, leadership, well-roundedness, or other traits Asian-Americans were not thought to possess. DALTON, *supra* note 45, at 68–69.

[364] A necessary prerequisite to asking our students to take responsibility for conferred dominance is our willingness to do the same. Most law teachers have substantial privilege, be it race, gender, class, sexuality or professional. We must be aware of the ways in which our own privilege blinds us to injustice and may affect the ways we treat our clients and our students. Mahoney describes this project as it relates to racism:

> Necessary steps toward change include attacking the power of whiteness as an invisible, dominant social norm; participating in the project (necessarily repeated) that reiterates the existence of subordination and privilege by revealing the ongoing reproduction of white privilege and power; disputing the legal and social preference for colorblind approaches that reproduce color and power evasion, protect privilege, and deny cultural autonomy; and seeking points of unity and transformative potential.

Mahoney, *supra* note 49, at 1677.

skin color. This is difficult because it is easy to cross the line from sharing privilege to patronizing the person or at least being perceived as patronizing.[365] Nevertheless, when the situation will not allow an oppressed person to participate or even to have access, an individual permitted access by virtue of some characteristic can step in. Without such sharing of privilege there will be no access to the knowledge or power.[366] One example of this sharing often occurs in traditional law firms. A person of color enters a firm but is not told the unwritten rules that are needed to survive and succeed. A person in a privileged position shares those rules and provides the new arrival with the necessary knowledge. Without that "insider" information, there is a greater chance of failure.

When student attorneys represent poor clients, there are many opportunities for the students to witness the sharing of privilege. Because of their status as lawyer/representative and sometimes because of their skin and class privilege, they are given more credibility than their client, who may be saying the same thing but not be heard. These experiences offer teachers a chance to examine that phenomenon with their students and focus on the role of privilege in how one is heard.

Sharing privilege includes a willingness not to be silent in the face of behavior that subordinates a group. Stephanie Wildman offers a powerful example of how privilege can be exercised by silence. She describes being called for jury service. During the *voir dire,* the jurors were asked to introduce themselves, and the attorneys were allowed to ask supplemental questions. The defense attorney asked the Asian-looking jurors if they spoke English. No one else was asked. The judge did nothing. Wildman describes her response to the questioning:

> The Asian-American man sitting next to me smiled and flinched as he was asked the questions. I wondered how many times in his life he had been made to answer questions such as that one. I considered beginning my own questioning by saying, I'm Stephanie Wildman, I'm a professor of law, and yes, I speak English. I wanted to focus attention on the subordinating conduct of the attorney, but I did not. I exercised my white privilege by my silence. I exercised my privilege to opt out of

---

[365] Sometimes when privileged individuals seek to "share privilege," we attempt to speak for someone as if she were not there. Stephanie Wildman and Adrienne Davis describe this phenomenon vividly in their essay. Wildman & Davis, *supra* note 44.

[366] Not all privileges are created equal. Dalton distinguishes them by categorizing positive advantages as those which we can work to spread, and negative types of advantages as those which, unless rejected, will always reinforce our present hierarchies. The key word is hierarchies—we should not only be suspicious of advantages that reproduce the racial pecking order, but should also treat as candidates for redistribution those advantages that are acquired in part because of a person's favored position in the pecking order. No advance is possible until the existence of White skin privilege is acknowledged. Dalton, *supra* note 45, at 115–16.

engagement, even though this choice may not always be consciously made by someone with privilege.[367]

Striving to promote justice, fairness, and morality may require us to face the discomfort of not remaining silent.[368] It is these circumstances that may offer those of us who have privilege an opportunity to act, using our privilege and credibility to identify the injustice. In the educational context, as teachers, we have the ability to share our own power and privilege in the classroom. We do this through our curricular choices and the comments we choose to ignore and those that we develop and examine in class. As members of an institution, we share our privilege through our willingness to encourage diversity among the faculty and the student body. We, like our students, can recognize that our choice not to speak may reinforce privilege and contribute to others' pain.

As legal educators, our own privilege—be it skin, class, professional, heterosexual, or male privilege—imbues us with certain power that we can use to confront the privilege itself. One of my sad realizations when teaching about race as a white woman is that my opinion about race is given more credence by white people than opinions about race offered by fellow black teachers. This is due to skin privilege and the assumption that I do not have an ax to grind or the faulty assumption that I do not have a vested interest.[369] Because I know this, I feel a responsibility to

---

[367] Wildman & Davis, *supra* note 44, at 892.

[368] We should not be satisfied with increasing our students' *pro bono* hours. We should strive for more. Thomas Shaffer and Robert Rhodes describe it vividly:

> The burdens of poverty are fashioned in Wall Street offices faster and more effectively than legal services and public interest offices can lift them. If you spend the day on corporate takeovers and plant closings without thinking about the people you put out of work, you cannot make up for the harm that you do by giving a woman free legal advice in the evening when her unemployed husband takes out his frustration by beating her.

Thomas L. Shaffer & Robert E. Rhodes, Jr., *A Christian Theology for Roman Catholic Law Schools,* 14 U. DAYTON L. REV. 5, 18 (1988).

Whites must accept joint ownership of America's race problem. First, they must unlearn the many ways they commonly disown race which is done by: heightened rhetoric of Black responsibility (Blacks need to become more ambitious, take education seriously. . . .); treating Blacks as if they were fully in control of their own fate (Why don't they just get a job. . . .); and turning the tables (the notion that White men have suffered greatly at the hands of people of color and White women). Second, people disown the race problem by removing race from the picture (Black problems have to do more with class than race). This is flawed because it assumes that race and class are independent. The cause of many poor people's situation is not solely class but also the racial pecking order and race-related indifference, which play a role in our unwillingness to do what is necessary to improve the lot of the poor. Finally, rather than disown the race problem, many Whites make their participation conditional (I'd be willing to help if you would only . . . be less shrill, get your own house, meet me halfway. . . .). White and Black aspirations are not necessarily inconsistent and if we take joint responsibility for cleaning up the racial mess, we could search for creative solutions to expand opportunities for everyone. DALTON, *supra* note 45, at 117–25.

[369] At the same time, because I have skin privilege, I am less likely to have a full understanding and sensitivity to the effects of white supremacy. Harlon Dalton notes the phenomenon of discounting black voices: "When it comes to race, too often the opinions and judgments of people of color are regarded by Whites as subjective and self-interested, and therefore of dubious value. We need look no further than the legal academy to see this dynamic

discuss race and racism as much as possible. At the same time, as a woman, my voice about women's issues is characterized as shrill by many men because I am perceived to have a vested interest. A male's critique of sexism, however, is likely to be more persuasive to those same men. This is unfortunate because the phenomenon of privilege undermines the voices that are most familiar with the ways in which oppression affects us. For those of us who are deeply concerned about problems of oppression in society even when we are not the direct victims, this phenomenon offers us a role to play and a responsibility to play it. In essence, as teachers, we are helping our students take off their blinders and recognize the unearned power conferred upon them. Once the blinders are off, they will necessarily assume responsibility for the perpetuation of privilege because they will no longer be able to exercise it unknowingly.

POST-CLASS REFLECTION MEMO

Draft and submit a memo in response to the questions below:

- How will you take the lessons you have learned in class today and apply them to your work before you leave law school?
- How might you use these lessons after you graduate?
- Name one specific way you will you use the lessons you have learned in this class to change or challenge your own thinking about the meaning of justice and your professional role in delivering justice?

---

in action." DALTON, *supra* note 45, at 44. He cites some examples. In the legal academy people of color new to teaching are advised by concerned White colleagues to avoid dealing with issues of race in their scholarship so as to guard against problems with tenure, while White junior faculty can write about whatever they want. They are applauded for quality work that is supportive of the aspirations of people of color as well as for scholarship that is highly critical of positions associated with prominent scholars of color. *Id.*

APPENDIX

COPYRIGHT ACKNOWLEDGMENTS

■ ■ ■

Andrea Elliot, "Girl in the Shadows: Dasani's Homeless Life". From the New York Times, Dec. 9 © 2013. The New York Times. All rights reserved. Used by permission and protected by the Copyright Laws of the United States. The printing, copying, redistribution, or retransmission of this Content without express written permission is prohibited.

Andrew Dlugan, *25 Skills Every Public Speaker Should Have*, http://sixminutes.dlugen.com/25-skills-every-public-speaker-should-have/; Majorie Brody, *Presentation Power: Four Ways to Persuade*, http://sixminutes.dlugan.com/4-ways-persuasive/#more-5772; Andrew Dlugan, *Critique: Lessig Method Presentation Style (Dick Hardt, Identity 2.0, OSCON 2005)*, http://sixminutes.dlugan.com/presentation-20-hardt-executes-the-lessig-method/. Copyright © 2008 Six Minutes. Reprinted with permission.

Axam, Tony L. & Robert Altman, *The Picture Theory of Trial Advocacy*, LITIGATION MAGAZINE (April 1986) pp. 8–11. Copyright © 1986 Litigation Magazine. Reprinted with permission.

Brené Brown, *The Power of Vulnerability*, TED Talks http://www.ted.com/talks/lang/en/brene_brown_on_vulnerability.html. Copyright © 2010 TED Talks.

Bryan Garner, BETTER BUSINESS WRITING, Harvard Business Review Press, pp. 3–17 (2012). Copyright © 2012 Harvard Business Review Press. Reprinted with permission.

Carrie Menkel-Meadow, *When Winning Isn't Everything: The Lawyer As Problem Solver*, 28 HOFSTRA L. REV. 905 (2000) pp. 905–23. Copyright © 2000 Hofstra Law Review. Reprinted with the permission of the Hofstra Law Review Association.

Case Planning, in LEGAL SERVICES PRACTICE MANUAL: SKILLS (Benchmark Institute 2010) pp. 5–9. Copyright © 2010 Benchmark Institute. Reprinted with permission.

Charles H. Rose III, FUNDAMENTAL TRIAL ADVOCACY, Chapters 4, 5, 6, 7, 8, and 14, Appendix II (West 2nd Ed.). Copyright © 2010 West Academic. Reprinted with permission.

Clark D. Cunningham, *What Clients Want From Their Lawyers* (August 2006) pp. 1–6. Copyright © 2006 Clark D. Cunningham. Reprinted with permission.

Collaborative Justice: How to Collaborate, at collaborative justice.org/how/htm (2013 Center for Effective Public Policy) pp. 1–4. Copyright © 2013 Center for Effective Public Policy. Reprinted with permission.

Daniel L. Shapiro, *A Lawyer's Guide to Emotion: Four "Laws" to Effective Practice*, in DISPUTE RESOLUTION MAGAZINE (Winter 2001), pp. 3–8. Copyright 2012 © by the American Bar Association. Reprinted with permission. This information or any or portion thereof may not be copied or disseminated in any form or by any means or stored in an electronic database or retrieval system without the express written consent of the American Bar Association.

Danny Ertel, *Getting Past Yes: Negotiation as if Implementation Mattered*, HARVARD BUSINESS REVIEW (Nov. 1, 2004) pp. 454–465. Copyright © 2004 Harvard Business Review. Reprinted with permission.

David A. Binder, Paul Bergman, Paul R. Tremblay & Ian S. Weinstein, *Chapter 7 Theory Development Questioning—Pursuing Helpful Evidence*; and *Chapter 8: Theory Development Questioning Undermining Adversaries' Likely Contentions*, in LAWYERS AS COUNSELORS: A CLIENT-CENTERED APPROACH (3d ed. West 2012), pp. 151–169, 198–207. Copyright © 2012 West Academic. Reprinted with permission.

David A. Binder, Paul Berman, Susan C. Price & Paul R. Tremblay, *Principles Underlying Effective Counseling*, in LAWYERS AS COUNSELORS: A CLIENT CENTERED APPROACH (2nd ed., Thomson West 2004) pp. 270–292. Copyright © 2004 Thomson West. Reprinted with permission.

David Chavkin, Clinical Methodology, in Clinical Legal Education: A Textbook for Law School Clinical Programs (Lexis/Nexis). Copyright © Lexis/Nexis. Reprinted with permission.

David Dempsey, *Legally Speaking: 40 Powerful Presentation Principles Lawyers Need to Know*, (NY, Kaplan 2009) pp. 3–8. Copyright © 2009 David Dempsey.

Debbi Wilgoren, *Purchase of a Lifetime*, Washington Post (Dec. 14, 15, and 16, 2005). From the Washington Post, [December 14] © [2005] Washington Post Company. All rights reserved. Used by permission and protected by the Copyright Laws of the United States. The printing, copying, redistribution, or retransmission of this Content without express written permission is prohibited.

Donna St. George, "Murder in the Making," Washington Post (August 27, 2000). From the Washington Post, [August 27] © [2000] Washington Post Company. All rights reserved. Used by permission and protected by the Copyright Laws of the United States. The printing, copying, redistribution, or retransmission of this Content without express written permission is prohibited.

Edward A. Dauer, *Hurting Clients*, in THE AFFECTIVE ASSISTANCE OF COUNSEL, Majorie A. Silver, ed. (Carolina Academic Press 2007): 317–38. Copyright © 2007 Carolina Academic Press. Reprinted with permission.

Excerpts from EVERY PATIENT TELLS A STORY: MEDICAL MYSTERIES AND THE ART OF DIAGNOSIS by Lisa Sanders, copyright © 2009 by Lisa Sanders. Used by permission of Broadway Books, an imprint of the Crown Publishing Group, a division of Random House LLC. All rights reserved.

Excerpts from Jennifer K. Robbennolt and Jean R. Sternlight, PSYCHOLOGY FOR LAWYERS: UNDERSTANDING THE HUMAN FACTORS IN NEGOTIATION, LITIGATION, AND DECISION MAKING (2012 American Bar Association), pp. 7–27, 142–156. Copyright 2012 © by the American Bar Association. Reprinted with permission. This information or any or portion thereof may not be copied or disseminated in any form or by any means or stored in an electronic database or retrieval system without the express written consent of the American Bar Association.

Excerpts from Leigh Thompson, CREATIVE CONSPIRACY: THE NEW RULES OF BREAKTHROUGH COLLABORATION, (Harvard Business Review Press 2013), pp. 120–142. Copyright © 2013 Harvard Business Review Press. Reprinted with permission.

Excerpts from THE INVISIBLE GORILLA: HOW OUR INTUITIONS DECEIVE US by Christopher Chabris, copyright © 2010 by Christopher F. Chabris and Daniel J. Simons. Used by permission of Crown Books, an imprint of the Crown Publishing Group, a division of Random House LLC. All rights reserved.

Healey-Etten, Victoria & Shane Sharp, *Teaching Undergraduates How to Do an In-Depth Interview: A Teaching Note with 12 Handy Tips*, 38 TEACHING SOCIOLOGY 157–64 (April 2010). Copyright © 2010 Teaching Sociology. Reprinted with permission.

Higgins, Loraine & Lisa D. Brush, GETTING BY, GETTING AHEAD: WOMEN'S STORIES OF WELFARE TO WORK (National Institute of Justice 2002), http://www.pitt.edu/~lbrush/Getting_By.pdf. Copyright © 2002 National Institute of Justice. Reprinted with permission.

HOW DOCTORS THINK by Jerome Groopman, M.D. Copyright © 2007 by Jerome Groopman. Reprinted by permission of Houghton Mifflin Harcourt Publishing Company. All rights reserved.

James McElhaney, *More than Just Words: This is What it Really Means to Talk Like a Lawyer*, in ABA Journal, http://www.abajournal.com/magazine/article/more_than_just_words_this_is_what_it_really_means_to_talk_like_a_lawyer/. Copyright 2012 © by the American Bar Association. Reprinted with permission. This information or any or portion thereof may not be copied or disseminated in any form or by any means or stored in an electronic database or retrieval system without the express written consent of the American Bar Association.

Jane Aiken & Stephen Wizner, *Law as Social Work*, 11 Wash. U. J. L. & Pol'cy 63 (2003). Copyright © 2003 *Washington University Journal of Law and Policy,* Washington University School of Law. Reprinted with permission.

Jayne Seminare Docherty, *Culture and Negotiation: Symmetrical Anthropology for Negotiators*, 87 MARQUETTE L. REV. 711–22 (2004). Copyright © 2004 *Marquette Law Review,* Marquette University Law School. Reprinted with permission.

John Yarbrough, Jugues Herve & Robert Harms, *The Sins of Interviewing: Errors Made by Investigative Interviewers and Suggestions for Redress*, in Barry S. Cooper, Dorothee Driesel & Marguerite Ternes, Eds., APPLIED ISSUES IN INVESTIGATIVE INTERVIEWING, EYEWITNESS MEMORY, AND CREDIBILITY ASSESSMENT, (Springer Science and Business Media 2013), pp. 59–76, 77–79, 83–86, 88, 90–92. Copyright © 2013 Springer Science and Business Media. Reprinted with permission.

Justice William Quigley, *Revolutionary Lawyering: Addressing The Root Causes of Poverty and Wealth*, 20 Wash. U. J.L. & Pol'y 101 (2006). Copyright © 2006 *Washington University Journal of Law and Policy,* Washington University School of Law. Reprinted with permission.

Miriam Kass, *The Ba Theory of Persuasive Writing*, 12 LITIGATION 47 (1985–1986). Copyright © 1985-1986 Miriam Kass. Reprinted with permission.

Paul R. Tremblay, *Counseling Community Groups*. 17 CLINICAL LAW REVIEW 389 (2010). Copyright © 2010 Clinical Law Review. Reprinted with permission.

Peter De Jong & Scott D. Miller, *How to Interview for Client Strengths*, 40 Soc. Work 6 (1995): 729–36. Copyright © 1995 Social Work. Reprinted with permission.

Roald Hoffmann, *Why Buy That Theory?*, 91 AMERICAN SCIENTIST 9 (Jan. 2003), pp. 9–11. Copyright © Roald Hoffmann. Reprinted with permission.

Ronda Muir, *The Importance of Emotional Intelligence in Law Firm Partners*, 33(5) Law Practice Magazine 60–64 (July/Aug. 2007). Copyright © 2007 Ronda Muir. Reprinted with permission by Ronda Muir, Esq., founder and principal of Law People Management, LLC, www.LawPeopleManagement.com.

Sarah Burns, Central Park Five (Knopf Doubleday 2001), pp. 9; 18–19; 21–27; 31–32; 37–38; 39–41; 50–51; 161; 162–163; 174–175; 185; 188–189; 194–196; 208–209. Copyright © 2001 Random House. Reprinted with permission. Any third party use of this material, outside of this publication, is prohibited. Interested parties must apply directly to Random House LLC for permission.

Stephen Denning, *Telling Tales*, HARVARD BUSINESS REVIEW (May 2004), pp. 115–130. Copyright © 2004 Harvard Business Review. Reprinted with permission.

Sternlight, Jean R. & Jennifer Robbennhold, *Good Lawyers Should Be Good Psychologists: Insights for Interviewing and Counseling Clients*, 23 Ohio St. J. On Dis. Resol. 437–548 (2007–08). Copyright © 2007–2008 *Ohio State Journal on Dispute Resolution,* Moritz College of Law—The Ohio State University. Reprinted with permission.

Steven Lubet, *Murder in the Streets of Tombstone: A Legendary Theory of the Case*, 27 LITIGATION 35-36 (Fall 2000). Steven Lubet is the author of *Murder in Tombstone: The Forgotten Trial of Wyatt Earp* (Yale University Press). Copyright © 2000 Litigation Magazine. Reprinted with permission.

Sue Bryant & Jean Koh Peters, *Five Habits for Cross Cultural Lawyering*, in Kimberly Holt Barnett & William H. George, RACE, CULTURE,

PSYCHOLOGY AND LAW (Sage 2005), pp. 47–60. Copyright © 2005 Sage. Reprinted with permission.

Wayne C. Booth, Gregory G. Colomb & Joseph M. Williams, *Chapter 7, Making Good Arguments*, in MAKING GOOD ARGUMENTS (University of Chicago Press 2008), pp. 108–119. Copyright © 2008 University of Chicago Press. Reprinted with permission.